Writing History in the Middle Ages
Volume 3

Medieval Cantors and their Craft

Writing History in the Middle Ages
ISSN 2057-0252

Series editors

Dr Henry Bainton, University of York
Professor Lars Boje Mortensen, University of Southern Denmark

History-writing was a vital form of expression throughout the European Middle Ages, and is fundamental to our understanding of medieval societies, politics, modes of expression, cultural memory, and social identity. This series publishes innovative work on history-writing from across the medieval world; monographs, collections of essays, and editions of texts are all welcome.

Other volumes in the series are listed at the back of this book.

Medieval Cantors and their Craft

Music, Liturgy and the Shaping of History, 800–1500

Edited by
Katie Ann-Marie Bugyis,
A. B. Kraebel and Margot E. Fassler

THE UNIVERSITY *of York*

YORK MEDIEVAL PRESS

First published 2017
Paperback edition 2019

A York Medieval Press publication
in association with The Boydell Press
an imprint of Boydell & Brewer Ltd
PO Box 9, Woodbridge, Suffolk IP12 3DF, UK
and of Boydell & Brewer Inc.
668 Mt Hope Avenue, Rochester, NY 14620–2731, USA
website: www.boydellandbrewer.com
and with the
Centre for Medieval Studies, University of York

ISBN 978 1 903153 67 3 hardback
ISBN 978 1 903153 92 5 paperback

A CIP catalogue record for this book is available
from the British Library

The publisher has no responsibility for the continued existence or accuracy
of URLs for external or third-party internet websites referred to in this book,
and does not guarantee that any content on such websites is,
or will remain, accurate or appropriate

This publication is printed on acid-free paper

Typeset in Palatino LT by David Roberts, Pershore, Worcestershire

In memory of Olivia Remie Constable

Contents

Illustrations

Frontispiece

Figures

Tables

Music Examples

The editors, contributors and publishers are grateful to all the institutions and persons listed for permission to reproduce the materials in which they hold copyright. Every effort has been made to trace the copyright holders; apologies are offered for any omission, and the publishers will be pleased to add any necessary acknowledgement in subsequent editions.

Contributors

Cara Aspesi is doctoral candidate and Instructor in the Department of Theology at the University of Notre Dame concentrating in Liturgical Studies. She is completing her dissertation on Lucca, Biblioteca Arcivescovile MS 5, a Crusader breviary and partial pontifical that provides insight into many aspects of life and thought in the Latin Kingdom of Jerusalem in the twelfth century. She also works on the influence of early Christian liturgical reading on the emergence of the concept of a Scriptural canon.

Anna de Bakker is PhD student at the Medieval Institute of the University of Notre Dame, working on the intersections of music, liturgy, and culture in the high to late Middle Ages. She holds a Master of Arts in Religion from Yale Divinity School, with a certificate from the Institute of Sacred Music, and an AB in History from Harvard College. Her dissertation explores the late medieval office in the Lowlands.

Alison I. Beach is Associate Professor of history at the Ohio State University. In 2004 she published *Women as Scribes: Book Production and Monastic Reform in Twelfth-Century*. In 2002, she organized a conference at Stift Admont in Steiermark, Austria, which brought together medieval scholars from both the English- and German-speaking traditions. Prof. Beach then edited a volume based partially on the conference entitled *Manuscripts and Monastic Culture: Reform and Renewal in Twelfth-Century Germany*, published in 2007.

Katie Ann-Marie Bugyis is Assistant Professor in the Program of Liberal Studies at the University of Notre Dame. Her research focuses primarily on the liturgical and intellectual histories of communities of women religious in the central and late Middle Ages. She is currently working on a book on the pastoral roles and liturgical practices of Benedictine women religious in England during the central Middle Ages, entitled, *In Persona Christi: Benedictine Women's Ministries in Central Medieval England*.

Margot Fassler, Keough-Hesburgh Professor of Music History and Liturgy, and Director of the Program in Sacred Music, University of Notre Dame, is also Tangeman Professor of Music History, Emerita, Yale University. Recent books include *Music in the Medieval West* and its accompanying *Anthology* (2014) and (with Jeffery Hamburger, Eva Schlotheuber, and Susan Marti) *Life and Latin Learning at Paradies bei Soest, 1300–1425: Inscription and Illumination in the Choir Books of a North German Dominican Convent*, 2 vols. (2016). Fassler is Vice President of the Medieval Academy of America and a fellow of the American Academy of Arts and Sciences.

David Ganz studied in Oxford, Tubingen and Munich and wrote his thesis on Corbie in the Carolingian Renaissance. He was Professor of Medieval Latin in Chapel Hill, whence he moved to the Chair of Paleography in the University of London. In 2011 he gave the Lowe lectures in Oxford, and in 2012 he became a Visiting Professor of Paleography at the University of Notre Dame. He has worked on Latin manuscript books before 900, and is an advisor to Digital Scriptorium and to the St Gall Plan website.

James Grier is Professor of Music History at the University of Western Ontario. Author of *The Critical Editing of Music* (1996) and *The Musical World of a Medieval Monk: Adémar de Chabannes in Eleventh-Century Aquitaine* (2006), he has also published an edition of music written in the hand of Adémar in CCCM (2012), the first music to be published in that series, and articles on music and liturgy in medieval Aquitaine, textual criticism and editing music, and the music of F. J. Haydn, Frank Zappa, and Bob Dylan and Roger McGuinn.

Paul Antony Hayward is senior lecturer in history at Lancaster University. He works on historiography, the cult of saints and political practice in Latin Christendom, *c.* 400–1150. Recent publications include *The Winchcombe and Coventry Chronicles: Hitherto Unnoticed Witnesses to the Work of John of Worcester*, Medieval and Renaissance Texts and Studies 373, 2 vols. (2010), and 'The Importance of Being Ambiguous: Innuendo and Legerdemain in William of Malmesbury's *Gesta regum* and *Gesta pontificum Anglorum*', ANS 33 (2011), 75–102. He is presently writing *Power, Rhetoric and Historical Practice in Medieval England: From William of Malmesbury to Geoffrey of Monmouth*.

Peter Jeffery is the Michael P. Grace II Chair of Medieval Studies at the University of Notre Dame, and Scheide Professor of Music History Emeritus, Princeton University. He is presently completing an annotated translation of *Ordo Romanus Primus*. Among his many grants and awards are those from the Guggenheim Foundation, the MacArthur Foundation, the National Endowment for the Humanities, and the American Musicological Society.

Claire Taylor Jones is Assistant Professor of German at the University of Notre Dame. She is currently completing a monograph on convent literature for German Dominican women and translating a major work by Johannes Meyer, a mid-fifteenth-century Dominican friar whose German-language chronicles are the object of her contribution to this volume.

A. B. Kraebel is Assistant Professor of English at Trinity University, San Antonio, Texas. His research focuses on book history and religious literature in the later Middle Ages, especially as they relate to scholastic commentary and biblical translation. He is currently completing a monograph on the subject, tentatively entitled *The Appeal of the Academic: Biblical Commentary and Translation in Later Medieval England.*

Lori Kruckenberg is Associate Professor of Musicology at the University of Oregon, where she teaches courses in medieval and Renaissance music. Her scholarship focuses on Latin monophonic song in the Middle Ages, especially sequences, tropes and the so-called new song tradition. More recent work centers on traditions of the cantrix in German-speaking lands, *c.* 900–1400, and on the *Casus sancti Galli.* She has twice held fellowships from the Fulbright Commission and recently won the Noah Greenberg Award.

Rosamond McKitterick is Professor Emerita of Medieval History in the University of Cambridge and Fellow of Sidney Sussex College and currently Chair of the Faculty of History, Archaeology and Letters of the British School at Rome. Her books include *History and Memory in the Carolingian World* (2004); *Perceptions of the Past in the Early Middle Ages* (2006); *Charlemagne: the formation of a European identity* (2008); *Old Saint Peter's, Rome* (ed. with J. Osborne, C. Richardson and J. Story) (2014); and *The Resources of the Past in the Early Middle Ages* (ed. with C. Gantner and S. Meeder) (2015). Her current work within the field of the early medieval history of Europe focuses on a people's (re)construction, knowledge and use of the past, especially the Roman past.

Henry Parkes is Assistant Professor of Music at the Yale Institute of Sacred Music and Department of Music. A professional church musician turned academic, his current research deals broadly with the lived experience of chant and liturgy at the turn of the first millennium. A particular interest in the material and intellectual histories of liturgical codices stands behind his first book, *The Making of Liturgy in the Ottonian Church,* published in 2015.

Susan Rankin is Professor of Medieval Music at the University of Cambridge. She studied at Cambridge, King's College London and Paris (EPHE IV). Her research engages with music of the middle ages through its sources and notations, and through its place and meaning within ritual. A special focus has been the paleography of early medieval musical sources, and she has edited facsimiles of two Sankt Gallen tropers and the Winchester Troper, demonstrating how the earliest European repertory of two-part polyphony can be recovered. She is now working on the relation between musical sound and notations in the ninth century.

Charles C. Rozier is Lecturer in Medieval History at Swansea University. His work examines the collection and composition of historical texts in Anglo-Norman monasteries. He is co-editor of *Orderic Vitalis: Life, Works and Interpretations* (2016) and is currently writing a monograph which explores the multi-layered uses of the past at Durham Cathedral Priory, *c.* 995–1130 (forthcoming).

Sigbjørn Olsen Sønnesyn received a Cand. Philol. degree in history, English, and Latin from the University of Bergen in 2002, and a PhD in history from the same University in 2007. He was lecturer at the department of history, University of Bergen, from January to November 2007, and between 2008 and 2013 he held a post-doctoral fellowship at the University. From January 2011 he has also held a post-doctoral fellowship at the Saxo Institute, University of Copenhagen, Denmark. His main publication is *William of Malmesbury and the Ethics of History* (2012).

Teresa (Tessa) Webber is University Reader in Paleography at the University of Cambridge and a Fellow of Trinity College. She is the author of *Scribes and Scholars at Salisbury Cathedral c. 1075– c. 1125* (1992) and co-editor of *The Libraries of the Augustinian Canons*, CBMLC 6 (1998) and *The Cambridge History of Libraries in Britain and Ireland, Volume I: To 1640* (2006). She is currently preparing for publication her Lyell Lectures, delivered in Oxford in 2016, on public reading and its books in English monastic practice, *c.* 1000–*c.* 1300.

Lauren L. Whitnah is Lecturer in the Marco Institute for Medieval and Renaissance Studies at the University of Tennessee, Knoxville. Her research examines the cults of Anglo-Saxon saints in northern England and southern Scotland in the twelfth century, exploring the impact of political upheaval on local religious practice. Her current book project, tentatively entitled *Patrons of that Place*, is an interdisciplinary study of the relationship between saints' cults and sacred place in twelfth-century Northumbria.

Acknowledgements

In a book with nineteen chapters, edited by three scholars, there are countless people and institutions that should be acknowledged – especially the libraries where each of us have worked, the universities and foundations that have supported us, and the many people who have helped along the way, including the requisite kinds of spousal support. Out of all these, most greatly to be thanked are the Medieval Institute of the University of Notre Dame and its friend and supporter Robert M. Conway. Through Mr. Conway's generosity we were able to begin work on this book with a superb conference at the Notre Dame London Centre in October 2013. At this conference, curated by Katie Bugyis and Margot Fassler, scholars from the University of Notre Dame and other institutions in the USA and Canada joined colleagues from universities in the UK to share the ideas from which this book developed. We thank the Notre Dame London Centre and its staff, especially Charlotte Parkyn, for their hospitality and assistance, the students from the University of Notre Dame who helped curate the conference, especially Emily Kirkegaard and Anna de Bakker, and the scholars who chaired sessions: Emma Dillon, Nicholas Bell and Helen Deeming. Giles Constable of the Institute for Advanced Study in Princeton attended at our invitation and enlivened our conversations with his ideas. Professor Remie Constable, the then Conway Director of the Medieval Institute and Professor of History at the University of Notre Dame, must be credited with the initial inspiration for our work. Her support, constant enthusiasm and kindness made this book possible, and we dedicate it to her memory.

We wish to express our particular gratitude to the Institute for Scholarship in the Liberal Arts at the University of Notre Dame for financial support in the book's production and printing. Caroline Palmer of Boydell and Brewer and Professor Pete Biller of York Medieval Press have been helpful and supportive at every turn. We are thankful to them and to all the authors in our book who have faithfully answered every query. Collaborating with our contributors has been a joy.

Some of those contributors wish to acknowledge individual debts. In addition to thanking the conference organizers, David Ganz expresses his gratitude for the valuable feedback provided by Charles Rozier and Julie Barrau. For their efforts in helping him locate and consult the primary sources behind his chapter, Henry Parkes extends his thanks to the staff of the Hochschul- und Landesbibliothek Fulda, the Württembergische Landesbibliothek in Stuttgart and the Universitäts- und Landesbibliothek Darmstadt, as well as Michael Kuthe of the Stadtarchiv Konstanz. Teresa Webber thanks Michael Gullick for his careful reading of her chapter. Lauren

Acknowledgements

Whitnah acknowledges the generous suggestions made by Anna Siebach Larsen, Hildegund Müller, Julia Schneider and John Van Engen.

KAB
MEF
ABK

Abbreviations

AASS   *Acta Sanctorum*

AH   *Analecta Hymnica Medii Aevi*

ANS   *Anglo-Norman Studies*

ASE   *Anglo-Saxon England*

BHL   *Bibliotheca Hagiographica Latina, Antiquae et Mediae Aetatis*

BL   London, British Library

BLB   Karlsruhe, Badische Landesbibliothek

BnF   Paris, Bibliothèque nationale de France

Bodl   Oxford, Bodleian Library

Can   CANTUS: A Database for Latin Ecclesiastical Chant

CBMLC   Corpus of British Medieval Library Catalogues

CCCC   Cambridge, Corpus Christi College Library

CCCM   Corpus Christianorum, Continuatio Mediaevalis

CCM   Corpus Consuetudinem Monasticorum

CCSL   Corpus Christianorum, Series Latina

CCT   Corpus Christianorum in Translation

CP   *Casus Monasterii Petrihusensis*, ed. O. Abel and L. Weiland, MGH Scriptores 20

CSEL   Corpus scriptorum ecclesiasticorum Latinorum

CUL   Cambridge, University Library

Decreta   Lanfranc, *The Monastic Constitutions of Lanfranc*, ed. D. Knowles and C. Brooke (Oxford, 2002)

DUL   Durham, University Library

EadLD   *Vita S. Dunstani*, in *Eadmer: Lives and Miracles*, ed. A. J. Turner and B. J. Muir (Oxford, 2006)

EadMD   *Miracula S. Dunstani*, in *Eadmer: Lives and Miracles*, ed. A. J. Turner and B. J. Muir (Oxford, 2006)

EEA   *English Episcopal Acta*

EHR   *English Historical Review*

ELD   *Early Lives of St Dunstan*, ed. M. Winterbottom and M. Lapidge (Oxford, 1991)

    A   Adelard of Ghent, *Lectiones in Depositione S. Dunstani*

    B   *Vita S. Dunstani*

Fass A   M. E. Fassler, 'Office of the Cantor in Early Western Monastic Rules and Customaries: A Preliminary Investigation' *Early Music History* 5 (1985), 29–51

Fass B	M. E. Fassler, *Gothic Song: Victorine Sequences and Augustinian Reform in Twelfth-Century Paris* (Notre Dame, IN, 1993 and 2011)
Fass C	M. E. Fassler, *The Virgin of Chartres: Making History through Liturgy and the Arts* (New Haven, CT, 2010)
Fass D	M. E. Fassler, 'The Liturgical Framework of Time and the Representation of History', in *Representing History, 900–1300: Art, Music, History*, ed. R. A. Maxwell (University Park, PA, 2010), pp. 83–123
GPA	William of Malmesbury, *Gesta pontificum Anglorum*, ed. M. Winterbottom and R. M. Thomson, 2 vols. (Oxford, 2007)
GRA	William of Malmesbury, *Gesta regum Anglorum*, ed. R. A. B. Mynors, M. Winterbottom and R. M. Thomson, 2 vols. (Oxford, 1998, 1999)
HBS	Henry Bradshaw Society
HE	Bede, *Ecclesiastical History of the English People*, ed. B. Colgrave and R. A. B. Mynors (Oxford, 1969)
Heads	*The Heads of Religious Houses, England and Wales, 940–1216*, ed. D. Knowles, C. N. L. Brooke and V. C. M. London (Cambridge, 1972)
HLB F	Hochschul- und Landesbibliothek Fulda
JAMS	*Journal of the American Musicological Society*
LC	*Le Liber Censuum de l'église romaine*, ed. Fabre
LdE	Symeon of Durham, *Libellus de Exordio*, ed. D. Rollason (Oxford, 2000)
LP	*Le Liber Pontificalis*, ed. L. Duchesne, 2 vols. (Paris, 1886–92)
MGH	Monumenta Germaniae Historica
	Capit. — Capitularia regum Francorum
	Epp. — Epistolae
	Libri Mem. NS — Libri Memoriales et Necrologia, Nova series
	SRG NS — Scriptores rerum Germanicarum, Nova series
	SRM — Scriptores rerum Merovingicarum
	SS — Scriptores (in Folio)
OsLD	Osbern, *Vita Sancti Dunstani*, in *Memorials of St Dunstan*, ed. W. Stubbs, Rolls Series (London, 1874)
OsMD	Osbern, *Liber Miraculorum Beatissimi Patris nostri Dunstani*, in *Memorials of St Dunstan*, ed. W. Stubbs, Rolls Series (London, 1874)
PL	*Patrologia Latina*
PPTS	Palestine Pilgrims' Text Society
RB	*Revue Bénédictine*
SG	Stiftsbibliothek Sankt Gallen
ULB D	Universitäts- und Landesbibliothek Darmstadt
WilLD	*Vita Dunstani (Life of Dunstan)* in William of Malmesbury, *Saints Lives: Lives of SS. Wulfstan, Dunstan, Patrick, Benignus and Indract*, ed. M. Winterbottom and R. M. Thomson (Oxford, 2002)
WLB	Stuttgart, Württembergische Landesbibliothek

Historiated initial depicting the cantor Osbern of Canterbury:
British Library, MS Arundel 16, fol. 2

Introduction

Katie Ann-Marie Bugyis, Margot E. Fassler and A. B. Kraebel

'History', as it was understood by medieval Christians, was a broad concept with many meanings. It could be defined as a written record, compiled through processes inherited from classical Greek and Roman authors. But even when it proclaimed itself to be 'factual', the work of those who shaped the past in the Latin Middle Ages was different from that of their pagan ancestors. Although they often made claims about veracity, even when dealing with the miraculous, they did not 'absolutize' history (as de Lubac put it). Although they had a sense of universal history, time instead related to and unfolded within a framework conditioned by the Incarnation of the Word, and by the moral sense that this history-transforming event could impart to listeners and readers. The biblical orientation of history gave time a clear beginning and also predicted an apocalyptic end. But even as time moved relentlessly forward in this cosmic sense, the liturgy made it constantly spiral backward, rendering past sacred events present through ritual commemoration. Such liturgical celebration of time had many layers, mingled and arranged according to the calendar, with its varying and its fixed cycles of feasts, voiced through psalmody, readings from the Old and New Testaments and the lives of the saints.

How the past was known, both by individuals and within communities, varied from one specific local community to another, for the liturgy was ever changing, especially as new feasts, and feasts of new saints, were added to suit particular needs. Some knew about certain past events from what they read, as had long been the case, but in the Middle Ages many more knew about the past from various reenactments: ritual actions, dramatic productions, sermons and tales they heard about biblical characters and saints, encounters with art and architecture and from contact with shrines and relics.

Much of medieval history-making was thus memorial in nature, bringing the past forward, again and again, to recall its individual or communal significance. At the heart of the medieval Christian understanding of the past was a simple, foundational command from Christ: 'Hoc facite in meam commemorationem' ['Do this in remembrance of me'] (Luke 22. 19). Recreate the past for me, through the liturgy of the Mass, with its chants, readings from Scripture and communion service, as well as through the eight hours of communal prayer sung in both monasteries and cathedrals at set times throughout the day, with appropriate chants, Psalms and readings complementing those recited at Mass to distinguish any particular feast.

After the hour of Prime there was a chapter meeting, where, in addition to the Benedictine practice of reading from the Rule, both monastic and cathedral communities heard daily readings from the martyrology, a fixed collection of remembrances of the saints and figures from the Bible, and the necrology, which preserved the names of people from the community who had died on that day (or within the week or month), sometimes with statements from their wills. The liturgy, whether the Mass or the Divine Office, not only saved and preserved the past, but it taught its meanings to all who were involved in its observance, hour by hour, day by day, season by season, year by year, through text, music, matter and movement.

History is not known without effort. If the past is not recorded, recreated and reimagined, it dissipates from memory and ceases to exist. In the Latin Middle Ages many different kinds of people were required to undertake the complex processes of remembering the past and fostering its many ways of being taught and sounded out in public and private ceremonies. The past was never static, but was always being reshaped, often to suit political conditions as well as spiritual needs. This book is about medieval cantors, the people who were among the most responsible for shaping history in this period, and the many and varied activities they performed. We have observed their work and their characters, beginning with the Carolingian period and moving forward until the very late Middle Ages. And although many of the following chapters focus on Anglo-Norman England, where the evidence is especially abundant, we have taken up case studies from history-makers on the Continent as well, signalling that, although our book is the first to treat this complicated subject from our particular perspective, the authors hope to encourage further study.

The initial idea behind the gathering of scholars that produced this volume centered upon the individual in medieval monastic life who 'kept the time'. This person was the medieval cantor, *precentor* or *armarius* – these three being common names for the same office-holder in the late tenth, eleventh and twelfth centuries. There is a profile for this individual, especially in the central Middle Ages, and it is outlined in medieval customaries, those books that flesh out the various duties of monastic and, sometimes, of cathedral officers. There was also a profile for the kind of book(s) the cantor required in order to do the work of marking time.[1]

One of the fullest descriptions of the many duties performed by the *armarius* is found in the pages of the *Liber ordinis* of the abbey of St Victor in

---

[1] For example, excellent studies of the so-called 'Durham cantor's book' are found in two seminal articles: A. Piper, 'The Durham Cantor's Book (Durham, Dean and Chapter Library, MS B.IV.24)' in *Anglo-Norman Durham (1093–1193)*, ed. D. Rollason et al. (Woodbridge, 1994), pp. 79–92; and M. Gullick, 'The Scribes of the Durham Cantor's Book and the Durham Martyrology Scribe', in *Anglo-Norman Durham*, ed. Rollason et al., pp. 93–109.

Paris, a customary with the earliest copies dating *c.* 1200. The portrait that emerges from this source is of a figure who was in charge of the liturgy and its music at the abbey. He assigned readings and chants and made sure that lectors and singers were prepared for their liturgical assignments; he ensured that liturgical books were ready for use and could be consulted in a timely fashion. He was the monastic librarian, and all the books, both those for the liturgy and for other communal and private uses, were in his keeping. He was in charge of the scriptorium, and the procurement of the materials needed for making books was within his remit, as was their proper and timely repair. In monastic scriptoria, the production of liturgical books was by far the most common of the tasks; thus, the liturgical knowledge and authority of the *armarius*/cantor was crucial. His role was also ceremonial: some chants were intoned by him, and he held the book when the abbot read or sang. Although not mentioned in the Victorine source, the *armarius*/cantor may have written tonaries and other materials needed for instruction in singing, given his musical expertise.

In monastic institutions throughout Europe there were men and women charged with these duties, and their work prepared them to be intimately involved in the keeping of the history of the places they served. Insofar as they were in charge of liturgical materials, including calendars and martyrologies, they were responsible for recording death dates and for sending out notices to communities and individuals within their confraternity of prayer to request prayers for the dearly departed. Insofar as establishing the date of Easter, which fell to them, they were skilled in the use of the *computus* and the mathematical calculations required to mete out festal time. In line with their responsibilities, many medieval cantors composed new music and texts for the veneration of saints, especially those of unique local significance. Institutional history was shaped in and through hagiography, and cantors, time and again, did the work to foster, translate and maintain their communities' treasured cults. Many cantors moved back and forth across the thin or fuzzy line separating history and hagiography, registering the deeds of saints as well as of popes, bishops, kings, queens and other renowned personages, both past and present. There were many medieval figures who fit this profile, who took on one or more of the aspects of the assignments commonly belonging to the *armarius*/cantor; some of them will be featured in this book.

In creating a description of medieval librarians, Richard Sharpe advises, 'the diversity and inconsistency of their activities must warn against easy generalization'.[2] Whereas our book is about the processes of shaping history in the Middle Ages, with an emphasis upon the history-makers

---

[2] R. Sharpe, 'The Medieval Librarian', in *The Cambridge History of Libraries in Britain and Ireland, Vol. 1: To 1640*, ed. E. Leedham-Green and T. Webber (Cambridge, 2006), pp. 218–41 (p. 241).

and their various roles within their communities, it is not solely a book about the medieval cantor/*armarius*, and easy generalizations have indeed been avoided. Sometimes it seems as if we are deliberately deconstructing this office, pointing to the many ways in which the cantors we discuss do not fit the profile recovered from the Victorine *Liber ordinis*. We also take up the kinds of history-making that were not solely the work of cantors, even in monasteries, and the question of whether their textual and musical productions should even be considered works of 'history'. To establish a framework for understanding the chapters that follow, our study begins with definitions of 'history' presented by David Ganz, challenging the reader at the outset to consider what history was to those who wrote it – those who 'made' it.

Some authors in our book have written on figures who fit the description of the cantor-chronicler given above: Lori Kruckenberg's study of Ekkehard IV of St Gallen, Alison Beach's work on the cantor of Peterhausen, Charlie Rozier's study of Symeon, the cantor-historian of Durham, Sigbjørn Sønnesyn on William of Malmesbury, Cara Aspesi on the cantors of the Holy Sepulchre in Jerusalem, and Peter Jeffery on the twelfth-century cantor-chronicler Benedict of St Peter's basilica in Rome. Others have looked at the ways that liturgy shaped historical texts and that saints' cults, in turn, promoted historical understanding and regional identity: Rosamund McKitterick on the *Liber pontificalis*, which includes study of various local recensions, Margot Fassler on the cult of Dunstan, Lauren Whitnah's work on liturgy and identity in an office for St Æbbe, Claire Jones's study of Johannes Meyer's chronicles and his defence of reformed Dominican nuns, and Anna de Bakker's work on the cantor Goswin of Bossut and an office created for the Cistercian monastery of Villers.

Several chapters in the book have expanded our understanding of the work that musicians did for their libraries and their liturgies, inspiring the reader to think about the many activities of musicians, whether they held the office of cantor or not: Susan Rankin's study of Notker of St Gallen, James Grier's account of Adémar of Chabannes, Henry Parkes on various officials working at Constance, Katie Bugyis's study of English Benedictine women religious, including not only cantors but also sacristans, Teresa Webber on the shared duties of cantors, priors and sacristans, A. B. Kraebel on William of Newburgh's shorter writings in relation to his larger exegetical and historical projects, and Paul Hayward's analysis of William of Malmesbury, which charges that his work as cantor actually had little to do with his history-writing (a point of view with which two other authors disagree).

This volume, when compared with scholarship on medieval history-writing that appeared around a generation ago, demonstrates that a steady transformation has taken place in the way the subject is studied. Our book is near in spirit to *The Writing of History in the Middle Ages: Essays Presented to Richard William Southern*, ed. R. H. C. Davis and J. M. Wallace-Hadrill (Oxford,

1981). In their foreword, Davis and Wallace-Hadrill claim that their book is about historiography, 'not only the writing of history by medieval men but the way they looked at the past and the influences that led to that looking' (p. v). Foundational to this exploration is the study of how history relates to monastic identity, to hagiography, to schools of thought, to confession, to sermons and to law. But all of these activities are perceived only as textual – that is, they lack the idea that liturgy, the liturgical arts and the people who were responsible for their production were also deeply engaged in history-writing and in history-making, and that their activities influenced their work as composers of history, hagiography and music. More recently, this idea has come to the fore in the need to understand not only how history was written, but how it was made and performed.[3]

Our book is in sympathy with these attempts to redefine history as both a written phenomenon and a way of sounding, representing and reenacting the past. But we aim not only to examine the role of the liturgy in the making of history, but also to attend closely to the individuals who shaped history through their textual and musical compositions, and to the kinds of training and knowledge these compositions required. We have tried to define the medieval cantor as a history-maker, and, in doing so, we have found a richer and fuller understanding of this office (and related ones) than we initially imagined was possible. The cantor-historian that emerges from the pages of medieval customaries is an idealized official. But, as many of our contributors confirm, this ideal often was transformed (or abandoned) to fit the needs of particular communities, and, indeed, the different roles that the customaries describe could be performed by an individual cantor at different stages in his career. Many contributors, citing paleographical and codicological evidence, vividly demonstrate the kinds of books cantors copied, and how they copied them, and some are even able to hint at the quirks of a cantor's personality through the very corrections or annotations that he or she made. Others show that other monastic officers (often priors or sacristans), depending on their talents and their communities' needs, assumed some of the responsibilities envisioned for a cantor. And one suggests that the liturgy might not always have been the primary shaping force behind a cantor's history-writing – classical historical sources could be greater influences, at least at certain stages in the career, to speak to the interests and tastes of patrons and intended audiences. By allowing concrete case studies to complicate, broaden

---

[3] This change can be seen in many studies, but especially in the following: *Medieval Concepts of the Past: Ritual, Memory, Historiography*, ed. G. Althoff et al. (Cambridge, 2002); S. Boynton, *Shaping a Monastic Identity: Liturgy and History at the Imperial Abbey of Farfa, 1000–1125* (Ithaca, NY, 2006); *Representing History, 900–1300: Art, Music, History*, ed. R. A. Maxwell (University Park, PA, 2010); and *Contextualizing Miracles in the Christian West, 1100–1500: New Historical Approaches*, ed. M. M. Mesley and L. E. Wilson (Oxford, 2014).

and pluralize our initial idealized definitions of the medieval cantor, we have uncovered more nuanced portraits of monastic and cathedral history-makers. It is our hope that readers of this volume will come away impressed by this diversity and encouraged to search for other shapers of the medieval past.

PART I
The Carolingian Period

1

Historia: Some Lexicographical Considerations

David Ganz

Introduction to the term 'historia'

This chapter seeks a clearer understanding of what medieval historians said about the nature of history, especially in the period before 1200. The two essential studies of the meaning of history in the Middle Ages are the chapter by Gert Melville in the volume *Formen der Geschichtsschreibung* and Peter von Moos's prodigiously learned monograph, *Geschichte als Topik*[1] They both seem to me to have been largely ignored by English readers, but they offer unrivalled guidance about medieval ideas of the nature and function of history. Lastly, but by no means least, in English there is the recent book by Matthew Kempshall, *Rhetoric and the Writing of History, 400–1500*.[2]

The questions I shall address include: What is the purpose of history? What is its literary genre? How does human history relate to divine history? And lastly, what is the place of hagiography in history? Many of the chapters in this volume are concerned with views of the past and the shaping of the past in various kinds of writing, ranging from chronicles to saints' lives, and the roles that musically and liturgically trained authors played in these many understandings of the past. My work looks instead at the term 'historia' in a narrower sense, one rising out of classical antiquity – an understanding that I believe continued to be important in the Middle Ages, especially in the Carolingian period.

I begin with a quotation from Burckhardt, which defines my own position: 'While philosophers of history see the past as a contrast and a preliminary stage to our development, we look at what is constant and recurrent as something echoing in us and so comprehensible.'[3] The sense of historical

---

[1] G. Melville, 'Wozu Geschichtsschreibung? Stellung und Funktion der Historie im Mittelalter', in *Formen der Geschtsschreibung*, ed. R. Koselleck et al. (Munich, 1982), pp. 86–146; von Moos, *Geschichte als Topik: das rhetorische Exemplum von der Antike zur Neuzeit und die historiae im 'Policraticus' Johanns von Salisbury* (Hildesheim, 1988).

[2] M. S. Kempshall, *Rhetoric and the Writing of History, 400–1500* (Manchester, 2011).

[3] J. Burckhardt, *Über das Studium der Geschichte*, in *Jacob Burckhardt Werke: kritische Gesamtausgabe*, 28 vols. at present (Munich, 2000–), X, 356: 'Die Geschichts-philosophen betrachten das Vergangene als Gegensatz und Vorstufe zu uns als

constants, so ably explored by Burckhardt in his lectures on the study of history, is absent from most courses of study today, but it was a medieval commonplace. The ways in which God had treated earthly powers were always instructive, and they followed a pattern. Orosius, for example, writes, 'Multa convenienter inter Babylonam, urbem Assyrirorum tunc principem gentium, et Romam, acque nunc gentibus dominantem, conpacta conscipsi' ['I noted the many points of similarity between the Assyrian city of Babylon, which was the leading nation at the time, and Rome, which dominates the nations in a similar way today'].[4] Likewise, Hrabanus Maurus believed that kingdoms were transferred from one people to another because of injustice and wickedness, and this was, for him, the enduring lesson of the history of every nation.[5]

To preface the following sketch of a very complicated subject, it should be noted that history was never a formal discipline in classical or medieval education; indeed, as a literary genre history was always subordinate in the scheme of the liberal arts. Clio was considered one of the nine Muses who feature in Martianus Capella, but medieval commentators explained that she represented rhetoric. Philosophy put the Muses to flight. The earliest placing of Clio would seem to be Hugo of Mâcon's mid thirteenth century *Gesta militum*, and he merely dedicated a book of his work to each Muse.[6] In 1243 Richard of St Germano, a Monte Cassino notary, began his Chronicle by quoting the verse, 'Explicat ingenio res gestas ordine Clio' ['Clio sets events forth in an ingenious order']. Because history was never exactly defined, it risked a vague and contingent status. But, as Melville has shown, there were clear rules about different categories of history which all might be contrasted with other expressions of human experience. Human institutions and their development might be understood as a part of the order of times, and an understanding of the literal meaning of Scripture was the basis for any exploration of its spiritual meaning.[7]

Entwickleten. Wir betrachten das sich Wiederholende Constante, Typische, als ein in uns Anklingendes, und Verständliches.'

4 *Pauli Orosii Historiarum Adversum Paganos Libri VII* VII, 2, ed. K. F. W. Zangemeister (Leipzig, 1889), p. 235; for the English, see *Seven Books of History Against the Pagans*, trans. A. T. Fear (Liverpool, 2010), p. 320.

5 Cf. Hrabanus's gloss on Ecclesiasticus 10. 8, PL 109, 827: '*Regnum a gente in gentem transfertur, propter iniustitias, et iniurias, et contumelias, et diversos dolos. Huius sententie veritatem omnium pene gentium notant historie, et causas diversorum populorum ostendunt. Nec hoc ignorare potest, qui Chaldeorum et Persarum Grecorumque potentissima regna subversa legit, et Romanorum regnum vacillare conspicit, nec stabile aliquid in mundo esse perpendit.*'

6 See *De Gesta militum des Hugo von Mâcon: ein bisher unbekanntes Werk des Erzählliteratur des Hochmittelalters*, ed. E. Könsgen, 2 vols. (Leiden, 1990).

7 The most familiar statement of this last commonplace is found in the writings of Hugh of St Victor, admirably set out by B. Smalley, *The Study of the Bible in the Middle Ages*, 3rd rev. edn (Oxford, 1983), pp. 97–106.

To understand what the term 'historia' meant in the early Middle Ages, we may start with the excellent entry in the *Thesaurus linguae latinae* by Wolfgang Schmid.[8] He distinguishes between the knowledge of events through experience, knowledge of geography or natural history and types of knowledge of past events, which might be mythical or true (in which case one might speak of *historia vera, historie veritas*). History was distinguished from annals in that it was told by those who had been present. It might be reliable information about a person, it might be the title of a book and it might be the precepts learned from such works, *brevis et aperta et probabilis*. In a more abstract sense, the idea of tradition was central, but that might mean that it was different from what could be understood rationally. It was composed or woven using verbs more elaborate than merely 'to write'. But it could also be the story of someone's life.

With these general considerations in mind, the remainder of this chapter traces the use of 'historia' in a variety of Latin authors, for convenience divided into two major parts: first, writers in antiquity, beginning in pre-Christian Rome, and, second, writers in the early Middle Ages, up to *c.* 1200, though on occasion straying later. Throughout these many centuries, this particular strain of meaning for the term 'historia' remains remarkably consistent.

'Historia' in classical and late antiquity

In some ways medieval understandings of the term 'historia' were rooted in classical and late antiquity. History offers not only truthful information, but the lessons which the informed reader can reach. And the concern for clarity and brevity remind us that history was written for oral delivery as much as for the study. Cicero and Quintilian argued that history may present the greatest task for the orator in terms of fluency and variety of language. As forensic oratory came to play a less obvious part in civic life, 'history was the one branch of rhetoric that had lost none of its ancient opportunities'.[9]

The concern with clarity and brevity is often stressed by historians in their prefaces. Sallust in the *Catiline War* had commented on the diffculty of writing history because the style and diction must be equal to the deeds recorded.[10] Some medieval authors followed suit. Fredegar wanted to write

[8] *Thesaurus linguae latinae*, 11 vols. at present (Leipzig, 1900–), VI, cols. 2833–40.
[9] R. W. Southern, 'Aspects of the European Tradition of Historical Writing, I: The Classical Tradition from Einhard to Geoffrey of Monmouth', in *History and Historians, Selected Papers of R. W. Southern*, ed. R. J. Bartlett (Oxford, 2004), p. 18.
[10] Sallust, *Bellum Catilinae* III.2, ed. L. D. Reynolds (Oxford, 1991), pp. 6–7: 'Tamen in primis arduum videtur res gestas scribere; primum quod facta dictis exaequanda sunt; dehinc, quia plerique, quae delicta reprehenderis, malevolentia et invidia

in an appropriate style and as concise a manner as possible and hoped for eloquence.[11] Freculf wanted to be clear and concise in his compilation of whatever pertains to the truth of history.[12] Lupus in the preface to his *Vita Wigberti* alludes to the problem of style in historical narrative: 'historiam quae se obscurari colorum obliquitatibus rennuit' ['he disapproves of history which is obscured by the oblique effects of rhetorical colours']. Marius Victorinus, echoed by Hrabanus, explained that grammar was the science of explaining poets and historians. And Homer, Virgil and Lucan might be considered historians.

The kind of narrative based on the exposition of the facts presents three forms: legendary, historical and realistic. The legendary tale comprises events neither true nor probable, like those transmitted by tragedies.[13] Servius famously said that Lucan was a historian and not a poet, most probably because he excluded the gods from his epic,[14] and his verdict was repeated by Isidore (*Etymologies* VIII.vii.9) and in the Bern commentary on Lucan.[15]

The *Rhetorica ad Herrenium* contrasts the historical narrative, an account of exploits actually performed, but removed in time from the recollection of our age, and those realistic narratives recounting imaginary events, which nevertheless could have occurred, like the plots of comedies.[16] This view was adapted by Bede. Events always needed to be probable, and this seems to be Bede's chief concern when he referred to laws of history, as Cicero had done:

dicta putant; ubi de magna virtute atque gloria bonorum memores, quae sibi quisque facilia factu putat, aequo animo accipit, supra ea veluti ficta pro falsis ducit.'

[11] Fredegar, *Chronica*, MGH SRM II, 123: 'Cum aliquid unius verbi proprietate non habeo quod proferam nisi prestitum ab Altissimo. ... Vernaculum linguae huius verbi interpretatur, absorde resonat: si ob necessitate aliquid in ordine sermonum mutavero, ab interpretis videor officio recessisse.' This passage has been linked to Jerome's translation of Eusebius (*PL* 19, 313: 'Accedunt hyperbatorum anfractus, dissimilitudines casuum, varietates figurarum; ipsum postremo suum, et, ut ita dicam, vernaculum linguae genus'), but Jerome is talking about translation, while Fredegar is talking about his own language.

[12] Freculf, *Historiarum Libri XII*, ed. M. I. Allen CCCM 169A (Turnhout, 2002), p. 17.

[13] *Ad Herrenium* I.viii.13, ed. F. Marx (Leipzig, 1894), p. 195: 'Id quod in negotiorum expositione positum est tres habet partes: fabulam, historiam, argumentum. Fabula est quae neque veras neque veri similes continet res, ut eae quae tragoediis tradite sunt. Historia est gesta res, sed ab aetatis nostrae memoria remota.'

[14] *In Virgilii Carmina Commentarii, ad Aen.* I.382, ed. G. Thilo, 3 vols. (Leipzig, 1883–1902), I, 129: 'Lucanus namque ideo in numero poetarum esse non meruit, quia videtur historiam compuisse, non poema.'

[15] P. von Moos, 'Poeta und historicus im Mittelalter. Zum Mimesis-Problem am Beispiel einiger Utreile über Lucan', *Beitrage zur Geschichte der deutschen Sprache und Litteratur* 98 (1976), 93–130.

[16] *Ad Herrenium* I.viii.13, p. 195.

Lectoremque suppliciter obsecro, ut si qua in his que scripsimus aliter quam se veritas habet posita repererit, non hoc nobis imputet qui, quod vera lex historie est, simpliciter ea que fama vulgante collegimus ad instructionem posteritatis litteris mandare studuimus.[17]

[I humbly beg the reader, if he finds anything other than the truth set down in what I have written, not to impute it to me. For in accordance with a true law of history I have simply sought to commit to writing what I have collected from common report, for the instruction of posterity.]

Likewise, in his commentary on Luke, Bede claimed that 'opinionem vulgi exprimens, que vera historie lex est, patrem Ioseph nuncupat Christi' ['expressing the common belief, which is the true law of history, he [the Evangelist] called Joseph the father of Christ'].[18] Bede is here quoting Jerome, *Adversus Helvidium*,[19] and Bede himself would, in turn, be quoted by William of Malmesbury and Henry of Huntingdon.[20]

The contrast between theological truth and common perception was an issue for authors in late antiquity. For Jerome, *lex historie* is the legitimation of oral tradition. A truthful narrator may sometimes use vulgar opinion even if it is false, as when Joseph was called the father of Jesus. Evangelists spoke *veritatis historie* because of eyewitness information. Isidore rejected oral sources in favour of what was seen, a feature which Einhard later grasped and employed. Einhard claims that no one could write more truthfully than he had done, since he was present at the events which he described and as an eyewitness he is reliable: '**oculata** ut dicunt **fide**', with his reference 'as they say' indicating that he is quoting. The expression goes back to Cyprian, referring to Paul's ascent to heaven, when he saw Christ, 'qui **occulata fide** Ihesum Dominum vidisse se gloriatur' ['who boasts that he saw the Lord Jesus as an eyewitness'].[21] It is also found in Roman law: eyewitness accounts

---

[17] *HE* Pref., pp. 6–7. See further R. Ray, 'Bede's *Vera lex historiae*', *Speculum* 55 (1980), 1–21; W. Goffart, 'Bede's *Vera lex historae* Explained', *ASE* 34 (2005), 111–16; T. J. Furry, *Allegorizing History: The Venerable Bede, Figural Exegesis and Historical Theory* (Cambridge, 2013).

[18] *In Lucae Evangelium Expositio* I.2, ed. D. Hurst, CCSL 120 (Turnhout, 1960), p. 67; translation taken from Goffart, 'Bede's *Vera lex*', p. 112.

[19] Jerome, *Adversus Helvidium* IV, PL 23, 197.

[20] *GRA* V.445, p. 796–7; Henry of Huntingdon, *Historia Anglorum* IV.14, ed. D. Greenway (Oxford, 1996), p. 235.

[21] Cyprian, *Ad Fortunatum* 13, in *Cypriani Opera Omnia*, ed. G. Hartel, CSEL III.1 (Vienna, 1868), p. 346; and II Cor. 12. 1–10; cf. the miracles of St Stephen: *visibus vestris occulata fide* (PL 41, 837).

were superior to hearsay evidence,[22] and in the *Historia Tripartita*: 'et hoc **oculata fide** cognoscens'.[23]

An anonymous medieval commentary on Matthew, spuriously attributed to Bede in Cologne, Dombibliothek MS 16, makes clear the imporance of oral testimony. Herod is described in Matthew 14. 9 as very sorrowful (*contristatus*), and though the commentator thinks this was feigned, he explains that historians tell events as they seemed to the people who were present.[24]

History could be national: Augustine frequently talks of Roman history and of Christian history, and national histories were to have a long future.[25] Augustine's approach to historical events depended on his distinction between the literal and the spiritual truth of a particular event, and involved a necessarily unending struggle to be free from the effects of imperfect human understanding.[26] For Augustine, the deeds of God are also history, in line with St Paul's dictum that the history of Exodus is an allegory of the Christan people: 'All these things happened to them in figure, and they are written for our correction' (I Corinthians 10. 11). These ideas will be considered at greater length below, but it should be noted that history is not a Hebrew concept: the Old Testament talks of Chronicles but apparently there is no term corresponding to history.[27]

---

[22] Justinian, *Institutes*, III.vi.9, trans. P. Birks and G. McLeod (Ithaca, NY, 1987), pp. 98–9: 'Cum magis veritas **occulata fide** quam per aures animis hominum infigatur.' (Birks and McLeod include a facsimile reprint of Krueger's Latin edition.)

[23] *PL* 69, 894. For further discussion, suggesting that the expression goes back to what Isidore says about history in the *Etymologies*, see Kempshall, 'Some Ciceronian Models for Einhard's Life of Charlemagne', *Viator* 26 (1995), 11–37 (p. 17).

[24] *PL* 92, 71: 'Nequaquam enim Herodes pro huiusmodi petitione contristatus est; sed mos est historicorum ita res narrasse sicut tunc a presentibus facta fuisse videbantur: simulabat enim tristitiam in facie, cum letitiam haberet in mente.' The passage is quoted by the late Carolingian commentator known as 'Christian of Stavelot', see *Expositio super Librum generationis*, ed. R. B. C. Huygens, CCCM 224 (Turnhout, 2008), pp. 80, 283.

[25] H.-W. Goetz, '*Gens*: Terminology and Perception of the "Germanic" Peoples from Late Antquity to the Early Middle Ages', in *The Construction of Communities in the Early Middle Ages: Texts, Resources and Artefacts*, ed. R. Corradini et al. (Leiden, 2003), pp. 39–61; see too the essays collected in *Die Suche nach den Ursprüngen: von der Bedeutung des frühen Mittelalters*, ed. W. Pohl (Vienna, 2004).

[26] C. Ligota, 'La foi historienne, histoire et connaissance de l'histoire chez s. Augustin', *Revue des études augustiniennes* 43 (1997), 111–72.

[27] See the essays collected in *Das Alte Testament–ein Geschichtsbuch?*, ed. E. Blum et al. (Münster, 2005).

13

Medieval developments of 'historia'

As already suggested, medieval discussions of the disciplines had no separate place for history. Isidore of Seville treated history at the end of his book on grammar 'because it commits to letters whatever is worthy of memory'.[28] In his grammar, Alcuin defined twenty-six *genera*, including Letters, Syllables, Figures and Tropes, Prose and Verse, Fables and History.[29] But what is not a category of literature can be a category of bibliography. Alcuin's account of the authors at York included the *historici veteres* Pompeius Trogus and Pliny.[30] Carolingian librarians often regarded history as a separtate category, and the ninth-century Lorsch catalogue in Vatican Libary MS Pal. lat. 1877, fol. 3 lists the *Historia eccelesiastica Eusebii, Historia Iosephi, Historia Orosii, Chronica Eusebii, Hieronimi et Bede, Gesta Pontificum Romanorum, Gesta Francorum Gregorii Toronensis, Historia Iordanis, Pompeii Trogi Epitoma, Excidium Troie et Historia Daretis Frigii, Florus, Julius Hilarionis, Hieronimi, Idacii, Solini, Iosephi Libri antiquitatum*.[31] Likewise, the ninth-century Murbach catalogue has a section *de historiis*.[32]

To discover what history was, a medieval writer could turn to glossaries and encyclopedias. The *Liber glossarum* entries begin *Historia compositionis rei geste* and end *Historicus pantomimus qui historias scribit*, but they chiefly quote from Isidore's *Etymologies*.[33] Isidore distinguished between history, argument and fable and explained that history is the narrative of things which have happened, and through such narratives things done in the past are made known:

> Historia est narratio rei geste, per quam ea que in preterito facta sunt dignoscuntur. Dicta autem Grece *historia*, ἀπὸ τοῦ ἱστορεῖν, id est a *videre* vel *cognoscere*. Apud veteres enim nemo conscribebat historiam, nisi is qui interfuisset, et ea que conscribenda essent vidisset. Melius enim oculis que fiunt deprehendimus, quam que auditione colligimus.[34]

---

[28] *Etymologies* I.xli.1–2, ed. W. M. Lindsay, 2 vols. (Oxford, 1911). (Note that Lindsay's edition is unpaginated.)

[29] Alcuin, *De grammatica*, PL 101, 858. Cf. M. Sot and Y. Coz, 'Histoire de écriture de l'histoire dans l'œuvre d'Alcuin', in *Alcuin de York à Tours: écriture, pouvoir et réseaux dans l'Europe du haut Moyen Âge*, ed. P. Depreux and B. Judic (Rennes, 2004), pp. 175–91.

[30] Alcuin, *The Bishops, Saints and Kings of York*, ed. P. Godman (Oxford, 1982), p. 124.

[31] A. Häse, *Mittelalterliche Bücherverzeichnisse aus Kloster Lorsch: Einleitung, Edition und Kommentar* (Wiesbaden, 2002), p. 137, with commentary on pp. 189–94. In some cases several texts were collected in one manuscript volume.

[32] Wolfgang Milde, *Der Bibliothekskatalog des Klosters Murbach aus dem 9. Jahrhundert. Beihefte zum Euphorion* 4 (Heidelberg, 1968), p. 47.

[33] I have used the Lorsch copy, Vatican Library MS Pal. lat. 1773, fol. 147.

[34] *Etymologies* I.xli.1; trans. S. Barney et. al (Cambridge, 2006), p. 67. See further A. Borst, 'Das Bild der Geschichte in Enzyklopädie Isidors von Sevilla', *Deutsches*

[A history is a narration of deed accomplished; through it what occurred
in the past is sorted out. History is so called from the Greek term [meaning
'inquire', 'observe'], that is, from 'seeing' or from 'knowing'. Indeed, among
the ancients no one would write a history unless he had been present and
had seen what was to be written down, for we grasp with our eyes things
that occur better than what we gather with our hearing.]

Isidore explains what needs to be considered: person, action, time and
place – a supplement to theology. It was important that the events narrated
had actually happened, and the role of history was to narrate them:
monumenta quod memoriam tribuunt rerum gestarum.[35] The events are told
for the instruction of men of the present. Henry of Huntingdon was clear
about that function: making the past present again was a way to transmit
values.[36] The past served to teach how to judge the future, and it provided a
source of new understanding.[37] (More on this below.) 'Historia' transmitted
knowledge which would otherwise trickle away, in a process which Melville
calls *Entgegenwärtigung*, or making the past present.

Isidore might also have chosen to treat history as a branch of rhetoric,
and it is worth considering why he failed to do so. Ancient rhetorical theory
affirmed that the rhetoricians have not furnished it with rules, for its rules
are obvious. According to Cicero, 'Who does not know history's first law to
be that an author must not dare to tell anything but the truth? And its second
that he must make bold to tell the whole truth? ... The nature of the subject
needs chronological arrangement'.[38] We can find a more rhetorical account
than Isidore's preserved in a late eighth century Monte Cassino florilegium
containing over fifty texts dealing with metre, grammar and rhetoric, with a
progymnasmata sequence including works by Emporius and Priscian, clearly
designed to train pupils in various genres of prose composition.[39] This
includes a discussion of history which encapsulates the Roman rhetorical
traditon:

> Historia est rerum gestarum et dignarum memoria relatio: ea versatur aut in
> rebus bellicis aut in negotiis civilibus, id est pacis. Historici officii sunt tria:
> ut vera res, ut dilucide, ut breviter exponat. Vere res sunt, si rerum actarum
> vetustas et obcsuritas diligentur exploretur, si explorata libere, id est sine

Archiv für Erforschung des Mittelalters 22 (1966), 1–62.

[35] *Etymologies* I.xli.2.

[36] Melville, 'Wozu Geschichte schreiben?', pp. 96–7.

[37] Kempshall discusses the categories for judging the usefulness of past events and
the prominence given to understanding events of the past within deliberative
rhetoric: *Writing of History*, pp. 237–48.

[38] Cicero, *De Oratore* II.xv.62, trans. E. W. Sutton and E. Rackham (Cambridge, MA,
1942), pp. 243, 245.

[39] L. Holtz, 'Le Parisinus Latinus 7530, synthèse cassinienne des arts libéraux', *Studi
Medievali* 16 (1975), 97–152.

metu aut gratia aut invidia referatur. Lucida fit historia, si ut oportet res pro temporibus, pro locis, pro activis structura simplici et perfecta explanetur: brevis autem, si nihil vel supervacaneum vel leve interponatur, si singulis verbis sentventie exprimantur, si non longo circuitu elocutio terminetur. Est et illa virtus ut grata sit, quod fieri solet, si varietate si translationibus, si figures, si novis verbis, si cultu sententiarum, si concinnatiore structura concinnetur. Opus historie est, ut nos notitia rerum instruat, finis autem, id est to telos, ut ex ea sequendas aut fugiendas res cognoscamus aut ad usum eloquentie adiuvemur.[40]

[History is the account of events worthy of memory and it covers matters of war and civil affairs, that is peace. The duties of a historian are threefold, that he expounds true matters, that he writes clearly and that he writes briefly. Matters are true if the age and obscurity of events is carefully explored and what is discovered is reported freely, that is without fear or favour or envy. History is made clear if the matter is explained as it should be according to times, places and deeds. It is brief if nothing superfluous or light is inserted, if the opinions are expressed in the individual words and if the utterance does not end in a long periphrasis. Its virtue is that it should be pleasing. The task of history is that it instruct us by the knowledge of events, its end, or *telos*, is that from them we may know what is to be followed or avoided or that we be helped to the use of eloquence.]

Complementing this rhetorical tradition, discussions of 'historia' also proliferate in exegetical theory. In this context, history was the base of all understanding, as set out by 'Christian of Stavelot' in his commentary on Matthew:

Studui autem plus historicum sensum sequi quam spiritalem, quia irrationabile mihi videtur spiritalem intelligentiam in libro aliquo querere, et historicam penitus ignorare: cum historia fundamentum omnis intelligentie sit et ipsa primitus querenda et amplexanda, et sine ipsa perfecte ad aliam non possit transiri.[41]

[I have endeavoured to follow the historical sense more than the spiritual, for it seems to me irrational to seek after a spiritual understanding in any book while being thoroughly ignorant of the historical, since history is the foundation of every understanding, and is itself to be sought after

---

[40] C. Halm, *Rhetores Latini Minores* (Leipzig, 1863), p. 588; the translation also appears in my essay, 'The Astronomer's Life of Louis the Pious', in *Rome and Religion in the Medieval World: Studies in Honor of Thomas. F. X. Noble*, ed. V. L. Garver and O. M. Phelan (Farnham, 2014), pp. 129–48 (p. 134). The text is discussed by J.-P. Callu, 'Ecrire l'histoire à la fin de l'empire', in his *Culture profane et critique des sources de l'antiquité tardive* (Rome, 2006), pp. 7–23; see too M. Sehlmeyer, *Geschichtsbilder für Pagane und Christen: Res Romanae in den spätantiken Breviarien* (Berlin, 2009), pp. 17–24.

[41] *Expositio super Librum generationis*, pp. 52–3.

and embraced first, and without it one cannot perfectly go on to another understanding.]

According to one version of the familiar schema, history is when things done by God or man are recounted; allegory, when they are understood as being said figuratively; analogy, when the harmony of the old and the new covenants is being deomonstrated; etiology, when the causes of things are presented. Is the making of heaven and earth only historical?[42] No; it is also a science. We can see this in the Carolingian scheme of the divisions of philosophy into the practical and the investigative sciences which moved from the visible to the divine, with quotations from Scripture showing examples of each one. The investigative sciences are divided into history (simply exposition of doctine in which nothing is secret save that the words resound) and spiritual understanding, itself divided into the tropological, allegorical and anagogical.[43]

The role of the divine in establishing history is most clearly set out by Folcuin in his history of the monastery of Lobbes, composed between 965 and 990:

> Vis enim Deitatis omnipotentissima, cuique quod est, esse perfectum est, rerum formas per principales quasdam materias penes se semper perfectas habuit, sed quando voluit et ubi voluit nobis visibiles fecit … et ipse in tempora cuncta ordinaverit. Nam quando voluit, regna statuit, et quando voluit, mutavit.[44]

> [The omnipotent power of God, for whom what is is perfect, has the forms of things through certain principal materials which are for him always perfect, but when he wills and where he wills, he makes them visible to us … and he himself ordered all things in time. For when he wills he establishes kingdoms, and when he wills he changes them.]

Orosius explains that studious men wrote down the deeds of kings and peoples to preserve an eternal memory.[45] At the end of the Carolingian age, Regino said it seemed unworthy that since historians had transmitted

---

[42] Augustine, *De Genesi ad litteram* II.5, ed. J. Zycha, CSEL 28.1 (Vienna, 1894), pp. 38–9.

[43] B. Bischoff, 'Eine verschollene Einteilung der Wissenschaften' in his *Mittelalterliche Studien*, 3 vols. (Stuttgart, 1966–81), I, 273–88; see Valenciennes, Bibliothèque municipale MS 404, fols. 58r–59v; Munich, Bayerische Staatsbibliothek MS Clm 14456, fols. 68r–69r; and Bamberg, Staatsbibliothek MS Hist. nat. 1, fol. 44rv.

[44] MGH SS 4, pp. 54–5. Cf. G. Simon, 'Untersuchungen zur Topik der Widmungsbriefe mittelalterliche Geschichtschreiber bis zum Ende des 12 Jahrhunderts', *Archiv für Diplomatik* 4 (1958), 59–119 and 5/6 (1959–60), 73–153. For full translations, see J. Lake, *Prologues to Ancient and Medieval History: A Reader* (Toronto, 2013).

[45] *Historiarum Adversum Paganos* I.1, p. 5: 'Et quoniam omnes propemodum tam apud Grecos quam apud Latinos studiosi ad scribendum viri, qui res gestas regum populorumque ob diuturnam memoriam verbis propagaverunt.'

the events of Hebrews, Greeks, Romans and other peoples to our own age, his own age should be stuck in a perpetural silence, as if all human activity had ceased or nothing was worthy of memory.[46] Historical narrative offered coherence, the only remedy to the incoherence of events scattered through time.

The usefulness of history comprises an understanding of the sequence of events in time, and this was very important for the medieval use of the term, as taken over from antiquity. The historian does not compose that order but narrates it: it may involve human constructions, but what has happened is created and controlled by God. In the *City of God*, Augustine dismantled an idealized history of Rome: virtue and liberty were unmasked as greed for praise and a desire for domination. But there were clear hermeneutic problems in any understanding of history. As he writes in *On the Trinity*,

> In omnium istarum quas commemorauimus temporalium rerum scientia quaedam cognoscibilia cognitionem interpositione temporis antecedunt sicut sunt ea sensibilia quae iam erant in rebus antequam congnoscerentur uel ea omnia quae per historiam cognoscuntur; quaedam uero simul esse incipiunt uelut si aliquid uisibile quod omnino non erat ante nostros oculos oriatur, cognitionem nostram utique non precedit, aut si aliquid sonet ubi adest auditor, simul profecto incipiunt esse simulque desinunt et sonus et eius auditus. Verumtamen siue tempore precedentia siue simul esse incipientia cognoscibilia cognitionem gignunt, non cognitione gignuntur.[47]

> [In the knowledge of all these temporal things which we have mentioned, there are some knowable things which precede the acquisition of the knowledge of them by an interval of time, as in the case of those sensible objects which were already real before they were known, or of all those things that are learned through history; but some things begin to be at the same time with the knowing of them – just as, if any visible object, which did not exist before at all, were to rise up before our eyes, certainly it does not precede our knowing it; or if there be any sound made where there is some one to hear, no doubt the sound and the hearing that sound begin and end simultaneously. Yet nonetheless, whether preceding in time or beginning to exist simultaneously, knowable things generate knowledge, and are not generated by knowledge.]

[46] MGH SS 1, p. 543: 'Indignum etenim mihi visum est, ut, cum Hebreorum Grecorum et Romanorum aliarumque gentium historiographi res in diebus suis gestas scriptis usque ad nostram notiatiam transmiserint, de nostris quamquam longe inferioribus temporibus ita perpetuum silentium sit, ut quasi in diebus nostris aut hominum actio cessaverit aut fortassis nil dignum, quod memorie fuerit commendandum, egerint aut, si res digna memoratu gestae sunt, nullus ad hec litteris mandata idoneus invetus fuerit, notariis per incuriam otio torpentibus.'

[47] *De Trinitate* XIV.x.13, ed. W. J. Mountain, CCSL 50–50A (Turnhout, 1968), II, 440; trans. A. W. Haddan (Edinburgh, 1873), pp. 360–1.

Likewise, in *On Christian Doctrine*:

> Narratione autem historica cum preterita etiam hominum instituta narrantur, non inter humana instituta ipsa historia numeranda est, quia iam que transierunt nec infecta fieri possunt, in ordine temporum habenda sunt, quorum est conditor et administrator Deus.[48]

> [History itself is not to be reckoned among human institutions, because things that are past and gone and cannot be undone are to be reckoned as belonging to the course of time, of which God is the author and governor.]

In his letter *On Seeing God*, Augustine asserts that past events, most notably the Resurrection, can only be known by faith. Things seen by the mind need no bodily senses to let us know that they are true, but those seen through the body cannot become our knowledge without a mind to which these incoming messages can be referred.[49] Indeed, God's temporal arrangement by means of his changeable creation is designed to make the soul recall its origin and perfect nature.[50] Dispersal in time is counteracted by the temporal structure of the narrative.

Augustine insists that historical events could only be believed and never understood by men.[51] When he attempts to formulate how God might know history he draws on the analogy of singing:

> Certe si est tam grandi scientia et prescientia pollens animus, cui cuncta preterita et futura ita nota sint, sicut mihi unum canticum notissimum, nimium mirabilis est animus iste atque ad horrorem stupendus, quippe quem ita non lateat quidquid peractum et quidquid reliquum seculorum est, quem admodum me non latet cantantem illud canticum, quid et quantum eius abierit ab exordio, quid et quantum restet ad finem. Sed absit, ut tu, conditor universitatis, conditor animarum et corporum, absit, ut ita noveris omnia futura et preterita. Longe tu, longe mirabilius longeque secretius.[52]

> [Surely, if there be a mind, so greatly abounding in knowledge and foreknowledge, to which all things past and future are so known as one psalm is well known to me, that mind is exceedingly wonderful, and very astonishing; because whatever is so past, and whatever is to come of after ages, is no more concealed from him than was it hidden from me

---

[48] *De Doctrina Christiana* II.xxviii.44, ed. J. Martin, CCSL 32 (Turnhout, 1962), p. 63; trans. J. F. Shaw (Edinburgh, 1873), p. 63.

[49] *De videndo Deo* 38, in *Epistulae*, ed. A. Goldbacher, CSEL 44 (Vienna, 1904), pp. 312–13.

[50] *De vera religione* X.19, ed. K.-D. Dauer, CCSL 32 (Turnhout, 1962), pp. 199–200.

[51] *De diversis quaestionibus* XLVIII, ed. A. Mutzenbecher, CCSL 44A (Turnhout, 1975), p. 75: 'Alia sunt que semper creduntur et numquam intelleguntur, sicut est omnis historia temporalia et humana gesta percurrens.'

[52] *Confessiones* XI.xxxi.41, ed. L. Verheijen, CCSL 27 (Turnhout, 1981), p. 215; trans. J. G. Pilkington (Edinburgh, 1886), pp. 317–18.

when singing that psalm, what and how much of it had been sung from the beginning, what and how much remained unto the end. But far be it that thou, the Creator of the universe, the Creator of souls and bodies – far be it that thou shouldest know all things future and past. Far, far more wonderfully, and far more mysteriously, thou knowest them.]

This notion of some mysterious, divine understanding of historical events helps to explain the medieval penchant for reading history in a moralizing vein. History was regarded as a branch of Ethics according to William of Malmesbury:

Iam uero ethice partes medullitus rimatus, illius maiestati assurgo, quod per se studentibus pateat et animos ad bene vivendum componat; historiam precipue, que iocunda quadam gestorum notitia mores condiens, ad bona sequenda vel male cavenda legentis exemplis irritat.[53]

[As for ethics, I explored parts in depth, revering its high status as a subject inherently accessible to the student and able to form good character; in particular I studied history, which adds flavour to moral instruction by imparting a pleasurable knowledge of past events, spurring the reader by the accumulation of examples to follow the good and shun the bad.]

A similar account in Henry of Huntingdon is considerably more elaborate, a passage later taken up by John of Salisbury in his *Policraticus* VII.9:

Ubi autem floridius enitescit virorum fortium magnificentia, prudentium sapientia, iustorum iudicia, temperatorum modestia, quam in rerum contextu gestarum? Audivimus quidem Homericam laudans historiam Flaccus intimaverit, dicens: 'Qui quid sit pulchrum, quid turpe, quid utile, quid non, / Plenius et melius Crisippo et Cantore dicit' [*Epistles* I.2, 3–4]. Cantor siquidem et Crisippus, circa morum doctrinam philosophantes, multis codicibus desudarunt, Homerus autem velut speculo eliquans prudentiam Ulixis, fortitudinem Agamennonis, … honestum et utile, ad his contraria, lucidius et delectabilius philosophis historiando disseruit.[54]

[Where does the grandeur of valiant men shine more brightly, or the wisdom of the prudent, or the discretion of the righteous, or the moderation of the temperate, than in the context of history? Indeed, we have heard what Horace said, in praise of Homeric history, that it 'defines what is noble and what is infamous, what is proper and what is not, more fully and better than Chrysippus and Crantor'. Whereas Crantor and Chrysippus sweated to produce many volumes of moral philosophy, Homer showed, as clearly as in a mirror, the prudence of Ulysses, the fortitude of Agamemnon, … and in his narrative he discussed what is right and proper more clearly and agreeably than the philosophers.]

---

[53] *GRA* II.prol., pp. 150–1.
[54] *Historia Anglorum*, pp. 2–3.

The exemplum, according to Isidore (*Differentiae* 191) was made credible through history,[55] and von Moos has rightly challenged the view that only with the Renaissance are these exempla used to learn concrete modes of behaviour rather than to prove and convince. Indeed, medieval exempla are said to convey, elucidate and didactically strengthen a doctrine which is already known. To return to Augustine:

> Non modo querimus utrum sit factum, sed utrum fuerit faciendum. Sane quippe ratio etiam exemplis anteponenda est, cui quidem et exempla concordant, sed illa, que tanto digniora sunt imitatione quanto excellentiora pietate.[56]

> [We are not inquiring whether it has been done, but whether it ought to have been done. Sound judgment is to be preferred even to examples, and indeed examples harmonize with the voice of reason; but not all examples, but those only which are distinguished by their piety, and are proportionately worthy of imitation.]

Sound reason and morality must determine the choice of exempla.

The question of exemplarity leads us, finally, to the status of saints' lives. As Paul Lehmann noted, throughout the Middle Ages the term 'historia' could be used to refer to books of the Bible, saints' lives, versified offices and even schoolbooks such as the *Historia Scholastica*.[57] 'Historia' came to categorize those biblical passages which were used for responses, and for the liturgical groupings of responses themselves.[58] In a similar sense, 'historia' was frequently used for the lives of the saints – but there the word means 'story'. Thus Bede and Alcuin both describe their hagiographical writings as 'historia'.[59] Ardo, in his life of Benedict of Aniane, links the traditional practice of learning from histories and annals with his hagiographical

---

[55] *Differentiae* 191, *PL* 83, 1329: 'Exemplum historia est, similitudo approbatio.' Cf. von Moos, *Geschichte als Topik*, pp. 58–60.

[56] *De Civitate Dei* I.22, ed. B. Dombart and A. Kalb, CCSL 47 (Turnhout, 1955), p. 24; trans. (Edinburgh, 1871), I, 33. This passage was quoted by Gratian, *Decretum* IX.11.

[57] P. Lehmann, 'Mittelalterliche Büchertitel', in his *Erforschung des Mittelalters* (Stuttgart, 1959–62), V, 1–93. Cf. H.-W. Goetz, 'Die "Geschichte" im Wissenschaftssystem des Mittelalters', in F.-J. Schmale, *Funktion und Formen mittelalterlicher Geschichtsschreibung* (Darmstadt, 1985), pp. 165–213.

[58] For detailed discussion of the term as applied to liturgical sources (often traced back to Amalarius of Metz), see also Ritva Jonsson (Jacobsson), *Historia: Études sur la genèse des offices versifiés* (Stockholm, 1968), pp. 9–25.

[59] Bede, *Vita Felicis confessoris*, *PL* 94, 789: 'Felicissimum beati Felicis triumphum, quem in Nola Campanie civitate, Domino adiuvante, promeruit, Paulinus eiusdem civitatis episcopus versibus hexametris pulcherrime ac plenissime descripsit; qui quia metricis potius quam simplicibus sunt habiles lectoribus, placuit nobis ob plurimorum utilitatem, eamdem sancti confessoris **historiam** planioribus dilucidare sermonibus.' Alcuin, *Vita Willibrordi*, *PL* 101, 695: 'Hanc **historiam** sanctissimi patris et summi sacerdotis Willibrodi.'

enterprise.[60] Likewise, the *exempla sanctorum* were contrasted with Hector and Socrates by Sulpicius, since their exempla comfort us through grace and not heroics.

As von Moos concluded: 'In the great majority of cases, "historia" has the sense of an authorized "history", narrated and in a particular written form, and it can then blend into derived meanings like "history-book" and historiographical works.'[61] In the words of Beryl Smalley: 'The saint's life offered a tempting model of dateless history.'[62] But a longer narrative, even though it offered examples – and in Christian times examples shaped by grace – also showed God's purposes.[63] In this regard, if they are not always instances of 'historia' in the stricter sense traced above, the saints' lives discussed in the following chapters can share with 'historia' a complex commitment to rhetorical invention, exemplarity and, of course, the recording of *res gestae*.

---

[60] *Subsidia Anianensia:* Überlieferungs- und textgeschichtliche Untersuchungen zur Geschichte Witiza-Benedikts, seines Klosters Aniane und zur sogenannten 'anianischen Reform'; mit kommentierten Editionen der 'Vita Benedicti Anianensis', 'Notitia de servitio monasteriorum' des 'Chronicon Moissiacense/Anianense' sowie zweier Lokaltraditionen aus Aniane, ed. W. Kettemann (Duisburg, 2000), pp. 141–3: 'Esto occulendam esse decrernerit, veniam de meo posco errore: Sin vero utilem, qui libenter parverunt viventi, immitari satagant vitam absentis. Perantiquam siquidem fore consuetudinem, et actenus regibus usitatam, queque geruntur acciduntve annalibus tradi posteris cognoscenda, nemo, ut reor, ambigit doctus. Et quoniam mens diversis rebus partita oblivione cecatur, divinitus credimus esse consultum, ut que oblivio prolixa procurrente tempore poterat aboleri, litteris mandarentur servanda, quarum lectione iocundantur, hylarescunt totosque se ad gratiam inflectunt. Hi qui talia concupiscunt legere: nec ab his temerarius iudicatur, auctor scripture, etiam si contingat minus politis perstrepere verbis; ad quam avide cognoscendam desudant. Concedant igitur nobis et precedentium legere vitam, et posteris mandare que ipsis nostris temporibus vidimus, vel audivimus, ad augmentum animarum profutura: nec condemnemur de imperitis sermonibus, et rusticitatis vitium redolentes, quoniam ratum ducimus normam salutiferam licet rudibus depromere.'

[61] Von Moos, *Geschichte als Topik*, p. 150: 'Im weitaus den meisten Fällen hat *historia* den Sinn einer erzählten, insbesondere schriftlich fixierten, autorisierten "Geschichte" und kann darum mit der abgeleiteten Bedeutung des "geschichtenbuchs" oder des historiographischen Werks verschmelzen.'

[62] Smalley, *Study of the Bible*, p. 49.

[63] Kempshall brings this out in his discussion of Gregory's *Regula Pastoralis*. See *Writing of History*, pp. 409–10.

2

Liturgy and History in the Early Middle Ages

Rosamond McKitterick

The Frankish historians responsible for the *Annales regni francorum* charted Charlemagne's visits to particular saints' burial places to honour their cults. The regular record of where the king spent Easter and Christmas, and thus the framing of the ruler's movements within Christian time, is also a striking feature of the contemporary annalists' account of his reign.[1] They underscored the place of religious devotion in Charlemagne's conception of his role as ruler within his realm. Major political occasions and royal demonstrations of power, from Charlemagne's royal coronation on the feast of St Denis in 768 onwards, were orchestrated within an essentially liturgical framework. That reality underpins the narrative itself, for the celebration of Christmas and Easter provides the impetus for each successive year, recorded furthermore according to the year of the Incarnation. The Frankish representation of Charlemagne and his deeds is thus unconditionally Christian and accords significant prominence to liturgical observance.

So much is well known. Stating the obvious nevertheless prompts the questions of how and why both the Christian era and the liturgical celebration were established as possible and accepted features of an historical narrative, as instrumental in the representation of particular protagonists and their success, and as part of the literary structure of an historical text.[2] Other eighth-century narratives of the Franks, notably the *Liber historiae francorum* and the Continuations of the Chronicle of 'Fredegar', lack such liturgical emphasis. In the *Liber historiae francorum* at least, the liturgy played a decisive part in the narrative only twice. The account of the attack on Vienne when Bishop Mamertus was celebrating Mass and the royal palace was burnt relates that the bishop thereupon declared a three-day fast and the 'three-day litany' that the author claims is now 'practised everywhere'.[3] A reference to a three-day

[1] R. McKitterick, *Charlemagne: the Formation of a European Identity* (Cambridge, 2008), pp. 321–6.

[2] S. Foot, 'Finding the Meaning of Form: Narrative in Annals and Chronicles', in *Writing Medieval History*, ed. N. Partner (London, 2005), pp. 88–108; G. Declercq, *Anno Domini: Les origines de l'ère chrétienne* (Turnhout, 2000).

[3] *Liber historiae francorum* c. 16, ed. Bruno Krusch, MGH Scripotores rerum merovingicarum 2 (Hannover, 1888), p. 266.

period of prayers and fasting is included in the Chronicle of Fredegar as part of the story about the remarkable (in every respect) discovery by the bishops of Antioch, Jerusalem and Constantinople of the Lord's garment from the Passion, inserted as an event in the thirtieth reign of the Frankish king Guntramn, in the same year that war broke out between Franks and Bretons.[4] Certainly a three-day fast is also subsequently associated with the Avar campaigns in 791/3,[5] and the process which produced the *Ordinatio imperii* in 817, even if the narrative sources do not tell us this.[6]

The *Liber historiae francorum* also refers to Chlotild's proposal to her husband Clovis that they build a church in Paris dedicated to St Peter, prince of the apostles, so that he will help Clovis in his war against the Arian Goths. That same chapter records how Clovis's campaign against Alaric II, king of the Visigoths, brought him to Tours, and Clovis asked for a sign at the basilica of St Martin. When his messengers crossed the threshold was the moment when the *primicerius* was leading the antiphon from Psalm 18. 37–8 that was presumably part of the night office in the church that day: 'Precinxisti me Domine, virtutem ad bellum, subplantasti insurgentes in me subtus me et imimicorum meorum dedisti mihi dorsum et odientes me disperdedisti' ('You have girded me Lord with the strength in battle. You have subjected under me those who rose up against me. You have made my enemies turn their backs to me and you have destroyed those who hate me'). This was the message that was brought to Clovis and, by implication, helped him to secure his victory at Vouillé. Clovis subsequently gave gifts to the church of St Martin at Tours.[7]

Although the Paris church's dedication to St Peter is the *Liber historiae francorum*'s own contribution to the narrative about Clovis, the story about the pointed choice of antiphon is taken from Gregory of Tours's *Historiae* II.37.[8] The Psalm text at this point of the narrative acts as an affirmation of God's support, and effectively as prophecy.

Communicating the appreciation of God's special support for the Franks has long been recognized as a major element of the annalists' agenda,[9] and the use of biblical language is also a familiar and effective literary device

---

4 *The Fourth Book of the Chronicle of Fredegar and its Continuations*, ed. J. M. Wallace-Hadrill (London, 1960), c. 11, p. 9.

5 MGH Epp. IV, ed. E. Dümmler (Berlin, 1895), pp. 528–9. See D. Bachrach, *Religion and the Conduct of War, c. 300–c. 1215* (Woodbridge, 2003), pp. 34, 39.

6 *Ordinatio imperii*, ed. A. Boretius, MGH Cap. I (Hanover, 1883), no. 136, 270–1.

7 *Liber historiae francorum*, ed. B. Krusch, MGH SRM 2 (Hanover, 1888), c. 17, p. 268.

8 Gregory of Tours, *Historiarum libri decem*, ed. B. Krusch, MGH SRM 1 (Hanover, 1951), p. 86.

9 M. Garrison, 'The Franks as the New Israel? Education for an Identity from Pippin to Charlemagne', in *The Uses of the Past in the Early Middle Ages*, ed. Y. Hen and M. Innes (Cambridge, 2000), pp. 114–61.

by writers of history and political polemic.[10] The particular deployment of liturgical texts and the framing of the narrative to make the antiphon the climax of the story, however, suggest the conjoining of liturgical language and historical thinking on the part of both Gregory and the *Liber historiae francorum* author. This antiphon was more than an apt biblical phrase. It placed the anecdote of Clovis's subsequent victory over the Arians in a precise commemorative context of the weekly liturgical ritual not just of Tours, but of all the ecclesiastical communities that celebrated the Office of the church. Above all, it articulated the entire ideology of Clovis's campaign in liturgical language.

One source of narrative inspiration for both the deployment of the liturgy in this way and for liturgical information for Gregory of Tours was the *Liber pontificalis*. Gregory's knowledge of the *Liber pontificalis* is clearly affirmed by his inclusion of a summary *gesta* of the bishops of Tours in Book X of his *Historiae*.[11] The *Liber pontificalis*, moreover, arguably established not only the appropriateness of the topic of liturgy in an historical narrative but also its symbolic importance for the author of the *Liber historiae francorum* and the later Frankish annalists.

The transmission of the text of the *Liber pontificalis*, the history of the bishops of Rome from St Peter to the ninth century, is strikingly Frankish in its concentration.[12] Many of the earliest extant manuscripts were produced at the end of the eighth century and in the early ninth century in Francia. Distinctively Frankish redactions of the eighth-century lives in particular were created, probably after the Frankish conquest of Lombardy, and possibly in two stages. The first was in Rome itself by someone who might have been able to consult documents in the *vestiarium*, and the second stage was in Francia, possibly at the court.[13] Certainly a Frankish audience was envisaged, and knowledge of the text at the Carolingian court can also reasonably be supposed.[14]

---

[10] M. de Jong, 'Carolingian Political Discourse and the Biblical Past', in *The Resources of the Past in the Early Middle Ages*, ed. C. Gantner, R. McKitterick and S. Meeder (Cambridge, 2015), pp. 87–102.

[11] R. McKitterick, 'Rome and the Popes in the Construction of Institutional History and Identity in the Early Middle Ages: the Case of Leiden Universiteitsbibliotheek Scaliger MS 49', in *Rome and Religion in the Medieval World: Studies in Honor of Thomas F. X. Noble,* ed. O. Phelan and V. Garver (Aldershot, 2014), pp. 207–34; and M. Sot, 'Introduction. Auxerre et Rome: *Gesta pontificum* et *Liber pontificalis*', in Liber, Gesta, *Histoire*. Écrire l'Histoire des Évêques et des Papes, de l'Antiquité au XXIe siècle, ed. F. Bougard and M. Sot (Turnhout, 2009), pp. 5–20.

[12] F. Bougard, 'Composition, diffusion et réception des parties tardives du *Liber Pontificalis* romain (VIIIe–IXe siècles)', in Liber, Gesta, *Histoire*, pp. 127–52.

[13] Ibid., p. 138; and C. Gantner, 'The Lombard Recension of the *Liber Pontificalis*', *Rivista di storia del cristianesimo* 10 (2013), 65–114 (p. 71).

[14] M. Buchner, 'Zur Überlieferungsgeschichte des "Liber pontificalis" und zu seiner Verbreitung im Frankenreich im 9. Jahrhundert. Zugleich ein Beitrag zur Geschichte

The most crucial aspect of the *Liber pontificalis* in its later eighth-century biographies, however, is the integration of the Franks into Roman and papal history and the way in which Rome's past is made a relevant aspect of Frankish historical memory.[15] As I have suggested elsewhere, the Christian or Christianizing representations of Rome's past in the *Liber pontificalis* also became part of the Frankish memory of Rome in the eighth and the ninth centuries.[16] I have also linked that very particular memory with the liturgical readings incorporated into the lectionary that appears to have been compiled in Rome in the course of the late seventh century. The entire set of readings is orchestrated according to the stational liturgical readings of Rome, with the church specified. During Holy Week, for example, the Gospel for the day was read in sequence from Monday to Saturday at Santa Prassede, Santa Prisca, Sancta Maria,[17] the Lateran, Santa Croce in Gerusalemme, the Lateran, and Santa Maria Maggiore on Easter Sunday itself. The lectionary creates a virtual duplication of Rome within the framework of the liturgical readings. Liturgical time is mapped onto the sacred space of Rome and fused within the surviving copies of this lectionary, all of them extant from the Frankish realms and designed for performance within a Frankish church.[18]

The earliest and fullest example of such evocation of churches in detail is the Godescalc lectionary, produced by the scribe associated with Charlemagne's court and on commission from Charlemagne and his wife Hildegard to mark the baptism of their young son Pippin in Rome in 781.[19] Godescalc's elaboration of the many churches of Rome, so very much fuller than any other extant version of the church lectionary or *ordo* from the eighth century, suggests that one possible source for Godescalc was indeed the *Liber pontificalis* itself. The papal history may well have inspired Godescalc's imaginative extrapolation of the lectionary rubrics and deployment of the copious information about the special churches of Rome in that historical narrative to extend the sacred space in Francia in which these extracts from Scripture were read aloud.[20]

---

der karolingischen Hofbibliothek und Hofkapelle', *Römische Quartalschrift* 34 (1926), 141–26.

[15] R. McKitterick, 'Transformations of the Roman Past and Roman Identity in the Early Middle Ages', in *The Resources of the Past*, pp. 225–44.

[16] R. McKitterick, 'Charlemagne, Rome and the Management of Sacred Space', in *Charlemagne: les temps, les espaces, les hommes. Construction et deconstruction*, ed. R. Große (Turnhout, forthcoming).

[17] The church of St Mary is not further specified, though certainly in later sequences it is Santa Maria Maggiore as for Easter Sunday.

[18] McKitterick, 'Charlemagne, Rome'.

[19] L. Nees, 'Godescalc's Career and the Problems of Influence', in *Under the Influence: the Concept of Influence and the Study of Illuminated Manuscripts*, ed. J. Lowden and A. Bovey (Turnhout, 2007), pp. 21–43.

[20] C. Denoël, 'Die Perikopen', in *Das Godescalc-Evangelistar, Eine Prachthandschrift für Karl den Großen*, ed. F. Crivello, C. Denoël and P. Orth (Munich, 2011), pp. 98–125.

In this chapter therefore, with its possible function in mind as a model for a particular way of writing history, I should like to explore the degree to which the *Liber pontificalis* exploits the liturgy and music as a narrative strategy to highlight both actual and symbolic meaning in relation to papal representation. That empirical finding may then throw light on the wider issue of liturgy's place in medieval historical writing more generally, in terms of both the representation of time and the way liturgical memory might have enhanced historical imagination. Although the *Liber pontificalis* is so well known, it is worthwhile briefly highlighting those aspects of the text – its structure and composition – that are particularly germane to any enquiry about the way liturgy might have been used by the *Liber pontificalis*'s authors.

The *Liber pontificalis*, first composed in the sixth century and added to periodically from the seventh century until the later ninth century, presents a history of the popes in the form of serial biography in chronological sequence from St Peter (d. *c*. 64).[21] The text follows the model provided by the serial biographies of Roman emperors, namely, Suetonius' *Lives of the twelve caesars* and the brilliantly outrageous fourth-century concoction known as the *Historia augusta*, in order to substitute the Roman bishops historiographically for Roman emperors and to Christianize Roman history.[22] Like the imperial biographies, each life is formulaic in structure and content, with particular details offered, some more substantial than others, about the pope's origin and father, his election, events during his reign, his contributions to the religious life of Rome, political activities, endowments and building activity, death, burial and the number of ordinations he performed of bishops, priests and deacons. The Petrine chronology is an innovation as well as a political statement to reinforce not just the apostolic succession but also the primacy of the see of St Peter.[23]

---

[21] *Le* Liber pontificalis. *Texte, Introduction et Commentaire*, ed. L. Duchesne, 2 vols. (Paris, 1886–1892); 2nd edn + vol. 3 (Paris, 1955–57); *Liber pontificalis (Pars prior)*, ed. T. Mommsen, MGH SS Gesta pontificum romanorum I,1 (Berlin, 1898); H. Geertman, 'La Genesi del *Liber pontificalis* romano. Un Processo di Organizzazione della Memoria', in Liber, Gesta, *Histoire*, pp. 37–107; D. M. Deliyannis, 'The Roman *Liber pontificalis*, Papal Primacy, and the Acacian Schism', *Viator* 45 (2014), 1–16.

[22] R. McKitterick, 'Roman Texts and Roman History in the Early Middle Ages', in *Rome across Time and Space, c. 500–c. 1400: Cultural Translation and the Exchange of Ideas*, ed. C. Bolgia, R. McKitterick and J. Osborne (Cambridge, 2011), pp. 19–34. Some elements of this argument are also in R. McKitterick, 'La Place du *Liber pontificalis* dans les genres historiographiques du haut Moyen Âge', in Liber, Gesta, *Histoire*, pp. 23–35.

[23] M. Borgolte, *Petrusnachfolge und Kaiserimitation. Die Grablege der Päpste, ihre Genese und Traditionsbildung* (Göttingen, 1989); S. Scholz, *Politik- Selbstverständnis – Selbstdarstellung. Die Päpste in karolingischer und ottonischer Zeit* (Stuttgart, 2006), R. McKitterick, 'The Representation of Old St Peter's Basilica in the *Liber pontificalis*', in *Old St Peter's, Rome*, ed. R. McKitterick, J. Osborne, C. Richardson and J. Story (Cambridge, 2013), pp. 107–34; D. M. Deliyannis 'The Roman *Liber pontificalis*'.

Despite the multiple authorship and potential variety of perspectives on the history of the popes and Rome that were incorporated into the *Liber pontificalis* between the sixth and the ninth centuries, the text maintains a remarkable degree of thematic and narrative consistency. Unfortunately no agreement has been reached about the precise identity or official function of the authors. It is generally agreed that the authors were papal clerks of some kind. Some prefer to see the text as emerging from the notarial office of the *Primicerius notariorum* who made use of papal records in other offices, especially that of the *vestiarius*.[24] Others suggest that it was the *vestiarium* clerics themselves who composed the papal lives.[25] There is so much implied in the content of the lives about access to a comprehensive range of papal records, beyond the estate and church fabric records kept in the Registers in the *vestiarium*, that the papal writing office may indeed have been where the *Liber pontificalis* was compiled; there is no decisive evidence to help resolve this issue as yet. To account for the nature of the information in the text, some scholars have resorted to a degree of movement between the two offices by those responsible for its composition in a way that is difficult to envisage in practical terms.[26] The most revealing evidence, as Richard Pollard has demonstrated, is the deployment of the *cursus*, or prose rhythm in the writing style of the papal chancery, which indicates that whoever was writing the papal letters in the late sixth and the seventh century at least was not also responsible for the *Liber pontificalis*.[27] Taking up a suggestion made by Margot Fassler in the light of particular links between earlier medieval liturgical and literary and historiographical composition,[28] there is the possibility of a constructive association between those compiling the liturgical books with texts and *ordines* on behalf of the popes, the composers of chant, and the authors of the *Liber pontificalis*. This is perhaps reflected in the perspectives and occasional detail in the latter's text. Such a scenario is all the more plausible in the light of the apparently intense period of activity in the composition of liturgical texts in the later seventh and eighth centuries in Rome that can be surmised from the later

---

[24] L. Duchesne, *Étude sur le* Liber pontificalis, Bibliothèque des Écoles Françaises d'Athènes et de Rome 1 (Paris, 1877); T. F. X. Noble, 'A New Look at the *Liber Pontificalis*', *Archivum Historiae Pontificiae* 23 (1985), 347–58.

[25] H. Geertman, *More veterum. Il* 'Liber pontificalis' *e gli edifici ecclesiastici di Roma nella tarda antichità e nell'alto medioevo* (Groningen, 1975).

[26] F. Bougard, 'Composition, diffusion et réception'. See also C. Gantner, 'The Lombard Recension'.

[27] R. M. Pollard, 'The Decline of the *cursus* in the Papal Chancery and its Implications', *Studi Medievali* 50 (2009), 1–40; and R. M. Pollard, 'A Cooperative Correspondence: Papal Letters in the Age of Gregory the Great', in *A Companion to Gregory the Great*, ed. B. Neil and M. Dal Santo (Leiden, 2013), pp. 291–312.

[28] Fass A; Fass B.

manuscript evidence and the dissemination of liturgical books north of the Alps.[29]

The template provided by the first section of the *Liber pontificalis* was adopted by the subsequent authors, with an enhancement of established themes as well as new elements, not least the liturgy. The liturgical thread within the narrative plays a number of different roles. In the first place it anchors the liturgy within Rome as part of the new Christian identity of Rome itself. Some of the elements of the construction of that identity are equally pertinent for the deployment of the liturgy as a narrative and political strategy on the part of the authors.[30]

Certainly, too, the text of the *Liber pontificalis* constructs a history of the liturgy as a fundamental element of the narrative. In this respect the authors follow their imperial models. The secular imperial biographies had routinely presented the emperor's devotion to religious matters as central aspects of the imperial role. These contributions to the religious life of the city were reinterpreted within a Christian framework by the *Liber pontificalis* authors, but in historiographical terms the authors also incorporated a history of the liturgy as orchestrated by the pope himself. Whether or not any particular pope, especially those recorded in the pre mid sixth century section of the *Liber pontificalis*, can actually be credited with the innovations attributed to them is hardly the point. Too much credence may have been given hitherto to the chronology of liturgical development presented in the *Liber pontificalis*'s first sixty lives, but that is a topic not to be laboured here. The *Liber pontificalis* authors used the fact of papal innovation to enhance the popes' leadership in matters of Christian worship emanating from Rome, and thus the formative role of Rome and its bishop in the construction of the liturgy and liturgical observance overall. This manifests itself in contributions to the cycle of the liturgical year, to the structure and content of the Mass and accompanying

---

[29] See J. MacKinnon, *The Advent Project. The Later Seventh-Century Creation of the Roman Mass Proper* (Berkeley, 2000); the useful surveys in C. Vogel, *Medieval Liturgy: an Introduction to the Sources*, trans. and rev. W. G. Storey and N. K. Rasmussen (Washington D.C., 1986); and Y. Hen, *The Royal Patronage of Liturgy in Frankish Gaul to the Death of Charles the Bald (877)* (London, 2001). See also J. Dyer, 'Roman Processions of the Major Litany (*litaniae maiores*) from the Sixth to the Twelfth Century', in *Roma felix – Formation and Reflections of Medieval Rome*, ed. C. Neuman de Vegvar and É. Ó Carragáin (Aldershot, 2007), 113–38; and P. Jeffery, 'The Early Liturgy of Saint Peter's and the Roman Liturgical Year', in *Old Saint Peter's, Rome*, pp. 157–76.

[30] I have explored the question of Roman identity in relation to the liturgical evidence more fully elsewhere. See R. McKitterick, 'Romanness and Rome in the Early Middle Ages', in *Transformations of Romanness in the Early Middle Ages: Regions and Identities*, ed. W. Pohl, C. Gantner, C. Grifoni and M. Pollheimer (Berlin, forthcoming). Consequently there is some overlap between that chapter and this one and I have drawn on some sections of it in what follows.

prayers and readings, and specifications about the performance of the ritual documented in the *ordines*.

Some of the innovations noted in the *Liber pontificalis*, furthermore, concern the organization of the liturgy and clergy in Rome. Others have more general implications for liturgical observance in Britain, Frankish Gaul, Spain, Italy, Dalmatia and the German regions where papal authority was in the process of becoming established. A hint, too, of the understanding of the essentially commemorative function of the liturgy in relation to Christ's life and passion underlying all the texts and the creative purpose of their composition and assembly is the reference to the historical re-enactment of liturgical performance in the Life of Innocent I (401–17), who decreed a fast on Saturdays, since 'Hic constituit sabbatum ieiunium celebrari, quia sabbato Dominus in sepulchro positus est et discipuli ieiunaverunt' ('It was during a Saturday that the Lord had lain in the tomb and the disciples fasted').[31] Similarly Pope Silvester I (314–35) is said to have required the sacrifice on the altar to be on 'non in siricum neque in pannum tinctum, nisi tantum in lineum terrenum procreatum, sicut corpus domini nostri Iesu Christi in sindonem lineam mundam sepultus est' ('naturally produced linen [not silk or dyed cloth] just as the body of our Lord Jesus Christ was buried in a fine linen shroud').[32]

Examples of the construction of a history of the basic liturgy are the crediting to Pope Telesphorus (*c.* 125–*c.* 136) with the introduction of the Lenten period of fasting before Easter, the celebration of a night Mass on the Lord's birthday and the singing of the Gloria before the offering of the Eucharist in the Mass.[33] Pope Victor I (189–98) was said to be emulating Pope Eleutherius (*c.* 174–89) in saying Easter should be on a Sunday.[34] Pope Miltiades (311–14) forbade fasting on Thursdays and Sundays, 'quia eos dies pagani quasi sacrum ieiunium celebrabant' ('for those were days the pagans observed as a holy fast').[35] Pope Damasus I (366–84) decreed that 'psalmos die noctuque canarentur per omnes ecclesias; qui hoc precepit presbiteris vel episcopis aut monasteriis' ('in all the churches the psalms should be sung by day and night, a requirement he placed on priests, bishops and monasteries').[36] Pope Celestine I (422–32) is described as issuing a decree 'ut psalmi David CL ante sacrificium psalli antiphanatim ex omnibus, quod ante non fiebat, nisi tantum epistula beati Pauli recitabatur et sanctum evangelium' ('before the sacrifice

---

[31] Life 42, *LP*, I, 222; R. Davis, trans., *The Book of Pontiffs* (Liber Pontificalis). *The Ancient Biographies of the First Ninety Roman Bishops to AD 715*, 3rd edn (Liverpool, 2010), p. 32.

[32] Life 34, c. 7, *LP*, I, 171; *Book of Pontiffs*, p. 15.

[33] Life 9, *LP*, I, 129.

[34] Life 15, *LP*, I, 137.

[35] Life 33, *LP*, I, 168.

[36] Life 39, *LP*, I, 213; *Book of Pontiffs*, p. 29.

the 150 Psalms of David should be performed antiphonally by everyone, that this used not to be done, but only St Paul's Epistle and the holy Gospel were recited').[37] Leo I (440–61) introduced the prayer 'sacrum sacrificium' in the performance of the Mass; Pope Gelasius I (492–96) is credited with providing 'sacramentorum prefationes et orationes' ('prefaces and prayers for the sacraments'); and Pope Gregory I (590–604) added the prayer 'diesque nostros in tua pace dispone, et cetera' ('and dispose our days in thy peace etc.') to the recital of the canon.[38] Pope Simplicius (468–83) is praised for his provision for the liturgical observance in particular Roman churches, for 'hic constituit ad sanctum Petrum apostolum et ad sanctum Paulum apostolum et ad sanctum Laurentium martyrem ebdomadas ut prebyteri manerent, propter pentitentes et baptismum: regio III ad sanctum Laurentium, regio prima ad sanctum Paulum, regio VI vel septima ad sanctum Petrum' ('he fixed the weekly turns at St Peter's, St Paul's and St Lawrence's so that priests should remain there for penitents and for baptism – from region three at St Lawrence's, region one at St Paul's, regions four through seven at St Peter's).[39] According to the *Liber pontificalis*'s authors John III (561–74) took this further by insisting that 'oblationem et amula vel luminaria in easdem cymiteria per omnes dominicas de Lateranis ministraretur' ('every Sunday at the martyr's cemeteries the offering, the vessels, and the lighting should be serviced from the Lateran').[40] Symmachus (498–514) decreed the singing of the Gloria every Sunday and martyr's feast day.[41] The Feast of SS Peter and Paul on 29 June is attributed to Pope Cornelius (251–53),[42] and the specific provision for the liturgical commemoration of St Peter and his shrine in St Peter's basilica was augmented by Pope Gregory I.[43] Devotion to the Cross was enhanced in the aftermath of Sergius I's (687–701) finding of a fragment of the Cross in St Peter's basilica.[44] Pope Sergius also introduced the singing of the *Agnus Dei* into the Mass.[45] Leo IV (847–55) added to the growing

---

[37] Life 45, *LP*, I, 230; *Book of Pontiffs*, p. 33. See P. Jeffery, 'The Introduction of Psalmody into the Roman Mass by Pope Celestine I (422–432): Reinterpreting a Passage from the *Liber Pontificalis*', *Archiv für Liturgiewissenschaft* 26 (1984) 147–65.

[38] Lives 47, 51, 66, c. 3, *LP*, I, 239, 255, 312; *Book of Pontiffs*, pp. 37, 42, 60.

[39] Life 49, *LP*, I, 249; *Book of Pontiffs*, p. 40.

[40] Life 63, c. 1, *LP*, I, 305; *Book of Pontiffs*, p. 58.

[41] Life 53, *LP*, I, 263.

[42] Life 22, *LP*, 150; and R. McKitterick, 'The Representation of Old Saint Peter's Basilica'.

[43] Life 66, *LP*, I, 312; and Jeffery, 'The Early Liturgy of Saint Peter's'.

[44] Life 86, c. 10, *LP*, I, 374: 'die Exaltationis sancte crucis in basilica Salvatoris que appellatur Constantiniana osculatur ac adoratur'; *Book of Pontiffs*, p. 83. See É. Ó Carragáin, 'Interactions between Liturgy and Politics in Old Saint Peter's, 670–741. John the Archanctor, Sergius I and Gregory III', in *Old Saint Peter's, Rome*, pp. 177–89 (pp. 185–7).

[45] Life 86, c. 1, *LP*, I, 376; and J. F. Romano, *Liturgy and Society in Early Medieval Rome* (Farnham, 2014), pp. 71–3.

number of Marian commemorations in Rome by introducing the Octave day of the Assumption, 'que minime Roma antea' ('never before kept at Rome').[46]

The founding, endowment or embellishment of new oratories and churches in Rome is often noted in association with liturgical observance, sometimes explicitly to emulate the liturgical observance of St Peter's basilica. Gregory III (731–41), for example, established a monastic community at S. Crisogono so that they would perform 'Deo laudes in eundem titulum, diurnis atque nocturnis temporibus ordinatum, secundum instar officiorum ecclesie beati Petri apostoli' ('God's holy praises, as arranged for daytime and nighttime, just like the offices of St Peter's).[47] The development of the institutional structure and personnel of the Roman church is a further element of the *Liber pontificalis*, by the simple device of recording for each pope how many bishops, priests and deacons were ordained during their reigns, on what became in due course, the Ember days – three days, Wednesday, Friday and Saturday – after each Feast of St Lucy (13 December), Ash Wednesday, Pentecost and Holy Cross Day (14 September) in the liturgical year.[48] Similarly the *Liber pontificalis* documents the organization of the church within the city of Rome as well as more generally, such as the establishment of the *tituli* and the seven deacons of Rome attributed to Pope Evaristus (*c.* 100–*c.* 109), the organization of the seven regions with notaries by Pope Clement I (*c.* 91–*c.* 101) and the definition of the grades of the clerical hierarchy credited to Pope Gaius (283–96).[49] The process for the election of the pope is recorded from St Peter's designation of his successors Linus (*c.* 66–*c.* 78) and Anacletus (*c.* 79–*c.* 91) onwards, and the obligation imposed on the bishop of Ostia to consecrate the bishop of Rome.[50]

More general points are also made by the authors by means of the liturgy. Sergius I's addition of the *Agnus Dei* and litanies for the feast days of Mary – the Annunciation, Dormition and Nativity – serve to enhance papal and Roman leadership, and round off the narrative of Sergius's firm stance against doctrinal interference from Byzantium and the sequence of papal endowments within Rome.[51] The liturgical renewals of 'ancient ritual for the various grades of the clergy' by Stephen III (768–72),[52] and the innovations

---

[46] Life 105, c. 26, *LP*, II, 112.

[47] Life 92, c. 9, *LP*, I, 418; R. Davis, trans., *The Lives of the Eighth-Century Popes*, 2nd edn (Liverpool, 2007), p. 24.

[48] For details see McKitterick, 'Romanness and Rome'.

[49] Lives 6, 4, 29, *LP*, I, 126, 123, 164.

[50] Life 35, *LP*, I, 202, though the bishops of Porto and Albano joined the bishop of Ostia as the three bishops customarily designated as the consecrators of the new pope.

[51] Life 86, c. 14, *LP*, I, 376.

[52] Life 96, c. 27, *LP*, I, 478: 'Erat enim hisdem prefatus beatissimus presul ecclesie traditionis observator; unde et pristinum ecclesie in diversis clericatus honoribus renovavit ritum. Hic statuit ut omni dominico dei a septem episcopis cardinalibus

with respect to the establishment of litanies before Ascension Day by Leo III (795–816),[53] not only assist in the creation of the image of the pope at the heart, and as the fount, of the religious organization and ritual of the church, but also reinforce, by the placement of these references in the biographies of each pope, his political legitimacy. Thus in Stephen's case, his establishment of the *xenodochia* is part of the statement of his character at the beginning of his Life, and the claim to have restored ancient ritual with the provision for the seven 'cardinal bishops' to celebrate Mass and recite the Gloria in the Lateran comes after the long episodes concerning Pope Constantine II and the attempts to force the pope to consecrate the *scriniarius* Michael as archbishop of Ravenna.[54] In Leo III's case, the references to his endowments and liturgical practice are placed after his trial and reinstatement by Charlemagne's *missi*.

References to the liturgy in the *Liber pontificalis*, therefore, are significant in both their quantity and their function, and references to music no less so. Most are simply part of the liturgy, such as processions accompanied by 'cum ymnis et canticis spiritalibus' ('with hymns and spiritual chants'), and the chanting of the psalms. Paul I established a monastery for monks to chant in the Greek manner.[55] But the wish of Pope Hadrian I (772–95) that the community of SS Bartholomew and Andrew should celebrate the Office in two choirs was also designed for his own commemoration: 'quatenus piis laudibus naviterque psallente, hymniferis choris Deique letis resonent cantibus, reddentes Domino glorificos melos pro sepius memorati venerandi pontificis nomen, scilicet in secula memorialem eius pangentes carminibus' ('in this way they should diligently chant their psalms of pious praise, re-echoing with chants in hymn-singing and God-pleasing choirs, and render glorious melody to the Lord in this venerable pontiff's name, composing his memorial in song forever').[56] The scattering of references to singing as well as to liturgical prayer and procession, moreover, all suggest that liturgy and its performance were presented as a distinctive mark of papal virtue, at least from the late seventh century onwards. Every day, for example, Stephen V (885–91) is said to have celebrated the ceremonies of the Mass: 'Nocte et die orationi insistebat, et numquam psalmodiis cessabat nisi cum utilitatem populi ad se reclamantis perficere cupiebat, ut oppressos sublevaret et afflictis subveniret' ('night and day he devoted himself to prayer and he

---

ebdomadariis, qui in ecclesia Salvatoris observant, missarum solemnia super altare beati Petri celebraretur et "Gloria in excelsis Deo" ediceretur.'; *Eighth-Century Popes*, p. 102.

[53] Life 98, c. 43, *LP*, II, 12.

[54] R. McKitterick, 'The *damnatio memoriae* of Pope Constantine II (747–768)', in *Italy and Medieval Europe: Papers for Chris Wickham on the Occasion of his 65th Birthday*, ed. Ross Balzaretti, Julia Barrow and Patricia Skinner, Past and Present Supplementary Series (Oxford, 2016).

[55] Life 95, c. 5, *LP*, I, 465.

[56] Life 97, c. 68, *LP*, I, 506; *Eighth-Century Popes*, p. 157.

never ceased the chanting of the psalms except when he wanted to fulfil the need of the people that called to him in order to raise up the crushed and help the afflicted').[57] A few popes – Leo II (682–3), Benedict II (684–5), Sergius I, possibly Gregory III, Leo III, Paschal I (687) and Sergius II (844–7) – are distinguished for their skill as singers,[58] but the *scola cantorum* is mentioned only in the Lives of Sergius II and Stephen V.[59]

So far I have suggested that the *Liber pontificalis* maintains the theme of liturgical commemoration, innovation and organization as a major aspect of the pope's role. This in itself serves to reinforce both the continuities and contrasts in the early medieval conception of the papal successors to the imperial rulers of Rome. The pope's public display takes the form, at least within the narrative of the *Liber pontificalis*, primarily of religious observance and liturgical commemoration, not least the performance and processions of the stational liturgy.[60] But the punctuation of the text with particular forms of liturgical celebration also demonstrates the pope's responsibility for his people as an intercessor with God and the saints, and thus the liturgy's essential role as the formal and ritualized mode of communicating with God as well as with the Christian populace. In the violent and politically charged context in which Pelagius I (556–61) became pope after the death of Vigilius (537–55) his predecessor, recorded in the mid seventh century reconstruction of the previous century's events in the second section of the *Liber pontificalis*,[61] Pelagius and the Byzantine military general Narses made an attempt to appease the populace by liturgical means. No bishops had been willing to ordain Pelagius. His consecration was in the end performed by the bishops John of Perugia and Bonus of Ferentinum along with Andrew, 'a priest from Ostia'.[62] The litany and procession 'cum ymnis et canticis spiritalibus' ('with hymns and spiritual chants') to St Peter's was followed by 'Pelagius tenens evangelia et crucem Domini super caput suum' ('Pelagius holding the Gospels and the Lord's cross above his head'); he then 'in ambone ascendit, et sic satisfecit cuncto populo et plebi quia nullum malum peregisset contra Vigilium' ('went up to the ambo; in this way he satisfied the entire populace and *plebs* that he had caused Vigilius no

---

[57] Life 112, c. 8, *LP*, II, 192; R. Davis, trans., *The Lives of the Ninth-Century Popes* (Liverpool, 1995), p. 301.

[58] Lives 82, c. 1; 83, c. 1; 86, c. 1; 92, c. 1; 98, c. 1; 100, c. 1; 104, c. 2, *LP*, I, 359, 363, 371, 415; II, 1, 52, 86.

[59] Lives 104, c. 2; 112, c. 17, *LP*, II, 86, 195. See C. Page, *The Christian West and Its Singers. The First Thousand Years* (New Haven, 2010), pp. 243–60.

[60] J. F. Baldovin, *The Urban Character of Christian Worship; the Origins, Development, and Meaning of Stational Liturgy*, Orientalia Christiana Analecta 228 (Rome, 1987).

[61] Lives 62–72, *LP*, I, 303–24. R. McKitterick, 'The Papacy and Byzantium in the Seventh- and Early Eighth-Century Sections of the *Liber pontificalis*', *Papers of the British School at Rome* 84 (2016), 1–33.

[62] Life 62, c. 1, *LP*, I, 303; *Book of Pontiffs*, p. 57.

harm').[63] In the late seventh century the celebration of Mass in Santa Maria Maggiore was made the dramatic scene of the formal rejection of a doctrinally unacceptable 'synodic' letter from the patriarch of Constantinople. The people and clergy of Rome prevented Pope Eugenius I (654–57) from finishing the celebration of Mass until he had promised to reject it.[64] Even more overtly political was the ambivalent description, given the context, of the leave given to the papal legate Bishop John of Porto, in attendance at the council in Trullo (680), to celebrate Mass in Latin, before the emperor and patriarchs, on the Octave of Easter in the church of Santa Sophia in Constantinople. Praise, also in Latin, 'victoriis piisimorum imperatorum' ('for the victories of the pious emperors') (possibly a reference to the *laudes*) was offered by the congregation.[65]

Liturgical invocation against enemies, both natural and human, is also deployed in the *Liber pontificalis*. Daily litanies were inaugurated in the aftermath of the death of Pope Adeodatus II (672–76) 'to placate the Lord' and avert yet more dreadful weather that was destroying crops and preventing the threshing and storing of grain.[66] For the province's safety and that of all Christians, Pope Stephen II (752–57) decreed a litany should take place every Saturday.[67] Perhaps the most famous instance of a protective liturgy so that 'this city might stand firm and strong forever', however, is the blessing of the newly constructed Leonine city and walls encircling St Peter's basilica ordered by Pope Leo IV:

> ut omnes cum eo episcopi pariter ac sacerdotes, immo levite et universi ordines clericorum sancte catholice et apostolice Romane ecclesie, post letanias et psalterium decantatum, cum hymnis et canticis spiritalibus per totum murorum ambitum, nudis pedibus, cinerem portantes in capite, circuirent; et inter cetera episcopis cardinalibus aquam fieri benedictam precepit, ut inter orationum officia, aquam ipsam transeuntes per murum sanctificationes gratia iactare omnimodis studuisset. Qui ab eo iussum fuerat humiliter peregerunt. Ipse autem venerabilis pontifex ore suo tres super eundem murum orationes multis cum lacrimis ac suspiriis dedit, rogans ac petens ut sepedicta civitas et Christi conservaretur in evum auxilio et sanctorum omnium angelorumque presidio ab universo inimicorum secura et inperterrita perduraret incursu.[68]

---

[63] Life 62, c. 2, *LP*, I, 303; *Book of Pontiffs*, p. 58. On the consecration of a pope compare note 50 above.

[64] Life 77, c. 2, *LP*, I, 341.

[65] Life 81, c. 15, *LP*, I, 354: 'et omnes unanimiter in laudes et victoriis piisimorum imperatorum idem latine vocibus adclamarent.

[66] Life 79, c. 5, *LP*, I, 467.

[67] Life 94, c. 13, *LP*, I, 443.

[68] Life 105, cc. 72–3, *LP*, II, 124–5; *Ninth-Century Popes*, pp. 142–3.

[All the bishops, *sacerdotes*, deacons and all the orders of the clergy of the holy catholic and apostolic Roman church, should, after litanies and the chanting of the psalter, with hymns and spiritual chants, go with him round the whole circuit of the walls, barefoot and with ash on their heads. Among other things he enjoined that the cardinal bishops should bless water, so that during the offices of the prayers they might be zealous in casting that water in every direction to hallow the wall as they crossed it. They humbly fulfilled what he had ordered. The venerable pontiff himself pronounced three prayers over this wall, with much weeping and sighing, asking and beseeching that this city might both be preserved for ever by Christ's aid and endure safe and unshaken from every incursion of its enemies by the guardianship of all the saints and angels.]

The *Liber pontificalis* then included three newly composed papal prayers in the narrative, one to be said over the gate which looks towards St Peregrinus (one of the Frankish hotels), one over the postern which overlooks the Castle s. Angelo, and the third over the postern which looks towards the *Schola saxonum*. Initially presented as a reaction to a Saracen attack, the narrative uses the liturgy and the texts of the prayers to create a dramatic staging of the ritual and the prayers to emphasize the apostolic succession from St Peter and the pope's duty to preserve the holy apostolic and catholic church from enemies, as well as to proclaim the work Leo IV had carried out for the sake of God's protection of Rome and St Peter's.

This threefold blessing is then further reinforced by the singing of a Mass for the safety of the people (so-called from the opening words of the introit 'Salus populi') in the basilica. The fact that it was the day before the vigils of the apostles Peter and Paul was of further significance: 'And throughout the whole city of Rome there were celebrations of unbounded gladness and unmeasured rejoicing.' The author then called on all readers – for Leo IV was apparently still living when this section of the biography was written – to pray for the pope himself.[69] This liturgical exhortation is the climax of this biography, for the next section of the Life is devoted to an itemization of Leo IV's embellishments of, and gifts to, various churches in Rome, interspersed with a brief account of the Synod of 853 and the approval of forty-two canons pertaining to 'the salvation and gain of all Christian men'.[70] The narrative was clearly designed to reach an immediate audience and is a significant instance of the expectations of both writers and readers as far as the effectiveness of liturgical prayer is concerned.[71]

Even the popes' meetings with secular rulers are reinforced liturgically. Perhaps the most famous of these are, first of all, the account in the Life of Hadrian I, which notes how Charlemagne was welcomed with shouts of

---

[69] Life 105, c. 74, *LP*, II, 125.
[70] Life 105, cc. 90–1, *LP*, II, 129.
[71] See Davis, *Ninth-Century Popes*, p. 150, notes 131–3.

acclamation and praise 'laudem Deo et eius excellentie decantates universus clerus et cuncti religiosi Dei famuli, extensa voce adclamantes: "benedictus qui venit in nomine Domini"' ('and the whole clergy and all God's servants the monks chanted praise to God and his Excellency, loudly acclaiming: "Blessed is he who cometh in the name of the Lord"').[72] Similarly, the Life of Sergius II describes when Louis II was only a mile or so away from the city, 'universas militie scolas una cum patronis direxit, dignas nobilissimo regi laudes omnes canentes, aliosque militie edoctissmos Grecos, imperatorias laudes decantantes, cum dulcisionis earundem laudium vocibus, ipsum regem glorifice susceperunt' ('he sent all the *schole* of the militia, along with the *patroni*, all chanting praises worthy of the noble king, and with other most learned Greeks of the militia chanting the imperial praises with these sweet sounds of praise they gloriously welcomed the king').[73]

In conclusion, the extraordinary creativity in modes of representing the past in eighth- and ninth-century Francia and Italy has long been recognized, but the role of liturgy within historical narrative and understanding of the past in a way that goes beyond the record of incidents or even the use of liturgical or biblical language needs to be more fully acknowledged. At a basic level, Roman historians emerge in the *Liber pontificalis* as no less creative than their Frankish confrères north of the Alps, and it is no surprise to find them influencing each other, particularly from the second half of the eighth century onwards. Some Frankish historians, for their part, undoubtedly registered and demonstrated their absorption of the presentation of the liturgy and music in the *Liber pontificalis* and appreciation of its potential. Indeed, they augmented it, as the telling Frankish interpolations into the full texts and also preserved in various Frankish epitomes clearly reflect.[74] The association between liturgy and virtue, for example, appears to have been accepted by some at least among its readers and copyists. The singing of the Sanctus described as an innovation made by Pope Sixtus I (*c.* 116–*c.* 125) is a Frankish interpolation made in the late eighth century. Sixtus had allegedly decreed that within the performance of the Mass with the priest beginning it, the people should sing the hymn Holy Holy Holy Lord God of Sabaoth.[75]

This dynamic connection between liturgy and history was an important legacy for writers of history in eleventh- and twelfth-century Europe. I offer two instructive examples here – one from the beginning and one from the end of the *Liber pontificalis* in an eleventh-century epitome of the *Liber pontificalis*

---

[72] Life 97, c. 38, *LP*, I, 497; *Eighth-Century Popes*, p. 139.

[73] Life 104, c. 9, *LP*, II, 88; *Ninth-Century Popes*, p. 78.

[74] C. Gantner, 'The Lombard Recension'; and R. McKitterick, 'Perceptions of Rome and the Papacy in Late Merovingian Francia: the Cononian Recension of the *Liber pontificalis*', in *East and West in the Early Middle Ages: the Merovingian Kingdoms in Mediterranean Perspective*, ed. S. Esders and Y. Hen (Berlin, forthcoming).

[75] Life 8, *LP*, I, 128; *Book of the Pontiffs*, p. 35.

attributed to Adémar of Chabannes of the *Liber pontificalis* in Paris BnF lat. 2400. There a claim is added to the Life of Peter that Peter had been the 'primus missam constituit celebrare in commemoratione passionis domini in pane et vino aqua mixto cum sola oratione dominica et sanctificatione sancte crucis quam ceteri sancti apostoli imitati sunt in hac celebratione' ('first to lay down that the Mass be celebrated to commemorate the Lord's passion in bread and wine mixed with water, using only the Lord's prayer and hallowing with the holy cross; this the other holy apostles copied when celebrating it').[76] The epitome of the *Liber pontificalis* (fols. 138–51) is part of a composite manuscript.[77] The whole codex exemplifies the integration of liturgical practice and history. Besides the special redaction of the *Liber pontificalis*, it includes a version of Amalarius of Metz's *Liber de divinis officiis*, canons from a number of different canon law collections, and texts on heresies, bishops, the burial places of the patriarchs, apostles and fathers, a Carolingian version of Bede's *De sex etatibus mundi* and extracts from the *Annales Engolismenses*.[78] The *Liber pontificalis* epitome also includes a long account of the liturgical work of Hadrian II (867–72), extant only in this manuscript. The papal official responsible for the original life had provided a full account of the singing and chanting that had taken place on the Friday of Septuagesima and how Hadrian had invited the Greek monks and others attending the (possibly special) service to take refreshment. He not only served his guests with his own hands but made a break with tradition by reclining with them and 'cum illis Deum in hymnis et canticis spiritalibus ibi per totum spatietem iugiter concrepantium laudans' ('joining with them in praising God with hymns and spiritual chants [going through] the whole vast company of them there as they kept up a constant chorus [of praise]').[79] In the original life this dramatic display of humility is set within the context of Hadrian's succession to Pope Nicholas and the opposition to Photius of Constantinople.

It appears to have been Adémar himself who added a detailed account of the Gregorian antiphoner. The full text is provided in Duchesne's edition and Davis translated it as follows.[80]

---

[76] Life 1, *Liber pontificalis*, ed. T. Mommsen, p. 4.

[77] *LP*, I, clxxxii–clxxxiv.

[78] R. Landes, *Relics, Apocalypse, and the Deceits of History. Adémar of Chabannes, 989–1034* (Cambridge MA, 1995), pp. 362–5.

[79] Life 108, cc. 16, 19, *LP*, II, 176.

[80] *LP*, I, clxxxii. This story was also included by Adémar of Chabannes in his Chronicle; see *Ademari Cabannensis Chronicon*, ed. P. Bourgain (Turnhout, 1999), p. 89; and *Adémar de Chabannes, Chronique*, trans. Y. Chauvin and G. Pon (Turnhout, 2003), pp. 147–9. See also A. Haug, 'Noch einmal: Roms Gesang und die Gemeinschaften im Norden', in *Nationes, Gentes und die Musik im Mittelalter*, ed. F. Hentschel and M. Winkelmüller (Berlin, 2014), pp. 103–46. Adémar's contributions to the history of music are discussed further in Chapter 5 in this volume.

Like the earlier Hadrian he confirmed the Gregorian antiphoner in many places and he laid down that a second prologue in hexameter verses was to be sung at the high Mass on the first day of our Lord's Advent; this begins like the proemium of the earlier Hadrian, which he had composed very carefully for all Masses on the same first Sunday of the Lord's Advent, but it consists of more verses. He laid down that in the monasteries at high Mass on special solemnities not only were those interpolated hymns that they call 'praises' be sung in the angelic hymn 'Glory be to God on high', but also in the psalms of David that they call 'introits' there were to be sung the inserted chants which Romans call 'festival praises' and Franks call 'tropes', which means figured adornments in praise of God. He also handed down the melodies for singing before the Gospel, those which they call 'sequences' because the Gospel 'follows' them. And because these festival chants had been established and composed by lord pope Gregory I and afterwards by Hadrian together with Abbot Alcuin the favourite of Emperor Charles the Great (and this Caesar Charles took great delight in them), but they were now being omitted by the neglect of the singers, they were so confirmed to our Lord Jesus Christ's praise and glory by this bounteous prelate of whom we speak, that through the care of scholars the troper also should thenceforth be kept in use alongside the antiphoner for honourable chants on solemn days at high Mass. He laid down that Roman clerics should instruct our brethren the poor of our Lord Jesus Christ that for three days before Holy Easter Sunday, that is, on the day of the Lord's Supper, the day of Preparation, and the day of the Lord's being in the tomb, they should beg alms in this city of Rome in no other way than by singing this chant loudly in the streets and in front of monasteries and churches: 'Kyrie eleison, Christe eleison, Lord have pity on us, Christ the Lord became obedient unto death'. He performed two ordinations in December and March, eight priests, five deacons; for various places sixty bishops.[81]

Davis notes that these ordination statistics are recorded nowhere else, but what they do indicate is Adémar's own reproduction of what he felt to be the most important themes of the *Liber pontificalis*. Like the Mainz/Fulda epitomizer of the *Liber pontificalis* whose work is extant in Leiden Universiteitsbibliothek Scaliger 49, Adémar also registered the importance of the liturgical innovation that was so integral a part of the pope's history, the emphasis on succession and continuation of the church by the simple means of ordination of priests to perform the ministry, and above all the intertwining of liturgy and history in the perception of the past in the early Middle Ages.[82]

The authors of the *Liber pontificalis* clearly understood liturgy as an essential component of the history of Rome and the popes. I have suggested that with its particular representation of the past, the *Liber pontificalis* provided a historiographical as well as an actual model for liturgy's place in

---

[81] *Ninth-Century Popes*, pp. 293–4.
[82] McKitterick, 'Rome and the Popes'.

history. The pope's liturgical functions were a specific means of defining and symbolizing his leadership of the church. As I have commented elsewhere, moreover, 'liturgy in the *Liber pontificalis* increasingly served as an historical anchor as well as an essential reminder and memory of the continuity of the papal institutions and the Petrine succession in the *Liber pontificalis*, especially in the eighth- and ninth-century sections. In this sense the pope in the *Liber pontificalis*'s historical representation is at the junction of cyclical liturgical time, which he himself orchestrates, and of linear historical time, in which he is an active player'.[83] The *Liber pontificalis* played a crucial role in establishing the Christian era and liturgical celebration as both possible and accepted features of a historical narrative.

Yet the literary deployment of descriptions of liturgical ritual and the inclusion of liturgical prayers to chart major political positions and notable phases in the narrative structure overall, to reinforce the actions of particular protagonists, and to account for their success all suggest that the liturgy was indeed one of the formative strands of early medieval historiography. Authors wanted to make sure that their readers understood their place in contemporary Christian history as well as within a more comprehensive past. Drawing on a liturgy that was a central and familiar element of their own religious devotion was a vital and evocative means of connecting past and present.

---

[83] McKitterick, 'Romanness and Rome'.

3

Notker Bibliothecarius

Susan Rankin

DE PASSIONIBUS SANCTORUM

Preter ea debes agones et uictorias sanctorum martyrum diligentissime perquirere, ut eorum exemplo non tantum inlecebras mundi respuere, sed et animam pro Christo ponere et cruciatus corporis pro nihilo ducere dei gratia et sancti spiritus inhabitatione consuescas; primumque precipuorum apostolorum Petri et Pauli, Andreae et Iacobi fratris Iohannis, sed et Iacobi fratris domini … Post apostolos sequitur passio uel hystoria de sancto Clemente. Dehinc mirabilis de sancto Alexandro, Euentio, Theodolo, Hermete et Quirino et ceteris …[1]

[ON THE PASSIONS OF THE SAINTS

In addition you should most assiduously go through the struggles and the victories of the holy martyrs, that, by their example, you should not only spurn the delights of the world but you should place your soul for Christ and grow accustomed to think nothing of the troubles of your body except for the indwelling of the grace of God and the Holy Spirit. Firstly the chief apostles Peter and Paul and Andrew and James the brother of John and James the brother of the Lord … After the apostles follows the passion of St Clement and then wonders about St Alexander, Eventius, Theodolus, Hermes and Quirinus and the rest …]

This is but the tenth part of a substantial account of literature about the passions of the saints of the Christian Church, set out in chronological order and with explanations of the contributions of individual writers – including Eusebius, Jerome and Cassiodorus – to this body of texts. The letter of which it forms a part begins with the admonition 'miror te res ineptas appetere' ('I am amazed that you are looking at unsuitable things'), continuing 'si me audisses, omnes auctores nostros notissimos haberes' ('had you listened to me, you would have known all of our authors very well').[2]

---

[1] E. Rauner, 'Notkers des Stammlers "Notatio de illustribus uiris". Teil I: Kritische Edition', *Mittellateinisches Jahrbuch* 21 (1986), 34–69 (pp. 67–8). On the *Notatio* see also B. Kaczynski, 'Reading the Church Fathers: Notker the Stammerer's *Notatio de illustribus viris*', *Journal of Medieval Latin* 17 (2007), 401–12.

[2] Rauner, 'Notker des Stammlers', p. 58. This translation from Kaczynski, 'Reading the Church Fathers', p. 409.

The text is threaded through with commentary, often very personal observations, with the comments on authors and works cited described by Kaczynski as 'specific and rich in detail'.[3] The passage dealing with the passions of saints is shaped as a historical presentation of Christianity, and the place of individual figures within it:

> Occidens etiam ipse licet sero, tandem tamen aliquando in germen erupit: Martinum Pannoniis ortum et non solum Italiam uel Germaniam seu Gallias sua presentia inluminantem, sed etiam omnes orientales ipsis testibus claritate luminis superantem.[4]

> [But in the west, though it was late, at last at some time, the seed burst forth: Martin, born in Pannonia, and illuminating not only Italy and Germany or Gaul by his presence, but also conquering all the easterns, according to their testimony, by his clarity of light.]

Begun with the apostles, the passage about saints and martyrs is drawn to a close with a series of names presented in plural form and chosen to cover many parts of Europe – rendering the list all-inclusive.

> Comgellos, ..., Columbas, Columbanos, Gallos, Gregorium V. nomen Chrisostomi Grecis auferentem, Benedictos, Honoratos, Libertinos, Otmaros nostrum et Belgicum.[5]

> [the Comgalls, ..., Columbas, Columbanuses, Gauls, Gregory or the name of Chrysostom brought over from the Greeks ... Benedicts, Honoratuses, Libertines, Otmars – ours and the Belgian one.]

If it were not otherwise known, this closing list would have identified the institution where this Christian literary schedule was composed. Including St Comgall, the Irish founder of the abbey of Bangor, from where St Gall had set out on missionary activity, then Columbanus, Gall's master, as well as the older St Columba, and ending with 'our Otmar', first abbot of the abbey of Sankt Gallen, the letter was self-evidently written at that abbey. Composed by Notker Balbulus, it was addressed to his pupil Salomo at some time in the 880s.[6] The passage on passions of the saints invites us to reflect not only on Notker's own awareness of and attitude toward such literature, but also on the wider campaign of study and compilation of the deeds of the saints at Sankt Gallen.

---

[3] Kaczynski, 'Reading the Church Fathers', p. 410.

[4] Rauner, 'Notker des Stammlers', pp. 68–9.

[5] Ibid.

[6] The earliest manuscript source of the letter is Vienna, Österreichische Nationalbibliothek, MS lat. 1609, copied at Freising in the early tenth century, probably directly from a St Gallen exemplar: see N. Daniel, *Handschriften des zehnten Jahrhunderts aus der Freisinger Dombibliothek* (Munich, 1973), pp. 70–2.

Notker Balbulus of Sankt Gallen

We are used to thinking of Notker as a composer of sequences, extremely artful in their craft;[7] as the writer of an account of the Deeds of Charlemagne;[8] and as the author of a life of St Gall in verse.[9] There are many other bits and pieces composed by him: hymns to Stephen, copied by Notker himself in SG 242 (pp. 3–9);[10] some tropes in verse;[11] a collection of letter and charter models;[12] and several charters.[13] Edited mainly in the *Monumenta Germaniae Historica* that is, apart from Wolfram von den Steinen's *Notker der Dichter* these texts have led us to imagine that Notker is largely mastered: we know him, because we have read his words. But there are two serious gaps in our knowledge of Notker as a learned and creative figure. For the sequences, astonishingly, no modern edition with music has yet been published. Happily this lacuna will shortly disappear.[14]

[7] The texts (but not the melodies) are edited in W. den Steinen, *Notker der Dichter*, 2 vols. (Bern, 1948).

[8] *Notker der Stammler. Taten Kaiser Karls des Grossen*, ed. H. F. Haefele, MGH Scriptores n.s. 12 (Berlin, 1959); *Two Lives of Charlemagne: Einhard and Notker the Stammerer*, trans. D. Ganz (London, 2008).

[9] W. Berschin, 'Notkers Metrum de vita S. Galli. Einleitung und Edition', in *Florilegium Sangallense: Festschrift für Johannes Duft zum 65. Geburtstag*, ed. O. P. Clavadetscher et al. (Sigmaringen, 1980), pp. 71–121.

[10] *Poetae Latini aevi carolini*, ed. P. Winterfeld, MGH Antiquitates 4.1 (Berlin, 1864), pp. 337–9. Manuscripts in the Stiftsbibliothek at Sankt Gallen will be cited as SG followed by a number; all may be seen in digital facsimile on the e-codices website, unless otherwise noted.

[11] These are preserved on pages set before the *Notatio* in Vienna 1609 (fols. 4r–8v): see S. Rankin, 'Notker und Tuotilo: Schöpferische Gestalter in einer neuen Zeit', *Schweizer Jahrbuch für Musikwissenschaft* n.s. 11 (1991), 17–42.

[12] *Das Formelbuch des Bischofs Salomo III von Konstanz aus dem 9. Jahrhundert*, ed. E. Dümmler (Leipzig, 1857); see also Rauner, 'Notker des Stammlers'; A. Rio, *Legal Practice and the Written Word in the Early Middle Ages. Frankish Formulae, c. 500–1000* (Cambridge, 2009), 152–60; and P. Erhart, 'Notker Balbulus, Othere und Adalbert der Erlauchte in Oberwinterthur', in *Schaukasten Stiftsbibliothek St. Gallen. Abschiedsgabe für Stiftsbibliothekar Ernst Tremp*, ed. F. Schnoor et al. (St Gallen, 2013), pp. 104–13.

[13] On the identification of charters copied by Notker himself, see Susan Rankin, 'Ego itaque Notker scripsi', *RB* 101 (1991), 268–98, proposing four individual examples; for a list of charters of which the text was composed by a 'Notker' or 'Notger', with notice of two further charters copied by Notker, see Erhart, 'Notker Balbulus', Appendix 2. Reproductions of the charters are now published in the series *Chartae Latinae Antiquiores: Facsimile Edition of the Latin Charters, 2nd series, Switzerland, Sankt Gallen*: see especially vols. 106–7, Switzerland IX–X, Sankt Gallen VII–VIII, ed. P. Erhart et al. (Dietikon-Zurich, 2013–14). On the total œuvre of Notker see W. Berschin, 'Notker I. von St. Gallen (d. 912) überlieferungsgeschichtlich gesehen', in *Mittellateinische Studien* (Heidelberg, 2005), pp. 193–202.

[14] C. Bower, *Notker Balbulus* Liber Ymnorum, forthcoming as HBS 121–2 (Woodbridge, 2016).

The other unnecessary gap in our understanding is cognizance of his intellectual formation – what books were available to him and how he used them – gathered from extant materials. Such information about any creative figure is desirable, but more often than not elusive. Yet for Notker Balbulus, awareness of the texts he knew well and cared about need not be vague, since there is a wealth of information about it still surviving in material form.[15] Identified in a charter of 890 as 'Notker bibliothecarius',[16] Notker also wrote of himself as 'having accumulated much' for the library of St Gallen, 'by the grace of God'.[17] The traces of Notker's activity as scribe and as organizer of other scribes are omnipresent in the surviving books of the abbey. As a young man, he was often set to copy texts; later – whether or not named as librarian – he had extensive responsibility for the abbey's books; in this role, he can be seen renewing deteriorated materials, procuring texts not present in the library, compiling volumes necessary for the daily life of the community, organizing teams of scribes to copy, providing paratextual resources to explain the contents of those volumes, and generally caring for this enormously important resource on which his monastic community depended.

In the context of the discussion of cantors, and of the variety of activities undertaken by such office-holders – including, besides liturgical organization and composition, the writing of history – the nature and spread of the enterprises at the centre of which Notker sat is extremely interesting. It is doubtful that he had responsibility for liturgical organization at any stage of his life, and I have not seen evidence of his involvement with the copying of books of chant for the liturgy;[18] yet his participation in the copying of homiliaries – and his potential contribution to their structuring and adaptation for St Gallen – cannot be underestimated. There is no evidence that Notker held the office of cantor, yet he was much more than a competent musician, as becomes clear through study of the *Liber ymnorum*.[19] He was certainly a historian, yet writing the chronicle of his own abbey's history was

---

[15] The same questions are raised by Rauner, 'Notker des Stammlers', p. 35, who writes: 'The answer to this is only to be found in the St Gallen library, in its manuscripts and medieval book catalogues' ('Gerade hierzu ist Antwort nur in der St Galler Bibliothek zu finden, in ihren Handschriften und mittelalterliche Bibliothekskatalogen').

[16] H. Wartmann, *Urkundenbuch der Abtei Sanct Gallen 2: 849–920* (Zurich, 1866), no. 679 (890 VIII 1).

[17] SG 14, p. 331: 'nefas putaui si illa bibliothecę sancti Galli . cui dei gratia multi accumulaui . scribere negligendo defrudauerim ·', a notice written into the book by Notker himself.

[18] In the context of a collection of materials for the liturgy of the dead, now in SG 152 (pp. 280–336) for which he had the main responsibility, Notker copied the incipits of responsories and their verses under the heading 'RESP[ONSORIIS] IN COMMEM[ORATIONE] FRATRU[M] · DE IOB ET PSALMIS ·' (p. 336).

[19] See the introduction to Bower, *Notker Balbulus Liber Ymnorum*, vol. 1.

not consigned to him but to his colleague, Ratpert.[20] Finally, his compilation of a martyrologium and concern with the copying of saints' passions provide a material evidential backdrop to his remarks in the *Notatio de illustribus viris* – this was a monk for whom the drama of Christian history had a significant place in daily life. If then we are to think about the activities of liturgical musician, chronicler and historian as linked and undertaken by the same person, Notker earns his place rather easily.

Notker as scribe and maker of books

Notker's hand is identifiable on the basis of an autobiographical passage ('Ego Notkerus...') written into SG 14 (p. 331), and the clear likeness of this hand with that writing a series of charters copied by a scribe named Notker.[21] The identity of the hand is confirmed by a further association, between the note in SG 14 and another codex in the Stiftsbibliothek. That note refers to the fact that Notker had had the book of Baruch together with a letter of Jeremiah copied at the end of a book of the prophets. The copy can be found at the end of SG 39 (pp. 453–67), with its title and the first two lines (p. 453, lines 1–6) copied by the same hand. As many as thirty-one codices in which Notker can be found writing substantial portions, or leading the work of a team of scribes, or simply correcting text as he read it, have been identified; there may be more.[22] He can be seen copying large portions of text in the Martyrology of Hrabanus (SG 458), including the prose and verse dedications (pp. 4–8) and the whole of the first gathering (up to p. 18). There are several instances where he is found copying the same text into different codices; these include, for example, a narration ('relatio') for the feast of St Michael the archangel (*Memoriam beati archangeli Michaelis toto orbe venerandam*),[23] copied into SG 432 (pp. 464–7) and then into SG 433 (pp. 402–10). His first copy was appended

---

[20] *Ratpert St. Galler Klostergeschichten (Casus sancti Galli)*, ed. and trans. H. Steiner, MGH Scriptores rerum germanicum 75 (Hannover, 2002): this covers the period 614–884. A contemporary copy of Ratpert's text is still in the library at St Gallen (SG 614, pp. 78–134): of this Notker copied the first three lines on p. 79, that is, the beginning of the main text.

[21] On the identification of Notker's hand see Susan Rankin, 'Ego itaque Notker scripsi', with previous bibliography. There are several charters in the Stiftsarchiv at St Gallen with the subscription 'Notker', but not all were actually written by Notker Balbulus: see Rankin, 'Ego itaque Notker scripsi', and for a complete list, with some new additions, see Erhart, 'Notker Balbulus', Appendix 2.

[22] The resources of the *codices electronici sangallenses* have enabled this task in a way unimaginable before the advent of digital photography. I have not yet carried out a comprehensive search for Notker's work in the Stiftsbibliothek holdings. Much of the Notker copying known to me will be mentioned in this paper, but there is more beyond this.

[23] BHL 5948–9; Notker attributes the text to Bede.

at the end of an homiliary to which he added a substantial supplement; at that stage he added at the end of this long account 'Ego Beda hanc hystoriam tortuosissimam . ad normam ueritatis correxi ·' ('I, Bede, corrected this very convoluted history to the standard of truth') (SG 432, p. 467b, lines 16–17). The source of this note is unknown, but Notker's interest in passing it on is typical of his concern with Christian history and authorship. In SG 432 that text was followed by the homily *Celebritas hodierne diei admonet*, written in honour of the Blessed Virgin and attributed to Augustine (pp. 467–9). Later, in the homiliary he largely organized and copied himself, this homily was placed in the appropriate position in sequence between homilies for St Lawrence (10 August) and St Bartholomew (24 August), as the first of a series for the feast of the Assumption on 15 August (SG 433, pp. 282–7). Notker's concern with the preservation of texts, and understanding their status, is well illustrated by the introductory title in SG 39 (p. 453): 'Liber iste qui Baruc nomine praenotatur · in librorum canone non habetur · nisi tantum in uulgata editione · similiter epistola Hieremiae · propter notitiam autem legentium hic scripta sunt · quia multa de Christo · novissimisque temporibus indicant ·' ('This book which is entitled by the name of Baruc. It is not in the canon of books. Unless, however, in the vulgate edition. Similarly the letter of Jeremiah. For the notice of readers these things are written because they proclaim many things about Christ and the last days').

Notker's interactions with other scribes take many forms. In the simplest cases, he sets the style and module of script and hands over to another scribe. In the contemporary copy of Ratpert's *Casus sancti Galli*, Notker wrote out the first three lines on the first page, and then never reappeared (SG 614, pp. 78–134, at p. 79). In contrast, in the copy of the Martyrology of Ado (SG 454), a more supervisory presence is revealed: on the grand title page (SG 454, p. 24) someone drew three large decorated initials (for IN NOMINE DOMINI, QUO GENERE and POPULUS CHRISTIANus).[24] Then, in the first column, Notker wrote the rest of the title, in rustic capitals using red ink, and then, after Q, in black ink; following P at the top of the second column, he wrote one line in rustic capitals, and then continued the main text in his typical Caroline hand, up to line 10 'marty', the next scribe taking over to finish this word 'rum'.[25] (This may have been a deliberate act of disguise, in a situation in which the scribe to whom Notker handed over was also expert, and wrote

---

[24] A. von Euw considered these initials to be the work of Notker: see his *Die St. Galler Buchkunst vom 8. bis zum Ende des 11. Jahrhunderts*, 2 vols. (St Gallen, 2008), I, 444. This is difficult to demonstrate, other than through their proximity to the script of Notker. The ink used to draw these initials is slightly darker than that used to write the rustic capitals which sit alongside. The same is true of the decorated initial and rustic capitals at the beginning of the dedicatory letter on p. 2 of the codex.

[25] It should be noted that, in l. 6 of this column, the word 'meritis' has been corrected, with only 'me' representing the first copying campaign.

a hand very close to Notker's own.) This second scribe continued working up the end of the introduction, including the hymn *Aeterna Christi munera* (p. 27); then Notker wrote (in rustic capitals in red ink) the title for the next passage ('In nomine Domini · Incipit libellus de festiuitatibus apostolorum · et reliquorum qui discipuli aut uicini · successoresque ipsorum apostolorum fuerunt ·'). And then at the top of the next page (p. 28) Notker wrote out the rubric and the rest of lines 1–2, and his expert colleague took up the reins again. Notker's script appears elsewhere in the volume, above all in the compilation of the prefatory material on pp. 2–22, the dedicatory letter and then the Kalendar-Martyrologium.[26]

As head of a team of scribes, Notker also corrected passages copied by those whose work he directed – and he was an inveterate corrector. If the problem were substantial he could erase, or write passages into the margin, but more usually the corrections are simply written into the main text, with dots to signal deletion, or even crossings out. On the first three lines of SG 152, p. 294 the first scribe wrote:

1   Non enim

2 diceret celestia . dixit autem . et ter

3 restria corpora

Notker corrected this to:

1   Non enim de car

2 ne diceret cęlestia . dixit autem . et ~~ter~~

3 ~~restria~~ corpora cęlestia ·

And as corrector Notker can be discovered not only sorting out the passages copied under his direction, but also texts copied long before. Such an example is the homily *Audiens a domino Petrus quia dives difficile* in SG 553 (pp. 151–62), copied in Sankt Gallen in the mid-ninth century, as an adaptation of Bede's homily for Benedict Biscop for the feast of St Gall.[27] Notker worked his way through this text, making constant adjustments, and then copied it out, with all those corrections, into the homiliary now SG 433 (pp. 447–57).

Notker's working procedures and his title of librarian (in 890 at least) suggest the value of juxtaposition with Reginbert, librarian at Reichenau until his death in 846, and involved in copying at least thirty-five extant manuscripts.[28] As scribes in charge of other scribes, Reginbert's and

---

[26] Von Euw has, quite rightly, corrected my attribution of the whole of p. 2 to Notker (*Die St. Galler Buchkunst*, I, 444): Notker wrote only up to column a, line 7, 'fuisse'.

[27] Although he was active on p. 159, Notker was not responsible for the long interjection in the lower margin of this page.

[28] On Reginbert see K. Preisendanz, 'Reginbert von der Reichenau. Aus Bibliothek und Skriptorium des Inselklosters', *Neue Heidelberger Jahrbücher* n.s. (1952/53),

Notker's engagement with the processes and tasks of copying appear very similar, and the older librarian may well have been a direct model for the younger. Reginbert can be found copying long stretches of text, as in BLB Aug. perg. 18, where he was the main scribe for a collection of texts, including commentaries on the Lord's Prayer and on creeds; on pages filled by other scribes (some writing Caroline rather than Alemannic scripts), Reginbert's very characteristic rustic capitals may often be seen in the headings or other interjections into the text. At the other end of the spectrum, his work may appear only in titular material, as in BLB Aug. perg. 144, where he wrote in red, and in rustic capitals on fols. 2v, 13v, 14r and 16r, and nowhere else in the book. The point of handover from Reginbert to another scribe can be more visually evident than in Notker's work, that is, when the other scribe writes a Caroline minuscule, in contrast to Reginbert's own stylish Alemannic minuscule.[29] But in many cases, as Maag has demonstrated for the so-called Wolfcoz-Evangelistar in Sankt Gallen, the handover from Reginbert to another scribe writing Alemannic minuscule can be hard to spot, unless the detail of the ductus of individual letters is carefully traced. Where his intervention is easily as obvious as Notker's is in the correction of errors. Within a heading written in red capitals in BLB 94 (fol. 39r) he supplied words and endings missing from the first scribe's work (shown here in italics). On this occasion Reginbert's intrusion is rendered more obvious through his use of brown ink:

FINIT LIBER EUSEB*II* HIERONIMI *PRIMUS*
INCIP*IUNT CONTRA IOVINIANUM · CAPITULATIONES DE LIBRO ·II · do ·*

Reginbert's hand reappears in syllables, words and phrases between lines and in the margins on many pages of this codex.

Of course, the geographical closeness of the two abbeys and the fact of considerable exchange between them means that Notker – working one generation after Reginbert's death in 846 – may have had a teacher who had himself learnt from the model of Reginbert. Whether or not Notker could recognize the difference between the hands of Reginbert and Wolfcoz – one working in Reichenau, the other in Sankt Gallen, in the first half of the ninth century, and both writing Alemmanic minuscule – he will have had these

---

1–49. The most comprehensive list of material copied by Reginbert is now N. Maag, *Alemannische Minuskel (744–846 n. Chr.)*, Quellen und Untersuchungen zur lateinischen Philologie des Mittelalters 18 (Stuttgart, 2014), pp. 203–5; see also M. Tischler, 'Reginbert-Handschriften, mit einem Neufund in Kloster Einsiedeln', *Scriptorium* 50 (1996), 175–83, and pl. 12. On the famous ex-libris added by Reginbert see W. Berschin, 'Vier karolingische Exlibris', in *Mittellateinische Studien*, pp. 169–78; and F. Heinzer, '*Ego Reginbertus scriptor* – Reichenauer Büchersorge als Spiegel karolingischer Reformprogrammatik', in *Klosterreform und mittelalterliche Buchkultur im deutschen Südwesten* (Leiden, 2008), pp. 17–31.

[29] As, for example, in BLB Aug. perg. 144, fol. 5r, where Reginbert wrote out the first fourteen lines, followed after this by another scribe who wrote Caroline minuscule.

heavy and clear hands as constant visual models. In his explanation written into SG 14 – a collection of Old Testament books – he referred directly to having read the extract he would copy into the codex in a very old book at Reichenau ('in quodam antiquissimo augiensium libro').[30] Large portions of this codex were copied by Wolfcoz,[31] including the passage after which Notker added a note, an excerpt from Augustine's *De civitate Dei* and the riddle from the apocryphal book Esdras III. The work of these two important scribes was before Notker's eyes, their handling of texts part of his everyday experience.

The juxtaposition of Reginbert and Notker throws into relief the differing achievements of the two and calls attention to specific interests followed up by Notker. Among books copied by Reginbert or organized by him we find patristica, contemporary biblical commentaries, canon law and history, and even a book of Office liturgy including chants.[32] Also related to daily worship are several volumes of saints' lives.[33] Our knowledge of Reginbert's range as a scribe can be extended beyond extant books, since he made a list of what he had copied (or had organized to have copied). It includes an 'antiphonarius gradualis' with 'antiphone de litaniis vel de quacunque tribulatione'; in other words, a gradual with an appendix of processional chants.[34] Then there is a 'libello continetur cantus gradualis et nocturnalis' and collections of hymns for the whole year ('et hymni festis diebus per circulum anni').[35] The span of Reginbert's commissions as librarian and scribe is vast, including much *liturgica*, but it also includes the Reichenau Confraternity book and inscriptions on the famous St Gallen plan. I think that means that, if you needed something copied at Reichenau and wanted the best scribe, you got Reginbert.

Those ways in which Notker's copying activity differs from Reginbert's are informative. What I have found copied or organized by him covers a wide sweep of monastic reading, including Augustine, Isidore and accounts of church councils and monastic rules, but the dominating theme is *liturgica* – there are no less than seven collections of homilies, as well as homilies copied into other books, three martyrologies (not including the one he himself composed) and a collection of saints' lives, with which he was involved. While we do not yet know just how much can be attributed to Notker, we

---

[30] On this see p. 45 above.

[31] Maag, *Alemannische Minuskel*, pp. 107–9.

[32] Nuremberg, Germanisches Nationalmuseum, Kupferstichkabinett, Kapsel 536/SD 2815, 2816 (two folios).

[33] BLB 32 (passions of saints), 136 (fols. 21–46, several saints' lives) and 202 (fols. 87–152, passions and lives of saints); WLB Cod. Theol. et phil. 2o 95 (saints' lives).

[34] P. Lehmann, *Mitterlalterliche Bibliothekskataloge Deutschland und der Schweiz I: Die Bistümer Konstanz und Chur* (Munich, 1918), p. 260.

[35] Ibid., p. 261.

can see immediately that he was *not* copying the grand manuscripts made at St Gallen during his lifetime – the Folchart Psalter (SG 23, in which the hand is very like Notker's, but it is not his), books of Gospel readings (SG 53 and 54), the lives of SS Gall and Otmar (SG 562) and many other books. For these high-grade books, it was the habit at the abbey of Sankt Gallen to entrust each to a single good scribe. Notker's time and energy seem to have been directed in other ways, managing the work of teams of scribes – including many who appear to be embarking on their first task of copying, ordering the parts of codices, producing paratextual material and sometimes working closely with the text.

Such an example of close work with a text is in a copy of the *Indiculum* of the works of St Augustine produced in association with the saint's *vita* by Possidius. It was argued by François Dolbeau that Possidius's *indiculum* was not an isolated work, but an integral part of the *vita* of Augustine; indeed, Augustine himself may be behind the preparation of the list, as a preliminary to 'publishing' his complete works.[36] The list was copied into SG 571 (pp. 1–48), with the heading 'INCIPIT INDICIUM LIBRORUM SANCTI AUGUSTINI EPISCOPI · QUOD POSSIDIUS CALAMENSIS EPISCOPI COLLEGIT · QUI ET VITAM IPSIUS COMPOSUIT ·',[37] followed immediately by the *vita* (pp. 50–178). The *Indiculum* and the *vita* are in physically separate gatherings, with a list of chapter headings for the *vita* in between,[38] and they could have been bound in either order, at the time of their manufacture; these texts are now bound with others copied in the eleventh and twelfth centuries. It was Notker who organized, oversaw and corrected these three textual entities.[39]

Notker's work on Possidius's *vita* involved the correction of passages copied by scribes whose comprehension of the text was weak, or who left

[36] F. Dolbeau, 'La survie des œuvres d'Augustin. Remarques sur l'Indiculum attribué à Possidius et sur la bibliothèque d'Anségise', in *Du copiste au collectionneur. Mélanges d'histoire des textes et des bibliothèques en l'honneur d'André Vernet*, Bibliologia 18 (Turnhout, 1998), pp. 3–22 (pp. 6, 12). Possidius' list is edited by A. Wilmart, 'Operum S. Augustini elenchus', *Miscellanea Agostiniana* 2 (Rome, 1931), pp. 149–208. On various assessments of the status of the *Indiculum* see W. Geerlings, ed., *Possidius Vita Augustini* (Paderborn, 2005), pp. 109–11.

[37] 'Here begins the list of the books of St Augustine, bishop, which Possidius, bishop of Calama, assembled, and who also wrote his life.' The use of 'Indicium' rather than 'Indiculum' was relatively common.

[38] The *Indiculum* is written out in three quaternios, followed by a list of chapter headings for the *vita* written into a binio, from which the first folio has been removed; then four quaternios, a ternio (pp. 151–62), and two further quaternios for the *vita*.

[39] I thank Hartmut Hoffmann † for his identification of this manuscript as one of those in which Notker's hand can be seen.

out phrases in error.[40] Having written out the first lines of the *vita* (p. 55, lines 1–5), and then the first lines on the subsequent page (p. 56, lines 1–6), Notker then seems to have considered this model enough for the other scribes who were to copy out the text; from this point on he intervened in the *vita* only as a corrector. For the other two parts of this Augustinian enterprise his participation was of a quite different kind. The list of chapter headings for the *vita* was substantially copied by him,[41] and he was probably responsible for all of the numbers set into the left-hand margin throughout the four pages occupied by these *tituli* (pp. 50–3). It is not known whether this *Capitulatio* belonged to the original text of the *vita*, or represents an early medieval addition,[42] nor are the specific divisions of the *vita* made here replicated elsewhere.[43] Whence Notker got these divisions and *tituli* is currently unknown.

The manuscript transmission of the *Indiculum* of Augustine's writings is more easily followed,[44] and it would be possible to consider Notker's interventions in that light. Without going so far, however, it is possible to see Notker working through this list, not only to correct the text copied by the other scribe with whom he collaborated to produce the *Indiculum*, but also attempting to sort out a certain amount of chaos in the numbering, and, in addition, using the list as a way of checking what was and what was not in the library at St Gallen. Many of his interventions, following his writing out of the title (p. 1, lines 1–4) and first three entries (p. 1, lines 5–7), are immediately identifiable through the use of red ink (then corroborated by details of script). Since he was working through the list adding numbers in red ink to the left of entries, he commonly came across situations in which correction was needed. These corrections were supplied by him using the pen which was in his hand at the time; thus, for example, the additions of 'muliere' and 'supra' (as well as others) on p. 42 are in his characteristic hand. On many pages he marked 'rq.' or 'r' (*require*) in the margin, seemingly reminding himself of the need to identify copies of specific texts.[45] Other remarks (as opposed to corrections) in red include 'hos libros alii capitula vel titulos dicunt' (p. 7); 'sine numero'

---

[40] As for example on p. 161, where the scribe left out phrases between two occurences of 'Magis timeamus' (*Vita*, c. 30); these were added by Notker in the lower margin.

[41] p. 50 in total; p. 51, lines 1–3, 'quomodo'; p. 52, lines 1–8, and all the chapter numbers.

[42] This list of chapter headings is edited by Walter W. Berschin: 'Possidius, Vita Sancti Augustini. Eine patristische Biographie mit klassischem Hintergrund', in *idem.*, *Mittellateinische Studien* (Heidelberg, 2005), pp. 1–7.

[43] On the manuscript transmission see H. T. Weiskotten, *Sancti Augustini vita scripta a Possidio episcopo* (Princeton, 1919), pp. 23–32; the *Vita* is also edited by A. A. R. Bastiaensen, *Vita di Cipriano, Vita di Ambrogio, Vita di Agostino* (Milan, 1975), pp. 130–240.

[44] See Wilmart's edition (n. 36 above).

[45] As, for example, three times on p. 27.

(p. 13); 'si decadas attenderis ' si uero tractatus · inferius numera ·' (p. 23); 'absque num .' (p. 28); and at the end of the list 'hec de plurimis pauca sunt adnotata' (p. 48). To make sense of these annotations would require proper philological study. For now, it can be observed that the exemplar(s) available to Notker were deficient in the way in which the entries were numbered. His interventions reveal the extent to which he attempted to put order into this text and its numbering system, presumably as a basis for checking the Augustinian holdings of the abbey's library. His work with the *Indiculum* and *vita* did not stop there; in the large passional whose preparation he oversaw (SG 577), he began the *tituli* for the *vita* (p. 451a, lines 3–8) and the *vita* itself (p. 453a, lines 1–4). The text of the *Indiculum* which follows the *vita* was copied directly from SG 571, with Notker's corrections in red incorporated (sometimes rendering nonsense). Finally, he added at the end (p. 513b, lines 12–16): 'Hęc de plurimis pauca sunt adnotata · Ita ut in his ipsis multa sint de numeris omissa · Idcirco et iam capitulatio uidetur imperfecta' ('From here on few are listed; thus many are left out of the numbers; therefore the chapterizing is seen to be imperfect').

Martyrologies, saints' lives and homiliaries

One of the most sustained campaigns of book-making at St Gallen in the second half of the ninth century was dedicated to the assemblage of codices for formal reading, principally during liturgical celebrations. This led to the copying as well as creation of martyrologies, to the construction of collections of saints' lives and to the production of several collections of homilies. This work had begun while Notker was still young; in the earliest of the homiliaries, he was certainly not in charge. More significantly, the drive may have been led by the most influential figure associated with St Gallen in this period: Grimald. Hrabanus Maurus had dedicated his own martyrology to Ratleik, abbot of Seligenstadt and chancellor to Louis the German, and to Grimald, abbot of St Gallen (841–872) and archchaplain to Louis the German; that dual dedication probably dates from the period when Ratleik and Grimald were both at court before Ratleik's death in 854.[46] Yet Notker was deeply involved in this campaign, at many points acting to put into action plans which may have been conceived by others and, in the last years of his life, composing a new martyrology. This new martyrology survives in a copy made in the early tenth century (SG 456), possibly after Notker's death; there is no sign

---

[46] See B. Bischoff, 'Bücher am Hofe Ludwigs des Deutschen und die Privatbibliothek des Kanzlers Grimald', in *Mittelalterliche Studien* 3 (Stuttgart, 1981), pp. 187–212 (p. 195). In a list of books owned by Grimald and given to the monastic library on his death, a 'martyrologium Rhabani in volumine I' is listed (SG 267, p. 31); this was probably the current SG 457.

anywhere in this book of his own hand (and the text was left incomplete). But Notker had already organized the copying of other martyrologies from which his own version drew; his most important textual source was that by Ado of Vienne (d. 875), and the SG copy of the second version (SG 454) was both begun and finished by him.[47] In a copy of the martyrology made by Hrabanus Maurus, Notker inscribed the whole of the verse dedication from Hrabanus to Grimald in rustic capitals, giving it more prominence than the preceding (prose) dedication to Ratleik (SG 458).[48] The St Gallen library also possessed the martyrology composed in verse by Wandalbert of Prüm (SG 250, pp. 28–65), for which Notker had copied the first three pages (pp. 28–31),[49] and an older copy of Bede's martyrology (SG 451).[50] Notker's work in preparing these martyrologies was merely the starting point for a further campaign of study of their content, evidence for which survives in copious detail. John McCulloh's investigations into the relation between Notker's own text and those of his main models, Ado and Hrabanus, have demonstrated significant characteristics of Notker's approach, above all, his ways of dealing with conflicting dates. As elsewhere, Notker was articulate about what he was actually doing: 'What does make Notker unusual is the surprising number of notices in which he announced to his audience that his sources disagreed or in which he actually refuted the errors in his sources.'[51] Very often the textual versions presented in Notker's martyrology can be traced back to annotations made in the earlier books, allowing the compositional process documented in text form by McCulloh to be seen in process, as Notker sat before those books.

Among copies of saints' lives with which Notker was involved, his most sustained contributions appear in the 'passionarium novum', SG 577 (as the codex was described in the contemporary lists in SG 566).[52] In this book his presence is all-pervasive as the writer of chapter lists (p. 5 for the *Vita sancti*

---

[47] See above, p. 46, and Rankin, 'Ego itaque Notker scripsi', pp. 289–90. On martyrologies in this period see especially J. McCulloh, 'Historical Martyrologies in the Benedictine Cultural Tradition', in *Benedictine Culture 750–1050*, ed. W. Lourdaux and D. Verhelst (Leuven, 1983), pp. 114–31, with previous bibliography.

[48] On this manuscript see *Rabani Mauri Martyrologium*, ed. J. McCulloh, CCCM 44 (Turnhout, 1979), xliii–xlvi; McCulloh links the work of the main corrector of this manuscript with corrections made to SG 457, describing the hands as identical – and this was certainly Notker's hand.

[49] Without knowledge of Notker's involvement as scribe, it was Von Euw's view that Notker was responsible for the compilation of this whole 'astronomical-computistic encyclopedia' during the period when he was librarian (set by Von Euw as 880–90) (*Die St. Galler Buchkunst*, I, no. 120).

[50] Bischoff, *Katalog* III, no. 5752 dates the manuscript to the first quarter of the ninth century.

[51] McCulloh, 'Historical Martyrologies', p. 126.

[52] See P. E. Munding, *Das Verzeichnis der St. Galler Heiligenleben und ihrer Handschriften in Codex Sangall. No. 566*, Texte und Arbeiten I/3–4 (Beuron, 1918).

Ermenlandi; p. 242 for the *Vita sancti Cassiani*; p. 451, lines 3–8, for the *Vita sancti Augustini*); as the scribe who could write the beginnings and endings of individual parts, so as to set them out clearly (as on p. 45b, lines 1–15, the end of the *Vita sancti Ermenlandi* and the beginning of the *Vita heremite Meginrati*, and on p. 374b, the end of the *Passio sancti Thrutberti* and the beginning of the *Passio sancti Andeoli*); and as the scribe who added headings (above all in the *Vita sancti Ermenlandi*, but also as on p. 174a, lines 20–7) or showed how to write out a hymn composed by St Hilary of Poitiers (p. 158b, l. 22 to p. 159a, l. 4). At one point Notker wrote out a whole page, including a passage of fourteen lines written in rustic capitals, alternately red and black – why the *Vita sancte Marie Egyptiacae* deserved this special treatment is unclear, unless it was because it had been translated by Paul the Deacon.[53] Notker can also be found working in a volume of saints' lives (SG 551), and making corrections in much older copies of texts (as in the *Passio sancti Leudegarii* in SG 548, pp. 67–116), preparatory to their being recopied.

There is one type of book of liturgical readings for which, over time, Notker seems to have become the main overseer of design and creation: the homiliary. In extant homiliaries, it is possible to follow his scribal work from a period when he was working to the orders of someone else, to a time when he was in charge and making serious decisions about what should be copied and how, and finally, to a time when, as an older man, he was simply commissioned by one of his ex-students to make a homiliary for use elsewhere. SG 431 is a winter homiliary, the second of a pair, and consequently containing homilies for feasts from Septuagesima to Tuesday in Holy Week. Unlike all of the copying work so far considered, in this book Notker copied long passages of text on series of pages; he was also responsible for the table of contents (pp. 2–4). That Notker was working to someone else's orders can be inferred further from the opening page of text (p. 6), where, in contrast to his work in such a book as SG 454, he was not the scribe who wrote out the introductory heading in *capitalis*, but the scribe of the main text (column b, l. 8 onwards). Moreover, the hand seen in SG 431 is thin and upright, as in the charter dated 873;[54] this is manifestly Notker's 'young' hand.

A series of collections drawing on the homiliary prepared by Paul the Deacon was made at St Gallen between the second quarter and the end of the ninth century.[55] As a group SG 430–434 offer an almost complete compilation of homilies for the *temporale* and *sanctorale*, as follows:

---

[53] SG 577, p. 269a, 'Huius imitabilis conuersionis · actuumque et morum uitam · et poenitentie magnum uirileque certamen uenerabilis Mariae Egyptiacę · qualiter in heremo expleuerit tempora uitae · de Greco transtulit in Latinum Paulus uenerabilis diaconus · sanctae Neapolitanae ecclesiae ·'

[54] Sankt Gallen Stiftsarchiv III.310.

[55] I leave out of consideration here two St Gallen homiliaries: SG 422 (made in the first half of the ninth century, and possibly before SG 432), with a selection and

Winter I (Advent to Sundays after Epiphany, Purification and Annunciation):
SG 430

Winter II (Septuagesima to Tuesday before Easter): SG 431

Summer I (Easter Vigil to 26th Sunday after Pentecost, including Proper of
Saints): SG 432

Summer II (Sundays after Pentecost, 26 in number): SG 434

Proper of Saints (St Andrew, 30 November, to St Clement, 23 November,
and Common of saints): SG 433[56]

Of these the oldest is SG 432, probably begun in the 830s;[57] this reproduces,
largely, the collection of texts prepared by Paul the Deacon at the request of
Charlemagne for these parts of the liturgical year, ending with the homily
'Clementissimus omnipotens Deus pietate' *in letania quando volueris*.[58] As in
other copies of this centrally prepared and disseminated book, the way in
which SG 432 is arranged mixes feasts of the *temporale* and *sanctorale*, and
names Sundays after Pentecost in relation to saints' feasts; thus, on p. 193, we
find the homily 'Dominus Deus cum David regem' with the rubric 'Dominica
I post natale apostolorum' (thus the Sunday after the feast of SS Peter and
Paul on 29 June), and on p. 224 the homily 'Surdus ille et mutus' with the
rubric 'Dominica I post sancti Laurenti' (thus the Sunday after 10 August).

The other codices were all made later, and in all four this older system
of reference has been abandoned; thus, 'Dominus Deus cum David regem'
is now set for the fourth Sunday after Pentecost (SG 434, p. 64) and 'Surdus
ille et mutus' for the twelfth Sunday (SG 434, p. 186).[59] More importantly,
the arrangement of material sequentially through the year, with all of the
problems caused by the constantly changing relation between fixed and
moveable feasts, was now altered in favour of a separation between *temporale*
and *sanctorale* feasts: SG 434 was dedicated to the Sundays after Pentecost

---

ordering of homilies unrelated to the later collections considered below; and Basel
Universitätsbibliothek B.III.2, on which Zachary Guiliano (see n. 58 below) will
report. It is clear from numerous annotations (as on fol. 118v, end of lines 12–17)
that Notker had access to this manuscript, and may have used it in the preparation
of other books.

[56] From p. 60: the preceding section was added (in the late ninth or early tenth
century) to the original corpus.

[57] Von Euw, *Die St. Galler Buchkunst*, p. 375.

[58] In as much as the content of Paul's collection can currently be checked using
R. Grégoire, *Homéliaires liturgiques médiévaux: analyse de manuscrits* (Spoleto, 1980).
A detailed study of the composition, dissemination and use of Paul the Deacon's
homiliary from the late eighth to the mid ninth century is currently being prepared
by Zachary Guiliano at the University of Cambridge. I am grateful to him for many
useful conversations about the St Gallen homiliary material.

[59] At some time during the preparation of SG 434 the listing of Sundays after Pentecost
slipped, so that the numbering in the main codex is one behind the numbering in
the contents pages, which begins with the second Sunday after Pentecost. In the
case of 'Surdus ille et mutus' the Sunday named in this list (p. 3) is the thirteenth.

and SG 433 to the saints' feasts. With the exception of its last four pages (pp. 337–40) SG 434 was copied in its entirety by Notker; the same is true of the main body of SG 433 (pp. 60–632). In these two volumes, besides the separation of the two festal series, another new design element emerges: in the collection circulated under Paul the Deacon's name, only a small number of saints' feasts were linked with specific homilies, leaving users to select from a large number of others for the *sanctorale* of an individual institution. In SG 433, instead of retaining that large unspecific collection, individual homilies are selected for each saint's feast.

It is clear from the contents of SG 430 and 431 – containing the winter readings up to Easter – that a programme of expansion of the main Paul the Deacon series had been undertaken, with about a quarter to a third as much again drawn primarily from sermon collections by John Chrysostom, Maximus of Turin, Pope Leo, Pope Gregory, Bishop Gregory of Tours and Bede.[60] (The inclusion of this extra material explains why the winter part of the homiliary was broken into two volumes.) This suggests the presence of a senior directing hand, seeking out and choosing material. At that stage, Notker was not in charge, and it was surely too early for him to have had such a charge. In the case of SG 433 and 434, however, it may well have been Notker who had to identify and extract any specifically named saints' feasts with homilies from earlier collections; who then had to construct an appropriate list of the many saints' feasts for whom homilies were required (including not only the main Roman saints but also St Gall, and the new feast of All Saints); and who finally, before beginning to copy, had to choose appropriate homilies for each individual *temporale* and *sanctorale* feast. For the feast of St Gall, for example, four homilies were copied in SG 433:

p. 438: 'Ad sancti ac beatissimi istius patris nostri' (Maximus)
p. 444: 'De se ipso Dominus' (Bede)
p. 447: 'Audiens a Domino' (Bede)
p. 457: 'Sancti euangelii fratres karissimi aperta uobis est' (Gregory)

Three of these were drawn directly from Paul the Deacon's collection, but 'Audiens a Domino' was based on Bede's homily for St Benedict, rewritten so that it could apply to St Gall. That rewriting had already been achieved long before Notker got his hands on the text; he was merely responsible for correcting it (SG 553, pp. 151–62) and then recopying it in SG 434. Likewise, for the feast of All Saints, six homilies were proposed, beginning with three drawn from Paul's collection, and then sermons by Gregory, and two attributed to Hrabanus and Walafrid Strabo:

---

[60] Other material includes selections from Origen's *Commentary on Romans* (quite rare at this time), the *Revelatio Sancti Stephani*, and some Augustine and ps-Augustine, a sermon by Jerome and St Cyril's letter to Nestorius (attributed to Leo).

p. 504: 'Qui sanctorum merita' (John Chrysostom)
p. 510: 'Et si generaliter omnibus loquitur' (Bede)
p. 515: 'Iste locus evangelii' (Augustine)
p. 515: 'Quia enim superna' (Gregory)
p. 656: 'Legimus in ecclesiasticis historiis' (Hrabanus)
p. 669: 'Hodie dilectissimi omnium sanctorum' (Walafrid)[61]

Such choices surely required a good knowledge of individual saints (or knowledge of how to find out about them) as well as comprehension of these mainly patristic homilies. One clear demonstration of Notker's knowledge of the homilies of Gregory the Great is in a supplement provided for SG 432 (pp. 464–538); this includes thirteen homilies, of which only one was not begun by Notker (beginning on p. 484).[62] Of these thirteen, nine are attributed to Gregory.

It is in the copying of homiliaries that Notker's interest in the saints is likely to have been grounded. He would have known of the spiritual benefits of studying saints' lives and deaths on earth – from reading Hrabanus's words directed to Grimald, if not elsewhere, since 'the sufferings of the martyrs were a direct result of their Christian commitment', and 'readers and hearers' of these stories would thus be convinced that they might 'ask with confidence for assistance from the saints in their own struggle for eternal life'.[63] That is the background against which Notker's words directed to Salomo in the *Notatio de illustribus viris* should be set. By the example of the martyrs, Salomo should not only spurn the delights of the world, but place his soul for Christ and grow accustomed to think nothing of the troubles of his body. Notker's pride in the book of homilies for saints that he himself made is observable in the grandeur of its first main opening (SG 433, pp. 60–1), where as much of the written area is occupied by decorated letters in red as text written in minuscule letters and in black (see plate X).

Late in his life Notker oversaw the preparation of a short homiliary which may well have been intended for Salomo: in WLB HB VII 57, the impressive opening page (fol. 1r) is unmistakeably his work.[64] The hands of other scribes involved suggest that this book was made in the early tenth century, and must thus belong to the late work of Notker, long after he had sorted

---

[61] These last two attributions are of unclear value, although they are among the earliest ones: see J. E. Cross, '"Legimus in ecclesiasticis historiis": A Sermon for All Saints and its Use in Old English Prose', *Traditio* 33 (1977), 101–35 (pp. 127–8), though he does not catch all the relevant manuscripts.

[62] A further group of two homilies was copied on pp. 538–41, with no evidence of involvement on Notker's part.

[63] McCulloh, 'Benedictine Historical Martyrologies', p. 131.

[64] Reproduced in H. Hoffmann, *Buchkunst und Königtum im Ottonischen und frühsalischen Reich*, 2 vols. (Stuttgart, 1986), II, pl. 209. I am grateful to Professor Hoffmann for communicating this identification (as well as several others) to me.

out homiliaries for the abbey itself; here he made a selection for a beloved pupil, who might himself have often experienced Notker at work on his homiliary tasks. Finally, Basel Universitätsbibliothek B.IV.26 is, like the Stuttgart collection, a shortened selection of homilies; in this codex Notker has a supervisory presence, beginning sections, sometimes writing out whole pages, or simply headings.[65] That these last two homiliaries both escaped from St Gallen is due, I think, to their having been made to be sent out; both are shorter than the St Gallen house collections, and, in as much as can be judged from what has survived, may have provided homilies for the whole year in one volume.

In all of this work on homilies, martyrologies and saints' lives, Notker was making books for his monastic community, books which had a central place in the daily life of that community, including its liturgical celebrations. These books are not sacramentaries, with prayers addressed to God, or antiphoners, with chants sung in praise of God; they are books of instruction, holding texts which expound the meaning of scripture or invoke models of Christian life. Notker was creating materials for teaching his community, for their meditation in the long hours of the night Office, or while they ate. Of scribes Cassiodorus had said: 'et Domini precepta scribendo longe lateque disseminant . Felix intentio laudanda sedulitas . manu hominibus predicare . digitis linguas aperire . salutem mortalibus tacitum dare . et contra diaboli subreptiones inlicitas calamo atramentoque pugnare ·' ('by writing they spread the Lord's teachings far and wide. A blessed purpose, a praiseworthy zeal, to preach to men with the hand, to set tongues free with one's fingers and in silence to give mortals salvation and to fight with pen and ink against the unlawful snares of the devil').[66] These are lofty claims, not to be lightly regarded. And it is in this vision of profound individual responsibility that I believe Notker used his abilities to support and to shape the spiritual life of the monks of Sankt Gallen: each individual book made by him should have strength as a weapon in the fight for salvation.

---

[65] The Basel manuscript opens with the rubric 'a natiuitate domini usque in octauam pentecostes', and that is indeed the period that it covers. In the Stuttgart manuscript, the evidence is ambiguous: the opening rubric 'in diebus dominicis uel aliis festiuitatibus per circulum anni' implies that it is intended for reading throughout the whole circle of the year, but it seems to be drawing to a close by the time it reaches Holy Week, with only a very brief *commune sanctorum* following.

[66] *Institutiones* I.30 (SG 199, p. 102).

4

Singing History:
Chant in Ekkehard IV's *Casus sancti Galli*

Lori Kruckenberg

The collected writings of the monk Ekkehard IV of Sankt Gallen (*c.* 980–*c.* 1060) reveal a medieval polymath at work.[1] Among his *opera omnia* are two series of versified 'blessings' and two sets of poetic inscriptions for wall paintings. His lifelong literary activities also include scores of epitaphs, 'carmina varia', translations and paraphrases, a guide for writing and hundreds of glosses. Moreover, in addition to a group of office antiphons and responsories, several non-liturgical Latin songs, proper tropes and a revised saint's *vita* seem likely to be his work.

It is, of course, Ekkehard's monastic history – the *Continuatio casuum sancti Galli* (*c.* 1050) – that has garnered him the greatest attention in scholarship of the last two centuries and helped to secure his legacy as a chronicler.[2] For musicologists and liturgical historians, the rich discussion of ecclesiastical chant in Ekkehard's *Casus sancti Galli* is one of the great sources on early medieval musical practice, and his approximately sixty references to liturgical song in the *Casus* are unparalleled in medieval documents in terms of the number and scope of named chant composers

---

[1] In English-language and German-language scholarship, 'Ekkehardus' can be rendered as either 'Ekkehard' or 'Ekkehart'; I use 'Ekkehard' throughout this chapter. For a helpful overview of the life and work of Ekkehard IV, see H. F. Haefele, 'Ekkehard IV. von St. Gallen', in *Die deutsche Literatur des Mittelalters. Verfasserlexikon*, ed. K. Ruh, et al. 2nd edn, 12 vols. (Berlin, 1977–2007), II, cols. 455–65; and J. Duft, 'Der Geschichtenschreiber Ekkehart († um 1060)', in *Die Abtei St. Gallen: ausgewählte Aufsätze in überarbeiteter Fassung*, ed. J. Duft, 3 vols. (Sigmaringen, 1991), II, 211–20. While useful, these overviews do not reflect several recent re-evaluations, attributions and bibliographic summaries; e.g. the work of E. Tremp, S. Weber, H. Eisenhut and M. Klaper cited in nn. 6, 8, 13 and 19 below.

[2] See Ekkehard IV, *Casus sancti Galli*, ed. and trans. Haefele (Darmstadt, 1980). Since there are other chronicles known as instalments of *Casus sancti Galli*, the *Continuatio casuum sancti Galli Ekkehardi IV* is the more accurate title. In the current study Ekkehard's Sankt Gallen history is the one under consideration and I will hereafter use its accepted shortened form *Casus sancti Galli*, or simply *Casus*.

and compositions, and as regards how musical detail is enlisted in the narrative.[3]

As Margot Fassler has shown, for medieval historians, liturgy often 'formed the framework for historical understanding', and this framework is evident in a myriad of ways.[4] Furthermore, because liturgy was the purview of cantors in particular, it is not uncommon to find that historians were often cantors, and vice versa.[5] Certainly in the case of Ekkehard, it is clear that his musical-liturgical knowledge very much informed how he viewed history. Thus, in this chapter, rather than treat Ekkehard's activities as historian and musician separately, I will explore how he merges the perspectives of chronicler and cantor by analysing a key moment in an episode found in Chapters 51–56 in the *Casus*. I will propose, moreover, that in addition to aspects of the liturgy providing a natural underpinning for how Ekkehard writes history, he describes sung acts and cites specific chants as an effective means of shaping his narrative and telling his story.

One of Ekkehard's central aims in the *Casus* was to provide proof that, over the centuries and up to his day, the monks of Sankt Gallen lived in accordance with the Rule of Benedict.[6] In effect, the *Casus* was to serve as

---

[3] L. Kruckenberg, 'Ekkehard's Use of Musical Detail in the *Casus Sancti Galli*', in *Medieval Music in Practice: Studies in Honor of Richard Crocker*, ed. J. A. Peraino (Neuhausen-Stuttgart, 2013), pp. 23–57 (pp. 28–30). In that study, I listed fifty-nine references to liturgical song; I have subsequently counted one more reference, the sung response *Tu autem* (Ekkehard IV, *Casus*, pp. 222–4, i.e., chap. 113), which fits the category of 'sung occurrence' (consult Table 3.1 in Kruckenberg, 'Ekkehard's Use of Musical Detail', pp. 28–9). A revised list of references can be found in the table in Appendix 1 of the current chapter. For an overview of chants attributed to medieval composers, see: T. F. Kelly, 'Medieval Composers of Liturgical Chant', *Musica e storia* 14 (2006), 95–125; M. Fassler's chapter in *The Cambridge History of Medieval Music*, ed. M. Everist and T. F. Kelly (Cambridge, forthcoming), studies modes of attribution.

[4] Fass D, pp. 157, 167–8.

[5] Ibid.

[6] Ekkehard's repeated assertion that Sankt Gallen adheres to the Rule, and his insistence that external monastic reform was unnecessary, are noted by E. Dümmler, 'Ekkehart IV von St Gallen', *Zeitschrift für deutsches Alterthum* n.s. 2 (1869), 1–73, further pursued by K. Hallinger, *Gorze-Kluny: Studien zu den monastischen Lebensformen und Gegensätzten im Hochmittelalter*, 2 vols. (Rome, 1950–51), I, 187–99. See also H. E. Feine, 'Klosterreformen im 10. und 11. Jahrhundert und ihr Einfluß auf die Reichenau und St. Gallen', in *Aus Verfassungs- und Landesgeschichte: Festschrift zum 70. Geburtstag von Theodor Mayer*, ed. H. Büttner et al., 2 vols. (Lindau-Konstanz, 1955), II, 77–91. More recently, see S. Patzold, *Konflikte im Kloster: Studien zu Auseinandersetzungen in monastischen Gemeinschaften des ottonisch-salischen Reichs* (Husum, 2000), 190–200; E. Hellgardt, 'Die *Casus Sancti Galli* Ekkeharts IV. und die *Benediktsregel*', in *Literarische Kommunikation und soziale Interaktion: Studien zur Institutionalität mittelalterlicher Literatur*, ed. B. Kellner et al. (Frankfurt, 2001), pp. 27–50; E. Tremp, 'Ekkehart IV. von St. Gallen († um 1060) und die monastische Reform', *Studien und Mitteilungen zur Geschichte des Benediktinerordens und seiner*

a contemporary defence against past, putative and potential initiatives of monastic reformers from outside the cloister. I suggest, furthermore, that Ekkehard 'instrumentalized' his cloister's musical and liturgical tradition in order to authenticate the legitimacy of the abbey as a keeper of the Rule.[7] To that end I will consider how the sung act plays a key role in the narrative of Chapters 51–56. Here Ekkehard describes how, in the face of tragedy, a monk's faith in his sacred chant and its efficacy brings about a wondrous change. At the same time, the chronicler proves that this monk, under the most trying of circumstances, fulfilled his monastic obligation of performing the *opus Dei*. Before turning specifically to Ekkehard as historian-cantor, however, let us briefly review his life as poet, glossator, reader and teacher – aspects of his work that surely informed his thinking as chronicler and musician.

Ekkehard as poet, glossator, reader and teacher

The *Liber benedictionum* is a powerful testament to Ekkehard's lifelong work as poet and his ongoing interest in redacting such writings, some dating from his youth.[8] In this collection, a variety of poetic types, genres and uses are represented, with two sets of 'blessings', the *Benedictiones super lectores per circulum anni* and the *Benedictiones ad mensas*, forming the cornerstone of the compendium. There are also two sets of *tituli*, the *Versus ad picturas domus domini Moguntinae* and the *Versus ad picturas claustri sancti Galli*, which were intended to accompany a series of wall paintings in Mainz Cathedral and one at Sankt Gallen, respectively.[9] Also found are over a dozen epitaphs, several occasional pieces and Ekkehard's Latin translation of Ratpert's Old

---

Zweige 116 (2005): 67–88; Tremp, 'Tradition und Neuerung im Kloster: Ekkehard IV. von St. Gallen und die monastische Reform', in *Tradition, Innovation, Invention: Fortschrittsverweigerung und Fortschrittsbewusstsein im Mittelalter*, ed. H.-J. Schmidt (Berlin, 2005), pp. 381–97.

[7] The monks' observance of the Rule is a strong element in the tale of Craloh and Victor as well; see Kruckenberg, 'Ekkehard's Use of Musical Detail', pp. 38–51.

[8] The *Liber benedictionum* is SG 393, an autograph of Ekkehard. See S. Weber, *Ekkehardus poeta qui et doctus: Ekkehart IV. von St. Gallen und sein gelehrt poetisches Wirken* (Nordhausen, 2003). As is often pointed out, many of Ekkehard's earliest works were later revised when he was an adult, with many of these youthful efforts serving as a source of pride. Ibid., p. 74.

[9] Ibid., pp. 41–51. See also H. Leithe-Jasper, 'Beobachtungen zur Arbeitsweise Ekkeharts IV. in seinen *Versus ad picturas domus domini Moguntinae*', in *Latin Culture in the Eleventh Century: Proceedings of the Third International Conference on Medieval Latin Studies*, ed. M. W. Herren et al., 2 vols. (Turnhout, 2002) II, 51–60; Leithe-Jasper, '*Umbra, figura, praefigurator*: Typologie bei Ekkehart IV. von St. Gallen', in *Text und Bild: Tagungsbeiträge*, ed. V. Zimmerl-Panagl and D. Weber (Vienna, 2010), pp. 289–304. Ekkehard spent most of his life at Sankt Gallen, but from *c.* 1022 to *c.* 1031 he taught in the cathedral school at Mainz, serving there until Archbishop Aribo's death in 1031.

High German *Galluslied*. Other examples of poetry not attached to the *Liber benedictionum* include his tract on poetics, the *De lege dictamen ornandi*, itself in rhymed leonine verse.[10] In the past century and half, modern assessments of Ekkehard's poetic abilities have frequently been negative, but as Stefan Weber makes clear, Ekkehard delighted in writing poetry, and these pieces resound with his humour and wit.[11] Moreover, as regards style and diction, many of these poems likely had a pedagogic function, and thus were designed for pupils with limited Latinity.[12]

Ekkehard's activities as glossator are also well documented, and hundreds of glosses, marginalia, corrections, emendations and a few drawings in over sixty sources have been identified in his hand.[13] Thus, his reception of and interaction with all manners of text can be traced, revealing the wide range of subjects that confronted and preoccupied this learned monk. Among the many works for which he provided glosses are writings on rhetoric, dialectics, the quadrivial arts and histories. Martyrologies, saints' lives, homilies, sermons, biblical commentaries, theological tracts – all foundational sources for the materials for the Mass and canonical Hours – also constitute a large portion of the works he glossed. He reworked and revised writings by others, as is likely the case with the oldest *Vita sancte Wiborade*, probably penned by Ekkehard I (d. 973). Like his predecessor, Ekkehard IV took a keen interest in the promotion of this local saint's cult.[14]

In sum, Ekkehard's poetic works and glosses point to a learned scholar, teacher and bibliophile.[15] Certainly it comes as no surprise that Ekkehard

---

[10] Other examples of his verse include SG 146, 168, 174, 176, 211, 279, 342, 621, 626, 830 and 915. For a discussion and listing of these and sources outside of the Stiftbibliothek's holdings, see Weber, *Ekkehardus poeta*, pp. 62–7, 87–95.

[11] Ibid., pp. 68–74, 80–1.

[12] See, for instance, A. Grotans, *Reading in Medieval St. Gall* (Cambridge, 2006), p. 78.

[13] For a recent assessment of Ekkehard as glossator, examples of his editing processes and an extensive bibliography and tables on the identification of his hand and relevant manuscripts, see H. Eisenhut, *Die Glossen Ekkeharts IV. von St. Gallen im Codex Sangallensis 621* (St Gallen, 2009); Eisenhut, 'Ekkehart IV. von St. Gallen–Autor, Korrektor und Glossator von Codex Sangallensis 393', in *Medieval Autograph Manuscripts: Proceedings of the XVIIth Colloquium of the Comité International de Paléographie Latine*, ed. N. Golob (Turnhout, 2013), pp. 97–110. Ekkehard added drawings of diagrams and maps as yet another way to 'gloss' texts. See N. Lozovsky, 'The Uses of Classical History and Geography in Medieval St Gall', in *Mapping Medieval Geographies: Geographical Encounters in the Latin West and Beyond, 300–1600*, ed. K. D. Lilley (Cambridge, 2013), pp. 65–82.

[14] For revisions attributed to Ekkehart IV and a discussion on his contributions to the cult of St Wiborada, see *Vitae Sanctae Wiboradae: Die ältesten Lebensbeschreibungen der heiligen Wiborada*, ed. and trans. W. Berschin (St Gallen, 1983), pp. 13–16, 108–9; Berschin, 'Das sanktgallische Wiborada-Offizium des XI. Jahrhunderts', in *Studies in Medieval Chant and Liturgy in Honour of David Hiley*, ed. T. Bailey et al. (Budapest and Ottawa, 2007), pp. 79–85.

[15] Weber, *Ekkehardus poeta*, pp. 80–1.

was steeped in works representing the curriculum of the seven liberal arts as well as theological tracts and histories, such as those by Flavius Josephus and Paulus Orosius as well as Notker Balbulus.[16] Yet he was also immersed in works used for and supporting the liturgy, and he thought and wrote accordingly, as can be seen his collection of verses for readings, which, as with the items of the Mass and the Office, was ordered by Ekkehard to follow the liturgical year: 'Incipiunt benedictiones super lectores per circulum anni'. Indeed, the oldest extant copy of these blessings – in Ekkehard's hand – shows his clear liturgical conceptualization of this cycle, with his rubrics indicating liturgical seasons (for example, 'De adventu Domini', 'In Quadragesima'), feast days ('In natale Domini', 'In natale Sancti Sephani Protomartyre') as well as specific moments in the liturgical rites ('In prima nocturna', 'in secunda nocturna', 'in evangelio').

Ekkehard as historian and cantor

While Ekkehard's work as poet and glossator present him as a multifaceted writer, informed reader and devoted teacher, his most famous and fascinating literary achievement is his monastic history, the *Casus sancti Galli*.[17] Written sometime in the mid eleventh century, the *Casus* recounts the history of the monastery of Sankt Gallen between c. 890 and 972, and, as a 'continuatio', its primary and official purpose was to resume the chronicle where Ekkehard's predecessor, Ratpert (d. c. 911), had left off.[18] Even so, as already noted,

---

[16] Notker Balbulus of Sankt Gallen (d. 912), himself a composer of liturgical chant, was the author of the history *On the Deeds of Charlemagne*, which also includes numerous references to chant and liturgical matters. See Notker Balbulus, *Gesta Karoli Magni Imperatoris*, ed. Haefele, MGH SRG NS 12 (Berlin, 1959); for an English translation, see *Einhard and Notker the Stammerer: Two Lives of Charlemagne*, trans. D. Ganz (New York, 2008). Notker mentions music and liturgy in Book I, Chapters 1, 5, 7, 8, 10, 18–19, 22, 31 and 33, and in Book II, Chapters 7 and 21. Although the current study emphasizes the importance of liturgy as a framework in Ekkehard's historical writing, it goes without saying that other historical writings influenced and served as models for him as well. See Lozovsky, 'Uses of Classical History and Geography', pp. 65–82.

[17] The prominence of the *Casus* is attested by its two nineteenth-century editions (in 1826 and 1877), and by an early novel loosely based on it: J. V. von Scheffel, *Ekkehard: Eine Geschichte aus dem zehnten Jahrhundert* (Frankfurt am Main, 1855). Subsequently, the *Casus* has been mined by scholars for both its historical content and its highly engaging narrative, illustrated well by the seven selections found in *Life in the Middle Ages*, trans. G. G. Coulton, 4 vols. (Cambridge, 1928–30), IV, 50–84.

[18] Ekkehard states in the prologue that he intends to treat the years of eight abbots, beginning with Salomon III (r. 890–919) and continuing up through his own time, i.e., with the abbatiate of Norbert (1034–72). See *Casus Sancti Galli*, p. 16. In actuality, Ekkehard seems not to have completed the projected chronological span, and extant versions of the *Casus* end in 972. See Haefele, 'Zum Aufbau der *Casus Sancti Galli*

modern historians have often observed that Ekkehard uses the assembled tales on late ninth- and tenth-century life in the Gallus cloister as evidence for his house's adherence to and unremitting preservation of the Rule of Benedict in his own day, an important aspect to which I will return more fully below.

Rivalling Ekkehard's legacy as historian is his legacy as composer, musician, music scribe/neumator and, most of all, as chronicler of past musical events, including the musical works and deeds of others.[19] Indeed, the *Casus* has long been hailed as one of the most informative contemporary witnesses to early medieval musical and liturgical practices in the Latin West, and it contains references to sixty chants (see Appendix 2). Among these, Ekkehard names thirteen composers of chant, ascribing to them collectively forty-two chants or groups of chants,[20] with named authors including such Sankt Gallen notables as Notker Balbulus, Tuotilo and Ratpert, as well as 'outsiders' such as Emperor Charles the Fat and the duchess Hadwig of Swabia. Ekkehard's attributions, though they should often be treated with scepticism, were likely intended to assert the relevance of Sankt Gallen with regard to chant. (Certainly, these attributions, together with his story of the Roman cantors Petrus and Romanus, have helped to shape the late medieval and modern views that Sankt Gallen prevailed as an important centre of early medieval liturgical song.[21]) Additionally, Ekkehard mentions chant

---

Ekkehards IV.', in *Typologia litterarum: Festschrift für Max Wehrli*, ed. S. Sonderegger et al. (Zurich, 1969), pp. 155–66 (pp. 156–7). Ekkehard does incorporate several details from earlier in the ninth century, and he makes a few references to eleventh-century events as well. Cf. Ratpert, *St. Galler Klostergeschichten/Casus sancti Galli*, ed. and trans. H. Steiner (Hannover, 2002), and the next instalment, the *Casuum sancti Galli continuatio anonyma: Textedition und Übersetzung*, ed. and trans. H. Leuppi (Zurich, 1987).

[19] A standard assessment of Ekkehard IV's musical contributions is A. E. Planchart, 'Ekkehard of St Gallen', *The Grove Dictionary of Music and Musicians Grove Music Online*, http://www.oxfordmusiconline.com/subscriber/article/grove/music/08676pg4 (accessed 8 June 2015). To supplement Planchart's overview, see M. Klaper, 'Ekkehart IV. und die liturgische Musikpraxis des Gallusklosters: Das Beispiel der *Te Deum*-Tropen', in *Ekkehart IV. von St. Gallen*, ed. N. Kössinger et al. (Berlin, 2015), pp. 303–21.

[20] For a summary of musical references and a discussion of types of references, see Kruckenberg, 'Ekkehard's Use of Musical Detail', pp. 26–32. Ekkehard is both specific and general when identifying the works of named composers. In the case of the composer Notker Medicus, for example, he writes, 'Then [Notker Medicus] composed beautiful antiphons for [St] Otmar and the hymn 'Rector eterni metuende secli', and certain [verses for the] reception of kings and a hymn for a non-martyred virgin, that is, a hymn to a blessed virgin' (translation mine). See *Casus sancti Galli*, p. 238.

[21] When, in 1512, the humanist Joachim Cuontz completed his massive anthology of sequences for the 600-year commemoration of the death of Notker Balbulus, he included names of composers and the supposed place of origin for numerous

as part of the action in the *Casus*: this is the case for twenty-one references, with three serving simultaneously as an attribution and as a sung act in the narrative.

A handful of scholars have offered compelling reasons for identifying Ekkehard as the author of chant texts, melodies, or (in some examples) both. These include antiphons and responsories for an office for St Otmar,[22] the office antiphon 'Gaudia de geminis' for St Wiborada[23] and several *Te Deum* tropes.[24] In some sources, Ekkehard served as both text scribe and neumator: not only did he supply the neumes for his translation of Ratpert's *Galluslied* (as seen in SG 168, 174 and 393), but he also likely composed the tune for his Latin version of the text – or at least he adapted a pre-existing melody used for the Old High German original.[25] Ekkehard has also been identified as the notator of 'Gratia de celis', his Christmas song for the pupils of Sankt Gallen,[26] and it seems likely that he composed its melody as well.

Finally, Ekkehard has often been treated not simply as a practising musician, but, on the basis of one particular passage in the *Casus*, as a *de facto* cantor.[27] In his eyewitness account of Easter Mass in 1030, celebrated in the presence of Emperor Konrad at Ingelheim, Ekkehard states that a monk of

---

sequences, clearly relying on Ekkehard IV's attributions. Cf. F. Labhardt, *Das Sequentiar Cod. 546 der Stiftsbibliothek von St Gallen und seine Quellen*, 2 vols. (Bern, 1959–63). The combined testimony of the monastery's unusually large cache of notated sources and Ekkehard's claims have helped to position Sankt Gallen—rightly or wrongly—as a leading centre of Latin monophony. See A. Schubiger, *Die Sängerschule St. Gallens vom 8. bis 12. Jahrhundert* (Einsiedeln, 1858); W. von den Steinen, *Notker der Dichter und seine geistige Welt*, 2 vols. (Bern, 1948); S. Rankin, 'Ways of Telling Stories', in *Essays on Medieval Music in Honor of David G. Hughes*, ed. G. M. Boone (Cambridge MA, 1995), pp. 371–94; A. Haug, 'Sankt Gallen', in *Die Musik in Geschichte und Gegenwart*, ed. L. Finscher et al., 2nd rev. edn, 29 vols. (Kassel, 1998), VIII, cols. 948–69.

[22] W. Berschin, P. Ochsenbein and H. Möller, 'Das Otmaroffizium: Vier Phasen seiner Entwicklung', in *Die Offizien des Mittelalters: Dichtung und Musik*, ed. W. Berschin and D. Hiley (Tutzing, 1999), pp. 25–57 (pp. 31–9). As the title of the article indicates, the creation of the office for Otmar occurred in phases, beginning with the *Historia sancti Otmari* (c. 900), a late tenth-century expansion attributed to Notker Medicus by Ekkehard (see n. 20 above), additional chants by Ekkehard and a later version from the second half of the eleventh century.

[23] W. Berschin, 'Das sanktgallische Wiborada-Offizium'.

[24] For the most recent and comprehensive evaluation of Ekkehard's compositional output, Klaper's recent article is essential (see above, n. 19). I am grateful to the author for providing me with a copy in advance of its publication.

[25] Ibid.

[26] Weber, *Ekkehardus poeta*, p. 84. Compare the neumes of the *Galluslied* on SG 393, pp. 247–51 to those of the 'Gratia de celis' on SG 393, p. 253.

[27] E.g., Planchart, 'Ekkehard of St Gallen'; Planchart, 'Ekkehard von St. Gallen', in *Die Musik in Geschichte und Gegenwart*, ed. L. Finscher, 2nd rev. edn, 29 vols. (Kassel, 1998) VII, cols. 214–16 (col. 215), where he is referred to as 'choirmaster' and 'Chorleiter' respectively. Likewise Haefele speculates in a footnote to his edition

Sankt Gallen was in charge of leading the *schola cantorum* of Mainz.[28] Since this event coincides with Ekkehard's own tenure at Mainz, scholars have presumed that he is the unnamed Gallus choirmaster. Yet, as Haefele and Weber have noted, the identity of the choirmaster is far from unambiguous.[29] I know of no extant document formally naming Ekkehard IV (or anyone else, for that matter) as holding the office of cantor at Sankt Gallen in the eleventh century.[30] It is clear, however, that in addition to serving as a teacher in Mainz and at Sankt Gallen, Ekkehard had extensive access to his cloister's library, as well as to the musical and liturgical books kept and used in the choir. As Fassler has shown, the duties of *armarius* and librarian were often combined with those of the cantor as well as of the historian,[31] and the many types of texts that occupied Ekkehard as reader and glossator – *vite*, martyrologies, other hagiographical writings, biblical commentaries, sermons, homilies – were frequently the kinds of texts that engaged cantors and historians alike. Indeed, it is hard to imagine a figure of the Ottonian-Salian era who was more thoroughly enmeshed in the liturgy and music of his community than Ekkehard IV.

Ekkehard can thus be referred to as a cantor in the more generic sense of the word – that is, as an ecclesiastical singer, rather than as the holder of a particular clerical or monastic office. And, despite Haefele's and Weber's legitimate caution, the evidence of the Ingelheim episode might still allow us to consider Ekkehard as a 'cantor' in a narrower sense, that is as a musical leader of some kind. In any event, we can be certain that Ekkehard possessed a deep knowledge of the tradition and practice of music and liturgy at

that Ekkehard IV is presumably the director in question. See *Casus sancti Galli*, p. 140, n. 98.

[28] *Casus sancti Galli*, pp. 140–2: 'vidi egomet ipse Chuonrado imperatore Ingilinheim pascha agente, sancti Galli monacho scolas Magontie curante, officium, ut solitum est, in medio chori crebro coronati inspectu agere.' Ekkehard continues to describe how this monk lifted his hand to depict the melody of the sequence ('Cumque manum ille ad modulos sequentie pingendos rite levasset') and how three bishops who were also present requested that they might once again sing with their former teacher, having studied with him at Sankt Gallen. This cantor was moved to tears. Finally, when the mass had concluded the unnamed cantor was brought before Emperor Conrad and Empress Gisela in order to receive a gift of gold, and to be presented with a ring by the emperor's sister Mathilde.

[29] Haefele, 'Ekkehard IV. von St. Gallen', in *Verfasserlexikon*, col. 456; Weber, *Ekkehardus poeta*, p. 8.

[30] While C. Page cites examples of named cantors found in documents from Latin Antiquity and the early medieval period, Fassler has demonstrated that the offices of the cantor, *precentor* and *succentor* were more properly phenomena of the late of eleventh century and after. Thus that Ekkehard IV is not formally cited as 'cantor' does not prevent him from having acted in some related capacity. Cf. C. Page, *The Christian West and Its Singers: The First Thousand Years* (New Haven, 2010), and Fass A.

[31] Fass A and D.

Sankt Gallen. His authorship of chant texts and melodies and his proven notational literacy (attested in his neumed entries in multiple manuscripts) suggest that he had more than a passing acquaintance with chant. Finally, his *Weltanschauung* concerning music and liturgy thoroughly complemented and indeed infused his historical writing.

Let us turn now to one of the many examples revealing how thoroughly music and liturgy informed Ekkehard's historical narratives. As we will see, his intersecting sensibilities as an historian and as a cantor-liturgist are clearly on display in Chapters 51–6 of the *Casus*, the tale of Heribald and the Hungarians.

Heribald and the Hungarians

Chapters 51–65 of the *Casus* recount the dramatic years of 926–37, a time when bands of Hungarian raiders attacked not only Sankt Gallen, but also settlements throughout the southern German lands and beyond, killing many. Ernst Tremp helpfully divides the overarching story of the Hungarian invasion into three sections; I caption these sections:

(i) The evacuation and occupation of Sankt Gallen and the Hungarians' interaction with Heribald (chaps. 51–6)

(ii) An *excursus* before 926: the visits of a young St Ulrich (later bishop of Augsburg) to the anchoress St Wiborada (chaps. 57–61)

(iii) The defeat and repelling of the Hungarians (chaps. 62–5)[32]

It is the first section, the Hungarians' arrival at and subjugation of Sankt Gallen, that will be considered here. In particular, we will explore how Ekkehard closes this section with a vocalized prayer – the antiphon 'Sanctifica nos' – and how this chant acts as a kind of numinous catalyst, marking a crucial shift in the narrative and signalling deliverance through divine intervention.

According to Ekkehard, though Abbot Engilbert of Sankt Gallen initially attempted to hold off the Hungarians, he was ultimately forced to retreat. Meanwhile many of the Gallus brethren hastily removed what property they could, transporting most valuables to the nearby fortress at Weissburg and to the abbey of Reichenau. With evacuation complete and the marauders drawing ever closer, Ekkehard writes: 'Ingruunt tandem pharetrati illi, pilis minantibus et spiculis asperi' ['Finally, bearing quivers, with menacing spears

---

[32] E. Tremp, 'Eine Randfigur im Rampenlicht: Heribald von St. Gallen und die Ungarn', in *Scripturus vitam: Lateinische Biographie von der Antike bis in die Gegenwart: Festgabe für Walter Berschin zum 65. Geburtstag*, ed. D. Walz (Heidelberg, 2002), pp. 435–41 (p. 435).

and sharpened arrows, they violently broke in'].[33] Moving stealthily through the cloister with intent to kill, the Hungarians found the abbey abandoned – with the sole exception of Heribald, a slow-witted monk of noble birth. Despite the repeated pleas of his fellow coenobites, Heribald had refused to leave the cloister, since he had not yet received his annual allotment of shoe leather. The Hungarians were puzzled to find this untroubled simpleton at the monastery, and through an interpreter (a cleric captured along the way) they finally came to realize the nature of his naïvety. They spared his life, and Heribald became something of a company pet, tolerated as a figure of ridicule and a source of amusement.

The invaders, discovering a nearly emptied treasury and church, set about plundering what little remained, finding only candlesticks and golden candleholders. When they came upon two intact wine barrels, however, Heribald shooed them away, scolding that the wine must remain until his confrères returned. Though they howled with laughter, the Hungarians finally relented and left the cellar unmolested, with one of them bidding that the wine casks of their fool must remain untouched.[34]

Though the Hungarians' treatment of Heribald seems at times almost benevolent, Ekkehard recounts several dishonourable and horrific actions. Two invaders, taking the cloister's name ('Gallus') as a reference to the avian creature (*gallus*, rooster) rather than its missionary-founder, presumed that the weathercock atop the abbey was a kind of titular totem, and, thinking it to be made of some precious material, they scrambled up the tower to retrieve it. One of them, reaching with his lance for the *gallus*, lost his balance and fell to his death below. His compatriot then moved toward the cross of the eastern spire, and, with the intent of defiling the temple, he proceeded to empty his bowels from the pinnacle. Falling backwards, he plunged to his death and his body shattered. Under the threshold of the church the invaders built a funeral pyre for the fallen duo. While the church was greatly in peril – the flames grew to reach the ceiling and even left singe marks on the lintel – miraculously neither the *templum Galli* nor the nearby Church of St Mangen succumbed to the fire.[35]

Ekkehard depicts the marauders as heathens, eating raw meat, gnawing on bones and drinking immoderately. (Though they left the abbey's cellar untouched, they had brought their own wine reserves.) They boxed, taunted and beat their imprisoned cleric-interpreter and Heribald, who seems to have taken little offence at this. At the close of Chapter 54, Ekkehard depicts a mad scene: having eaten and drunk to excess, the Hungarians then

[33] *Casus sancti Galli*, p. 116.
[34] Ibid., pp. 116–18.
[35] Ibid.

horridissime diis suis omnes vociferabant. Clericum vero et fatuum suum id ipsum facere coegerant. Clericus autem lingue bene eorum sciolus, propter quod etiam eum vite servaverant, cum eis valenter clamabat.[36]

[all cried out in the most frightful manner to their gods. Indeed they gathered around the cleric and their fool to force them to do the same. The cleric, able to speak their language fairly well (for which reason they kept him alive), began then to robustly howl with them.]

Ekkehard goes on:

Cumque iam satis lingua illorum insanisset, antiphonam de sancta cruce, cuius postera die inventio erat, 'Sanctifica nos' lacrimans inceperat. Quam Heribaldus cum eo, quamvis voce raucosus, et ipse decantabat. Conveniunt omnes, qui aderant, ad insolitum captivorum cantum, et effusa leticia saltant coram principibus et luctantur.[37]

[Now when the cleric had wildly raved in their tongue long enough, weeping he intoned 'Sanctifica nos', an antiphon for the Holy Cross, since the following day was the feast of its discovery. And Heribald, though rough in voice, sang the antiphon to completion with him. All came together to the unknown song of their captives, and in their rambunctiousness they danced and wrestled before their chieftains.]

As the story concludes, the cleric-interpreter begged for mercy at the feet of the leaders, taking the soldiers' sport as an opportune moment to seek his release. The chieftains mocked him and ordered the warriors to seize him. They flew upon the cleric and began to poke their knives into his tonsured pate, a ritual of torture before decapitation. Just as the terrified cleric was to be beheaded, from the forest's edge horns sounded, signalling a warning to the Hungarians that local defenders were in the vicinity. The Hungarians made a hasty retreat, the cleric's life was spared and he and Heribald were left behind.

At first blush, this episode blends elements of an adventure story and an account of war with a few humorous touches, and it might therefore simply be considered an entertaining or diverting anecdote. Yet this is also a story of a steadfast monk and, in some sense, a set of miracles, arguably intended to edify its readers – for Ekkehard uses this dramatic event to testify, in the person of Heribald, to Sankt Gallen's continuity as an intact Benedictine community. Thus this simpleton, who may seem an unorthodox and even unfit representative of monastic life, manages nonetheless to uphold the general Benedictine principle of *stabilitas* amid the most trying and chaotic of circumstances.

[36] Ibid., p. 120.
[37] Ibid.

To be sure, Heribald might not have understood the subtleties of religious life, but he had absorbed and internalized its rules, and he stood by them in the face of a cruel enemy. His seemingly bizarre refusal to leave the abbey without his yearly ration of shoe leather is, in fact, an attempt to live in accord with the Rule, for, according to Chapter 55, monks are to be provided with suitable clothing and shoes are to be replaced.[38] Similarly, while his preference to guard the wine cellar instead of any other treasures may seem dim-witted or fickle, it can be taken to suggest Heribald's concern with Chapter 40 of the Rule, which deals with the daily apportioning of wine. Even when Heribald is given meat to eat – a victual forbidden save for emergencies – he respects monastic customs for meals, setting chairs for himself and the cleric.[39] By contrast, his heathen captors ate with their bare hands while reclining on the ground, rather than with the benefit of utensils and vessels.

In line with this reading, the final scene with the sung antiphon might be understood as Heribald and the cleric tending to the *opus Dei*, though in an abbreviated fashion. The Hungarians had attempted to compel the pair to sing to their gods, and the cleric sang along while Heribald was silent. Afterwards, ashamed for his lack of faith, the cleric tearfully began the 'Sanctifica nos', and now Heribald – though of a voice raw or unskilled – joins him. Uncertain of what this music is, the Hungarians become frenzied, wrestling, leaping and drawing their weapons, and the cleric, losing faith in the potency of his sung prayer, prostrates himself before the warriors, begging them for his release rather than continuing to call on his own God. He is nearly killed. In contrast, Heribald remains steadfast, and then miraculously in the distance, a rescue draws nigh and the Hungarians flee. Might this sung action, together with the ensuing events, be understood as the final part of a series of occurrences that suggest divine intervention?

To develop this suggestion, we must consider more carefully the potential significance of 'Sanctifica nos'. Focusing on the liturgical context, text and melodic tradition of this antiphon at Sankt Gallen, as well as on the manner of singing and the efficacy of the song that Ekkehard describes, will help to clarify why this cantor-historian might have chosen to refer to this particular chant.

---

[38] *The Rule of Saint Benedict*, ed. and trans. B. L. Venarde (Cambridge MA, 2011), pp. 178–9.

[39] Fitting comportment during mealtime is stressed in numerous places throughout the Rule; cf. e.g., Chapters 32 and 35. Heribald's setting out chairs seems somewhat reminiscent of duties described in Chapter 35 of the Rule, i.e., concerning kitchen servers, though his later boasts of feasting on meat contradict someone following the guidelines of set out by the cellarer. Tremp, 'Eine Randfigur', p. 438, notes that none of the known Heribalds found in confraternity lists and necrologies match Heribald the fool, and, as Tremp surmises, Heribald may better be understood as a construct, useful for Ekkehard's storytelling but not an actual person.

The musical-liturgical tradition and context of 'Sanctifica nos'

According to the two oldest surviving antiphoners from the cloister, 'Sanctifica nos' was one of forty-nine office chants for the Feast of the Finding of the Cross, and was specifically assigned to Second Vespers.[40] Might Ekkehard have meant his citation of this one antiphon to serve, synecdochically, as a stand-in for the whole of Second Vespers, or indeed the whole Office for this feast? 'Sanctifica nos' was neither the first nor the final chant of its respective hour, nor of the day, these being the positional placements typical in such cases of synecdoche. And though 'Sanctifica nos' was the last relatively lengthy chant of Second Vespers in the Sankt Gallen sources, nevertheless there are still four more versicles and three additional short responsories (*responsoriola*) with verses that conclude the office.[41] (See Table 4.1 for chants of the *Inventio crucis* in the Sankt Gallen tradition, following the arrangement found in SG 391, from *c.* 990–1000.) Based on the liturgical placement of 'Sanctifica nos', it would be difficult to argue that the intent of Ekkehard's reference to this single antiphon is synecdochic.

Setting aside the four versicles and the three concluding short responsory-verse items, there are forty-two chants, namely thirty antiphons and twelve responsories, that can be described as moderately lengthy and comparable to 'Sanctifica nos'. The texts of these chants can be grouped according to three basic textual themes: (1) Paschaltide, (2) the legend of Helena and the finding of the cross and (3) the cross as abstract cultic object.[42] Chants in the first category are often assigned to more than one day in the liturgical year, especially for the *tempore paschali*, and their texts make no explicit mention of the cross. This is the case, for example, with 'Surrexit pastor bonus', the third responsory for the first nocturn of Matins in the early Sankt Gallen antiphoners, and first assigned to the Thursday after Easter, as well as 'Ecce vicit leo', the second responsory for the second nocturn of Matins, and first assigned to the Wednesday after Easter. They read:

Surrexit pastor bonus qui posuit animam suam pro ovibus suis et pro suo grege mori dignatus est. alleluia alleluia alleluia.

---

[40] These are SG 390, p. 65 (i.e., the first volume of the 'Hartker codex'), from the very end of the tenth century, and SG 388, p. 236. In some liturgical traditions, 'Sanctifica nos' was also sung on the Feast of the Exaltation of the Cross, but that is not the case in the Sankt Gallen books. However, in the second part of the Hartker codex (SG 391, p. 22), sometime in the thirteenth century a scribe added 'Sanctifica nos' as a cue for St Magnus.

[41] I am basing the genre designations on those used in the CANTUS database, with some modifications.

[42] For an indispensible source on the themes found in this and related liturgies for the cross, see L. van Tongeren, *Exaltation of the Cross: Toward the Origins of the Feast of the Cross and the Meaning of the Cross in Early Medieval Liturgy* (Leuven, 2000).

[Risen is the Good Shepherd, who gave his life for his sheep and for his flock is worthy to die. Alleluia, alleluia, alleluia.]

Ecce vicit leo de tribu Iuda radix David aperire librum et solvere septem signacula eius alleluia alleluia alleluia.

[Behold, the Lion of the tribe of Judah, the root of David has conquered to open the book and to loosen its seven seals, alleluia, alleluia, alleluia!]

With its references to the resurrection, 'Surrexit pastor bonus' typifies the Easter focus often found in chants of this category, while 'Ecce vicit leo', with its clear reliance on Apoc. 5. 5, exemplifies the eschatological dimension present in many of these chants.

References to the cross are common to chants of both the second and third categories, though they occur in distinct manners in each group. In the second category, texts refer to the cross as the object whose discovery is described in the fifth-century legend of St Helena. Save for the Gospel antiphon 'Helena desiderio plena orabat', used for the Vigil to First Vespers, all of the texts in this category are assigned to Lauds. They are organized sequentially, collectively forming a narrative, and these texts often include reported speech and the names of Helena and Judas Cyriacus.[43] In the final category, the texts typically panegyrize properties of the cross, and they are thus filled with evocative imagery, often drawing on or paraphrasing hymns atributed to Venantius Fortunatus – 'sweet nails' (*dulces clavos*), 'precious wood' (*lignum preciosum*), 'wood of cedars' (*ligna cedrorum*) or 'the blessed cross glitters' (*crux benedicta nitet*). In texts in this category, the cross is expressly hailed as a symbol of life and succour to those in need. It is to this final category which 'Sanctifica nos' belongs, made clear in both its initial phrase, 'Sanctifica nos Domine signaculo sancte crucis' ['Sanctify us, Lord, through the sign of the holy cross'], and in its concluding clause, 'Defende nos Domine per lignum sanctum et per pretium iusti sanguinis tui cum quo nos redemisti, alleluia' ['Defend us, Lord, through the holy wood and through the price of your righteous blood, with which you have redeemed us. Alleluia'].

Yet, despite these similarities, the middle clause of 'Sanctifica nos' sets it apart from nearly all chants assigned to the *Inventio crucis* at Sankt Gallen: 'ut fiat [crux] nobis obstaculum contra seva iacula inimicorum' ['that for us [the cross] might be a shield against the cruel arrows of the enemies']. Only three

---

43 See, e.g., the second antiphon for Lauds: 'Helena sancta dixit ad iudam comple desiderium meum et vive super terram ut ostendas mihi qui dicitur calvarie locus ubi absconditum est pretiosum lignum dominicum Alleluia.' ['St Helena said to Judas, "Fulfill my desire, and remain among the living on earth, so that you may show me on earth that place that is called Calvary, where the precious wood of the Lord is hidden." Alleluia.']

Table 4.1 Chants and psalms for the Office of *Inventio Crucis* in SG 391, pp. 61–6

Rubrics (in small caps), *genre abbreviation and chant incipit (in roman type)*	CANTUS *number*
IN SANCTAE CRUCIS INVENTIONE . IN VIGILIA AD VESPERUM R. Hoc signum crucis *	006845
IN EVANGELIO A. Helena desiderio plena orabat	003023
AD INVITATORIUM A. Surrexit dominus vere*	001166
IN I NOCTURNO Psal. Domine dominus noster* Conserva me* Domine in virtute [tua]* Domini est terra* Magnus dominus* Iubilate deo* R. Hoc signum crucis V. Cum sederit filius	006845, 006845a
R. Agnus dei Christus*	006065
R. Surrexit pastor bonus*	007742
IN II NOCTURNO Psal. Confitebimur* Notus in iudea* Bonum est confidere* Cantate domino i* Dominus regnavit ex[u]ltet* Cantate [domino] ii* R. Dulce lignum dulces clavos V. Hoc signum crucis erit	006530, 006530a
R. Ecce vicit leo*	006616
R. Dignus es domine accipere*	006448
IN III NOCTURNO R. Crux fidelis inter omnes V. O crux admirabilis evacuatio	006351, 006351c
R. Crux benedicta nitet V. O crux gloriosa o crux adoranda	006350, 006350b
R. O crux benedicta que sola fuisti V. Mihi autem absit	007265, 007265a
R. O crux gloriosa o crux adoranda V. Mihi autem absit	007266, 007266a
IN MATUTINIS LAUDIBUS A. Helena constantini mater	003022
A. Helena sancta dixit ad iudam	003024
A. Mors et vita apposita sunt	003809
A. Cumque ascendisset iudas	002056
A. Orabat iudas deus deus meus	004172
A. Cum orasset iudas	002020
IN EVANGELIO A. Tunc precipit eos omnes igne	005249
AD VESPERAM R. O crux benedicta*	007265

Table 4.1 *continued*

Rubrics (in small caps), genre abbreviation and chant incipit (in roman type)	*CANTUS* number
IN EVANGELIO	
A. Lignum vite in cruce tua	003628
A. Ecce crucem domini fugite	002500
A. Per signum crucis de inimicis	004264
A. Dulce lignum dulces clavos dulce pondus sustinuit	002432
A. O magnum pietatis opus mors mortua tunc est	004035
A. Salva nos Christe salvator per virtutem	004686
A. O crux benedicta quia in te	004017
A. O crux gloriosa o crux adoranda	004018
A. Nos autem gloriari oportet	003953
A. O crux benedicta que sola fuisti	004016
A. Tuam crucem adoramus domine	005227
A. Adoramus te Christe	001287
A. Salvator mundi salva nos qui	004690
A. Crux benedicta nitet dominus	001961
A. Super omne ligna cedrorum crux	005061
A. Crux fidelis inter omnes	001962
A. Adoremus crucis signaculum	001292
A. O crux viride lignum	004020
A. O crux splendidior cunctis astris	004019
A. Crux alma fulget	001960
A. Sanctifica nos domine	004744
VERSUS UNDE SUPRA .	
Psal. Mihi autem absit gloriari* Omnis terra adoret te deus* Dominus regnavit a ligno* Surrexit dominus de sepulchro*	
RESPONSORIOLA UNDE SUPRA .	
R. Omnis terra adoret te et psallat V. Psalmum dicat nomini tuo domine	007322, 007322a
R. Dominus regnavit a ligno V. Laetentur insulae multe	006525, 006525a
R. Surrexit dominus de sepulchro V. Qui pro nobis pependit	007738, 007738a

Key:

R.   responsorium; responsoriolum

V.   versus; versiculus

A.   antiphona

Psal. psalmus; psalmi

*   cued entry, incipit only

Spelling, capitalization and punctuation follow SG 391.

of the *Inventio* chants in the Sankt Gallen antiphoners make direct reference to 'enemies',[44] but the text of 'Sanctifica nos' is unique in its reference to the cross as a shield and in its reference to the enemies' weapons. The 'savage arrows' (*seva iacula*) of the chant recall Ekkehard's description of the invaders' arrival with quivers, sharpened arrows and javelins ('pharetrati illi, pilis minantibus et spiculis asperi'). Likewise, the symbol of the cross as a shield (*obstaculum*) evokes the scene of the invader's attempt to defile the cross atop the church tower. The cross prevails as God's shield, and Sankt Gallen is spared – the Hungarian climbers are toppled, and their cohorts fail to set the monastery ablaze.

The significance of 'Sanctifica nos' for Ekkehard's narrative is further complicated by consideration of its melodic tradition. Though the antiphon's mode 4 melody is fairly stable, there is one significant melodic variant: the antiphon concludes in one of three different ways. (For a list of sources surveyed and their ending types, see the table in Appendix 2.)[45] The first basic type concludes with the word *redemisti*, which consists of groups of one to six notes, all limited to a range of *D* to *a* before cadencing on *E* – as seen in the version in Graz, Universitätsbibliothek MS 30 (St Lambrecht, fourteenth-century) in Fig. 4.1. The second type concludes with a brief or medium-length Alleluia. In a pair of manuscripts from Augsburg, *c.* 1580 (Copenhagen, Det kongelige Bibliotek Slotsholmen MSS Gl. Kgl. S. 3449 8° VI and Gl. Kgl. S. 3449 8° XI), this nearly syllabic Alleluia is little more than an extension of the aforementioned *deuterus plagalis* cadence on *redemisti*. More common to second-type sources are cadential figures ranging from as few as ten or

---

44 These are the antiphon 'Ecce crucem domini', which includes the phrase, 'Ecce crucem Domini: fugite partes adverse', and the antiphon 'Per signum crucis', with the phrase, 'De inimicis nostris libera nos'. The antiphon 'O crux gloriosa', and a responsory with the identical text, both name *diabolus* as a vanquished agent, but the word *inimicus* is not used. The text reads in full: 'O crux gloriosa, o crux adoranda, o lignum pretiosum et admirabile signum, per quod et diabolus est victus et mundus Christi sanguine redemptus, alleluia.'

45 As of 21 August 2015, the CANTUS database listed forty-five entries for 'Sanctifica nos' (cued incipits and full-scale repetitions included) in thirty-six sources. In addition, I was able to locate this antiphon in another seven sources not at that time surveyed by CANTUS: a thirteenth-century antiphoner from Sankt Gallen (SG 389), as well as sources from Einsiedeln (eleventh-century), Stift St Nikola in Passau (twelfth-century), St Vanne Abbey in Verdun (thirteenth-century) and Stift Schäftlarn (fourteenth-century). It is also found in a late tenth-century miscellany from St Alban in Mainz, where it occurs in the midst of processional antiphons, and finally in a thirteenth-century gradual from Fontevrault, where it has been rubricated as an offertory and assigned to the Mass for the *Inventio crucis*. My study of this melody was greatly facilitated by the collection found at the Bruno-Stäblein-Mikrofilm-Archiv at the Institut für Musikwissenschaft (Universität Würzburg). In all I consulted thirty-one sources and transcribed the melodies from twenty-seven of these, the basis for my melodic analysis. Consulted sources are listed in Appendix 2.

Fig. 4.1 Graz, Universitätsbibliothek MS 30, fol. 251v (selection)

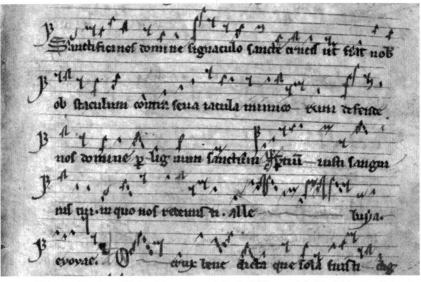

Fig. 4.2 Verdun, Bibliothèque municipale MS 129, fol. 86r (selection)

eleven notes to as many as twenty-seven notes. In almost all readings of this ending-type, the Alleluia remains in the lower part of the modal range – generally within the compass of C to G – as can be seen in a thirteenth-century antiphoner from St Vanne in Verdun (Fig. 4.2).[46]

The third type of reading closes with an elaborately set Alleluia – as in the Sankt Gallen sources, where we find a sixty-note 'coda'. (See, for instance, the version in SG 391, Fig. 4.3.) The melodic reading in SG 391 and two later Sankt Gallen antiphoners are found in a subset of mainly German sources. While the Sankt Gallen manuscripts are notated with adiastematic neumes and thus give no pitch referents, according to the diastematic readings in this subset the final phrase extends well beyond the tessitura found in the Alleluia of the second type.[47] In the prolix Alleluia reading of type three, the final phrase moves into the upper register of the mode 4 range. It climbs twice to c, the highest note of the entire antiphon and otherwise sounded only twice preceding this coda – first in the rising figure *D–a–c* on the first syllable of *signaculo* at the clause '<u>through the sign</u> of the holy cross', and a second time in the same figure at the word *defende* in the petition '<u>Defend</u> us, Lord'. Yet the Alleluia of the third ending type goes even higher, reaching high *d*, and thus exceeding the upper bounds of the other versions of 'Sanctifica nos'. As a consequence, the type-three ending actually shifts the melodic climax of the entire chant, not only raising it by a whole step, but more importantly delaying the musical highpoint until the last few notes of the Alleluia.

This florid ending had initially been copied in a twelfth-century manuscript from Klosterneuburg (Klosterneuburg, Augustiner-Chorherren-stiftsbibliothek CCl. 1013), but, as can be seen in Fig. 4.4, it was subsequently erased (though many of the original notational figures can still be read). In yet another Klosterneuburg antiphoner (Augustiner-Chorherrenstifts-bibliothek CCl. 589) ample space had been left for entering a long Alleluia, as indicated by the inscribed text underlay *ae ... uia*, but the final word was never completed notationally.[48]

---

[46] The version of 'Sanctifica nos' found in Limoges, Bibliothèque municipale MS 2 was transposed up–mostly up a fourth with some phrases or events up a fifth, perhaps indicating the use of partial transposition or *conjuncta*. However, if this reading is 're-transposed' down to E, the concluding Alleluia falls in the range of E to b-natural.

[47] Diastematic readings are found in a twelfth-century antiphoner from Zwiefalten (Karlsruhe, Badische Landesbibliothek Aug. perg. 60) but notated anew in the thirteenth century, and fourteenth-century antiphoners from Einsiedeln and Klosterneuburg bei Wien (respectively Einsiedeln, Stiftsbibliothek Codex 611 and Klosterneuburg, Augustiner-Chorherrenstiftsbibliothek CCl. 1018).

[48] The bibliography on the Klosterneuburg chant tradition is extensive, but I point especially to three recent studies: D. Lacoste, 'The Earliest Klosterneuburg Antiphoners' (PhD diss., University of Western Ontario, 2000); R. Klugseder, 'Studien zur mittelalterlichen liturgischen Tradition der Klosterneuburger Augustinerklöster St Maria und St Magdalena', *Musica Austriaca* 27 (2008), 11–42; M. L. Norton and A. J. Carr, 'Liturgical Manuscripts, Liturgical Practice and

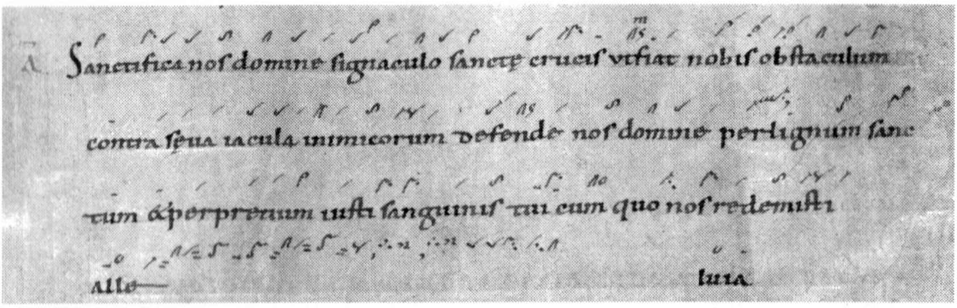

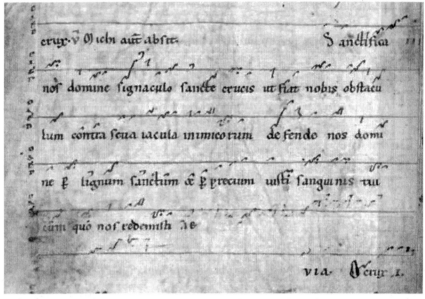

Fig. 4.3 St Gallen, Stiftsbibliothek Cod. Sang. 391, p. 65 (selection)

Fig. 4.4 Klosterneuburg, Augustiner-Chorherrenstiftsbibliothek CCl. 1013,
fol. 160r (selection)

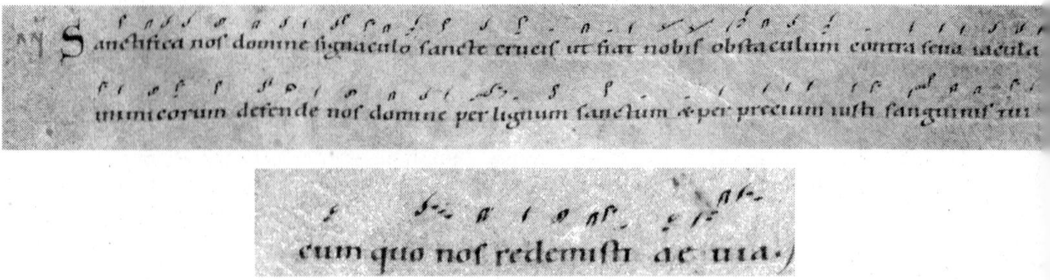

Fig. 4.5 Einsiedeln, Stiftsbibliothek Codex 83:
(a, *above*) fol. 56r (selection); (b, *below*) fol. 56v (selection)

A melodic survey of 'Sanctifica nos' as centred on the three ending-types shows that the elaborate Alleluia *explicit* of the Sankt Gallen tradition was not universal. Indeed, it may have been 'contested' in some places – as the three aforementioned antiphoners from Klosterneuburg indicate – or the antiphon's ending may have been subject to change over time – as the differing solutions in the Einsiedeln books show. Based on my survey of thirty-one sources, the transmission of this melismatic ending does not appear to be tied especially or exclusively to the monastic cursus (as can be observed in Appendix 2). Neither does this ending seem especially local or regional – for it is not limited to the *Bodenseeraum*, Swabia or, more generally, the southern German regions – nor is it more typical of earlier or later sources. Thus, for instance, the antiphoner that is now Einsiedeln, Stiftsbibliothek MS 83 offers an example of the more modest Alleluia conclusion (see Fig. 4.5). This eleventh-century antiphoner is roughly contemporaneous with both the oldest Sankt Gallen antiphoner and the writing of the *Casus sancti Galli*. Moreover, this manuscript belonged to the neighbouring Benedictine cloister of Einsiedeln, about 60 miles (100 kilometres) from Sankt Gallen, and, as we know from other tenth- and eleventh-century liturgical manuscripts from Einsiedeln, that abbey's chant tradition was often similar to that of the Gallus cloister, if not dependent upon Sankt Gallen.[49]

There is thus no way of knowing whether Ekkehard was aware that the long concluding flourish of 'Sanctifica nos' sung in his house was unusual or far from standard. At the same time, Ekkehard had experienced life beyond his cloister's walls, spending a decade at Mainz and, according to a passage in the *Casus*, having travelled some distances (as, for example, to Longemer in the Vosges Mountains, about 50 kilometres west of Colmar).[50] Furthermore, we know he encountered liturgical traditions elsewhere, as his Ingelheim Easter report makes clear.[51] It is also worth noting that in his

the Women of Klosterneuburg', *Traditio* 66 (2011), 67–169. As several authors have noted, the differences among chant manuscripts from the double house at Klosterneuburg may in part have something to do with their destined uses in either the liturgy of the canons or in that of the canonesses. The Klosterneuburg sources also show different strains of influences (diocesan, Augustinian, Swabian, Hirsauian), and of interest for the current study are MSS CCl. 1013, 589 and 1018, which Norton and Carr note to show different mixtures and degrees of influences of Swabian and/or Hirsau-related *Visitatio sepulchri* traditions. See M. L. Norton and A. J. Carr, 'Liturgical Manuscripts', pp. 96–105, 120–37. One might ask if a similar sort of relationship could explain the presence in far-away Klosterneuburg of the type-three ending of 'Sanctifica nos' known mainly in Swabian sources from Sankt Gallen, Zwiefalten/Reichenau and fourteenth-century Einsiedeln.

[49] See, for instance, the various contributions to the commentary of *Codex 121 Einsiedeln. Faksimile und Kommentarband*, ed. O. Lang, 2 vols. (Weinheim-Basel, 1991).

[50] *Casus sancti Galli*, pp. 162–4.

[51] Ibid, pp. 140–2.

description of Heribald's singing, Ekkehard uses the word *decantare* ('et ipse decantabat'), a verb that stresses that the antiphon was sung all the way through or to its end.[52] Is it possible that, as with the text of the antiphon and its unusual mention of enemies and weaponry, Ekkehard alluded to the melodic elaboration of Sankt Gallen's 'Sanctifica nos' conclusion – the most prolix Alleluia of all of the *Inventio crucis* chants in Gallus antiphoners – to help explain the miraculous rescue of Heribald and the cleric? To that end, it might be helpful to consider alongside the words and melody of the antiphon Ekkehard's description of the 'performance' of the chant in his narrative.

In addition to the possible significance of *decantare*, Ekkehard's description of the cleric's singing includes a particular use of *incipere*: 'antiphonam de sancta cruce ... "Sanctifica nos" lacrimans inceperat.'[53] Certainly *incepere* is a common verb, yet in musical-liturgical writings it has a more technical meaning ('to intone'), and it indicates the learnedness of the singer in a hierarchy of musical abilities.[54] In contrast, Heribald, 'rough with voice' (*voce raucosus*) exemplifies sonic qualities most certainly *not* prized in a singer. As expressed by Isidore of Seville and Aurelian of Réôme (among other medieval writers), the voice of the ideal cantor should never be raw, raucous, husky, hoarse or dissonant, but always resonant, clear, illustrious, melodious, sweet, liquid and sharp.[55]

Ekkehard adds that when the Hungarians heard 'Sanctifica nos', they were drawn to this 'unknown song' and reacted first with frenetic leaps and swordplay. Their games, however, turned violent when the cleric abandoned his sung prayer to the cross to implore his captors. Here, Ekkehard could be suggesting the steadfastness of Heribald's petition to the cross was the cause of the cleric's ultimate rescue, for Chapter 19 of the Rule of St Benedict instructs singers on the following points:

---

[52] Ibid, p. 120.

[53] Ibid.

[54] Verbs used to express 'to intone' include *incipere, inchoare* and *imponere*. Ekkehard also (unusually) employs *levare* to mean 'to intone' in a pair of passages in the *Casus*, perhaps to connect the cantors to the great psalmist and cantor King David. See Kruckenberg, 'Ekkehard's Use of Musical Detail', pp. 42–7. See also H. E. Loth, 'A Study of the Lexicography of the "Casus sancti Galli" of Ekkehardus IV' (PhD diss., University of Chicago, 1936). For extensive catalogues of 'singing verbs' as found in liturgical poetry, see G. Iversen, '*Verba canendi* in Tropes and Sequences', in *Latin Culture in the Eleventh Century*, ed. Herren et al., I, 444–73.

[55] Isidore, *Etymologies* III.xx.10–14, ed. W. M. Lindsay, 2 vols. (Oxford, 1911). For a new English translation, see *Etymologies of Isidore of Seville*, trans. S. Barney et al. (Cambridge, 2002), pp. 96–7. Isidore provides an abridged version of this in his chapter on the 'Psalmist' in *De ecclesiasticis officiis* II.12, *PL* 83, 792; for the English, see *De ecclesiasticis officiis*, trans. T. L. Knoebel (New York, 2008), p. 83. In the ninth century, Aurelian of Réôme adopts similar language; see Aurelianus Reomensis, *Musica disciplina*, ed. L. Gushee, Corpus scriptorum de musica 21 (Rome, 1975), pp. 69–70.

Ubique credimus divinam esse praesentiam et *oculos Domini in omni loco speculari bonos et malos*. Maxime tamen hoc sine aliqua dubitatione credamus, cum ad opus divinum adsistimus. Ideo semper memores simus quod ait propheta: *Servite Domino in timore* [Ps. 2. 11], et iterum *Psallite sapienter* [Ps. 46. 8], et *In conspectu angelorum psallam tibi* [Ps. 137. 1]. Ergo consideremus qualiter oporteat in conspectu divinitatis et angelorum eius esse, et sic stemus ad psallendum ut mens nostra concordet voci nostre.[56]

[We believe that the divine presence is everywhere and that *the eyes of the Lord observe the good and the wicked in every place*. Let us believe this most of all, without a trace of doubt, when we are present at the divine office. Therefore let us always remember what the prophet says: *Serve the Lord in fear*, and again, *Sing psalms sagely*, and *I will sing to you in the sight of the angels*. So let us consider how we ought to behave in the sight of the divinity and his angels, and stand to sing psalms in such a way that our spirits and voices are in harmony.]

Heribald, though lacking in vocal refinement or advanced musical abilities, nevertheless fulfils the monastic charge: *psalle sapienter*. As a trusting servant, he harmonized heart, mind and voice as he offered up his chanted petition, never losing faith or forgetting his God.

Conclusion: Reading Cited Chants

Ekkehard's citation of 'Sanctifica nos' is just one of twenty-one examples of 'sung action' in the *Casus sancti Galli*. Based on the analyses of eight other examples completed thus far, I hypothesize that Ekkehard achieves a variety of things when he cites such acts in his narration: chant can serve as speech or thought; present an argument or support a cause; anticipate a change of heart or accompany a divine intervention; supply a subtext; or offer intentional misdirection and finesse a wished-for set of outcomes.[57] In all cases studied thus far, Ekkehard uses song to assert his cloister's continuing adherence to the Rule of Benedict, as well as the brothers' vows to maintain monastic discipline. Cited chants therefore seem to have carried meaning for the

---

[56] *Rule of Benedict*, ed. and trans. Venarde, pp. 90–1.

[57] I have discussed two examples ('Deus qui sedes' and 'Laus tibi sit, O fidelis Deus') at length in Kruckenberg, 'Ekkehard's Use of Musical Detail', pp. 38–51, and a third example ('Pater iuste') briefly in the same study, pp. 31–32. In studies currently underway, I explore Ekkehard's pairing of the chants 'Cives apostolorum' and 'Summi conatibus' in a story challenging an external attempt to reform Sankt Gallen, and his citation of the contrafact 'Thalassi ke potami' [*sic*] of 'Maria et flumina' as the oldest known composition by a female composer in the tradition of the Latin West, as well as his possible allusion, by means of the 'Deus in adiutorium' in *Casus*, Chapter 57, to a *vita*'s description of St Wiborada learning chant as a sign of particular holiness and girding against temptation.

intended audience of monks, oblates and pupils, and these references tapped into the audience's musical sensibilities and aural recall, drawing on his readers' reservoir of musical knowledge.

In his critical edition of 1980, Hans Haefele helpfully provided extensive footnotes indicating more than 300 quotations, paraphrases and allusions to a variety of literary sources, including Scripture, Isidore, Benedict, and various *vite*, as well as Terence, Virgil, Lucan, Ambrose and Sedulius. In only four places in the *Casus* does Haefele identify cited chant or some aspect of musical-liturgical contexts of the chant in question – yet the sixty references to musical texts in the *Casus* illustrate another important portion of Ekkehard's 'library', namely chant books kept there and in the choir. Understanding the meaning and tradition of the liturgical song 'Sanctifica nos' and other 'cantorial' references in the *Casus*, then, may provide yet another variety of 'textual' references, and these sung acts underscore the close, interlocking relationship that chroniclers, historians, cantors and liturgists enjoyed at medieval Sankt Gallen. In such cases, Ekkehard the chronicler is clearly also Ekkehard the singer, a monk who is steeped in the liturgy of his cloister and who relies on his 'cantorial' knowledge to help tell his story.

Appendix 1
Sixty references to chants and melodies in
Ekkehard IV's *Casus sancti Galli*

This table reflects a chant reference identified in the *Casus sancti Galli* since the publication of my study, 'Ekkehard's Use of Musical Detail', pp. 26–30. For additional information on several of Ekkehard's unspecified chant references and named composers, as well as references provided with neumes in the oldest copy of the *Casus*, see Tables 3.1 and 3.2 of that study. In what follows, italic print indicates a textual incipit; small capitals a melody name.

Chapter	Cited music	Use of musical citation in narrative	
		As attribution	As sung occurrence or act
6	*Humili prece*	x	
6	*Ardua spes mundi*	x	
6	*Hodie cantandus est*	x	
6	unspecified sequences	x	
14	unspecified praises for the reception of a king	(x)	x
24	*Pater iuste*		x
30	*Kyrieleison* (Easter morning)		x
34	unspecified verses and melodies	x	
37	unspecified melodies	x	
42	*Deus in adiutorium meum intende*		x
44	*Te deum laudamus*		x
46	*Hodie cantandus* [*est*]	x	
46	*Omnium virtutum gemmis*	x	
46	*Quoniam Dominus Ihesus Christus*, etc.	x	
46	*Omnipotens genitor fons origo*, etc.	x	
46	*Gaudete et cantate*	x	
46	unspecified tropes	x	
46	*Viri Galilei* (offertory)	x	
46	*Sollempnitatem huius devoti filii ecclesie*	x	
46	unspecified chants	x	
46	unspecified sequences and tropes	(x)	

Chapter	Cited music	Use of musical citation in narrative	
		As attribution	As sung occurrence or act
47	METENSES (i.e. MINOR and MAIOR)	x	
47	ROMANA	x	
47	AMOENA	x	
47	unspecified textings of METENSES		
47	unspecified texting of ROMANA	x	
47	unspecified texting of AMOENA	x	
47	FRIGDORA	x	
47	OCCIDENTANA	x	
47	unspecified texting of FRIGDORA	x	
47	unspecified texting of OCCIDENTANA	x	
54	Sanctifica nos		x
57	Deus in adiutorium		x
59	Kyrie eleison (unspecified)		x
66	unspecified sequence (Easter Sunday)		x
74	Deus qui sedes		x
76	Laus tibi sit, o fidelis Deus		x
80	Prompta mente canamus	x	
80	Summum preconem Christi	x	
80	Qui benedici cupitis	x	
80	A solis occasu	x	
80	unspecified antiphons (St Afra)	x	
80	unspecified sequence (St Afra)	x	
80	O martyr eterni patris	x	
80	Ambulans Ihesus	x	
80	Adoremus gloriosissimum	x	
80	texting 'in lidio Charlomannico'	x	
86	Te Deum laudamus		x
94	Maria et flumina		x
94	Thalassi ke potami	x	x
102	Cives apostolorum		x
108	Summis conatibus	x	x
111	unspecified hymns of blessing		x

Chapter	Cited music	Use of musical citation in narrative	
		As attribution	As sung occurrence or act
113	*Tu autem*		x
119	unspecified antiphons (Assumption BVM)		x
123	unspecified antiphons (St Otmar)	x	
123	*Rector aeterni metuendi secli*	x	
123	unspecified verses (reception of kings)	x	
123	unspecified hymn (unmartyred virgin)	x	
133	*Te Deum laudamus*		x
146	act of composing of unspecified chants		(x)

Appendix 2
Sources of 'Sanctifica nos' consulted, transcribed and analysed

Source	Provenance	Date	Cursus*	Ending type			
				'redemisti'	*short/medium 'Alleluia'*	*long 'Alleluia'*	*unknown*
Aachen, Domarchiv, G 20, fol. 259v	Aachen, Marienstift	XIII²ᐟ²	S	x			
Berlin, Staatsbibliothek, Preussischer Kulturbesitz, Mus. Ms. 40047, fol. 78v	Quedlinburg, St Servatius	XIⁱⁿ	S			x	
Cologne, Erzbischöfliche Diözesan- und Dombibliothek, Cod. 215, fol. 100rv	Franconia (Würzburg?)	XII²ᐟ²	M	x			
Copenhagen, Det kongelige Bibliotek Slotsholmen, Gl. Kgl. Samling, 3449 8° VI, fols. 181v–182v	Augsburg	1580	S		x		

* M = monastic   S = secular

Source	Provenance	Date	Cursus*	Ending type			
				'redemisti'	*short/medium 'Alleluia'*	*long 'Alleluia'*	*unknown*
Copenhagen, Det kongelige Bibliotek Slotsholmen, Gl. Kgl. Samling, 3449 8° XI, fols. 104v–105r	Augsburg	1580	S		x		
Einsiedeln, Stiftsbibliothek, Codex 83, fol. 56rv	Einsiedeln	XI²/²	M		x		
Einsiedeln, Stiftsbibliothek, Codex 611, fol. 10/v	Einsiedeln	XIV¹/²	M			x	
Graz, Universitätsbibliothek, MS 30, fol. 251v	Sankt Lambrecht	XIV	M	x			
Karlsruhe, Badische Landesbibliothek, Aug. perg. 60, fol. 148v	Zwiefalten, later Reichenau	XII^ex/ XIII	M			x	
Klosterneuburg, Augustiner Chorherren-stiftbibliothek, CCl. 589, fol. 20r	Kloster-neuburg	XIV	S			(x)^a	
Klosterneuburg, Augustiner Chorherren-stiftbibliothek, CCl. 1012, fol. 68r	Kloster-neuburg	XII	S				inc.^b
Klosterneuburg, Augustiner Chorherren-stiftbibliothek, CCl 1013, fol. 160r	Kloster-neuburg	XII	S			(x)^c	
Klosterneuburg, Augustiner Chorherren-stiftbibliothek, CCl. 1018, fol. 36v	Kloster-neuburg	XIV¹/²	S			x	

* M = monastic   S = secular

Source	Provenance	Date	Cursus*	Ending type			
				'redemisti'	*short/medium 'Alleluia'*	*long 'Alleluia'*	*unknown*
Limoges, Bibliothèque municipale, MS 2, fol. 137r	Paris for Fontevrault	XIII^med	(M)		x		
Munich, Bayerische Staatsbibliothek, Clm 6423, fol. 13r	Freising or diocese	XIII	S	x			
Munich, Bayerische Staatsbibliothek, Clm 17010, fol. 175r	Schäftlarn	XIII/ XIV	S	x			
New Haven, Beinecke Library, MS 481–51, fol. 102v	Lambach	XII^ex	M	x			
Bodl, Canon. Lit. 202, fol. 66v	S. Germany, later Sondrio	XIII	S?	x			
Bodl, Laud. misc. 284, fol. 56r	Würzburg	XII	M?	x			
BnF, nal 1535, fol. 105r	Sens	XIII	S				inc.^d
Piacenza, Biblioteca Capitolari, c. 65, fol. 347v	Piacenza	XII	S		x		
Rouen, Bibliothèque municipale, MS 248, fol. 84v	Jumièges	XIII	M	x			
SG 388, p. 236	Sankt Gallen	XII	M			x	
SG 389, pp. 187–8	Sankt Gallen	XIII^2/2	M			x	
SG 391, p. 65	Sankt Gallen	c. 990– 1000	M			x	
Utrecht, Universiteitsbibliotheek, Hs 406, fols. 111v–112r	Utrecht, Mariakerk	XII^2/2	S		x		

* M = monastic   S = secular

Source	Provenance	Date	Cursus*	Ending type			
				'redemisti'	*short/medium 'Alleluia'*	*long 'Alleluia'*	*unknown*
Valenciennes, Bibliothèque municipale, MS 114, fol. 151v	St Amand	XII	M	x			
Verdun, Bibliothèque municipale, MS 129, fol. 86r	Verdun, St Vanne	XIII	M		x		
Vienna, Österreichische Nationalbibliothek, Cod. 1888, fol. 195r	Mainz, St Alban	X^{ex}	(M)			x	
Vienna, Österreichische Nationalbibliothek, Cod. 1890, fol. 267rv	Augsburg, St Ulrich and Afra	XIII	M	x			
Vorau, Stiftsbibliothek, MS 287, fol. 174v	Salzburg	XIV$^{1/2}$	S	x			

a 'Alleluia' ending (presumably the long type) was prepared with text underlay but never notated.

b Entered in source as incipit only: no ending given.

c 'Alleluia' ending (long type) was entered but subsequently erased.

d Entered in source as incipit only: no ending given.

* M = monastic   S = secular

PART II
The Eleventh Century

5

Adémar de Chabannes (989–1034) as Musicologist

James Grier

Today, Adémar de Chabannes, monk of the abbey of St Cybard in Angoulême during the early eleventh century, is famous for two things: he was the most respected historian of his day in Aquitaine and he advocated the apostolicity of St Martial, patron saint of the abbey that bears his name in Limoges, where Adémar, due to his strong family connections, spent a good deal of time over the early decades of the eleventh century. These accomplishments are well known to modern scholarship principally through the work of Richard Landes, Daniel Callahan and Pascale Bourgain. The third book of Adémar's *Chronicon* remains an essential primary source for Aquitanian history of the tenth and early eleventh centuries, and historians continue to mine his sermons for information about the abbey of St Martial.[1] A third

---

[1] The principal text is Adémar de Chabannes, *Chronicon*, ed. P. Bourgain et al., *Ademari Cabannensis Opera Omnia Pars I*, CCCM 129 (Turnhout, 1999). The seminal study of his historical writing is R. Landes, *Relics, Apocalypse, and the Deceits of History: Ademar of Chabannes, 989–1034*, Harvard Historical Studies 117 (Cambridge, MA, 1995); see also D. F. Callahan, 'The Sermons of Adémar of Chabannes and the Cult of St Martial of Limoges', *RB* 86 (1976), 251–95; Callahan, 'Adémar de Chabannes et la paix de Dieu', *Annales du Midi* 89 (1977), 21–43; Callahan, 'Adémar of Chabannes, Apocalypticism and the Peace Council of Limoges of 1031', *RB* 101 (1991), 32–49; P. Bourgain, 'L'Aquitaine d'Adémar de Chabannes', in *L'Aquitaine des littératures médiévales (XIe–XIIIe siècle)*, ed. J.-Y. Casanova and V. Fasseur, Cultures et Civilisations Médiévales 51 (Paris, 2011), pp. 97–107; P. Depreux, 'Adémar de Chabannes et le souvenir des abbés de Saint-Martial de Limoges', *Bulletin de la Société Archéologique et Historique du Limousin* 137 (2009), 5–23; Depreux, 'Réforme monastique et discours historiographique: L'évocation par Adémar de Chabannes de la dédicace de la basilique du Sauveur et de l'introduction de l'observance bénédictine à Saint-Martial de Limoges au IXe siècle', in *Rerum gestarum scriptor: Histoire et historiographie au Moyen Âge, Mélanges Michel Sot*, ed. M. Coumert et al., Cultures et Civilisations Médiévales 58 (Paris, 2012), pp. 435–52. On Adémar's advocacy of the apostolicity of St Martial, see additionally L. Saltet, 'Une discussion sur Saint Martial entre un Lombard et un Limousin en 1029', *Bulletin de Littérature Ecclésiastique* 26 (1925), 161–86, 279–302; Saltet, 'Une prétendue lettre de Jean XIX sur Saint Martial fabriquée par Adémar de Chabannes', *Bulletin de Littérature Ecclésiastique* 27 (1926), 117–39; Saltet, 'Les faux d'Adémar de Chabannes: Prétendues décisions sur Saint Martial au concile de Bourges du 1er novembre 1031', *Bulletin de Littérature Ecclésiastique* 27 (1926), 145–60; Saltet, 'Un cas de mythomanie historique bien documenté: Adémar de Chabannes (988–1034)', *Bulletin de Littérature Ecclésiastique* 32 (1931), 149–65.

area of endeavour has more recently attracted attention, namely Adémar's contributions to the musical community at St Martial during his sojourns there, the subject of my own research.[2]

Adémar emerges from his writings as a knowledgeable and sophisticated historian, intimately familiar with texts that remain central primary sources for the history of the early Middle Ages, including Gregory of Tours, the *Gesta regum Francorum* (which he used as the source of Book I of his *Chronicon*), the Royal Frankish Annals and the *Liber pontificalis*.[3] Moreover, his historical writing contains a host of references to musical practices in Aquitaine and elsewhere that unequivocally demonstrate his detailed knowledge of the art. He bases the second book of his *Chronicon* on the Royal Frankish Annals, into which he interpolated a narrative of the debate between the Frankish and papal cantors that occurred in Rome during Charlemagne's visit to the papal curia of Adrian I at Easter 787.[4] He in turn borrows this narrative from the biography of Gregory the Great written in Rome by John the Deacon between 873 and 875. Adémar sharpens the historical details of John's account by correcting him – John, for example, states that Adrian was not yet pope when Charlemagne first visited Rome in 774, but Adémar knew better from a comparison of the *Liber pontificalis*, which he had just edited for Bishop Roho of Angoulême, with the Royal Frankish Annals, the source of his Book II – and by placing the debate in the context of the Frankish reform of chant, the motivation for which Adémar attributes to this incident.[5]

In several other literary works, Adémar uses technical terms for genres of liturgical music that exhibit an intimate knowledge of musical practices – for example, his account of the music sung at Mass in the abbey of St Jean d'Angély at the public acknowledgement of the newly discovered skull of John the Baptist; his interpolation into the notice of Pope Adrian II in the *Liber pontificalis* in which he details the musical innovations of the pontiff; and his narrative of the music sung at the Council of Limoges in 1031, the setting for Adémar's fictional debate regarding the apostolicity of St Martial.[6] In all of these, he identifies musical genres with technical terms such as

---

[2] The music is now available in modern editions: Adémar de Chabannes, *Opera liturgica et poetica: Musica cum textibus*, ed. J. Grier, 2 vols., *Ademari Cabanensis Opera Omnia Pars II*, CCCM 245, 245A (Turnhout, 2012). See also Grier, *The Musical World of a Medieval Monk: Adémar de Chabannes in Eleventh-Century Aquitaine* (Cambridge, 2006).

[3] On his use of historical sources, see 'Introduction' to Adémar, *Chronicon*, ed. Bourgain et al., pp. lxiii–lxv.

[4] Adémar, *Chronicon* II.8, pp. 89–90.

[5] See J. Grier, 'Adémar de Chabannes, Carolingian Musical Practices, and *Nota Romana*', *JAMS* 56 (2003), 43–98.

[6] St Jean d'Angély: Adémar, *Chronicon* III.56, p. 176. Adrian II: *Le liber pontificalis: Texte, introduction et commentaire*, ed. L. Duchesne, 2nd edn, 3 vols. (Paris, 1955–57), I, clxxxii(b) n. 1. Council of 1031: [Adémar de Chabannes], *Acta concilii Lemovicensis* II, PL 142, 1353–1400 (1377D–8A). See Grier, *Musical World*, pp. 277–80.

tropi, laudes (meaning tropes of the Gloria) and *sequentiae*. These terms not only vivify his narrative prose by creating a more precise context for the presentation of musical events, but they also verify the author's own technical expertise.

Similarly, Adémar shows sophisticated historical acumen in the way he shapes the texts for the chants that constitute the Offices for SS Valérie and Austriclinian. The cults of these two saints held strong associations with Martial, the saint for whom Adémar strove to assert an apostolic identity. Austriclinian accompanied Martial across the Alps on his mission to evangelize Limoges, a journey that included six other clerics dispatched to cities in Gaul, most notably Denis, the eventual martyr of Paris. Valérie was Martial's first convert in Limoges. Adémar composed the Offices to convince Jordan, bishop of Limoges, to endorse his eccentric campaign to win apostolic status for Martial, making Austriclinian the first bishop of the city and therefore Jordan's distinguished predecessor. Owing to John A. Emerson's pioneering work on these two Offices, we know that Adémar created the texts for the chants by drawing on his own sermons. But behind those texts, whether the chant texts or the sermons from which he extracted them, lies a critical appreciation of the available historical sources for the lives of these two saints: the *uitae* of Martial and Valérie herself, but above all, the history of Gregory of Tours.[7]

Beyond his deep knowledge of these texts, Adémar also exhibited a fine critical acuity as a historian, reconciling errors of fact in John the Deacon and establishing his own narrative from a judicious reading of his sources.[8] When he turned to the production of music manuscripts during two of his stays at St Martial, he applied many of the same critical tools to the establishment of the musical texts, evincing the attributes of a sophisticated music historian, combining his expertise in history and music to create extraordinary documents in a way that makes him deserving of the anachronistic epithet, musicologist.

The crowning achievement of these endeavours, of course, is his advocacy for the apostolic status of Martial, whose tomb became the site of the abbey that bears his name in Limoges, an important pilgrimage destination already in the fifth century. Adémar, despite his knowledge of Gregory of Tours, who identifies Martial as a third-century Roman missionary to Limoges, recast him as a first-century Jew, intimate of Jesus, attendee at the Last Supper, companion of St Peter and his personal delegate to

---

7 J. A. Emerson, 'Two Newly Identified Offices for Saints Valeria and Austriclinianus by Adémar de Chabannes (MS Paris, Bibl. Nat., Latin 909, fols. 79–85v)', *Speculum* 40 (1965), 31–46; Grier, 'Hoax, History, and Hagiography in Adémar de Chabannes's Texts for the Divine Office', in *Representing History, 900–1300: Art, Music, History*, ed. R. A. Maxwell (University Park, PA, 2010), pp. 67–72.

8 Grier, 'Adémar and *Nota Romana*', pp. 56–61.

Gaul.[9] He packaged this radical revision of biblical history as told by Gregory in an elaborate liturgy that he confected for the saint's feast day, as well as those of several of his companions, including Austriclinian and Valérie. These liturgies involved the adoption of existing texts, to maintain continuity with prevailing liturgical practices, the adaptation of chants whose texts identified Martial as a bishop and the creation of entirely new chants, demonstrating his abilities as a composer and musician.[10]

Our pathway to an appreciation of these achievements lies in the musical manuscripts Adémar produced at the abbey of St Martial. During the period 1027–29, Adémar twice fled difficult personal situations at his home abbey in Angoulême for refuge at St Martial. On these visits, he inscribed the musical notation for two elaborate liturgico-musical manuscripts in the abbey's scriptorium, now BnF lat. 1121 and 909.[11] Why would the monks of the scriptorium entrust this task to a monk from another abbey? Adémar, of course, was well known at St Martial because of previous visits there, especially his prolonged stay around 1010 when he pursued advanced education under the tutelage of his paternal uncle Roger de Chabannes, who eventually became the abbey's cantor.[12]

The disciplines he studied with Roger would have included the liturgy, its music and the notation used to record it. Moreover, Roger participated in a major project to record all the liturgical music in use at the abbey, a campaign I suspect (but cannot prove) he directed as cantor. Earlier attempts, around the turn of the millennium, to produce music manuscripts had failed. A fragmentary proper troper survives as the endpapers of BnF lat. 1834 and the remnants of a processionale form the lower text of a palimpsest in the last gathering of BnF lat. 1085.[13] In the face of these apparent failures, the musical community at St Martial renewed their efforts to create a permanent record of their repertories early in the eleventh century, I think in its second decade. This attempt succeeded and its results survive in BnF lat. 1085, an abbreviated antiphoner that preserves the chants of the Divine Office, and in BnF lat. 1120, a manuscript arranged in *libelli* that correspond to the liturgical

---

[9] For a brief summary of the evidence for Martial's life and the early history of the abbey, see Grier, *Musical World*, pp. 4–6.

[10] Grier, *Musical World*.

[11] On BnF lat. 1121, see Grier, 'The Musical Autographs of Adémar de Chabannes (989–1034)', *Early Music History* 24 (2005), 125–68 at 134–56; on BnF lat. 909, see Grier, '*Scriptio interrupta*: Adémar de Chabannes and the Production of Paris, Bibliothèque Nationale de France, MS latin 909', *Scriptorium* 51 (1997): 234–50; Grier, 'Musical Autographs', pp. 156–9.

[12] Grier, 'Roger de Chabannes (d. 1025), Cantor of St Martial, Limoges', *Early Music History* 14 (1995), 53–119.

[13] On BnF lat. 1834, see Emerson, 'Fragments of a Troper from Saint Martial de Limoges', *Scriptorium* 16 (1962), 369–72; on the project as a whole, see Grier, 'Roger de Chabannes', pp. 70–81.

Table 5.1 The *Libelli* of BnF lat. 1120 and 1121

Libelli in BnF lat. 1120	*Libelli* in BnF lat. 1121
Proper tropes	Proper tropes
Ordinary tropes	Ordinary tropes
Prosae	*Sequentiae*
Processional antiphons	Tracts
Offertories	Offertories
Antiphons	Processional antiphons
	Alleluias
	Antiphons
	Prose
	Tonary
	Antiphons
	Office of the Trinity
	Antiphons

repertories it preserves (see Table 5.1).[14] In other publications, I characterize this succession of genres as *gradus ad parnassum*, a progressive programme of study for the young singer who aspires to become a soloist in the monastic musical community, culminating in the ornate Offertories with their verses.[15]

Adémar, then, received his invitation to provide the musical notation, first for BnF lat. 1121 and then BnF lat. 909, because he was well known to the monks of the scriptorium, who could always be assured of the quality of his musical training, and, as the nephew of the cantor Roger, he was associated with his uncle and the success of the project to codify the abbey's musical repertories. In fact, the St Martial monks received a good deal more than they were anticipating, since Adémar used the opportunity to introduce the key concept of accurate heighting to the Aquitanian notation in use at the abbey.[16] Previously, in BnF lat. 1120, for example, Aquitanian notation used the vertical axis of writing to indicate melodic direction. Notes written

---

[14] Grier, 'Roger de Chabannes', pp. 82–119.

[15] Grier, *Musical World*, pp. 45–7; Grier, 'Adémar de Chabannes (989–1034) and Musical Literacy', *JAMS* 66 (2013): 605–38 at 621–2.

[16] P. Evans, *The Early Trope Repertory of Saint Martial de Limoges*, Princeton Studies in Music 2 (Princeton, 1970), pp. 48, 121–5, first identified BnF lat. 1121 as the earliest Aquitanian manuscript with precise relative pitch information; see also A. E. Planchart, 'The Transmission of Medieval Chant', in *Music in Medieval and Early Modern Europe: Patronage, Sources and Texts*, ed. I. Fenlon (Cambridge, 1981), pp. 347–63 (355). I identified Adémar as the music scribe of this manuscript, in 'The Musical Autographs', pp. 134–56.

higher above the sung text sound higher on the gamut than those written lower and closer to the text. Adémar, by regulating the height of the note according to the musical distance from its neighbours, introduced relative pitch information to Aquitanian notation.

Whatever the source of this innovation might have been, it is here, in its imposition, that Adémar used many of the tools we would associate with modern musicology. Many of the repertories for which Adémar provided the melodies in BnF lat. 1121 also occur in lat. 1120: tropes of the Proper and the Ordinary, processional antiphons, *prosae* (although the proser in lat. 1121 is fragmentary) and Offertories. He could well have used the neumations in lat. 1120 as at least a guide for those he inscribed in lat. 1121.[17] But many of the repertories in lat. 1121 have no parallel in lat. 1120: *sequentiae*, Tracts and Alleluias. Where did he get the melodies for these chants? We shall see that his procedure did not fundamentally differ between the two groups.

Figs. 5.1 and 5.2 show the opening of the Offertory 'Tollite portas' from BnF lat. 1120 and 1121. First, 1120 gives only the incipit of the refrain, whereas 1121 provides the entire refrain, a decision made by the different text scribes of these two manuscripts. But a comparison of the two neumations with a transcription into modern notation (Ex. 5.1) makes it clear that the heighting of 1120 offers only directional guidance, not specific information about pitch relationships, while Adémar's neumation in 1121 does show firm intervallic data.[18] The scribe of 1120 indicates direction with precision and, when the melody moves in conjunct motion, provides accurate information, but he writes intervals larger than a third without accuracy. It is important to note that, for the purposes of the scribe and the users of this manuscript, this form of notation is entirely sufficient. Those who used 1120 retained these melodies in their memory, and from the notation derived information about the direction of the melodic motion.

Adémar provides an entirely different graphic representation of the melody, exploiting the vertical axis of writing to indicate precise intervallic relations. To derive these data, it seems like that, in the first instance, he would draw on his own memory of the chant, using the neumation of BnF lat. 1120 for a supplement. In this regard, his procedure probably resembles that of most music scribes of the era, coordinating their own recollection of the

---

[17] On Adémar's use of BnF lat. 1120 as an exemplar for BnF lat. 1121 and 909, see Grier, *Musical World*, pp. 159–82.

[18] Compare the transcriptions in *Offertoriale triplex cum versiculis* (Solesmes, 1985), no. 7 pp. 14–15; R. Hankeln, *Die Offertoriums Prosuln der aquitanischen Handschriften: Voruntersuchungen zur Edition des Offertoriumscorpus und seiner Erweiterung*, 3 vols., Regensburger Studien zur Musikgeschichte, 2 (Tutzing, 1999), III, 18; R. Maloy, *Inside the Offertory: Aspects of Chronology and Transmission* (New York, 2010), online edition, no. 6, with commentary, pp. 253–6; and F. Ackermans et al., 'Vorschläge zur Restitution von Melodien des Graduale Romanum, Teil 29', *Beiträge zur Gregorianik* 51 (2011), 11–56 (no. 97.4 pp. 36–7).

Fig. 5.1 BnF lat. 1120, fol. 186r (selection)

melody with whatever written support was available. But more was at stake. It would be unfair to characterize Adémar as an outsider in the scriptorium at St Martial, but he did lack the indispensable credential to be regarded as an insider: membership in the monastic community. So, he could not rely on his reputation and the association with his uncle alone to convince his peers in the scriptorium of the reliability of his neumations.

In constructing the sequentiary, the *libellus* of untexted and partially texted sequences for the full liturgical year, over which he had sole discretion, Adémar clearly strove to make his collection accord with practice at St Martial, in regard to both the choice of pieces for each feast and the melodic fabric of each chant.[19] I strongly suspect that he canvassed the members of the

---

[19] Grier, 'Adémar de Chabannes and the Sequence and the Sequence at Saint-Martial in the Early Eleventh Century', in *Medieval Music in Practice: Studies in Honor of Richard Crocker*, ed. J. A. Peraino (Middleton, WI, 2013), pp. 59–84.

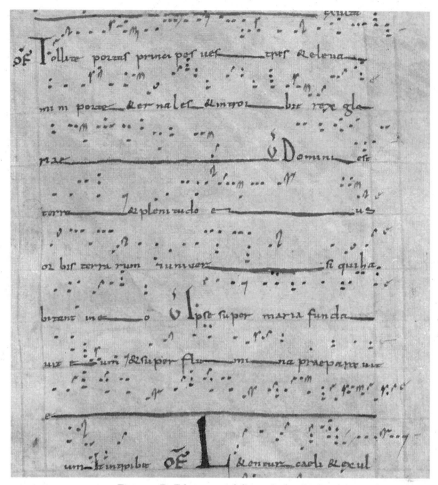

Fig. 5.2 BnF lat. 1121, fol. 93r (selection)

Ex. 5.1 Offertory 'Tollite portas' (opening refrain and first verse only)

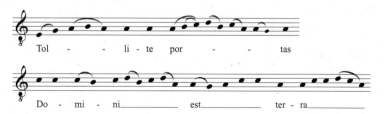

(a)

(b)

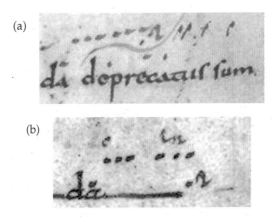

Fig. 5.3 (a) BnF lat. 1120, fol. 201v (selection);
(b) BnF lat. 1121, fol. 118r (selection)

abbey's musical community to supplement, confirm and complement the available written information regarding this repertory. So too, then, with the Offertories, Adémar augmented his own memory and the spare written data in BnF lat. 1120 with melodic information gleaned from his peers. Where BnF lat. 1120 lacked a repertory, the Alleluias, for example, Adémar was obliged to rely on memory alone to construct his neumation – his own memory and the institutional memory of members of the community, without benefit of a written exemplar.

Furthermore, in several places, Adémar supplements the intervallic information he provides with indications of performing nuances. Fig. 5.3 shows a passage from the second verse of the Offertory 'Confitebor tibi' that consists of six repeated notes. The scribe of BnF lat. 1120 writes them all in a continuous row, whereas Adémar, in BnF lat. 1121, first separates them into two groups of three notes each, and then characterizes the performing style of each group with *litterae significatiuae c*, meaning *celeriter*, 'fast', and another abbreviation (not encountered in Notker's epistle about these *litterae*) *ln*, presumably standing for *lene* or *leniter*, 'gently' or 'mildly'.[20] However one was to interpret these two markings – and they do not seem to me to be opposites – Adémar clearly envisages a contrast between the two groups, of which there is no indication in 1120.

One final example further illustrates the nature of his accomplishment. The Office of the Holy Trinity obviously held great importance for the community at St Martial. The scribes of BnF lat. 1085, the abbey's abbreviated antiphoner, originally reserved one complete folio, the current fol. 70, for the Office. When it did arrive at the abbey, a new set of scribes undertook to enter

[20] For an edition of Notker's letter, see J. Froger, 'L'épitre de Notker sur les "lettres significatives": Édition critique', *Études Grégoriennes* 5 (1962), 23–71.

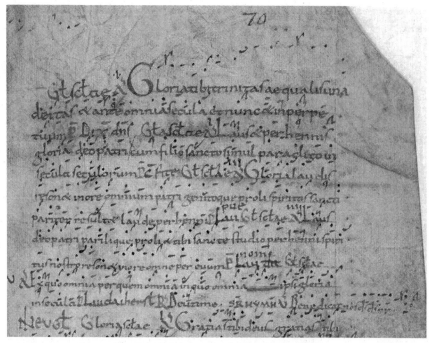

Fig. 5.4 BnF lat. 1085, fol. 70r (selection)

it into the manuscript and simultaneously decided to provide full texts and neumations, unlike the practice of the original scribes, who throughout the manuscript provide for the most part only the incipits of the chant texts and very sparing musical notation (see Figs. 5.4 and 5.5). Still, the music scribe used heighting, as in BnF lat. 1120, that provides only directional information, which the manuscript's users would need to supplement with orally transmitted information, but Adémar constructs a neumation that transmits accurate relative pitch information, presumably, again, from his memory and that of his peers.

We know he succeeded in this endeavour because of events of the following year. Adémar remained at St Martial for the second half of 1027 and probably into the early months of 1028; we have no evidence of his presence in Angoulême before 6 April, when he witnessed the mysterious death of Count William of Angoulême. In the dynastic strife that followed, Adémar fled for Limoges and refuge, once more, in the abbey of St Martial.[21] In the meantime, the scriptorium there had embarked on an ambitious new project, a commission of an elaborate troper-proser for the abbey of St Martin

---

[21] Landes, *Relics, Apocalypse, and the Deceits*, pp. 178–93; and Grier, *Musical World*, pp. 25–6.

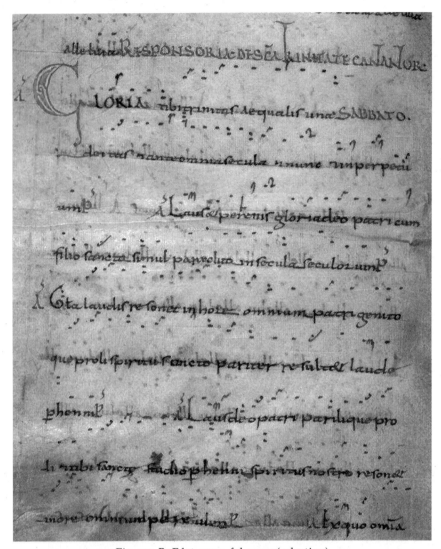

Fig. 5.5 BnF lat. 1121, fol. 223v (selection)

in Limoges, recently reformed under the Benedictine rule.[22] The first scribe to whom they assigned the inscription of the musical notation could not replicate Adémar's accurate heighting. So, when Adémar reappeared, probably in the late spring or early summer 1028, the monks of the scriptorium immediately set him to work writing the notation in this important manuscript, now BnF lat. 909.

[22] Grier, '*Scriptio interrupta*', pp. 237–9.

Fig. 5.6 (a) BnF lat. 1120, fol. 5or (selection);
(b) BnF lat. 1121, fol. 3or (selection); (c) BnF lat. 909, fol. 43r (selection)

They had two reasons for inviting Adémar to complete BnF lat. 909. The achievement of introducing accurate heighting was impressive enough on its own merits, but I believe they were even more satisfied with the melodic fabric of the neumations he provided for BnF lat. 1121.[23] So, Adémar went one important step beyond the accomplishments of Roger and his colleagues in compiling the liturgical music used at the abbey in BnF lat. 1120 and 1085; he created an accurate historical record of many of those melodies through the precise and consistent imposition of accurate heighting to the notation, showing the intervallic content of the melodies.

To achieve this result, Adémar must have applied many of the same tools modern musicologists use to create a critical recension of a musical text. In particular, he stole a page from the modern ethnomusicologist's book of strategies, and did field work among his peers in the musical community at St Martial, consulting their individual and collective memories alongside his own. For he could not rely on his memory alone, as well respected in the community as he may have been on account of his own accomplishments and the association with his uncle, Roger the cantor. On this collected material, however, he also imposed his own critical awareness of the melodic tradition.

[23] Grier, 'Adémar and Musical Literacy', pp. 624–5.

I close with two brief examples. In the *prosae,* the scribe of BnF lat. 1120 uses liquescence not to facilitate the enunciation of diphthongs or awkward combinations of consonants, as most scribes do, but instead as melodic ornaments. Adémar, exhibiting a much more utilitarian view of liquescence, suppresses them.[24] Second, he has altered the melodic fabric a number of times to create a slightly different effect on a local level, reflecting the essentially conservative environment in which he worked. Fig. 5.6 presents the end of a trope element from the Mass for St Martial. It closes with the under-second cadence familiar from the sequence repertory. On the second syllable of *uota,* the scribe of BnF lat. 1120 extends the phrase with an anticipation of the note a second below the final. Adémar, in BnF lat. 1121 and 909, suppresses this note in order to articulate the cadential figure more cleanly. The modification does not alter the melodic structure of the chant, and affects only this cadence, but is the result of Adémar's personal critical evaluation of the melodies practised at the abbey and recorded in BnF lat. 1120.

To ensure the success of his project, Adémar needed, in the first instance, to capture in writing the corporate memory of the St Martial community. And he was confronting a much more difficult audience than that which the modern musicologist does: the active participants and contributors to the living musical tradition of the abbey. To succeed, he had to apply a critical appraisal of that tradition in its historical context.

[24] Grier, *Musical World,* pp. 169–74.

6

Cantor or *Canonicus*? In Search of Musicians and Liturgists in Eleventh-Century Constance

Henry Parkes

In seeking to understand the disposition of personnel within early medieval religious communities, we can do far worse than to consult the famous confraternity books of Carolingian Reichenau and Sankt Gallen. In the lands around Lake Constance, where the modern states of Germany, Austria and Switzerland now converge, groups of ninth-century monks assembled (and their successors expanded) extensive inventories of the members of other Christian communities, both living and departed.[1] The purpose of these compilations was to faciliate networks of reciprocal intercession right across Europe, in locations as widely dispersed as Provence, Normandy, Saxony, Bavaria and Lombardy, and as far from Constance as Jerusalem. Many of the entries were also accompanied by the specific ranks of those for whom prayer was offered: not only the monks we might expect, but also monarchs, dukes and counts, laymen, doctors, nuns, anchorites, priests, deacons, archpriests, chancellors, chaplains, clerics, deans, priors, bishops, popes, patriarchs – and cantors.

Confraternity books are not especially informative, as it turns out, about the specific role of cantors within religious communities of this early period. But what they lack in historical insight they make up for in methodological counsel, because their pages exemplify an important point of ambiguity. When we encounter the individual Purchart, who is titled 'can', or the individual Ruadheri, titled 'ca', there is more than one possibility for the expansion of these respective abbreviations.[2] Does 'can' refer to the high office of 'cantor', who, as later medieval descriptions tend to concur, took charge of music and liturgy within a given institution?[3] Does it simply refer to the lowly rank of 'cantor', literally 'singer', to which young clerics were sometimes ordained prior to the traditional entry-level position of

---

[1] R. McKitterick, *The Carolingians and the Written Word* (Cambridge, 1989), pp. 156–73; see also J. Hendrix, 'Liturgy for the Dead and the Confraternity of Reichenau and St Gall, 800–950' (unpublished Ph.D. dissertation, University of Cambridge, 2007).

[2] *Der Verbrüderungsbuch der Abtei Reichenau*, ed. J. Autenrieth et al., MGH Libri Mem. NS 1 (Hanover, 1979), p. 223, facsimile pp. 4, 126.

[3] Fass A.

door-keeper?[4] Or might it refer instead to a 'canonicus' (or 'canon'), a member of a community of priests associated with a cathedral or collegiate church, whose coveted existence had a reputation – at least until the reform movements of the eleventh and twelfth centuries – as a sinecure for the sons of the nobility?[5] I cite this point of confusion not as a challenge to existing readings of confraternity books, but as a cause for reflection in this important collection of cantor-historian studies. To what extent can we be confident that the 'cantor' we find documented in a particular historical source was always in a position of high authority? Can we be sure that all 'cantors' had the same broad remit within their respective communities, and that the normative body of monastic customs from which our working definition of 'cantor' comes was indeed the norm? And how often, as the entries of Purchart and Ruadheri gently suggest, might historical evidence of a 'cantor' appear simply because we wish to find it?

The value of these questions will become clear in a chapter which tries to shed light on the lives of early medieval canon-cantors. The intention is not only to flesh out our incomplete understanding of musical and liturgical activity within early communities of priests, but also to seek redress for a historiography dominated by the achievements of monks, and by the narratives of monks who chose to present their clerical counterparts in an unfavourable light.[6] Whether or not we accept those narratives, undisputed is the fact that canons sang together in church. As we find out in the *Regula canonicorum* of Chrodegang of Metz, an eighth-century template for canonical life which draws heavily on the Benedictine Rule, canons were expected

---

[4] R. E. Reynolds, 'The *De officiis vii graduum*: Its Origins and Early Medieval Development', *Mediaeval Studies* 34 (1972), 113–51; R. E. Reynolds, ' "At Sixes and Sevens" – and Eights and Nines: The Sacred Mathematics of Sacred Orders in the Early Middle Ages', *Speculum* 54 (1979), 669–84.

[5] For a sense of the tensions, familial and financial, among both canons and canonesses, see H. Fichtenau, *Living in the Tenth Century: Mentalities and Social Orders*, trans. P. Geary (Chicago, 1991), pp. 224–30. Further bibliography on canons is cited below.

[6] A recent and most welcome corrective to this is J. Barrow, *The Clergy in the Medieval World: Secular Clerics, Their Families and Careers in North-Western Europe, c. 800–c. 1200* (Cambridge, 2015). Among existing studies which consider 'cantors' among communities of priests see G. Vecchi, 'L'Insegnamento e la Pratica Musicale nelle Communità dei Canonici', in *La Vita Comune del Clero nei Secoli XI e XII. Atti della Settimana di Studio: Mendola, Settembre 1959*, 2 vols. (Milan, 1962), II, 26–39; M. Schuler, 'Zur Geschichte des Kantors im Mittelalter', in *Bericht über den Internationalen Musikwissenschaftlichen Kongress, Leipzig 1966*, ed. C. Dahlhaus et al. (Leipzig, 1970), pp. 169–73. Focused accounts of musical canons include Fass B; Fass C; and B. Brand, *Holy Treasure and Sacred Song: Relic Cults and Their Liturgies in Medieval Tuscany* (New York, 2014). See also H. Parkes, *The Making of Liturgy in the Ottonian Church: Books, Music and Ritual in Mainz, 950–1050* (Cambridge, 2015), chs. 2, 4.

to perform both the Mass and the Office in community.[7] Chrodegang was famous for his musical initiatives, indeed, having been responsible for an early attempt to import Roman chant to his cathedral at Metz. And when his Rule was repackaged and ratified for all of Francia at the Council of Aachen in 816, one of the proclamations was concerned very specifically with canonical 'cantors', requiring that junior singers use their musical skills not to vaunt their pride but to 'encourage the people around them to meditate lovingly upon heaven, not only by the sublime texts but also through the harmonious sounds they produce'.[8]

This passage is sometimes construed as evidence for a musical official, but there is nothing to suggest that musicians had a *de facto* place within the hierarchy of clerical communities before the middle of the tenth century. Among the earliest references to an official is that found in a disciplinary document sent to the canons of Aschaffenburg in 976.[9] An irrascible cantor named Gozmar had lashed out in anger, we are told, resulting in the tragic death of a school pupil who was standing too close. The story has been taken as a symptom of the less than perfect standards in canonical communities to this point, but no less important is the frame for this cautionary tale. Willigis of Mainz, Gozmar's bishop, documented the tragic events not only to confirm the cantor's punishment (a spell in a monastery) but also to sort out a disfunctional community, much as bishops of the time were doing in dioceses right across Europe.[10] The new energies being injected into the clerical life in this period help to explain a sudden profusion of references to canon-cantors: from 986 onwards charters from Lucca Cathedral consistently list the cantor near the top of the canonical hierarchy;[11] the chronicler Richer was in later centuries credited with having been both 'cantor and canon' in late tenth-century Reims;[12] necrologies list two of the earliest cantors at

---

[7] M. A. Claussen, *The Reform of the Frankish Church: Chrodegang of Metz and the Regula canonicorum in the Eighth Century* (Cambridge, 2004). The relevant texts are edited and translated in J. Bertram, *The Chrodegang Rules: The Rules for the Common Life of the Secular Clergy From the Eighth and Ninth Centuries* (Aldershot, 2005).

[8] Bertram, *Chrodegang Rules*, p. 164.

[9] K. H. Rexroth, 'Der Stiftsscholaster Herward von Aschaffenburg und das Schulrecht von 976', in *1000 Jahre Stift und Stadt Aschaffenburg: Festschrift zum Aschaffenburger Jubiläumsjahr 1957*, ed. W. Fischer, 2 vols. (Aschaffenburg, 1957), I, 203–30.

[10] C. Dereine, 'Vie commune, règle de Saint Augustin et chanoines réguliers au XIe siècle', *Revue d'histoire ecclésiastique* 41 (1946), 365–406; J. Siegwart, *Die Chorherren- und Chorfrauengemeinschaften in der Deutschsprachigen Schweiz vom 6. Jahrhundert bis 1160, mit einem Überblick über die Deutsche Kanonikerreform des 10. und 11. Jh*, Studia Friburgensia NF 30 (Fribourg, 1962).

[11] E. Kittel, 'Der Kampf um die Reform des Domkapitels in Lucca im 11. Jahrhundert', in *Festschrift Albert Brackmann*, ed. L. Santifaller (Weimar, 1931), pp. 207–47 (p. 237).

[12] J. Glenn, *Politics and History in the Tenth Century: The Work and World of Richer of Reims* (Cambridge, 2004), p. 21.

Notre Dame as Lisiernus (d. 990) and Adelelmus (d. 1035);[13] Margot Fassler has brought to light an intriguing cantor's book from the circle of Fulbert of Chartres (d. 1028);[14] and in the years around 1065 an individual named Stephen identified himself in his own liturgical pocket-book as priest, cantor and canon at Verona.[15] In this period cantors (and precentors) also begin to be named regularly as signatories in cathedral charters, with prominent French examples including Tours (933), Chartres (950), Toul (971) and Poitiers (1016).[16] Just as seems to have happened in monastic communities during the same period, canonical communities of the tenth and eleventh centuries increasingly placed musically trained officials near the top of their hierarchies.

It is not clear, however, how far the monastic parallel goes. The duties of clerical cantors are not really described in any detail before to the end of the eleventh century, when the new wave of disciplined, ascetic communities – including the celebrated foundations of Saint-Ruf (founded in 1039), Rottenbuch (1073), Marbach (*c.* 1090), Saint-Victor (1113) and Prémontré (1120) – began to produce customaries which clearly take after monastic models.[17] We might wish to project these models of existence back onto previous centuries, were it not for an intriguing eleventh-century anomaly. In the customary which Delamare attributed to the cathedral of Rouen, the musical, liturgical and educational responsibilities of the community are distributed in a quite unmonastic manner, based loosely upon the *Epistula ad Leudefredum*, a seventh- or eighth-century description of clerical orders

---

[13] G. V. Birkner, 'Notre-Dame Cantoren und Succentoren vom Ende des 10. bis zum Beginn des 14. Jahrhunderts', in *In Memoriam Jacques Handschin*, ed. H. Anglès (Strasbourg, 1962), pp. 107–26 (p. 112); H. Tischler, 'The Early Cantors of Notre Dame', *JAMS* 19 (1966), 85–7 (p. 85).

[14] Fass C, pp. 96–106.

[15] *L'orazionale dell'arcidiacono Pacifico e il Carpsum del cantor Stefano*, ed. G. G. Meersseman, E. Adda and J. Deshusses, Spicilegium Friburgense 21 (Fribourg, 1974).

[16] This information comes from a combination of the TELMA, http://www.cn-telma. fr/originaux/index/ (accessed 1 December 2014) and ELEC, http://elec.enc. sorbonne.fr/ (accessed 1 December 2014) databases. For detailed personnel lists, and for evidence of cantors' relatively late arrival in cathedral chapters, see D. S. Spear, *The Personnel of the Norman Cathedrals during the Ducal Period, 911–1204* (London, 2006). A useful survey of English evidence is presented in D. Greenway, 'The False *Institutio* of St Osmund', in *Tradition and Change: Essays in Honour of Marjorie Chibnall*, ed. D. Greenway et al. (Cambridge, 1985), pp. 77–101 (p. 84).

[17] On these developments see, principally, C. Dereine, 'Vie commune'; J. Siegwart, *Die Chorherren- und Chorfrauengemeinschaften*; S. Weinfurter, 'Neuere Forschung zu den Regularkanonikern im deutschen Reich des 11. und 12. Jahrhunderts', *Historische Zeitschrift* 224 (1977), 379–97. For evidence of canons borrowing their customs from monasteries, see J. Siegwart, *Die Consuetudines des Augustiner-Chorherrenstiftes Marbach im Elsass (12. Jahrhundert)*, Spicilegium Friburgense 10 (Fribourg, 1965); Fass B.

sometimes attributed to the milieu of Isidore of Seville.[18] This rare survival from a pre-1100 canonical community raises the serious possibility that clerics structured their communities in different and hitherto unpublicized ways. That finding does not play a prominent role in this chapter, except that it gives legitimacy to the unusual approach which follows. Acknowledging that monastically tinged customs laid down in later centuries may say nothing of earlier practice, this chapter probes the world of the early canon-cantor from another direction. Instead of seeking out normative job descriptions, it seeks out the biographies of named individuals, whose musical, liturgical, scribal, codicological and historical competencies can help us understand how responsibilities were shared within a single institution. The fact that we can even countenance this approach is because of the remarkable testimony of our subject, the eleventh-century cathedral community at Constance, located but a few miles from the Sankt Gallen and Reichenau monks with whose books we began.

The cathedral of Constance and its scribes

In his two attempts to survey choral traditions at Constance, Manfred Schuler demonstrated the difficulty of identifying named cantors from Constance's early medieval cathedral.[19] Although the Reichenau confraternity book tells us of at least thirty canons living there during the time of Bishop Salomon (d. 871), there is no written evidence of a musical official there before 1158. What we do have, however, is a readily reconstructible eleventh-century library. Ordinarily, the reconstruction of such collections is fraught with difficulty, for paleography informs us principally about writing, not reading, and surviving catalogues are notoriously difficult to match up with the material which survives. But the Constance collection is delimited with unusual clarity, as Johanne Autenrieth was able to show in her brilliant doctoral thesis of 1952, because in the years around 1070 a handful of local scribes suddenly devoted themselves to the glossing and annotation of their books.[20] Autenrieth traced almost fifty volumes which had passed through

---

[18] R. Delamare, Le 'De officiis ecclesiasticis' de Jean d'Avranches, Archevêque de Rouen (1067–1079): étude liturgique et publication du texte inédit du manuscrit H. 304 de la Bibliothèque de la Faculté de Montpellier (Paris, 1923); R. E. Reynolds, 'The "Isidorian" Epistula ad Leudefredum: An Early Medieval Epitome of the Clerical Duties', Mediaeval Studies 41 (1979), 252–330.

[19] M. Schuler, 'Die Anfänge der Konstanzer Domkantorei', Freiburger Diözesan-Archiv 99 (1979), 45–68. For a good introduction to the Constance cathedral community, see Siegwart, Die Chorherren- und Chorfrauengemeinschaften, pp. 204–10; see also H. Maurer, Die Konstanzer Bischöfe vom Ende des 6. Jahrhunderts bis 1206 (Berlin, 2003).

[20] J. Autenrieth, Die Domschule von Konstanz zur Zeit des Investiturstreits: Die wissenschaftliche Arbeitsweise Bernholds von Konstanz und zweier Kleriker dargestellt auf

their hands, the majority being Carolingian books produced at Reichenau or in the general Lake Constance area, and in the years since this list has been expanded considerably.[21] Even the most conservative tally of the annotations numbers well into the thousands.

The importance of this glossing evidence from Constance is that it informs scholars not only of the array of authors and texts present in an eleventh-century community, but also of the manner in which they were being read. Since the publication of Autenrieth's thesis, historians have feasted upon this information, using the glosses to explore local attitudes to the burning issues of the Investiture Controversy, among them questions of celibacy, simony and ecclesiastical authority.[22] One of the glossators identified was none other than Bernold of Constance, one of the most vocal supporters of the Gregorian cause.[23] But this political dimension was only one part of Autenrieth's work. She also happened to find occasional evidence that her scribes had copied liturgical music. These sporadic additions, usually a chant or two squeezed opportunistically into a margin, amount to the earliest known witnesses to musical activity at Constance, and through their notation they reveal a strong level of musical competence within this community.[24] While the glosses and musical additions have justly received attention as separate categories of intellectual activity, no one has yet addressed their remarkable confluence. If

Grund von Handschriftenstudien (Stuttgart, 1956). Also identifiable are some fifteen to twenty books produced in the cathedral scriptorium in the eleventh century, as described in W. Irtenkauf, 'Die Dombibliothek', in *Die Bischöfe von Konstanz*, ed. E. L. Kuhn et al., 2 vols. (Friedrichshafen, 1988), II, 205–13; H. Hoffmann, *Buchkunst und Königtum im ottonischen und frühsalischen Reich*, 2 vols., Schriften der MGH 30 (Stuttgart, 1986); H. Hoffmann, *Handschriftenfunde*, MGH Studien und Texte 18 (Hanover, 1997), pp. 97–101. Many (but not all) of these were also glossed. For a comparable case study see T. Webber, *Scribes and Scholars at Salisbury Cathedral c. 1075–c. 1125* (Oxford, 1992).

[21] J. Autenrieth, *Die Handschriften der ehemaligen Hofbibliothek Stuttgart, III: Codices Iurdici et Politici (HB VI 1–139). Patres (HB VII 1–71)* (Wiesbaden, 1963); H. Spilling, 'Konstanz oder Weingarten? Ein Exemplar der Moralia Gregors des Großen aus der Zeit des Investiturstreits', in *Litterae medii aevi: Festschrift für Johanne Autenrieth zu ihrem 65. Geburtstag*, ed. M. Borgolte and H. Spilling (Sigmaringen, 1988), pp. 165–82; Hoffmann, *Handschriftenfunde*; H. Hoffmann, *Schreibschulen des 10. und des 11. Jahrhunderts im Südwesten des Deutschen Reichs*, 2 vols., Schriften der MGH 53 (Hanover, 2004).

[22] Examples include I. S. Robinson, 'Zur Arbeitsweise Bernolds von Konstanz und seines Kreises: Untersuchungen zum Schlettstädter Codex 13', *Deutsches Archiv* 34 (1978), 51–122; I. S. Robinson, 'The Bible in the Investiture Contest: The South German Gregorian Circle', in *The Bible in the Medieval World: Essays in Memory of Beryl Smalley*, ed. K. Walsh and D. Wood (Oxford, 1985), pp. 61–84; Spilling, 'Konstanz oder Weingarten?'; Maurer, *Die Konstanzer Bischöfe*.

[23] J. Autenrieth, 'Bernold von Konstanz und die erweiterte 74-Titelsammlung', *Deutsches Archiv* 14 (1958), 375–94; Autenrieth, *Die Domschule*, pp. 24–6, 118–34.

[24] For a first attempt at an inventory, significantly expanded here, see M. Schuler, 'Die Musik am Konstanzer Dom um 1100', *Freiburger Diözesan-Archiv* 109 (1989), 131–39.

our scribes were politically motivated *and* musically active, what else might we surmise about their canonical lives? Drawing on the insights of Autenrieth, the many scholarly contributions since her work appeared in the 1950s, as well as some recent discoveries of my own, I shall introduce these individuals one by one.

Wolferad

One of Autenrieth's most breathtaking achievements was to deduce the names of her scribal subjects. Identifying the hand of Bernold, already extremely well known for his scholarly writings, was clearly the headline grabber. But no less interesting was the discovery of a learned figure named Wolferad, who signed his name at least once, and whose work leaps from the page with its small, sharp-edged letterforms and backward-leaning aspect.[25] This individual was almost certainly a Constance canon. Marshalling evidence which she had collected from a dozen or more manuscripts, Autenrieth was able to demonstrate Wolferad's likely clerical status (on two occasions he commented with the words 'nostri ordinis'), his detailed knowledge of the Constance Cathedral chapter in the 1080s (in an extended annotation which I shall consider at the end of this chapter), his sense of regret about 'erring' with the royalist Bishop Otto (who was finally replaced by the pro-Roman candidate Bishop Gebhard III in 1086) and his interest in the Constance patron St Pelagius, whose name he glossed as 'noster patronus'.[26] Wolferad also copied several inventories of property, whose existence conforms to the Aachen proclamation of 816 that only canons could 'lawfully draw on their own resources as well as those of the Church'.[27] We may also detect a streak of anti-monastic feeling in one gloss which, referring to a passage about abbots being held accountable on the Day of Judgment, exclaims: 'audiant hoc abbas Augensis et qui dicitur Gallensis et contremiscant' ('the abbots of Reichenau and Sankt Gallen should hear this and tremble').[28]

There are thirty or so books on Wolferad's reading list as it survives, of which two-thirds are either scriptural or patristic, with as many as nine

---

[25] For a more sophisticated characterisation, see Autenrieth, *Die Domschule*, pp. 22–3.

[26] This information is drawn directly from ibid., pp. 143–9. On St Pelagius and his expanding eleventh-century cult, see K. S. Frank, 'St. Pelagius, der unbekannte und vergessene Diözesanpatron', *Freiburger Diözesan-Archiv* 110 (1990), 5–21; also K. Becker, 'Über die Herkunft der Reliquien des hl. Pelagius, des zweiten Patrons der Konstanzer Bischofskirche', *Freiburger Diözesan-Archiv* 96 (1976), 358–60; F. Meyer, *Sankt Pelagius und Gregor der Grosse: Ihre Verehrung im Bistum Konstanz* (Munich, 2002).

[27] Bertram, *Chrodegang Rules*, p. 145. See HLB F Aa 15, fols. iir, 215v; HLB F Aa 3, rear endleaf; and BNF Lat. 11638, fol. 238v.

[28] Autenrieth, *Die Domschule*, pp. 167, 177.

volumes by Augustine: the tractates on John's Gospel (two volumes), the expositions of the Psalms (three volumes), *De baptismo, De quantitate anime, Enchiridion* and *Civitas Dei*.[29] Our scribe was also greatly interested in history, judging by his attention to Eusebius' *Historia ecclesiastica* in its Latin translation by Rufinus (two copies) and the *Historia tripartita* of Cassiodorus, as well as two non-Christian texts, the *De bello Judaico* of Flavius Josephus (now only a fragment) and Justinus's epitome of the Philippic histories.[30] The antique flavour of these works is underlined by Wolferad's own propensity to cite classical proverbs and witticisms from Virgil, Martial, Juvenal, Cicero, Horace and Terence.[31]

This much speaks of an erudite scholar, but that is not all. Wolferad was also a musician. In the margins of a ninth-century copy of Augustine on Psalms 101–50 (HLB F Aa 24) he added two offertories with full notation: 'Portas celi aperuit' for Easter Wednesday (fol. 183v; Can g01030) and 'Intonuit de celo' for Easter Tuesday (fol. 197v; Can g01024). The two annotations are fascinatingly close to each other, both liturgically and in manuscript position, suggesting that, even if Augustine's Psalm commentaries had no obvious place at Mass during Easter Week, Wolferad may have been reading them at that time. Perhaps the act of notation even served as a means of preparing a performance in his mind. Tellingly, Wolferad also copied 'Portas celi aperuit' into another book (WLB HB VII 43), where it appears with almost identical notation among a large group of chants added to spare parchment on fol. 147r–v. The book in question is an incomplete ninth-century witness to the *De ecclesiasticis officiis* and letters by Amalarius of Metz, whose very incompleteness was Wolferad's opportunity. Next to 'Portas celi aperuit' he copied two further chants for Easter Week: 'Christus resurgens' (the communion for Easter Wednesday; Can g01031) and 'Erit vobis hic dies' (the offertory for Easter Friday; Can g01042). Although that concentration of Easter music is not sustained among the remaining musical additions – which collectively reveal no discernible ritual, musical or theological pattern (Table 6.1) – these two occurrences of notations alongside glosses point towards a scenario in which liturgical singing and monastic *lectio* were coming into direct daily contact.

Wolferad's decision to gloss Amalarius is itself interesting, for it reveals his investment in the context and interpretation of the liturgy. It appears from his glosses that he was interested in, among other things, liturgical

---

[29] All manuscripts described in Autenrieth, *Die Domschule*, with the exception of BNF Lat. 11638 (*Civitas dei*), as identified in Hoffmann, *Schreibschulen* I, 174.

[30] All manuscripts described in Autenrieth, *Die Domschule*, with the exception of Einsiedeln, Stiftsbibliothek, Cod. 346 (Eusebius/Rufinus), as identified in Hoffmann, *Schreibschulen* I, 125.

[31] See especially WLB HB VII 38, on which see Autenrieth, *Die Domschule*, pp. 79–80. A copy of Juvenal survives from Constance, on which see ibid., p. 148.

Table 6.1 Chants in the hand of Wolferad

MS page	Chant	Genre	Feast[†]
WLB	Benedicta sit sancta trinitas	Introit	Trinity
HB VII 43,	Omnes gentes plaudite	Introit	Pentecost VII
fol. 147r	Exsurge domine non	Gradual	Lent III
	Inmittit angelus domini	Offertory	Lent I, Thursday
	V. Benedicam domino	Offertory verse	Lent I, Thursday
	Sepe expugnaverunt me	Tract (v. 1 only)	Lent V
WLB	Benedictus sit deus	Offertory	Trinity
HB VII 43,	Benedicite deum celi	Communion	Trinity
fol. 147v	V. Qui pro mundi salute in ligno	Offertory verse	Holy Cross
	Alleluia V. Ave Maria gratia plena	Alleluia	Feasts of Mary
	Iustus non conturbabitur	Introit	SS Hermetis/
			Chrysogonus
	Portas celi aperuit	Offertory	Easter Wednesday
	Christus resurgens	Communion	Easter Wednesday
	Erit vobis hic dies	Offertory	Easter Friday
	Sedit angelus ad sepulcrum	Procession	Easter Day
	V. Recordamini quomodo	Procession verse	Easter Day
HLB	Portas celi aperuit	Offertory	Easter Wednesday
F Aa 24,			
fol. 183v			
HLB	Intonuit de celo	Offertory	Easter Tuesday
F Aa 24,			
fol. 197v			

[†] Where there is a discrepancy I follow the assignment in Einsiedeln, Stifts-bibliothek, Cod. 121.

procedure (comments on baptism, on processions) and discipline (a comment on why Matins must not be skipped), as well as in Amalarius's unusual analogy between the singing of Graduals and Alleluias and 'active' and 'contemplative' life (fol. 60r). That last passage might well have piqued the interest of a canon in this period of canonical revival, caught as these individuals were between their outward-looking pastoral ministry and inward-looking communal life. We know that communal life was an interest of Wolferad's, because he chose to gloss a copy of Hildemar's commentary on the Benedictine Rule (Engelberg, Stiftsbibliothek, Cod. 142). Among various glosses, Wolferad contributed one on fol. 145r which addresses the question of whether one sings Psalmody with mouth or voice. Although the comment is largely lost to trimming, the sentiment adds to an impression, already apparent from the copy of Amalarius, that Wolferad's interest in communal life found a particular focus in matters of daily liturgy. Further musical and liturgical concerns surface in a third manuscript, a copy of John the Deacon's

Life of Gregory (WLB HB XIV 3) in which Wolferad's words point out the iniquity of John's famous description of Alpine voices (Wolferad's riposte: 'the inconsiderate and false mockery of the Romans, whose voice is like the hen pecked at by her mate') and clarify the histories of the Gregorian and Gelasian recensions of the sacramentary.[32]

To comment on the liturgy or even to add musical chants is not itself proof of any particular institutional responsibility, for these are skills which any individual could learn (and perhaps even use the margins to practise) over an extended period of time. But Wolferad also had scribal responsibilities. Autenrieth reported how he had applied interlinear corrections to a local Constance copy of Jerome's commentary on Isaiah (WLB HB VII 7).[33] Better still, at the front of an apparently unfinished portion of Augustine's *De quantiate anime* (now part of ULB D 896) Wolferad took on the role of scribe, borrowing the preceding blank page and shifting into a more formal script, in order to copy Augustine's retractation (a kind of postscript) to *De quantitate anime*.[34] Most authoritative of all was Wolferad's role in completing the aforementioned ninth-century copy of Amalarius (WLB HB VII 43), to which he had added miscellaneous chants on fol. 147r–v. At a later stage he returned to sort out the lacunae in the text. Beginning to copy on fol. 148r, he added the missing Amalarius letters before completing the volume with *De ecclesiasticis officiis* book IV. Two further scribal hands contributed to this effort, and this allows us to deduce that Wolferad was more than just a copyist. Taking over for short bursts, frequently at the heads of pages or gatherings (among them fols. 149r, 150r, 156r and 158r), he clearly had a supervisory, coordinating role. This division of labour is all but confirmed by a colophon on the last page, fol. 189v, penned by one of his co-scribes in three knotted lines of hexameter:

> Est a Wolverado semper mundana secuto
> Quarta remissa prius pars scripta voluminis huius.
> Addideram quartum tribus his ego Stelio librum.

> [The fourth part of this volume, ever worldly
> [and] previously incomplete, has been written with Wolferad's support.
> I, Stelio, had appended the fourth book to these three.]

The adjective 'worldly' makes good sense of *De ecclesiasticis officiis* book IV, with its emphasis on daily worship; and while I have translated 'remissa' as 'incomplete' (literally 'slackened off'), an equally plausible reading holds

---

[32] 'Inconsiderata Romanorum irrisio et falsa, quorum vox similis quo mordetur gallina marito', with veiled reference to Juvenal, *Satura* III.91; fols. 45r and 49v, respectively.

[33] Autenrieth, *Die Domschule*, p. 93.

[34] Ibid., p. 82; the text is Augustine, *Retractiones* I.8.

that a portion had been 'sent back', perhaps to a neighbouring library. As for 'Stelio', this may be a name or nickname, or it may have been a learned form of self-deprecation: Proverbs 30.28 lists the 'stelio' (or 'lizard') among creatures which are 'small but ... exceedingly wise'; and in the eyes of Pliny the Elder 'stelio' could, by extension, denote a roguish figure.[35] Autenrieth found it strange that this colophon should appear to attribute scribal agency to Wolferad and yet not be written in his hand. ('A Wolverado' has an active connotation which is not preserved in my rendering above, and confusingly Wolferad *did* copy the line 'addideram ... librum' into two other books.)[36] But I would suggest that in this instance Autenrieth had not appreciated the coordinated nature of the copyists' collaboration, nor the reptilian professions of an apparently subordinate scribe.

Anonymous A

A single Wolferad figure ought perhaps to have sufficed within the Constance scriptorium. Remarkably, however, our subject was not alone. Another individual, writing in a similar but slightly plumper script, was also busy working in the margins of Constance's books. Autenrieth named him 'Anonymus A' (which I anglicize here for the avoidance of confusion) and she presented convincing evidence that he had interacted with Wolferad's glosses, and vice versa, as if they were colleagues or close contemporaries.[37] Although there is no firm evidence that Anonymous A was musical, his scribal activities have so much in common with Wolferad's that they throw both individuals valuably into relief.

Among the books to which Anonymous A applied his pen we can trace at least twenty-five volumes to Wolferad's thirty, among which patristic texts number just under half, with a notable predilection for Gregory's *Moralia* (annotations in six of the seven surviving Constance volumes).[38] The remaining books divide into legal texts (a notable absence in Wolferad's work), computistic and astronomical texts, hagiography and works relating to the liturgy or communal life. Like Wolferad, Anonymous A glossed Hildemar's commentary on the Benedictine Rule (using a second copy, Karlsruhe, Badische Landesbibliothek, Aug. perg. 203), and his unusually barbed comments about its somnolent qualities add weight to the idea that

---

[35] Pliny, *Natural History* XXX.27.

[36] HLB F Aa 15, fol. iir; WLB HB VII 38, fol. 1r. In both cases the poetic addition is one among many.

[37] On the distinctive features of his script see Autenrieth, *Die Domschule*, p. 24; on their collaboration see ibid., pp. 146–7.

[38] All manuscripts described in Autenrieth, *Die Domschule*, with the exception of certain copies of the *Moralia*, on which see Spilling, 'Konstanz oder Weingarten?'.

he too was operating outside of a monastic context: 'nescio quid iste somniet' ('I know not what this man is dreaming'), he says at one stage; at another, 'fateor lectori quia hec legendo dormitavi' ('I confess to the reader that I felt drowsy reading these things').[39] Anonymous A's institutional standing is also suggested by the annotations (here represented in italics) with which he clarified Hildemar's interpretation of an abbot's office: 'Abbas non potest esse sine regula. Nam si alteram *canonicalem* vitam duxerit, illius *monachi* ordinis, non est abbas sed eius cuius vitam duxerit' ('The abbot cannot exist without a rule for if he leads another, *canonical* life he is not an abbot of that *monastic* order, but of this in which he leads his life').[40] Anonymous A corrected this volume vigorously, in fact, often openly advertising his text-critical credentials: on one occasion he noted that 'aut hic deesse, aut quod melius credo hoc versum, id est cum invocarem, post sequentem textum inseri debere' ('either [something] is missing here or, which I better believe, this verse "cum invocarem" ought to be inserted after the text which follows').[41] Just like his colleague Wolferad, Anonymous A, too, had scribal responsibilities which also extended to a supervisory role. In one of the *Moralia* volumes (HLB F Aa 31a) he began a new gathering on fol. 96r, only to cede to another scribe after fifteen lines.[42] He also worked as text scribe in two more *Moralia* copies (WLB HB VII 24 and HB VII 27), the latter of which he appears to have begun.[43] And in a local collection of saints' lives (WLB HB XIV 16) he was involved in texts for St Sebastian (fols. 17r–24r, seemingly over-extensive erasure), the Invention of the Holy Cross (fols. 61r, 66r) and SS Marcus and Marcellus (fols. 128v–89r, 131r).[44]

Further mirroring the work of his colleague Wolferad, Anonymous A was also interested to point out matters of liturgical procedure, both in the margins of Amalarius' *De ecclesiasticis officiis* and in relation to a specific Bede text found in a homiliary (WLB HB VII 58, fols. 304v–7v).[45] Many of these comments relate to the contours of the liturgical year, including issues such as when to sing the Alleluia, the timing of Septuagesima and Lent, the giving of alms before Holy Week and the role of the archdeacon (a key figure in clerical communities) in preparing the wax *Agni* for Easter Week. But within those contours one aspect of the year received a particular cluster of annotations: the Lenten scrutiny rituals for baptismal candidates on fols. 12r–13r. Here Anonymous A noted in the margin all the salient

---

[39] Fols. 51r and 84r, respectively.
[40] Fol. 54v (with other corrections incorporated).
[41] Fol. 29v.
[42] Hoffmann, *Handschriftenfunde*, p. 100.
[43] Spilling, 'Konstanz oder Weingarten?', pp. 168–9, 174–7. Autenrieth omitted these manuscripts from her initial survey.
[44] As reported in Hoffmann, *Handschriftenfunde*, p. 100.
[45] Autenrieth, *Die Domschule*, p. 103; Bede, *Homilies* II.16.

organizational features of the ritual – the responsories, the lessons and the Gospel reading – as if pondering a schema for performance. A subsequent comment on fol. 40r, on the readings assigned to catechumens at the vigils of Easter and Pentecost, raises the possibility that Anonymous A himself had responsibility for initiates within his own community, perhaps as an educator or schoolmaster. That hypothesis contextualizes two further aspects of his work. First, Anonymous A was a prominent contributor to the many local copies of Gregory's *Moralia*, which Herrad Spilling suggested to have been cultivated for classroom use.[46] Second, Anonymous A contributed any number of annotations to the aforementioned Hildemar commentary (Aug. perg. 203) which suggest pedagogical intent: not only several observations on points of grammar, noted by Autenrieth, but also the marking up of multiple portions concerning discipline and, intriguingly, a passage on fols. 57v–8r on the need to give due prominence to junior clerics who excel in grammar, reading or singing.[47]

All of this feeds most interestingly into existing speculation about the identity of Anonymous A, for when Ian Robinson examined these glosses he discovered one remarkable correspondence.[48] An impressive number of the scribe's additions, even though spread across several books, correspond to the content of the *Liber ad Gebehardum*, a tract written by the Alsatian intellectual Manegold of Lautenbach. With admirable restraint Robinson stopped short of proclaiming that which the evidence so tantalizingly suggests, noting that 'if [further] investigation does not demonstrate that Anonymous A and Manegold of Lautenbach are one and the same, it will at least show that they were remarkably unanimous about what was most relevant in the codices of the cathedral library of Constance'.[49] Further in support of his theory, Robinson also noted Manegold's subsequent reputation as an author of biblical glosses and Psalm commentary, as reported by Wolfger of Prüfening.[50] To my knowledge, however, no one has ever accepted the invitation to explore this association further. In the light of the deductions about Anonymous A made above, four aspects of Manegold's biography immediately jump out in favour of Robinson's thesis. First, Manegold was renowned as an educator, described by Pope Urban II in 1096 as a 'magister scholarum'.[51] Second, he was a cleric and reformer who lived in several canonical communities, who may have come into conflict with monks and

[46] Spilling, 'Konstanz oder Weingarten?', esp. p. 167.
[47] On the grammatical annotations see Autenrieth, *Die Domschule*, pp. 149, 176–7.
[48] Robinson, 'The Bible', pp. 69–72, 83–4.
[49] Ibid., pp. 71–2.
[50] Ibid., pp. 83–4.
[51] Manegold of Lautenbach, *Liber contra Wolfelmum*, ed. and trans. Robert Ziomkowski (Leuven, 2002), pp. 23–7, 114.

whose scathing *Liber ad Wolfhelmum* was directed at one monk in particular.[52] Third, what Ivo of Chartres described as the 'many winding paths' of Manegold's career suggest a life of itineracy, and evidence of his appointment both as dean of Rottenbuch in the 1080s and as prior of Marbach in the 1090s (both communities of canons) makes it quite possible that he sojourned at Constance, the eminent institution located exactly midway between the two.[53] Fourth, Manegold knew and cited Bernold of Constance, who himself addressed Manegold as 'frater noster' in a letter dated to before 1084.[54] All of this is a most promising fit for the glosses which we find.

Heremann

My third Constance scribe is one whom Autenrieth never properly identified, chiefly because she was distracted by the similarity of his hand to Wolferad's. Noticing a small group of additions to HLB F Aa 15, a book otherwise full of Wolferad glosses, she pondered why on fol. 214v this individual had signed off in another name: 'Hec Heremannus scripsit non scriptor ineptus' ('These things Heremann wrote, not inept as a scribe').[55] As Hausmann and Schuler later retorted, the obvious answer is that these additions were *not* penned by Wolferad's hand.[56] The script appears to be younger, with a rounder, more even appearance than that of Wolferad's, and with distinctive features including a teardrop-shaped 'O', 'Q' and 'D', prominent wedges on the ascenders, backward-curving descenders and the habitual use of a 'v' shape in a terminal 'us'. Of the six books in which I have so far been able to find Heremann's work, no fewer than four were glossed by Wolferad, implying that they worked in proximity, while the remaining two were probably assembled in the Constance area. In all six manuscripts Heremann devoted himself to the copying and notation of music.

This strong musical focus explains two of the most striking features of Heremann's annotations. First, almost all of his contributions were applied, upside down, to the lower margins of their respective books. Since this orientation obstructs the simultaneous reading of text and annotation, the implication is that Heremann was not a glossator – as Wolferad seems to have been – who occasionally flexed his musical musculature but simply a

---

[52] Ibid., pp. 4–5, 21. On the conflict, between the canons of Rottenbuch and the monks of Schaffhausen, see pp. 3, 114–15.

[53] Ibid., pp. 20–3, 112–13.

[54] Ibid., pp. 16–7, 106–8. As the author cautions, however, this salutation needs not have any institutional connotation.

[55] Autenrieth, *Die Domschule*, p. 52.

[56] R. Hausmann, *Die theologischen Handschriften der Hessischen Landesbibliothek Fulda bis zum Jahr 1600* (Wiesbaden, 1992), p. xxix; Schuler, 'Die Musik', p. 137.

musician in search of blank parchment. Second, unlike Wolferad, Heremann restricted himself to very specific genres of chant. Among the forty or so distinct pieces or portions of pieces which I have identified in his hand among Constance manuscripts, a remarkable thirty-two belong to the melismatic, soloistic genres of graduals, alleluias, offertories and responsories (Table 6.2).[57] Indeed, among Heremann's contributions for the Mass I can find just one chant which is *not* melismatic: a single Advent introit on fol. 224r of ULB D 896. With such an emphasis on difficult, elaborate chants, it appears that Herman's self-proclaimed 'not-ineptness' went far beyond his role as scribe.

The remaining pieces in Heremann's hand are no less focused in their identity, for all are Office chants and all pertain to the veneration of two saints, Pelagius and Nicholas. This is a most revealing pairing on two counts. First, since the chants for these saints lay outside the main 'Gregorian' canon – that is, they were more regional in cultivation and more reliant on specific local expertise – they were also likely candidates for being recorded opportunistically on local parchment. Second, both saints demonstrably had a role in Constance's liturgy in this late eleventh century period. St Pelagius was none other than a patron saint of the community, whose appearance in Cassiodorus's *Historia tripartita* was glossed by Wolferad with the words 'noster patronus'.[58] St Nicholas was notoriously the flavour of the moment, his relics having been stolen from Asia Minor and brought to Bari in 1087. It was in this very same period that the prior of Constance, a man named Henry, reorganized part of the cathedral interior, apparently with the purpose of accommodating some newly acquired relics. As the anonymous local *Vita Conradi* explains:

> Prioris locum monumenti altius exstructum celebri memoria decoravit, capellam etiam antiquitus inibi constructam, sed tunc desolatam, destruxit, aliamque in sublimi edifficavit [*sic*], quam in honore sancti Nicolaï dedicari fecit.[59]

> [He adorned the area of the old monument, of celebrated memory, this having been raised higher up; he also pulled down a chapel which had been built in olden times but which was now unused; and he built another in that lofty place, which he dedicated in honour of St Nicholas.]

This rearrangement took place in the time of Bishop Gebhard III (1086–1110), and it is therefore most likely to have taken place after St Nicholas's translation in 1087. Only two years after that famous event, Gebhard rededicated

---

[57] Verses are counted separately, since Heremann often copies them alone. An earlier inventory may be found in Schuler, 'Die Musik', pp. 136–7.
[58] Autenrieth, *Die Domschule*, p. 64.
[59] Transcribed from HLB F D 11, fol. 35v. See also *Vita Conradi altera*, ed. G. Pertz, MGH SS 4 (Hanover, 1841), p. 441.

Table 6.2 Chants in the hand of Heremann

MS page	Chant	Genre	Feast[†]
ULB D 896, fol. 223r	Universi qui te expectant	Gradual	Advent I
	V. Vias tuas domine notas	Gradual verse	Advent I
	Alleluia V. Ostende nobis domine	Alleluia	Advent I
ULB D 896, fol. 224r	Ad te levavi animam meam	Introit	Advent I
ULB D 896, fol. 226v	Alleluia V. Surrexit pastor bonus	Alleluia	Eastertide?
ULB D 896, fol. 232r	Alleluia V. Christus resurgens	Alleluia	Easter Tuesday
ULB D 896, fol. 233v	Alleluia V. Domine deus meus in te speravi	Alleluia	?
WLB HB VII 29, fol. 5r	Oratio mea munda est	Offertory	Vigil of St Laurence
	V. Probavit me dominus sicut	Offertory verse	Vigil of St Laurence
	Timete dominum omnes sancti	Gradual	St Cyriac
	V. Inquirentes autem dominum	Gradual verse	St Cyriac
	Alleluia V. Surrexit pastor bonus	Alleluia	Eastertide?
WLB HB VII 29, fol. 5v	Alleluia V. Christus resurgens	Alleluia	Easter Tuesday
WLB HB VII 37, fol. 37v	die [melisma from 'Mirabilis in excelsis']	Offertory verse	Christmas Day, Second Mass
	V. Dominus regnavit decorum	Offertory verse	Christmas Day, Second Mass
	Alleluia V. Non vos reliqua orphanos	Alleluia	Pentecost
WLB HB VII 37, fol. 78r	Tenuisti manum decretam	Gradual	Palm Sunday
	V. Quam bonus Israel	Gradual verse	Palm Sunday
WLB HB VII 37, fol. 85v	Eripe me domine	Gradual	Lent V
	V. Liberator meus domine	Gradual verse	Lent V

Table 6.2 *continued*

MS page	Chant	Genre	Feast[†]
WLB HB VII 37, fol. 86r	V. Quia factus [es] adiutor	Offertory verse	Lent V, Wednesday
	Herusalem [melisma from 'Memento domine']	Offertory verse	Lent V, Thursday
WLB HB VII 37, fol. 92v	Ave sancte egregie	Antiphon	St Pelagius
WLB HB VII 37, fol. 147v	in lo[n]gitudine dierum [melisma from 'Mirabilis in excelsis']	Offertory verse	Christmas Day, Second Mass
WLB HB VII 37, fol. 162v	Videns autem [tyrannus]	Responsory	St Pelagius
	V. Cumque athleta fortis	Responsory verse	St Pelagius
WLB HB VII 37, fol. 177v	Stetit angelus iuxta aram	Offertory	St Michael
	V. In conspectu angelorum	Offertory verse	St Michael
WLB HB VII 37, fol. 180r	Alleluia V. Concussum est mare	Alleluia	St Michael
WLB HB VII 37, fol. 180v	Videns autem tyrannus	Responsory	St Pelagius
WLB HB VII 37, fol. 181r	Ingressus Pilatus	Responsory	Palm Sunday
	V. Tunc agit illis Pilatus	Responsory verse	Palm Sunday
WLB HB VII 37, fol. 181v	['ora' melisma from 'Ave sancte egregie']	Antiphon	St Pelagius
	['ora' melisma from 'Ave sancte egregie']	Antiphon	St Pelagius
	ora [melisma from 'Ave sancte egregie']	Antiphon	St Pelagius
	ora [melisma from 'Ave sancte egregie']	Antiphon	St Pelagius
	Ave sancte egregie	Antiphon	St Pelagius
HLB F Aa 3, fol. 1r	O Christi pietas omni	Antiphon	St Nicholas

Table 6.2 *continued*

MS page	Chant	Genre	Feast[†]
HLB F Aa 15, fol. ii[r]	Audiens Christi confessor	Responsory	St Nicholas
HLB F Aa 15, fol. 189r	Alleluia V. Letamini in domino	Alleluia	Feast of a martyr
	fabrice mundi [melisma from 'Descendit de celis']	Responsory	Christmas Day
HLB F Aa 15, fol. 214v	O Christi pietas omni	Antiphon	St Nicholas
	O per omnia laudabilem	Antiphon	St Nicholas
WLB HB VII 62, fol. 176v	Dixit do[minus mulier]i Chananee	Antiphon	Lent II
	[Hodie] sacratissimus	Antiphon	St Pelagius

[†] Where there is a discrepancy I follow the assignment in Einsiedeln, Stiftsbibliothek, Cod. 121.

Constance's cathedral, during which ceremony patronal relics customarily played a major part.[60] If the cults of SS Pelagius and Nicholas had been subject to renewed energy and exposure in the later eleventh century, much in the way that clerics across Christendom were busy promoting their cults in this period, it would be a surprise if musical practices had not followed suit.[61]

Heremann may even have been involved in their creation. While the Office chants for St Nicholas have a complicated history which antedates the translation of 1087, those for St Pelagius are unknown prior to Heremann's annotations.[62] There are no further witnesses to these chants, indeed, until the early thirteenth century, when a complete set was copied into a breviary from the abbey of Kreuzlingen (Heidelberg, Universitätsbibliothek, Cod. Sal. IX.61, fols. 170r–2v), whose community of Augustinian canons had been founded by a former bishop of Constance a little over a mile from the cathedral church.[63] The full and complete concordance of the Kreuzlingen breviary with Heremann's annotations concentrates the local flavour of this musical repertory, as does the telling mention of the 'urbs preclara Constancia'

[60] A. Knoepfli, 'Beiträge zur Baugeschichte des Konstanzer Münsters im 10. und 11. Jahrhundert', *Freiburger Diözesan-Archiv* 109 (1989), 27–84.

[61] For further examples of music and cult promotion see, among many, Fass C; Brand, *Holy Treasure*.

[62] C. Hohler, 'The Proper Office of St. Nicholas and Related Matters with Reference to a Recent Book', *Medium Aevum* 36 (1967), 40–8.

[63] See Meyer, *Sankt Pelagius*, p. 43, who also lists a scattering of later medieval sources, all from the Lake Constance area.

Ex. 6.1 Heremann's five different attempts at the 'ora' melisma from the chant 'Ave sancte egregie' in WLB HB VII 37, set against a later medieval version from Kreuzlingen, now Heidelberg, Universitätsbibliothek, Cod. Sal. IX.61

fol. 92v

fol. 181v (1)

fol. 181v (2)

fol. 181v (3)

fol. 181v (4)

o - ra

Kreuzlingen

('shining city of Constance') in the chant 'Ave sancte egregie'. What hints at our scribe's specific responsibility is the mutable shape of the chants as recorded by his pen. The responsory 'Videns autem tyrannus' appears once with the word 'tyrannus' and once without, and Heremann copied the antiphon 'Ave sancte egregie' in two distinct versions, along with no fewer than four separate attempts to copy its distinctive exhortatory melisma on 'ora'. Although all four attempts coexist on the very same page, they are identical neither in melody nor in the manner of their neumatic notation, yielding the impression that our author was exploring multiple actuations of that one phrase (Ex. 6.1). (No pitch-specific copy of this chant survives.) If this is not concrete evidence of a composer at work, it is at least evidence that Heremann exerted creative freedoms with respect to this repertory. That points towards a situation in which he was in charge.

Until now Heremann has not been celebrated as a text scribe, but two pieces of evidence point in that direction. The first is a ninth-century copy of the *Quadripartitus* canon law collection (WLB HB VII 62), whose final page, though highly damaged, contains an interesting mix of opportunistic annotations, all apparently by Heremann.[64] With the help of the ink offset onto the rear binding board it is possible to identify an antiphon for St Pelagius ('Hodie sacratissimus'), as well as one intriguing extract of canon law:

[Cum excommunicato] nullus loquatur neque qualibet eum compassione vel miseratione refoveat.

[Nothing should be spoken with an excommunicate, nor should anything revive him with sympathy or compassion.]

---

[64] See Autenrieth, *Die Handschriften*, pp. 219–20; L. Kéry, *Canonical Collections of the Early Middle Ages (ca. 400–1140): A Bibliographical Guide to the Manuscripts and Literature* (Washington, DC, 1999), p. 168.

The text appears earlier in the *Quadripartitus*, which means that Heremann had probably copied out a passage of interest while reading through. Such behaviour would align him not only with the scholarly activities of Bernold and Anonymous A, both highly active canon lawyers, but also with the methods of Wolferad, who frequently copied one-line extracts from other texts. Several of these extracts are interwoven among Heremann's chants on the endleaves of HLB F Aa 15.

A second observation on Heremann's scribal activity is that, just like Wolferad and his colleague Stelio, he too composed a colophon in rhyming hexameters. At the conclusion of a late tenth or early eleventh century copy of Jerome on Isaiah (WLB HB VII 6, fol. 141v), Heremann's hand proclaims:

> Omnibus expletis arcem subit ille quietis.
> Gloria sit Christo pax et qui scripserat
> hec qui scribebat Herimannus nomen habebat.

> [Now that everything is complete, he climbs the citadel of calm.
> Glory be to Christ, and peace to he who had written.
> He who wrote these lines goes by the name of Heremann.]

The 'lines' to which Heremann refers are not his – for he had no part in copying this manuscript – but those of the poem. The 'completion' is not the scribal task, therefore, but the act of reading. Hence with his combination of scholarly engagement, marginal intervention and, as here, self-advertising hexameters, Heremann's pursuits turn out to be most hamonious with those of his Constance colleagues. Were we to perform Autenrieth's survey anew, we might well find that Heremann had contributed further.

The chapter of Constance Cathedral *c.* 1080

For each of the three scribes under consideration, the wide range of comptencies on show constitutes the classic raw material for some kind of 'cantor' position, and doubtless we would describe it as such if there were an appropriate customary to corroborate that thesis. But the individual-centred approach of this chapter has now pushed us in another direction. For as much as these scribes had a huge amount in common, as glossators, text scribes, overseers and general all-round intellectuals, perhaps the most striking finding is just how distinctly their personalities and interests shine through. Anonymous A preferred Augustine, while Wolferad preferred Gregory; the one focused on canon law, the other history, while Heremann specialized in music. The first and third also had a penchant for poetry, as well as for the copying of one-line aphorisms at the beginnings and ends of manuscripts. It is also worth mentioning that many other scribes, as yet unidentified, also added music to Constance manuscripts, and plenty more added markings and annotations for liturgical reading.[65] What we seem to find, therefore, is not one model 'cantor' operating in late eleventh century Constance, but a variety of individuals exercising distinctly 'cantorial' responsibilities.

That point takes on an extra lustre when we examine the largest and most celebrated annotation of Wolferad. On the final page of a ninth-century copy of Augustine on the Psalms (ULB D 897), he listed the names of some sixty members of the clergy in order of rank. The addition was always understood as a roll call of the cathedral chapter in 1080s until, in a comprehensive rereading, Karl Schmid argued that Wolferad had been manipulating the names to take a very particular stance on local internal politics, the community having wrestled in these very years with the competing claims of imperially and papally appointed bishops.[66] Be that as it may, three names on the list stand out: 'Wolferat presbiter' (no. 22), 'Manegolt presbiter' (no. 30), and 'Hereman presbiter' (no. 34). We have encountered all three. These were all popular appelations in German-speaking lands, it should be said, and plenty of the other names in Wolferad's list are themselves duplicates. Nonetheless, with evidence of Manegold of Lautenbach's mysterious itineracy in the 1080s, and with the suggestion of Heremann's marginally junior status (remembering that his script and hagiographical contributions point more towards the 1090s than the 1070s or 1080s), there is a very serious possibility that all three subjects were colleagues.

The hypothesis may be impossible to prove, but it is valuable because behind much of our scholarship on cantors and precentors lies an assumption, informed principally by monastic custom, that in every religious institution there was probably a single authority figure in whose hands lay the various responsibilities of the liturgy, music, library and making of history. Constance suggests otherwise. Indeed, it now beckons us to explore how the unique structures of canonical life, and in particular the role of education within clerical communities, might have required different abilities and responsibilities, going beyond the norms which later medieval customaries imply. Perhaps the aforementioned Rouen arrangement, with its distinctive division of labour between a 'precentor primicherius', 'corepiscopus' and 'succentor', was much more widely known.[67] While that line of research is beyond the scope of the present study, in this chapter our clerical expectations have already gained a vivid redress: for every Gregorian polemicist, it

---

[65] On the latter see H. Parkes, 'Biblical Readings for the Night Office in Eleventh-Century Germany: Reconciling Theory and Practice', in *Reading the Bible in the Middle Ages*, ed. J. Nelson and D. Kempf (London, 2015), pp. 77–100.

[66] K. Schmid, 'Zu den angeblichen Konstanzer Gegenbischöfen während des Investiturstreites', *Freiburger Diözesan-Archiv* 109 (1989), 189–212. Earlier interpretations can be found in E. Dümmler, 'Mittheilungen aus Handschriften', *Neues Archiv* 11 (1886), 404–13 (p. 408) and Autenrieth, *Die Domschule*, pp. 59–61. Recall Wolferad's comment about 'erring' with Bishop Otto, mentioned above.

[67] Delamare, *Le 'De officiis ecclesiasticis'*, p. liii.

turns out, there was a canon busily practising his offertory verses; for every learned scriptural exegete there was probably a poet, or Church historian, or scriptorium supervisor or composer of patronal music; and for all of these high-flyers there were also the glossators bored by the tedium of their texts, strewing the margins impulsively with the comments which Autenrieth would later dismiss as 'uninteressant'. Just like the confraternity books of Reichenau and Sankt Gallen, Wolferad's list of cathedral dignitaries also assigns clerical ranks. At the top of the page we find bishops, followed by priests, deacons and subdeacons, and then at the bottom appear the names Landolt 'can', Adelpret 'c', Willebolt 'c', Ödelrich 'c' and Henrich 'c'. Although we may now have our own ideas of how to expand those abbreviations, whether *canonicus, cantor* or something else entirely, the experience of Constance cathedral suggests that this is beside the point. The work of an eleventh-century polymath was an occupation which did not always need a name.

7

Shaping the Historical Dunstan:
Many Lives and a Musical Office

Margot E. Fassler

O Magnum gloriosi presulis meritum, qui meruit vivens videre angelorum visiones vocesque mirabiles eorundem audire!

[How great the deserts of this glorious bishop, who found fit while still alive to see visions of angels and hear their wonderful voices!][1]

The early evidence and the first lives of Dunstan

Two Dunstans (d. 988) walk through eleventh and early twelfth century England as the most venerated of saints. One emerges through the study of contemporary historical sources, while the other is a character that developed over time, known through liturgical celebration as well as in folklore and oral traditions. There is rich evidence for the transformation of the first Dunstan into the second, evidence of changing character traits and descriptions of historical events associated with his life. Several manuscripts can be associated with him and his students, while letters and charters are eyewitnesses to his life; at the same time, there are five *vite* from the late tenth, eleventh and early twelfth centuries to document his saintly attributes, as well as an office copied *c.* 1230 (See Table 7.1 and Appendix 1). His character is also reflected in other contemporary histories and hagiography. This chapter explores how a historical understanding of the saint developed over time, from the tenth to the early thirteenth century. Throughout this long period, several cantor-historians have roles to play, including the musician who finally put the tradition together in its final (and only surviving) musical office.

The outline of known milestones in the saint's life recently sketched by Michael Winterbottom and Michael Lapidge draws on the two earliest surviving *vite*, which they edit and translate, as well on other documents and charters (see Table 7.2).[2] The tenth-century life by a writer called simply B, someone who knew Dunstan and was, early in the saint's life, an eyewitness to some of the events he reported, is justly privileged as evidence, a case study of the major role of hagiographical writings for understanding the

[1] *ELD* B 35, pp. 98–101.
[2] *ELD*, pp. xiii–lxiii.

Table 7.1 The prose *vite* of Dunstan (up to the twelfth century)
and their probable dates of composition

1	B, of Glastonbury and Liege (=*ELD* B) Two versions: one that was kept at Glastonbury and another revised in the first half of the eleventh century at Canterbury (see St Gall, Kantonsbibl. 337). A possible name for B is Byrhthelm, a deacon once in Dunstan's entourage.	995–1005
2	Old English version of B This version does not survive, but it was known to both Osbern (4) and to William (6). It seems to have expanded B considerably.	(unknown)
3	Adelard of Mont St Blandin, Ghent (=*ELD* A) A life arranged in twelve lections for the Divine Office commissioned by Abbot Ælfheah, dependent on B.	c. 1006-11
4	Osbern of Canterbury, *Life and Miracles* Osbern's work is dependent on Adelard (3), B (1) and B's later recension (2). It is the most extensive of the lives, reflecting Osbern's times and the people he knew.	1089-93
5	Eadmer of Canterbury, *Life and Miracles* A reworking of Osbern (4).	by 1116, probably before 1109
6	William of Malmesbury, *Life* William attacks Osbern (4) even as he uses much of his material; in fact it is usually impossible to say if William was drawing directly from Eadmer (5) or Eadmer's source, Osbern.	c. 1129-30

past. Information concerning Dunstan's childhood and early upbringing shows him to have been well born (Wessex aristocracy), a member of the royal entourage in his twenties and appointed abbot of Glastonbury during the reign of King Edmund, while still apparently very young.[3] After a brief time of exile, he returned to be a bishop, though retaining his relationship to Glastonbury. As can be seen from the lack of later significant personal events, as detailed in Table 7.2, the final twenty years of Dunstan's life are poorly attested; the evidence of B breaks off when Dunstan returned from exile because the author was apparently no longer associated with him. As a result, B created his narrative primarily from knowledge of Dunstan's early career, mentioning a few things he had heard about the very end of his life to finish up the job. The work was an attempt to earn favour with Ælfric, then archbishop of Canterbury, and it formed the basis of all later *vite* and much

---

[3] Ironically, despite B's emphasis on Dunstan's early life, little is known about his parents except their names.

Table 7.2 Timeline of the career of Dunstan and other major events

Date*	Event
by 910	Born
mid 920s	In minor orders in Glastonbury, which is apparently not yet Benedictine
c. 934–39	Became a monk
c. 939–46	Made abbot of Glastonbury by King Edmund I (r. 939–46)
946	Eadred succeeds his brother Edmund as king
953–55	Dunstan acts as a kind of vice-regent due to the king's illness
late 955	Death of Eadred
956	Eadwig succeeds his brother Eadred, instead of Edgar, Eadred's son; Dunstan driven into exile by King Eadwig; on the continent, Dunstan learns to write Caroline minuscule and is at St Peter's in Ghent (reformed Benedictine)
957	Edgar becomes king of some parts of England; Dunstan is restored to favour and named, in quick succession, bishop of Worcester and of London
959	Eadwig dies; Edgar becomes king of all the territory; Dunstan is named Archbishop of Canterbury and retains his post as abbot of Glastonbury, as well as his positions as bishop of Worcester and London
960	Travels to Rome to accept the pallium from John XII (r. 955–64)
961	New bishops installed at Worcester and London
later career	Dunstan was a very successful administrator and something of a scholar, but much of the evidence for his work as a monastic reformer is late and circumstantial (the reform of Westminster being an exception)
975	Edgar dies, succeeded by his son Edward
978	Murder of Edward
979	Coronation of King Æthelred
988	Death of Dunstan

* Many of these dates and ranges are estimates, as found in the Introduction to *ELD*.

of the history of Dunstan's early life. But there was from the very beginning a serious lacuna in the later part of the historical narrative. Some saints' lives evolved over time, as did the life of Dunstan, and many people with a variety of needs and strategies shaped historical understanding of Dunstan's times through their written and sung contributions.

As a result of the partial nature of B's *vita*, much of the commonly held understanding of Dunstan's role as a monastic reformer was based not on tenth or early eleventh century sources, but on the third *vita Dunstani*, penned by Osbern of Canterbury (d. *c.* 1090) in the late eleventh century, and on other twelfth-century hagiographers and historians. It was apparently John of Worcester (d. *c.* 1140) and Osbern who shaped the reforming aspect of the saint's character, bringing Dunstan into line with descriptions found in *vite* of SS Oswald and Æthelwold.[4] Winterbottom and Lapidge examined charters and various contemporary documents, and, confirming the work of Nicola Robertson and other recent scholars, found no firm evidence that Dunstan ever reformed any monasteries, with the exception of his actions at Westminster. In fact, he seems to have been content to work both with secular canons and with monks. Other features of his character are harder to discern. As a man of letters, it can be said that his Latin was good and he was a competent poet, but no significant writings by him survive.[5] The extent to which 'Hand D' (sometimes identified as his) actually corrected and glossed a small group of manuscripts has yet to be firmly established. Likewise, though he seems to have been a capable preparer of royal charters and to have cared about the liturgy, the extent of his activities in both these realms has not been precisely determined.[6] The portrait of him in the so-called 'classbook' is sometimes thought to have been drawn by Dunstan himself (see Fig. 7.1). It is clear that he was a man of 'prodigious' energy, and that 'a clear sense emerges from the evidence –paleographical, liturgical, computistical – that what we now see is merely the tip of an iceberg'.[7] This early evidence shows that Dunstan was a significant historical figure, a highly placed administrator exercising great influence on the politics and on the religious life of his times, but saints are not made from such profiles alone.

The second life of Dunstan, by Adelard of St Peter's, Ghent, is actually a series of twelve liturgical readings dedicated to Archbishop Ælfheah (commonly spelt 'Elphege', r. 1006–12), demonstrating that Dunstan was already venerated as a saint by the early eleventh century – at least in Canterbury, and on the occasion of his deposition (19 May).[8] Winterbottom

---

[4] For detailed arguments and further bibliography, see N. Robertson, 'Dunstan and Monastic Reform: Tenth-Century Fact or Twelfth-Century Fiction?', *ANS* 28 (2006): 153–67.

[5] Dunstan's known corpus of Latin poetry is transcribed and translated in *ELD*, Appendix IV, pp. 163–72.

[6] The evaluation of liturgical evidence by Winterbottom and Lapidge is tantalizing, especially as it concerns the so-called Dunstan Pontifical, BnF lat. 943; see *ELD*, pp. xl–xli; and J. Rosenthal, 'The Pontifical of St Dunstan', in *St Dunstan, His Life, Times and Cult*, ed. N. Ramsay et al. (Woodbridge, 1992), pp. 143–63. On the papal privilege that is part of the book, see *ELD* B, p. 84 n. 247.

[7] *ELD*, p. xliii.

[8] Adelard's lections were apparently composed in Ghent: see *ELD*, p. cxxvii. For a summary of the documents demonstrating the early development of Dunstan's cult, see A. Thacker, 'Cults at Canterbury: Relics and Reform under Dunstan and his Successors', in *St Dunstan*, ed. Ramsay et al., pp. 221–45.

Fig. 7.1 Bodl Auct. F.4.32, fol. 1r.
The additions related to Dunstan date to the tenth century

and Lapidge suggest the likelihood that the readings were commissioned by the archbishop in an attempt to shift emphasis from Glastonbury (as in B) to Canterbury and to supply more details worthy of a saint's cult in his place of burial.[9] Elphege himself would become the second most venerated saint at Canterbury, and, unlike Dunstan, he would be deemed a martyr, killed at the hands of the Danes. Adelard's set of readings had a long shelf-life, as it were, known by all subsequent hagiographers, but the set of chants he apparently provided to travel with them does not survive.[10] These chants would have been composed at a time when pitch notation in the region was not secure, and therefore they could only have been transmitted by a singer who could have brought them from Ghent to England in person.[11]

Late eleventh and early twelfth century lives

Different kinds of hagiographical materials must have been circulating in the century following the composition of the two earliest lives of Dunstan, both at Canterbury, where Dunstan was archbishop for over twenty years, and at Glastonbury, where he was abbot, at least in name, for the greater part of his life. There must have been something specific, then, motivating the new life and series of miracles for Dunstan written by Osbern, mentioned above, especially given that Adelard's lections were doubtless well established there as office readings. As Jay Rubenstein notes, in his assessment of Osbern's career, Christ Church, Canterbury, had burned in 1067, and with it went the tombs of both Elphege and Dunstan.[12] New building projects always required new or restored saints' cults, and the young Osbern would eventually rise to the occasion at Canterbury by supplying hagiographical materials for two of its major saints. The story of Osbern's opening a shrine to see what was inside it (accompanied by Eadmer) is an example of his predilections and curiosity. When he was sent to Bec to study with Anselm (archbishop of Canterbury,

---

[9] *ELD*, pp. cxxvii–cxxx. Of the four main sources for Adelard's readings, three are from passionals, including the main source used for the new edition, BL Cotton Nero C. vii, fols. 60–79. See *ELD*, pp. cxxxi–cxxxiv.

[10] The number of lections was abbreviated to eight for *The Monastic Breviary of Hyde Abbey, Winchester*, ed. J. B. L. Tolhurst, 6 vols. (London, 1932–42), III, fols. 256r–7v; for other appearances in English medieval sources, see *ELD*, pp. cxlii–cxliii.

[11] The non-appearance of the responsories in early sources is attested by J. Billet, *The Divine Office in Anglo-Saxon England, 597–c. 1000* (London, 2014), p. 194. An overview of notation in the period is offered by S. Rankin, 'Neumatic Notations in Anglo-Saxon England', in *Musicologie médiévale: Notations et Séquences*, ed. M. Huglo (Paris, 1987), 129–44; and Rankin, 'Music Books', in *The Cambridge History of the Book in Britain, Volume 1: c. 400–1100*, ed. R. Gameson (Cambridge, 2012), pp. 482–506.

[12] J. Rubenstein, 'The Life and Writings of Osbern of Canterbury', in *Canterbury and the Norman Conquest: Churches, Saints, and Scholars, 1066–1109*, ed. R. Eales and R. Sharpe (London, 1995), pp. 27–40.

1076–80) and to be disciplined for a severe but unknown fault, it might seem that his interest in Canterbury saints and their cults was rubbing off on his master. In a letter to Abbot Lanfranc from the period, Anselm expressed joy at Osbern's progress: 'Your Dom Osbern, in fact, daily develops admirably, both in his fervour for prayer seasoned with a sense of joy and in his progress in knowledge through perseverance in study, coolness of thinking, and a tenacious memory.'[13] Anselm felt compassion for Osbern because he was quite ill at the time and, in addition to other symptoms, when singing he often experienced vertigo.[14]

In the same letter, immediately after describing the symptoms of Osbern's sickness, Anselm said that he had heard about St Dunstan's 'Rule of Life' (this would be Æthelwold's *Regularis Concordia*, often attributed to Dunstan) and asked Lanfranc to send him a copy, in addition to Dunstan's *vita*. After Osbern returned to Canterbury in 1080, he said that Abbot Lanfranc asked him to compose music for a *historia* for the martyred Bishop Elphege, and that later he wrote the *vita* for the saint to complement his musical composition.[15] Rubenstein suggests that the character Elphege in the *vita* may include several features of Osbern's dearly beloved master, Anselm, as well as of the abbot of the latter's monastery, in his youth, Lanfranc. There was certainly little else upon which to base his writing, for this saint had no early *vite*. There is history in hagiography; when an author like Osbern has first-hand knowledge of two great contemporary men, but no historical materials for the saint for whom he was writing a life, he, of course, drew upon his own times and people he knew and respected. Aspects of the characters of Lanfranc and Anselm were thus woven into the *vita* of a bishop who had died nearly a century before them.

In contrast, Osbern had far more material on which to draw when establishing a cult and recreating a *vita* for Dunstan than for Elphege. But as the comparative study of musical and liturgical events found in the lives below will show, Osbern's work is especially rich in details about the saint's life in Canterbury, and this is material he had to gather from oral tradition

---

[13] *The Letters of St. Anselm of Canterbury* 39, trans. W. Fröhlich (Kalamazoo, 1990–94), I, 139–141 (p. 140); for the Latin, see *Anselmi cantuariensis archiepiscopi opera omnia*, ed. F. S. Schmitt, 6 vols. (Edinburgh, 1946–61), III, 149–51 (p. 150).

[14] Ibid.

[15] Although the life and translation survive, both the text and the music of the office have been lost. The life and the translation are found in *PL* 149, 371–94; the *translatio* is edited and translated in A. R. Rumble, *The Reign of Cnut: King of England, Denmark and Norway* (London, 1994), pp. 294–315. For discussion, see P. Hayward, 'Translation-Narratives in Post-Conquest Hagiography and English Resistance to the Norman Conquest', *ANS* 21 (1998): 67–93 (pp. 70–3). Rubenstein, 'The Life and Writings', p. 35, comparing the life of Elphege to that of Dunstan, assumes that the second is later since it is more polished in style and assured in its understanding of the genre.

or invent from his own experiences.[16] Osbern, who spent his boyhood as a chorister at Canterbury, was surely well supplied with knowledge of circulating tales and associations found in the religious and liturgical culture of his times, and he would use these to enliven the cult associated with Dunstan's tomb. The miracle of Dunstan protecting the choristers from a cruel whipping traditionally administered in the week before Christmas provides evidence that he and the boys prayed to the saint when in need of help (which was apparently very often). Osbern reported other incidents of beatings, one of which regularly occurred in August, and put the Advent beating slightly closer to Christmas than does Eadmer in his retelling of Osbern's miracle story. The terror of the young choristers is worth recording (here following both Osbern's and then Eadmer's adaptation of Osbern), together with Dunstan's intercession to prevent an annual beating, administered apparently for no cause except to provide an opportunity for teachers to vent spleen. Both Osbern and Eadmer had been child choristers themselves and knew well the customs associated with punishment; Osbern provided more details and tended toward repetition in his choice of phrasing; Eadmer adapted his same story, but truncated it.

Osbern: Surgentes ergo pueri ut intrarent domum martyrii, transierunt ante primos magistros; dormierunt. Transierunt ante secundos; dormierunt. Transierunt ante tertios et quartos; domierunt. Post paulum vero evigilantes et derisos se graviter dolentes, versi in furorum, statuunt sevissimam tertia diei hora de pueris ultionem sumere, quos protegente Dunstano mane non potuerunt contingere. Talis enim mos in ecclesia tunc temporis erat, ut quos prima diei hora sine vindicta servaret, eos hora tertia durius puniret. Sed Dunstanus … .

[And so the boys rising up that they might enter the house of their martyrdom, crossed before the first group of teachers: they slept; they crossed before the second group of teachers: they slept; they crossed before the third and the fourth: they slept. A little while later waking up, greatly pained to feel themselves tricked, the teachers turned in rage, and set up the most cruel revenge for the third hour of the day for the boys who with Dunstan protecting, they were not able to touch earlier. In those times the custom in the church was that if punishment was escaped in the first hour, it would be ever more severe in the third. But Dunstan … .]

[16] Unlike the other medieval *vite* of Dunstan, only Osbern's, the most widely copied and important for adding flesh to Dunstan's bones, does not exist in a modern critical edition or English translation. For Osbern's life and miracles of Dunstan, one still must cite the text provided in *Memorials of Saint Dunstan*, ed. Stubbs (hereafter abbreviated *OsLD* for the *vita* and *OsMD* for the *miracula*). D. Townsend, 'The Current Questions and Future Prospects of Medieval Latin Studies', in *The Oxford Handbook of Medieval Latin*, ed. D. Townsend and R. Hexter (Oxford, 2014), p. 15, laments the lack of serious attention paid to Osbern's Latinity, which he rightly notes was highly influential.

Eadmer: Iam aurora, id est hora tremenda, advenerat, cum magistri, flagris taureis et nodatis corrigiis armati, locis sibi opprotunis pueros illo transituros prestolabantur. Sed malivolos illos subito gravissimus sopor simul involuit, et qui pueros per medium illorum transeuntes retineret, vel in aliquo lederet, nullus fuit. Hinc magistros non sevitia qua fervebant contra innocentes, sed ipsorum innocentum cantus et congratulatio a somno excitavit et alta dies. Confusi ergo, quod effectum sevitate sue a qua nullius prece discedere passi sunt dormiendo perdiderant, sero doluerunt.[17]

[And now, dawn, that is the dreaded hour, had arrived; armed with bull-hide whips and knotted lashes the teachers stood waiting in opportune places for the boys to pass by there. But suddenly all at once a most deep sleep enveloped those malevolent men, so that none of them was able to stop the boys passing through their midst, nor to inflict injury upon anyone. It was not the viciousness which they bore against the innocent children that roused the teachers from their slumber, but the singing and rejoicing of these innocents, and the high feast itself. They were confused, and regretted too late that by falling asleep they had lost their chance to indulge their savagery.]

This example shows Osbern to be an able storyteller, transcending the narrow range of inherited written material concerning Dunstan, and drawing on his first-hand knowledge of the miracle tales and lives that unfolded at Canterbury in the eleventh century, before and after the Conquest. He was given an open window for incorporating angelic interventions as well by B, who claimed that Dunstan 'often learned from his divine inspirers the melodies of sacred songs', and by Adelard's lofty twelfth reading, which places Dunstan among the ranks of the saints in heaven.[18]

Osbern takes us on the scene, with an ear to popular culture, to what people in the late eleventh century were interested in hearing about the past of the institution where they prayed every day near the tomb of blessed Dunstan. Such a story would have resonated well with the children who served in the church as well. We cannot determine with precision when Osbern composed his new life and the set of miracles to accompany it, but it was surely at some point after 1080 and before his apparent death date of 1093 – by the time Osbern wrote his *vita et miracula*, that is, he had already been named precentor of the cathedral, a highly respected member of the community. He was known widely for his musical gifts, as can be seen from a comment by William of Malmesbury, who seemingly respected Osbern for little else (although he helped himself liberally to his hagiographical materials in the creation of his own life of Dunstan).[19]

[17] *OsMD* 15, pp. 141–2; and *EadMD* 14, pp. 174–5.
[18] *ELD* B 31.1, pp. 90–1; *ELD* A 12, pp. 140–5.
[19] *WilLD*.

Osbern's *vita* and miracles 'served as a source and model for most subsequent hagiography of Dunstan'.[20] He was the first to make Canterbury the seat of a lion's share of the life and miracles, highlighting Dunstan's tomb and events near to it, and, as noted above, he is responsible for making Dunstan a champion of monastic reform. Osbern's account was rewritten and reworked, with an eye to B and Adelard as well, by two other twelfth-century hagiographers, Eadmer, precentor of Canterbury (who wrote a set of miracles in addition to a *vita Dunstani*) and William, precentor of Malmesbury (who wrote a *vita* alone). Eadmer probably carried out his work while on the continent with Anselm in the years 1097–1100 and 1103–6, and surely finished by 1116.[21] It is difficult to provide hard and fast motivations for Eadmer's redaction of Osbern, but it is likely that he wished to remake Dunstan more in the mould of Anselm, and thereby give honour to his teacher and friend.[22] He did correct a few details, made the prose less purple while omitting long biblical quotations, and in general showed himself more of a Norman than an Anglo-Saxon. In his revising of wording, he often preferred B or Adelard over Osbern, and he sometimes omitted names of people and of places that Osbern supplied.[23] William of Malmesbury, like his friend Eadmer, was highly critical of Osbern, but used Osbern's materials and their narrative structure as the framework for his own offering, tweaking numerous details, but making few major changes.[24] William's life was commissioned by the monks of Glastonbury, who were then advancing the preposterous claim that Dunstan was buried in their abbey, and William probably wrote the work *c.* 1120–30.[25] It is not surprising that William apparently never finished the book of miracles they also wished him to write; he was 'keen to fit his characters into a convincing historical framework and to get the non-miraculous facts right'.[26]

---

[20] *ELD*, p. cliv.

[21] Ibid., pp. clvi–clvii; *Eadmer of Canterbury: Lives and Miracles of Saints Oda, Dunstan and Oswald*, ed. and trans. A. J. Turner and B. J. Muir (Oxford, 2006), pp. lxvii–lxix.

[22] S. A. Vaughn, 'Among these Authors are the Men of Bec: Historical Writing among the Monks of Bec', in *Essays in Medieval Studies 17: The Uses of History*, ed. J. A. Frantzen (Chicago, 2000), pp. 1–18.

[23] For a more detailed comparison, see *Eadmer: Lives and Miracles*, pp. lxix–lxxvii.

[24] *ELD*, pp. clvii–clviii and *WilLD*, pp. 159–63, with a table comparing William's life to that of Osbern.

[25] William of Malmesbury, *Saints' Lives: Lives of SS. Wulfstan, Dunstan, Patrick, Benignus and Indract*, ed. and trans. M. Winterbottom and R. M. Thomson (Oxford, 2002), p. xv.

[26] Ibid., p. xxxviii.

The role of music in the lives of Dunstan

The three lives of Dunstan from the late eleventh and early twelfth centuries were written by cantors, and two of these cantors wrote significant histories as well as hagiography, a typical profile for those who 'managed time' in Anglo-Norman book culture. William of Malmesbury, although known among recent scholars for his comparative rigour as an interpreter of past events,[27] was engaged in strengthening some musical dimensions of Dunstan's character even beyond Osbern, who also made Dunstan another David in his love of music.[28] William says of Dunstan's training at Glastonbury (particularly at the hands of Irish teachers):

> musica que appendent, gratanter addidicit et diligenter excoluit. ... Quapropter cum ceterarum tum maxime musice dulcedine captus, instrumenta eius cum ipse libenter exercere, tum ab aliis exerceri dulce habere. Ipse citharam si quando litteris vacaret sumere, ipse dulci strepitu resonantia fila quatere. Iam vero illud instrumentum quod antiqui barbiton, nos organa dicimus, tota diffudit Anglia. ... Hoc porro exercebatur non ad lenocinium voluptatum sed ad divini amoris incitamentum ... .[29]

> [he learned music with pleasure and worked at it diligently ... Hence Dunstan was captivated by music in particular; he took delight in playing musical instruments, and thought it agreeable when they were played by others. Whenever he had time left over from reading, he took up the harp, and in person 'struck the resounding strings with pleasant noise' [cf. Statius, *Achill.* II. 157]. He spread through England knowledge of what the ancients call *barbiton* and we 'organs'. ... Dunstan practised on this instrument not because of its enticing pleasures, but to arouse his love for God ... .]

Because many hagiographers and historians from the central Middle Ages were also trained in music and liturgy, these two subjects often loom larger than might be expected in historical writings. Helgaud of Fleury, who in the early eleventh century wrote the life of King Robert I of France, known as the Pious, began the tendency to ascribe musical gifts and liturgical understanding to the king, a motif which only developed over time as more cantors continued to recreate his character.[30] The same cumulative development can be seen in the stages of Dunstan's figure, for though B and Adelard mention Dunstan's training as a young scholar, there is no music

---

[27] See Winterbottom and Thomson, n. 25, above.

[28] *OsLD* 8, p. 78.

[29] *WilLD* I.iv.2–4, pp. 178–81.

[30] M. E. Fassler, 'Helgaud of Fleury and the Liturgical Arts: The Magnification of Robert the Pious', in *Magnificence and the Sublime in Medieval Aesthetics: Art, Architecture, Literature, Music*, ed. C. S. Jaeger (New York, 2010), pp. 102–27.

in the curriculum they describe. Osbern, by contrast, transformed Dunstan into a student of music and a player of many instruments, taking another opportunity to create parallels between Dunstan and the psalmist David, who made music for the religiosity of the art, and adding a long warning from Amos 6. 4–6 against those who luxuriate in sounds.[31] Eadmer said that Dunstan used his musical gifts to move others 'to meditation of celestial harmony as much by the sweetness of the words (both in his mother tongue and another language) interwoven in the musical measure, as by the harmonious music he produced through them'.[32] And then William, as we have seen, added even more information, depicting Dunstan as an advocate for organs all over the land. William, as cantor-historian, defended organ playing by means of a newly created attribute of the man who was at that point England's most famous and beloved saint.

Comparative work in the lives of Dunstan from the perspective of music and musical-liturgical understanding provides evidence for the ways that cantors who managed the cults of the saints furthered respect for their own expertise as musicians and promoted popular historical understanding as a result. A handful of examples will suffice, including one showing Dunstan involved in music and music-making at the time of miraculous intervention, and another focusing on Dunstan's ability to hear angelic hosts and their music in visionary experiences, occasionally bringing the sounds he heard back to earth – an idea initially put forward by B.

B's *vita* is filled with miraculous moments occurring while Dunstan prayed and sang, giving Dunstan's character a musical dimension that was later exploited by the cantors who wrote new histories and *historie* for the saint. His emphasis reveals that B was steeped in chant and liturgy, and that he manipulated this knowledge in subtle ways. Singing Compline, Dunstan and his companions were spared from a falling stone (*ELD* B 8.3). When Dunstan sang a delayed Vespers, fulfilling his obligation to sing the office, a dove miraculously appeared from heaven (*ELD* B 11). When the devil came to Dunstan in the form of a bear while the saint was at prayer, he scared him off by singing Psalm 67, 'Exsurgat Deus' (*ELD* B 17). The devil threw an enormous rock at Dunstan and a pupil walking outside singing psalms (*ELD* B 18). In exile, Dunstan dreamed of his community back at Glastonbury singing Vespers, but were unable to complete the Magnificat antiphon, although they tried again and again; Dunstan rebuked them in the dream, and God answered explaining that this meant the plot to expel Abbot Dunstan would not be completed (*ELD* B 23).[33] Although B wrote primarily about

[31] *OsLD* 8, p. 78.
[32] *EadLD* 7, pp. 58–61.
[33] *ELD* B 23.3–5, pp. 72–5. It is not without meaning that the Magnificat antiphon the community tried repeatedly to sing was 'Quare detraxistis', the text of which is based upon Job 6. 25–28 (Can 004448). The final two words of the antiphon, which

Dunstan's early life, he also describes the saint as archbishop of Canterbury singing psalms as he walks along late at night (*ELD* B 36), in keeping with his earlier musical attributes.

A dramatic example of miraculous music-making in these *vite* is the story of Dunstan's singing harp, which became well established in the hagiographical tradition. Although later authors name the instrument a *cithera*, B uses two terms; when the young Dunstan, a skilled artisan, came to the house of a noble lady to help her design a liturgical vestment, 'sumpsit secum ex more citharam suam quam lingua paterna *hearpan* vocamus' ('he brought with him as usual his harp, which we call in our fathers' tongue *hearpa*').[34] The instrument was hung on the wall while the assembled group of women was working on the cloth with Dunstan, and it began to play, of its own accord, the antiphon 'Gaudent in celis anime sanctorum qui Christi vestigia sunt secuti ... '.[35] The text promises that saints who walk in Christ's footsteps will reign with him forever, since they have shed their blood for his love. B describes Dunstan taking the instrument's warning to heart, but he does not mention this incident later, even though the eventual exile is apparently the trouble it portends. Perhaps this is why Adelard moved the story to later in his set of readings, placing it just before the events that would lead up to Dunstan's death, thereby giving the antiphon's message greater narrative weight.[36]

Later cantors reused B's material in their *vite*, keeping various elements but integrating them into the narrative. Osbern, continuing with his favoured Old Testament conceit, has Dunstan play the same instrument for the king, a David to a Saul. This is followed by the episode with the self-playing harp, and immediately after that, as various jealousies abound at court, Dunstan is accused of practising 'sinister arts' and it was said that his skills were used 'for deception of simple people rather than any kind of religion'.[37] As a result, soon after the harp incident Dunstan was nearly murdered, thrown into a pit, like a Joseph, and the prophecy of the miraculously

---

could not be sung, are 'cogitis explete' ['finish what you have begun']. The chant would have been sung at second Vespers during the Old Testament *historia* for Job, rendered at Matins with some other Old Testament books in the month of September; see *Ordo Romanus* XIIIA 9, in M. Andrieu, *Les Ordines Romani du haut Moyen Age*, 5 vols. (Louvain, 1956–61), II, 484–5. This chant appears primarily in Italian and occasionally in French sources, as can be seen from its circulation among manuscripts represented in the CANTUS database, so it is somewhat strange that B emphasized it.

[34] *ELD* B 12.2, pp. 42–3. Dunstan was also known as a metalworker; a bell he supposedly cast was hung by his tomb in Canterbury.

[35] Can 002927, widespread throughout all Europe, was sung in the office for several feast days, including for individual saints and for All Saints.

[36] *ELD* A 9, pp. 134–5.

[37] *EadLD* 9, pp. 60–3. In B the incident of near murder takes place before the harp plays.

rendered antiphon rang true.[38] Eadmer and William follow Osbern's arrangement.[39]

The tale of the harp suggests another important aspect of the place of music in these *vite*, namely the relationship between Dunstan's musical gifts and the music of the heavenly hosts.[40] In Osbern's version, the harp's music offered the listeners a foretaste of heaven.[41] In Eadmer's version, Dunstan realized the heavenly source of the antiphon and its prophetic power: 'He accepted that the performance was truly brought about by the music of angels so that he might be taught as if in the actual presence of God what ought to be done by him in the future.'[42] The angelically produced antiphon sounded by the harp is just one of a number of incidents in which Dunstan is privy to the sounds of angelic song – in fact this ability became one of his chief characteristics as he is depicted by later cantors. One of the pieces Dunstan heard on high and brought back to earth, which seems not to have survived, is the antiphon 'O rex dominator gentium'. This is a surprising omission in the liturgical sources, since, as Eadmer tells the story, Dunstan insisted that the work be written down, and according to William Dunstan teaches the piece to his community – both common strategies used by cantor-historian-hagiographers to establish new pieces in the liturgy.[43]

While 'O rex dominator gentium' is unfortunately lost, another piece featured in the Dunstan lives can be traced in the history of English liturgical music, that is, a Kyrie that is mentioned first by Adelard in his ninth lesson:

quod nocte quadam sancto sopori deditus, tanquam ad superna raptus, angelicis mulcebatur concentibus; ibi sanctos spiritus sanctissime Trinitati in laudem et hominibus in salutem audivit modulantes et dicentes 'Kyrie eleison, Christe eleison, Kyrie eleison'.[44]

[One night, while deep in holy slumber, as though rapt to the heavens he [that is, Dunstan] was soothed by angelic harmonies. He heard there the holy spirits singing in praise of the Holy Trinity and for the salvation of men, saying 'Kyrie eleison, Christe eleison, Kyrie eleison'.]

---

[38] *OsLD* 10, 11, pp. 80–1.

[39] But Eadmer brings the piece in a second time closer to the end of his *vita*, and in this case he includes Osbern's radiant light, *EadLD* 53, pp. 130–1.

[40] See especially D. Hiley, 'What St Dunstan Heard the Angels Sing: Notes on a pre-Conquest *Historia*', in *Laborare fratres in unum: Festschrift László Dobszay zum 60. Geburtstag*, ed. D. Hiley and J. Szendrei (Hildesheim, 1995), pp.105–15.

[41] *OsLD* 10, pp. 80–1.

[42] *EadLD* 8, pp. 60–61. William emphasized the prophetic rather than the angelic: *WilLD* I.6.2, pp. 182–3.

[43] *EadLD* 51, pp. 128–9; *WilLD* II.27, pp. 284–7.

[44] *ELD* A 9, pp. 134–5.

Osbern tells of the angelic Kyrie as part of Dunstan's vision of his mother in heaven, and he says that the chant resounded in organum.[45] Eadmer tells of a royal hunting party on Sunday morning, for which Dunstan was instructed to delay Mass past the usual hour; instead, he falls asleep in church and has Mass with the heavenly host who teach him a Kyrie, which he in turn gives to others to learn, 'and today the holy church in many places sings it during the solemn rites of the Mass'.[46] William repeats this information, but not in his *vita Dunstani*, though there he does note that Dunstan 'many times heard the heavenly choirs sweetly singing Kyrie eleison'.[47] Instead, William uses the story in his history of English bishops, where he writes: 'I believe, and it is no empty belief, that he also heard the song of the angels as they chanted the Kyrie eleison, which is now gladly taught and gladly learned in the churches of the English.'[48]

The end of Dunstan's life was also filled with musical allusions, beginning with Adelard's tenth lesson, which told that Dunstan was called to celebrate the celestial Mass in heaven by throngs of angels. But as Ascension Thursday was imminent and the people needed him to celebrate Mass and preach on this holy day, he asked them to delay so he could fulfil his priestly duties, and the heavenly host agreed to do without him until Saturday. The angels' speech to Dunstan in Adelard was repeated by Osbern and both Eadmer and William, with only minor alterations – 'Hail, our Dunstan! Come if you are ready, and be so kind as to join our company' – and after Dunstan's request for a slight delay: 'Be ready on Saturday, to pass with us hence to Rome, for with us you must forever chant before the highest bishop, "Holy, holy, holy".'[49]

The Dunstan office in Worcester F. 160

Worcester, Cathedral Library MS F. 160 is a compilation made up of various liturgical books, among them both an antiphoner and a gradual. The antiphoner, the earliest section of the manuscript, has been dated *c.* 1230.[50] As several scholars have observed, this central source for the study of chant of the Sarum Use contains many offices for English saints, some of which, including that of Dunstan, survive only because this book escaped

---

[45] *OsLD* 40, pp. 117–18.
[46] *EadLD* 52, pp. 128–31.
[47] *WilLD* II.26, pp. 284–5.
[48] *GPA* i.19.11, pp. 40–41.
[49] *ELD* A 10, pp. 136–9; *OsLD* 41, pp. 120–1; *EadLD* 63, pp. 150–1; *WilLD* II.30, pp. 288–9.
[50] For a facsimile, see *Antiphonaire monastique: XIIIe siècle, codex F. 160 de la Bibliothèque de la Cathédrale de Worcester*, ed. L. McLachlan, Paléographie musicale 12 (Tournai, 1922).

the near-total destruction of the Worcester liturgical books in the sixteenth century.[51] The Dunstan office is a complicated work, as medieval offices so often are, with several historical layers and with numerous connections to the *vite* studied above. The full office in F. 160, fols. 220r–223r, is catalogued on the CANTUS database, beginning with first Vespers on the eve of the 19 May feast and ending with second Vespers on the day of the feast.[52]

Several characteristics are immediately notable. This is a monastic office, and so it has twelve readings, twelve responsories and two sets of antiphons (six each) for the night office. The 'mode' column on the CANTUS catalogue shows that the two sets of antiphons for Matins are modally ordered, and the texts of these are in fact rhythmic poetry, doubtless composed no earlier than the second half of the twelfth century. The responsories, however, are a different matter, not modally ordered and not expressed in accentual poetry (see Appendix 1). The same is true for the set of five antiphons sung at Lauds. The office thus has at least two layers, earlier and later.

To investigate the entire office is beyond the scope of this chapter, but it is clear from Appendix 1 that the texts of the responsories were to a large degree based on Adelard, though their language and structure also suggest the influence of Osbern's *vita* and, in one instance, Eadmer's.[53] In addition, several of the 'musical incidents' in Dunstan's life studied above are re-enacted through the texts and their musical settings. The two earlier parts of the office, for example, the responsories and Lauds antiphons, are closely tied to the *vite* of Dunstan, but they also provide a new view of the saint – one that is sung and thus embodies ideas about music's role in his life. The twelve readings of Adelard, which were employed in one guise or another for the Sarum Use, shortened for a cathedral office or perhaps because some of them were taken from Scripture, are the fundamental source for the texts of the responsories, as can be seen in Appendix 1 (in which the responsories are matched with their probable readings).

When one of Adelard's readings did not suit the larger scheme of the Worcester office, it was apparently cut; Adelard's fifth reading, for example, which concerns the burial of a king at Glastonbury, had little interest for this

---

[51] D. Hiley, 'The Music of Prose Offices in Honour of English Saints', *Plainsong and Medieval Music* 10 (2001), 23–37.

[52] David Hiley and I are preparing a fully transcription and translation of the office, with commentary, for the series *Historiae*, published by the Institute of Mediaeval Music.

[53] There is also a truncated *vita* for Dunstan in BL Cotton Nero E. i, part of a passional from Worcester dating from the early thirteenth century. This manuscript will feature in my future work, and I intend to check these readings against the F. 160 responsories more closely. Readings in Nero are labeled with the day of his feast, and they are unusually long, including about half of Eadmer's *vita*, as well as a few texts from William. The set shows the prominence of both of these authors' materials at Worcester in the period before F. 160 was copied.

Canterbury office, and so apparently would not have been read with these responsories. It would seem that the tenth reading was divided, allowing for one entire nocturn to be devoted to the several miracles that were associated with Dunstan's final celebration of Mass on Ascension Thursday at Canterbury and his reception into the heavens on the Saturday following this grand feast. In this way, the story of Dunstan's life in the *historia* has three major parts: (1) his miraculous birth and early life, (2) miraculous events beginning with the end of his exile and his time as Archbishop of Canterbury and (3) the end of his time at Canterbury – this especially fitting for a feast that honoured the shrine at the centre of his cult at Canterbury. The history of his life is reshaped to suit the place and the architecture of the new church.

The comparisons in Appendix 1 demonstrate that the sources for the responsory texts create a historical narrative for Dunstan, inviting the singers (and their audience) to enter into Dunstan's musical imagination and experiences. Great responsories have two sections, a respond and a verse, and since the final section of the respond is sung again after the verse, the two must be constructed so that there is a smooth connection between the verse and the last part of the respond which follows it. The words in parentheses at the end of the text in Appendix 1 show where to begin the part of the respond that serves as a refrain after the verse. In responsories that close out the end of a nocturn, the refrain is repeated twice, once after the verse, and once after the doxological statement that is traditionally sung. Responsory 1 is an example of the way the form of the genre has been exploited by the composer to add depth and new dimensions to Dunstan's saintly character. The text of the opening describes Dunstan as a pillar of the church, taking up that light (Christ) which, upright in the heavens, sustains the earth, and it then contains another statement about Dunstan as a bulwark of apostolic faith who shines with the heavenly light mentioned in the respond. As the respond ends with the words 'alleluia, alleluia', the sound of the heavenly host, this creates an angelic refrain, bringing the sound of heaven down into the celebration of Dunstan and his light, described through a miracle in the first reading. In this way the chant embodied the miraculous tale of the reading.

Responsory 8 forms a musical high point of this magnificent office. As can be seen from Ex. 7.1 the chant has been structured to emphasize the word 'organis' as the final section of the respond (see also Appendix 1, R.2.4). This section was sung after the verse and again after the doxological statement. And then, in a most unusual and dramatic musical gesture, a Kyrie chant was sung, a mode 8 chant that was set polyphonically in the Winchester troper. Since it was Osbern who, in his life of Dunstan, introduced the idea that the chant was sung with organum, it is just possible that this masterful musician may have had a hand in writing the responsories copied in F. 160. Another musical tour de force is found in the antiphons for Lauds. The final responsory, which depicts Dunstan feasting at the heavenly banquet of the lamb with all the saints (cf. Apoc. 19), was an introduction to Lauds, where

Ex. 7.1 Responsory 'Dunstanus archiepiscopus' (transcribed by Margot Fassler and David Hiley and engraved by Benjamin A. Stone)

et__ spi - ri - tu - i__ san - cto._____

Or - ga - nis._____

Ky-ri - e - - - - - ley - son.

Chri-ste - - - - - - -

- - ley - son. Ky - ri - e - - -

- - - - -

- - ley - son. al - le - lu - ya._

each antiphon celebrates a rank of saints (see Table 7.3). When coupled with the designated psalmody, this set of chants provides commentary on the great heavenly feast and places Dunstan at the table.

In his history of the bishops of England, William of Malmesbury describes Dunstan's many miracles, making it clear that they cannot be disassociated from his character. William thus draws on his knowledge of the lives of the saint, and surely also on his knowledge of Dunstan's liturgical veneration, bringing both together as he shapes an aspect of England's past. As in the case of Dunstan, to understand how the past was understood and recreated in the Middle Ages often requires knowledge of three kinds of materials – written histories and chronicles, lives of the saints, and the chants and readings of the liturgy – and this is especially true because the cults of the saints played a major role in the process of history-making. The three kinds of sources worked interactively in the intellectual, religious and artistic understandings,

Table 7.3 Subjects of Lauds antiphons for the Feast of Dunstan, Worcester F. 160

Antiphon 1	Patriarchs and Prophets (with 'Dominus regnavit', Ps. 98)
Antiphon 2	Apostles (with 'Iubilate', Ps. 99)
Antiphon 3	Martyrs (with 'Deus Deus meus', Ps. 62)
Antiphon 4	Confessors (with 'Benedicite', Ps. 102)
Antiphon 5	Virgins (with 'Laudate Dominum', Ps. 150)

especially of monks and clerics who sang and heard the office, and joined in the musical events of Dunstan's life as part of his history.

All three types of materials were subject to various kinds of transformation, and the ways in which chronicles interact with saints' lives, and the ways in which chants were incorporated into histories, must be assessed on a case-by-case basis. Early materials composed for Dunstan lacked significant information about the Canterbury years, and since this was to become a major site for his cult, something had to be done. Osbern of Canterbury filled the gap initially, and his work most likely included new chants with texts drawn from his new set of life and miracles. Eadmer of Canterbury followed suit. The Sarum office in Worcester F. 160 shows complex dependencies on the early lives and on the later work of the Canterbury cantors, fleshing out Dunstan's character so he could be understood and his miracles could be relived through musical re-enactment. Dunstan was England's greatest saint in the pre-Becket centuries, and his character grew slowly and steadily from early eyewitness observations, to Canterbury, to a Sarum office –an example of the ways in which the past was both known and made, especially at the hands of cantors, who sang, wrote offices and penned histories.

Appendix 1
The responsories for Dunstan's historia in Worcester 160 (first half of the century), with comparative references to the readings by Adelard and to other *vite* of Dunstan

First Nocturn

Reading 1 The miracle of the candles on the feast of the purification before his birth. All candles are suddenly extinguished, but then Dunstan's pregnant mother has her candle miraculously lit, and from its flame all the others are reignited.

R. 1.1 (mode 1)

Presul Christi Dunstanus **sanctis parentibus ortus claruit quorum animas inter angelos post excessum eorum videte promeruit** alleluia. V. Sancti sanctum genuere et **regi regum Christo** optulere. [quorum ...]	Prelate of Christ, Dunstan, was singled out, a man born of saintly parents, whose souls he merited to see among the angels after their death alleluia. V. To bear a holy man for the Holy One, and to offer to Christ, the king of kings.

Commentary Miracle not in B; the R is very close to Adelard (bold, with some alterations); greatly expanded in Osbern; in Eadmer and William. Language in the verse (emboldened) is found in Osbern's description of the miracle at the Purification: *OsLD* 4, 14, p. 72.

Reading 2 His education and illness at Glastonbury. He is preserved by climbing the walls of the church, and is found sleeping at the altar.

R. 1.2 (mode 3)

Pius adolescens Dunstanus florem iuuentutis flore induit virginitatis per quem complacuit et Deo et angelis allleuia alleluia. V. Puri cordis munditie casti corporis sociavit pudiciam. [Per ...]	The holy young man Dunstan clothed the flower of his youth with the flower of virginity through which he was pleasing to God and to the angels, alleluia, alleluia. V. He joined chastity of the chaste body to the modesty of the pure heart.

Commentary The emphasis on chastity in R1.2 is not found in B, but it is at the very end of Adelard's lections: see *ELD/A* 12, pp. 144–5 and for Osbern, see *OsLD* 40, p. 119, which is paraphrased in the Responsory text.

Reading 3 King Edmund makes Dunstan head of Glastonbury and pleads his support, and Dunstan becomes like a pillar of light for monasticism diffused through the entire English sphere.

R. 1.3 (mode 4)

Preciosus vir Domini Dunstanus splendidum ecclesie ornamentum factus columpna lucis effulsit que erecta in celum orbem terre sustinuit alleluia alleluia. V. O robur apostolice fidei plenum lumine celi [Alleluia ...]

Dunstan, the godly man of great worth, made into a splendid decoration for the church, shines forth with a magnificent pillar of light which upright in the heavens sustains the orb of the earth, alleluia alleluia. V. O bulwark of apostolic faith, full with the light of heaven.

Commentary The text in Adelard is the closest, but Osbern and Eadmer follow. Adelard (*ELD*/A,3, p.118) reads: 'ut sicut dixi de lampande pregnantis genetricis sue ceterorum per omnem ecclesiam lampades accensas, ita per eum ex hoc loco columen religionis monastice toto Angelorum orbe diffusum sit.'

Reading 4 Dunstan has a vision in which Peter, Paul and Andrew appear to him, offering him symbols of protection.

R. 1.4 (mode 4)

In visione sancta apparuere beato Dunstáno principes regni Dei et iudices seculi singuli offerentes ei gladium et armaturam **Spiritus** sancti alleluia, alleluia. V. Petrus ergo et Paulus cum sancto Andrea effulsere ei que gratiam apostolice benedictionis contulere. [singuli ...] V. Gloria Patri et Filio et Spiritui sancto. [singuli ...]

In a holy vision, the leaders of the kingdom of God and the judges of the age appeared to blessed Dunstan one by one, offering him a sword and the armour of the Holy Spirit, alleluia alleluia. V. Peter therefore and Paul with blessed Andrew shone forth to him and conveyed the grace of an apostolic blessing. V. Glory to the Father and to the Son and to the Holy Spirit.

Commentary This responsory is a paraphrase of Adelard (the vision is also in B). The king interprets the vision (*ELD*/ A,4, p. 122): 'Cum gladii quos ex apostolica benedictione suscepisti armaturam pretendant spiritus Sancti ...'. Hiley ('What St Dunstan Heard', p. 111) shows that the melisma on *spiritus* is based on phrases from the sequentia 'Ostende maior' commonly sung with 'Salus eterna'.

Adelard Reading 5 Dunstan buries King Eadred, as he had previously buried Edmund at Glastonbury.

No responsory relates.

Second Nocturn

Reading 5 (Adelard 6)   Dunstan is sent into exile at Mont Blandin, where he is under the protection of Arunulf of Flanders. He is visited by the Apostle Andrew.

R. 2.1 (mode 6T)

Beatus Dunstanus exilio pro iusticia est ascriptus ubi crebra sanctorum consolatione a Deo est relevatus. Alleluia. V. Cui pro veritate exulanti per sanctam Andream apostolam astitit piissimiis Deus. [Ubi ...]

Blessed Dunstan was consigned to exile because of his righteousness where he was sustained by God with strong consolation of the saints, alleluia. V. For whose exiled truth most holy God had stand the blessed Apostle Andrew.

Commentary   B does not know the location of the exile and makes no mention of St Andrew. The responsory text and verse is a paraphrase of Adelard, *ELD/A* 6, pp. 128–9.

Reading 6 (Adelard 7)   Dunstan is recalled to England and becomes bishop of London (Paul) and of Worcester (Peter) and archbishop of Canterbury (goes with Rochester, which is of St Andrew), fulfiling the vision of the three apostles.

R. 2.2 (mode 7)

Misertus Dominus destitute ecclesie Dunstanum patrem cum gloria revocauit et ei patriarchatum prime metropolis Anglorum magnifice concessit alleluia. V. Respexit Dominus populum suum tum beatum Dunstanum patrie redonavit. [Et ei ...]

The Lord feeling pity for the destitute church recalled father Dunstan with glory and magnificently conceded to him the patriarchy of the first metropolitan in England, alleluia. V. The Lord cared for his people when he gave back Dunstan to the homeland.

Commentary   Responsory text emphasizes Canterbury, as does Osbern, another indication that the chant texts represent a Canterbury reworking of the sense of Adelard. Several of the words found in the responsory text are found in Osbern, *OsLD* 32, pp. 108–9.

Reading 7 (Adelard 8)   Dunstan sees the mystical dove twice during liturgical celebrations.

R. 2.3 (mode 8)

Celestium contemplator Dunstanus angelica atque apostolica visione et visitatione dignissimus columbam a Iohanne in Christi baptismate visam sibi in letitia cordis sui exultavit ostensam alleluia. V. Dunstanus columbe Dei filius cordis munditie et sancte innocentie deditus. [Columbam ...]

Dunstan, a contemplator of the heavens and most worthy of angelic and apostolic vision and visitation, celebrated in the joy of his heart, a dove shown to him by John the Baptist in Christ, alleluia. V. Dunstan, a son of the dove of God, given over to purity of the heart and to holy innocence.

Commentary Not in B. The responsory refers to the apostolic vision of the sword of Andrew and the vision of the dove with reference to John the Baptist. These are together Adelard: *ELD/A* 8, pp. 132–3; see also *OsLD* 33, p. 109 and *WilLD* i.13.2, pp. 196–7.

Reading 8 (Adelard 9)   Dunstan has a vision of heaven in which the angels sing to the Trinity, 'Kyrie eleison, Christe eleison, Kyrie eleison'; the saint's harp miraculously plays the antiphon 'Gaudent in celis anime sanctorum qui Christi vestigia sunt secuti' and so on.

R. 2.4 (mode 8)

Dunstanus archiepiscopus sancto sopori deditus angelicis mulcebatur organis sic modulantibus: Kyrie eleison alleluia. V. Sancti Spiritus psallebant insullimi et clare modulando preces offerebant sancte Trinitati. [organis …] V. Gloria Patri et Filio et Spiritui sancto. [organis …] Kyrie eleison. Christe eleison. Kyrie eleison. Alleluia.

Dunstan the archbishop, given over to holy sleep, was soothed by organized (that is, set in organum) modulations: Kyrie eleison, alleluia. V. Those of the Holy Spirit on high psalmodized and offered with bright modulation to the Holy Trinity. V. Glory to the Father and to the Son and to the Holy Spirit. Kyrie eleison. Christe eleison. Kyrie eleison. Alleluia.

Commentary   Not in B; Adelard emphasizes the Trinitarian aspect of the Kyrie sung by the angelic hosts. At this point in Adelard, Dunstan's harp plays the antiphon 'Gaudent in celis anima' and so on. In Osbern the Kyrie is sung in organum, and text proves what other materials only suggest: Osbern's hand (or that of someone dependent on him) is present in the development of the chant texts; see OsLD 40, p.117. The phases of the chant relate to a mode 8 Kyrie that was sung at Winchester in organum. (Note: The word *insullimi* is here taken as a version of *insublimi*, 'those on high', which as a nominative third-person plural noun makes grammatical sense.)

Third Nocturn

Reading 9 (Adelard 10.1)   On the Ascension, Ælfgar, afterwards bishop of Elmham, has a vision of cherubim and seraphim calling Dunstan away. (Note: Reading 10 has been divided to make lessons 10 and 11.)

R. 3.1 (mode 8)

Transiens ex hoc mundo venerandus pontifex **angelicis choris ducentibus migravit ad Christum qui ei factus est corona et perhenne premium** alleluia. V. Cumque exitum suum dominicis muniret sacramentis translatus est ab angelis ad auctorem luminis. [Qui ei …]

The venerable bishop crossing from this world with angelic choirs leading the departed to Christ who made for him a crown and an everlasting reward, alleluia. V. And, so his leaving might fortify the Sunday sacraments, he was carried by angels to the author of light.

Commentary In Adelard, the bishop Ælfgar has a vision, seeing Dunstan on high with the angels and seated in a pontifical throne. Part of the text of this responsory is found in Eadmer, relating to the day of Dunstan's death, thereby breaking the chronology found in Adelard: 'Et responso a cunctis Amen, transit, et angelicis eum choris ducentibus, migravit ad Christum qui ei factus est corona et perenne premium' (*EadLD* 67, pp. 156–7). This is yet another sign of an ongoing Canterbury influence on the chant texts.

Reading 10 (Adelard 10.2) Dunstan is asked if he is ready to depart; he answers affirmatively and the angels say: Be ready on Saturday to come with us, where you will sing 'Holy, Holy, Holy' in the presence of the great high priest forever.

R. 3.2 (mode 4)

Exultemus et letemur in Domino: ecce beatus Dunstanus unus candidati gregis in albis agnum sequentis 'Sanctus, sanctus, sanctus' clamare non cessat alleluia alleluia. V. Conscriptus numero eorum qui sequuntur agnum Dei quocumque ierit. [Sanctus …]	Let us rejoice and be glad in the Lord. behold blessed Dunstan, one of the gleaming flock in white following the lamb, does not cease to cry 'Holy, holy, holy', alleluia, alleluia. V. Enrolled in the number of those who follow the lamb of God wheresoever he goes.

Commentary From Adelard: The angels said to Dunstan: 'Paratus esto die Sabbati nobiscum hunc Romam transire, quia opertet te coram summo pontifice nobiscum "Sanctus, Sanctus, Sanctus" eternaliter canere' (*ELD*/A, 10, pp. 138–9). The same is paraphrased in Osbern, *OsLD* 41, p. 121, and quoted from Adelard in Eadmer (*EadLD* 63, 150–1); the text is not in William.

Reading 11 (Adelard 11) Last sermons; last farewell; Dunstan celebrates last communion.

R. 3.3 (mode 1)

Translate ad celestia benigne pater Dunstane suspirantes ad te filios noli deserere sed ad te transferre satage ut tecum coram Christo mereamur gaudere alleluia. V. Dum enim in corpore peregrinamur a Domino tuo quesumus non destituamur auxilio. [Ut tecum …]	Taken to heaven, blessed father Dunstan, do not desert your sons sighing to you but be energetic to bring them to you so that with you in the presence of Christ we may merit eternal joy. V. For while we journey in the body we beg your Lord that we not be left without help.

Commentary Adelard emphasizes his care for the people. Osbern expands Dunstan's farewell speech.

Reading 12 (Adelard 12) Dunstan enters into the company of the angels, patriarchs, prophets, martyrs and virgins (as is made clear in the antiphons, see below).

R. 3.4 (mode 1):

Beatus es care Dei Dunstane qui in cena nuptiarum agni discumbis qui gaudio Domini tui letus perfrueris gaudebis ergo cum angelis et in ligno vite cum sanctis epulaberis alleluia. V. Ecce sicut sol in conspectu Dei emicas ubi cotidie 'Sanctus' clamare non cessas. [gaudebis ...] V. Gloria Patri et Filio et Spiritui sancto.[gaudebis]

You are blessed and beloved of God, Dunstan, who recline at the nuptial meal of the lamb, who joyful has full enjoyment of the praise of your Lord, therefore you will rejoice with the angels and feast with the saints on the tree of life. V. Behold you shine forth as the sun in the view of God where daily you do not cease to cry 'Holy'. V. Glory to the Father and to the Son and to the Holy Spirit.

Commentary: Compare Adelard: 'Et ideo cum hiis qui non inquinaverunt vestimenta sua agnum Dei sequeris. Ideo in cena nuptiarum agni letus discumbis. Ergo cum talibus et tot civibus in perpetuum feliciter gaudebis, et in ligno vite eternaliter epulaberis' (*ELD*/A, 12, pp. 144–5).

8

Female Monastic Cantors and Sacristans in Central Medieval England: Four Sketches

Katie Ann-Marie Bugyis

Until Margot Fassler's study of the multifaceted office of the medieval monastic cantor, this office had received little scholarly attention.[1] Through her investigation of extant monastic rules and customaries from the ninth through the eleventh centuries, Fassler was able to uncover the development of this office over the course of the central Middle Ages. Though the Benedictine Rule made no explicit provision for the cantor as a monastic officer, later customaries written in the tenth and eleventh centuries as elaborations on the Rule, particularly those issued from the abbey of Cluny, increasingly articulated and expanded upon this office so that it encompassed a variety of liturgical and scriptorial responsibilities.

Fassler's study focused exclusively on the office of the cantor in communities of male Benedictine religious. Not until Anne Yardley's recent study did the office of *cantrix* in communities of women religious receive sustained consideration.[2] Yardley devoted a chapter to detailing not only the liturgical responsibilities of the *cantrix*, but also those of the abbess, sacristan (*editva* or *secretaria*) and weekly *cantrix*, as they were described in monastic rules, customaries, ordinals and visitation records from Benedictine, Bridgettine, Dominican and Franciscan houses. Given the nature of the extant sources, she limited the scope of her study to the fourteenth through the sixteenth centuries, though a few sources from the twelfth and the thirteenth centuries were referenced when instructive. In her discussion of the *cantrix*, she divided this officer's responsibilities under four headings: general oversight of liturgical practices, regulation of music, vocal instruction of community members and soloistic roles.[3] And her account of the sacristan's responsibilities attended primarily to the maintenance of the community's liturgical space, eucharistic vessels, vestments, books, candles and reliquaries, as well as to her keeping of time during the daily *cursus*.[4]

---

[1] Fass A.

[2] A. Yardley, *Performing Piety: Musical Culture in Medieval English Nunneries* (New York, 2006).

[3] Ibid., pp. 53–66.

[4] Ibid., pp. 69–72.

Yardley's work has done much to reveal the liturgical histories of late medieval English women religious, but those of women religious from earlier centuries must still be recovered. Though the sources for this earlier period are often more scarce, fragmentary and male-mediated, they nonetheless contain *tesserae* that can be pieced together to form a mosaic of the liturgical lives of women religious and the monastic officers who directed them. Mortuary rolls, saints' lives, miracle collections and calendars bear traces of the cantors and sacristans who commissioned or undertook their initial production. They offer glimpses of the various ways that these women created, preserved and passed on their communities' *memoria* through the copying of liturgical books, the writing and preservation of charters and other documents, the maintenance of necrologies and mortuary rolls, the creation of texts and music for the Divine Office and Mass, the ornamentation of sacred spaces, the production of *vite* and *miracula* for patron saints, the custody of their relics and the proper observance of both the calendar and the *hore* of prayer throughout the year's liturgical *cursus*.

Though some of the women engaged in these activities were explicitly identified as cantors or sacristans, more often the titles of their offices and even their names were not recorded. Thus simply searching for the incidence of those invested with the title of cantor or sacristan and then detailing the activities that these women performed will yield only a partial account of how the liturgy was orchestrated in women's monastic houses; attention must also be given to the women who performed the kinds of liturgical activities scripted for these offices in monastic rules and customaries, even if they are untitled or unnamed. Taking this dual approach will ensure that the contributions of many more of the women figured as their communities' custodians of the liturgy are culled for consideration. Determining whether they were 'officially' cantors or sacristans, in many respects, matters less than showing that they performed the cantor- or sacristan-like duties of directing the music of the liturgy, preparing the Eucharist, guarding saints' shrines and serving as scribes for their communities.

Three women were explicitly assigned to the office of cantor or sacristan in the extant sources: Eadburh of Nunnaminster, Wulfruna-Judith of Barking and Edith of Nunnaminster. In the *Life* of Eadburh by Osbert of Clare (d. *c.* 1158), he names the mid tenth century saint as the 'precentrix' of her community.[5] And though Susan Ridyard questions the historical accuracy of his attribution, wondering whether it simply means that 'her love of singing was such that she seemed to be *like* a precentrix', it is clear from his references to the liturgical responsibilities that Eadburh assumed that she exercised both cantor- *and* sacristan-like roles.[6] Goscelin of Saint-Bertin (b. *c.* 1040, d. after

---

[5] Ridyard provides an edition of Osbert's text in *The Royal Saints of Anglo-Saxon England* (Cambridge, 1998), pp. 255–308 (p. 281).

[6] Ibid., p. 34 n. 89 (emphasis mine).

1107) identifies the eleventh-century woman religious Wulfruna-Judith as an 'editva' at Barking.[7] In his *Lives of two of the abbey's abbess-saints*, Æthelburh (d. *c.* 693) and Wulfhild (d. after 996), Goscelin features Wulfruna-Judith as a central character in and witness to various miracles, and his accounts of these miracles provide rich evidence for the range of liturgical and scribal duties entrusted to her care. Finally, Nunnaminster's *titulus* for the mortuary roll for Vitalis, abbot of Savigny (d. 1122), lists among the obituaries of the community the name 'Edita', and in the interlinear space above her name, the title of her office was supplied: 'cantrice'.[8] The importance of her office is revealed by the high rank accorded her within the litany of Nunnaminster's departed; her name was listed immediately after the names of the abbess and prioresses and before the names of the other sisters that bear no title.

Liturgical leaders

Review of the extant sources relating the life of Eadburh of Nunnaminster provides the most comprehensive, though admittedly idealized, portrait of a *precentrix*'s musical leadership and ability. In Osbert's *Life*, the first hints of her devotion to the performance of the Divine Office are found in the chapter concerning her practice of the virtue of patience. He claims that the saint was so steadfast in her dedication to the hours of sung prayer that 'psalterium David nusquam minibus virgineis excidit, nusquam decacordum legis divine ab eius intentione recedit' ('David's Psalter never was taken from her virginal hands, and the ten-stringed instrument of the divine law never departed from her intention').[9] Both night and day she was dedicated to the *cursus* of prayer, 'et siquid minus impletum in Dei laudibus diurna luce meminerat, nocturnis excubiis devota sedulitate' ('and if she remembered that anything was unfulfilled in the praises of God during the day, she supplied the night watches with devout assiduity').[10] According to Osbert, early in her formation, Eadburh was so zealous in her devotions that she often remained in the

---

[7] M. L. Colker, 'Texts of Jocelyn of Canterbury which Relate to the History of Barking Abbey', *Studia Monastica* 7 (1965), 383–460 (pp. 412, 433).

[8] *Rouleau mortuaire du B. Vital, abbé de Savigni*, ed. L. Delisle (Paris, 1909), no. 184. For the edition of this mortuary roll, see *Recueil des rouleaux des morts (VIIIe siècle–vers 1536)*, ed. J. Dufour, 4 vols. (Paris, 2005), I, 580, no. 122.184. Edita may also be the 'Ediva' named among the dead remembered in Nunnaminster's *titulus* for Matilda, abbess of La Trinité, Caen (d. 1113), listed among the 'monache' (ibid., I, 405, no. 114.11). The identification of Edita and Ediva is strengthened by the fact that all the other names listed among Nunnaminster's deceased in the *rotulus* for Vitalis also appear in the *rotulus* for Matilda, but it must be emphasized that in the *rotulus* for Matilda, Ediva was not identified as a *cantrix*.

[9] *Royal Saints*, p. 266. Unless otherwise noted, all translations are my own.

[10] Ibid., p. 267.

oratory beyond the hours of the Office in order to continue praying in private. The prioress of the community ultimately had to punish Eadburh for this practice, because she wished to teach the community 'ut nulla earum privatis in oratorio vacaret officiis, neque publicis abesset conventibus eiusdem congregationis' ('that no one should be idle in private offices in the oratory and be absent from the public gatherings of the congregation').[11] Though the prioress came to repent of her action after discovering that Eadburh was the daughter of the king, the saint vowed 'nec ultra transcurrere, nec instituta regule aliqua prevaricatione transire' ('neither to hasten farther nor to pass over anything instituted by the rule through transgression').[12] Osbert insists that Eadburh remained faithful to her vow, and when he next praises her devotion to prayer, he marvels: 'nocteque ac die horis insistens canonicis' ('day and night she persevered in the *canonical* hours').[13]

A unique reference to Eadburh's devotion to the performance of the Office appears in an anonymous Latin *vita* found in an early fourteenth century collection of saints' lives from Romsey Abbey (BL Lansdowne 436). It not only recounts her strict discipline of psalmody, but also claims that she expressed divine praise through the singing of hymns:

> Macerabat namque corpus suum vigiliis et orationibus, psalmos assidue canens nocte ac die, intendens animum ad Psalmiste dictum: 'Septies in die laudem dixi tibi'. Studebat per septenarium numerum hymnorum cotidie perficere.[14]

> [For she wore down her body in vigils and prayers, assiduously singing psalms day and night, exerting her soul according to the dictum of the Psalmist: 'Seven times a day have I praised you'. She strove to complete seven hymns daily.]

Only the Lansdowne *vita* refers to Eadburh's hymnody, which fact likely reveals that the author of this *vita* did not depend on Osbert's exclusively. Though the number of daily hymns credited to Eadburh may reflect hagiographical hyperbole, it could be the case that the author of the *vita* had recourse to other source materials, perhaps a *Life* written at Nunnaminster, and enriched Osbert's portrait of the saint as a model *precentrix* with details composed and/or preserved by her *consorores*.

[11] Ibid.

[12] Ibid. It should be noted that the Benedictine Rule does permit the practice of private prayer in the oratory beyond the hours of the Divine Office: see *La Règle de saint Benoît*, ed. A. de Vogüé and J. Neufville, Sources chrétiennes 181–6 (Paris, 1971–7), II, 610.

[13] *Royal Saints*, p. 274 (emphasis mine).

[14] L. Braswell, 'Saint Edburga of Winchester: A Study of her Cult, AD 950–1500 with an Edition of the Fourteenth-Century Middle English and Latin Lives', *Mediaeval Studies* 33 (1971), 292–333 (p. 330). Cf. Ps. 118. 164.

Eadburh's exemplarity in the performance of the Office may have merited her the office of *precentrix*, since, in the same scene in which Osbert mentions the office which she held, he recalls that, even near the moment of her death, she directed her community in song: 'Ceteras in antiphonis sorores preveniens inchoandis, Daviticos ructabat favos in psalmis, horam sue imminentis prestolans migrationis' ('Coming before the other sisters in antiphons to be sung, awaiting the hour of her imminent passing, she poured out the Davidic honeycombs in psalms').[15] For 'quamdiu vitalis spiritus lingue loquentis habuit instrumentum' ('as long as her vital spirit had the instrument of a speaking tongue'), she would not cease to sing the praise of God.[16] Even after she was no longer physically present to lead her sisters, they continued to honour her memory by persevering in the singing of psalms during her burial.[17]

Eadburh was remembered as having been more than just a leader of liturgical song; she was also a highly skilled singer of chants that were assigned to cantors in earlier and contemporary monastic customaries and liturgical books. According to Osbert, once during a banquet held at Nunnaminster for the saint's father, King Edward the Elder (899–924), he commanded her 'ut aliquod celeste melos suavi modulatione concinat, alleluia videlicet cuius vocali concordia celestis aula Dei terrestrisque resultat' ('to sing some heavenly melody with sweet modulation, namely the alleluia, whose vocal harmony resounds in the heavenly and earthly court of God').[18] Despite her initial resistance, both the crowd's encouragement and her father's promise of a fitting reward ultimately persuaded Eadburh to accede to their request. She sang: 'Alleluia, eripe me de inimicis meis', the Alleluia and verse based on Psalm 58, which was often listed as the chant to be sung at Mass before the Gospel reading on one of the Sundays following Pentecost.[19] So resonant was Eadburh's voice 'cum harmonie celestis organum, omnium

---

[15] *Royal Saints*, p. 281.

[16] Ibid.

[17] Ibid., p. 283: 'Curat exequias virginis caterve plebs congrua virginalis, et dum iste modulis insistunt et psalmis, lacrimis ille et querulis suspirant in lamentis.'

[18] Ibid., p. 272.

[19] Ibid. No manuscript containing the repertory of Proper chants for the Mass survives from Nunnaminster; thus it is difficult to determine when 'Alleluia, eripe me de inimicis meis' was to be sung during the liturgical year there in the second half of the tenth century, if it was indeed to be sung at all. The Alleluia series found in Bodl Bodley 775, a mid eleventh century manuscript from nearby Old Minster and one of the famous Winchester tropers, may shed light on when 'Alleluia, eripe me de inimicis meis' was to be sung at Nunnaminster. According to Bodley 775, it was to be sung on the thirteenth Sunday after Pentecost. Notably this assignment conflicts with the Proper repertory found earlier in the manuscript, which designates 'Alleluia, Dominus regnavit' (Ps. 92) for this Sunday instead. Susan Rankin has discussed this inconsistency, along with many others that can be detected through comparative analysis of the cycles of Proper chants in Bodley 775, in 'Making the

in se rapuit animos auditorum' ('with the organum of celestial harmony, she seized the souls of those listening to her').[20] With her audience held captive by the beauty of her singing, the saint was able to make a successful plea to the king on her community's behalf. Suffering from want of sufficient material provision, Nunnaminster required additional financial support. To impress upon the king his obligations toward the community, Eadburh reminded him of the responsibility that he had inherited from his mother, Ealhswith (d. 902). This 'virago' had initiated the construction of Nunnaminster but was unable to complete it before her death, and it consequently fell to the king to finish the good work begun by his mother.[21] Roused by Eadburh's speech, Edward granted in perpetuity a tract of land at All Cannings in Wiltshire, which had recently come into his possession. Even in Osbert's day, Eadburh's successors at Nunnaminster enjoyed the benefits of this tribute.[22]

Eucharistic ministers

While Eadburh seems perfectly to have embodied (or was later fashioned to embody) the normative ideal for the office of cantor, her liturgical activities were also believed to extend beyond those prescribed for this office in monastic rules and customaries. Osbert reports that she performed an important role in the celebration of the Eucharist in her community too. He describes this role in his account of the first translation of the saint's relics at Nunnaminster. After the women had learned through a series of miracles that they had not buried Eadburh's body in a location befitting her sanctity, they decided to translate her relics to a site near the choir so that she could be near the place where she had spent so much time in prayer. Apparently the plan was agreeable to all, except to the saint herself. While her sisters were sleeping, Eadburh appeared to them in a vision to identify her preferred resting place: 'Secus mensam collocari dominicam appetebat cui dum carnem circumferret spirituales cibos ipsa paraverat' ('She desired to be positioned alongside the Lord's table for which she herself had prepared spiritual foods when she was still moving about in the flesh').[23] Though Osbert's seemingly euphemistic use of 'spirituales cibos' for the eucharistic elements of bread and wine deflects the full force of what Eadburh allegedly communicated in her vision, it is still evident that her ministry of the altar was viewed as significant enough to her community to justify the translation of her relics to a location

Liturgy: Winchester Scribes and their Books', in *The Liturgy of the Late Anglo-Saxon Church*, ed. H. Gittos and M. B. Bedingfield (London, 2005), pp. 29–52 (p. 47).

[20] *Royal Saints*, p. 272.
[21] Ibid., p. 273.
[22] Ibid., p. 274.
[23] Ibid., pp. 288–9.

proximate to it. What the saint's eucharistic ministry entailed is difficult to recover from Osbert's oblique language. *Preparare* could encompass a range of activities related to the eucharistic rite: Eadburh may have performed the sacristan-like duties of making the hosts and ensuring that hosts, wine and water were readily accessible before every Mass; she may have brought forward the hosts and wine at the offertory; she may have assisted with the consecration of the Eucharist and helped to distribute it at communion; or she may have taken out the Eucharist held in reserve for communion in the absence of a priest.

Near the *vita*'s beginning, in Osbert's account of Eadburh's vocation to the religious life as a child, he mentions that her father gave Nunnaminster gifts of a gospel book and chalice – the very ecclesiastical ornaments that his daughter had chosen over secular riches – in anticipation of when she would be committed to the care of this monastic community.[24] Though perhaps King Edward intended for all these gifts to be used by the chaplains or visiting clerics associated with Nunnaminster – if he did indeed grant these gifts at all – the possibility that they were meant for and used by the women religious themselves should not be ruled out. Evidence from manuscripts of gospel books and prayerbooks, other saints' lives and wills bequesting patens and chalices indicates that some women religious did assume the liturgical roles of proclaiming the gospel and preparing the Eucharist.[25] It is not implausible, then, to suspect that Eadburh made good use of the very gifts with which her father had endowed her community when she prepared spiritual foods for the altar.

In its reference to eucharistic preparation, Osbert's account of Eadburh bears comparison to what we know of Margaret, the biological and spiritual sister of the twelfth-century holy woman, Christina of Markyate. The *Life* of Christina relates a series of miracles in which Christ appeared as an unknown pilgrim at both Markyate and St Albans. His telling of the pilgrim-Christ's second appearance at Markyate seamlessly conflates Luke's accounts of Christ's visit to the home of Martha and Mary in Bethany and Christ's appearance to two apostles on the way to Emmaus. Through this conflation, the writer transforms Christina and Margaret into both 'aliam Mariam et Martham' and hosts at a eucharistic meal.[26] Like another Martha, Margaret 'laboriosius circa necessaria discurrit' ('ran about more busily concerned with the necessary things'), while her sister, like another Mary, 'attentius assidet

---

[24] Ibid., p. 265. Cf. William of Malmesbury's accounts of the same episode; *GPA* ii.78.3–6, p. 274; *GRA* ii.217.1–2, p. 400.

[25] This evidence is examined in Bugyis, 'Ministers of Christ: Benedictine Women Religious in Central Medieval England' (unpublished Ph.D. dissertation, University of Notre Dame, 2015), chs. 5 and 7.

[26] *The Life of Christina of Markyate: A Twelfth Century Recluse*, ed. C. H. Talbot (Oxford, 1959; repr. Toronto, 1998), p. 182.

viro' ('attended to the man more intently').[27] But unlike Luke, the writer of Christina's *Life* does not value the saint's repose over her sister's busyness; both ministries are shown to be necessary in the offering of hospitality to the pilgrim (cf. Luke 10. 42). In fact, the writer's description of both the setting of the table and the feeding of the pilgrim suggests that Margaret not only prepared the bread for the meal but also placed it in the pilgrim's mouth, just as she would have done had she been administering the Eucharist: 'mensa parata ori panis apponitur et quasi cibum sumere videbatur' ('when the table was prepared, the bread was placed in his mouth, as if he was seen to accept the food').[28] Though the writer of Christina's *Life* does not explicitly name Margaret as Markyate's sacristan, or show her performing other eucharistic roles in a less allegorical mode, its figuration of her as 'another Martha' in the account of the pilgrim-Christ's visit to her community may hint at the other sacristan-like roles that she assumed. Margaret thus merits mention in the litany of *cantrices* and *editve* from central medieval England.

Guardians of shrines

As noted above, the only woman explicitly named as an 'editva' in the extant sources is Wulfruna-Judith of Barking. In the prologue to Goscelin's *vita* of Wulfhild, Barking's late tenth century abbess-saint, he singles out Wulfruna-Judith as a witness of singular importance to the holy deeds he recorded.[29] Though she was not always remembered as having performed her duties as sacristan perfectly – the *Life* of Wulfhild recalls an occasion when she lost the keys to the sacristy and had to pray to Æthelburh for their miraculous recovery – two features of her office seem to have enhanced her credibility in Goscelin's estimation: she was the custodian of the saints' shrines and therefore a first-hand observer of and even a participant in a number of miracles, and she was a scribe of a deluxe liturgical book.[30] Goscelin recounts her special care of the relics of Barking's abbess-saints in the *Lives* of both Æthelburh and Wulfhild. In the *Life* of Wulfhild, during the rebuilding of the abbey's church after the Danish invasions in the early eleventh century, Wulfruna-Judith questions Æthelburh about the construction of her shrine compared to those housing her *consorores*: 'Quare sancte Hildelithe sancteque

---

[27] Ibid.

[28] Ibid.

[29] 'Texts of Barking Abbey', p. 418. See too the discussion of her role as scribe below. Wulfruna-Judith's contributions to the literary culture at Barking Abbey during the eleventh century have attracted recent scholarly interest. See especially the essays by Stephanie Hollis and Thomas O'Donnell in *Barking Abbey and Medieval Literary Culture: Authorship and Authority in a Female Community*, ed. J. N. Brown and D. A. Bussell (York, 2012).

[30] Ibid., pp. 433–4.

Vulfilde porticus solummodo est cortinata et circa te pauperascit domus nuda? Acquire, inquam, tibi unde et tua parentur loca' ('Why is only the portico of St Hildelith and St Wulfhild vaulted while the naked house around you is scantily endowed? Acquire for yourself whence your place may also be furnished').[31] Seemingly in response to Wulfruna-Judith's command, the next day, a certain matron presented Æthelburh's shrine with a vault that amply covered her choir.[32] Goscelin does not moralize the significance of Wulfruna-Judith's solicitude for Æthelburh's proper memorial, but so cast, Wulfruna-Judith's efforts not only exemplify the office of sacristan for her later successors at Barking, but also encourage future lay donors to be as prompt and generous in their gifts to the abbey as the anonymous matron.

In one of the miracles recorded in the *Life* of Æthelburh, in which the saint heals a girl with a severe physical disability, Wulfruna-Judith appears as a kind of gatekeeper to the saint's shrine. The girl's parents frequently took her to Barking so that they could pray to Æthelburh for their daughter's health, but on the vigil of the saint's feast day, the girl especially wished to pray before Æthelburh's shrine. The girl is said to have asked Wulfruna-Judith for permission to spend the night in prayer before the shrine, but the sacristan denied her request, saying, 'Foris ora, foris te curet sancta Ethelburga si vult, nam interius te non admittemus' ('Pray outside. May holy Æthelburh cure you outside, if she wishes, for we may not admit you inside').[33] Wulfruna-Judith's reasons for denying the girl's request are not specified, but her actions do not elicit negative commentary from Goscelin. In the sentence building to her direct speech, he calls her 'admirabilis fidei femina' ('a woman of admirable faith'), motivated to act 'quasi pio zelo indignata' ('as if indignant with pious zeal').[34] Perhaps Wulfruna-Judith's seemingly callous response to the girl's request was considered justifiable, even necessary, to guard against unfettered access to Barking's most sacred spaces by visitors, especially at night, for the safety of the women religious (and the girl, too) depended on such security measures. External threats to Barking's sanctuary were real and, indeed, a part of the community's not-too-distant past. In the chapters of the *vita* preceding this one, Goscelin recounts the Danes' plundering of Barking.[35] The devastation of this hostile invasion was likely recalled by the women religious at Barking because, even in Goscelin's day, the damage that Æthelburh's shrine suffered 'adhuc conspicuum est in ipso lapide' ('was still visible in the stone itself').[36] With the possibility of unwanted

---

[31] Ibid., p. 434.

[32] Ibid.: 'Hec ea suggerente sequenti die quedam matrona cortinam honorificam beate Æthelburge optulit que chorum suum late ambiit'.

[33] Ibid., p. 415.

[34] Ibid.

[35] Ibid., pp. 413–15.

[36] Ibid., p. 414.

visitors threatening, entrance to the saints' shrines had to be controlled, and Wulfruna-Judith, as sacristan, may have been charged with this responsibility. Fortunately for the girl seeking healing, Æthelburh's power could extend easily beyond the monastery's doors and restored her that very night to 'rectos gressus' ('right steps').[37]

Wulfruna-Judith's *cura* of Barking's shrines also seems to have included ensuring that relics were transported properly during translation. Exactly thirty years after the deposition of Abbess Wulfhild's body, *c.* 1030, her community decided to translate her relics to a location next to the principal altar, but on the vigil of the proposed translation, the saint appeared to a certain woman in the community and asked, 'Cum proxime tumba mea in translatione reserabitur, hanc mihi fac gratiam ut ea tuo panno operiatur ne corpus meum a turba conspiciatur' ('When my tomb is nearly opened in the translation, please do me this favour, that it is covered with your cloth, lest my body be seen by the crowd').[38] On the following morning, the woman reported the vision to her fellow sisters, whereupon Wulfruna-Judith, that 'mirabilis fidei soror' ('sister of marvelous faith'), immediately took action.[39] For the translation, she is said to have 'maforam quam habebat optimam ac nitidissimam in votivum parat obsequium' ('prepared in vowed obedience the best and brightest kerchief that she had'),[40] and when the lid to the tomb was removed, she stepped in front of the crowd to place the white cloth over the saint's body. To the amazement of all, the body was discovered to be incorrupt, and though several of the sisters and their abbess, Leofflæd, beheld this marvel with their own eyes, 'sola Iudith fidelissima ausa contingere cognovit solidum corpus mira integritate' ('only the most faithful and daring Judith knew to touch the intact body with wonderful integrity').[41] Whether Wulfruna-Judith intervened in Wulfhild's translation in her capacity as Barking's sacristan is not made clear in the *vita*, but her fellow sisters apparently did not question her authority or ability to do so. The service Wulfruna-Judith rendered to the saint was deemed so faithful that Wulfhild later miraculously provided her handmaid with money to purchase a new vestment for herself, during the time when Barking desperately suffered from lack of provisions in the wake of the Danish depredation.[42]

The *vita* of Eadburh of Nunnaminster also contains hints of another woman religious's custody of a saint's shrine. Though unnamed, the woman is identified as 'custos sacrorum vasorum' ('the guardian of the holy

---

[37] Ibid., p. 415: 'At illa orans forinsecus ante ianuam monasterii subito in rectos gressus restituta est.'
[38] Ibid., p. 432.
[39] Ibid.
[40] Ibid.
[41] Ibid.
[42] Ibid., chap. 15, p. 433.

vessels').[43] Osbert's use of this epithet suggests that this woman exercised a sacristan-like role at Nunnaminster, and his characterization of her care of Eadburh's first burial site as an *officium* lends greater plausibility to this conclusion.[44] Eadburh was initially buried along with the other departed from Nunnaminster in an atrium beside the monastery's church, where there was a window that overlooked the saint's grave. It was the responsibility of the *custos* to make sure that this window was opened during the day and closed at night, likely to prevent anyone from plundering or desecrating the graves. One night, when the woman tried to perform her office, she found that she could not close the window; her hand itself seemed to be repelled from the act by some force. Unable to find a natural cause for the window's resistance, she prayed for a spiritual explanation. Through her attentive vigils, she (and later her fellow sisters) learned that they were 'gloriose corpus Edburge de loco ad locum celebriorem transferre' ('to translate the glorious body of Eadburh from that place to a more celebrated place').[45] Owing to the guardian's zealous care of Eadburh's grave and her faithful reading of the miraculous sign, the saint's relics were translated, ultimately to the very location that Eadburh desired – next to the church's altar.

Scribes and authors

Wulfruna-Judith also captivated Goscelin's interest as a renowned scribe of liturgical books. A missal that she copied is prominently featured in the final miracle recounted in his *Vita Æthelburge*. During the Conquest, when a band of Norman soldiers descended on Barking, the women fled to London, leaving behind their community's greatest treasures. Among the possessions left exposed to plundering was a missal, 'quem memorabilis Vulfruna scripserat' ('which the famous Wulfruna had written'), visibly displayed on the altar dedicated to Æthelburh.[46] A priest accompanying the band of troops is said to have found this missal and stolen it; he took it back to his parish in Normandy and dared to celebrate Mass with the holy object, even though it had become sacrilegious by his theft.[47] After eight years, he decided to return to England, not to return the missal, but to visit another parish. During his voyage across the Channel, a violent storm unexpectedly erupted and threatened to capsize his ship. The storm persisted for five days, and it was not until the priest remembered his guilt, prayed to Æthelburh for forgiveness, and vowed to return the missal to its rightful home that it finally

---

[43] *Royal Saints*, p. 286.
[44] Ibid.: 'Huius officii sedula quedam virtutis erat femina flameo Christi insignita ...'
[45] Ibid., p. 287.
[46] 'Texts of Barking Abbey', p. 416.
[47] Ibid.

relented. Once his ship landed in Dover, he immediately set out for Barking. At the saint's shrine, he took off his shoes and assumed the posture of a penitent. There, he prayed to the saint for forgiveness, returned the missal to its proper place on the altar dedicated to her name, and gratefully explained to all the miracle that had transpired. Upon recovering the stolen treasure,

> Fit ingens cunctis ecclesie pignoribus exultatio maximaque Deo laus et gratiarum actio, non tantum pro optimi codicis officio sed et longe eminentius pro materno miraculo, que tam in pelago et longinquis terris adest rogata quam ubi corporali rutilat presentia.[48]

> [Mighty exaltation was made for all the relics of the church, and the greatest praise and act of thanks was made to God, not only for the office of the best codex but also, by far more eminently, for the maternal miracle, who, when asked, was as present in the sea and in remote lands as where she blazed with her bodily presence.]

Goscelin's use of the adjective *optimus* to describe the missal is striking, especially since he probably had seen it, maybe even used it to celebrate Mass at Barking. From first-hand experience, he would have been able to attest to the quality of Wulfruna-Judith's craftsmanship as a scribe. The restoration of the stolen book occurred *circa* 1074, just over a decade before Goscelin wrote the *vite* of Barking's abbess-saints *circa* 1086. Undoubtedly this event was still fresh in the memories of the women that Goscelin enlisted for information about the abbey's history. Wulfruna-Judith likely provided her own recollection of what had transpired, given that she outlived the reign of at least William the Conqueror (1066–87).[49] The spiritual value of her *optimus codex* surely increased appreciably after its allegedly miraculous recovery, becoming a relic of Æthelburh's vast power, but it should be recalled that the book already had been accorded a venerable position among the *ornamenta* of Barking's church prior to its theft; it was on perpetual display on top of the altar dedicated to the monastery's founding saint. The missal's prominence must have owed in part to its superlative making – it certainly caught the eye of the Norman priest, who probably had his pick of the plunder.

Wulfruna-Judith's missal is no longer extant. Most likely it was a casualty to the advance of time and liturgical innovation, but the devastation that Barking's library met during the abbey's dissolution in 1539 cannot be

---

[48] Ibid., p. 417.

[49] Ibid., p. 418: 'Notissima est adolescentioribus eius sanctimonialis discipula Vulfruna, Iudith cognominata, a primevo flore sub ipsa educata, que ad nostri regis Vuilielmi supervixit sceptra.' It is not clear whether the 'King William' Goscelin refers to here is William the Conqueror or William Rufus (1087–1100). If it were the latter, Wulfruna-Judith would have lived into very old age, since Abbess Wulfhild died near the beginning of the eleventh century.

ruled out as a culprit. Yet another liturgical book, dating to the time that she flourished, exhibits the kind of scribal skill and knowledge of the liturgy that she would have possessed: Bodl Bodley 155, an eleventh-century gospel book from Barking. Though none of the hands responsible for the initial copying and later correction, annotation, neumation and re-punctuation of this gospel book can be ascribed to Wulfruna-Judith with certainty, the paleographical and codicological analysis of this manuscript that I have detailed elsewhere shows that scribes similar in monastic office and training to Wulfruna-Judith must have been behind the later additions, for only scribes fully versed in the musical and dramatic performance of the liturgy would have possessed the skills necessary to supply them so expertly.[50]

The scribal handiwork and poetic creations of cantors and sacristans also may be preserved in the entries (*tituli*) from various cathedral chapters, schools, anchorholds and monastic houses on two twelfth-century mortuary rolls (*rotuli*) that travelled widely throughout France and England for Matilda, abbess of La Trinité, Caen (d. 1113), and for Vitalis, abbot of Savigny (d. 1122).[51] Among the extant *rotuli* from the central Middle Ages, these two are notable because they visited female monastic houses in England as well as neighbouring male ones in La Trinité's and Savigny's confraternities of prayer. Typically, a *titulus* includes a promise to pray for the soul of the person for whom the *rotulus* was issued and a request for prayer for the deceased of the community in which the particular *titulus* was composed. Most *tituli* list the names of their recently deceased, and some even contain elegiac poems. In the *rotulus* for Matilda, the *tituli* from Nunnaminster,

---

[50] See Bugyis, 'Ministers of Christ', chap. 5.

[51] The *rotulus* for Matilda has received considerably more scholarly attention than that for Vitalis. The *tituli* written on behalf of female monastic communities have been mined for prosopographical information as well as evidence of the scribal productions and poetic creations of women religious. See R. N. Sauvage, 'Rouleau mortuaire de Marie, abbesse de la Trinité de Caen', *Bibliothèque de l'école des Chartes* 61 (1910), 49–57; H. Feiss, 'The Poet Abbess from Notre-Dame de Saintes', *Magistra* 1 (1995), 39–54; D. Sheerin, 'Sisters in the Literary Agon: Texts from Communities of Women on the Mortuary Roll of the Abbess Matilda of La Trinité, Caen', in *Women Writing Latin: From Roman Antiquity to Early Modern Europe*, ed. P. Brown, L. Churchill and J. Jeffrey, 3 vols. (New York, 2002), II, 93–132; J. Stevenson, 'Anglo-Latin Women Poets', in *Latin Learning and English Lore: Studies in Anglo-Saxon Literature for Michael Lapidge*, ed. K. O'Brien O'Keeffe and A. Orchard, 2 vols. (Toronto, 2005), II, 86–107; and T. Leslie, '"Orate pro nobis": The Mortuary Roll Ritual and its Texts' (unpublished Ph.D. dissertation, Emory University, 2005). Though Leslie's dissertation focuses on the *rotulus* for Matilda, she also examines the *rotulus* for Vitalis in considerable detail. More generally, see G. Signori, 'Introduction: The *Rotulus*', in *Bruno the Carthusian and his Mortuary Roll: Studies, Text, and Translations*, ed. H. Beyer et al. (Turnhout, 2014), pp. 3–10, with further essential bibliography.

Amesbury and Shaftesbury incorporate such poems,[52] as did Wilton's *titulus* for Vitalis's *rotulus*.[53] In all four *tituli*, the names of the poems' authors were not disclosed, but in Nunnaminster's, a heading precedes its third and final poem and provides a clue regarding its authorship: 'versus cuiusdam neptis sue' ('verses of a certain female relative of hers').[54] This line reveals that the author of the verses was a woman, an admission which (when read alongside additional evidence from the *tituli* from French female monastic houses) helps to discredit the entrenched scholarly assumption that women religious enlisted their chaplains or outside scribes to craft these elegiac poems.[55] This heading also highlights the poet's personal connection with the deceased; she was Matilda's relative, perhaps her niece. Without the poet's name, it is difficult to determine the details of this relationship, but clearly it was close enough to motivate her to write the poem and to make known to her fellow sisters at Nunnaminster and to other viewers of the *rotulus* her affiliation with La Trinité's abbess. At the time when Nunnaminster appended its *titulus* to Matilda's *rotulus*, it was under the direction of a Norman abbess, as was Shaftesbury.[56] Indeed, after the Conquest, the population of many English monastic houses became increasingly Norman. Nunnaminster had at least one of Matilda's relatives among its members, but there may have been more women in the community, originally of Norman extraction, who were acquainted in some way with the deceased abbess and interested in honouring her *memoria*.

Though we cannot definitively ascribe the writing of either the *tituli* or elegiac poems from communities of English women to their cantors or sacristans, it should be noted that, according to the monastic customary

---

[52] *Recueil des rouleaux des morts*, I, 404–5 (no. 114.11), 406 (no. 114.13), and 407 (no. 114.18), respectively. Poems do not accompany the other surviving entries from communities of English women religious; see the entries from Wherwell (p. 405, no. 114.12) and from Wilton (p. 406, no. 114.15). The original roll is no longer extant, but most of the texts survive in a copy prepared for Jean Mabillon (BnF lat. 12652, fols. 87–132). The concluding *tituli* on the original roll, including those of Barking and Romsey, were not copied in full; thus, it is possible that the *tituli* of these two communities did include elegiac poems.

[53] Ibid., p. 571 (no. 122.153). Poems do not accompany the entries from Barking (p. 558, no. 122.99), Nunnaminster (p. 580, no. 122.184), Romsey (p. 580, no. 122.185) or Shaftesbury (p. 581, no. 122.187).

[54] Ibid., p. 405 (no. 114.11). The poem consists of twelve lines and employs antistrophe throughout. Each line ends with the vocative 'Maria'.

[55] See, for example, C. Fell et al. *Women in Anglo-Saxon England and the Impact of 1066* (Bloomington, 1984), p. 164.

[56] S. Elkins, *Holy Women of Twelfth-Century England* (Chapel Hill, 1988), p. 6; Leslie, 'Mortuary Roll Ritual', p. 207. For more general studies of the 'Normanization' of the English ecclesiastical hierarchy, see H. Loyn, 'Abbots of the English Monasteries in the Period Following the Conquest', in *England and Normandy in the Middle Ages*, ed. D. Bates and A. Curry (London, 1994), pp. 95–103; B. Golding, *Conquest and Colonisation: The Normans in Britain, 1066–1100* (New York, 1994), pp. 146–76.

composed by Lanfranc, archbishop of Canterbury (1070–89), the cantor was charged with the 'cura brevium', sending out a notice (perhaps a *rotulus*, if the deceased were an abbot or personage of significant status), requesting prayers for a deceased community member, and the sacristan was responsible for the burials of monks and lay affiliates.[57] Given their respective care for the community's dead, either the cantor or sacristan would likely have been held responsible for preparing a *titulus* when his community received a *rotulus*. Though he may have enlisted another scribe or pupil as a copyist, he still would have directed the task. A similar protocol for preparing a *titulus* likely obtained for communities of women religious. As we have seen, some of the women who held the offices of cantor and sacristan were versed in Latin (Eadburh) or trained as accomplished scribes (Wulfruna-Judith).[58] Internal evidence from the two twelfth-century *rotuli* also attests that there were women religious capable of performing the same literary and scribal tasks as their confrères; they could battle with keen metrical, rhetorical and allusive skill in the 'literary agon' of poetic creation, and this fact was not lost on their competitors.[59] The poems in *tituli* inscribed by male communities often contain veiled (or outrightly misogynistic) barbs against the poems that women religious penned. For example, the poem in the *titulus* for the students of Bath on Matilda's *rotulus* decries:

> Quid furitis nonne? Quid amastis carmen inane?
> ...
>
> Quid teritis tempus, ventosaque verba rotatis,
> Insuitis versus et ploratus pueriles?
>
> [Why do you rave, nuns? Why do you love inane poetry?
> ...
>
> Why do you waste time and wield windy words,
> And sew on verses and puerile laments?][60]

---

57 *The Monastic Constitutions of Lanfranc*, ed. D. Knowles, rev. C. N. L. Brooke (Oxford, 2002), p. 122.

58 See also the praise Muriel, a poet at Wilton Abbey, received in the letters of Baudri of Bourgueil (*c.* 1046–1130), Hildebert of Le Mans (*c.* 1055–1133) and Serlo of Bayeux (*c.* 1050–1113×22). A. Boutemy, 'Muriel: note sur deux poèmes de Baudri de Bourgueil et de Serlon de Bayeux', *Le Moyen âge*, 3rd ser. 6 (1935), 241–51; A. Wilmart, 'L'élégie d'Hildebert pour Muriel', *Revue bénédictine* 49 (1937), 376–80; *Baldricus Burgulianus Carmina*, ed. K. Hilbert (Heidelberg, 1979), pp. 137, 189–90. For a review of the surviving evidence on Muriel, but with a less than generous assessment of her presumed poetic abilities, see J. S. P. Tatlock, 'Muriel: The Earliest English Poetess', *PMLA* 48 (1933), 317–21. For a more insightful assessment, see J. Stevenson, *Women Latin Poets: Language, Gender and Authority from Antiquity to the Eighteenth Century* (Oxford, 2005), p. 124; Stevenson, 'Anglo-Latin Women Poets'.

59 The characterization of the poetic competition on *rotuli* as a 'literary agon' is Daniel Sheerin's ('Sisters in the Literary Agon', pp. 98–9).

60 *Recueil des rouleaux des morts*, I, 409 (no. 114.28).

Such invectives, though arguably riddled with elements of humour, become necessary only when engaging in a verbal contest against a worthy rival, and the *versatrices* provoked in this poem were viewed as just that by their male agonists.

One final piece of evidence, exhibiting the cantor- or sacristan-like scribal activities of a woman religious, warrants close examination: two additions made to the liturgical calendar that opens the St Albans Psalter (Hildesheim, Dombibliothek, MS St Godehard 1), a deluxe codex produced at St Albans *c.* 1123 and subsequently adapted for Christina of Markyate's use.[61] Three separate sets of scribal additions were made to the psalter's calendar. The earliest hand, identified as scribe 3 by Otto Pächt, Francis Wormald and C. R. Dodwell, entered the obituary for Christina's first spiritual mentor at Markyate, Roger (12 September), sometime after his death *c.* 1121.[62] Scribe 5, possibly the next earliest hand, added the feast days of St Margaret (20 July) and the dedication of Markyate Priory (27 May);[63] the inclusion of the dedication of Christina's community may help to date these additions to after 1145, the year in which Alexander, bishop of Lincoln (1123–48), performed the dedication. Scribe 4, likely the latest hand in the calendar, entered the obituaries of Christina's close relations: neighbouring men and women religious, family members (her father, mother, brothers and, possibly, aunt),[64] Geoffrey, abbot of St Albans (1119–46), and Christina herself.[65] This hand also

---

[61] The question of the psalter's production and ownership has enjoyed lively debate since Pächt, Dodwell and Wormald claimed Christina as the psalter's intended recipient: *The St Albans Psalter (Albani Psalter)* (London, 1960). For a recent detailed account of the scholarly arguments both for and against the assignment of a Markyate provenance to the psalter, see K. Bugyis, 'Envisioning Episcopal Exemption: The Life of Christina of Markyate', *Church History* 84 (2015), 32–63 (p. 48 n. 71). I am persuaded by arguments in favour of a Markyate provenance.

[62] Roger's obituary reads: 'Obiit Rogeri heremite monachi sancti Albani apud quemcumque fuerit hoc psalterium fiat eius memoria maxime hac die'; Hildesheim, Dombibliothek, MS St Godehard 1, p. 11. I agree with Jane Geddes that the words 'apud quemcumque' are 'quite neutral about both the location and ownership of the psalter', contrary to Donald Matthew's assertion that this obit 'proves unequivocally' that Christina was not the first owner of the psalter, and that Roger very likely was; Geddes, 'The Calendar and Liturgical Apparatus', *The St Albans Psalter Project*, https://www.abdn.ac.uk/stalbanspsalter/english/essays/calendar.shtml (accessed 2 June 2015); Matthew, 'Incongruities', p. 401.

[63] Hildesheim, Dombibliothek, MS St Godehard 1, pp. 7 and 9: see *The St Albans Psalter Project*, https://www.abdn.ac.uk/stalbanspsalter/english/commentary/page007.shtml, and https://www.abdn.ac.uk/stalbanspsalter/english/commentary/page009.shtml (accessed 2 June 2015).

[64] The identification of the obituary for 'Ailiva mater Michaelis', found on 23 January, as Christina's aunt, Alveva, mistress of Ranulf Flambard (*c.* 1060–1128), is more tentative. For the *Life*'s reference to Alveva, see *Life of Christina*, p. 40.

[65] Scribe 4's addition of Christina of Markyate's obit appears on p. 14 of Hildesheim, Dombibliothek, MS St Godehard 1: see *The St Albans Psalter Project*, https://www.

added the feast days of the Circumcision of the Lord, All Saints and several universal and more local Anglo-Saxon saints.

The additions of scribe 5 are particularly relevant to this discussion of cantor- and sacristan-like liturgical activities performed by women religious, since they may have been added by Christina's sister, Margaret. We have already seen that Margaret was figured as an important supporting character in Christina's *Life*, possibly as a kind of sacristan at Markyate, and elsewhere I have investigated the possibility of Margaret's contributions to the first written accounts consulted for and incorporated into the *Life*.[66] Despite the important role that Margaret exercises in the *Life*'s narrative and Markyate's history, however, her obituary was not added to the calendar along with those of Christina's other immediate family members. Perhaps Margaret was still alive when the last set of additions was copied in the calendar, and no effort was made at Markyate to record deaths after the date of these additions. But there is a hint in Christina's *Life* that suggests that Margaret died before her sister. The writer refers to her once as 'sororem beate memorie virginem .M.' [the virgin M[argaret], sister of blessed memory'].[67] This epithet is not used for any other character in the *Life*, including Christina. Thus the inclusion of Christina's obituary in the psalter's calendar and the exclusion of her sister's must be explained.

A possible explanation is that the feast day of St Margaret was to double as an obituary for Margaret of Markyate. Though the feast day of St Margaret appears in all the extant twelfth-century calendars from St Albans,[68] and its addition to the calendar opening Christina's psalter may thus have simply been an attempt to make Markyate's liturgical year conform more closely to St Albans', we know that the saint held special significance for Christina and possibly for her sister as well.[69] Notably, Christina's own obituary coincides with another important feast day – the Conception of Mary (8 December). Like Henrietta Leyser, I do not believe that the collocation of these memorials is accidental.[70] The Feast of the Conception of Mary was

---

abdn.ac.uk/stalbanspsalter/english/commentary/page014.shtml (accessed 2 June 2015).

[66] See Bugyis, 'Ministers of Christ', chap. 1.

[67] *Life of Christina*, p. 154. It is clear from the narrative context that the initial 'M' refers to Margaret.

[68] Extant twelfth-century St Albans calendars include: St Petersburg, Public Library, MS Q.v.I, 62 (s. xii^{med}); BL Egerton 3721 (s. xii^{med}); BL Royal 2.A.x (s. xii^{med}); Bodl Auct. D.2.6 (s. xii^{med}). These calendars are collated in *English Benedictine Kalendars after A.D. 1100, vol. I: Abbotsbury–Durham*, ed. Francis Wormald, HBS 77 (London, 1939), pp. 31–45.

[69] St Margaret makes a dramatic appearance in the only healing miracle included in the *Life* (pp. 118–20).

[70] See Leyser's introduction to *Christina of Markyate: A Twelfth-Century Holy Woman*, ed. S. Fanous and H. Leyser (New York, 2005), pp. 1–11 (p. 11 n. 20).

promoted increasingly in England beginning in the late eleventh century, especially at St Albans,[71] and the alignment of Christina's obituary with this feast day probably sought to enhance her sanctity further by placing it under the Virgin Mary's aegis. In the case of Margaret, the identity of her name and the saint's would have allowed for a more complete, even univocal, affiliation between the two holy women, and the Markyate community may therefore have simply allowed the entry for St Margaret's feast to double as Margaret's obituary. The celebration of the two holy women's memorials may have seemed fitting not only because Margaret was specially devoted to the saint, but also because Margaret herself may have added the saint's feast day to the calendar.

The hand in which both St Margaret's feast and the dedication of Markyate Priory were added does not appear elsewhere in the St Albans Psalter, nor does it feature in the two charters that pertain to Markyate's foundation and dedication in 1145,[72] nor can it be linked definitively with Margaret's own hand, since no written evidence explicitly ascribed to her name survives. But if she indeed effectively functioned as a sacristan at Markyate, then she could have been charged with properly accounting for the days of the liturgical year in both practice and writing, including making additions to any calendar of feast days and memorials that Markyate possessed. Certainly Margaret's involvement in the full range of liturgical and scribal activities that were incumbent on the office of sacristan should not be discounted without further paleographical evidence to the contrary, because this is the very reading of her duties within the Markyate community that her sister's *Life* promotes.

Conclusion

Sometimes explicitly named as cantors or sacristans, more often recognized by the fruits of their labours, the women highlighted in this chapter were liturgical directors, skilled singers, eucharistic ministers, custodians of saints' shrines, scribes of liturgical books and mortuary rolls, wardens of sacred space and time, and keepers of their communities' *memoria*. Uncovering the various responsibilities and activities of these women has been essential in my larger study of the liturgical and pastoral ministries of Benedictine women religious in central medieval England, from which this chapter is drawn.[73] They were the orchestrators of the very liturgical performances that

---

[71] R. M. Thomson, *Manuscripts from St Albans Abbey, 1066–1235*, 2 vols. (Cambridge, 1992), I, 38–9. See also K. D. Hartzell, 'The Musical Repertory of St Albans, England, in the Twelfth Century' (unpublished Ph.D. dissertation, University of Rochester, 1970), I, 68–73.

[72] BL Cotton Ch. xi.6 and Cotton Ch. xi.8, respectively.

[73] See Bugyis, 'Ministers of Christ'.

I examine in detail, and they likely contributed to the production of many of the manuscripts that offer the best witnesses to those performances. Though too often unsung in the histories of medieval women religious, they take centre stage in mine.

actually not very much about singers / teachers

But look up AB (Goscelin/) Osbert Bob

PART III
England in the Twelfth Century

9

Cantor, Sacrist or Prior?
The Provision of Books in Anglo-Norman England

Teresa Webber

The account of the office and duties of the cantor in the monastic customs compiled during the late 1070s or early 1080s by Archbishop Lanfranc for Henry, prior of Christ Church, Canterbury, ends by assigning to him general responsibility for the community's books: 'He takes care of all the books of the house, and has them in his keeping, if his interests and learning are such as to fit him for keeping them.'[1] By the later eleventh century it had become common in England and on the Continent for the duties of the cantor to be combined with those of the *armarius*, to whom several late tenth and eleventh century customaries had assigned custody of the community's books in addition to oversight of the liturgical and other readings, together with certain other duties.[2] For Anglo-Norman England, the norms described in customaries can be supported by other forms of documentary evidence from the twelfth century onwards, recording the allocation of revenues to the cantor for various purposes associated with the production, custody and upkeep of books.[3] The identification of the handwriting of a number of cantors acting at some point in their career as copyists, annotators and correctors has also been seen to reflect the close relationship between the cantor and the production and custody of books.[4] In a volume that examines the activities of those involved in the practice of the liturgy, its music and the writing of history, and seeks to understand and explain how such activities

---

[1] *Decreta*, pp. 122–3: 'De universis monasterii libris curam gerat, et eos in custodia sua habeat, si eius studii et scientie sit, ut eorum custodia ei commendari debeat'.

[2] See Fass A. For the description of the *armarius*'s responsibilities in the late tenth century customs of Fleury and those recorded in Einsiedeln, Stiftsbibliothek MS 235, fols. 1–19, see now also 'Consuetudines Floriacenses antiquiores', ed. A. Davril and L. Donnat, and 'Redactio Sancti Emmerammi dicta Einsidlensis', ed. M. Wegener and C. Elvert, in *Consuetudinum saeculi x/xi/xii monumenta non-Cluniacensia*, ed. K. Hallinger, CCM 7.3 (Siegburg, 1984), pp. 16–17 and 207.

[3] M. Gullick, 'Professional Scribes in Eleventh- and Twelfth-Century England', *English Manuscript Studies 1100–1700* 7 (1998), 1–24; R. Sharpe, 'The Medieval Librarian', in *The Cambridge History of Libraries in Britain and Ireland, Volume I: to 1640*, ed. E. Leedham-Green and T. Webber (Cambridge, 2006), pp. 218–41.

[4] Sharpe, 'Medieval Librarian', pp. 221–2. Additionally, in the present volume, see especially the contributions of Aspesi, Bugyis, Fassler, Hayward, Jeffery, Kruckenberg and Rozier.

might be connected, it may be helpful to consider in more detail to what extent and in what ways the duties of the combined office of cantor-*armarius* encompassed the provision of books within Anglo-Norman monastic communities, which other offices were associated with the provision of books and why the amalgamation of the roles of cantor and *armarius* continued to endure throughout the twelfth century and beyond.[5]

The production and custody of books

Lanfranc's assigning of the care of the community's books to the cantor, like much else in his customs, reflects the influence of the customs of Cluny.[6] That influence is also evident in the majority of customaries and other records of customs that survive from later medieval England, although it remains unclear to what extent it was Lanfranc's own customs (copies of which were in circulation before and after 1100) that were the channel for this diffusion,[7] or an earlier, presumably Norman, source from which Lanfranc also drew.[8] Common to all post-Conquest English customaries that describe the duties of specified officials is the allocation of general responsibility for the care and maintenance of the community's books to the cantor, assisted, in some instances, by a deputy, the *succentor*.[9] Lanfranc's customs, however, do not

[5] The discussion here is limited to Benedictine houses and thus excludes those of the new orders of monks and canons introduced to England during the twelfth century. For a comparison of the customs of the different orders regarding the office of cantor and the provision of books, see P. Lefèvre, 'A propos de la "lectio divina" dans la vie monastique et canoniale', *Revue d'histoire ecclésiastique* 67 (1972), 800–9; *Le coûtumier de l'abbaye d'Oigny en Bourgogne au XIIe siècle*, ed. P. F. Lefèvre and A. H. Thomas (Louvain, 1976), pp. l–liii.

[6] *Decreta*, pp. xxxix–xlii. The earliest surviving Cluniac customary, the mid eleventh century *Liber tramitis*, ed. P. Dinter, CCM 10 (1980), sometimes distinguishes between the duties of cantors and those of the *armarius*, but it also contains evidence indicating that the process whereby the two came to be combined was already underway during the first half of the eleventh century: Fass A, pp. 44–8.

[7] *Decreta*, pp. xxx–xxxiii.

[8] C. A. Jones, 'Monastic Custom in Early Norman England: The Significance of Bodleian MS. Wood Empt. 4', *RB* 113 (2003), 135–68, 302–36.

[9] Descriptions of the office of cantor and/or his duties or allocated revenues are found in customaries or records of more restricted scope from the following houses (listed chronologically). Abingdon abbey: a brief compilation of customs dating from the late twelfth century, appended to a thirteenth-century copy of the Abingdon Chronicle, printed as 'De obedientiariis abbatiae Abbendonensis' in *Chronicon monasterii de Abingdon*, ed. J. Stevenson, 2 vols. (London, 1858), II, 335–417 (pp. 371–4). Glastonbury abbey: revenues allocated to the cantor (but without specific mention of books or materials involved in their production and upkeep) recorded in an abbatial survey of 1189: *Liber de Henrici de Soliaco abbatis Glaston. et vocatur A*, ed. J. E. Jackson (London, 1882), p. 8. Evesham abbey: customs

elaborate as to how that responsibility was to be discharged. The greater detail found in some of the later English customaries displays a mixture of shared norms and variation in levels of specificity and in certain particulars. The limited nature of the evidence that survives from the twelfth century, and the number of houses from which no medieval customary survives at all, make it perilous to generalize unreservedly from what has survived, or to discount the possibility that different customs, deriving from earlier traditions, may have been followed in houses from which no such record survives, or persisted for some decades or more after the Conquest in those for whom the surviving customs are of a later date.[10]

Unfortunately, of all the English written customs that provide significant detail about the cantor's responsibility for book provision, only perhaps those from Abingdon Abbey demonstrably pre-date the thirteenth century. These, which are dateable to the late twelfth century, refer to oversight of the production and renewal of books as well as to the custody and maintenance of the book collections.[11] Provision for parchment, ink and everything else required was to be met from the revenues allocated to the cantor; if a professional scribe was employed, the cantor was to reward his labour.[12] He was permitted to inspect books during the canonical Hours and at Mass,

---

instituted by Abbot Randulf in 1214 and recorded in Thomas of Marlborough's *History of the Abbey of Evesham*, ed. J. E. Sayers, trans. L. Watkiss (Oxford, 2003), pp. 387–411 (pp. 394–5). These only specify the allocated revenues; the duties belonging to the office of precentor are recorded in a damaged fourteenth-century register (BL Cotton Vitellius E.xvii, fols. 226–52), quoted in *English Benedictine Libraries: The Shorter Catalogues*, ed. R. Sharpe et al., CBMLC 4 (London, 1996), pp. 132–3. Eynsham abbey: a thirteenth or early fourteenth century customary: *The Customary of the Benedictine Abbey of Eynsham in Oxfordshire*, ed. A. Gransden, CCM 2 (Siegburg, 1963), pp. 16 and 20 (for the date), pp. 164–8. Westminster abbey: a fourteenth-century customary probably transmitting customs drawn up in the 1260s: *Customary of the Benedictine Monasteries of St Augustine, Canterbury and St Peter, Westminster*, ed. E. M. Thompson, HBS, 23, 28 (London, 1902–4), II, vi–vii (for the date), 28–42. St Augustine's Abbey, Canterbury: an early fourteenth century customary, closely related to that from Westminster, and probably also transmitting customs drawn up some decades earlier: ibid., I, vi–vii (for the date), 90–101. A miscellaneous twelfth-century collection of notes on various monastic customs in Bodl Wood Empt. 4 (of unknown English origin and medieval provenance), only mentions the cantor in a note that briefly elaborates upon the regulation concerning the lists that he compiled of those appointed as readers, singers and other ministers of the liturgy: Jones, 'Monastic Custom', p. 314.

[10] Jones, 'Monastic Custom', p. 148.

[11] For the date of the text, see G. Lambrik, 'Abingdon Abbey Administration', *Journal of Ecclesiastical History* 17 (1966), 159–83 (p. 167 n. 7).

[12] 'De obedientiariis', pp. 370–1: 'De redditibus cantori assignatis cantor inveniet parcamenam, incaustum, et omnia que ad preparationem librorum conventus sunt necessaria. ... Si fuerit scriptor exterius dispositione abbatis et cantoris ad commodum ecclesie scribens, abbas inveniet victum corporis, cantor mercedem laboris.'

except those books assigned for Mass, and he was to repair damage to the book-cupboards and books, and find the cloth for the overcovers of the 'books of the library'.[13] The daily distribution of the books assigned to each monk at the start of Lent and the books of chant, however, was delegated to the *succentor*, who had custody of the keys to the relevant cupboards.[14] The cantor was also responsible for the writing of the names of the deceased in the martyrology and for the parchment and administration of the *breves* that provided notification of their demise (duties also recorded by Lanfranc),[15] as well as of all the abbey's charters.[16] Abbot Randulf's statutes of 1214 for Evesham Abbey indicate a similar range of responsibilities in their allocation of revenues to the cantor for ink for all the monastery's scribes, pigments for illumination and all necessary materials for binding the books (as well as for the repair of the organs), but do not elaborate further on this aspect of the cantor's duties.[17]

The surviving customaries of the abbeys of Eynsham, Westminster and St Augustine's, Canterbury, dating in their surviving copies from the early fourteenth century but probably all transmitting sets of customs drawn up in the thirteenth,[18] describe these same responsibilities but in greater detail. Passages common to all three may represent extracts from the source from which they all ultimately derive, which is unlikely to have been later than the mid twelfth century (and may have been somewhat earlier);[19] details present

[13] Ibid., p. 373: 'Bibliotheca erit sub cantoris custodia'. Ibid., pp. 370–1: 'Cantori licet sine reprehensione horis canonicis et ad missas in libros inspicere, exceptis libris ad officium misse assignatis. ... Cantor almaria puerorum, iuvenum, et alia in quibus libri conventus reponentur, innovabit, fracta preparabit, pannos librorum bibliothece reperiet, fracturas librorum reficiet.' On textile overcovers, see M. Gullick, 'The Binding Descriptions in the Library Catalogue from Leicester Abbey', in *Leicester Abbey: Medieval History, Archaeology and Manuscript Studies*, ed. J. Story et al. (Leicester, 2006), pp. 147–72 (150–1, 160).

[14] Ibid., p. 374: 'Claves armariorum, in quibus libri annuales et libri cantus recluduntur, custodie succentoris assignabuntur'.

[15] *Decreta*, p. 122: 'Cura brevium, qui foras mitti solent pro defunctis fratribus, et cura numerandi tricenaria, et septenaria, ad eum pertinet.'

[16] 'De obedientiariis', p. 372. See also the later *Customary of Eynsham*, p. 164: 'Percamenum et incaustum ad brevia defunctorum et ad cetera communia que necessaria fuerint a cantore invenire debent'. No such stipulation is included in the St Augustine's, Canterbury and Westminster custumals, in which responsibility for writing the death-notice *breves* is said to lie with the *succentor*: *Customary of St Augustine's*, I, 99–100, II, 40–1.

[17] Thomas of Marlborough, *History*, p. 394: 'Ad officium precentoris pertinet quedam terra in Hamptona de qua percipit precentor annuatim quinque solidos, et decime de Stokes, et quedam terra in Alincestre. De hiis invenire precentor incaustum omnibus scriptoribus monasterii, et colores ad illuminandum, et necessaria ad ligandos libros, et necessaria ad organa.'

[18] See above, note 9, and Jones, 'Monastic Custom', pp. 145–6.

[19] Jones, 'Monastic Customs', pp. 143–9.

in only one of these customaries or in only the textually very closely related customaries from St Augustine's and Westminster may represent later, local developments.

The Eynsham customary replicates almost word for word two prescriptions in the Abingdon customary regarding the cantor's oversight of the maintenance of the books: those permitting him to inspect all but the 'libris ad officium misse assignatis', and those that require him to provide from his revenues the parchment, ink and everything else necessary for the repair of books.[20] A subsequent clause adds that it was for the cantor to decide when parchment was to be manufactured and books were to be corrected or bound,[21] but allowance was also made for the repair of books to be assigned to a different individual (to be called *armarius*) should the cantor be deficient in carrying out these duties (an allowance that might also be inferred from Lanfranc's customs concerning the competence of the cantor in such matters).[22] The two closely related customaries from St Augustine's, Canterbury, and St Peter's, Westminster, are generally far more comprehensive in their scope, describing in great detail the administration of both liturgical and extra-liturgical ritual and other customs of each abbey. Both replicate the late eleventh century Cluniac customs' reference to the cantor's alternative name of *armarius* from his custody of the books in the *armaria*, and assign all those books to his custody.[23] As at Abingdon and Eynsham, he was to provide ink and parchment to the monks,[24] and was responsible for the renewal, binding and repair of all of the books in his custody, in the church or the choir, but with the specified exception of the psalters (or other 'necessary books') and antiphoners which at St Augustine's and Westminster were assigned to the

---

[20] *Customary of Eynsham*, pp. 164–5 (with verbal concordance with the Abingdon customs indicated in bold): '**Cantori licet sine reprehensione horis canonicis et ad missas libros inspicere exceptis libris ad officium misse assignatis,** quod aliis non licet. ... **De** redditu **cantori** assignato **inveniet** ipse **parcamenum et incaustum et omnia, que ad** reparacionem **librorum sunt necessaria.**' It is unclear here and in other sources that refer to 'reparatio' whether responsibility for the repair of the books encompassed more than the restoration of their binding and other exterior elements to include also their correction.

[21] Ibid., p. 168: 'Cantoris est providere quando parcamena incidenda sunt vel radenda vel libri emendandi aut ligandi aut aliquid huiusmodi, quod ad officium cantoris pertineat faciendum'.

[22] Ibid., p. 166: 'Sciendum tamen est quod, si cantor circa librorum reparationem librorum negligens fuerit, poterit abbas alicui diligentiori fratri curam librorum assensu capituli committere et ille frater armarius vocabitur.'

[23] *Customary of St Augustine's*, I, 90, 96, II, 28, 36: 'Cantor, qui et alio nomine armarius appellatur, eo quod de libris curam habere solet, qui in armario [armariis: *Westm.*] continentur. ... Et de [Et insuper: *Westm.*] universis armariorum libris curam geret, et eos in custodia habebit'. See Fass A, p. 48 and n. 86.

[24] Ibid., I, 96, II, 36: 'Cantor [Qui similiter: *Westm.*] incaustum fieri faciet, quotiens opus fuerit. ... Similiter [Atque: *Westm.*] fratrum necessitatibus de membrana providere tenetur.'

master of the novices.[25] At all three houses, as at Abingdon, a deputy, the *succentor*, was given responsibility for access to the books required on a daily basis (such as the books of chant and, as specified in the Eynsham customs, also those assigned at the annual Lenten distribution).[26] The St Augustine's customary also provides for the cantor and *succentor* to have their own seats and carrels by the *armarium* so that they can be on hand to respond to any request from one of the brethren. [27]

None of these three customaries, nor the briefer record from Abingdon, describe how the Lenten distribution of books itself was to be observed. Lanfranc's customs describe the ritual but refer to the person who presided by the more general description of 'librorum custos',[28] the wording perhaps reflecting the transitional period when the roles of cantor and *armarius* were still in the process of becoming combined.[29] The St Augustine's and Westminster customaries allude briefly to the observance but without mentioning the officer involved,[30] nevertheless one may assume that once the cantor had taken on the responsibilities of *armarius*, he would also have presided over the Lenten distribution, as is the case in the remarkably detailed description of the observance in a late fourteenth century customary from Peterborough Abbey.[31]

The Eynsham customary stands alone among surviving English Benedictine recorded customs in deriving certain elements of the cantor's role as *armarius* from the *Liber ordinis*, the twelfth-century customary of the Augustinian house of St Victor, Paris.[32] These comprise the requirement to record individually the titles of every book, to set out or make account of all the books and to examine them carefully once or twice a year to ensure

---

[25] Ibid., I, 96–7, II, 36: 'Omnes vero libros qui in sua et succentoris custodia sunt, tam in ecclesia quam in claustro, necnon psalteria [libros necessarios: *Westm.*] ac antiphonarios qui magistri noviciorum cure commendantur, renovare, ligare, et quotiens opus fuerit, sumptibus suis resarcire faciet. It is unclear whether 'renovatio' refers only to the renewal of the exterior of the books or more broadly to their repair, replacement and perhaps also correction.

[26] *Customary of Eynsham*, p. 166; *Customary of St Augustine's*, I, 98, II, 37–8.

[27] *Customary of St Augustine's*, I, 202–3. For a fourteenth-century description of how the precentor at Evesham Abbey was to discharge his responsibility for supervising the daily reading in the cloister, see *English Benedictine Libraries*, p. 132; Sharpe, 'Medieval Librarian', p. 223.

[28] *Decreta*, p. 30.

[29] For an apparent confusion of the two roles in the *Liber tramitis*, and for an apparent separation of duties of *armarius* and cantor in the Lenten distribution as described in the late eleventh-century customs of Fruttuaria, see Fass A, pp. 44–6, 48 n. 85.

[30] *Customary of St Augustine's*, I, 39, II, 90.

[31] A. Gransden, 'The Peterborough Customary and Gilbert de Stanford', *RB* 70 (1960), 625–38 (pp. 632–8), and *Peterborough Abbey*, ed. K. Friis-Jensen and J. M. W. Willoughby, CBMLC 8 (London, 2001), xxviii–xxix, xliii–xlvi.

[32] Fass A, p. 51 n. 102; *Customary of Eynsham*, pp. 164–8.

against damage or injury from insects or decay. The *armarium* itself was also to be lined with wood and partitioned to protect the books from damp and other damage.³³ It was also the cantor's responsibility to decide which books were to be made available for daily consultation for rehearsal of either the chants and readings of the daily services or for those which he deemed useful and necessary for the instruction and edification of the brethren.³⁴ These and other customs of St Victor were adopted not only by houses that were members of the Victorine congregation, but also by other communities that followed the Augustinian rule, including the Dominicans. It is impossible, however, to determine whether they had already been adopted at Eynsham before the thirteenth century.³⁵

Although all of the later medieval English customaries assign general oversight of the community's books to the cantor, one category of books is treated as an exception: those used by officiants in the liturgy of the Mass. The Abingdon customs, for example, allowed the cantor permission to inspect all the books during the canonical Hours and the Mass, except the Mass-books themselves, and exactly the same provision is also found in the Eynsham customary.³⁶ Elsewhere in the Eynsham customary and in the customaries of St Augustine's, Canterbury, and Westminster, it is explained that these books were reserved to the custody of the sacrist, who was also responsible for their

³³ Ibid., p. 166: 'Armarius omnium librorum titulum singillatim annotatum habere debet et libros, qui anno illo pre manibus non habentur, per singulos <annos> semel aut bis exponere aut recensere et, ne in eis aliquid vel tinea vel alia qualibet corruptela infectum vel excessum fuerit, diligenter considerare. Ipsum autem armarium intrinsecus ligno vestiri debet, ne humor parietum membranas rubigine aliqua sive humectatione inficiat, in quo etiam diversi ordines distincti et convenitenter coapti esse tenentur, in quibus libri separatim ita collocari possint et distingui ab invicem, ne vel nimia compressio ipsis libris noceat vel confusio aliquid in eis specialiter querenti moram afferat vel impedimentum.' Cf. *Liber ordinis Sancti Victoris Parisiensis*, ed. L. Jocqué and L. Milis, CCCM 61 (Turnhout, 1984), pp. 78–9 ('De officio armarii'); and *The Observances in Use at the Augustinian Priory of S. Giles and S. Andrew at Barnwell, Cambridgeshire*, ed. and trans. J. W. Clark (Cambridge, 1897), pp. xlii–xlvi, 62–3. The reference to the lining of the *armarium* suggests that it comprised a recessed wall cupboard. *Armaria* could also take the form of free-standing (and presumably wooden) cupboards.
³⁴ *Customary of Eynsham*, p. 167: 'Debet cantor sive armarius inter libros, qui ad cotidianum officium ecclesie necessarii sunt etiam de aliis, aliquos, quos ad instructionem vel ad edificationem fratrum magis commodos et necessarios esse perspexerit, in commune proponere.' Cf. *Liber ordinis*, p. 82, which specifies the following books: 'bibliothece et maiores expositores et passionarii et vite patrum et homeliarii.'
³⁵ *Customary of Eynsham*, p. 17, noting the proximity of Eynsham to the Augustinian communities at Osney and St Frideswide's, Oxford. For Victorine influence upon customs regulating the care of books, see D. Nebbiai-dalla Guarda, 'La bibliothèque commune des institutions religieuses', *Scriptorium* 50 (1996), 254–68 (pp. 257–60).
³⁶ *Customary of Eynsham*, p. 164: 'Cantori licet sine reprehensione horis canonicis et ad missas libros inspicere exceptis libris ad officium misse assignatis.'

repair and renewal, and more detailed specification is provided concerning the books in question. All three specify those that pertained to the service of the altar and were used by the celebrant, deacon and sub-deacon: the gospel-books, epistolaries, lectionaries and benedictionals.[37] The Eynsham customs include the (presumably liturgical) books of the guesthouse ('libri hospitii'),[38] while the St Augustine's and Westminster lists add a volume containing the rites for exorcisms and blood-letting, and the collectars. The Westminster customary also includes non-notated ordinals, a lectionary for the Saturday Ember Days and a martyrology, while at St Augustine's it was also the sacrist's responsibility to ensure that the high altar never lacked the gospel-book containing the community's *Liber vite*.[39] Perhaps in acknowledgment of the cantor's expertise and wider responsibility for the conventual books, the sacrist at both Westminster and St Augustine's was required to carry out his responsibility for assembling and repairing all these books with the advice and active assistance of the cantor.[40] At all three houses, the repair of these books was the responsibility of the sacrist, while the cantor saw to the repair of the other books of the choir as well as those in the *armaria*, with the exception of the cloth overcovers, which fell to the chamberlain.[41] Nevertheless, these general norms need not have precluded the sacrist's

---

[37] *Customary of Eynsham*, p. 165: 'Sacrista tamen de missalibus, evangeliariis, epistolariis curam gerat et lectionariis et libris hospitii et benedictionali'. *Customary of St Augustine's*, I, 106, II, 49: '... quotiens opus fuerit, sumptibus suis reparare et renovare tenetur omnia missalia, ... et quecumque alia [alia: *om. Westm.*] ad missas celebrandas fuerint necessaria, necnon et textos atque librum evangeliorum, epistolarium, librum exorcismorum, et quoscumque benedictionarios, collectaria, [ordinalia divini officii et consuetudinum plane videlicet scripta absque nota cantus,: *add Westm.*] librum minutorum, [librum super quem legi solet in nocte et in octabis Pasche, et librum super quem lectiones legi solent in Sabbatis quattuor temporum, atque martyrologium,: *add Westm.*] et si qua sunt alia ad altarium volumina [volumina ad altarium: *Westm.*] sive sacerdotum ministerium specialiter pertinentia, de cantoris consilio et industria, componere, et quotiens opus fuerit, decenter reparare tenetur.'

[38] These may have included books for the Office as well as the Mass: mentions of books in the guesthouse in twelfth-century booklists include volumes described as 'breviaria', i.e. books containing materials for the Office: for example, *English Benedictine Libraries*, B37.12, B71.146.

[39] *Customary of St Augustine's*, I, 112: '... et quod magnum altare nunquam debet esse, quod absit, sine ... libro continente quattuor evangelia et nomina fratrum nostrorum defunctorum et benefactorum in eo scripta, ut sacerdos in eo celebrans memoriam eorum habeat specialiter, sicut et omnium fratrum et benefactorum nostrorum defunctorum quorum nomina in presenti libro sunt scripta.'

[40] Ibid., I, 106, II, 49.

[41] *Customary of Eynsham*, 165: 'Pannosque et cetera omnia ad horum librorum reparationem necessaria inveniet. Cantor reparabit ceteros libros tam chori quam armariorum et corium in ceteris necessariis inveniet. Camerarius vero pannos tantum ad libros quorum cantor curam gerit in choro reperiet'. *Customary of St Augustine's*, I, 197, II, 150 (on the office of the chamberlain): 'Panniculos vero ad

revenues being used on occasion to meet expenses for other kinds of books, as when Hervey (sacrist at Bury St Edmunds from sometime after 1121 until *c.* 1136) provided the means for his brother, Prior Talbot, to commission a great Bible for their community.[42]

The assignment of responsibility to the sacrist for the books used by the celebrant, deacon and sub-deacon in the Mass in the Eynsham, St Augustine's and Westminster customaries may reflect a practice already recorded in the eleventh- or twelfth-century customary from which all three 'derive. In Lanfranc's customs the sacrist is assigned custody of 'all the ornaments and utensils and furnishings of the church',[43] but there is a hint that among these 'ornaments' may have been certain books associated with the altar, since it was the duty of the sacrist to transfer the gospel-book from the altar to the vestry during the night office on Sundays and major feasts (in readiness for its use by the abbot or weekly priest) and then return it to the altar.[44] A description of the duties of the sacrist among the various customs jotted down perhaps during the mid twelfth century at an unknown English house (now Bodl Wood Empt. 4),[45] goes further in specifying the *ornamenta,* among them the 'textus', a term used for the gospel-books used in liturgical and extra-liturgical ritual.[46] The minor differences in the more extended lists of books found in later English custumals may therefore reflect local applications of a widely shared practice of perceiving certain liturgical books to be among the *ornamenta* of the church, and hence the responsibility of the sacrist. One might speculate that it was the precious metals, ivories and jewels applied to the exterior of the bindings (to form treasure bindings) that provide the most obvious explanation for their inclusion. The St Augustine's and Westminster customaries reproduce a very similar list of *ornamenta* to that in Wood Empt. 4, including the *textus,* which is prefaced by the comment that all the ornaments

---

psalteria aliosque libros parvi voluminis ex eodem [ex eodem: *om. Westm.*] eisdem [ex gratia: *add West.*] invenire solet.'

[42] Recorded in the abbey's thirteenth-century *Gesta sacristarum,* in *Memorials of St Edmund's Abbey,* ed. T. Arnold, 3 vols. (London, 1890–6), II, 289–96 (p. 290): 'Iste Herveus frater Taleboti prioris omnes expensas invenit fratri suo priori in scribenda magna bibliotheca ...'; see R. M. Thomson, *The Bury Bible* (Woodbridge, 2001), pp. 25–7. A fifteenth-century Bury register precedes a record of this endeavour with a reference to the rents 'quos antiquo iure sacrista iam habet in villa Sancti Edmundi comparavit'; see *English Benedictine Libraries,* 94.

[43] *Decreta,* pp. 122–3: 'Ad secretarii officium pertinet, omnia ornamenta monasterii, et omnia instrumenta et suppellectilem, que ad ipsum monasterium pertinent, custodire; horas providere.'

[44] Ibid., and n. 313. On this reading, see also T. Webber, 'Monastic Space and the Use of Books in the Anglo-Norman Period, *ANS* 36 (2014), 221–40 (p. 231).

[45] Jones, 'Monastic Custom', 139–140, 315–6, §23.

[46] Ibid., pp. 315–6: 'Secretarius curam habere debet omnium ornamentorum totius ecclesie, immo super omnia que ad eam pertinent, id est cruces, philacteria, feretra, textos, candelabra, thuribula, et si qua sunt alia circa altare versentur.'

of the church were by ancient custom assigned to the sacrist – all the 'centum' or treasure in gold, silver and precious stones.[47] By the thirteenth century, if not before, however, that rationale had been supplemented or superceded by a more functional relationship between certain categories of book and the performance of sacerdotal roles in the Mass. As a result the books involved came to include not only those in treasure bindings but also more plainly bound volumes.[48]

The evidence provided by customaries for the Anglo-Norman cantor's responsibility for book provision can be supplemented by the more numerous records of grants allocating revenues or other resources to the cantor for this purpose that date from the twelfth century onwards.[49] Such records reflect the growing tendency to formalize and record in writing both arrangements already in existence and those arising from the gradual, piecemeal and sometimes acrimonious process whereby the property and revenues of the head of the house became more sharply distinguished from those of the community, and portions of the community's revenues became allocated to particular offices, including that of the cantor.[50] As with the surviving written customs, the extant records of grants vary in how much and precisely what aspect of book provision is specified, although in general the kinds of responsibility outlined correspond with the norms described in the customaries. Certain grants provide revenues for the making of books (for materials and/or scribes),[51] others specify their correction and

---

[47] *Customary of St Augustine's*, I, 101, II, 42: 'Secretarius sive sacrista ex veteri consuetudine curam habere debet omnium ornamentorum totius ecclesie, immo super omnia que ad eam pertinent; omnem ecclesie censum sive thesaurum tam in auro et argento quam in lapidibus preciosis. Cruces vero et philacterias, feretra, textos ...'

[48] A late twelfth century booklist from Reading Abbey differentiates between the missal with a silver-gilt cover used on the most important feasts, one with just a silver cover used on other major feasts and Sundays, one with an unspecified (presumably plain) cover used on ferial days, and another (also presumably with an unornamented binding) used for the morrow mass: *English Benedictine Libraries*, B71.152.

[49] The evidence is collated and assessed by Gullick, 'Professional Scribes', and Sharpe, 'Medieval Librarian'. No obedientiaries' account rolls survive from before the thirteenth century; for the later medieval rolls from Ely and Norwich cathedral priories, see M. Gullick, *Extracts from the Precentors' Accounts of Ely Cathedral Priory concerning Books and Bookmaking* (Hitchin, 1985); *English Benedictine Libraries*, pp. 291–2, 299; and J. Greatrex, *The English Benedictine Cathedral Priories: Rule and Practice, c. 1270–c. 1420* (Oxford, 2011), pp. 176–86.

[50] For the particular example of Ely, an abbey that had become a cathedral priory in 1109, see N. Karn, *EEA XXXI. Ely 1109–1197* (Oxford, 2005), pp. xcviii–xcix.

[51] For example: a grant of Bishop William Giffard of Wincester of the church of Wroughton (Wilts.) to the monks and cantor 'ad faciendos libros' in 1107 was subsequently restored and confirmed *c.* 1128, restored again by Bishop Henry of Blois in 1142–3 ('ad conscriptionem librorum et ad reparationem organorum') and

repair.[52] However, the greater specificity provided by the grants sometimes indicates variation from the norms recorded in the customaries. Arrangements put in place by one grant were sometimes subsequently discontinued and had to be restored (and perhaps revised). At Ely, for example, a grant of lands and tithes that had been made sometime between 1134 and 1144 by Bishop Nigel to Aluric the cantor 'for the making and correction of books of our church' was later renewed in perpetuity in slightly different terms, and allocated not to a named cantor nor to the office of cantor, but to the 'scriptorio ecclesie Elyensis ad libros eiusdem ecclesie faciendos et emendandos'.[53] In this instance, the change (as Nicholas Karn suggests) may reflect a deliberate decision not to assign certain property and revenues to the office of cantor. Other examples of restorations or reconfirmations of earlier grants may reflect fluctuations in need.[54]

Nevertheless, as Richard Sharpe has observed, such funds would not on their own have been sufficient to make provision for additions to the community's holdings on the scale that took place at so many religious houses in England at various times during the late eleventh and twelfth centuries. Additional resources must have come either from the unassigned revenues of the community or from those in the hands of the abbot or bishop, where a separation between the two had already taken place,[55] or from unspent

reaffirmed in 1171: Gullick, 'Professional Scribes', 2–3; M. J. Franklin, *EEA VIII. Winchester 1070–1204* (Oxford, 1993), nos. 17, 21, 126, 132.

[52] For example: revenue from Halstow (Kent) was assigned to the cantor at Christ Church, Canterbury 'ad emendationem et reparationem librorum', in an *actum* of Archbishop Hubert Walter (no longer extant but quoted in an *actum* of Archbishop Stephen Langton) that restored Halstow to the community some time between 1198–1205: Gullick, 'Professional Scribes', pp. 3–4; C. R. Cheney and E. John, *EEA III. Canterbury 1162–1190* (Oxford, 1986), no. 388. K. Major, *Acta Stephani Langton Cantuariensis Archiepiscopi AD 1207–1228*, Canterbury and York Society 50 (1959), no. 10.

[53] Karn, *EEA XXXI. Ely*, nos. 32, 'ad faciendos et emendandos libros ecclesię nostrę') and 44 (*c.* 1158×1169), 'in perpetuam elemosinam scriptorio ecclesie Elyensis ad libros eiusdem ecclesie faciendos et emendandos'.

[54] See, for example, Gullick, 'Professional scribes', pp. 3–4, on the history of Halstow (above n. 52), originally granted by Archbishop Theobald to Prior Wibert between 1153 and 1161 for unspecified purposes, but perhaps for the making of books, then, in 1186, granted by Archbishop Baldwin to John of London, nephew of Thomas Becket, before it was restored to the community over ten years later.

[55] For the institution of professional scribes to copy the works of the Fathers at Abingdon by Abbot Faritius (1100–17), see *English Benedictine Libraries*, pp. 4–7, and for his allocation of the tithes from the manor of Dumbleton to the purchase of parchment to renew the books of the church, 'Ad pergamenum emendum, pro librorum ecclesie renovatione', see *Historia Ecclesie Abbendonensis: The History of the Church of Abingdon*, ed. and trans. J. Hudson, 2 vols. (Oxford, 2002–7), II, 216–7. At this date, the revenues of the abbot may not yet have become fully separated from those of the community at Abingdon: ibid., II, lxxxiv–lxxxvii. For the acts of a series of late eleventh and twelfth century abbots of St Albans by which revenues were

revenues allocated to other obedientiaries.[56] Reference is also made in the documentary records from a number of houses to the involvement of the prior in the provision of books which may reflect his role as the abbot's deputy and, after the separation of the property and revenues of the community from those of the abbot, its effective head, and hence with an overarching responsibility for how the community's resources were deployed.

The Rule of St Benedict itself makes no mention of the production or acquisition of books, nor of a specific individual to whom their custody was assigned. Responsibility for the delegation of such duties lay with the abbot, presumably falling within the prescriptions of chapter 32 of the Rule, which states that 'the goods of the monastery, that is, its tools, clothing or anything else, should be entrusted to brothers whom the abbot appoints and in whose manner of life he has confidence. He will, as he sees fit, issue to them the various articles to be cared for and collected after use'.[57] In the following chapter, which elaborates upon the evils of private ownership, books and writing materials are used as examples, and the overarching responsibility of the abbot is reinforced: 'Without an order from the abbot, no one may presume to give, receive or retain anything as his own, nothing at all – not a book, writing tablet or stylus – in short, not a single item. ... For their needs, they are to look to the father of the monastery, and are not allowed anything which the abbot has not given or permitted.'[58]

The prior, as the abbot's deputy, might also act on the abbot's behalf in distributing the community's resources, including books. This may account for the role assigned to the prior by the Aachen decrees of 23 August 816 (and repeated in subsequent legislation) in both carrying out the Rule's prescription for the Lenten distribution of books and having responsibility for all other personal use of books.[59] It may also lie behind the 'ancient custom'

---

assigned for professional scribes and their sustenance, the fabric of a designated space for producing books was maintained and books were commissioned, see the evidence from the *Gesta abbatum sancti Albani* assembled in *English Benedictine Libraries*, pp. 538–41, and discussed by R. M. Thomson, *Manuscripts from St Albans Abbey 1066–1235*, 2 vols. (Woodbridge, 1982).

[56] See, for example, Abbot Randulf of Evesham's customs, which made allowance for such viring of unspent income: Thomas of Marlborough, *History*, pp. 388–91.

[57] *RB 1980: The Rule of St Benedict in Latin and English with Notes*, ed. T. Fry (Collegeville, 1981), pp. 228–9: 'Substantia monasterii in ferramentis vel vestibus seu quibuslibet rebus prevideat abbas fratres de quorum vita et moribus securus sit, et eis singula, ut utile iudicaverit, consignet custodienda atque recolligenda.'

[58] Ibid., pp. 230–1: 'ne quis presumat aliquid dare aut accipere sine iussione abbatis, neque aliquid habere proprium, nullam omnino rem, neque codicem, neque tabulas, neque graphium, sed nihil omnino ... omnia vero necessaria a patre sperare monasterii nec quicquam liceat habere quod abbas non dederit aut permiserit.'

[59] 'Synodi primae Aquisgranensis decreta authentica', ed. J. Semmler, in *Initia consuetudinis Benedictinae, consuetudines saeculi octavi et noni*, ed. K. Hallinger, CCM 1 (Siegburg, 1963), p. 461: 'Ut in Quadragesima libris de bibliotheca secundum

recorded in the late thirteenth century Westminster customary whereby the cantor would bring the ink he had made to the prior for inspection,[60] as well as the charging of numerous expenses for parchment, books and scribes to the master of the cellar at Norwich Cathedral Priory (who kept the record of the prior's expenses) in the 'camera prioris' section of his accounts.[61]

Several examples can be cited of twelfth-century priors acquiring books for their communities, including three from the abbey of Bury St Edmunds, the most well known being the commissioning of the famous Bury Bible by Prior Talbot (with resources provided by his brother, Hervey, the sacrist).[62] The two others are manuscripts that contain inscriptions attributing responsibility for their production to Baldwin, prior from *c.* 1112 to *c.* 1125.[63] One may have been produced by a professional scribe, but the other, a copy of three works of Anselm, was produced in-house by several scribes whose hands are found in other Bury manuscripts of the first quarter of the twelfth century and who are more likely to have been monks. In this latter case, therefore, the prior presumably provided the material resources for producing the manuscript. At Evesham, the prior was formally allocated specified revenues in connection with the production of books in the customs instituted in 1214 by Abbot Randulf, and recorded in the history of the abbey by Thomas of Marlborough, himself then prior: 'To the prior's office belong the tithes of Bengeworth, the great as well as the small, from all the lands and men of the monks, and these are for parchment and the maintenance of the scribes who write the books.'[64] Thomas also recorded in his history the books that he had had made for the community after becoming prior, including a large breviary, a large psalter and four notated antiphoners (these last written by members of the community), as well as books he had purchased, among them several glossed books of the Bible.[65]

prioris dispositionem acceptis aliis nisi prior decreverit expedire non accipiant'; Fass A, p. 35 and nn. 25 and 26.

[60] *Customary of St Augustine's*, II,19: 'Antiquitus vero cantor, quando incaustum erat facturus, illud priori claustri premonstrare consuevit.'

[61] *English Benedictine Libraries*, ed. Sharpe, 292–9.

[62] See above, n. 42.

[63] Cambridge, St John's College MS D. 19 (94) and Bodl e Musaeo 112: P. R. Robinson, *Catalogue of Dated and Datable Manuscripts c. 737–1600 in Cambridge Libraries*, 2 vols. (Woodbridge, 1988), I, no. 298; A. G. Watson, *Catalogue of Dated and Datable Manuscripts c. 435–1600 in Oxford Libraries*, 2 vols. (Oxford, 1984), I, no. 657.

[64] Thomas of Marlborough, *History*, pp. 392–3: 'Ad prioratum pertinent decime de Beningwrthe tam maiores quam minores de omnibus terris et hominibus monachorum ad parcamenum et exhibitionem scriptorum pro libris scribendis.'

[65] Ibid., pp. 490–3.

The cantor-*armarius* and the provision of books for public reading

The descriptions of the duties of variously the *armarius*, cantor and cantor-*armarius* from the eleventh century onwards are dominated less by detail concerning their role as librarians[66] than by prescriptions for the correct performance of the liturgy and other rituals.[67] In this context, the 'provision' of books has a meaning that extends beyond the range of duties more usually associated with the management of libraries to include the preparation of both books and readers for reading aloud to the assembled community in the church, refectory and chapterhouse.

Lanfranc's customs require the cantor to ensure in advance ('providere') that nothing, whether sung or read, should be done negligently, to rehearse the readers and singers if necessary and to select each week the readers and singers based upon his own judgment of their suitability for the task in hand:

> Quicumque lecturus aut cantaturus est aliquid in monasterio, si necesse habet, ab eo priusquam incipiat debet auscultare. Ipsius est omni hora sollicite providere, ne eveniat neglegentia in quocumque obsequio quod fit in monasterio. ... Ipsius est omnes fratres in tabula ad omnia officia annotare, non considerato conversionis ordine, aut voluntate eorum, sed secundum quod ei visum fuerit, honestatem et edificationem in hoc vigilanter consideranti.[68]

> [Whenever anyone is to read or chant anything in the church the cantor shall, if need be, hear him go over his task before he perform it in public. It is the cantor's business to watch carefully at all times, so that no negligence occurs in any service in the monastery. ... It is his task to put down the brethren for all duties (that is, chants and readings) on the tabula, paying no attention to their seniority or their personal wishes, but according to his best judgment having careful regard only to good performance and edification.]

Supervision of the liturgical readings was one of the duties of the *armarius* which, over the course of the eleventh century, had become combined with the cantor's oversight of the chant.[69] Correct performance of monastic observance, and especially the liturgy, was a recurrent concern of monastic reformers throughout the Middle Ages, although what it was understood to involve and how it was to be achieved, might differ. Lanfranc's own stipulation that the cantor's choice of readers (and singers) should be based on their suitability may reflect an extrapolation from the Rule's teachings in

---

[66] Sharpe, 'Medieval Librarian', p. 224.
[67] For the eleventh-century background and continental evidence, see Fass A, pp. 42–9.
[68] *Decreta*, pp. 118–21.
[69] Fass A, pp. 39–46.

chapter 38 on the weekly reader in the refectory: 'the reader should not be the one who just happens to pick up the book, but someone who will read for a whole week, beginning on Sunday. ... Brothers will read and sing, not according to rank, but according to their ability to benefit their hearers.'[70] Elsewhere (and perhaps also, in practice, at Canterbury), it was commonly the custom for the readings of the Mass and the night office to be assigned to specific ranks and officers within the community, usually in ascending order of importance.[71]

Customaries also vary in their requirements concerning rehearsal, insofar as those who were no longer novices were concerned.[72] The late tenth century customary in Einsiedeln, Stiftsbibliothek MS 235 had gone so far as to insist that no one might deliver a reading in the church, refectory or in chapter without previously being heard by the *armarius* or someone else.[73] Lanfranc's customs, however, allow the cantor some discretion, an allowance also reflected in the later customaries of St Augustine's, Canterbury, and Westminster.[74]

The cantor's duty to correct the community's books, mentioned frequently in the records assigning revenues to his office, must have been associated especially with their preparation for oral delivery. This is made explicit, and coupled with a requirement to punctuate them appropriately, in the Eynsham customary, in a passage derived from the Victorine *Liber ordinis* concerning the 'libri communes', the books of chants and readings that were to be made available each day for consultation in some suitably accessible place. It was these books in particular that the cantor or *armarius* was to correct and

---

[70] *RB 1980*, pp. 236–8: '... nec fortuito casu qui arripuerit codicem legere ibi, sed lecturus tota hebdomada dominica ingrediatur. ... Fratres autem non per ordinem legant aut cantent, sed qui edificant audientes.' William of Hirsau, in his customs for Hirsau, extended this requirement to the evening reading at collation, *Willehelmi abbatis Constitutiones Hirsaugienses*, ed. C. Elvert and P. Engelbert, 2 vols., CCM 15 (2010), I, 382: 'Cavendum est armario, ne umquam cuiquam minus sciolo id iniungat, ut ad collationem legat; sed tam convenienti et intelligenti persone que ita legat, ut audientes edificet.'

[71] Fass A, p. 41.

[72] For the rehearsal of readings as part of the training of the novices, see S. Boynton, 'Training for the Liturgy as a Form of Monastic Education', in *Medieval Monastic Education*, ed. G. Ferzoco and C. Muessig (London, 2000), pp. 7–20 (pp. 9–13).

[73] 'Redactio Einsidlensis', p. 207: 'Nullus in ecclesia, in refectorio, in capitulo vel quolibet conventu audeat quicquam legere inprovise, quod ante non habuerit ab armario vel ab aliquo auscultatum. Similiter cantare non presumat, quod a cantore prius non audiatur'. See also Fass A, p. 47 and n. 81, for the same, albeit differently worded, stipulation in the *Liber tramitis*.

[74] *Customary of St Augustine's*, I, 90, II, 28: 'Quicumque lecturus est in conventu aut aliquid cantaturus, si necesse habet, ab eo priusquam incipiat debet ascultari. Ipsius est omni hora solicite providere ne aliqua in obsequio divino eveniat negligentia.'

punctuate lest the brethren stumble when singing or reading aloud.[75] The reading in question comprised not only the lections of the liturgy of the Mass and the Office but also those delivered in the refectory at mealtimes and in the chapterhouse during the morning chapter-office and the evening collation. The volumes involved likewise went beyond those specially produced for liturgical purposes (gospel-books or gospel-lectionaries, epistolaries, plenary missals, office lectionaries and breviaries) and those regularly used for the night office readings – Bibles, homiliaries and passionals – to include books now more usually associated with a modern conception of library: patristic and later exegesis and doctrinal exposition, ecclesiastical history, works of spiritual advice and monastic edification and smaller compilations of saints' lives,[76] all of which needed to be properly corrected and marked up as required prior to the rehearsal and/or delivery of the passages allocated by the cantor to be delivered as readings.

In her study of the evolution of the office of the cantor in the period up to the end of the eleventh century, Margot Fassler suggested that it was the introduction and increasing use of notated chant books during the eleventh century that contributed to the combining of responsibility for the chant with that of oversight of the library and scriptorium.[77] A further practical consideration may have played a part. Whereas the pericopes for the readings of the Mass had become more or less established by at least the eleventh century (with the important exception of the sanctoral, which remained more variable), the readings for the Office were not yet fixed but were determined locally in accordance with a common framework of an annual cycle of reading the books of the Bible, related patristic exegesis, a choice of gospel homilies corresponding to the pericope of the day, and, as considered appropriate to the feast, hagiography. Within these parameters, the decision as to where to begin and end each reading had come to be the responsibility of the *armarius*. In late tenth and early eleventh century customaries, for example, his task of correcting the books is commonly coupled with a requirement to determine the length of the readings.[78]

---

[75] *Customary of Eynsham*, p. 167; *Liber ordinis*, pp. 81–2: 'Libri communes, [id est: *Lib. ord.*] qui cotidie ad manum habendi sunt sive ad cantandum sive ad legendum, in loco competendi reponendi [exponendi: *Lib.ord.*] sunt, ut [ubi: *Lib.ord.*] competens accessus omnium fratrum esse possit. Quos precipue cantor vel [cantor vel: *om. Lib.ord.*] armarius diligenter emendare debet et punctare, ne fratribus [fratres: *Lib.ord.*] in cotidiano officio ecclesie, sive in cantando sive in legendo aliquod impedimentum faciant [inveniant: *Lib.ord.*].'

[76] I am preparing a study of public reading and its books in English monastic practice to be delivered as the Lyell Lectures in Bibliography in the University of Oxford in 2016. For a preliminary survey, see Webber, 'Monastic Space'.

[77] Fass A, p. 46.

[78] For example, 'Consuetudines Floriacenses', p. 17: 'Emendatio librorum et termini lectionum et responsio fidei catholice et hereticorum confutatio et, si quid sane

The issue was not simply one of judgment concerning length but also of coordination. In principle, the scriptural readings of the night office (and those of the refectory which dovetailed with and supplemented them) had to be made to fit within the framework of the annual cycle of reading the books of the Bible, as recorded (with minor variations) in a number of *ordines*.[79] Coordinating this programme of readings was not easy, involving both the negotiation of a number of variables (the length of time each year between Epiphany and Septuagesima, the length of the hours of darkness, the number of Sundays in the summer months) and a flexible response to progressive incremental change to festal observance, which might entail the substitution of the seasonal biblical readings with readings proper to the feast. But in addition to all of this, the organization of the biblical readings not only in the Office but also in the refectory needed to be coordinated as far as possible with the longer-established liturgical cycle of scripturally derived responsories that dovetailed with each set of readings within the night office. In the early thirteenth century ordinal of the Norman abbey of Fécamp, even the timing of the *ordo* of refectory reading is signposted in several places with the incipits of the series of responsories. The commencement of the reading of the Apocalypse after Easter, for example, is cued to the responsory 'Dignus es domine' (cf. Apoc. 5. 9), and the Canonical Epistles, which were to follow, to 'Si oblitus fuero tui'.[80]

In view of the problems of coordination that might arise in adapting the cycle of biblical reading to the broadly similar but not identical cycle of chants, it is easy to see why the custom of having a single master of ceremonies, in charge of assigning both chants and readings, became widespread within monastic practice, and why it endured. Even the readings of the evening collation, which usually comprised a diet of texts advocating or exemplifying the monastic virtues,[81] had sometimes to be coordinated with the festal liturgy. In the customary drawn up by William of Hirsau, for example, the prompt used to signal such exceptions is the manner of performance of the

---

doctrine obstiterit, illum attinet'; 'Redactio Einsidlensis', pp. 200–1: 'Breve cantorum et lectorum seu servitorum pridie antequam in capitulo recitetur scribi debet. ..... Similiter lectiones ab armario pridie ante sint terminate vel correcte.'

[79] For a detailed examination of the complexities involved and the fluidity of practice that could arise at the local level, see H. Parkes, 'Biblical Readings for the Night Office in Eleventh-Century Germany: Reconciling Theory and Practice', in *Reading the Bible in the Middle Ages*, ed. J. Nelson and D. Kempf (London, 2015), pp. 77–100. As Parkes shows, these complexities were not only a matter of concern for monastic communities, but for cathedral clergy as well.

[80] *The Ordinal of the Abbey of the Holy Trinity Fécamp (Fécamp, Musée de la Bénédictine, Ms 186)*, ed. D. Chadd, HBS 111–12 (London, 1999–2002), II, 675. For issues of coordination arising from differences in the ordering of the New Testament books of the Bible in the period between Easter and Ascension, see Parkes, 'Biblical Readings'.

[81] Webber, 'Monastic Space', pp. 235–6.

chants: 'On the major feasts on which the Venite is sung by four, or on feasts 'in cappis', a proper sermon is to be read at collation, if there is one.'[82] In such circumstances, combining the roles of cantor and *armarius* made good sense, and thus ensured, as Ulrich of Zell put it in the chapter on the cantor-*armarius* in the customary he compiled at William's request, 'what he should wish to be sung shall be sung, what he should wish to be read is to be read, in the church, in the refectory and at collation, and all should be obedient to him in this regard'.[83]

[82] *Willehelmi abbatis Constitutiones Hirsaugienses*, I, 382: 'In precipuis festivitatibus, in quibus quattuor Venite cantant, aut etiam in cappis, si habent proprium sermonem, inde legitur ad collationem ...'

[83] Ulrich, *Consuetudines Cluniacenses*, PL 149, 749: 'Quod voluerit ut cantetur, cantatur; quod voluerit ut legatur, legitur et in ecclesia, et in refectorio, et ad collationem; et ad huiuscemodi omnes debent semper ei esse obedientes.'

10

Symeon of Durham as Cantor and Historian at Durham Cathedral Priory, *c.* 1090–1129

Charles C. Rozier

The discussion which follows examines Symeon of Durham's activities as cantor and as historian at the cathedral priory of Durham, *c.* 1090–1129. By analysing Symeon's additions to Durham manuscripts of the late eleventh and early twelfth centuries, it seeks to augment our understanding of Symeon's work as Durham cantor, and considers some of the possible links between his roles as cantor and historian. In order to do so, it is divided into two main parts. The first part reconstructs Symeon's work as cantor. It suggests that, having worked alongside the previous incumbent from the 1090s onwards, before his likely appointment as cantor *c.* 1115–20, Symeon practised a form of cantorship which appears to have been closely related to that outlined in the *Decreta* of Archbishop Lanfranc, comprising responsibilities for supervising the accurate delivery of the liturgy, commemorating the dead, measuring time and for co-ordinating the acquisition, production and care of books. Following this, the second part links these duties with Symeon's work in copying, compiling and composing historical texts. It will be argued that Symeon's work as both cantor and historian made a number of essential contributions to the development and consolidation of the institutional identity of Durham's cathedral priory – an identity which was informed by the carefully selected and officially ratified vision of the community's past as featured in Symeon's writings, and which was broadcast and enhanced by the forms of liturgical commemoration to which Symeon contributed as cantor.

This study contributes to a wider discourse surrounding historical consciousness in medieval Durham, attempting to understand how much of the past was known by Symeon and his contemporaries, how they learned of their past, how they adapted this knowledge for use in their present and why their past mattered to them.[1] Analysis of Symeon's role as cantor at Durham

---

[1] A. J. Piper, 'The First Generations of Durham Monks and the Cult of St Cuthbert', in *St Cuthbert, his Cult and his Community to AD 1200*, ed. G. Bonner, D. W. Rollason and C. Stancliffe (Woodbridge, 1989), pp. 437–46; W. M. Aird, *St Cuthbert and the Normans: the Church of Durham, 1071–1153* (Woodbridge, 1998); essays in *Symeon of Durham: Historian of Durham and the North*, ed. D. W. Rollason (Stamford, 1998), especially A. J. Piper, 'The Historical Interests of the Monks of Durham', pp. 301–32; Charles C. Rozier, 'Contextualizing the Past at Durham Cathedral Priory,

provides an ideal focus for developing this line of enquiry. It will be seen that much of his work, both before and after the earliest known date of his cantorship, appears to have been directed towards an overarching aim to present a historically informed vision of what the community of St Cuthbert believed it was, where it came from and what it stood for. The discussion which follows aims to demonstrate that the cantor and the historian played a leading role in this initiative, and will suggest that by serving in both roles, Symeon was ideally suited to the cultivation and consolidation of Durham's place at the forefront of secular and ecclesiastical politics in Anglo-Norman Northumbria.

Symeon of Durham is best known to modern scholars as an author of historical texts which record events of northern English history during the Anglo-Saxon and Anglo-Norman periods.[2] Of these, the most famous is his account of the community of St Cuthbert produced between 1104 and 1115, and which, following the incipit to the two earliest manuscripts, is now usually referred to as the *Libellus de exordio atque procursu istius, hoc est Dunhelmensis ecclesie* (*Tract on the Origins and Progress of this, the Church of Durham*).[3] Other historically oriented texts attributed to Symeon include a set of annals added to the margins of Easter tables,[4] and a longer collection of annals relating to English and Frankish history,[5] both of which were copied in his hand. During the 1120s, Symeon also co-ordinated the production of a more substantial chronicle of English history down to 1129 known according to the rubric within the earliest surviving manuscript as the Durham *Historia de regibus Anglorum et Dacorum* (1129).[6]

---

c. 1090–1130: 107 Uses of History in the Annals of Durham, Dean and Chapter Library, MS Hunter 100', *Haskins Society Journal* 25 (2013), 107–23.

[2] The authoritative studies of Symeon's life and works are A. J. Piper, 'The Durham Cantor's Book (Durham, Dean and Chapter Library, MS B.IV.24)', in *Anglo-Norman Durham, 1093–1193*, ed. D. W. Rollason, M. Harvey and M. Prestwich (Woodbridge, 1994), pp. 79–92; Piper, 'The Scribes of the Durham Cantor's Book (Durham, Dean and Chapter Library, MS B.IV.24)', pp. 93–109; Piper, 'The Hand of Symeon of Durham: further reflections on the Durham Martyrology Scribe', in *Symeon: Historian*, ed. Rollason, pp. 14–31; *LdE*, pp. xliii–l.

[3] Symeon, *LdE*, p. 16, note a.

[4] Now Glasgow, University Library, MS Hunterian 85 (T.4.2), edited in W. Levison and H. Eberhard Meyer, 'Die *Annales Lindisfarnenses et Dunelmenses*: kritisch untersucht und neu herausgegeben', *Deutsches Archiv für Erforschung des Mittelalters* 17 (1961), 447–506. For discussion, see J. E. Story, 'Symeon as Annalist', in *Symeon: Historian*, ed. Rollason, pp. 202–13.

[5] Durham, Dean and Chapter Library, MS B.iv.22, fols. 3–5; Story, 'Symeon as Annalist'.

[6] For the text, see *Symeonis monachi opera omnia*, ed. T. Arnold, 2 vols. (London, 1882–5), II, 3–284, and the forthcoming edition by M. Lapidge and D. W. Rollason, Symeon of Durham, *Historia de regibus Anglorum et Dacorum, incorporating Byrhtferth of Ramsey, Historia Regum, with John of Hexham, Historia xxv annorum, and Anonymous, De obsessione Dunelmi et de probitate Uhtredi comitis, et de comitibus qui ei successerunt,*

The paleographical research of Michael Gullick has greatly augmented our knowledge of Symeon's life and the wider corpus of his works.[7] Gullick suggested that the character of Symeon's hand suggests that he was of northern French, probably Norman, origin, and noted that the earliest evidence dates his arrival in Durham to the early 1090s.[8] Identifying Symeon's additions to over forty extant manuscripts and documents, Gullick has shown Symeon as one of the most prominent scribes within the surviving corpus of late eleventh and early twelfth century Durham manuscripts, profiling his work as the main scribe, editor and rubricator of around thirty manuscripts containing patristic and medieval theology and biblical exegesis,[9] observing Symeon's production of seven extant charters on behalf of the monastic community and Bishops of Durham,[10] and noting his various additions of names and confraternity agreements in Durham's *Liber vitae*. Gullick also highlighted Symeon's additions to a number of manuscripts incorporating historical and hagiographical texts, including two manuscripts containing Bede's *Vita Cuthberti*, the *Historia Lausiaca*, William of Jumièges's *Gesta Normannorun ducum* and one small marginal addition to Durham's copy of Bede's *Historia ecclesiastica*.[11]

Symeon's status as cantor is known from two principal sources. The earliest is a letter dated to November 1126, which records the vision of a young boy named Orm, and which was sent to Durham addressed to 'Symeon, precentor of the church of Durham'.[12] No other Symeon is known to have been present in Durham at this time. Only one individual of this name features in the list of Durham monks which was added to one of the two earliest manuscripts of the *Libellus de exordio*, and in the near-contemporary list found in Durham's commemorative *Liber vitae*.[13] It is almost certain that Symeon, author of the

and *De primo Saxonum aduentu siue de eorundem regibus*, Oxford Medieval Texts (Oxford, forthcoming). For discussion of Symeon's role, see Symeon, *LdE*, p. xlviii; P. Hunter Blair, 'Some Observations on the *Historia Regum* attributed to Symeon of Durham', in *Celt and Saxon*, ed. N. K. Chadwick (Cambridge, 1963), pp. 63–118; Story, 'Symeon as Annalist'; and D. W. Rollason, 'Symeon of Durham's *Historia de regibus Anglorum et Dacorum* as a product of twelfth-century Historical Workshops', in *Long Twelfth-century Views of the Anglo-Saxon Past*, ed. M. Brett and D. A. Woodman (Aldershot, forthcoming).

7 Gullick, 'Scribes' and 'Hand'. See also the summary in Symeon, *LdE*, pp. xliv–l.

8 Ibid., pp. 18–19.

9 For a list of Symeon's manuscript additions, see ibid., pp. 24–31.

10 Ibid., pp. 26, 28, 30, items 12, 13, 24, 32, 33, 35 and 36.

11 Ibid., p. 24 items 1, 2 and 4; p. 27 item 18; and p. 41 item 41. Gullick locates Symeon's note in Durham's copy of Bede's *Historia ecclesiastica* on fol. 38v, when in fact it appears on fol. 39v.

12 Symeon, *LdE*, p. xliii; D. H. Farmer, 'The Vision of Orm', *Analecta Bollandiana* 75 (1957), 72–82.

13 DUL Cosin V.ii.6, fol. 7v, printed in Symeon, *LdE*, pp. 8–9, and also in Piper 'Lists', pp. 176–85 and BL Cotton Domitian A.vii, fol. 45r, printed in Piper 'Lists', pp. 176–85. For the Durham *Liber vitae* see also, *The Durham Liber Vitae: London,*

Libellus de exordio and scribe at Durham, was the intended recipient of this letter and, therefore, that he had been appointed cantor some time before 1126.

The second record of Symeon's cantorship is a rubric which appears at the beginning of a late twelfth century copy of his *Libellus de exordio*, now CUL Ff.1.27, p. 123. The text reads: 'Here begins the preface of the holy Symeon, monk and precentor of the church of St Cuthbert, in Durham.'[14] Rollason underlined the reliability of this rubric by concluding that the manuscript had almost certainly been produced at Durham in or just after 1188, and therefore by Symeon's successors, the oldest of whom may just have known him active in the cantor's role.[15]

Although the letter of 1126 gives a *terminus post quem* for Symeon's cantorship, the precise date of his appointment is more difficult to establish. Gullick has argued that Symeon was probably not cantor before 1104 due to the fact he is not named as such in Reginald of Durham's later twelfth-century account of the translation of Cuthbert. While Reginald noted Symeon's presence and gave others their due rank, Symeon was mentioned by name alone, with no accompanying note of office, and so it follows that he probably had none at that time.[16] The identification of Symeon's likely predecessor in the role sheds some further light on this issue. Gullick identified him as the individual recorded in Symeon's additions to the Durham martyrology as 'Willelmus cantor', and observed that like Symeon, this William had also been brought to Durham at the beginning of the 1090s.[17] Gullick noted that William's additions within the calendar and martyrology of the Durham 'Cantor's Book' (now Durham, Dean and Chapter Library, MS B.iv.24) and within the Durham *Liber vitae* suggest that William had been Durham's cantor before Symeon took over after William's death between *c.* 1110 and 1120.[18]

As is the case with many of the medieval cantor-historians discussed in this volume, assessing Symeon's activities as Durham cantor requires a judicious reading of the available evidence. Despite recent progress, it is still difficult to know exactly what the cantor's role entailed within a specific religious

British Library MS Cotton Domitian A.VII, ed. D. W. and L. Rollason with A. J. Piper, 3 vols. (London, 2007).

[14] 'Incipit prefatio reuerendi Symeonis monachi et precentoris ecclesie sancti Cuthberti Dunemli'. See also Symeon, *LdE*, pp. xxiv–vii, 16–17.

[15] Ibid., pp. xxvi–xxvii, xliii.

[16] Gullick, 'Hand', p. 21. For the text, see *Reginaldi monachi Dunelmensis libellus de admirandis beati Cuthberti uirtutibus quae novellis patratae sunt temporibus*, ed. James Raine, Surtees Society 1 (London, 1835), p. 84.

[17] Durham, Dean and Chapter Library, MS B.iv.24, fol. 37r; Piper, 'Lists', p. 200.

[18] Gullick, 'Hand', pp. 20–1. See also M. Gullick, 'The Scribe of the Carilef Bible: a new look at some late eleventh-century Durham Cathedral manuscripts', in *Medieval Book Production: Assessing the Evidence*, ed. L. Brownrigg (Los Altos Hills, 1990), pp. 61–83 (pp. 68–9 and n. 44).

community in the early and high Middle Ages.[19] While much can be learned by amalgamating descriptions of the role within contemporary customaries, the level of detail provided by these texts is frequently low, and is insufficient when seeking to reconstruct the hourly, or even the daily, routine of the medieval cantor. In addition, attempts to reconstruct the cantor's remit through the study of manuscript additions in known cantors' hands carry the potential to mislead due to the fact that it is often quite impossible to prove that any additions were made only as a direct result of his or her cantorship. As a consequence, the following reconstruction of Symeon's work as Durham cantor reads his contributions to the manuscript evidence with caution in this attempt to provide tentative conclusions about the office during his probable years of service.

A copy of Archbishop Lanfranc's *Decreta* arrived in Durham at the beginning of the 1090s, with large sections having been written by another leading Anglo-Norman cantor-historian, Eadmer of Canterbury.[20] At Durham, this copy of the *Decreta* was soon bound together with two copies of the *Rule of St Benedict* (one in Latin and one in Anglo-Saxon English) and a martyrology, to form what is now Durham, Dean and Chapter Library, MS B.iv.24. Piper christened the manuscript the 'Durham Cantor's Book', on account of its contents and the additions by Symeon and his predecessor, William.[21] The fact that Symeon and William added to the contents of the volume, which at that time is likely to have already included Lanfranc's *Decreta*, allows a speculative examination of the extent to which Symeon attempted to follow the recommendations relating to the cantor's role as featured therein.

[19] F. Wormald, 'The Monastic Library', in *The English Library before 1700*, ed. F. Wormald and C. E. Wright (London, 1958), pp. 15–31; Fass A; D. Hiley, 'Thurstan of Caen and Plainchant at Glastonbury: Musicological Reflections on the Norman Conquest', *Proceedings of the British Academy* 72 (1986), 57–90; J. Grier, 'Roger de Chabannes (d. 1025), cantor of St Martial, Limoges', *Early Music History* 14 (1995), 53–119; J. Grier, *The Musical World of a Medieval Monk: Adémar de Chabannes in Eleventh-Century Aquitaine* (Cambridge, 2006), especially chapter 6; A. Yardley, *Performing Piety: Musical Culture in Medieval English Nunneries* (New York, 2006).

[20] Durham, Dean and Chapter Library, MS B.iv.24, fols. 47r–71v. This manuscript provided the base-text for *The Monastic Constitutions of Lanfranc*, ed. D. Knowles with C. N. L. Brooke (Oxford, 2002) in which the manuscript is discussed at p. xliv. On Eadmer's role in copying the text, see M. Gullick, 'The Scribal Work of Eadmer of Canterbury to 1109', *Archaeologia Cantiana* 118 (1998), 173–89 (p. 183). On Eadmer's status as cantor, see Margot Fassler's essay in this volume and *The Historical Woks of Gervase of Canterbury*, ed. W. Stubbs, 2 vols. (London, 1879–80) I, 7; II, 374. For discussion, see R. W. Southern, *Anselm and his Biographer: a study of Monastic Life and Thought, 1059–c. 1130* (Cambridge, 1963), p. 237; Southern, *Saint Anselm: a Portrait in a Landscape* (Cambridge, 1990), pp. 418–21; Eadmer, *The Lives and Miracles of Saints Oda, Dunstan and Oswald*, ed. A. Turner and B. Muir (Oxford, 2006), p. xxvi.

[21] Piper, 'The Durham Cantor's Book'.

The type of cantor depicted in chapter 86 of Lanfranc's *Decreta* was one primarily responsible for the planning and accurate delivery of the liturgy. His main duties were to provide rehearsals of readings and chants prior to performance in church, to lead and to correct immediately any errors in readings and chant in church, where necessary to choose readers, and to distribute special copes on feast days.[22] Due to the ephemeral nature of these tasks, it is almost impossible to know how far Symeon followed Lanfranc's prescriptions in these areas. A generally poor survival rate of liturgical manuscripts from Anglo-Norman Durham, coupled with an absence of additions by Symeon in those which do exist, prevents further conclusions on Symeon's exact role in supervising the delivery of Durham's liturgy.[23]

In contrast to his poorly attested liturgical role, the remainder of Symeon's likely cantorial duties are better represented in the surviving evidence, most prominently in his additions to obit-lists and confraternity records and apparent supervisory role in the production and care of books. Lanfranc's description of the role concluded with the following short instructions in these areas:

> It also pertains to his office to supervise the letters sent out to ask for prayers for the dead brethren and to keep count of the week's and month's mind. He takes care of all the books of the house, and has them in his keeping, if his interests and learning are such as to fit him for keeping them.[24]

Symeon's involvement in the care of Durham's books is recorded in several surviving manuscripts. He compiled the first inventory of Durham's books, listing all those given to the monastic community by Bishop William of Saint-Calais on the front flyleaf of a large two-volume Bible, under the heading: 'Here are the names of the books which Lord Bishop William gave to St Cuthbert.'[25] In addition, Gullick has shown that Symeon corrected and

---

[22] Lanfranc, *Constitutions*, pp. 118–23.

[23] The surviving manuscripts are Durham, Cathedral Library, MSS B.iii.10, inside cover (fragments of a breviary, s. xi[ex]); B.iii.11, fols. 136–159 (antiphonal, s. xi[ex]); B.iii.32 (collection of hymns and canticles glossed in English, s. xi[ex]) and DUL Cosin V.v.6 (gradual, s. xi[ex] with additions to s. xii[1/4]). See R. A. B. Mynors, *Durham Cathedral Manuscripts to the End of the Twelfth Century* (Oxford, 1939); Richard Gameson, *Manuscripts of Early Norman England, c. 1066–1130* (Oxford, 1999). Symeon's list of books present in Durham by 1096 records the possession of two breviaries, two antiphonals, one gradual, three missals, two books of readings for Matins and three missals.

[24] Lanfranc, *Constitutions*, pp. 122–3.

[25] Durham, Cathedral Library, MS A.ii.4, fol. 1r: 'Ista sunt nomina librorum quos dominus Wilelmus episcopus sancto Cuthberto dedit'. The list was edited with commentary in A. C. Browne, 'Bishop William of St Carilef's Book Donations to Durham Cathedral Priory', *Scriptorium* 42 (1988), 140–55. A facsimile of the list appears in plate 15. The present manuscript is the first of two volumes, with the second now lost.

added incipits and explicits and short introductory sections of text to a total of nineteen surviving manuscripts.[26] This apparent supervisory role in the upkeep and production of Durham's books is strongly reflective of Lanfranc's stipulation that the cantor should 'take care' of books and, moreover, echoes the more detailed instructions on armarius-style cantorship found in other near-contemporary customaries such as the *Liber ordinis* and the *Liber tramitis*.[27]

Knowing the exact points in time by which Symeon was carrying out this activity has strong implications for the analysis of his role as a cantor at Durham. Gullick dated much of Symeon's correcting and editing to an intensive period of book production and acquisition which lasted from *c.* 1090 to 1110.[28] He dated Symeon's composition of the William of Saint-Calais's book-list to just after the death of the bishop in 1096.[29] This would suggest that Symeon supervised the care and production of books before the death of his likely predecessor, William (d. *c.* 1110–20), perhaps as an assistant-cantor, or as part of a small team of experienced bibliophile-scribes whose activities were similar, but not necessarily directly linked, to those depicted in Lanfranc's *Decreta*.

Several of Symeon's manuscript additions show him carrying out work which fits Lanfranc's instruction that cantors should 'supervise the letters sent out to ask for prayers for the dead brethren'.[30] Although no such letters survive in Symeon's hand, his involvement in similar processes of memorialization and commemoration can be seen in the pages of Durham's *Liber vitae* and martyrology. The *Liber vitae* is an elaborate confraternity book containing over 3,000 names arranged according to secular and ecclesiastical rank, and which was first made in an unknown ninth-century Northumbrian monastery, likely Lindisfarne or Wearmouth-Jarrow.[31] The book may have been inherited by the Durham community at any point, but was certainly

---

[26] These are Cambridge, Jesus College, MSS Q.A.14 (14) and Q.B.8 (25), fols. 1–18; Durham, Cathedral Library, MSS A.i.10; A.iv.16, fols. 6–109; B.ii.6; B.ii.7; B.ii.8; B.ii.21; B.iii.9; B.iv.5; B.iv.7; B.iv.12; B.iv.13; B.iv.16, fols. 110r–190v, and Durham, Dean and Chapter Library, MS Hunter 100; BL Harley 491; 526; 3864 and 4688; Bodl Bodley 819; Edinburgh, National Library of Scotland, MS Advocates 18.4.3, fols. 1r–122v; and Glasgow, University Library, MS Hunterian 85 (T.4.2). For discussion, see Gullick, 'Scribes' and 'Hand'.

[27] *Liber tramitis aevi Odilonis abbatis*, ed. P. Dinter, CCM 10 (Siegburg, 1980); *Liber ordinis Sancti Victoris Parisiensis*, ed. L. Jocqué and L. Milis, CCCM 61 (Turnhout, 1984).

[28] Gullick, 'Hand', pp. 15–28.

[29] Ibid., p. 25.

[30] Lanfranc, *Constitutions*, pp. 122–3.

[31] J. Gerchow, 'The Origins of the Durham *Liber Vitae*', in *The Durham* Liber Vitae *and its Context*, ed. D. W. Rollason, A. J. Piper, M. Harvey and L. Rollason (Woodbridge, 2004), pp. 45–61; L. Rollason, 'History and Codicology', in *The Durham Liber Vitae*, ed. Rollason, I, 5–42 (pp. 31–4).

there by *c.* 1099, when Cantor William added, amongst other sections, the names of the three earliest Norman bishops of Durham, including Ranulf Flambard, appointed in 1099, and a list of the monks who made up the cathedral priory (fols. 45r–45v).[32] Like William, Symeon also added to the list of Durham monks and recorded confraternity agreements such as the following entry featured on fol. 36v:

> Hec est conventio inter Dunelmensem conventum et Wilfravenum canonicum ecclesie Sancti Pauli Lundonie, ut pro singulis monachis defunctis Dunelmensis ecclesie dicat .xxx. missas, et pro eo defuncto singuli monachi dicant .xxx. missas.[33]

> [Here is the agreement between the monastery of Durham and *Wilfravenus*, Canon of the Church of Saint Paul in London. For each dead monk of the Durham church, *Wilfravenus* will say thirty masses, and upon his death, each monk will say thirty masses.]

Durham's martyrology now occupies fols. 12r–39v of the Durham Cantor's Book.[34] Like William, Symeon also added a number of obits in the margins, including individuals from within the community such as 'David the monk, subdeacon' (fol. 18v), the aforementioned 'William, cantor' (fol. 37r) and of those from without, including 'King Alexander of Scotland and his sister Matilda, Queen of England' (fol. 21r).[35] The similarities in the nature of Symeon's and William's additions to the martyrology and *Liber vitae*, suggest that both may have been working in their capacity as Durham's cantor. Since Gullick judged William to have been working in these books before Symeon, it seems likely that William led this exercise, before Symeon took over at a later date after the death of William and his own appointment as lead cantor.[36]

There is strong evidence to support the suggestion that Symeon was able to carry out Lanfranc's precept that the cantor was 'to keep count of the week's and month's mind'. This essential requirement that Symeon should be a competent student of *computus*, can be demonstrated in several surviving sources. Durham, Dean and Chapter Library, MS Hunter 100 is a collection of *computus* materials originally bound in up to four separate booklets.[37] Symeon copied sections of a *computus* guide by Robert of Losinga, which

---

[32] Gullick, 'Scribe of the Carilef Bible', pp. 68–9; and 'Hand', p. 21.

[33] *Durham Liber Vitae*, fol. 36v. On the attribution of this addition to Symeon, see Gullick, 'Scribes', p. 106, n. 53.

[34] A comprehensive list of its contents is featured in Piper, 'The Durham Cantor's Book', p. 94.

[35] Gullick, 'Hand', p. 31, noting additions on fols. 18v, 20v, 21r, 23v, 26v, 31v, 33v, 37r and 38v.

[36] Ibid., p. 21.

[37] For discussion, see Mynors, *Durham Cathedral Manuscripts*, pp. 49–50; Gameson, *Manuscripts of Early Norman England*, pp. 86–7; Rozier, 'Contextualising the Past', pp. 108–10.

now appears on fol. 19v of the current volume, lines 11–26.[38] While this provides only a small hint of Symeon's possible knowledge of the discipline, his additions within Glasgow, University Library, MS Hunterian 85 (T.4.2) are much more substantial. He annotated and rubricated the bulk of the manuscript, and added annals within the Easter tables of fols. 18r–24v.[39] Symeon's compilation of the annals in particular provides firm evidence that he understood the machinations of the adjacent tables. As such, Symeon's work within these two Durham *computus* manuals suggests that he may have had a good working knowledge of the main treatises on the calculation of time, and that he would have been able to meet Lanfranc's stipulation that the cantor should be able to organize the liturgical cycle according to the Christian calendar.

Study of the manuscripts featuring the hands of Symeon and his likely predecessor, cantor William, facilitates several conclusions on the likely nature of the cantor's role at Durham cathedral priory in the period *c.* 1090–1129. Symeon and William both worked as lead scribes and editors of Durham manuscripts from the 1090s onwards. During this time, Symeon also wrote the list of Bishop William's book-donations, perhaps as chief custodian of Durham's books. William and Symeon both added to the cumulative storehouses of commemoration housed within the Durham martyrology and *Liber vitae*, and it appears that William may have had the leading role in this process until his death, at which point Symeon took on a similar role. Finally, Symeon's work as scribe, editor and compiler of annals within the Easter tables of Glasgow, Hunterian 85 confirms that he would have been able to co-ordinate the Durham calendar.

In conclusion, there is good evidence that first William, and then Symeon after him, practised a form of cantorship which was similar to that prescribed in the copy of Lanfranc's *Decreta* known to have been present at Durham by 1096. In addition, Symeon's work as editor, corrector and rubricator of Durham manuscripts, and compiler of Bishop William's book-list before the end of the 1090s, suggests that he may have been working towards the remit of an armarius prior to the death of Cantor William. Since this William was also engaged in the production of Durham books, Symeon may have worked alongside him, perhaps informally as an assistant to the cantor, or as an armarius-cantor to William, the head liturgical-cantor.

The second half of this chapter considers the potential significance of Symeon's status as both historian and cantor to the monks of Durham. In order to do so, it is first necessary to provide a brief outline of his work as historian. The evidence suggests that Symeon's activities in this area may be placed within two distinct phases. During the first, Symeon worked to provide texts which underlined the presentation of his community and

[38] Gullick, 'Hand', p. 27.
[39] Ibid., p. 29.

its past alongside several well-known narratives of Roman, Norman and Christian history dated *c.* 1090–1115. Having completed this work, Symeon then appears to have begun a second phase of historical studies in 1120, contributing to the production of shorter chronicles and annals until his death in 1129×30.

Symeon's earliest work as a historian was directed towards the production and circulation of materials related to the foundation and development of Northumbrian Christianity and the cult of Durham's patron, St Cuthbert.[40] Bede's *Historia ecclesiastica* provided an important foundation to this process following its acquisition at some point before the production of Bishop William's book-list in 1096.[41] Although Symeon had no role in the production of the only surviving contemporary manuscript of the text (now Durham, Cathedral Library, MS B.ii.35, fols. 38–118), his access to it is demonstrated by a small addition to the margins of fol. 39v and by his regular use of the text in the composition of the *Libellus de exordio*.[42] Gullick showed that Symeon led the production of two additional volumes of Cuthbert materials, also before *c.* 1096.[43] In Bodl Digby 175, he copied Bede's prose and verse *Lives* of St Cuthbert, and the *Lives* of SS Aidan and Oswald derived from Bede's *Historia ecclesiastica*.[44] Additions in Bodl Bodley 596 (fols. 175–214), again show Symeon copying Bede's prose *Life* of Cuthbert, which in this case was also included alongside extracts from Bede's verse *Life*, and the earliest surviving copy of the anonymous *Historia de Sancto Cuthberto*.[45]

Symeon's best-known work, the *Libellus de exordio*, must be read within this drive to refine and circulate the existing narratives of Cuthbert's life, posthumous cult and community. Dated by Rollason to the period 1104–1107×15, Symeon's *Libellus* amalgamated material from Bede's hagiographical texts and *Historia ecclesiastica*, alongside various localized chronicles, administrative documents and the eleventh-century cartulary-chronicle known as the *Historia de sancto Cuthberto*, into a narration of the history of Cuthbert's community from the seventh century down to the end of the 1090s, and will be discussed in more detail below.[46]

Symeon also made a number of additions in other Durham manuscripts of historical texts, which have been dated by Gullick to Symeon's earliest years

---

[40] On the history of the community, see *Historia de sancto Cuthberto: a History of Saint Cuthbert and a record of his patrimony*, ed. T. J. South (Woodbridge, 2002); Symeon, *LdE*; and Aird, *Cuthbert and the Normans*, pp. 9–59.

[41] Browne, 'William of St Carilef's Book Donations', p. 155.

[42] Gullick, 'Hand', p. 31, item 41, recorded Symeon's addition as fol. 38v.

[43] Ibid., p. 24.

[44] Ibid., p. 24, item 2.

[45] Ibid., p. 24, item 4.

[46] Ibid., p. xlii, where Rollason dated the text based on its narration of the translation of St Cuthbert in 1104 and observation that Prior Turgot had been in office at the time of its writing. On Symeon's sources, see ibid., pp. lxviii–lxxvi.

in Durham and may also be placed within this first initial phase of historical studies. He corrected the whole of William of Jumièges's *Gesta Normannorum ducum*,[47] and made minor scribal and editorial additions to Palladius's account of the Desert Fathers (the *Historia Lausiaca*) and Eutropius's *Breviarium historie Romane*.[48] Symeon's use of these grand narratives of Roman, Norman and Christian history sheds important light on his status as historian and the aims of his writing. While Bede provided the base narrative for much of Symeon's *Libellus*, Symeon made no use of the narratives of William of Jumièges, Palladius or Eutropius, despite their apparent availability in Durham at the time of writing, and his near-contemporaneous contact with them as scribe and editor. As such, his additions within these manuscripts may provide better evidence of Symeon's activities as Durham scribe and editor than they do of his work as historian.

The second stage of Symeon's historical studies saw him involved in the study and production of historical annals. As noted by Story, it is possible to identify a marked revival of interest in the study of early medieval annals during the first half of the twelfth century at Durham.[49] Symeon copied two sets of annals. One detailed series of records of English and Continental events included across six folios of Durham, Cathedral Library, MS B.iv.22, and a series of marginal notations within the Easter tables in Glasgow, Hunterian 85. On paleographical grounds, Gullick dated the former to *c.* 1115–30 and the latter to *c.* 1125.[50] A further text, which, until recently, has been usually referred to as the Durham *Historia regum*, is widely thought to have been produced under Symeon's supervision. It consists of a lengthy chronicle of Anglo-Saxon history from the death of King Ethelbert of Kent (616), comprising some noted events from wider early medieval European history, such as the life and successors of Charlemagne, and runs to 1129. Although the original manuscript is now lost, the *Historia de regibus Anglorum et Dacorum* has been commonly attributed to Symeon, largely thanks to incipit and explicit within the earliest surviving manuscript, and due to the fact that its termination in 1129 is directly contemporaneous with Symeon's probable date of death.[51]

Neither Lanfranc's *Decreta* nor any other near-contemporary monastic customary suggests that cantors were expected to write history. Despite this, Symeon ranks alongside a number of other Anglo-Norman authors of historical texts who were also named as cantors or who appear to have

---

[47] BL Harley 491; Gullick, 'Hand', p. 27, item 18.

[48] Edinburgh, National Library of Scotland, Advocates MS 18.4.3 and BL Harley 2729, respectively. Gullick, 'Hand', pp. 24, item 1; 31, item 43.

[49] Story, 'Symeon as Annalist'.

[50] Gullick, 'Hand', pp. 29–30, items 30 and 34.

[51] CCCC 139, fols. 51v and 129v. For discussion of Symeon's role, see Symeon, *LdE*, p. xlviii; Blair, 'Some Observations on the *Historia Regum*'; and Story, 'Symeon as Annalist'.

engaged in the kinds of activities which may reflect a possible cantor's remit, including Eadmer of Canterbury, William of Malmesbury and Orderic Vitalis, not to mention the numerous other authors whose works are discussed within this volume.[52] This consistency suggests that there may be grounds for linking the two roles, even if the precise nature of cantorship and the exact circumstances through which each figure came to write history may have differed across the various religious communities in which each individual operated. Although it cannot be concluded that Symeon wrote history because he was Durham's cantor, or that he was appointed cantor because he had experience in the study and writing of history, it is nevertheless clear that some of Symeon's historical works exhibit features which appear well-suited to the cantor's role or to have been the results of it, and that some of his duties as cantor were of obvious relevance towards the study and ordering of the past.

The annals added by Symeon to Durham, Cathedral Library, MS B.iv.22, and Glasgow, University Library, MS Hunterian 85 (T.4.2), in addition to his work on the Durham *Historia de regibus Anglorum et Dacorum*, were almost certainly produced after his appointment as Durham's main cantor in *c.* 1115–20. Since there is no surviving evidence to suggest that Symeon worked to produce any other known annals before his appointment as cantor, his role in producing these texts deserves to be considered as a potential offshoot of the duties of his office. Most importantly, all three texts may be linked with the cantor's responsibility for the study and calculation of time. Symeon's annals in Hunterian 85 appear in the margins of Easter tables whose primary function was to assist in the calculation of the dating of Easter. Appearing alongside Bede's, *De temporum ratione* and letter to Witchelm on the dating of Easter, Dionysus Exiguus's letter on the dating of Easter and Abbo of Fleury's *Computus*, the codicological context of the Easter-table annals in Hunterian 85 establishes that they functioned within the process of time-reckoning.[53] Hayward's identification of eleven comparable sets of Easter-table annals from Anglo-Norman contexts, all within *computus* manuals (including those in Durham, Dean and Chapter Library, MS Hunter 100, which are closely related to those in Hunterian 85), suggests that the compilation of such annals provided a regular element of studies in this area during the

---

[52] For Eadmer, see n. 21 above. For William as cantor, see Paul Hayward's and Sigbjørn Sønnesyn's essays in this volume and R. W. Hunt, 'English Learning in the Late Twelfth Century', *Transactions of the Royal Historical Society* 4th s. 19 (1936), 19–42 (pp. 31–2); R. M. Thomson, *William of Malmesbury* (Woodbridge, 2003), pp. 6, 74. For Orderic's activities in this area, see Charles C. Rozier 'Orderic Vitalis as Librarian and Cantor of Saint-Évroult', in *Orderic Vitalis: Life, Works and Interpretations*, ed. Charles C. Rozier, D. Roach, G. E. M. Gasper and E. M. C. van Houts (Woodbridge, 2016), pp. 61–77.

[53] For details on this manuscript, see Mynors, *Durham Cathedral Manuscripts*, p. 55.

period.[54] It is therefore possible to posit a hypothesis that Symeon added annals to the margins of these Easter tables because, as cantor, he was expected to engage in the study of time-reckoning, and that he added the annals as an aid or embellishment to this process.

By adding obits, confraternity agreements and names in lists of individuals associated with Cuthbert's community within the Durham martyrology and *Liber vitae*, it is likely that William and Symeon were working towards Lanfranc's stipulation that the cantor should co-ordinate the commemoration of the dead. While the primary function of such collections was to provide a symbolic representation of the host community in prayer, it has also been argued by Rosamund McKitterick that such commemorative lists served as basic historical records, in that each list recorded the names of numerous historical individuals, many in chronological order, and as such could be used to formulate a skeletal outline of the past.[55] Elements within Symeon's *Libellus de exordio* suggest that this relationship also worked in the opposite direction, and that sections of this ostensibly historical text could be used within the commemorative memorial of the dead, in a similar way to the contents of Durham's martyrology and *Liber vitae*. One of the two earliest copies of Symeon's *Libellus*, now housed in DUL Cosin V.ii.6, was produced at Durham and corrected by Symeon in various places.[56] It included on fols. 6r–8v, two lists, which are representative of Symeon's vision of the Durham community and its origins. The first, appearing on fols. 6r–6v, presents the names of all the bishops of Lindisfarne and Durham down to Ranulf Flambard (d. 1128). The second, which is featured on fols. 7r–8v, lists members of the cathedral priory from its foundation in 1083.[57] Prior to the list of Durham monks, a short preface explained its presence in the *Libellus* manuscript in the following manner:

Hic scripta continentur nomina monachorum in hac ecclesia ad incorrupti corporis sanctissimi Cuthberti presentiam iam professorum, quorum nominibus prescriptis etiam illorum nomina qui futuris temporibus annuente Christo ibidem professionem facturi fuerint, ut scribendo adiungat, posterorum quesumus sollertia semper meminisse studeat. Pretera lectorem petimus, ut tam pro illo qui hoc opus fieri iusserat, quam pro illis qui obediendo iussis id studio et labora perfecerunt, Domino Iesu Christo preces fundere dignentur. Sed et pro omnibus quorum hic nomina

---

[54] On this topic, see P. A. Hayward, *The Winchcombe and Coventry Chronicles: Hitherto Unnoticed Witnesses to the Work of John of Worcester*, 2 vols. (Tempe, 2010), I, 20–4; and Rozier, 'Contextualising the Past'.

[55] R. McKitterick, *History and Memory in the Carolingian World* (Cambridge, 2004), pp. 156–8.

[56] Symeon, *LdE*, pp. xvii–xxii, xliv, liii; Gullick, 'Hand', p. 27, item 17; M. Gullick, 'The Two Earliest Manuscripts of the *Libellus de exordio*', in *Symeon: Historian*, ed. Rollason, pp. 106–19.

[57] Symeon, *LdE*, pp. 4–15; Piper, 'Lists', p. 161.

viderit, divine pietatis abundantiam invocare meminerit, uiuis quidem postulans sancte professionis augmentum et bone perseverantie in futuro premium, et defunctis, ut precepta venia peccatorum mereantur videre bona Domini in terra viventium.[58]

[There now follows a list of the names of the monks who presently make profession in this church in the presence of the incorrupt body of St Cuthbert, and we urge that those who come after us may have the conscientiousness to remember to add to this list the names of those who, Christ willing, will have made profession in the same place in the future. Moreover, we beg the reader that he should deign to offer prayers to our Lord Jesus Christ, both for him who ordered this work to be composed and for those who, in obedience to him, laboured and studied to bring it to completion. May he also remember to invoke the abundance of God's mercy for all those names he will see here, asking for the living that they may adhere more fully to their holy profession and may in the future receive the reward of their virtuous perseverance, and for the dead that they may receive forgiveness for their sins and be found worthy 'to see the good things of the Lord in the land of the living' (Ps. 26. 13).]

The addition of these two lists at the beginning of Symeon's *Libellus* provided a highly visible reminder of the community whose story was described in the remaining pages of the manuscript. By adding the names of the first Anglo-Norman bishops to those of the bishops of Lindisfarne and Chester-le-Street, the lists summarized the main argument of Symeon's narrative from the outset, and provided a prelude to his claims to show the Durham community as rightful inheritors of the spiritual, cultural and political legacy of the seventh-century episcopal church of Lindisfarne. Furthermore, by requesting that the lists should be updated to include subsequent generations of Durham's monks, this opening section of the *Libellus* provided a visible reminder that the interests of the community depended on the successful transmission of the foundation-narrative depicted in the text which followed.

The list of Durham monks included in the copy of the *Libellus de exordio*, now contained in DUL Cosin V.ii.6, is almost identical to the near-contemporaneous additions which recorded the names of Durham monks in the Durham *Liber vitae*.[59] As noted above, these additions were begun first by Cantor William and undertaken later by Symeon, and may have been added as part of their duties as Durham's cantors. There is no precise indication of when the list of Durham monks was added to the Cosin manuscript of the *Libellus*. Although Piper judged it broadly contemporaneous with the completion of the main text, the absence of the list within BL Cotton Faustina

[58] Symeon, *LdE*, pp. 4–7.
[59] For extensive comparison of the two, see Piper, 'Lists'.

A.v suggests that it was not an original feature of the project.[60] The list, therefore, may have been a slightly later addition, which was inspired by the assimilation of the Durham *Liber vitae* into the project of presenting Durham's historical identity, and by Cantor William and/or Symeon's involvement in this. Like Symeon's *Libellus*, the resurrected *Liber vitae* presented the Durham monks as direct continuators of Northumbria's Anglo-Saxon church, thereby providing a textual representation of what they believed to be their historical identity. By simply adding to the lists of Anglo-Saxon monks to include those of Durham's cathedral priory, William, Symeon and the successors who continued their additions, provided the simplest representation of these claims.

Consideration of how DUL Cosin V.ii.6 and the *Liber vitae* were to be used sheds further light on the relationship between the two books. The late sixteenth century text known as the *Rites of Durham* provided a detailed description of the monastic church and cathedral priory before the reformation. Its anonymous author observed that the *Liber vitae* was kept on the high altar of Durham Cathedral, and described its intended purposes as follows:

> There did lye on the high altar an excellent fine booke verye richly covered with gold and silver conteininge the names of all the benefactors towards St Cuthberts church from the first originall foundation thereof, the verye letters for the most part beinge all gilded as is apparent in the said booke till this day the layinge that booke on the high altar did show how highly they esteemed their founders and benefactors, and the dayly and quotidian remembrance they had of them in the time of masse and divine service did argue not onely their gratitude, but also a most divine and charitable affection to the soules of theire benefactors as well dead as livinge, which booke is as yett extant declaringe the said use in the inscription thereof.[61]

It is entirely plausible that the *Liber vitae* was kept on the high altar of Durham Cathedral during both William and Symeon's tenures as cantor. It is not possible to know whether the list in the Cosin *Libellus* was used or kept in a similar way within the cathedral church. However, additions to the list of monks on fols.7r–8v suggest that the original instructions were followed, and that the book was updated down to at least the mid 1160s.[62] Given its evident importance in the cultivation of Durham's historical identity at that time, it is possible that the Cosin *Libellus* may also have served a symbolic and ceremonial role similar to that of the *Liber vitae*. It was written in a large neat

---

[60] Ibid., pp. 172–3.

[61] *Rites of Durham: being a description or brief declaration of all the ancient monuments, rites and customs belonging or being within the monastical church of Durham before the suppression, written 1593*, ed. J. T. Fowler, Surtees Society 107 (London, 1902), pp. 16–17 (spelling unaltered from original).

[62] Piper, 'Lists', pp. 174–5.

hand, with large coloured capitals introducing subdivisions within the text.[63] More importantly, a number of the numerals which appear in the main text were given an interlinear gloss, through which the figures in the numerals were then spelled.[64] This provides strong evidence that at least some of the text was being read aloud, and that like the *Liber vitae*, DUL Cosin V.ii.6 may have had a performative and ceremonial function.

Reviewing Symeon of Durham's likely activities as cantor and historian at Durham sheds important light on some of the main themes discussed in this book. Analysing the well-established corpus of Symeon's surviving manuscript additions has given flesh to the possible nature of the cantor's role at Durham during the period *c.* 1090–1130. It has been argued here that much of Symeon's work matches Lanfranc's description of the ideal cantor. However, the fact that much of this work predates the death of Cantor William (*c.* 1115–20) suggests that at least during William's and Symeon's tenures, Durham's cantors might be regarded as working within a team of scribes and administrators who were together responsible for the production, upkeep and, in some cases, including the *Libellus de exordio*, the composition of new texts.[65] His surviving manuscript additions suggest that Symeon was required to fulfil a broad range of scribal duties. He wrote out two grants from King Edgar of Scotland to the Durham monks in 1097 and 1107 (Durham Cathedral, Dean and Chapter Muniments Misc. ch. 556 and 558), copied two precepts from bishop Ranulf Flambard between 1122 and 1128 (Durham Cathedral, Dean and Chapter Muniments 2.1 Pont. 10 and Pont. 11) and two charters from Ranulf to Durham's monks in 1128 (Durham Cathedral, Dean and Chapter Muniments 2.1 Pont. 1 and Pont. 2).[66] This, in addition to his scribal and editorial work in around twenty Durham manuscripts featuring a range of texts including patristic and medieval theology and exegesis, computistics and history, suggests that Symeon seems to have been required to work on whatever was required whenever it was required.

Symeon's status as one of Durham's intellectual elite suggests that he may only have worked as a historian and cantor because his skills in reading, copying and original writing rendered him one of the few individuals qualified to meet the demands of the two roles. This does not, however, negate the importance of studying the two roles in tandem. Symeon's engagement with the cantor's tasks for the duration of his time at Durham provides an important reminder that his works were written within and for the monastic context. Study of Symeon's additions to Durham's *Liber vitae*, martyrology, *computus* guides and confraternity agreements highlight the various ways in which Durham's past was manifested in the daily life of the monastery.

---

[63] Examples of these are numerous, such as those on fols. 12r–13r, 14v, 15r, etc.

[64] See *Symeon: Historian*, plate 51, which shows the example on fol. 26v.

[65] Gullick, 'Hand', pp. 18–22; Rollason, 'Erasures', pp. 140–1.

[66] Gullick, 'Hand', pp. 26, 30.

Comparison with Symeon's historical texts suggests that as both cantor and historian, his work contributed to the formation and promotion of Durham's historically informed monastic institutional identity. As has been argued by W. M. Aird, the possession of Cuthbert's body and the promotion of his cult provided the essential 'corporeal title deed' to these inheritances through various manifestations of the community.[67] By emphasizing what Symeon described as the 'origin and progress' of Cuthbert's cult and community through the circulation of Cuthbert's *vita*, the assimilation of the *Liber vitae* and the production of his *Libellus de exordio*, Symeon and his contemporaries were able to formulate a substantive claim to the entire historical, cultural, intellectual, devotional and financial inheritance of all the previous embodiments of Cuthbert's community, dating back to its foundation in 635. Symeon himself claimed this in the opening preface to his text, which stated the following:

> Licet enim causis existentibus alibi quam ab ipso sit locata, nichilominus tamen stabilitate fidei, dignitate quoque et auctoritate cathedre pontificalis, statu etiam monachice habitationis que ab ipso rege et Aldano pontifice ibidem instituta est, ipsa eadem ecclesia Deo auctore fundata permanet.[68]

> [Although for various reasons this church no longer stands in the place where Oswald founded it, nevertheless by virtue of the consistency of its faith, the dignity and authority of its episcopal throne, and the status of the dwelling-place of the *monks* established there by himself and Bishop Aidan, it is still very much the same church founded by God's command.]

To prove this interpretation of Durham's origins, Symeon was required to use all of his skills in the judicious selection and presentation of historical evidence, and in adapting the sensibilities of his Anglo-Saxon predecessors, including Bede and the anonymous author of the *Historia de sancto Cuthberto*. In order to promote and consolidate this interpretation of the Anglo-Saxon past and the Anglo-Norman present, Symeon and his contemporaries drew on the deep cultural resonances of history and combined them with the symbolism of a commemorative liturgy, in order to provide a consistent presentation of who the Durham monks thought they were, where they had come from and what they hoped to be in the future. As historian, assistant to Cantor William and later cantor in his own right, Symeon's involvement in this process, and its successes, were assured.

---

[67] Aird, *Cuthbert and the Normans*, pp. 34–5.
[68] Symeon, *LdE*, pp. 16–17.

11

Reshaping History in
the Cult of Æbbe of Coldingham

Lauren L. Whitnah

In the early 680s a member of the monastic community at Coldingham named Adomnan had a vision. Because 'the cells that were built for praying and for reading have become haunts of feasting, drinking, gossip and other delights',[1] God's judgment would fall upon the double monastery and it would be destroyed. Coldingham's abbess, Æbbe, would be spared from these dire consequences, and she was assured that the destruction of the monastery would happen after her death. Events transpired as Adomnan had predicted; shortly after Æbbe's death, the monastery burnt to the ground. When he recounted the incident in his *Historia ecclesiastica*, Bede observed darkly that, although the fire seemed like an accident, 'tamen a malitia inhabitantium in eo, et praecipue illorum qui maiores esse videbantur, contigisse omnes qui novere facillime potuerunt advertere' ('all who knew the truth were easily able to judge that it happened because of the wickedness of those who dwelt there and especially of those who were supposed to be its leaders').[2]

This is hardly an endorsement of the holiness of the monastery's abbess. Yet in the twelfth century, Æbbe was the focus of a significant cult. Women and men, young and old, trekked up the steep paths along the North Sea, north of the river Tweed, and spent Saturday nights in prayer at an oratory on the site of her monastery, waiting for visions and healing through their devotion to the saint.[3] Æbbe often responded to their veneration, loosing knots in tongues tied by the devil,[4] opening clenched and crippled hands,[5] and miraculously removing a goose bone from the throat of a choking man.[6] In response, cripples left their crutches on the site 'as a memorial of this great miracle'.[7] The saint's reputation spread; at the end of the twelfth century, a

---

[1] *HE* IV.xxv, pp. 424–5: 'domunculae, que ad orandum vel legendum factae erant, nunc in comesationum, potationum, fabulationum et ceterarum sunt inlecebrarum cubilia conuersae.'

[2] Ibid., pp. 420–1.

[3] *The Miracles of Saint Æbbe of Coldingham and Saint Margaret of Scotland*, ed. and trans. R. Bartlett (Oxford, 2003), p. 38.

[4] Ibid., p. 50.

[5] Ibid., p. 52.

[6] Ibid., pp. 34–6.

[7] Ibid, pp. 40–1: 'ob tante virtutis memoriam.'

local monk at Coldingham priory, a dependency of Durham, observed that 'crowds throng here from nearby and from distant regions' for miraculous cures.[8] So how did an abbess with no particular reputation for holiness in the seventh and eight centuries – indeed, quite the opposite – become a popular saint in the twelfth century? How did worshippers and writers reshape history for the purposes of forming and promoting this cult?

There is virtually no evidence for an Anglo-Saxon cult, although Æbbe is well-attested in early historical sources. Stephen of Ripon describes her as *sanctissima* and *sapientissima* in his *Vita S. Wilfridi*, where he says that she interceded with the king for the rights of the embattled bishop Wilfrid.[9] Although Æbbe is simply mentioned as the head of the monastery of Coldingham in the anonymous *Vita S. Cuthberti*, she plays a larger role in Bede's rewritten *vita* of the bishop of Lindisfarne. Bede elaborates on the story related by the anonymous author, providing more detail both about Æbbe's biography and about her holy virtues, changes which are typical in Bede's transformation of the anonymous *vita*. He says that Æbbe, the 'mother of the handmaidens of Christ' was honoured both for her religious practice and for her status as the *soror uterina* of Oswiu, king of Northumbria.[10] She was not only the sister of kings and the friend of bishops, but the teacher of other monastics as well. Bede first mentions Æbbe in the *Historia ecclesiastica* as the mentor of Æthelthryth, the queen who entered monastic life under Æbbe's supervision at Coldingham and then went on to an illustrious and saintly abbatial career of her own at Ely.[11] However, the story of the prophecy and destruction of Coldingham is the most extensive discussion of Æbbe in the *Historia ecclesiastica*.

It is not surprising that an abbess whose monastery was destroyed as punishment for sin would be slow in developing a reputation for sanctity, even though she was credited with some virtues in early sources. Æbbe's name does not appear in the surviving litanies of Anglo-Saxon saints, in the resting-place lists or in calendars.[12] After the eighth century, the next mention of Æbbe comes in the history of Durham by its cantor, Symeon, who

---

[8] Ibid., pp. 42–3: 'Ad hunc quoque locum … plures tam de vicinis quam remotis aliarum regionum partibus, catervatim conveniunt.'

[9] Stephen of Ripon, *The Life of Bishop Wilfrid*, ed. and trans. B. Colgrave (Cambridge, 1927), p. 39.

[10] Bede, *Vita S. Cuthberti*, in *Two Lives of Saint Cuthbert*, ed. and trans. B. Colgrave (Cambridge, 1940), p. 188–9: 'erat sanctimonialis femina et mater ancillarum Christi nomine Ebbe, regens monasterium quod situm est in loco quem Coludi urbem nuncupant, religione pariter et nobilitate cunctis honorabilis.'

[11] *HE* IV.xix, p. 392.

[12] M. Lapidge, *Anglo-Saxon Litanies of the Saints*, HBS 106 (Woodbridge, 1991); R. Rushforth, *Saints in English Kalendars Before AD 1100*, HBS 117 (Woodbridge, 2010); D. Rollason, 'Lists of Saints' Resting-Places in Anglo-Saxon England', *ASE* 7 (1978), 61–93.

includes her relics in a list of the bones of saints brought to Durham in the early eleventh century.[13] However, Symeon simply includes Æbbe's name in a longer list and provides no direct evidence for any particular veneration or celebration.

Despite the paucity of evidence for veneration for nearly four centuries after Æbbe's death, the late twelfth century saw the rapid development of a cult at Coldingham and the production of liturgical and literary texts to accompany it. Some of the surviving liturgical calendars from Durham and Coldingham include Æbbe's name for 25 August or 2 November.[14] It is unclear which feast was the primary one. Bartlett draws attention to 2 November as a feast on the eve of the nativity of John the Baptist, mentioned in the miracle collection; he suggests that the feast on 25 August was a secondary and later development.[15] Bartlett's hypothesis is complicated, however, by the appearance of Æbbe's feast on 25 August in the Winchcombe calendar, copied in the middle of the twelfth century. Bartlett suggests that the Æbbe in this southern calendar should be identified with a different person altogether, but there is northern evidence for the feast on 25 August as well. Æbbe's name, like the names of many other Anglo-Saxon saints, was inserted in the margin of the martyrology in the manuscript known as the 'Durham Cantor's Book' (Durham, Chapter Library, MS B.IV.24) in the late twelfth or early thirteenth century for 25 August: 'item festivitas sancte Ebbe VIRGINIS'.[16] Her name does not appear in the martyrology in November. Although the origins of the

---

[13] *LdE* III.vii, p. 164. Æbbe's relics are included in Durham relic lists in Cambridge, Trinity College, MS O.3.55 (Durham, s. xii); CUL Ff.1.27 (Durham, s. xii); Bodl Digby 41 (Durham, s. xii); York, Minster Library MS XVI.I.12 (Durham, s. xiv). On relic lists, see I. G. Thomas, 'The Cult of Saints' Relics in Medieval England' (unpublished Ph.D. dissertation, University of London, 1974).

[14] The feast on 25 August is found in Cambridge, Jesus College MS Q.B.6 (23) (Durham, s. xii, although Æbbe's name seems to be inserted in an early thirteenth-century hand); BL Cotton Tiberius E.iv (Winchcombe, s. xii); BL Harley 4747 (Coldingham?, s. xiii); BL Harley 1804 (Durham, s. xv). Since Harley 4747 is missing the folio for November, it is not clear if it once included both feasts. Durham, Chapter Library, End Paper Frag. 17 (Durham, s. xiii), which was apparently unknown to Bartlett, includes Æbbe's name for 2 November, not for 25 August. Three feasts for Æbbe are noted in the 'Coldingham Breviary', BL Harley 4664 (Coldingham, s.xiii): 22 June, 25 August and 2 November. The 22 June feast, the dedication of the altar of Æbbe in the church at Coldingham ('dedicatio altaris sancte Ebbe in Coldisburh'), is attested nowhere else that I have found.

[15] *Miracles of Æbbe*, pp. xxvi–xxvii.

[16] On MS B.IV.24, generally, see A. J. Piper, 'The Durham Cantor's Book (Durham, Dean and Chapter Library, MS B.IV.24)', in *Anglo-Norman Durham, 1093–1193*, ed. D. Rollason et al. (Woodbridge, 1994), pp. 79–92; M. Gullick, 'The Scribes of the Durham Cantor's Book (Durham, Dean and Chapter Library, MS B.IV.24) and the Durham Martyrology Scribe' in *Anglo-Norman Durham*, pp. 93–109. For the additions to the martyrology specifically, see A. J. Piper, 'The Early Lists and Obits of the Durham Monks', in *Symeon of Durham: Historian of Durham and the North*, ed.

November feast are mentioned in the *miracula*, it seems that the August feast was celebrated in both Coldingham and Durham as well.

Not only is there calendrical evidence for the celebration of Æbbe's feast, but a full night office provides additional information about the liturgical celebration of the saint. Although it only survives in a mid thirteenth century manuscript, the Coldingham Breviary,[17] the evidence discussed below will suggest that the office was almost certainly compiled before the *Vita et miracula S. Ebbe virginis* was written at the end of the twelfth century. The office for Æbbe contains antiphons and responsories for Vespers, Matins, consisting of three nocturns, and Lauds, as well as eight prose lessons. Although the Coldingham Breviary contains musical notation elsewhere, Æbbe's office is not neumed. The office follows the general outline of Æbbe's life and death and the burning of the monastery as described by Bede, adding a brief mention of the first translation of the relics in the final reading.

The main surviving narrative source for the cult of Æbbe is a *Vita et miracula* dateable to *c.* 1190.[18] The text has four distinct sections: a preface, an account of the saint's life, a description of two translations of the relics and a collection of forty-three miracles which occurred at several shrines.[19] In the sole surviving manuscript, a fourteenth-century Durham compilation of saints' *vitae*,[20] the explicit says the text is taken 'ex compilatione Reginaldi Dun[e]lm[ensis]' monachi'.[21] Reginald of Durham, a prolific hagiographer, probably did not compose the text as it survives, but he may have been involved at an earlier stage of its production.[22] His hagiographical output includes *vitae*

D. Rollason (Stamford, 1998), pp. 161–201. See also Rozier's chapter on Symeon in this volume.

[17] BL Harley 4664, fols. 261r–263r.

[18] The author describes the vision that inspired the rebuilding of the oratory as occurring in 1188: 'anno ab incarnatione Domini millesimo centesimo octogesimo octauo, qui est annus deposicionis sancte Ebbe quingentesimus sextus', confirming the date of Æbbe's death as 683. He seems to be writing very shortly after the reconstruction of the oratory, referring to miracles at the oratory as occurring *nuper*. *Miracles of Saint Æbbe*, p. 30. Also, as Bartlett points out (p. xxii), the first miracle benefited the daughter of a local noble who appears in charters of Coldingham and St Andrews between 1160 and 1203.

[19] Several sites in the immediate vicinity of Coldingham were linked with Æbbe's cult: two *fontes* (a seasonal one at the top of the headland and a constant one at the bottom), the priory church of St Mary in Coldingham (about two miles from the headland) and the oratory constructed on the headland first by a layman and then rebuilt by monks from Coldingham shortly after 1188.

[20] Bodl Fairfax 6, fols. 146r–173v.

[21] The explicit dates from the sixteenth century. See A. I. Doyle, 'William Claxton and the Durham Chroniclers', in *Books and Collectors, 1200–1700: Essays Presented to Andrew Watson*, ed. J. P. Carley and C. G. C. Tite (London, 1997), pp. 335–55.

[22] For the evidence for and against Reginald's authorship of the *Vita et miracula Ebbe*, see V. Tudor, 'Reginald's Life of St Oswald', in *Oswald: Northumbrian King*

of the Anglo-Saxon king Oswald – Æbbe's half brother – and the twelfth-century hermit Godric of Finchale, as well as an extensive collection of miracles that occurred at the shrine of Cuthbert at Durham. Whether or not Reginald was responsible for the *Vita et miracula S. Ebbe virginis,* it is clear that the author had spent time in the monastic community of Coldingham's mother house of Durham and was writing for his brethren there. The author declares that the proximity of his readers to the incorrupt body of Cuthbert gives them protection, strength and delight; he says that he longs to be there with them, but since he cannot be, he seeks the patronage of Æbbe instead.[23] The author does not say who, if anyone specifically, commissioned the work; the *vos* of the preface are neither precisely named nor described in more detail.

Unfortunately, the sources employed by the author do not bring us closer to identifying him. He seems to have used sources that were widely available as well as some that were highly local and specialized, both written and oral. Like the author of the office, the author of the *Vita et miracula* certainly had access to – and quoted extensively from – Bede's *Vita S. Cuthberti* and *Historia ecclesiastica.* He mentions several other sources, including a 'liber ... de conuersatione et operibus eiusdem uirginis' ['a book ... about the virgin's life and works'], which has not been identified.[24] The author is ostensibly sceptical of the reliability of this *liber,* saying that 'quam multa uulgo tantum dictante uidebantur inserta; a nonnullis nostrorum ferebantur incerta, quia nulla maiorum auctoritate suffulta' ('a great deal seemed to be included only on the basis of popular report and was said by [some] of our people to be uncertain, because [it was] not supported by the authority of our predecessors').[25] Bede's account of the abbess would hardly have qualified as *vulgo dictante* and it certainly would not have been *incerta,* as the author describes the *liber.* In addition, the author mentions a *libellus* about Æbbe's first translation; this also has not been identified and seems likely not to have survived. His interest in Æbbe's family tree suggests that the author had genealogical sources beyond what appears in Bede, although it is uncertain precisely which texts he was able to access.[26] As we shall see, he knew the office and used it extensively.

---

to European Saint, ed. C. Stancliffe and E. Cambridge (Stamford, 1995), pp. 178–94 (p. 178 n. 4); V. Tudor, 'The Cult of St Cuthbert in the Twelfth Century: The Evidence of Reginald of Durham', in *Cuthbert, His Cult and His Community to AD 1200,* ed. G. Bonner et al. (Woodbridge, 1989), pp. 447–67 (p. 448); *Miracles of Saint Æbbe,* pp. xvii–xx; M. Coombe, 'Reginald of Durham's Latin *Life* of St Godric of Finchale: A Study' (unpublished D.Phil. dissertation, University of Oxford, 2011), pp. 172–203.

[23] *Miracles of Saint Æbbe,* p. 2.

[24] Ibid., pp. 2–3.

[25] Ibid., with modifications to Bartlett's translation signaled with square brackets.

[26] See ibid., p. xix.

The author of the *Vita et miracula* was well acquainted with the office and used it repeatedly in his text, sometimes quoting it directly, sometimes augmenting its language and sometimes borrowing its metaphors. Direct quotations occur periodically. For instance, the third antiphon verse for the first nocturn states:

> Claris exorta natalibus
> Mundum fide et formam moribus
> Et sexum vicit virtutibus.[27]

> [Born from illustrious origins, she conquered the world by faith, and beauty by character, and her sex by virtues.]

The author includes this verse completely in his biography of Æbbe, adding only a postpositive *siquidem*.[28] More frequently, the author of the *Vita et miracula* quotes from the office and then elaborates on the quotation, adding specific details or some interpretation. The final verse of the antiphon, for example, reads:

> Puellis matrem instancia
> Et viris patrem constancia
> Quam mira se dedit gratia.[29]

> [By wonderful grace he gave her the earnestness of a mother for the girls and the constancy of a father for the men.]

The author of the *Vita et miracula* both clarifies the virtues and adds specificity: the grace is one of 'wonderful powers of discretion', the frequency is of 'exhortation' and the constancy is 'of her mind'.[30] On one occasion, the author of the *vita* explicitly acknowledges that he is quoting another source. He observes, 'Sicut enim, ut ait quidam, vitis uvam profert in vinea aut florem ex se producunt lilia, sic ex nobili regum prosapia, felix Ebbam felicem protulit Britannia' ('Just as, as someone says, the vine brings forth grapes in the vineyard or lilies produce flowers from themselves, in the same way happy Britain brought forth happy Æbbe from a noble line of kings').[31] This is almost a direct quotation of the first antiphon for the first nocturn:

---

[27] BL Harley 4664, fol. 261v. The office is printed in *Historiae Rhythmicae*, ed. G. M. Dreves, AH 13 (Leipzig, 1892), pp. 114–17, but the shortcomings of this edition have made it preferable to quote from the manuscript.

[28] *Miracles of Saint Æbbe*, p. 6: 'Claris siquidem exorta natalibus mundum fide et formam moribus et sexum vicit virtutibus'.

[29] BL Harley 4664, fol. 261v.

[30] *Miracles of Saint Æbbe*, pp. 10–11: 'que se admirabili discrecionis gracia et puellis matrem exhortacionis instancia, et uiris patrem exhibuit animi constancia.'

[31] Ibid., pp. 4–5.

> Sicut florem vitis in vinea
> Sic Ebbam in stirpe regia
> Felix produxit Britannia.[32]

[As a vine in a vineyard produces a flower, so blessed Britain brought forth Æbbe from a royal lineage.]

However, it is also an expansion of the antiphon: the author adds the lilies, uses *felicem* to modify Æbbe and includes the *nobili regum prosapia*.

Even in instances where the *vita* does not quote directly from the office, the author of the *vita* still seems to have been using the office as a source for his work. For instance, where the final versicle of the second nocturn says, 'Relinquens terre corpusculum / et inferens celo spiritum' ('Leaving her body to the earth and rendering her spirit to heaven),[33] the author of the *vita* says 'et beatum celo spiritum, relicta terre sancti corporis gleba, intulerit' ('and [she] rendered her blessed spirit to heaven, leaving the clay of her holy body to the earth').[34] There are shared, albeit general, metaphors as well, such as when both the office and the *vita* transition from describing monastic life at Coldingham to recounting its destruction by a reference to the serpent in paradise.[35]

Likewise, though the prose readings of the office are primarily compilations of direct quotations and summaries of Bede's *Vita S. Cuthberti* and *Historia ecclesiastica*, the few instances of similarities between the office readings and the *Vita et miracula* also seem to reflect a quotation of the office by the *vita*. Thus, when the office reading states that Æbbe's monastery was 'edificiorum sublimitate preclarus, nunc in solitudinis planitiem conuersus' ('resplendent with tall buildings, now turned into a level wasteland'),[36] the author of the *vita* quotes, 'Erat olim mons ille edificiorum sublimitate preclarus postea a malicia habitancium in eo in solitudinis planitiem conuersus' ('That headland was once resplendent with tall buildings but afterwards was turned into a level wasteland by the wickedness of those who lived there').[37] More rarely, the similarities may reflect quotation of a shared source. For example, both the office readings and the *Vita et miracula* quote and expand upon Bede's *Vita S. Cuthberti*.[38] Finally, the office readings do not describe any of the

---

[32] BL Harley 4664, fol. 261v.

[33] BL Harley 4664, fol. 263r.

[34] *Miracles of Saint Æbbe*, pp. 10–11.

[35] BL Harley 4664, fol. 262r; *Miracles of Saint Æbbe*, p. 12.

[36] BL Harley 4664, fol. 262v.

[37] *Miracles of Saint Æbbe*, pp. 8–9.

[38] Bede declares that 'Nanque erat soror uterina regis Oswiu', while the first office reading states, 'Erat enim soror uterina noblissimi regis Oswiu qui sanctissimo regi et martyri Oswaldo successit in regnum', and the *Vita et miracula S. Ebbe* declares that 'Erat enim regis Oswyu soror uterina, Egfridi Deo devoti regis amita'. *Two Lives of Cuthbert*, p. 188; BL Harley 4664, fol. 261v; *Miracles of Saint Æbbe*, p. 4.

forty-three miracles that occur at the end of the *Vita et miracula*. The final reading declares that miracles occurred in the church after the relics were translated there in general terms, but no miracles are described.

It therefore seems clear that the entire office – antiphons, responsories, versicles and readings – was composed before the *Vita et miracula*. Rather than the narrative text operating as the foundation source for the office, the office is a critical source for the *vita*. Bartlett has suggested that Æbbe's cult conforms to a model of cult development articulated by Pierre-André Sigal: cults generally begin with lay devotion and are then appropriated by clerical communities.[39] However, the relationship between the office and the *Vita et miracula* complicates this model. Since the office was composed before the *vita* (and thus almost certainly before the rise of popular interest in Æbbe's cult prompted by the construction of an oratory in 1188), we can see evidence for monastic veneration before we can see direct evidence for lay devotion. Although 'spontaneous popular piety' may play a role in the development of cults, and although local tradition and lay veneration were important in Æbbe's cult, the monks who composed the office for Æbbe's feast were not merely responding to lay pressure or co-opting an existing cult. By composing the office, they were in fact producing a cult with their liturgy.

The author of the *Vita et miracula* not only used material from Bede, from written accounts of the translation, and from the office, but he seems to incorporate local oral knowledge about the saint as well. The author says in several places that he is reporting contemporary miracles described for him by their beneficiaries.[40] His remark that some components of the *liber* were *vulgo dictante* suggests some kind of ongoing local oral tradition. He also tells a story about Æbbe which he describes as 'vulgo tritum est et a maioribus traditum' ('a familiar story among the populace and has been handed down by our forefathers').[41] In that anecdote, Æbbe was pursued by a Scottish king, and when she fled to the rocky promontory, the sea rose up to protect her and cut her off from her pursuer.[42] The author is repeating a local oral tradition with detail and attention to his sources.

---

[39] *Miracles of Saint Æbbe*, p. xxii; Pierre-André Sigal, *L'homme et le miracle dans la France médiévale (XIe–XIIe siècle)* (Paris, 1985), pp. 167–76.

[40] *Miracles of Saint Æbbe*, pp. 38, 54, 56.

[41] Ibid., pp. 6–7. The event is mentioned in the office as well: BL Harley 4664, fol. 261v.

[42] The *Liber Eliensis*, probably composed in the 1170s, contains a remarkably similar story: Æthelthryth flees her husband, king Ecgfrith, and retreats to 'Coldeburcheschevet, quod Latine caput Coldeburci dicitur'. The sea rises, effectively shielding Æthelthryth and the nuns from Ecgfrith. There is an appeal to local knowledge in the *Liber Eliensis* as well: 'Hoc de scriptis Bede non cepimus, sed quicumque locum Coludi norunt cum assertione huius rei testes existunt'. It seems clear that this story is a local one, attributed to the holy women—whether Æbbe or Æthelthryth—who could leave imprints in the physical topography of the site itself. There is no evidence that the *Liber Eliensis* was known to the Coldingham

From evidence in the office and the *vita*, it is possible to reconstruct the major events in the twelfth-century development of the cult. Æbbe seems to have died in 683, and the monastery burned down shortly thereafter. The author of the *vita* says that 'post multa temporum curricula' ('after a long passage of time'), shepherds discovered Æbbe's tomb on the rocky promontory. They carried her wooden coffin into the church at Coldingham where it was examined by the *fratres* there. The land and church at Coldingham had been granted to the monks of Durham by Edgar, king of Scots (d. 1107), and the priory of Coldingham was established some time before 1139, when *monachi* are first mentioned in a charter,[43] so the finding of the relics by the shepherds and their subsequent internment in the church probably took place around or after 1139. This first translation is mentioned in the final reading for the office as well.[44] Sometime thereafter, the *maiores* of the community wrote a *libellus* about it.[45]

A second translation occurred in the church after the 'venerable abbess' spoke in a vision to 'a certain older monk, who is still alive' and encouraged him to undertake another translation.[46] Since the author of the *Vita et miracula* took care to note that the monk was still alive when he was writing, it is unlikely that the second translation, described in detail in the *Vita et miracula*, could have occurred much before 1160. The office was probably composed between the first and second translations – while the first is mentioned in the office, the second is not. From the extensive description in the *vita*, the second translation seems to have been a major event for the community. In 1188, a simple-minded peasant named Henry had a vision of Æbbe and built an oratory on the headland approximately two miles from Coldingham itself.[47]

hagiographer; rather, both authors seem to be retelling a popular oral story about a holy woman and the topography of that particular landscape. *Liber Eliensis* I.xi, ed. E. O. Blake, Camden 3rd ser. 92 (London, 1962), pp. 27–28.

[43] See J. Donnelly, 'The Lands of Coldingham Priory 1100–1300' (unpublished Ph.D. dissertation, Cambridge University, 1989), pp. 250–4, and *Miracles of Saint Æbbe*, p. xv.

[44] BL Harley 4664, fols. 262v–263r: 'Transiit autem beata Ebba temporibus Ægfridi regis, cuius mausoleum post multa tempora a pastoribus inuentum est, et a fidelibus in ecclesiam sancte Marie de Coldingham translatum et ad australem partem altaris positum.'

[45] *Miracles of Saint Æbbe*, p. 22: 'Et hec quidem quasi omnibus manifesta et veritati consentanea in libello maiores redegerant.'

[46] *Miracles of Saint Æbbe*, pp. 22–5.

[47] For the site itself, see L. Alcock et al., 'Reconnaissance Excavations on Early Historic Fortifications and Other Royal Sites in Scotland, 1974–84: 1, Excavations near St Abb's Head, Berwickshire, 1980', *Proceedings of the Society of Antiquaries of Scotland* 116 (1986), 255–79; S. Stronach, 'The Anglian Monastery and Medieval Priory of Coldingham: *Urbs Coludi* Revisited', *Proceedings of the Society of Antiquaries of Scotland* 135 (2005), 395–422; C. Ferguson, 'Bernicia and the Sea: Coastal Communities and Landscape in North-East England and South-East Scotland, c. 450–850 AD' (unpublished D.Phil dissertation, University of Oxford, 2010).

The oratory was the site of miraculous cures, and the monks of Coldingham then tore Henry's oratory down and built a new one in the same place. 'Cuius amplitudo prioris angustias dilataret et divinis obsequiis commodior' ('Its proportions were larger than the cramped spaces of the earlier one and more suitable for divine service'), according to the author of the *Vita et miracula*, implying that some of the Coldingham monks were praying the office at the oratory as well as at the priory.[48] Neither oratory is mentioned in the office, again suggesting it was composed before the construction of the first oratory in 1188. Shortly after the rebuilding of the oratory, the author of the *Vita et miracula* composed his text. In a fairly brief period, a cult with a full complement of liturgical materials, popular devotion and sophisticated literary output had emerged, a cult which was appealing to monks, the 'simple-minded peasant' and the many young women who were healed at the shrines.[49]

To return to the apparent conundrum with which we started: how does an abbess with no particular reputation for holiness in the eighth century become a major local saint in the twelfth century, inspiring this sort of liturgical production and popular devotion? The authors of the office and of the *vita* reworked the history they had been given (both as it was written, particularly in Bede, and as it was passed down orally) to fashion and refashion the cult. Both the creator of the office and the author of the *Vita et miracula* needed to account for the blatant fact of the monastery's destruction and make that event consonant with Æbbe's holiness. Bede, the main source of history available to the twelfth-century authors, was explicit about the didactic purpose of the incident: the monastery's destruction was to provide his readers with a salutary warning against sin generally. He included the story, Bede said, 'so as to warn the reader about the workings of the Lord': the wrath of God that could result in either 'temporal loss' or 'everlasting perdition' or both.[50] In this case, the divine wrath is stirred up because

> Nam et domunculae, quae ad orandum uel legendum factae errant, nunc in comesationum, potationum, fabulationum et ceterarum sunt inlecebrarum cubilia conuersae; uirgines quoque Deo dictae, contemta reuerentia suae professionis, quotiescumque uacant, texendis subtilioribus indumentis

---

[48] *Miracles of Saint Æbbe*, pp. 30–1.

[49] Bartlett has drawn attention to the fact that the cult was 'marked by the unusual prominence of pilgrims who were female, poor and young'. *Miracles of Saint Æbbe*, p. xxv.

[50] *HE* IV.xxv, pp. 426–7: 'Hec ideo nostre historie inserenda credidimus, ut admoneremus lectorem operum Domini, quam terribilis in consiliis super filios hominum; ne forte nos tempore aliquot carnis inlecebris servientes, minusque Dei iudicum formidantes, repentina eius ira corripiat, et vel temporalibus damnis iuste seviens affligat vel ad perpetuam perditionem districtius examinans tollat.'

operam dant, quibus aut se ipsas ad uicem sponsarum in periculum sui status adornent, aut externorum sibi uirorum amicitiam conparent.[51]

[And the cells that were built for praying and for reading have become haunts of feasting, drinking, gossip, and other delights; even the virgins who are dedicated to God put aside all respect for their profession and, whenever they have leisure, spend their time weaving elaborate garments with which to adorn themselves as if they were brides, so imperiling their virginity, or else to make friends with strange men.]

In part, as Hollis observed, the sin is 'monastic women's involvement with secular society'.[52] However, there is also a liturgical failure here: both men and women are failing to keep the appropriate vigils. Bede draws a contrast between the holy man Adomnan, who has the vision of future destruction while praying the middle of the night, and the somnolent monks and nuns who neglect their vigils.[53] Although Bede hints at sexual misconduct between the men and women of the community, it is worth noting that he does not explicitly list it in his catalogue of offences. Feasting and inadequate liturgical discipline seem to be greater concerns.

Bede's history was shaped and reshaped by the authors who wrote about Coldingham in the twelfth century. Symeon of Durham revises Bede's interpretation of the story by emphasizing that the interaction between monastic men and woman is the primary sin. Although he quotes extensively from Bede's description of Coldingham, Symeon adds a brief account of the double monastery and cites the interaction between men and women in the monastic house as the primary sin:

Erant siquidem in eodem loco diversis tamen separate mansionibus monachorum sanctimonialiumque congregationes, qui paulatim a regularis discipline statu defluentes, inhonesta invicem familiaritate decipiendi occasionem inimico prebuerant.[54]

[There were congregations of monks and nuns, albeit living separately in different dwellings, who had gradually fallen away from the discipline of the Rule and had by their improper familiarity with each other given the Enemy the opportunity of ensnaring them.]

Symeon says that the destruction of Coldingham inspired Cuthbert's twofold prohibition: no interaction between the monks of his community and women

---

[51] Ibid., pp. 424–7.
[52] S. Hollis, *Anglo-Saxon Women and the Church: Sharing a Common Fate* (Woodbridge, 1992), p. 245.
[53] However, as Hollis points out, the *malitia* that sparked the devastation was apparently not conspicuous enough for Æbbe or for Adomnan to be aware of it without divine revelation. Hollis, *Anglo-Saxon Women*, pp. 101–2.
[54] *LdE* II.vii, pp. 106–7.

and no women present in his church.[55] Symeon goes on to provide several salacious stories about women who had violated the shrine of Cuthbert.[56]

The office modifies the moral of the story as well. It takes Cuthbert's prohibition against consorting with women for granted, but emphasizes that Æbbe is so worthy and so beloved by Cuthbert that he can relax his usually strict standards. In the first nocturn, the author of the office states:

> Cuthbertus Ebbam precipuo
> Amore complectens assiduo
> Subiectos sibi instruere
> Et hanc gaudebat inuisere
> Licet ut uirus consorcia
> Devitaret muliebria.[57]

[Constantly embracing Æbbe with particular love, Cuthbert rejoiced to visit her and to instruct those under her care, though he avoided fellowship with women like poison.]

There is no link in the office between the destruction of the monastery and Cuthbert's supposed strictures on women.

The *Vita et miracula* makes no such concession to virtue or friendship between a bishop and a nun, and it gives the interaction between the sexes as the explicit reason for the monastery's destruction. The author's concern with appropriate monastic practice is evident even in the description of Adomnan. According to Bede, Adomnan 'led a life devoted to God in austerity and prayer',[58] but the author of the *Vita et miracula* calls him a *uir exsimie sanctitatis* and adds that he was a priest.[59] By adding this information to his account, the author is bolstering Adomnan's visionary credentials and formalizing his role within the community. After describing the destruction of the monastery, the author announces, 'Liquet namque ex hiis quam uitanda sit bonarum etiam cohabitacio mulierum' ('It is clear from this how important it [is] to avoid living with women, even good women').[60] In fact, he follows Symeon in saying that the destruction of Coldingham was the impetus for Cuthbert's prohibition against women in his presence. The author declares:

Qui, accepto quanta facta fuit in domo Domini per feminas confusio, creditur, etsi non legitur, celebre condidisse decretum, lege perpetua seruis

---

[55] This prohibition has no evidence in the early sources for Cuthbert. See V. Tudor, 'The Misogyny of Saint Cuthbert', *Archaeologia Aeliana* 5th series 12 (1984), 157–67; Tudor, 'The Cult of Cuthbert in the Twelfth Century'.

[56] *LdE* II.viii–ix, pp. 108–11.

[57] BL Harley 4664, fol. 262r.

[58] *HE* IV.xxv, pp. 422–3: 'ducens uitam in continentia et orationibus multum Deo deuotam.'

[59] *Miracles of Saint Æbbe*, pp. 14, 16.

[60] Ibid., pp. 18–19.

suis obseruandum, quo non solum eis quocumque sui sancti corporis presencia fuerit consortia feminarum prohibuit, uerum etiam earum introitus et accessus et aspectus abscidit.[61]

[Learning of what great confusion had arisen in the house of the Lord through women, [Cuthbert] enacted the famous decree (as we believe, even though it is not recorded in writing), to be observed as a perpetual law by his servants, according to which not only was the company of women forbidden to them wherever his holy body was present but even the entry, access and sight of women were prohibited]

The monks were consciously overturning the past. The author of the *Vita et miracula* took what was a common expression of religious life in Anglo-Saxon England, the double monastery of men and women, and rejected it.

The authors of the office and the *Vita et miracula* had a challenging task: to demonstrate the holiness of a woman whose monastery was destroyed on account of the sin of its inhabitants. Both of these writers emphasize the fact that Æbbe was informed of the destruction before it happened as a sign of her virtue. They both make the connection even more explicit than Bede had done.[62] 'Think what her merit was', the *Vita et miracula* author declares, 'whom, for her consolation, the Lord deigned to inform through His servant of the desolation of her place'.[63] That is, for the author of the *Vita et miracula*, the revelation of the impending destruction had to become more spiritually significant than the destruction itself.

Not only was the community at Coldingham faced with the problem of a saint with very little claim to holiness in her biography, but they were not even the only claimants to the presence of her relics – and so history had to be reshaped, both textually and practically. The veneration of the saint, and particularly the miracles that occurred at her shrines, worked to overcome the dubious claims to sanctity in her biography. As we have seen, Symeon of Durham reported that Æbbe's relics were among those gathered by Alfred Westou and moved to Durham in the early eleventh century. Although the author of the *Vita et miracula* boldly declares that her 'mausoleum apud nos est' ('tomb is in our midst') at Coldingham, he goes on to admit that 'id suum profecto esse non tam ex traditione seniorum quam frequentia didicimus virtutum et beneficio consolationum' ('we have learned that it [i.e., the tomb] is indeed hers not so much from the tradition of our elders as from

---

[61] Ibid., pp. 20–1.

[62] BL Harley 4664, fol. 262v: 'Reuelabat Ebbe postea peritura flammis omnia sed id habebat solacii ipsa uiuente non fieri. Tanti quippe erat meriti quod possent casus tam miseri'.

[63] *Miracles of Saint Æbbe*, pp. 18–19: 'Pensandum itaque est cuius ista meriti fuerat, quam ad ipsius consolacionem de loci sui desolacione per servum suum Dominus dignatus est edocere.'

the frequency of miracles and the gift of aid').[64] The author acknowledges that the relics are disputed and addresses the doubters directly, charging them to consider the miracles at her shrine and the presence of the dust he has described.[65] The author of the *Vita et miracula* has to navigate between conflicting traditions about the location of Æbbe's relics and bemoans a lack of concrete evidence that her relics rest in Coldingham. However, he argues that the present miraculous events are enough to supplant any concerns about the past tradition of the relics' location. Regardless of the presence of the relics, the miracles provide a new incentive for veneration. The healing of a cripple is a demonstration of 'the duty of a new glorification of the virgin',[66] clearly implying both that the miracles were not entirely continuous with the past and that they ought to inspire devotion. So the present takes precedence over the past; the contemporary miracles become more compelling than the ambiguous sanctity in Æbbe's biography. Even the structure of the *Vita et miracula* bears this out; while the first three components of the text (the introduction, the account of her life and the descriptions of the two translations) occupy fols. 164r–168r in the manuscript, the forty-three miracles begin on fol. 168r and end on fol. 173r. That is, the author takes slightly more space to describe her miracles in the late twelfth century than he had used to introduce his subject, describe Æbbe's biography, narrate the two translations and account for the gap in time between her life and his own. Since the authority of the miracles mitigated against any uncertainty about the power of the relics or the sanctity of her life, ultimately the biography and the relics became less significant than the miracles for the development of the cult to those shaping it, both clerical and lay.

History was superseded by miracles. It was also intensely local. Æbbe was no longer a vague figure from the misty and unspecified past. Rather, she had become present, inhabiting the very landscape surrounding Coldingham. The authors of the office and the *Vita et miracula* took care to identify Æbbe with particular geographical and topographical features in the region, shaping her history into something deeply and intimately local. In the office *Britannia* is credited with producing such a saint, the sea and mountain protect her and the *locus* shines with her holiness and that of all the saints who lived with her.[67] The author of the *Vita et miracula* makes the connection between the saint and the place even more explicit, attributing the formation of particular

---

[64] Ibid., pp. 20–1.

[65] Ibid., p. 26: 'Alii igitur sacras eius reliquias sibi blandiantur et habere gaudeant et uenerari letentur; nos earum immunes non esse gaudeamus et manibus tractasse gratulemur, quos sua iugiter constat protectione muniri et in omnibus tribulacionibus nostris uberibus sue consolationis lactari.'

[66] *Miracles of Saint Æbbe*, pp. 50–1: 'et exhibendum uirgini noue exaltacionis obsequium'.

[67] BL Harley 4664, fols. 261r–262r.

geographical features in the landscape to God's power working through Æbbe. When he describes the sea rising up to protect her from the unwanted advances of the local lord, the author declares that the incident 'seems to have left a trace in the nature of the terrain'; the ebb and flow of the water carved out the headland.[68] The miracles Æbbe works in the twelfth century have the consequence of resanctifying the location. That author of the *Vita et miracula* links the miracles to the particular place; the faithful should understand that 'by the attestation of miracles, divine goodness had mitigated the state of sinfulness that had inflicted desolation upon the sacred places until now'.[69] The land is formed by the holiness of her life, corrupted by sin and ultimately restored by the miracles Æbbe works. Reshaping history meant emphasizing the saint in this particular locality. For the writers and the worshippers, Æbbe was powerful and she was *present*.

Liturgy, narrative and cultic practice all reshape history. The authors of these texts did not attempt to remove the destruction of Coldingham, the most conspicuous event in the history of the monastery and its abbess, from their celebration. Instead, they reworked it and reinterpreted it, and the lay beneficiaries of the miracles supplanted that history with their own stories of the saint's power. Ultimately, history itself mattered less than Æbbe's power in the late twelfth century present.

---

[68] *Miracles of Saint Æbbe*, pp. 6–7: 'cum etiam ex loci qualitate uideatur habere uestigium'. In the version of the story attributed to Æthelthryth and told in the *Liber Eliensis*, there is a similar impact on the local terrain: Æthelthryth's footprints left imprints in the rock. 'Insuper memoriale et pre ceteris mirabile est, quod vestigia pedum illius ascendentis et descendentis in latere montis infusa, tanquam in calida cera, nunc usque ostenduntur ad laudem domini nostri Iesu Christi.' *Liber Eliensis* I.11, ed. Blake, p. 28.

[69] *Miracles of Saint Æbbe*, p. 46: 'Quod culpam que hactenus sacris locis solitudinem intulit, divina bonitas signorum attestatione relaxavit' (my translation above).

12

William of Malmesbury as a Cantor-Historian

Paul Antony Hayward

William of Malmesbury would seem, at first sight, to represent the perfect example of a 'cantor-historian'. The author of three major histories, an extensive collection of Marian miracles and five finely constructed saints' lives, he is often acclaimed as one of the greatest historians of his era.[1] There is also no doubt that he spent some part of his career as his monastery's cantor. To be sure, William nowhere presents himself to his readers as such. The closest that he comes to doing so is in the preface to the *Historia novella*, where he styles himself as *bibliothecarius Malmesberie*, as 'the librarian of Malmesbury'.[2] Many customaries place the care of a monastery's book collection among the cantor's usual duties,[3] but this task was sometimes detached from the core role of managing the delivery of the liturgy. Lanfranc's decrees provide, for example, for the delegation of this job if the cantor lacks the skills and character to discharge it properly: 'De universis monasterii libris curam gerat, et eos in custodia sua habeat, si eius studii et scientie sit, ut eorum custodia ei commendari debeat' ('[The cantor] takes care of all the books of the house, and has them in his keeping, *if his interests and learning are such as to fit him for keeping them*').[4] It follows that the words which William has chosen leave open the possibility that he fulfilled the duties of librarian without being a cantor in the usual sense. Evidence that he was indeed his community's

---

[1] This is the view of historians such as J. Campbell, 'Some Twelfth-Century Views of the Anglo-Saxon Past', *Peritia* 3 (1984), 135–50 (p. 136); D. A. Carpenter, *The Struggle for Mastery: Britain, 1066–1284* (Harmondsworth, 2004), p. 543; V. H. Galbraith, *Historical Research in Medieval England* (London, 1951), p. 15; J. Gillingham, 'A Historian of the Twelfth-Century Renaissance and the Transformation of English Society, 1066–ca. 1200', in *European Transformations: The Long Twelfth Century*, ed. T. F. X. Noble and J. Van Engen (Notre Dame IN, 2012), pp. 45–74 (p. 46); P. Wormald, *The Making of English Law: King Alfred to the Twelfth Century*, 2 vols. (Oxford, 1999–2001), I, 137. William's career is also evaluated in the chapters by Fassler and by Sønnesyn in this volume.

[2] William of Malmesbury, *Historia novella*, pref., *The Contemporary History*, ed. E. King and trans. K. R. Potter (Oxford, 1998), p. 2. See also *GPA* v.271.2, p. 644.

[3] On the duties of the *armarius/cantor* in the eleventh and twelfth centuries, see Fass A; S. Boynton, 'Training for the Liturgy as a Form of Monastic Education', in *Medieval Monastic Education*, ed. G. Ferzoco and C. Muessig (London, 2000), pp. 7–20 (esp. pp. 9–10).

[4] *Decreta*, pp. 122–3 (emphasis mine).

cantor emerges from an external source, Robert of Cricklade. Writing in or soon after 1137, while William was still alive and active, Robert defines him as a monk and *cantor* of the *ecclesia* at Malmesbury.[5] Since he had read some of William's works and was a canon of Cirencester, a collegiate community located some twelve miles from Malmesbury, before going on to become abbot of St Frideswide's in Oxford,[6] it is reasonable to assume that he is an authoritative guide to the truth of the matter.

That being a cantor informed William's activities as an author and scribe also seems clear enough, but from texts and remains that might be considered peripheral to his achievement. Neil Ker detected William's hand in several books, one of which is especially relevant to the cantor's office, that is, Bodl Auct. F.3.14 (SC 2186).[7] As can be seen from this book's contents in Table 12.1, Bede's guides to the calculation of dates occupy the core of Auct. F.3.4, around which appear shorter, auxiliary tracts on the nature of the world, astronomy and problems in computus. This arrangement is typical of computistical collections produced in twelfth-century England.[8] The book is, more to the point, the sort of reference collection for which a cantor may well have felt a need. In the course of working out his community's liturgical programme he may often have had to remind himself of some of the more arcane aspects of time-reckoning, such as the problem of why the phases of the moon sometimes appear more advanced than the usual method of reckoning its progress would predict;[9] he will also have required such a volume when teaching computus to oblates and novices – a topic in the

---

[5] Robert of Cricklade, *De connubio patriarche Iacob*, ii.22, quoted from Bodl Laud. misc. 725, fol. 129va, in R. W. Hunt, 'English Learning in the Late Twelfth Century', *Transactions of the Royal Historical Society*, 4th s. 19 (1936), 19–42 (pp. 31–2 n. 1). This passage is quoted at length in the opening to Sigbjørn Sønnesyn's chapter. The dating depends on the preface, printed in T. E. Holland, 'The University of Oxford in the Twelfth Century', in *Collectanea*, ed. M. Burrows, Oxford Historical Society Publications, 16, vol. 2 (Oxford, 1890), pp. 137–92 (pp. 161–2), with further variants in Hunt, 'English Learning', p. 31 n. 3. Here Robert says that he has just heard about the death of Godfrey, abbot of Winchcombe, an event which took place on 6 March 1137: *Heads*, p. 79, with R. M. Thomson, *William of Malmesbury*, 2nd edn (Woodbridge, 2001), pp. 74, 169 n. 8, 199.

[6] Robert was abbot of St Frideswide's from before 8 January 1141 until 1174 or soon afterwards: see *Heads*, pp. 180, 284.

[7] N. R. Ker, 'William of Malmesbury's Handwriting', *EHR* 59 (1944), 371–6 (esp. pp. 374–5). For a paleographical analysis, see Thomson, *William*, pp. 82–5. See also M. B. Parkes, *Scribes, Scripts and Readers: Studies in the Communication, Presentation and Dissemination of Medieval Texts* (London, 1991), p. 87 n. 48.

[8] For a discussion, based on fifteen examples, see *The Winchcombe and Coventry Chronicles: Hitherto Unnoticed Witnesses to the Work of John of Worcester*, ed. and trans. P. A. Hayward, Medieval and Renaissance Texts and Studies 373, 2 vols. (Tempe, 2010), I, 44–8.

[9] Bede covers this topic in *De temporum ratione* 43, ed. C. W. Jones, CCSL 123B (Turnhout, 1977), pp. 241–544 (pp. 412–8).

Table 12.1 Contents of Bodl Auct. F.3.14 (SC 2186)

Item	Text	Folios
1	Isidore of Seville, *De natura rerum*	1r–19v
2	Bede, *De natura rerum*	20r–27v
3	Bede, *De temporibus liber primus*	27v–33r
4	Bede, *Episola ad Wicthedum de pascha celebratione*	33r–35v
5	Bede, *De temporibus liber secundus* [*i.e. De temporum ratione*]	35v–102r
6	Helperic of Granval, *De calculatoria arte* [*i.e. De computo*]	102r–114r
7	Proterius of Alexandria, *Epistola ad papam Leonem primum de ratione pasche*	114r–115v
8	Paschasinus of Lilybeum, *Epistola ad papam Leonem de ratione pasche*	115v–116v
9	Dionysius Exiguus, *Epistola ad Petronum episcopum de ciclo quingentorum .xxxii. annorum*	116v–118v
10	Dionysius Exiguus, *Epistola de eodem ad Bonifatium primicerium*	118v–120ar
11	[*Argumenta titulorum paschalium*]	120av
12	[*Magnus cyclus paschalis cum annales*]	120av–132v
13	Robert de Losinga, *Exceptio*[*nes*] *de chronica Mariniani* [*i.e. Mariani Scoti*]	133r–148v
14	*Liber Igini de spera celesti*†	148v–153r
15	*Regule de astrolabio*‡	153r–157v

† Known as 'Hyginus Philosophus', this work comprises an epitome of Hyginus, *De astronomia*, ed. G. Viré (Leipzig, 1992), beginning 'Duo sunt extremi vertices mundi quos appellant polos …' and ending '…cuius et gubernaculum et rectam puppem secans ad octavam partem cancri redit'. A briefer version of the same text is printed in E. Maass, *Commentariorum in Aratum reliquiae* (Berlin, 1898), pp. 309–12. Cf. A. Dell'Era, *Una caeli descriptio d'età carolingia* (Palermo, 1974), pp. 41–70.

‡ This work comprises an assortment of items about the astrolabe and its uses, ultimately derived from Arabic sources: 'Quicumque astronomice discere … fabricare horologia' (fols. 153r40–156r20), comprises much, but not all, of a tract that N. Bubnov edits as a work of Gerbert of Aurillac in *Gerberti postea Silvestri pape opera mathematica* (Berlin, 1899), pp. 114–38, 146–7; the remainder, from 'Iarius Apollo dum sibi pariter in lucem …' to 'et lector relege et relectum iterate' (fols. 156r21–157v41), echoes a number of the tracts that J. Millàs Vallicrosa edits in *Assaig d'història de les idees fisiques i matemàtiques a la Catalunya medieval* (Barcelona, 1931), pp. 288–90, 324–5, 304–5, 307–8, 322–4.

monastic curriculum that often fell under the cantor's remit.[10] Ker thought that William was responsible for inserting the table of contents on folio ii^v and at least one entry among the annals in the margins of the Easter Tables that appear on folios 120br to 132v.[11] He suspected, moreover, that this book, whose texts were copied by no less than fourteen scribes, was produced under William's supervision – a theory that Rod Thomson has developed.[12] The likelihood that William himself added annals to the Easter tables is particularly interesting, because this practice seems to have been associated with the teaching of computus. That is, one of the most credible explanations for the insertion of chronological notes in such tables is that cantors put them there to clarify the significance of these opaque grids of numbers – to make their relationship to time-reckoning less abstract for the novices whom they were training to use them.[13]

In the prologue to the *Historia novella*, furthermore, William tells us that he wrote 'three little books' to which he has given 'the name *chronica*'. Here he tells Robert, earl of Gloucester (1121–47), that in this work, as well as in the fifth book of the *Gesta regum Anglorum*, he has set down many of the deeds of his illustrious father Henry I.[14] Judging by this reference to the coverage of the reign of Henry I, it seems almost certain that this chronicle is the same work as that discussed in the final paragraph of the final version of *Gesta regum* – in the version that was prepared for Earl Robert in the late 1130s. Here, speaking directly to the earl, he says that rather than continue to amend and extend *Gesta regum*'s coverage of his father's reign on a year-by-year basis, he has decided to begin a new work that will comprise these additions. The writing of this work will occupy, he says, the rest of his life: it 'will

---

[10] For an example of the former approach to the function of these books, see A. J. Piper, 'The Durham Cantor's Book (Durham, Dean and Chapter Library, MS B.IV.24)', in *Anglo-Norman Durham, 1093–1193*, ed. D. W. Rollason et al. (Woodbridge, 1994), pp. 72–92; for an example of the latter, see H. Bober, 'An Illustrated Medieval School Book of Bede's *De natura rerum*', *Journal of the Walters Art Gallery* 19–20 (1956–7), 65–97 (esp. pp. 73, 81–6). Cf. *Winchcombe and Coventry*, I, 47–8.

[11] The addition attributed to William appears at the foot of fol. 120vb: 'Henricus rex Anglorum, regnavit annis .xxxv. 7 super hoc a nonis Augusti usque ad kl. Decemb.', a note that echoes his *Historia novella* i.11, p. 22. W. H. Stevenson, 'A Contemporary Description of the Domesday Survey', *EHR* 22 (1907), 73–84 (pp. 81–2), printed the annals for AD 1066–1139 found on fols. 120br–120cv, and identified various parallels in Williams histories. Note: three folios bear the number 120 in Auct. F.3.14, distinguished as 120a, 120b and 120c.

[12] 'The "Scriptorium" of William of Malmesbury', in *Medieval Scribes, Manuscripts and Libraries: Essays Presented to N. R. Ker*, ed. M. B. Parkes and A. G. Watson (London, 1978), pp. 117–42; rev. in Thomson, *William*, p. 84: 'He was the initiator and supervisor, evidently deciding what was to go in it and supplying the exemplars; it is his collection.'

[13] *Winchcombe and Coventry*, I, 42–3.

[14] *Historia novella* prol., pp. 3–4.

end only with life itself'.[15] These details imply that this history was a set of annals – that is, a list of events arranged in chronological order according to the years in which they fell. Yet it seems not to have survived. Some residues may underpin the *Eulogium historiarum*, a vast world history in five books compiled at Malmesbury in the 1360s, but it is impossible to ascertain their precise extent.[16] Still, there is enough information in William's references to this work to suggest that it was typical of the annalistic chronicles associated with cantors, like the set of annals that was compiled at the neighbouring abbey of Winchcombe in the 1140s.[17] Chronicles of this sort seem, for the most part, to have been used to teach oblates and novices about the shape of history on a larger, macroscopic, scale – about the ways in which one reign, pontificate and abbacy gave rise to another, about the span of the Sixth Age of the World, and so on.[18]

That William took the time not just to abbreviate but also to revise the *Liber officialis* by Amalarius of Metz can also be read as evidence for an interest in the liturgical education of his abbey's *pueri* – a task over which cantors often presided.[19] To be sure, the preface implies that this work was written for one monk in particular – for a certain Robert whom William had observed picking up a copy of Amalarius, but then being deterred by 'the difficulty of the words and the complexity of the contents'. Yet the preface also places the work in a pedagogical context in which the priority was to equip a newcomer to the monastic 'profession' with a basic knowledge of the Divine Office:

In historicis nos narrationibus occupatos detorsit a proposito tua, Rodberte amice, voluntas. Nuper enim cum in bibliotheca nostra sederemus et quisque pro studio libros evolveret, impegisti in Amalarium *De ecclesiasticis officiis*. Cuius cum materiam ex prima statim tituli fronte cognosceres, amplexus es occasionem qua rudimenta nove professionis animares, sed

---

[15] *GRA* v.449, pp. 800–1.

[16] *Eulogium historiarum sive temporis: Chronicon ab orbe condito usque ad annum Domini M.CCC.LXVI.*, ed. F. S. Haydon, 3 vols. (London, 1858–63). The first book ranges from the creation to the ascension of Christ, the second covers the apostles and the saints, the third the 'four empires', but especially the Roman Empire, the fourth the geography of the world and the fifth the history of England to 1366. Brief extracts from the known works of William of Malmesbury appear in the third and the fifth books.

[17] *Winchcombe and Coventry*, II, 356–543.

[18] Ibid., esp. 37–42 and 60–1. See also D. E. Greenway, 'Historical writing at St Paul's', in *St Paul's: The Cathedral Church of London, 604–2004*, ed. D. Keene et al. (New Haven CT, 2004), pp. 151–6 (p. 151); and for the alternative theories, see S. Foot, 'Annals and Chronicles in Western Europe', in *The Oxford History of Historical Writing*, vol. 2, *400–1400*, ed. S. Foot and C. F. Robinson (Oxford, 2012), pp. 346–67, and the literature cited there.

[19] I say 'presided over' because it was normal for the cantor to assess the boys' performance while the actual training was delegated to his assistant, the *succentor*. See Fass A, pp. 44–6; Boynton, 'Training', pp. 9–11.

quia confestim animi tui alacritatem turbavit testimoniorum perplexitas et sermonum asperitas, rogasti ut eum abreviarem. Ego autem qui semel proposuerim deferre tibi ut homini dilectissimo munus iniunctum non aspernanter accepi. In quo experiare licebit quantum propter faciliorem intellectum in deiciendo sermone laboravi qui cultius fortassis loqui potui. Est enim res de qua tractatur per necessaria et cuius ignorantia sit cunctis sacerdotibus pudenda.[20]

[Your wish, my friend Robert, has diverted us, [formerly] occupied in historical narratives, with a purpose. For recently when we were seated in our library and someone was taking out books for study, you fastened on Amalarius's *On Ecclesiastical Offices*. Since you could tell its subject straightaway from the title on the front cover, you embraced an opportunity by which you might enliven the rudiments of your new profession; but because the difficulty of the words and the complexity of the contents swiftly threw the liveliness of your mind into turmoil, you asked that I might abbreviate it. And I, who intended there and then to set aside a gift for you as the dearest of men, accepted this obligation without disdain – in that I, who can speak perhaps more elegantly, have laboured for the sake of easier understanding in cutting the wording as much as is permissible. For it is a matter which needs to be investigated, and ignorance of it is shameful in every priest.]

The preface to the *Defloratio Gregorii*, a collection of extracts from the works of Gregory the Great, provides further evidence that William was concerned with the provision of educational materials for his fellow monks:

Dominis suis et fratribus Meldunensis cenobii monachis Willelmus fide frater, professione conservus. Ad instructionem communem deflorationes ex libris precellentissimi pape Gregorii in hoc volumine compegi, ea potissimum intentione ut si quis nostrum vel valetudine vel occupatione vel etiam desidia impediente multis legendis non vacat, hic impromptu inveniat, quibus et animam pascat et vitam componat.[21]

[To our lords and brothers, the monks of the monastery of Malmesbury, William your brother in faith, a fellow-servant by profession. For general instruction I have compiled in this book flowers from the books of the most excellent pope, Gregory, with the intention of the strongest that if any of our own should be without the capacity for much reading – infirmity, business, or furthermore, slackness being an obstacle – he may readily find here that with which he may feed his soul and compose his life.]

---

[20] William of Malmesbury, *Abbreviatio Amalarii* prol., ed. R. W. Pfaff, *Recherches de théologie ancienne et médiévale* 48 (1981), 128–71 (p. 128). Pfaff details the extent of William's editing and revision of the *Liber officialis* in the introduction to his edition: idem, 'The "Abbreviatio Amalarii" of William of Malmesbury', ibid. 47 (1980), 77–113.
[21] CUL Ii.3.20, fol. 1r; D. H. Farmer, ed., 'William of Malmesbury's Commentary on Lamentations', *Studia monastica* 4 (1962), 283–311 (p. 309).

The inclusion of material that defines the proper extent of episcopal authority associates the *Defloratio Gregorii* with a core issue of William's histories of the English, *Gesta regum* and *Gesta pontificum*, and raises the possibility that this work may also have been aimed at external readers – at an audience, say, of bishops and canons[22] – but the educational agenda set out in the preface and largely fulfilled in what follows align the work with the cantor's role as a manager of books and provider of materials for the edification of his community.

There survive, then, a number of compositions that William might well have produced in order to fulfil the obligations of a cantor. It is hard, however, to identify passages in his narrative works where he has invested his text with allusions to the liturgy of the sort that one might expect from an author who was also a cantor, a finding that is especially true of the three great monographs on which his reputation rests: *Gesta regum Anglorum*, *Gesta pontificum Anglorum* and *Historia novella*.

It cannot be denied that there are passages in these works where he cites liturgical or musical materials, but these are relatively rare, and these citations typically turn out to have been required by the story that is being told – they turn out to have been unavoidable. Music figures strongly, for example, in *Gesta pontificum*'s account of the life of Archbishop Dunstan. William reports that the saint heard his harp, hanging on its peg, playing the antiphon 'Gaudent in celis anime sanctorum' without anyone touching it;[23] that during a visit to St Augustine's Abbey Dunstan had a vision of the Mother of God leading a choir of women in singing Sedulius's hymn *Cantemus Domino sotie;*[24] and that he had a vision of the angels singing a version of the *Kyrie eleison* that he passed on to his companions and which is still sung in English churches.[25] But Dunstan, his subject in this passage, was famed for his interest

---

[22] Note esp. how William refers to these passages in his preface (ibid.): 'de tolerandis uel ammonendis proximis, subeci sententias de prelatis et subditis, in quibus discant prelati *quantum* tuitionis et ammonitionis debeant subiectis imponere' ['next to [the sections] on toleration and on admonition I have appended passages about prelates and their subjects, in which prelates may learn about *how much* protection and admonition they ought to impose on their subjects'] (emphasis mine).

[23] *GPA* i.19.3, pp. 40–1; for the antiphon, see Can 002927. William's sources were Osbern of Canterbury, *Vita S. Dunstani* (BHL 2344) 10, *Memorials of St Dunstan, Archbishop of Canterbury*, ed. W. Stubbs (London, 1874), pp. 69–128 (p. 80); and Eadmer of Canterbury, *Vita S. Dunstani archiepiscopi et confessoris* (BHL 2346) 8, *Lives and Miracles of Saints Oda, Dunstan and Oswald*, ed. and trans. A. J. Turner and B. J. Muir (Oxford, 2005), pp. 44–159 (pp. 60–1).

[24] *GPA* i.19.10, p. 40, quoting from Sedulius, Hymn 1, lines 1–2; *Sedulii opera omnia*, ed. J. Huemer, CSEL 10 (Vienna, 1885), p. 155. William's sources were Osbern, *Vita Dunstani* 40, pp. 118–9; and Eadmer, *Vita Dunstani* 54, pp. 132–3.

[25] *GPA* i.19.11, p. 36, following Eadmer, *Vita Dunstani* 52, pp. 128–31. For the possibility that this episode refers to 'Kyrie rex splendens', a trope associated with the saint, see Stubbs's introduction to his *Memorials of St Dunstan*, pp. cxiv–cxv.

in music,[26] and the hagiographical tradition had long illustrated this element in his piety with these episodes. The stories about the harp and the vision of the Virgin leading a choir, for example, first appeared in B's *Vita Dunstani*, a work composed between 997 and 1002,[27] within two decades of its subject's death. Though he reworks Sedulius's verses a little, William's versions of these scenes scarcely suggest a deep interest in the liturgy.[28]

In general, William's histories favour the rhetorical devices, style and attitude of the classical historian.[29] This is true even of the hagiographical passages in his work – even of the passages where he is writing about saints. Consider, for example, the digression on English royal saints which appears in *Gesta regum* (§§ 207–19); it incorporates allusions to Virgil, but none to any liturgical text.[30] The way in which William's *res gestae* favour classical and poetic rather than biblical allusions stands in sharp contrast, moreover, to much high-medieval historiography. There are, of course, many passages where William references verses or scenes in the Bible,[31] but they are greatly outnumbered by those in which he quotes from or alludes to literary texts, especially ancient Roman texts.[32] Orderic Vitalis, in contrast, often quotes from the Bible and adduces parallels between its stories and recent events – a practice which seems to have been central to his understanding of history: 'Multa intueor in diuina pagina, quae subtiliter coaptata nostri temporis euentui uidentur similia' ('I see many things in divine Scripture which, if they are subtly accommodated, appear similar to the happenings in our own time').[33] William nowhere expresses a similar view. He tends to avoid biblical

---

[26] See William of Malmesbury, *Vita S. Dunstani* (*BHL* 2348) 4.3, *Saints' Lives*, ed. and trans. M. Winterbottom and R. M. Thomson (Oxford, 2002), pp. 166–303 (p. 178): 'cum ceterarum tum maxime musice dulcedine captus'; Osbern, *Vita Dunstani* 8; *Memorials of St Dunstan*, p. 78.

[27] *ELD* B 12, 36.2–3 (pp. 40–3, 100–1). William went on to develop the three scenes in greater detail in his own *Vita Dunstani* i.6.1–2 and ii.26.5–28, pp. 182–3, 284–9.

[28] For further discussion of William of Malmesbury's *Vita Dunstani*, see Margot Fassler's chapter in this volume.

[29] Cf. *GRA* i.prol.4, p. 14, where he declares that his aim was 'exarata barbarice Romano sale condire' ('to season the barbaric jottings [of English History] with Roman salt').

[30] Quotations from Virgil's *Georgics* iv.529, and *Aeneid* vi.835, appear in *GRA* 213.5–6, p. 396. There is also a faint echo of Prudentius, *Peristephanon* iii.5, in *GRA* 218, p. 402. It is worth noting also that William's preference was for quantitative rather than the rhythmic verse forms: see M. Winterbottom, 'William of Malmesbury *versificus*', in *Anglo-Latin and its Heritage: Essays in Honour of A. G. Rigg on his 64th Birthday*, ed. S. Echard and G. R. Wieland (Turnhout, 2001), pp. 109–27.

[31] E.g. *Historia novella* i.20, p. 38, quoting from Gen. 16. 12. King Stephen had to fight against so many enemies 'that what was said of Ishmael might justly be applied to him, having "every man's hand against him and his hand against every man"'.

[32] See further the *indices* of sources in *GRA* II, 457–68; *GPA* II, 389–94.

[33] Orderic Vitalis, *Historia Ecclesiastica* viii.16, ed. M. Chibnall, 6 vols. (Oxford, 1968–80), IV, 228; but for the translation, E. Mégier, '*Divina pagina* and the Narration of

quotations and allusions. Compare, for example, his treatment of the siege of Jerusalem with that found in Baudri of Bourgueil's *Historia Ierosolimitana*, a work drafted in 1105. Whereas William invests an account based on Fulcher of Chartres with quotations from Vegetius and Lucan,[34] Baudri populates an account based on the *Gesta Francorum* with six allusions to the Bible as well as two to classical texts – one to Sallust's *Iugurtha* and one to Virgil's *Eclogues*.[35]

The classicism of William's histories is clearest, however, in the passages where they use loaded alternatives and innuendo – devices that were crucial to rhetorical history.[36] Consider, for example, the much misunderstood passage in the preface to book three of *Gesta regum* where William says that he will maintain an even-handed approach when speaking about the Conqueror, because he draws his blood from both peoples – because he is Norman as well as English.[37] Some scholars read this aside as a statement of neutrality, but in William – as in Sallust and Tacitus – declarations of balance and objectivity signpost innuendo, and this passage is true to this tradition. For William goes on to declare that he will bring forth the king's good deeds without applying make up (*sine fuco*), that he will touch on his wrongful acts only as far as is necessary, and 'nec illum nota inuram censoria cuius *cuncta pene*, etsi non laudari, excusari certe possunt *opera*' ('he will not brand with a censorious note a man *almost all* of whose works can certainly be excused, even if they cannot be praised').[38] The insinuation is that deeds which needed to be defended vastly outnumbered those that could naturally or easily be praised – a damning comment.

The provocative content of many passages in William's histories would seem, moreover, to be at odds with the propriety expected of a monk. *Gesta regum* tells, for example, about how crusaders forced their Turkish captives

---

History in Orderic Vitalis' *Historia ecclesiastica*', *RB* 110 (2000), 106–23 (p. 108).

[34] *GRA* iv.369, pp. 646–50, reworking Fulcher of Chartres, *Historia Hierosolymitana* i.27, ed. H. Hagenmayer (Heidelberg, 1913), pp. 292–301. William adds quotations from Lucan, *Pharsalia* ii.227–8, 655–6; vi.88–89; and Vegetius, *De re militari* iv.15. There is also a faint echo of Sidonius Apollinaris, *Carmina* ii, 69–72. There are no allusions to the Bible. See Thomson's commentary in *GRA* II, 326–7.

[35] Baudri of Bourgueil, *Historia Ierosolimitana* iv.9–14, *Recueil des Historiens des Croisades: Historiens occidentaux*, ed. C. Thurot, vol. 4 (Paris, 1879), pp. 1–111 (pp. 96–103). See, likewise, Robert the Monk, *Historia Iherosolimitana* ix, ed. D. Kempf and M. G. Bull (Woodbridge, 2013), pp. 96–100, whose account of the same events has three biblical references as opposed to one allusion to Ovid.

[36] The present author treats William's use of these devices in greater detail in 'The Importance of Being Ambiguous: Innuendo and Legerdemain in William of Malmesbury's *Gesta regum* and *Gesta pontificum Anglorum*', *ANS* 33 (2011), 75–102; and *Power, Rhetoric and Historical Practice in Twelfth-Century England: From William of Malmesbury to Geoffrey of Monmouth* (forthcoming), ch. 3.

[37] *GRA* iii.pref.1, p. 424: 'Ego autem, quia utriusque gentis sanguinem traho, dicendi tale temperamentum seruabo'.

[38] Ibid. (my emphasis). See, likewise, *GRA* ii.228.12, p. 422.

to give up the coins that they had hidden on their persons – a tale which implies that these good Christians went about hitting women to force the coins from their vaginas.[39] He tells a tale, in a more playful mode, about three monks at Lanfranc's school in Caen who cast oracles to see who among them would become an abbot or a bishop by flipping the pages of a Bible. The outcome generated resounding laughter! One of the monks, Gundulf, went on to become bishop of Rochester (1077–1108); another, Walter, went on to become abbot of Evesham (1077–1104); and the third returned to the world – as predicted.[40] Here William chooses to mock Gundulf and Walter in a gentle fashion; elsewhere he destroys reputations. All that is reported, for instance, about Hugh d'Orival, bishop of London (d. 1085), is a tale about how he had himself castrated:

> The royal sickness covering his entire body with purulent ulcers, and he was brought to a shameful remedy. For, believing those asserting that his one and only recourse would be to have his scrotum, the receptacle of his humours – plainly, that which ought to be feared – removed, he did not refuse. Thus, a bishop bore the shame of the impotent, and he found no remedy: [he remained] leprous while he lived.[41]

The fat-shaming of Samson, bishop of Worcester (1096–1112), and his son Thomas II, archbishop of York (1109–14), is equally aggressive:

> From adolescence [Archbishop Thomas II was] free, so it was believed, of women and also of every obscenity. In his example to everyone [he was] feast-providing (*dapsilis*), and of fatty and loathsome corpulence, such that, breathing heavily, he could hardly walk.

> Not meagrely educated, but urging his stomach forward with extreme feasting, [Bishop Samson] was said to be the one and only gorge for meals (*unicus gurges escarum*) in this age! He would never leave un-bought anything that was up for sale if it would enable him to fill a space in his stomach with something rather spicy. He would have placed before him plates holding twenty-four chickens and a side of pork so that, when his greed had been indulged from the middle [of the plate], he might send out or give away to bystanders the rest that was on the dish without impropriety.[42]

These are just a few of the many passages where William uses literary invention and rhetorical artifice to ridicule and denounce the failings and pretensions of the higher clergy – an activity that scarcely aligns his work with the normal duties of a cantor.

[39] *GRA* iv.380.4, p. 678.
[40] *GPA* i.72.12–14, p. 218.
[41] *GRA* ii.73.18–19, p. 230.
[42] *GRA* iii.121.2β and iv.150β.1–2, pp. 398, 440.

William's evolution as a monk would seem, at first sight, to provide a way of explaining the contrast between his histories and his 'monastic works', the hypothesis being that his grasp of his vocation deepened over time leading him towards literary activities that were more fully informed by monastic ideals and eventually his work as a cantor at Malmesbury. *Gesta regum* and *Gesta pontificum* can be dated relatively precisely: their first editions were completed in late 1125.[43] A number of the works that seem to reflect the preoccupations of a cantor can be placed, on the other hand, in the 1130s – in the middle phase of his career. The 'three little books' that he called *chronica* were certainly written after the histories. There is nothing to say exactly when the *Abbreviatio Amalarii* was compiled, allowing us to infer that it may post-date these histories, even if we cannot rule out the possibility that it pre-dates them.[44] Since Robert of Cricklade mentions the *Defloratio* in the same passage where he identifies William as a cantor,[45] it has to be dated to before March 1137, but it may nevertheless post-date *Gesta regum* and *Gesta pontificum* by several years.

There is, moreover, a passage in the preface to book two of *Gesta regum*, which suggests that William acquired his love of history prior to entering the monastery:

> It is a while since I became accustomed to books, owing to my parents' care and my own persistence. Their pleasures have been with me ever since, from my childhood, and their seductions have matured just as I have. For I had been so informed by my father that, if I turned away to contrary pursuits, it would be at the expense of my soul and perilous to my reputation ... I expended labour on many kinds of study, but on some rather than others ... Again, I investigated aspects of ethics in depth: I surged towards its majesty, because it lays itself open to students and composes souls for living well. But history especially because, seasoning habits with an agreeable knowledge of definite deeds, it spurs readers to follow the good and to guard against the bad. Thus, when I had obtained with my private funds (*domestica sumpta*) not a few histories of foreign peoples, I proceeded in my household leisure (*familiaris otium*), to ask if something memorable could be discovered about our people for posterity...[46]

---

43 In the final section of *GPA* (v.278.3) William notes a series of events that happened 'in 1125', the latest of them being the death of the Emperor Henry V (23 May 1125). The latest event mentioned among the passages that belonged to the first edition of *GRA* is the release of King Baldwin II of Jerusalem from captivity, an event which took place on 29 August 1124 (*GRA* iv.386). See further Thomson's comments in *GRA* II, xvii–xviii, 343.

44 Cf. Pfaff, 'The "Abbreviatio Amalarii"', pp. 79–80.

45 See n. 5 above.

46 *GRA* ii.prol.1–2, p. 150.

This is not the only in the preface in *Gesta regum* in which William presents himself in as a private gentleman, one accustomed to the privileges of great wealth. In the preface to book four he speaks about how retreated to a life defined by the Roman concept of *otium* – of private, philosophical, leisure – rather than face the hostile responses of his critics or the efforts of others to force him to adopt this or that interpretation:

> I had long since retired to a life of leisure (*in otium concesseram*), content to remain silent; but after a period of idleness, my old love of study (*amor studium*) plucked me by the ear and laid its hand on my shoulder for I was incapable of doing nothing, and knew not how to devote myself to those business cares (*ista forenses*) that are so unworthy of a man of letters.[47]

Much of this clashes with a monastic context; monks were not supposed to own books, nor did they have their own 'domestic funds', nor was their education and reading unsupervised.[48] Of course, later records, book lists and commemorative texts, suggest that it was normal for erudite monks like William to retain books within their own control while they lived – typically books housing texts which they had copied for their own use.[49] But since the Rule expressly forbade the possession of books,[50] it seems unlikely that this practice was ever regarded as ownership. This preface would seem to imply, therefore, that William acquired and developed his passion for history while still in his father's household and at a time when he still had access to private funds which he could spend on the acquisition of books – and that William entered his monastery, not as a child-oblate, but as a young adult, in his late teens or twenties.[51]

With its account of how, having reached forty years of age, he has decided to abandon history in order to pursue exegesis and spiritual enquiry, the preface to the *Commentary on Lamentations*, a work that William finished

---

[47] *GRA* iv.prol.1–2, p. 540.

[48] For the strict supervision of 'private' reading in the cloister, see Benedict, *Regula* 48, ed. R. Hanslik, CSEL 75, 2nd edn (Vienna, 1977), pp. 125–30.

[49] Nigel Wireker, for example, retained and glossed his own copy of Peter Comestor's *Historia Scholastica* (Cambridge, Trinity College, MS B.15.5): see Nigel of Canterbury, *The Passion of St Lawrence, Epigrams and Marginal Poems*, ed. and trans. J. M. Ziolkowski, Mittellateinische Studien und Texte 14 (Leiden, 1994), pp. 282–3. For other examples, see L. Cleaver, 'The Monks' Library at Christ Church, Canterbury c. 1180–c. 1250', in *Medieval Art, Architecture and Archaeology at Canterbury*, ed. A. Bovey (Leeds, 2013), pp. 156–66; *St Augustine's Abbey, Canterbury*, ed. B. C. Barker-Benfield, CBMLC 13, 3 pts. (London, 2008), I, lxiii.

[50] Benedict, *Regula* 33.3, p. 99.

[51] Cf. the introduction to William of Malmesbury, *De gestis regum Anglorum libri quinque*, ed. W. Stubbs, 2 vols. (London, 1887–9), I, xii, and the final paragraph below.

before March 1137,[52] seems to provide further evidence for his evolution towards a more spiritual outlook:

> In the past, when I amused myself with histories, the charm of the subject suited my greener years and happy lot. Now advancing age and worsening circumstances demand a different type of expression (*aliud dicendi genus*). The ideal will be something able to warn me off the world and set me on fire towards God. Hitherto I have lived for myself, enough and more than enough. Henceforth I must live for my Maker. It is only right to show my gratitude to Him who has granted me life for so many years without punishing me too severely. ... This is why, from the whole range of possible topics, you have chosen for me the Lamentations of the prophet Jeremiah, that through their exposition the grace of compunction might be more abundant and the flame of divine love more inspiring ...[53]

It is worth noting also that liturgical references figure in this *Commentary* to a much greater extent than in William's histories. The prologue refers at one point, for example, to 'the splendid lament of David for Saul and Jonathan' whose 'fame can never be dimmed, so often is it sung by the choirs of the Church'.[54] That William's attitudes were gradually transformed by the performance of his duties as a monk and cantor seems, then, like a promising explanation.

There are, however, significant problems with this hypothesis, perhaps the most glaring being the existence of *Historia novella*, the third of William's pseudo-classical monographs. Here he took up once again many of the stylistic devices that characterize *Gesta regum* and *Gesta pontificum*, and there is no question that the *Historia* was one of his final works. It was begun in about 1140, and the latest event mentioned in it is the Empress Matilda's escape from the siege of Oxford in December 1142.[55] So, the chronology of William's career is at odds with the idea of a single direction of travel; he would seem to have switched back and forth from one mode of historical expression to another. There are hints, furthermore, that William's work as a cantor began at an early stage, well before he embarked on the composition of *Gesta regum* and *Gesta pontificum*. The immaturity of the hands found in Auct. F.3.14, for example, led Thomson to infer that William's computus collection was copied at an early stage in the organization

---

[52] Robert of Cricklade also names the commentary as one of the three works by William that he has read: see n. 5 above.

[53] William of Malmesbury, *Liber super explanationem Lamentationum Ieremiae* prol., lines 7–21, ed. M. Winterbottom and R. M. Thomson with S. O. Sønnesyn, CCCM 244 (Turnhout, 2011), p. 3. The present translation modifies that found in William of Malmesbury, *On Lamentations* prol.1–2, trans. M. Winterbottom, CCT 13 (Turnhout, 2013), p. 35.

[54] *Explanatio Lamentationum* prol., lines 45–8, p. 4.

[55] *Historia novella* prol. and iii.79, pp. 2, 132.

of his *scriptorium* – at a time when his scribes were still learning their craft.[56]

Another issue is that there are good grounds for doubting the claims that William makes about himself in his prefaces. There is no sign, for example, that he ever had the domestic funds to purchase his own manuscripts: all of the sixteen manuscripts that he is known to have added to the library at Malmesbury seem to have been produced in a monastic *scriptorium* – none of them appear to have been made by a professional scribe.[57] It is a mistake, moreover, to read any of these prefaces as a guide to William's life story. For the function of the preface in the classical rhetorical tradition was not to give a plain account of what is going on, but to render the intended audience receptive to the opinions that will follow. As Cicero says in his *De inventione* – a rhetorical manual that informed much twelfth-century practice – the purpose of a *prooemium* was to make the listener *benevolus*, *docilis* and *attentus*, 'well-disposed', 'tractable' and 'attentive'.[58] Flattering the audience was one way of doing this; expressing concern for the audience by declaring a commitment to brevity – by expressing the desire to avoid causing boredom – was another. Constructing an image of the author himself as a like-minded soul with whom the reader could identify and sympathize could be even more effective.[59] The author might talk about the adversities that have delayed the completion of the work till now, about the immense difficulties involved in doing justice to the subject matter and about his fear of rejection – his fear

---

[56] Thomson, *William*, pp. 84–5; idem, 'The Manuscripts of William of Malmesbury (*c.* 1095–*c.* 1143)', in *Manuscripts at Oxford: An Exhibition in Memory of Richard William Hunt*, ed. A. C. de la Mare and B. C. Barker-Benfield (Oxford, 1980), pp. 27–9 (p. 27). It cannot be considered certain, however, that William derived the account of Robert de Losinga's acts at Hereford which appears in *GPA* i.164.1, p. 458 from this manuscript's copy of his *Excerpta Mariani*. Its exemplar might also have had the peculiar variant ('MariNani') which has given rise to this theory: see Stevenson, 'Contemporary Description', pp. 83–4, together with A. G. Watson, *A Catalogue of Dated and Datable Manuscripts, c. 435–1600, in Oxford Libraries*, 2 vols. (Oxford, 1984), I, 10.

[57] Consider, for example, Oxford, Lincoln College, MS lat. 100, a book containing Vegetius's *De re militari*, Julius Frontinus and Eutropius. The work of six scribes, its contents were corrected by William himself as though it were produced under his supervision. William's hand appears on fols. 3 (verses and table of contents) and 91b7–93r (genealogical tables). See Ker, 'Handwriting', p. 375; Thomson, *William*, pp. 86–7.

[58] Cicero, *De inventione* i.15.20, ed. H. M. Hubbell (Cambridge MA, 1949), p. 40. See, likewise, Quintilian, *Institutio oratoria* iv.1.5, ed. H. E. Butler, 4 vols. (Cambridge MA, 1920–2), II, 8.

[59] See T. Janson, *Latin Prose Prefaces: Studies in Literary Conventions* (Stockholm, 1964), esp. pp. 67, 70–1, 120–1; C. W. Mendell, *Tacitus: The Man and his Work* (New Haven CT, 1957), pp. 109–19; D. den Hengst, 'The Preface to Livy's *Ab urbe condita*', in *Emperors and Historiography: Collected Essays on the Literature of the Roman Empire*, ed. D. W. P. Burgersdijk and J. A. van Waarden (Leiden, 2010), pp. 52–67.

that his work will be received with derision and contempt – and so on. Many of the usual tricks can be found in William's prefaces. Sometimes they are deployed in a perfunctory fashion. In the preface to book one of *Gesta regum*, for example, William borrows and reworks a brief version of the rejection theme found in the preface to Justin's epitome of the *Historia Philippice*.[60] But William goes well beyond mechanical recycling of the usual topoi. In the manner of the best rhetoricians, of Quintilian and Cicero, he constructs and sustains throughout his histories an image of himself, an authorial voice, that is precisely tailored to the values and prejudices of the intended audience.

It is clear from the dedicatory letters that were discovered and first printed by Ewald Könsgen in 1975 that the monks of Malmesbury presented copies of *Gesta regum* to two leading figures at the court of Henry I – namely, his daughter the Empress Matilda (1102–67) and his brother-in-law David, king of Scotland (1124–53).[61] A revised text was presented to Robert, earl of Gloucester (1121/2–47), at some point in the mid to late 1130s.[62] It is clear from the letters to Matilda and David that William was hoping that they would intervene on the monks' behalf in their dispute with Roger, bishop of Salisbury (1102–39), who had usurped the abbacy. That is, *Gesta regum* was addressed to certain lords who were chosen largely because they could present the monks' concerns to the king without having to go through Roger, who was then second only to the king.[63] Elsewhere, also, William praises both David and Robert for being well-bred gentlemen devoted, not just to military pursuits, but to good manners and, in Robert's case, literature and philosophy.[64] Much less is known about the actual reading habits of twelfth-century lords than is known about those of contemporary religious,[65] but the evidence, such as it is, confirms that there were some bibliophiles among

---

[60] Compare *GRA* i.prol.8, p. 16, with Justinus, *Epitoma historiarum Philippicarum Pompei Trogi* pref., ed. O. Seel (Stuttgart, 1972), p. 2. The verbal echoes were first noticed by B. Guenée, 'L'Histoire entre l'éloquence et la science: Quelques remarques sur le prologue de Guillaume de Malmesbury à ses *Gesta regum Anglorum*', *Comptes rendus des séances de Académie des inscriptions et belles-lettres* 126 (1982), 357–70 (pp. 359–63).

[61] *GRA* epp. i and ii, pp. 2–9. Cf. E. Könsgen, 'Zwei unbekannte Briefe zu den *Gesta regum Anglorum* des Wilhelm von Malmesbury', *Deutsches Archiv* 31 (1975), 204–14.

[62] *GRA* ep. iii, pp. 10–12.

[63] See Hayward, 'The Importance of Being Ambiguous', esp. 93–6; idem, *Power, Rhetoric and Historical Practice*, chs. 1–2.

[64] *GRA* epp. i.1–2 and iii.2, pp. 2–4, 10; ii.228.2, p. 416; v.400.2 and 446–9, pp. 726, .798–800. For David's grasp of the conventions of *amicitia*, see also William of Saint-Denis, *Vita Sugerii abbatis* i, *Suger: Œuvres*, ed. and trans. F. Gasparri, 2 vols. (Paris, 2008), II, 292–373 (p. 311).

[65] On the private libraries in England and France and the difficulties involved in reconstructing their contents, see J. Stratford and T. Webber, 'Bishops and Kings: Private Book Collections in Medieval England', in *The Cambridge History of Libraries in Britain and Ireland*, vol. 1, *To 1640*, ed. E. Leedham-Green and T. Webber (Cambridge, 2006), I, 178–217 (esp. pp. 178–83, 197–9).

them. Hue de Rotelande says, for instance, that his patron Gilbert fitz Baderon, lord of Monmouth (1176/7–1190/1), had many books in his castle *e de latyn e de romaunz*, 'in both Latin and French'.[66] There are even grounds for thinking that the surge of interest in Senecan ethics – one of the century's most important cultural trends – owed much to the enthusiasms of the secular elite.[67]

No dedicatory letters survive for *Gesta pontificum*, but from its design it seems likely that it was intended, in the first instance, for an audience of higher clergy, and in the mid 1120s, when it was completed, that meant an audience which included many bishops. Most of the bishops who presided in England and Wales at this time were unreconstructed secular clerics: Chichester was the only diocese to have a monk as its bishop (Seffrid I); Canterbury had a regular canon (William de Corbeil); sixteen were ruled by seculars.[68] The preference of the later Anglo-Saxon kings for electing monastic bishops had been almost entirely reversed. Many of these bishops had concubines;[69] a few maintained large military retinues;[70] and several built castles in the style of great country houses – that is, symmetrical structures with courtyards and towers arranged as much for decorative as for defensive purposes, and furnished with deer parks so that they and their guests could indulge the pleasures of the hunt.[71]

That William presented himself as a quasi-secular figure in works directed at these sorts of readers – that he hardly appears here as a monk, let alone as a cantor – is surely no coincidence. In these rhetorical histories he was trying, at least at the outset, to elicit the sympathies of a secular elite by presenting himself as a self-driven gentleman with a love of books and the Roman ideal

---

[66] Hue de Rotelande, *Protheselaus* lines 12707–11, ed. A. J. Holden, Anglo-Norman Texts 47–9, 3 vols. (London, 1991–3), II, 174.

[67] See P. A. Hayward, 'The Earls of Leicester, Sygerius Lucanus and the Death of Seneca: Some Neglected Evidence for the Cultural Agency of the Norman Aristocracy', *Speculum* 91 (2016), 328–55.

[68] This analysis is based on the evidence assembled in the relevant volumes of *EEA*; and *Fasti Ecclesiae Anglicanae 1066–1300*, ed. D. E. Greenway et al. (London, 1968–). The figures exclude St Asaphs, owing to its uncertain status at this time. Cf. R. Bartlett, *England under the Norman and Angevin Kings, 1075–1225* (Oxford, 2000), pp. 395–9; E. U. Crosby, *The King's Bishops: The Politics of Patronage in England and Normandy, 1066–1216* (New York, 2013), esp. pp. 38–9.

[69] See Crosby, *King's Bishops*, pp. 54–8.

[70] For Bishop Roger's bodyguard, see *Gesta Stephani* i.34, ed. and trans. K. R. Potter and R. H. C. Davis (Oxford, 1976), p. 72.

[71] For Bishop Roger's castles, see *Historia novella* ii.22, p. 44; R. A. Stalley, 'A 12th-Century Patron of Architecture: A Study of the Buildings Erected by Roger, Bishop of Salisbury, 1102–39', *Journal of the British Archaeological Association*, 3rd s. 34 (1971), 62–83 (pp. 65–70). On the secular clergy's enthusiasm for aristocratic pastimes, such as hunting and courtly love, see also H. M. Thomas, *The Secular Clergy in England, 1066–1216* (Oxford, 2014), pp. 42–8.

of *otium* – as a kindred spirit with whom a great prince might happily share an irreverent joke about the eunuch-bishop of London or about how the crusaders dealt with Turks who hid coins in their 'unmentionables'. But in the works that he wrote for religious audiences – and here the intended audience would seem, on the evidence of Robert of Cricklade's comments,[72] to have extended beyond his own house to include other religious communities – he attempts to render his readers receptive by presenting himself as a fatherly advisor sincerely motivated by monastic ideals. The contrast between William's histories and his monastic works is best explained, in short, not by bringing in his personal evolution, but by considering the audience, context and purpose of each text. The histories were written during periods in his career when his concerns as a cantor had to be set aside.

For the purposes of the present volume there is a useful conclusion to be taken from this case study. One of the core issues before us concerns the ways in which being a cantor may have shaped certain historians' approaches to the past: to what extent did it favour certain methods and styles of history? It is tempting to simplify the problem by arguing that cantors had a particular *mentalité*, that holding this office channelled them towards definable ways of thinking about the past that we can reconstruct and use to control the interpretation of their texts.[73] The work of some cantor-historians, not least those who confined their literary activities to the production of saints' lives and annals, lends itself to this approach; but it is hardly adequate for the purposes of comprehending William's work. Armed with an agile mind, he had the capacity to move from one way of processing ideas and observations to another as the needs of the moment required.[74] As Lanfranc himself recognized when he provided for the delegation of various duties associated with the role, the abilities of those who fulfilled the office of cantor could and did vary.[75]

---

[72] Notice also that Robert makes no mention of *GRA* or *GPA*: see n. 5 above.

[73] On the construction of 'con-texts', see R. M. Stein, 'Literary Criticism and the Evidence for History', in *Writing Medieval History*, ed. N. Partner (London, 2004), pp. 67–87; and for a critique of the concept of *mentalité*, see S. Reynolds, 'Social Mentalities and the Case of Medieval Scepticism', *Transactions of the Royal Historical Society*, 6th s. 1 (1991), 21–47.

[74] On literary genres as expressions of differing 'modes of thought', 'interpretive frameworks', and 'patterned', 'narrativised' or 'rule-governed forms of thinking', see C. F. Feldman, 'Genres as Mental Models', in *Psychoanalysis and Development: Representations and Narratives*, ed. M. Ammaniti and D. N. Stern (New York, 1994), pp. 111–21. See also C. F. Feldman and D. A. Kalmar, 'Autobiography and Fiction as Modes of Thought', in *Modes of Thought: Explorations in Culture and Cognition*, ed. D. R. Olson and N. Torrance (Cambridge, 1996), pp. 106–22 (esp. pp. 113–18); J. Bruner, 'Frames for Thinking: Ways of Making Meaning', in *Modes of Thought*, pp. 93–105 (esp. pp. 97–8, 102).

[75] See n. 4 above.

Another point follows from these findings. William's ability to vary his mode of expression so radically may have been unusual, but there are good grounds for thinking that he acquired his skills in his own monastery – not in a private, non-monastic context, as suggested by the preface to book two of *Gesta regum*. It seems almost certain that he had become a Benedictine in the usual manner for this time: as an oblate whose parents had given him to his community in his infancy.[76] He all but admits as much at one point in *Gesta regum*,[77] and his comments about the improvements in teaching that took place at Malmesbury under Abbot Godfrey (1087×91–1101×5) suggest that he himself witnessed this development.[78] It seems unlikely that many monasteries could offer an education as empowering as that provided at Malmesbury, but William's intellect and range show that they could, if their abbots and teachers were sufficiently adept and open-minded, do much to enrich and expand the imaginative world and literary skills of their monks. The present case study suggests, then, that we should be open to the possibility that monasteries were enabling environments that could help individuals to broaden their minds rather than as structures that worked to confine thought to particular channels – even though that complicates the task of explicating their histories.

---

[76] On the practice of oblation, see M. Chibnall, *The World of Orderic Vitalis* (Oxford, 1984), pp. 73–6; and for its origins, see M. de Jong, *In Samuel's Image: Child Oblation in the Early Medieval West* (Leiden, 1995).

[77] *GRA* ii.170.1, p. 288.

[78] *GPA* v.271.3, p. 644. In several chapters he says that he himself witnessed a miracle which took place during Godfrey's abbacy (*GPA* v.272.10, 273.6–7, 274.3–4), but if the images of himself found in his prefaces are questionable, then these claims must also be considered vulnerable. Cf. Thomson, *William*, pp. 4–5.

13

Lex orandi, lex scribendi?
The Role of Historiography in the
Liturgical Life of William of Malmesbury

Sigbjørn Olsen Sønnesyn

In the late 1130s, the Augustinian canon Robert of Cricklade found cause to underscore his credentials as a reader of monastic works of devotion.

> Nam et que in manus nostras venerunt scripta venerabilis abbatis Clarisvallensis legi; et viri summe eruditionis Guillelmi Meldunensis ecclesie monachi et cantoris preclarum opus quod super Lamentationes Ieremie compilavit non tantum legi, verum ut et in nostra ecclesia scriptum haberetur exegi.[1]

> [I have read whatever writings of the venerable abbot of Clairvaux that has come into my hands; and the brilliant work that the man of supreme learning, William, monk and cantor of Malmesbury, compiled on the Lamentations of Jeremiah I not only read, but even caused to be copied for our church.]

Robert goes on to praise William's miracles of the Virgin and his florilegium of Gregory the Great. This is, as far as I know, the only preserved reference to William of Malmesbury written in his own lifetime, and the focus and emphasis of Robert's portrayal offers a striking contrast to the prevailing image of William found in contemporary scholarship.[2] Though in recent

---

[1] Robert of Cricklade, *De connubio Patriarche Iacob* II, 22; Bodl Laud. misc. 725, fol. 129v. Printed in R. W. Hunt, 'English Learning in the Late Twelfth Century', *Transactions of the Royal Historical Society* 4th s. 19 (1936), 19–42 (p. 32).

[2] The fundamental study of William of Malmesbury remains R. M. Thomson, *William of Malmesbury*, 2nd edn (Woodbridge, 2003). For William as a historian and man of letters see also e.g. J. Gillingham, 'Civilizing the English? The English Histories of William of Malmesbury and David Hume', *Historical Research* 74 (2001), 17–43; R. M. Thomson, 'William of Malmesbury and the Latin Classics Revisited', *Proceedings of the British Academy* 129 (2005), 383–93; N. Wright, '"Industriae Testimonium": William of Malmesbury and Latin Poetry Revisited', *RB* 103 (1993), 482–531; N. Wright, 'William of Malmesbury and Latin Poetry: Further Evidence for a Benedictine's Reading', *RB* 101 (1991), 122–53; P. A. Hayward, 'The Importance of Being Ambiguous: Innuendo and Legerdemain in William of Malmesbury's *Gesta Regum* and *Gesta Pontificum Anglorum*', *ANS* 33 (2011), 75–102; A. Plassmann, 'Bedingungen und Strukturen von Machtausübung bei Wilhelm von Malmesbury

times William has been known and perceived mainly through his historical works, his monumental works on the deeds of the kings and bishops of the English are not even mentioned by Robert. Rather William the historian is overshadowed by William the cantor and monk, placed alongside no less a figure than Bernard of Clairvaux as a supreme exponent of monastic spirituality and devotion. The apparent tension between William the empirical, classicizing historian as we know him today and William the spiritual and liturgical master highlights the question I will address in what follows: to what extent did William's liturgical and other monastic practices and obligations influence, inform and direct his work as a historian and collector of classical literature? We know that William performed many of the tasks commonly associated with the office of cantor in this period, such as directing the library at Malmesbury.[3] But what interests me is not the exact extent of his activities as cantor, but the extent to which these informed his historiographical works, that is to say, the extent to which the principles and aims inherent in the role of *monachus et cantor* are commensurate with the principles and aims of his writing of history.[4]

The question of how and even if we may reconcile these two seemingly divergent perceptions of William is, of course, crucial to our understanding of his celebrated historiographical works, but it also has more general import given William's position as arguably the most accomplished of the great wave of monastic historians active in the first half of the long twelfth century. Though William's historiography has been studied in great detail, his theology has received comparatively scant attention.[5] In what follows I

und Heinrich von Huntingdon', in *Macht und Spiegel der Macht*, ed. N. Kersken and G. Verchamer (Wiesbaden, 2013), pp. 145–71; J. Gillingham, 'A Historian of the Twelfth-Century Renaissance and the Transformation of English Society, 1066–c.1200', in *European Transformations: The Long Twelfth Century*, ed. T. F. X. Noble and J. Van Engen (Notre Dame, 2012), pp. 45–74. For a somewhat different approach see e.g. K. A. Fenton, *Gender, Nation and Conquest in the Works of William of Malmesbury* (Woodbridge, 2008); B. Weiler, 'William of Malmesbury, Henry I, and the *Gesta Regum Anglorum*', ANS 31 (2009), 157–76; and S. O. Sønnesyn, *William of Malmesbury and the Ethics of History* (Woodbridge, 2012).

3 See Thomson, *William*, pp. 5–8; cf. Fass A, as well as many of the chapters featured in this volume, especially Paul Hayward's chapter on William of Malmesbury and Charles Rozier's and Teresa Webber's chapters on other twelfth-century English cantors.

4 I have set out what I take to be the guiding principles of William's writing of history in Sønnesyn, *Ethics of History*. See also the perceptive analysis in S. Bagge, 'Ethics, Politics, and Providence in William of Malmesbury's *Historia Novella*', *Viator* 41 (2010), 113–32.

5 The most comprehensive studies of William's theology are found in the context of editions of his theological works. See in particular D. H. Farmer, 'William of Malmesbury's Commentary on Lamentations', *Studia Monastica* 4 (1962), 283–311; William of Malmesbury, *De Laudibus et Miraculis Sanctae Mariae*, ed. J. M. Canal, *El libro 'De Laudibus et Miraculis Sanctae Mariae' de Guillermo de Malmesbury* (Rome,

will argue that William's scattered comments on the liturgy and its role in the monastic life amounts to a strong affirmation of a theology of liturgy that was central to monastic spirituality in the early and high Middle Ages and, furthermore, that his historiography can be, and even needs to be, seen in the light of this organic, comprehensive concept of the good monastic life. The structure of theology and ethics that William invokes issues from and is consummated in a spirituality of living and embodied faith expressed and nourished in prayer, especially in the singing of the Divine Office and the reading of Scripture. It is within such an overarching scheme, I will argue, that the apparent incommensurability of liturgy and history in William's works may be overcome.

William's collected œuvre offers rich materials for analysing the principles and tendencies of his thought on the liturgy and its significance for what he conceived of as the good and upright life. The notion of the good human life arguably played a guiding and fundamental role in William's intellectual and literary endeavours. The richness and comprehensiveness of this notion means that a full exposition of its constituent parts would be beyond the scope of this chapter; for our present purposes, the key feature of William's concept of the good human life is the embodiment of the virtues that actualize the human potential for goodness, and that direct and order the human love of and search for God.[6] While William drew on his extensive knowledge of classical thought to conceptualize and express his ethical ground views, the substance of his notion is summed up in the Christian concept of holiness. Throughout William's collected œuvre, strict, devout and assiduous liturgical observance is presented both as the supreme outward sign of individual and communal holiness, and as the most efficacious way through which such holiness is attained. A clear example here is William's surprisingly detailed and laudatory account of the emergence of the Cistercian way of life, the *religio Cistellensis*, which constitutes a substantial digression in the fourth book of his *Gesta regum Anglorum*. William was clearly impressed with these monks' renouncement of material possessions, but certainly also with their liturgical observance:

> Vestiti dormiunt et cincti, nec ullo tempore post matutinas ad lectos redeunt; sed ita horam matutinarum temperant ut ante laudes lucescat, ita regule incubantes ut nec iota unum nec apicem pretereundum putent. Statim

---

1968); and William of Malmesbury, *Abbreviatio Amalarii*, ed. R. W. Pfaff, 'The "Abbreviatio Amalarii" of William of Malmesbury', *Recherches de théologie ancienne et médiévale* 48 (1981), 128–71. See also S. O. Sønnesyn, 'Theology', in William of Malmesbury, *Liber super Explanationem Lamentationum Ieremiae Prophetae*, ed. R. M. Thomson and M. Winterbottom, with Sigbjørn Sønnesyn, CCCM 244 (2011), pp. xviii–xxiii.

[6] See Sønnesyn, *Ethics of History*, pp. 21–95 for a fuller exposition of William's moral outlook.

post laudes primam canunt, post primam in opera horis constitutis exeunt; quicquid fatiendum vel cantandum est, die sine aliena lucerna consummant. Nullus ex horis diurnis, nullus ex complectorio umquam deest, preter infirmos ... Horas canonicas indefesse continuant, nulla appenditia extrinsecus aditientes preter vigiliam pro defunctis. Cantus et himnos Ambrosianos, quantum ex Mediolano addiscere potuerunt, frequentat in divinis officiis. Hospitum et infirmorum curam habentes, importabiles corporibus suis pro animarum remedio comminiscuntur cruces.[7]

[They sleep fully clothed and wearing their girdles, and do not return to their beds anytime after Matins, but so arrange the time of Matins that daybreak may precede Lauds, keeping so closely to the Rule that they think it wrong to diverge by one letter, one iota. Immediately after Lauds they sing Prime, and after Prime go out to work for the prescribed number of hours; all work or singing in choir is completed by daylight without artificial light. No one ever misses the day-hours or Compline except the sick. ... They maintain the canonical hours without flinching, adding nothing further from outside sources except the Vigils of the Dead. In the Divine Office they normally use the chants and hymns of the Ambrosian rite, so far as they have been able to learn them from Milan.]

Here, William shows some insight into the reforms of Cistercian music underway in the 1120s,[8] but he does not commend the Cistercians for the aesthetic beauty of their liturgical celebration, but rather for their quest for authenticity and devotion, markers of identity that are also prominently featured in the documents preserving the Cistercians' own articulations of reform.[9] It is clear that it is this austere and intensely focused way of life that is much admired by William.

In keeping with the Benedictine tradition within which he lived and worked, William insisted that the Divine Office – and particularly its backbone, the Psalter – was crucial for proper monastic observance.[10] In the same way that strict and devout liturgical observance marked out the Cistercian way of life as particularly holy, so too William consistently uses this feature as a marker of holiness in individuals. Unfailing devotion to the Psalter and the canonical hours was a main feature of the lives of such important figures as Wilfrid and Bede, William's chief model.[11] William's lengthy depiction of Bishop Wulfstan

---

[7] *GRA* iv.336, pp. 581–4.

[8] See in particular C. Waddell, 'The Origin and Early Evolution of the Cistercian Antiphonary: Reflections on Two Cistercian Chant Reforms', in *The Cistercian Spirit: A Symposium in Memory of Thomas Merton*, ed. M. B. Pennington (Washington, 1973), pp. 190–223.

[9] See Waddell, 'Origin and Early Evolution'.

[10] See all the essays collected in *The Divine Office in the Latin Middle Ages: Methodology and Source Studies, Regional Developments, Hagiography*, ed. M. E. Fassler and R. A. Baltzer (Oxford, 2000).

[11] See, respectively, *GPA*, I, 328–49 and *GRA* i.59–60, pp. 88–91.

of Worcester, both in the *Gesta pontificum* and in the *vita* dedicated to the saint, will suffice as a representative sample. William emphasizes that Wulfstan 'non enim, ut tunc et nunc quidam, missa cursim mane cantata, tota die post hec gule vel questibus inhiabat, sed morosiore cura debitum consummans offitium orationes cotidianas et diuturnas aditiebat' ('did not, as some then and still do, sing the Mass cursorily in the morning, and proceed to spend the rest of the day intent on appetite and profit; instead, he completed the set office with scrupulous care, and supplemented it with prayers for long periods of the day').[12] As this statement illustrates, exterior observance of communal prayer was dependent upon and organically linked to interior devotion. Only in so far as it was sincerely and devoutly performed could the liturgy fulfil the central role William marks out for it in his narratives.

The role played by the liturgy in William's conception of the good and upright life is consistently and explicitly emphasized in this way in his narrative works. He privileges the practice of *religio* as the crucial constituent of moral and political progress.[13] As we have seen, the supporting pillar of the *religio Cistellensis* was the liturgy, and this is a crucial feature of William's usage of the term. The sense of *religio* centring on a life of prayer is recurrent in his depictions of individual holiness, and in general it would not unduly strain evidence or etymology to say that, to for William, the ligature of *religio* was the *lex orandi*.[14]

This also emerges from William's account of the importance of learning, both in a monastic context and in a broader social and political milieu. From an early age William worked closely with a certain Godfrey, who was abbot from 1081 to 1107 and brought the vibrant Norman monasticism from his native Jumiéges to Malmesbury.[15] William informs us that his prodigious efforts to continue Abbot Godfrey's labours to expand the library at Malmesbury was ordered towards providing the requisite level of learning for carrying out the Opus Dei:

> ego ad legendum multa congessi, probitatem predicandi viri in hoc dumtaxat emulatus. Ipsius ergo laudabili cepto pro virili portione non defui. Utinam sit qui labores nostros foveat! Monachi, qui vulgares tantum litteras balbutiebant, perfecte informati. Servitium Dei institutum liberaliter, actitatum instanter, adeo ut monasterium per Angliam nullum Malmesberiensi excelleret, multaque cederent.[16]

---

[12] *GPA* iv.137, pp. 422–3.

[13] Most notably in his depiction of the progress of the English before their slide into decadence prior to the Norman Conquest; see *GRA* iii.245, p. 456–7.

[14] Cf. the aphorism, *lex orandi, lex credendi*, often misatributed to Prosper of Aquitaine. See e.g. E. Palazzo, 'Foi et croyance au Moyen Âge: Les méditations liturgiques', *Annales. Histoire, Sciences Sociales*, 53 (1998), 1131–54 (p. 1135).

[15] Cf. Thomson, *William*, pp. 5–7.

[16] *GPA* v.271, pp. 644–5.

[I have collected much material for reading, approaching the prowess of my excellent predecessor at least in this respect; I have followed up his laudable start as best I could. Let us hope there may be someone to cherish the fruits of our labours! The monks, who had been mere stutterers in common or garden learning, were now given a proper education. The service of God was liberally endowed and put into effect as a matter of urgency, with the result that no monastery in all England excelled Malmesbury, and many yielded precedence to it.]

This passage is crucial in several respects. It quite clearly subordinates William's hard work as a librarian to the needs of the liturgy, and presents the rejuvenated observance at Malmesbury as the most important fruit of this labour. This not only illustrates how and why it had become expedient to merge the offices of cantor and *armarius* in this period,[17] but it also shows the importance William attached to the monastery as a space dedicated to a living tradition focused on communal, informed and devout worship. The entire length of the substantial fifth book of the *Gesta pontificum* is devoted to an account of Malmesbury Abbey from its origins, through its growth to maturity under Aldhelm's leadership, and finally to the resurgence of learning and prayer in William's own time. William's obvious pride and veneration for the tradition with which he was entrusted, and his fervent desire for this tradition to continue after his own time, suggest the motivation behind his various activities and the aim toward which these activities were directed.

The Bible may seem to occupy a radically relegated position within the scheme I have outlined so far. But nothing, indeed, could be farther from the full picture I am trying to sketch out here. The Word of God was absolutely central and fundamental to William, as it was to the monastic tradition he strove to maintain and develop, but the liturgy and the reading of the Bible formed one organic whole, rather than distinct and competing practices. Biblical exegesis was never an academic discipline in monastic culture – never aimed purely at adding to a reified body of knowledge. On the contrary, reading – and in particular the reading of Scripture – was a discipline oriented toward the total transformation of the reader.[18] The model of the multiple senses of Scripture that dominated medieval exegesis saturates William's

---

[17] See Fass A.

[18] See in particular D. Robertson, *Lectio Divina: The Medieval Experience of Reading* (Collegeville, MI, 2011); cf. E. Morgan, *The Incarnation of the Word: The Theology of Language of Augustine of Hippo* (London, 2010); J. Leclercq, *The Love of Learning and the Desire for God: A Study of Monastic Culture*, trans. Catharine Misrahi (New York, 1961), particularly pp. 15–22; and H. de Lubac, *Medieval Exegesis: The Four Senses of Scripture*, trans. E. M. Macierowski, 3 vols. (Grand Rapids/Cambridge, 1998–2009), here e.g. I, 230–67. See also B. Stock, *Augustine the Reader: Meditation, Self-Knowledge and the Ethics of Interpretation* (Cambridge MA, 1996).

works in the very way that it saturated his intellectual culture.[19] As Henri de Lubac has shown, medieval exegesis started out from the historical or literal meaning of Scripture as a necessary and inescapable starting point, but the goal of exegesis was to uncover the spiritual senses, the ways in which the Spirit spoke through the text to the heart of the Church and of the individual believer to effect inner reformation.[20] The spiritual senses of Scripture were not reached through philological, historical and reductively rational analysis, but through *lectio divina,* an ascent of the individual spirit to a contemplation of God and subsequent transformation of life.[21]

As the research of Susan Boynton has shown, the performance of the Bible in liturgy was a crucial part of the how the Word of God was embodied in a monastic context,[22] and in William's various works we find numerous examples of this.[23] William took great pains to show that the unceasing, responsive reading of Scripture was held to be constitutive of monastic life in England from the arrival of Christianity onwards.[24] But this study of Scripture is never described as an academic pursuit producing abstract knowledge; on the contrary, it is always presented as issuing from a life lived in Christ. Reading, prayer and meditation form an indivisible whole ordered towards reforming the soul. This comes to the fore in William's portrait of Bede. William quotes Bede's own account of his life: 'omnem meditandis scripturis operam dedi, atque inter observantiam discipline regularis et cotidianam cantandi in ecclesia curam, semper aut discere aut docere aut scribere duce habui' ('I devoted all my pains to the meditation on Scripture. In the intervals of regular monastic observance and the daily task of singing in choir, to learn, to teach or to write have ever been my joy').[25] William

---

[19] The fundamental account here is of course de Lubac, *Medieval Exegesis.* William employs the tripartite division of senses found, for instance, in Gregory I and Bede, but, as de Lubac clearly shows, the superficial differences between a threefold and a fourfold scheme of meanings rest on a fundamental unity of purpose and method (*Medieval Exegesis,* I, 132–4).

[20] See, again, de Lubac, *Medieval Exegesis,* I, 266–7 and passim.

[21] Robertson, *Lectio Divina,* passim; Leclercq, *Love of Learning,* pp. 15–22.

[22] S. Boynton, 'The Bible and the Liturgy', in *The Practice of the Bible in the Middle Ages: Production, Reception, and Performance in Western Christianity,* ed. S. Boynton and D. J. Reilly (New York, 2011), pp. 10–33. Cf. I. Cochelin, 'When Monks Were the Book: The Bible and Monasticism (6th–11th Centuries)', in Boynton and Reilly, ed., *The Practice of the Bible,* 61–83.

[23] The most explicit example here is the *Abbreviatio Amalarii,* in which William shows how the liturgical unity of the individual Sundays and feast days bring out the implications of the Biblical readings. In light of the practice set out in the *Abbreviatio,* see also e.g, the singing of Psalms mentioned in *GPA* ii.94, pp. 314–15; iii.100, pp. 330–1; v.213, pp. 538–9.

[24] See for instance the constitutions of the council at Clovesho in 743, extensively quoted in *GPA* i.5, pp. 10–13 (esp. pp. 12–13).

[25] *GRA* i.55, pp. 86–7.

places Bede's attitude to Scripture squarely within the monastic tradition of meditative reading described by Jean Leclercq and, more recently, by Duncan Robertson.[26] William's portrait of Bede illustrates well that the framework within which such meditation was carried out was liturgical. William adds: 'Nam et fidei sane et incuriose sed dulcis fuit eloquentie, in omnibus explanationibus divinarum scripturarum magis illa rimatus quibus lector Dei dilectionem et proximi combiberet quam illa quibus vel sales libaret vel lingue rubiginem limaret' ('His faith was sound, his style unpretentious but agreeable; in all his biblical commentaries he sought out material from which his reader might absorb the love of God and his neighbour, rather than the means of displaying a pretty wit or sharpening a rusty pen').[27] The purpose of studying the Bible was to be called and equipped to serving God and the wider community.

This approach to the Bible is not restricted to William's reports of the teachings of others; it recurs throughout his own teachings. William echoes his description of Bede in the preface to his Commentary on Lamentations, stating that while he had spent his youthful years playing at history, he penitently vowed to devote his more mature years to another kind of writing, the sort that, more than any other, could enflame the heart with the love of God.[28] William's commentary is certainly modelled on those of Bede in that it does not primarily provide analytical, abstract knowledge of the text; rather, it is a spiritual exercise, a protracted meditation on the text, guiding the reader to engage with the text as something interior, to let the soul be moved with the movements of the lament.[29]

Closely paralleling the methods of biblical exegesis are William's allegorical interpretations of the prayers, ceremonies and sacraments of the liturgy.[30] His *Abbreviatio Amalarii* offers the clearest example of such allegoresis. Here, he repeatedly shows how the set prayers, chants and readings for specific days in the liturgical calendar form organic wholes that reciprocally enhance the mysterious sense hidden in the texts:

> In sexagesima vero sicut septuagesima tribulationibus premimur. Unde et introitus est Esurge quare obdormis Domine. Oratio, Deus qui conspicis, quia ex nulla nostra virtute subsistimus. In epistola bonus athleta nos

---

[26] See Leclercq, *Love of Learning*; Robertson, *Lectio Divina*.

[27] *GRA* i.5, pp. 88–9.

[28] *Liber super explanationem Lamentationum*, p. 3.

[29] See Sønnesyn, 'Theology'.

[30] J. Monti, *A Sense of the Sacred: Roman Catholic Worship in the Middle Ages* (San Fransicso, 2012); Claude Barthe, 'The "Mystical" Meaning of the Ceremonies of the Mass: Liturgical Exegesis in the Middle Ages', in *The Genius of the Roman Rite: Historical, Theological, and Pastoral Perspectives on Catholic Liturgy*, ed. Uwe Michael Lang (Chicago, 2010), pp. 179–97.

hortatur exemplo qui tribulationes patienter suffere. ... Et qui in evangelio septuagesime missi sumus in vineam Domini, in evangelio ammonemur sexagesime ut simus boni agricole tale semen iaciendo quod afferat fructum in patientia. Sic de ceteris potest studiosus lector intelligere quod constitutor officiorum nostrorum nichil otiosum in eis voluit constituere.[31]

[On Sexagesima Sunday, as on Septuagesima, we are pressed down by tribulations. Therefore the introit is 'Arise; why do you sleep, O Lord', and the collect is 'God, you who see', because we are not in any way sustained through our own virtue. In the Epistle the good athlete who suffers tribulations patiently exhorts us through his example. ... And we, who in the Gospel for Septuagesima are sent into the vineyard of the Lord, are in the Gospel for Sexagesima admonished to be like the seed scattered by the good farmer that brings forth fruit in patience. In the same way may the assiduous reader understand that the composer of our Office would not compose anything idle in them.]

The liturgy, then, is the framework within which the Gospel is understood and applied in the lives of the monks – the various parts of the liturgy guide the devout soul through a set of movements designed to allow the Word of God to take root in the individuals who take part in it. And just as the various parts of the liturgy for individual days mutually inform each other, so does the recurring, rhythmical pattern within which these parts find their appointed place. Concerning the construction of the liturgical cycle, William writes:

Item lectio significat vetus testamentum quod non multum clare auditum est dum tantum in iudea notus Deus. Responsorium designat novum testamentum, cuius sonus exivit in omnem terram. Sicut cantus dulcior est auditu quam lectio, ita evangelium quod promittit vitam eternam dulcius est lege que promittit felicitatem caducam.[32]

[Likewise the reading signifies the Old Testament which is not heard very clearly while God is known only in Judea. The responsory designates the New Testament, the sound of which goes out to all the ends of the earth. Just as singing is sweeter than reading to the hearing, so too the Gospel that promises eternal life is sweeter than the law that promises perishable happiness.]

William goes on to explain that while the responsory answers the reading of the Old Testament law with the teaching of the Gospel, the verse in the responsory requires the inward application of the Gospel teaching: 'in versu

---

[31] *Abbreviatio Amalarii* I.ii, pp. 132–3.
[32] Ibid., II.ix, p. 156.

ad nos versi nos ipsos castigamus'.[33] The Alleluia then signifies the joy of the life to come, not in hope but in actuality.[34]

> Pulcherrimus ergo ordo, ut qui in lectione didicimus, in responsorio docuimus, in versu teneamus disciplinam, in Alleluia pro talibus studiis perpetuam habeamus letitiam. Quod ideo repetitur, quia duplex letitia erit ibi anime et corporis.[35]

> [This is therefore the most beautiful order, that we who learn in the reading, teach in responsory and maintain discipline in the verse, possess perpetual joy on account of these pursuits in the Alleluia.]

Again, William highlights how the liturgy guides and motivates the movements of the participant's soul. In the jubilant melismas of liturgical song one experiences a foretaste of the perfect felicity of the life to come:

> Cantus quem vocant sequentiam, quem sine ullis verbis quondam uibique, nunc in aliquibus ecclesiis post Alleluia, solent canere, illam laudem figurat qua in futura vita sancti Deum laudabunt, magis conscientie puritate quam sono articulato.[36]

> [The song that they call the sequence, which, without any words was once performed everywhere, and now in some churches after the Alleluia, is a figure of the praise with which the saints worship God in the life to come, more through the purity of their conscience than through the sound they make.]

It is always for the sake of this inner disposition, and not for exterior conformity, that the liturgy is performed. The choir should not merely sing with their voice, but fulfil the sense of the song through their voice;[37] their song acquired mystical meaning not through the sound they made, but through the purity of their conscience.

This reference to purity of conscience should also remind us that, for William, participation in the liturgy and meditation on Scripture had an irreducible moral component. Again his portrayal of Bede offers an instructive example. Bede's ability to penetrate into the mysteries of Scripture within the framework of liturgical observance rested precisely on

---

[33] Ibid.: 'Quod ideo responsorium dicitur, quia respondet et consonat veteri legi, ut impleat spiritualiter quod illa carnaliter prefigurat. Habet et versum, quia omnis bonus predicator postquam aliis predicaverit ad mentem quam convertitur, ne cum aliis predicat ipse reprobus inveniatur. In lectione ergo discimus, in responsorio aliis predicamus, in versu ad nos versi, nos ipsos castigamus.'

[34] Ibid.: 'Alleluia vero significat gaudium future vite non in spe sed in re.'

[35] Ibid.

[36] Ibid., p.157.

[37] Ibid.: 'Tenent ergo cantores tabulas, ut ammoneantur non solum voce canere sed etiam sensum cantus voce explere.'

the purity of his character. In fact, his prodigious wisdom was proof of the blamelessness of his character, just as the biblical adage that into a malicious soul Wisdom shall not enter promises. Bede's moral purity allowed him to penetrate into the deepest mysteries in meditation, and to pour forth the fruits of these meditations in his teaching: 'defecatus itaque vitiis subibat in interiora velaminis, que intus exceperat in animo fora efferens sermone castigato' ('purified from his sins he entered within the veil, and what he received within it in his heart, he brought forth to the world with disciplined speech').[38]

In the tradition of thought and spirituality to which both Bede and William belonged, the liturgy, and particularly the cyclical and unceasing repetition of the Psalms, was both the supreme method for attaining the purity of spirit which made Bede so receptive to the promptings of the Spirit, and the best approximation, in this temporal existence, to the ultimate goal for human development. Such a convoluted statement is in need of some unpacking. The Christian Middle Ages had inherited from classical moral philosophy a conception of ethics aimed at realizing the *telos*, the highest good and ultimate aim of human nature.[39] In the most influential incarnations of this mode of thought the ultimate end of human nature was not the satisfaction of the passions or full possession of reified goods, but by a good way of life, a good way of being-in-act.[40] By inculcating the virtues, that is, stable habits of character disposing those who embodied them to act in accordance with their *telos*, one could institute a way of life that would realize the full potential and the ultimate end of human nature.[41] While this fully realized mode of human life in classical thought was attainable by human resources alone and in temporal immanent human communities, Christian dogma had entailed the transposition of this ultimate end to the transcendent realm, which could only be attained through the gift of divine grace.[42] The perfection of human existence was no longer a life of civic virtue in a political community, but communion with God through

---

[38] *GRA* i.59, pp. 90–1.

[39] I have described this in detail in Sønnesyn, *Ethics of History*, pp. 21–41.

[40] It would be beyond the present scope to go into detail here. My reading of medieval ethics on this point is laid out in Sønnesyn, 'Ut sine fine amet summam essentiam: The Eudaemonist Ethics of St. Anselm', *Mediaeval Studies* 70 (2008), 1–29; and 'Qui Recta Quae Docet Sequitur, Vere Philosophus Est: The Ethics of John of Salisbury', in *A Companion to John of Salisbury*, ed. C. Grellard and F. Lachaud (Leiden, 2014), pp. 307–38.

[41] See e.g. I. P. Bejczy, *The Cardinal Virtues in the Middle Ages: A Study in Moral Thought from the Fourth to the Fourteenth Century* (Leiden, 2011).

[42] On this I am fundamentally influenced by the thesis argued in H. de Lubac, *The Mystery of the Supernatural* (London, 1967); see Sønnesyn, 'Ethics of John of Salisbury', pp. 323–30.

grace – in a glass darkly during earthly life and face to face in the life to come.[43]

For our present purposes, it is crucial to note that prayer, and particularly liturgical prayer centred on the Psalms, constituted the closest approximation to human beatitude within temporal existence.[44] Catherine Pickstock has suggested that ancient as well as Christian moral philosophy was consummated not in a system of doctrine, but in liturgical praise, and the Church Fathers, to whom William constantly professed his allegiance, certainly saturated their written works with references to such an idea.[45] Augustine, who more than any other single thinker translated classical eudaimonism into a Christian framework, emphasized the uniquely transformative power of liturgical prayer, and described liturgical praise as the only adequate response on the part of human beings to the salvific, gratuitous love offered by God.[46] Benedict admonished his monks to put nothing above the Opus Dei, and this admonition was in turn based on the scriptural injunction to pray unceasingly. William, in his role as cantor, will have been responsible for translating this into practice at Malmesbury. In the fifth and final book of the *Gesta pontificum* William's pride in the tradition of prayer and learning established by Aldhelm shines through, and there is every reason to believe that William was familiar with the theological underpinnings and implications of liturgical celebration. For example, William likely knew the following passage from Gregory the Great's Homilies on Ezekiel also disseminated to medieval monks through Alcuin's *de usu psalmorum*:

Vox enim psalmodie cum per intentionem cordis agitur, per hanc omnipotenti Domino ad cor iter paratur, ut intente menti vel prophetie mysteria vel compunctionis gratiam infundat. Unde scriptum est: Sacrificium laudis honorificabit me, et illic iter est quo ostendam illi salutare Dei ... In sacrificio igitur laudis fit Iesu iter ostensionis, quia dum per psalmodiam compunctio effunditur, via nobis in corde fit per quam ad Iesum in fine pervenitur.[47]

---

[43] Cf. Sønnesyn, *Ethics of History*, pp. 24–30.

[44] See R. Fulton, 'Praying with Anselm at Admont: A Meditation on Practice', *Speculum* 81 (2006), 700–33; M. A. Edsall, 'Learning from the Exemplar: Anselm's Prayers and Meditations and the Charismatic Text', *Mediaeval Studies* 72 (2010), 161–96; S. Boynton, 'Prayer as Liturgical Performance in Eleventh- and Twelfth-Century Monastic Psalters', *Speculum* 82 (2007), 896–931.

[45] See Catherine Pickstock, *After Writing: On the Liturgical Consummation of Philosophy* (Oxford, 1998).

[46] Among an enormous number of relevant passages, cf. e.g. Augustine, *Enarrationes in Psalmos* XLIX.21, CXXXIV, ed. D. E. Dekkers and J. Fraipont, 2 vols. (Turnhout, 1990), I, 590–1; II, 1937–57.

[47] Gregory the Great, *Homeliae in Hiezechihelem propheta*, 1.1.15, PL 76, 793.

[When the voice of the Psalms is expressed from the intention of the heart, a path is made for God to the heart through this act, so that he may fill the attentive mind with the mysteries of prophecy or compunction. Thus it is written: *The sacrifice of praise shall glorify me, and there is the way by which I will show him the salvation of God* (Ps. 49. 23). In the sacrifice of praise, then, a path or way of showing is made for Jesus; for while compunction is poured out through the psalmody, a way is made through our hearts by which we may ultimately reach Jesus.]

Thus, the life of praying the liturgy and meditating on Scripture was, within monastic thought, envisioned as the supreme way to inculcating virtue and embodying the Word of God, to opening up one's own life to the workings of grace. In this way, the monk participating in the singing of the Divine Office devoutly, with proper interior disposition, cooperates with divine grace in a movement of the soul that allows it to reach its appointed end in an encounter with the living Word of God. The liturgy was a school of prayer, an apprenticeship of virtue – the adage 'lex orandi, lex credendi' points to the symbiotic unity of liturgical prayer and the faithful Christian life. And it was not only in the practice of the psalmody, but also in the Eucharist that the Church effected the union of individual believers into one body.[48]

Ultimately, William's consistent emphasis on a way of life informed by and centred on the liturgy needs to be read in the context of the tradition of thought illustrated by the passage from Gregory. On several occasions William refers to the movement of the soul made possible through participating in the liturgy. In the *Abbreviatio*, concerning the prayers recited after the readings, William explains: 'post lectiones sequuntur orationes in quibus rogat sacerdos spiritualiter in nobis complendum quod lector dixit corporaliter factum' ('after the readings follow prayers, in which the priest asks that what the lector has spoken of as a corporeal fact be fulfilled in us in a spiritual way').[49] He also mentions reports of Bishop Ælfwold of Sherborne, who was especially devoted to St Cuthbert: 'Peneque semper antiphonam illam de Sancto tenebat corde, ruminabat ore, exercebat opere: "Sanctus antistes Cuthbertus, vir perfectus in omnibus, in turbis erat monachus, digne cunctis reverendus"' ('The well-known antiphon concerning the saint he would almost always have in mind, rehearse aloud, and put into practice: "Holy Bishop Cuthbert, a man perfect in all things, was a monk amid such crowds and worthy of respect from all"').[50] William's terminology here is resonant with the theology of prayer and liturgy that was revitalized in

---

[48] See e.g. H. de Lubac, *Corpus Mysticum: The Eucharist and the Church in the Middle Ages*, trans. Gemma Simmonds (London, 2006); Monti, *A Sense of the Sacred*; Barthe, 'The "Mystical" Meaning of the Ceremonies of the Mass'.

[49] *Abbreviatio Amalarii* I.xii, p. 143.

[50] *GPA* ii.82.4–5, pp. 282–5. For the antiphon, 'Sanctus antistes Cuthbertus', cf. Can 204487.

Benedictine monasticism during the twelfth century: *tenebat corde, ruminabat ore, exercebat opere*. By devoutly internalizing Scripture and the prayers of the liturgy, by meditating repeatedly on these texts and by making it *the* rule for living, one could develop the virtues that led to true happiness. The purpose of the whole exercise was not the perfunctory and mechanical repetition of a set of texts, but the incarnation of the Word in the lives of believers.

Still to be addressed is the purpose that the writing and reading of history serves within such a framework. William's scholarly pursuits need not be disengaged from his spiritual life, for the liturgical life, to which he was evidently committed, readily accommodated his historiographical enterprises. It would be far beyond the present scope to demonstrate that William's scholarly endeavours can be harmonized with the monastic theory and practice of Opus Dei, although I have made a beginning here. I would instead like to suggest for future work some elements of what a resolution of the apparent tension between history and liturgy should contain.

Firstly, we should remember what the ultimate purpose of writing and reading history was according to William. History's primary function was moral. The formation of character and a good way of life was the chief benefit William wanted his readers to attain through the reading of his works.[51] As we have seen, the theology of liturgy underpinning liturgical observance within the tradition to which William belonged presented the transformation of character and the attainment of the supreme good for human beings as the ultimate purpose of liturgical prayer as well. The two practices, then, converge in their ultimate purpose.

Secondly, history and liturgy relied on the same didactic principles and methods to attain their aims. I have argued elsewhere that the only way in which history could realize its purported moral-didactic function was through being embodied in practice by the reader through imitation of examples and meditation leading to new and reformed ways of living based on a deeper understanding of the human condition in time.[52] Such *imitatio* and *meditatio* correspond very closely to the mode through which the *lectio divina* and the liturgy exercise their perfective functions. The liturgy was not merely aimed at teaching the best possible way of human activity and living; it *was* the perfect way of being human.   History and liturgy also converge in their methods. It was only through embodiment in practice that their fruits could be harvested. While the liturgical life represents the grace-filled fullness of human existence, history could still play an important role as a discipline preparing human beings for the lofty heights of meditative contemplation through inculcating the virtues necessary for informed participation in the liturgy.

---

[51] See *GRA* ep. iii, pp. 10–13; *GRA* ii. prol., pp. 150–3; *Polyhistor*, ed. H. T. Oullette (Binghampton, NY, 1982), p. 37; cf. Sønnesyn, *Ethics of History*, pp. 82–3, 89–95.
[52] See Sønnesyn, *Ethics of History*, passim.

Thirdly, the liturgy provided a framework within which history could be understood, and within which the moral lessons of history could be discerned. Historical narratives could be included within the liturgical framework, as readings for Matins and possibly for Chapter.[53] But even narratives unsuitable for liturgical usage could and, I would argue, would have been read within the powerful overarching matrices of interpretation formed by the liturgy and scriptural exegesis.[54] The same God could be seen active in secular affairs just as much as in overtly spiritual events, and the meaning of God's providential acts and its significance for human lives could be extracted from historical narratives using the interpretive framework developed in the monastic way of life.[55]

A liturgical rhythm governed monastic life in a fundamental, all-embracing way. In monasteries, the writing of history and the pursuit of learning often unfolded within liturgical contexts. The theological tradition to which William was heir presented a theology of liturgy capable of governing one's entire life, of using the services of learning and scholarship to progress towards the ultimate end of humankind. History, on the other hand, was consciously written and read in order to guide readers towards these ultimate ends, using didactic methods that prepared its audience for participation in the transformative practices of liturgical prayer. The basic principles of the liturgy thus converge with the basic principles of the reading and writing of history, but the actual unity of the two disciplines are not found on the level of principles and concepts, but only in the organic wholes of human lives. It was ultimately in its practice within an overall conception of the monastic life that history could be placed at the service of liturgy.

The temporal sphere of history was, in and of itself, incommensurable with the transcendent and eternal aims of the liturgy, but it was an explicit aim and joyful hope of the monastic life that this incommensurability could be overcome through grace and the transformative efficacy of prayer. The view of liturgy that emerges from William's writings, read in the light of his theological context, suggests that the *lex orandi* that governed his life as *monachus et cantor* was also the *lex scribendi* in his historiographical practice.

---

[53] As David Ganz's chapter in this volume demonstrates, it is difficult to draw strict boundaries between historiographical texts and other genres dealing with events and people of the past. For the use of historical material in a liturgical context, see e.g. R. D. Ray, 'Orderic Vitalis and his Readers', *Studia Monastica* 14 (1972), 17–33.

[54] See Robertson, *Lectio Divina*; Stock, *Ethics of Reading*.

[55] See Bagge, 'Ethics, Politics, and Providence'.

14

Of the Making of Little Books:
The Minor Works of William of Newburgh

A. B. Kraebel

Among the most celebrated historians of twelfth-century England, William of
Newburgh (1135/6–c. 1200) has a long-standing reputation for bookishness.
According to Rachel Fulton: 'The world came to William in books, and it was
through books that he was most comfortable making sense of it.'[1] Fulton
follows the Rolls Series editor, Richard Howlett, in adducing a long list of
sources used by William in his *Historia Anglorum*, including the histories of
Symeon of Durham (d. after 1129) and Henry of Huntingdon (d. *c.* 1157).[2] Yet
there is good reason to doubt whether William's reading was as extensive as
Howlett suggested – and this not just because of the apparently negligible
size of Newburgh's library.[3] Indeed, John Gillingham has demonstrated that
many of William's alleged sources, Symeon and Henry included, almost
certainly reached him second-hand, mediated through the compiling
efforts of another Yorkshire historian, Roger of Howden (d. *c.* 1201).[4] This
dependence on another northern writer, one whose history could be found
in the library at nearby Rievaulx (now London, Inner Temple, MS 511.2),
suggests the local and limited nature of William's bibliographical resources.
This sense of regional limitation is reinforced by his other major work, a
Marian commentary on the Song of Songs. Though he could find in patristic
writings 'quomodo ... vel in ecclesiam vel in excellentis meriti animam
idem nuptiale carmen intelligi debeat' ('how this nuptial song should be

---

[1] R. Fulton, *From Judgment to Passion: Devotion to Christ and the Virgin Mary, 800–1200*
(New York, 2002), p. 433.

[2] Ibid., citing *Chronicles of the Reigns of Stephen, Henry II and Richard I*, ed. R. Howlett,
Rolls Series, 4 vols. (London, 1884–5), I, xxv–xxxvi. See, similarly, N. F. Partner,
Serious Entertainments: The Writing of History in Twelfth-Century England (Chicago,
1977), pp. 60–1; J. Burton, *The Monastic Order in Yorkshire, 1069–1215* (Cambridge,
1999), pp. 294–5.

[3] In addition to the manuscript of William's *Historia*, discussed below, only two other
extant volumes can be tied to Newburgh, and all three Newburgh books date from
around the time of William's death. See N. R. Ker, *Medieval Libraries of Great Britain:
A List of Surviving Books*, 2nd edn (London, 1964), p. 133; A. Lawrence-Mathers,
Manuscripts in Northumbria in the Eleventh and Twelfth Centuries (Cambridge, 2003),
p. 269.

[4] J. Gillingham, 'Two Yorkshire Historians Compared: Roger of Howden and William
of Newburgh', *Haskins Society Journal* 12 (2002), 15–37.

understood either in regard to the Church or a soul of distinguished merit'), William was apparently unaware of the more recent Marian commentaries on the Song by such writers as Rupert of Deutz (d. *c.* 1129) or Honorius Augustodunensis (d. 1154).[5] In light of these limitations, William's elaborate historical and exegetical writings are all the more impressive, revealing that even with a small library one can still be bookish.

Were he to be judged solely on the basis of these two major works, William might seem to present a split authorial personality. At the very least, his *Historia* and his commentary could almost be read as unrelated productions, each composed in response to a specific request by a different Cistercian official: the *Historia* for Ernald, abbot of Rievaulx (r. 1189–99), and the commentary for Walter, abbot of Byland (r. 1142–96).[6] Working to overcome this division, Fulton has emphasized the degree to which, in William's commentary, Christ and the Virgin become 'historical actors' and the Marian reading of the Song is treated as 'not a figure of history but history itself'.[7] Yet, though there is certainly some validity to the continuities that Fulton seeks to trace, it is possible to trace them more precisely. In particular, consideration of William's minor works – three short texts that are designated *homilie* or *sermones* in the surviving manuscripts – reveals not only continuities, but also a sense of a developing career and of distinct, though at times overlapping, authorial interests.[8] The range of interests expressed in William's writings, especially British and English history (seen in the *Historia* and homily on St Alban) and liturgical song (seen in the commentary on the Song of Songs and the homily on the Trinity) suggests that William may have been his priory's cantor. Further, his short texts indicate that, lacking access to a larger supply of books, William became his own best source, and, across his full corpus, he tended to focus his efforts on elaborating a limited range of recurrent ideas.

Certainly the most prominent recurring concern in William's writing is, very generally, praise of the Virgin Mary. In addition to his commentary on the Song, one of his homilies is focused on giving literal and spiritual readings of Luke 11. 27, when an anonymous woman cries to Christ: 'Beatus venter qui te portavit et ubera que suxisti' ('Blessed is the womb that bore thee and the paps which gave thee suck'). Unsurprisingly, William borrows

---

[5] William of Newburgh, *Explanatio sacri epithalamii in matrem sponsi: A Commentary on the Canticle of Canticles*, ed. J. C. Gorman (Fribourg, 1960), p. 71. Throughout the following, I have silently repunctuated editions of Latin texts. William's Marian commentary is compared to these other works at length by Fulton, *Judgment to Passion*, esp. chapters 6 and 8.

[6] See the prefatory letters to the two works, *Explanatio*, pp. 71–2; *Chronicles*, I, 3–4. For the dates of Ernald and Walter's abbacies, see *Heads*, pp. 129, 140.

[7] Fulton, *Judgment to Passion*, p. 441.

[8] I provide an edition of these works in *The Sermons of William of Newburgh*, ed. A. B. Kraebel (Toronto, 2010).

images and phrases from one of his texts on this subject when composing the other. As part of his literal reading in the homily, for example, attempting to recover what the woman meant by her pithy exclamation, William writes:

> Beatus inquam ille venter non quia virgineus, nam multi sunt ventres virginei, nec quia plenus, nam multi sunt ventres pleni, sed quia virginea simul et plenus, quod scilicet nullus alius. Et beata illa ubera non quia virginea, nam multa sunt ubera virginea, nec quia plena, quia multa sunt ubera plena, sed quia virginea simul et plena, quod scilicet nulla alia.[9]

> [That womb is blessed not because it is virginal, for there are many virgin wombs, nor because it is full, for there are many full wombs, but because it is at once virginal and full, which is true of none other. And those breasts are blessed not because they are virginal, for there are many virgin breasts, nor because they are full, for there are many full breasts, but because they are at once virginal and full, which is true of no others.]

Similarly, in the prologue to his commentary, William explains that the Virgin alone is able to sing the Song of Songs,

> Non quia virgo est, quod commune habet cum multis, sicut nec quia mater est, quod itidem commune habet cum tam multis, sed quia fecunda virgo et virga puerpera, quod scilicet in ea unicum et singulare est.[10]

> [Not because she is a virgin, which she has in common with many, nor because she is a mother, which she similarly has in common with just as many, but because she was a fecund virgin and a flowering rod, which is unique and singular in her.]

Deferring for the moment the question of which of the two is the source for the other, it is apparent that some borrowing has occurred. The ideas expressed in each passage are conventional enough, but the common structure of the phrases – setting the Virgin apart from other women not because she has one or the other of two common though usually mutually exclusive features, but because she has both simultaneously – would seem to be one which William especially favoured.[11]

In the prologue to William's commentary, this notion of Mary's 'unique and singular' ability to sing the Song of Songs forms part of a larger discussion of the different types of song which creation offers in praise of the divine. William first distinguishes between what he calls the 'old song' and the 'new song':

---

9 *Sermons*, p. 68.
10 *Explanatio*, p. 75.
11 For other correspondences between the homily and commentary, see the notes to my edition.

Canticum vetus est ad quod invitatur omnis intellectualis creatura, cum dicitur: *Benedicite Domino omnia opera eius* (Ps. 102. 22). Canticum vero novum est ad quod invitatur tantummodo omnis terra, id est omnis ex redemptis hominibus ecclesia, cum dicitur: *Cantate Domino canticum novum: cantante Domino omnis terra* (Ps. 95. 1). Utrumque sane canticum cantat omnis terra, id est redempti homines, sed cum sanctis angelis canticum vetus cantat creatori; sola vero canticum novum cantat redemptori. Sola inquam terra cantat canticum novum, quia veritas de terra (non de celo) orta est, id est verbum caro (non angelus) factum est et habitavit in nobis (cf. Ps. 84. 12 and John 1. 14).[12]

[The old song is the one to which every intellectual creature has been invited, when it is said: *Let all his works bless the Lord* (Ps. 102. 22). The new song is the one to which the whole earth, i.e., the whole Church of those who have been redeemed, has been invited, when it is said: *Sing to the Lord a new song: sing to the Lord all the whole earth* (Ps. 95. 1). The whole earth, i.e., the redeemed people, sings both of these songs, but it sings the old song together with the holy angels to its creator, and it sings the new song alone to its redeemer. Indeed, the earth alone sings the new song, since the truth has sprung out of the earth (not out of heaven), i.e., the Word was made flesh (not angel) and dwelt among us (cf. Ps. 84. 12 and John 1. 14).]

While the general *canticum novum* is sung by all redeemed humanity, William goes on to describe a special form of this song which can only be voiced by the virgin chorus described in Apoc. 14. 3–4, 'qui non solum integritatem mentis cum ceteris sed etiam integritatem carnis pre ceteris agno mente et carne integro dicarunt' ('who dedicated to the Lamb, itself untouched in mind and flesh, not only the integrity of their mind like the rest of the redeemed, but also, beyond the rest, the integrity of their flesh').[13] Without doubt, William says, Mary is one of the virgins who follow the Lamb and recite this song, but she also stands apart from this crowd, singing (as we have seen) the Song of Songs, 'quod nemo potest dicere agno nisi illa que peperit agnum' ('which no one is able to sing to the Lamb except for the one who gave birth to the Lamb').[14] With this schema in mind, William can then begin his interpretation of the Song as a dialogue between the Virgin and her son.[15]

Beyond the suggestion that it is a song which humanity redeemed shares with the angels, William says very little about the *canticum vetus* in this prologue. A fuller treatment of this topic does appear, however, in the second of his minor works, a homily explaining the significance of the lesser doxology, 'Gloria Patri et Filio et Spiritui Sancto', together with another

---

[12] *Explanatio*, p. 73.

[13] Ibid., pp. 74–5.

[14] Ibid., p. 75.

[15] The distinction among different types of songs offered in the commentary's prologue is also discussed by Fulton, *Judgment to Passion*, pp. 436–7.

Trinitarian versicle, 'Benedicamus Patrem et Filium cum Sancto Spiritu'.[16] Though the phrase *canticum vetus* is never used in the homily, it seems clear enough that William is describing the same type of song in both of these works. It is a song, he says in the homily, shared by both humanity and the angels, though it is sung 'multo sollemnius atque suavius ab angelis quam ab hominibus' ('much more solemnly and sweetly by angels than by people').[17] In response to their creation, William writes, the angels 'in gratiarum actione se totos dederunt, et pro sue beatificationis letitia sollemnes choros ducentes claris vocibus cantare coeperunt: Benedicamus Patrem et Filium cum Sancto Spiritu' ('devoted themselves wholly to giving thanks, and, rejoicing over their beatification, they began to lead solemn choirs and with clear voices to sing: Let us bless the Father and the Son with the Holy Spirit').[18] At the opening of his homily, William suggests that, since the beginning of time, the angelic choirs have been singing a Trinitarian verse that is now, in his present, also sung by his fellow canons.

This assertion creates a problem for William, namely how it is possible to know that humanity and the angels share this specific song of praise. To address this problem, William turns to scriptural accounts of visionaries and prophets – writers who claim to have peered (or, indeed, to have been taken) into the heavens and who, therefore, must have some knowledge of angelic song. At the same time, William also adapts the interpretive commonplace of the three Augustinian modes of sight (*visionum genera tria*), using this schema to explain the discrepancies among the different visionary accounts and to weigh their relative authority accordingly.[19] William follows earlier commentators in identifying Paul as the most authoritative biblical seer, since, as the Apostle suggests in II Corinthians 12. 2, he was taken up into the third and highest heaven. Here, William writes, pushing the visual focus of the commentary tradition in a distinctly auditory direction, the Apostle 'interfuit choris angelicis et ... angelos audivit sollemniter canentes' ('was in the midst of the angelic choirs and ... heard the angels solemnly singing').[20] Paul heard in a purely intellectual and unmediated manner (the third Augustinian

---

[16] See *Sermons*, p. 10 n. 30, for the use of these texts in the liturgy.

[17] Ibid., p. 37.

[18] Ibid., p. 38.

[19] I discuss these modes of sight, and their adaptation in the early medieval commentary tradition, in the introduction to Richard of St Victor, 'On the Apocalypse of John (Selections)', in *Interpretation of Scripture: Theory*, ed. F. T. Harkins and F. A. Van Liere (Turnhout, 2012), pp. 329–70 (pp. 330–6); see too *Sermons*, p. 12. At various points in his homily, William's language indicates that he is adapting this visual scheme to suit his auditory interests: e.g., *Sermons*, p. 41, 'Ibi sane hoc ipsum audivit angelos canentes quod Paulus in tertio celo, sed aliter, sicut et hoc ipsum ibi vidit quod Paulus in tertio celo, sed aliter. ... Porro in medio celo corpus sed quasi corpus cernitur, nec sonus sed quasi sonus auditur.'

[20] Ibid., p. 39.

mode), but this lack of mediation also made it impossible to convey adequately in human language or with a human voice what he had heard – herein lies the difference between the clear singing of the angels (*canunt clare*) and human hoarseness (*canunt rauce*).[21] Despite these limitations, however, William believes that Paul was able to communicate something of the angelic singer's voice (*vox canentis*) and the heavenly song's form (*forma canendi*), and he suggests that the Apostle attempted this translation in Romans 11. 36, 'Quoniam ex ipso et per ipsum et in ipso sunt omnia, ipsi gloria in secula' ('For of him and by him and in him are all things, to whom be glory for ever').[22] Like the liturgical texts quoted at the beginning of the homily, Paul's rendering of angelic song is Trinitarian in its form and focus.

William supports this notion by turning to the accounts of Isaiah and John, visionaries who reached the second heaven and therefore perceived in the second Augustinian mode (called alternately spiritual or imaginary). In their case, William writes, 'per quantas imaginum figuras menti prophetice veritas refulgebat' ('the truth flashed in their prophetic mind by means of great figures of images').[23] This figural mediation, again in a specifically auditory form, is foregrounded in John's account, at Apoc. 14. 2, when he writes that he hears a voice *as* the voice of many waters, and *like* harpists harping on their harps. Responding to this verse, William comments:

> Non dicit se audisse vocem aquarum multarum aut tonitrui magni aut cytharedorum, sed per 'tanquam' et 'sicut' indicat se non tales sonos aure corporali, sed talium similitudines sonorum aure hausisse spirituali.[24]

> [He does not say that he heard the voice of many waters or of a great thunder or of harpists, but by means of 'as' and 'like' he indicates that he did not hear sounds with his bodily ear, but rather he imbibed similitudes of such sounds with his spiritual ear.]

The reference to a 'spiritual ear' indicates that John is hearing in the second Augustinian mode: he discerns heavenly (that is, non-bodily) things represented to him under the cover of sensory experiences derived from the physical (that is, bodily) world, though without any physical bodies actually being present. This level of mediation underscores the notion that Isaiah and John, like Paul, were not able to capture the words of true angelic song (there being no words as such to capture), but William can nevertheless use the threefold angelic *sanctus* reported in both Isaiah 6. 3 and Apoc. 4. 8 to confirm that the Trinitarian doxology of Romans 11. 36 was Paul's attempt to reproduce what he heard in the heavens. Admittedly, the liturgical texts which

---

[21] Cf. ibid., p. 37.
[22] Cf. ibid., p. 39.
[23] Ibid., p. 41.
[24] Ibid., p. 43.

William cites at the beginning of his homily represent more rudimentary forms of these angelic songs, written in this way 'propter simpliciores ... qui apostolicorum profunditatem verborum penetrare non poterant' ('on account of simpler people ... who were unable to grasp the depth of the Apostle's words').[25] Insofar as they preserve this Trinitarian quality, however, all of these different songs can fall under the category of the *canticum vetus*.

Though their content does not overlap in the same way as his Marian homily and his commentary on the Song, the Trinity homily does serve to complement the commentary's prologue, and taken together these two texts present William's full account of biblical, liturgical and heavenly song. Their interdependent quality suggests that one was composed with the other in mind – yet, before turning to address the order of their composition, it will be useful to give some consideration to the remaining homily as well.

William's third short text is an account of the conversion and death of the British proto-martyr, Alban, believed to have been killed *c.* 300 in the Diocletian persecutions. The homily alternates between brief descriptions of scenes from Alban's life (on which, more below) and longer passages developing the general theological or moral significance of those scenes. Perhaps somewhat surprisingly, in these elaborative reflections the content of the homily sometimes coincides with material in William's commentary on the Song. For example, after opening the homily by exclaiming, 'Inter rosas martyrum rutilat insigniter noster Albanus' ('Our Alban's redness shines brilliantly among the roses of the martyrs'), William then asks, 'Numquid rubet inter rosas et non candet inter lilia?' ('Could his redness shine among the roses and his whiteness not glow among the lilies?'). He finds his answer in the Song of Songs:

> Loquitur sponsa in Canticis de summo martyre, martyrum capite, *Dilectus*, inquiens, *meus candidus et rubicundus* (Song 5. 10). Quale autem caput, talia et membra. In tantum enim membra, in quantum similitudo capitis in eis. ... Ergo quale caput martyrum, tales et martyres. Ergo et ipsi non tantum rubicundi sed etiam candidi, distincte tamen. Quippe illi ideo candidi quia candidati, ille vero ita candidus quod non candidatus. Ille inquam candidus natus et ideo minime candidatus, illi vero tetri nati sed renascendo candidati. Quia ergo similitudo hominis in eis, illius inquam hominis de quo dicitur, *Dilectus meus candidus et rubicundus*, etiam ipsi sunt candidi et rubicundi. In vita candidi, in morte rubicundi. Candidi remissione peccatorum et munditia morum, rubicundi vero cruore martyrii.[26]

> [In the Song the Bride speaks of the highest martyr, the head of the martyrs, saying, *My beloved is white and ruddy* (Song 5. 10). As with the head, so with the members. For they are members insofar as they have the image of the

[25] Ibid., p. 40.
[26] Ibid., pp. 87–8.

head within them. ... Therefore as with the head of the martyrs, so with the martyrs. Therefore too they are not only red but also white, but with a difference. For they are white because they were made white, and he is white because he was not made white. He, I say, was born white and therefore was not at all made white, while they were born ugly but were made white in their rebirth. Therefore, because they have the similitude of that man within them (the man about whom it is said, *My beloved is white and ruddy*), they are white and red. In their life white, in their death red. White in the remission of their sins and the cleanness of their lives, red in the blood of their martyrdom.]

Indeed, the same language appears in William's commentary on Song 5. 10, with a similar (not to say similarly excessive) play on the differences between *candidus* and *candidatus*.

Candidus, id est sine macula peccati, *et rubicundus*, id est occisus pro peccatis nostris in similitudine carnis peccati. Ita candidus quod non candidatus, ita mundus quod non mundatus. ... Ideo autem non tantum est candidus sed etiam rubicundus, ne solus sit candidus. Rubuit enim sanguine passionis, et in eo laventur et super nivem dealbentur (Ps. 50. 9) quos preordinavit ad vitam, fiantque ex atris candidi, et ideo candidi quia candidati. Solus ergo est ita candidus, quod non candidatus, per quem et in quo alii candidantur. Solus est in semetipso singulariter candidus, qui ad candidandos alios salubriter est rubicundus.[27]

[*White*, i.e., without the stain of sin, *and ruddy*, i.e., killed for our sins in the similitude of the flesh of sin. Thus white, since he was not made white: thus clean, since he was not made clean. ... But he is therefore not only white but also ruddy, lest he alone be white. He was made red with the blood of his Passion, and in that blood those preordained to life are washed and made whiter than snow (Ps. 50. 9), and from their blackness they are made white, and therefore they are white because they have been made white. He alone is white without being made white, through whom and in whom others are made white. He alone is in himself singularly white, who is reddened to make others white for their salvation.]

The commentary's rationale for describing Christ as 'white' without qualification is matched, in the homily, by the account of Alban as 'white' only by virtue of Christ's whiteness and sacrificial redness: for everyone but Christ, being 'white' is (as it were) an acquired characteristic. Even in the homily, William is clear that Song 5. 10 should be understood as pertaining primarily to Christ, and it is descriptive of the martyrs, Alban included, only insofar as they present in themselves a *similitudo Christi*.

Though Fulton and the commentary's editor, John Gorman, take William at face value when he claims that his Marian reading offered 'novam et

---

[27] *Explanatio*, p. 249.

intentatam ab omnibus ... explanationem' ('a new exposition, untried by anyone'), his gloss on Song 5. 10 indicates the extent to which he could in fact depend on what he calls the 'egregios maiorum labores' ('exceptional work of older writers').[28] Whether these *maiores* identified the *sponsa* as the Virgin, the Church, or the individual pious soul, they would nevertheless agree with William that, in verses like this one, the *sponsa* was describing Christ – and this agreement is crucial, not least because it can help to indicate whether the commentary or the homily on Alban is the earlier of William's works. The interpretation of Song 5. 10 in William's commentary reflects an understanding of this verse found in the work of Bede (d. 735), whose exegesis was the source for similar interpretations in the commentary of Haimo of Auxerre (d. c. 878) and, in William's own century, the *Glossa ordinaria*.[29] In the *Glossa*, the verse is met with two brief interlinear notes, the first explaining that the Bridegroom is *candidus* 'quia peccatum non fecit' ('because he did not commit any sin') and the second that he is *rubicundus* 'quia in sanguine suo peccatores lavit' ('because he washed sinners in his blood'), as well as a slightly longer marginal gloss: 'Primo mundus et sanctus venit in mundum, postmodum passione cruentus exivit de mundo' ('He first came into the world clean and holy, and later he went out of the world bloody from his Passion').[30] William appears to have seized upon the ideas and language of traditional glosses like these and developed them in original ways in his commentary, and he subsequently extended this notion of Christ as *candidus et rubicundus* to describe Alban as well. William's commentary, that is, seems to have served as a source for his later homily on the British martyr.[31]

Sources like his commentary on the Song thus supplied William with material for reflecting on the significance of Alban's life, but they could not provide the details of the life itself. To that end, William turned to Bede's *Historia ecclesiastica* I.vii, a work which he calls 'veracis Bede historiam' ('the history of truthful Bede').[32] William's account of Alban's life and death appears to be drawn almost exclusively from the *Historia ecclesiastica*, and he often borrows words and whole phrases from this

---

[28] Ibid., pp. 364, 71. See, e.g., Fulton, *Judgment to Passion*, p. 434: 'William was left with only meditation and prayer to guide him.' Similarly, Gorman devotes only a single paragraph in his introduction to discussing William's sources, asserting (not incorrectly) that 'William shows a great deal of independence in his writing' (*Explanatio*, p. 35).

[29] For Bede, see *PL* 91, 1161cd; for Haimo, *PL* 70, 1085.

[30] *Glossa ordinaria in Canticum canticorum*, ed. M. Dove, CCCM 170, pars 22 (Turnhout, 1997), p. 299. As Dove indicates, all of these glosses are drawn, ultimately, from Bede.

[31] For a second example supporting this conclusion, compare the interpretations of Song 2. 16 in *Explanatio*, p. 141, and *Sermons*, p. 89.

[32] *Sermons*, p. 91. For Bede's account of Alban, see *HE* I.vii, pp. 28–35.

source.[33] His description of the pagan judge hearing rumours that Alban offered refuge to a Christian cleric –

> Pervenit ad aures nefandi presidis quod penes Albanum latere vir Dei, iussitque eum diligenter perquiri. Tum Albanus magistrum dimisit, ipsum quidem utilitati plurimorum servare intendens, se autem passioni pro eo constanter exponens.[34]

> [It reached the ears of the wicked ruler that the man of God was hidden in Alban's household, and he ordered him diligently to be sought out. Alban then sent his master away, resolutely putting himself forward to suffer in his place in the hope that his master could help many more people.]

– begins by following Bede closely, with the added reference to the priest's future utility anticipating William's next major elaborative passage, in which he discusses when it is appropriate to flee from such persecution.[35] In other cases, William seizes on small details in Bede's narrative and develops them imaginatively. While Bede simply notes, for example, 'Contigit autem iudicem ea hora qua ad eum Albanus adducebatur aris adsistere ac demonibus hostias offerre' ('It happened that, when Alban was taken to him, the judge was standing before the altars and offering sacrifices to demons'), William adds a description of the judge's anger at having his devotions interrupted by the captive Christian.[36] He writes:

> Exhibetur a militibus presidi aris tunc forte adsistenti atque immolanti demonibus. ... Impius enim iudex, funestis illis sacris specialiter intentus, in eorum contemptorem illo loco et illa sibi hora exhibitum gravius erat seviturus, ut quanto diis suis gratia loci et temporis videretur esse devotior, tanto etiam hostibus eorum ... infestior redderetur.[37]

> [The soldiers present him to the ruler, who was then by chance standing before the altars and offering sacrifices to demons. ... Especially intent on those deadly sacrifices, the impious judge, presented with someone who scorned them, became more gravely enraged, so that he might be made all the more threatening to the enemies of his gods, the more he appeared to be devoted to them.]

---

[33] At the end of the homily, however, William does quote the brief mention of Alban in a hymn by Fortunatus: see *Sermons*, p. 109.

[34] *Sermons*, p. 94.

[35] Cf. *HE* I.vii, p. 28: 'Pervenit ad aures nefandi principis confessorem Christi, cui necdum fuerat locus martyrii deputatus, penes Albanum latere; tugurium martyris pervenissent, mox se sanctus Albanus pro hospite ac magistro suo ipsius habitu, id est caracalla qua vestiebatur, indutus militibus exhibuit, atque ad iudicem vinctus perductus est.' Other instances of William's close adherence to Bede's text are noted in my edition.

[36] Ibid., p. 30.

[37] *Sermons*, p. 98.

Responding to Alban's obvious disbelief in the validity of his sacrifices, the judge's rage is either feigned or calculated, an attempt to appear more devout in order to intimidate his prisoner even before their interview begins. Such embellishments are common in the homily – William regularly enlivens the events described by Bede by imagining the complex thoughts that lie behind them.[38]

In its adherence to 'the history of truthful Bede', this homily bears comparison with the prologue of William's second major work, the *Historia Anglorum*, which includes a lengthy discussion of Bede as the *fons et origo* of all English historiography. The prologue begins, straightforwardly, by noting, 'Historiam gentis nostre, id est Anglorum, venerabilis presbyter et monachus Beda conscripsit' ('The venerable priest and monk Bede committed the history of our people, the English, to writing'), but this dry observation quickly gives way to effusive praise.[39] Bede is an historian 'de cuius sapientia et sinceritate dubitare fas non est' ('whose wisdom and honesty cannot be doubted'), and, though other writers have recorded the history of England after Bede, 'illi quidem minime comparandi' ('they pale in comparison to him').[40] One of these more recent historians is so mendacious and willfully deceptive that he must be singled out for censure. This, of course, is Geoffrey of Monmouth (d. *c.* 1155). William describes Geoffrey as writing 'impudenti vanitate' ('with shameless vanity'), such that 'quam petulanter et quam impudenter fere per omnia mentiatur nemo nisi veterum historiarum ignarus, cum in librum illum inciderit, ambigere sinitur' ('only someone ignorant of the old histories, were he to encounter his book, could be unsure of how insolently and shamelessly he lies throughout almost all of it').[41] According to Monika Otter, this 'celebrated attack' is based on the observation 'that there is simply no room in the accepted history of the country for Geoffrey's Arthurian stories'.[42] For William, that 'accepted history' has been provided by Bede:

> Hec cum iuxta historicam veritatem a Venerabili Beda expositam constet esse rata, cuncta que homo ille de Arturo et eius vel successoribus vel post Vortigirnum predecessoribus scribere curavit partim ab ipso, partim et ab aliis constat esse conficta.[43]

---

[38] Similarly, according to Gillingham, 'Two Yorkshire Historians', p. 24, in the *Historia Anglorum* William 'constructed his own very different history' around 'the essential skeleton of information provided by Roger of Howden's *Gesta Henrici II et Ricardi I*', treating that work 'as a useful repository of facts around which to weave his own interpretation'.

[39] *Chronicles*, I, 11.

[40] Ibid., p. 18.

[41] Ibid., pp. 11, 13.

[42] M. Otter, *Inventiones: Fiction and Referentiality in Twelfth-Century English Historical Writing* (Chapel Hill, 1996), p. 95.

[43] *Chronicles*, I, 14.

[Since these things [i.e., the succession of Anglo-Saxon kings] are shown to be authoritative, in accord with the historical truth expounded by the Venerable Bede, all of the things which that man [i.e., Geoffrey] took pains to write about Arthur, and about those who succeeded him and preceded him after Vortigern, are clearly fabricated, in part by him and in part by others.]

To find room for these figures in the historical record, Geoffrey has had to describe some Anglo-Saxons as the mere vassals of his fictitious British rulers, when the former in fact included some 'quos Venerabilis Beda fortissimos dicit fuisse reges Anglorum, universe Britannie nobiliter imperantes' ('whom the Venerable Bede says were the kings of the English, nobly wielding power over the whole of Britain').[44] As Nancy Partner writes, William regards Bede as 'the standard against which all other historians must be measured', and he has found Geoffrey wanting.[45]

William devotes the bulk of the *Historia*'s prologue to correcting various errors in Geoffrey's writing, and it seems possible that his homily on Alban could be related to this effort. In the *Historia regum Britannie*, Geoffrey includes a brief discussion of Alban's martyrdom, closely following the *De excidio Britannie* of Gildas (d. c. 570), and, though Geoffrey's account is quite short, it does introduce at least one unprecedented detail. The fugitive priest responsible for Alban's conversion had been anonymous in the writings of Gildas and Bede, but Geoffrey names him 'Amphibalus', perhaps punning on the garment that Alban borrows to impersonate him.[46] This name is subsequently taken up in the new legend of Alban and Amphibalus composed by another William, a monk of St. Albans, sometime during the abbacy of Simon (r. 1167–83).[47] The Benedictine William states that he found the name of Alban's priest 'in historia quam Gaufridus Arturus de Britannico

---

[44] Ibid., p. 18.

[45] Partner, *Serious Entertainments*, p. 63. Further excellent discussions of William's critique of Geoffrey are offered by D. Rollo, *Historical Fabrication, Ethnic Fable and French Romance in Twelfth-Century England* (Lexington, 1998), pp. 305–7, and Rollo, 'Three Mediators and Three Venerable Books: Geoffrey of Monmouth, Mohammed, Chrétien de Troyes', *Arthuriana* 8 (1998), 100–14.

[46] *Historia regum Britanniae*, ed. N. Wright and J. Crick, 5 vols. (Cambridge, 1985–91), I, 50. In the *Dictionary of Medieval Latin from British Sources*, ed. R. E. Latham et al., 17 vols. (London, 1975–2013), I, 79, 'amphibalus' is defined as a 'rough cloak'. Note, however, that neither Gildas nor Bede uses this word to describe the garment belonging to Alban's priest: Bede, *Ecclesiastical History* I.vii, p. 28, refers to it as a 'caracalla' ['long tunic'], and Gildas, *De excidio Britanniae* I.xi, ed. H. Williams (London, 1899), p. 28, simply says 'vestimenta' ['robes']. J. S. P. Tatlock, *The Legendary History of Britain: Geoffrey of Monmouth's Historia Regum Britanniae and Its Early Vernacular Versions* (Berkeley, 1950), pp. 235–6, suggests that the name may derive from Geoffrey's misreading of a later (and unrelated) portion of the *De excidio*.

[47] For the dates of Simon's abbacy, see *Heads*, p. 67.

in Latinum se vertisse testatur' ('in the history which Geoffrey Arthur swears he translated from the British language into Latin'), and he likewise adapts Geoffrey's infamous account of his supposed source, the 'Britannici sermonis librum vetustissimum' ('ancient book in the British language'), to justify his own historical fabrication. Addressing Abbot Simon, he begins his preface, 'Cum liber Anglico sermone conscriptus passionem beati martyris Albani continens ad nostram notitiam pervenisset, ut eum verbis Latinis exprimerem precepistis' ('You ordered me to translate into Latin a certain book that had come to our attention, written in English and containing the passion of the blessed martyr Alban').[48] William of Newburgh gives no indication that he was familiar with the other William's text when he wrote his Alban homily, and he likewise makes no mention of Geoffrey's *Historia regum*, but, in light of the criticisms he offers in the prologue to his own *Historia*, it is just possible that he had one or both of these texts in mind when he wrote his short work on the martyr. Showing the same deference to Bede that he expresses, at length, in the *Historia Anglorum*, William could have intended his homily as a corrective to this recent Galfridian tradition.[49]

Each of William's minor works can therefore be tied to one (or both, in the case of the Alban homily) of his major writings, whether through their shared language or their complementary discussions. Internal evidence has already indicated that the homily on Alban derives material from the commentary on the Song, but otherwise the nature of the relationships among the works remains to be established. In this regard, details of the manuscripts preserving William's texts can be especially helpful, though we must first eliminate one promising but ultimately misleading piece of evidence. London, Lambeth Palace Library 73 is an early thirteenth-century manuscript which contains the *Historia Anglorum* (fols. 1r–103r; 103v blank), William's three homilies (104r–121ra) and the Latin text of the *Shepherd of Hermas* (121rb–145v), all copied in what appears to be a single book hand. The manuscript was either prepared at the Cistercian house at Buildwas (Shropshire) or it was at least in that abbey's library soon after its production.[50] Before the second homily

---

[48] *AASS*, 5 June, 149. For Geoffrey's account of his source, see *Historia regum* I, 1. Convenient discussions of the larger hagiographic tradition surrounding Alban are offered in two editions of the Middle English verse life by John Lydgate: *The Life of Saint Alban and Saint Amphibal*, ed. J. E. Van der Westhuizen (Leiden, 1974), pp. 26–44, and *Saint Albon [sic] and Saint Amphibalus*, ed. G. F. Reinecke (New York, 1985), pp. xviii–xxiv.

[49] Other continuities between the Alban homily and the *Historia* must be passed over due to constraints of space. But note, for example, the indictment of British perfidy present in both texts: *Sermons*, p. 87; *Chronicles*, I, 11.

[50] For descriptions, see M. R. James and C. Jenkins, *A Descriptive Catalogue of the Manuscripts in the Library of Lambeth Palace* (Cambridge, 1930–2), pp. 117–29; J. Sheppard, *The Buildwas Books: Book Production, Acquisition and Use at an English Cistercian Monastery, 1165–c. 1400* (Oxford, 1997), pp. 114–19; *Sermons*, pp. 26–8.

in Lambeth, on fol. 110ra, the scribe has included a colophon: 'Item tractatus eiusdem ad eundem super hunc versum: Benedicamus Patrem et Filium cum Sancto Spiritu' ('A treatise by the same to the same on this verse: Let us bless the Father and the Son with the Holy Spirit'), and a similar note appears in the main scribe's hand before the final homily, on fol. 115va: 'Item tractatus eiusdem ad eundem de sancto Albano' ('A treatise by the same to the same on St. Alban'). In his discussion of Lambeth, Howlett concluded that these notes, which are preserved in none of the other manuscripts, demonstrate that the homilies were written to be presented, along with the *Historia*, to Ernald of Rievaulx (*ad eundem*), at whose request William undertook his history.[51] Since the *Historia* seems to have been left unfinished at William's death, breaking off abruptly after describing events dateable to May 1198, this would then indicate that the homilies were all late works – and that all three of them, like the Alban homily, share material or thematic interests with the Song commentary because they are all drawing on (or responding to) that earlier text.[52] Yet, as we will see, the evidence of the Lambeth colophons should not be trusted so readily, and any conclusions based on them are likely to be incorrect.

As Howlett himself recognized, Lambeth was almost certainly copied from BL Stowe 62, a manuscript prepared at the beginning of the thirteenth century at William's own priory of Newburgh.[53] That Stowe lacks the Lambeth colophons should already cast doubt on their authority, and this scepticism is reinforced by other details of Stowe's production. In what is likely an attempt to reproduce the appearance of his exemplar (near-facsimilar copying), the scribe of Lambeth planned his work with the *Historia* such that the text would end in the first column of a recto (fol. 103ra), and he then left the remainder of that recto and the entirety of the verso blank, beginning his copy of William's Marian homily at the top of the next recto (fol. 104ra; see Figs. 14.1 and 14.2).[54] The same pattern appears at the end of the *Historia* and the beginning of the homilies in Stowe (the *Historia* ends on fol. 158ra; 158rb–v blank; the homilies begin on 159ra; see Figs. 14.3 and 14.4), but while this arrangement is part of the Lambeth scribe's planned and uninterrupted copying of his exemplar (made clear by the observation that the break occurs in the middle of a quire), in Stowe the textual break reflects a material break, evidence of the manuscript's discontinuous production. That is, the recto on

---

[51] *Chronicles*, I, xli–xlii.

[52] On the incomplete state of the *Historia*, see *Chronicles*, I, xxiii–xxiv; Gillingham, 'William of Newburgh and Emperor Henry VI', in *Auxilia Historica: Festschrift für Peter Acht*, ed. W. Koch et al. (Munich, 2001), pp. 51–71 (pp. 68–70).

[53] *Chronicles*, I, xlii: 'There can be little doubt that L[ambeth] is a copy taken direct from S[towe].' For a description of Stowe, see *Sermons*, pp. 24–6.

[54] As is evident in Fig. 14.1, a later annotator has filled some of the blank space originally left on fol. 103r; on this addition, which helps to place the book at Buildwas, see Sheppard, *Buildwas Books*, pp. 117–18.

which the *Historia* ends in Stowe is the final folio of a quire and originally the end of the book, the scribe evidently having planned his work with care, and the homilies were added in a new and distinct fascicle, copied, as R. W. Hunt observed, 'in a later hand of the thirteenth century'.[55] The (presumably) Newburgh canon who assembled Stowe in its final form seems to have meant it as a collection of the then-deceased author's writings, drawing into a single volume works that could have been prepared at various points across William's career. The Lambeth scribe, however, must have regarded Stowe as a single, coherent production, and the colophons he added to the homilies are most likely his own invention, an attempt to reinforce this sense of coherence and explain the inclusion of the shorter texts.

Though Stowe is useful for discounting the claims made in Lambeth, it offers little evidence for the relative dating of homilies. Fortunately, the only other manuscript of William's short texts is more useful in this regard. Bodl Rawlinson C.31 is made up of what were originally three distinct booklets: William's Trinity homily is copied into a quire of three bifolia (fols. 1r–6v), the Marian homily occupies a separate quire of four bifolia with the last folio trimmed (7r–13v), and then the volume concludes (in its present form) with glosses on Peter Comestor's *Historia Scholastica* through Exodus 28, copied across two quires (14r–31v). The last item, in a small book hand from roughly the beginning of the thirteenth century, is clearly unrelated to the first two texts, copied in charter scripts which Rodney Thomson dates to the third quarter of the twelfth century.[56] Though, as Thomson notes, the hands of the

---

[55] R. W. Hunt, 'The Library of the Abbey of St Albans', in *Medieval Scribes, Manuscripts and Libraries: Essays Presented to N. R. Ker*, ed. M. B. Parkes and A. G. Watson (London, 1978), pp. 251–77 (p. 265 n. 77). The three sermons in Stowe were originally copied continuously across three quires, the second of which (between fols. 166 and 167) has been lost. The notion that Stowe's copy of the *Historia* was executed carefully and deliberately is challenged by Lawrence-Mathers, 'William of Newburgh and the Northumbrian Construction of English History', *Journal of Medieval History* 33 (2007), 339–57 (p. 343), who draws attention to 'signs of haste in the writing [of Stowe], with errors sometimes forthrightly marked in red, suggesting an attempt to complete this fair copy before the author's death'. This last claim is completely speculative, and it is probably misleading to interpret the errors highlighted and corrected by the scribe as signs that he was particularly rushed: useful on this point is D. Wakelin, *Scribal Correction and Literary Craft: English Manuscripts, 1375–1500* (Cambridge, 2014). Lawrence-Mathers's discussion of the apparent Cistercian influence on Stowe's execution remains extremely useful – indeed, the possibility that the small priory of Newburgh lacked its own house style (and, relatedly, did not produce many manuscripts) could help to explain the errors she observes in Stowe. See further Lawrence-Mathers, 'The Artistic Influence of Durham Manuscripts', in *Anglo-Norman Durham, 1093–1193*, ed. D. Rollason et al. (Woodbridge, 1994), pp. 451–69 (p. 469); Lawrence-Mathers, *Manuscripts in Northumbria*, pp. 187–8.

[56] R. M. Thomson, *Manuscripts from St Albans Abbey, 1066–1235*, 2 vols. (Woodbridge, 1982), I, 109; see also *Sermons*, pp. 22–4.

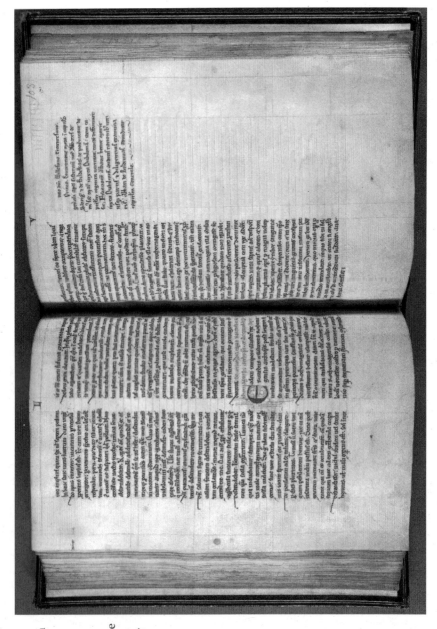

Fig. 14.1
The conclusion
to Book 5 of
the *Historia
Anglorum*
in London,
Lambeth Palace
Library MS 73,
fols. 102v–103r

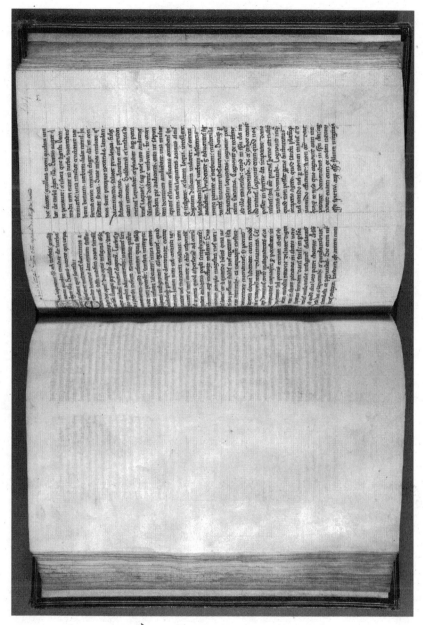

Fig. 14.2
The beginning
of the Luke
homily in
Lambeth 73,
fols. 103v–104r.
Note that
Lambeth is
quired in eights,
with fols. 103
and 104 being
the seventh and
eighth folios in
the thirteenth
quire

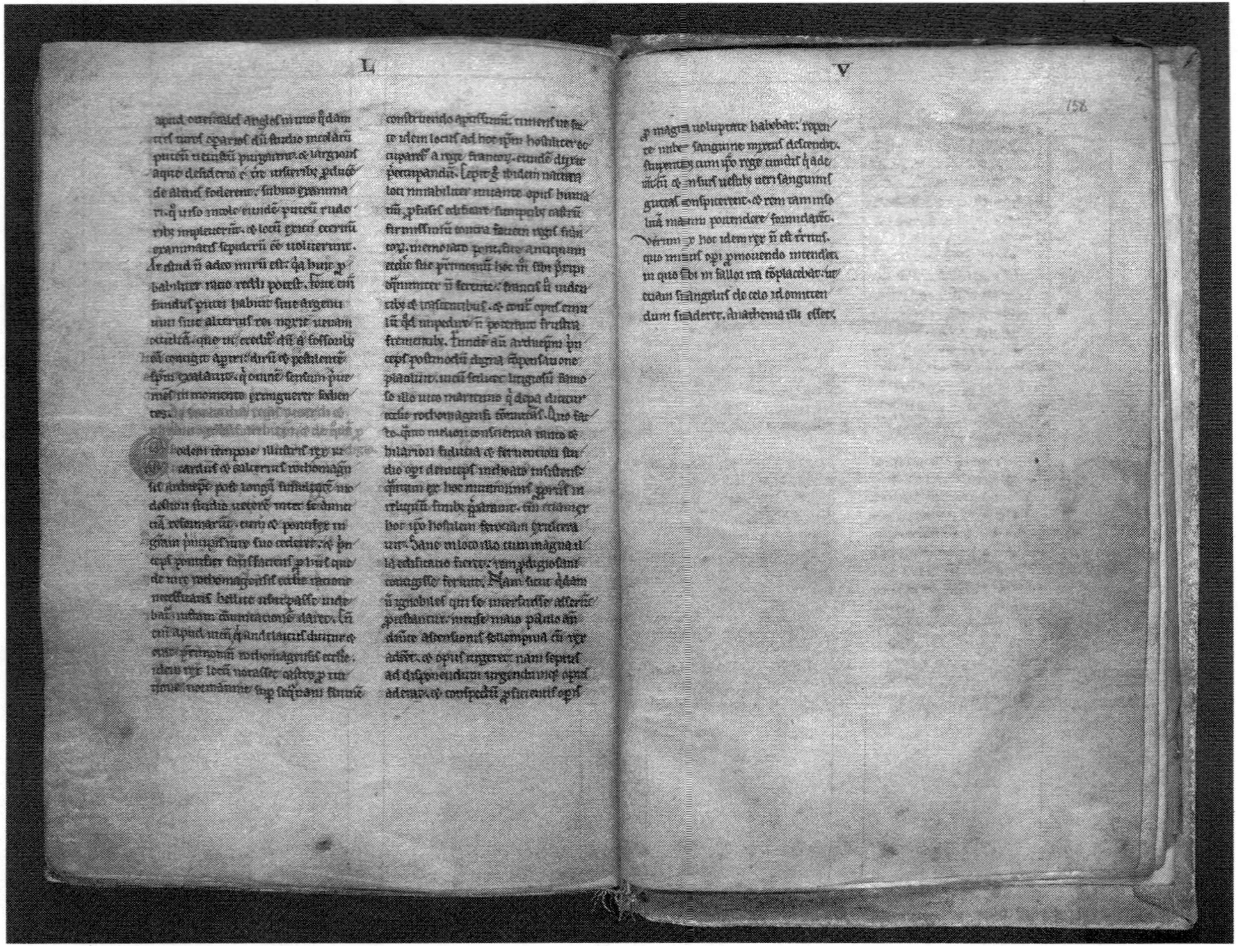

Fig. 14.3 The conclusion to Book 5 of the *Historia Anglorum* in BL Stowe 62, fols. 157v–158r

Fig. 14.4
The beginning
of the Luke
homily in
BL Stowe 62,
fols. 158v–159r.
Note that
fol. 159r starts
a new quire

273

two homilies are 'very similar', the differences between them are sufficient to indicate that, if they did belong to the same scribe, each represents a discrete stint of copying (see Fig. 14.5).[57] Although I suspect that Thomson's dating is slightly too early, the evidence of Rawlinson still makes it clear that these two homilies circulated as loose fascicles well before the composition of the *Historia Anglorum*.[58]

In light of what we can learn from Rawlinson, the details of William's career become somewhat clearer. Quite rightly, Fulton questions why the abbot of Byland would have turned to an Augustinian canon from a relatively small (if neighbouring) house with his request for a Marian commentary on the Song.[59] However, if Abbot Walter had been familiar with William's Marian homily, circulating as a little book like the second quire of Rawlinson, then the request becomes immediately explicable.[60] The abbot liked what he read in the homily, and he wanted more. As William wrote his commentary, he incorporated material from his Marian homily into his new interpretation of the Song, and he also built upon ideas explored in his Trinity homily, now classifying the liturgical texts discussed there as the *canticum vetus*, against which the *canticum novum* of the Song could be defined. In his third homily, as we have seen, William developed further some of the material previously included in his commentary, that is, the Alban homily was almost certainly written at least several years after the other two. The endpoint of William's career is, of course, the *Historia*, and yet it is difficult to tell whether the final homily predates that larger project or was composed in conjunction with it. The high esteem in which Bede is held in the homily could easily represent an extension of the discussion in the *Historia*'s prologue. Then again, if the

[57] Hunt, 'St Albans', p. 265, does not observe the scribal and material distinctions between the two homilies.

[58] Rawlinson seems to have been assembled in its present form by Fabian, subprior of St Albans from *c.* 1214 until his death in 1223, and it was Fabian who gave the manuscript to St Albans. On Fabian and his books, see Hunt, 'St Albans', p. 265; Thomson, *St Albans*, I, 46–7, 54, 63. Fascicular circulation has tended to be considered with regard to later medieval book history, but there are some notable recent exceptions: see esp. Richard Sharpe, 'Anselm as Author: Publishing in the Late Eleventh Century', *Journal of Medieval Latin* 19 (2009), 1–87; Sharpe and Teresa Webber, 'Four Early Booklets of Anselm's Work from Salisbury Cathedral', *Scriptorium* 63 (2009), 58–72. More generally, see Alexandra Gillespie, 'Medieval Books, Their Booklets, and Booklet Theory', *English Manuscript Studies, 1100–1700* 16 (2011), 1–29.

[59] Fulton, *Judgment to Passion*, pp. 302–3.

[60] Unfortunately, though this scenario seems especially likely, it cannot be established with complete certainty. The only criterion for dating the commentary is the dedication to Walter of Byland, whose abbacy was unusually long (1142–96, according to *Heads*, p. 129), and so, even if Rawlinson had been copied at the beginning of the range of dates proposed by Thomson (third quarter of the twelfth century), it would still be conceivable, though doubtful, that the commentary antedated the two homilies Rawlinson contains.

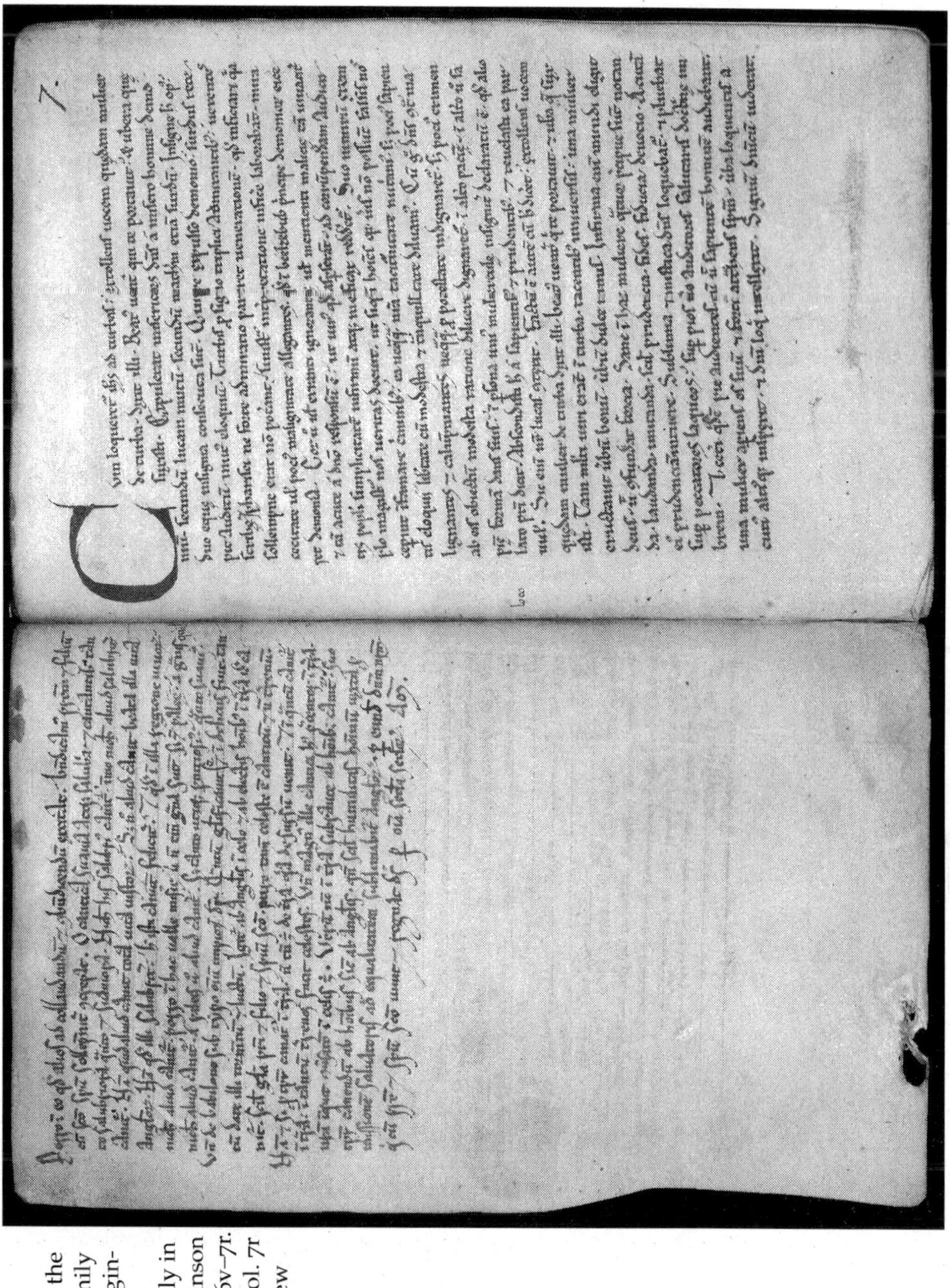

Fig. 14.5
The end of the Trinity homily and the beginning of the Luke homily in Bodl Rawlinson C.31, fols. 6v–7r. Note that fol. 7r begins a new quire.

homily were composed earlier and circulated in a loose fascicle like William's other short texts, it could have come to the attention of the abbot of Rievaulx in that form and inspired him to commission the *Historia*. Either option is conceivable.

The range of topics represented in William's writings, especially the liturgical exposition of the Trinity homily and his interest in English history, fit well with what we might expect from a late twelfth century cantor, and it seems possible that William held this office at Newburgh.[61] If he did, however, the reconstruction of his authorial career offered here should serve as a reminder that these interests need not always cohere in a single, unified *mentalité*. Indeed, though he apparently wrote about liturgical song from an early date, William's concern with historiography seems to have developed only later, perhaps in response to a specific request from Ernald of Rievaulx, or perhaps growing out of his engagement with the hagiographical content of Bede's *Historia ecclesiastica*. Very generally, then, William fits the description of a cantor offered long ago by David Knowles, who observed that, by William's lifetime, 'the post became the perquisite of the most gifted man of letters in the community, ... the intellectual leader of the house'.[62] Building from one text to the next, William's intellectual undertakings led him to return to, and elaborate upon, a narrow range of ideas, and his major works need to be understood in light of the little books that supported them.[63]

---

[61] In addition to the other chapters in the present volume, see Fass C, p. 24: 'Cantors and the scribes who were normally under their auspices had charge of two essential kinds of materials: those that belonged to the liturgy, including the obituaries and martyrologies, and the chronicles and other written histories.'

[62] D. Knowles, *The Monastic Order in England: A History of Its Development from the Times of St Dunstan to the Fourth Lateran Council, 940–1216*, 2nd edn (Cambridge, 1963), p. 428.

[63] After this chapter went to press, I discovered a previously unnoted fourth copy of William's sermons, in The Hague, Koninklijke Bibliotheek, MS 73 E 20, fols. 14vb–24vb. This copy appears to support my argument concerning the circulation of the sermons, and I plan to discuss its position in the textual history of the sermons more extensively in a separate essay.

PART IV
On the Continent:
Five Case Studies

15

The Cantors of the Holy Sepulchre and their Contribution to Crusade History and Frankish Identity

Cara Aspesi

The Western Christians who arrived to Jerusalem in June 1099 came as conquerors intent on freeing the holy places from Muslim rule. When they succeeded in taking Jerusalem on 15 July, they inflicted damage not only to Jerusalem's walls and buildings, but also to its existing social and religious infrastructure, slaughtering or expelling Jerusalem's Muslim and Jewish inhabitants, electing their own secular and religious rulers and appropriating most of the holy shrines of the city.[1] They also suppressed the rights of their co-religionists; the first act of the new Latin patriarch Arnulf of Chocques was to drive the Orthodox Christians out of the Holy Sepulchre and place the church entirely under the control of Latin clergy.[2] It was these very clergy, however – especially the cantors of the Holy Sepulchre Ansellus 'de

---

[1] Historians contemporary to the First Crusade testify to the enormous number slain in the siege, though the accounts may exaggerate, since they are written as religious narratives rather than historical reports. See B. Kedar, 'The Jerusalem Massacre of July 1099 in the Western Historiography of the Crusades', *Crusades* 3 (2004), 15–75. The following year the city was emptied of Muslims and Jews when Baldwin I banned all remaining non-Christians from the city. See William of Tyre, *Chronicon* XI.27, ed. R. B. C. Huygens, CCCM 63 (Turnhout, 1986), p. 536. The establishment of new leadership occurred immediately; eight days after the capture Godfrey of Bouillon was elected the first Latin ruler of Jerusalem, and, on 1 August, Arnulf of Chocques the first Latin patriarch. See J. Riley-Smith, 'The Title of Godfrey of Bouillon', *Historical Research* 52 (1979), 83–6; B. Hamilton, *The Latin Church in the Crusader States: The Secular Church* (London, 1980), p. 12. Daniel the Abbot, who visited between 1106 and 1107, reports that the Dome of the Rock was then used by the Franks as a church, named the *Templum Domini*, which accords with the report of William of Tyre, who attributed its foundation to Godfrey. See *The Pilgrimage of the Russian Abbot Daniel in the Holy Land*, trans. C. W. Wilson, PPTS 4 (London, 1895), pp. 20–1; William of Tyre, *Chronicon* IX.9, p. 431. The al-Aqsa Mosque became the royal residence in 1104 and later the headquarters of the Templars. See A. J. Boas, *Jerusalem in the Time of the Crusades: Society, Landscape, and Art in the Holy City under Frankish Rule* (New York, 2001), pp. 79–80. The Franks also began to administer all the major Christian shrines: the Church of the Assumption, Mount Sion and the church of the Ascension on the Mount of Olives. See Hamilton, *The Latin Church*, pp. 95–6.

[2] Hamilton, *The Latin Church*, p. 14.

Turre', Giraldus, Bernardus, Peter and Bartholomeus – who contributed significantly throughout the twelfth century to the reconstruction of Jerusalem and its fractured society. The cantors' tool in this regard was the liturgy, especially a new feast adopted by the canons of the Holy Sepulchre early in the century, the *Festivitas sancte Hierusalem*.[3] This feast, celebrated annually on 15 July in commemoration of the capture, presented a new vision of Crusade history. It referred explicitly to the capture by combining chants from the Latin liturgical repertory with selections from the *Historia Hierosolymitana* of Fulcher of Chartres, and it presented the conquest as the restoration of Jerusalem foretold in the Old Testament and the descent of the Heavenly Jerusalem foreseen by the Apostle John. This liturgical recasting of Crusade history had specific implications for Frankish identity, making the Franks the foretold vessels of God's saving power, liberators and heralds of the New Jerusalem.[4] Yet the Frankish identity constructed through the liturgy was not entirely stable, and the Jerusalem feast underwent two full revisions in the twelfth century. In the second version, the Franks were depicted as Jerusalem's righteous watchmen, while the third version portrayed the Franks as ordained ministers of Jerusalem, with the city interpreted as the Church. Insofar as these liturgically constructed views of the Franks had the potential to be transformative, shaping Crusader identity through the power of ritual performance, the cantors of the Holy Sepulchre can be considered some of the most influential history-writers and social architects of twelfth-century Jerusalem.

To determine the extent of the influence exercised by these cantors, we must first reconstruct their careers as fully as the surviving evidence will

---

[3] My work on the Jerusalem feast elaborates on and occasionally challenges that of Amnon Linder, who has provided the most extensive evaluation of the history, themes and significance of the Jerusalem feast. His analysis can be found in a number of articles including 'The Liturgy of the Liberation of Jerusalem', *Mediaeval Studies* 52 (1990), 110–31; and '"Like Purest Gold Resplendent": The Fiftieth Anniversary of the Liberation of Jerusalem', *Crusades* 8 (2009), 31–51. More recently, see S. Salvado, 'The Liturgy of the Holy Sepulchre and the Templar Rite: Edition and Analysis of the Jerusalem Ordinal (Rome, Bib. Vat., Barb. Lat. 659) with a Comparative Study of the Acre Breviary (Paris, Bib. Nat., Ms. Latin 10478)' (unpublished Ph.D. dissertation, Stanford University, 2011), pp. 171–81; and M. C. Gaposchkin, 'The Echoes of Victory: Liturgical and Para-Liturgical Commemorations of the Capture of Jerusalem in the West', *Journal of Medieval History* 40 (2014), 237–59. While carrying out independent research on the feast, I reached some conclusions similar to those expressed by Salvado and Gasposchkin, though my view of its developmental stages, thematic evolution, and implications (discussed below) is essentially different from theirs, and I remain extremely grateful to both scholars for their generosity in sharing their most recent work and ideas.

[4] This discussion adopts the legal definition of a 'Frank' as anyone who celebrated the Latin rite; see Hamilton, *The Latin Church*, p. 162.

allow. Once this is established, our attention can turn to one of the most elaborate examples of the cantors' ability to shape perceptions of the past, namely the liturgy for a new feast written to commemorate the Crusaders' capture of Jerusalem. Surviving manuscripts preserve this liturgy in a variety of forms, all clearly related and apparently representing the development of the feast over the course of the century. After reconstructing the stages of this development, we will see that all of the revisions to the feast can be tied to the Holy Sepulchre, most likely the work of different cantors. With the relative dating of each version tentatively established, it will then be possible to suggest which cantors were responsible for each stage in the feast's history, thereby indicating some of the ways in which specific cantors helped to shape Crusade history and Frankish identity.

The cartulary of the Holy Sepulchre provides the names of five of the twelfth-century cantors of the Holy Sepulchre: Ansellus, Giraldus, Bernardus, Peter and Bartholomeus. A sixth figure, William, may also have held the office. The most is known of Ansellus. In a charter of the Holy Sepulchre dated 1124, 'Ansellus de turre' is listed among the canons of the Holy Sepulchre who witnessed a gift made to the church of the Quarantaine in 1116, and 'Anselmus de turre David' subscribes another royal charter, this dated 1114.[5] It is likely, therefore, that Ansellus lived in the Tower of David in the north-west corner of Jerusalem,[6] at least until 1121, when he finally submitted to the reform of the canons instituted by Patriarch Arnulf seven years earlier.[7] Geneviève Bresc-Bautier points out that two letters sent from 'Ansellus, gloriosissimi Sepulcri cantor et presbyter' to Notre Dame in Paris indicate he had belonged to that church before departing on Crusade. In the first he recalls how he was 'nutritus et eruditus' there.[8] His fondest memories of his former chapter concerned celebrating the liturgy: 'I often dream that I am back with you, taking part in the processions on great feasts and singing the night office.'[9]

Recent scholarly consensus would indicate that Ansellus took up his

---

[5] See *Le Cartulaire du Chapitre du Saint-Sépulcre de Jérusalem*, ed. G. Bresc-Bautier (Paris, 1984), no. 94; *Regesta regni Hierosolymitani: Additamentum*, ed. R. Röhricht (Innsbruck, 1904), no. 76a.

[6] Many different people used the Tower was used as a residence, including Baldwin I. See Boas, *Domestic Settings: Sources on Domestic Architecture and Day-to-Day Activities in the Crusader States* (Boston, 2010), p. 72.

[7] The canons of the Holy Sepulchre were placed under the Augustinian Rule in 1114. See *Le Cartulaire*, ed. Bresc-Bautier, no. 20.

[8] These letters accompanied a fragment of the True Cross which Ansellus sent to Notre Dame. Formerly thought to date to 1108/09, Bresc-Bautier argued for a date of 1120. See Bresc-Bautier, 'L'envoi de la relique de la vraie Croix à Notre-Dame de Paris en 1120', *Bibliothèque de l'École des Chartes* 129 (1971), 387–97. Ansellus' letters can be found in *PL* 162, 729–32.

[9] Quoted in Hamilton, *The Latin Church*, p. 113.

office in 1112, but it is more likely he was cantor as early as 1099.[10] 'Ansellus, precentor' subscribed to a charter that can be securely dated to 1108 on the grounds of the absence of the subscription of the patriarch of Jerusalem and the presence of the dual subscription of the 'Evremar and Gibelin, archbishops', a state of affairs that existed only in 1108 when, due to the connivances of Baldwin I, the Patriarchate was disputed and therefore briefly unoccupied.[11] Ansellus was therefore acting cantor at least as early as 1108. Further, in the first letter Ansellus sent to Notre Dame in 1120, he mentions that he had been absent from them for twenty-four years. As Cristina Dondi points out, this suggests he left Europe in 1096 and was likely present at the siege of Jerusalem.[12] Corroborating this, Cecilia Gaposchkin notes that the readings for the Reception of the Cross in a fourteenth-century breviary of Notre Dame in Paris refer to the canon 'who joined the knights in the liberation of Jerusalem and who, after the city was captured and freed from "filthy idolatry", sent back the relic so that the church of Notre Dame and indeed all of "Gaul might shine more brightly".'[13] If Ansellus was present at the siege, then it is possible he was one of the twenty secular canons appointed by Godfrey of Bouillon in August 1099 to serve at the Holy Sepulchre, especially given the paucity of qualified clergy at the time.[14] He might have been made cantor immediately, for a charter of the Holy Sepulchre dating to 1102 refers to the cantor's wages (though without specifying who held the post).[15] If Ansellus was indeed the first Latin cantor of the Holy Sepulchre, he would have held the office for nearly forty years, from *c*. 1099 to sometime after 1138 when his name disappeared from charter subscriptions.[16]

Less is known about the careers of the remaining cantors. After Ansellus, no cantor of the Holy Sepulchre appears in the subscriptions of the documents of the Latin Kingdom of Jerusalem until 1151, when the cantor 'Giraldus' subscribed a charter of the Holy Sepulchre, witnessing charters again in 1153 and 1155.[17] This Giraldus may have been the canon who was once a deacon and on occasion a scribe, as indicated by a charter of 1130–33 ('Giraldus, S.

---

[10] This on account of Bresc-Bautier's redating of Ansellus' letters, with 1112 being the date of next documents of the Latin Kingdom that refer to him as cantor. See *Regesta regni Hierosolymitani*, ed. Röhricht (Innsbruck, 1893), no. 68; *Regesta: Additamentum*, no. 68a.

[11] The dispute over the patriarchate is discussed by Hamilton, *The Latin Church*, 56–7. The charter appears in *Regesta: Additamentum*, no. 56a.

[12] C. Dondi, *The Liturgy of the Canons Regular of the Holy Sepulchre of Jerusalem: A Study and a Catalogue of the Manuscript Sources* (Turnhout, 2004), p. 58.

[13] Gaposchkin, 'Echoes of Victory', p. 241.

[14] Hamilton, *The Latin Church*, pp. 113–14.

[15] *Cartulaire du Chapitre du Saint-Sépulcre*, no. 19.

[16] 'Ansellus, precentor' last appears in the subscriptions of a charter of February 1138. See ibid., no. 34.

[17] Ibid., nos. 69, 114 and 115.

Sepulchri diaconus, qui chartam composuit'), especially since the duties of a scribe and deacon would have prepared Giraldus to take up the tasks of the cantorship.[18] After Giraldus, Bernardus became cantor, almost certainly assuming the office sometime between 1155 and 1159, the year when Bernardus's name first appears in charters. His name only appears through 1160, however.[19] Peter was the next known holder of the office, appearing in the cartulary and other documents of the Latin Kingdom between 1170 and 1175.[20] Finally, the name 'Bartholomeus' appears with the title of cantor in 1178; he may have remained cantor until the fall of the city to Saladin in 1187.[21]

The largest gap in knowledge of the twelfth-century cantors of the Holy Sepulchre comes in the period between the cantorships of Ansellus and Giraldus, 1138–51. It is possible that Giraldus succeeded Ansellus directly, though it is equally possible that a certain William was cantor in the intervening period. One notes that a 'Willelmus, succentor' subscribed after Ansellus in a charter of 1112, confirming the rights of Patriarch Arnulf.[22] William's name and title then appear again in a charter of 1123.[23] He was therefore *succentor* under Ansellus for at least eleven years, and if he survived Ansellus, he could easily have succeeded him in the office of cantor. William, therefore, may have been the second cantor of the Holy Sepulchre, from 1138 to around the middle of the century.

Though further details of the cantors' careers are not known, as identifiable holders of the office they can be presumed to have been persons of both actual and ideological power within their sphere of liturgical influence. This is in part due to historical circumstance, since these men occupied their office at a time when the power of the cantor was waxing. As Margot Fassler has demonstrated in her study of medieval customaries, by the twelfth century, cantors had come to exercise significant authority over the liturgy in many places, both its production and performance. Over time, the offices of *armarius* and cantor had merged, so that by the twelfth century, the cantor was in charge of the library and often the scriptorium, overseeing the composition of liturgical books. He also controlled the presentation of the liturgy as a kind of liturgical 'master of ceremonies', correcting musical errors, controlling pitches, selecting the readers and singers, ruling the choir and ordering the processions, to name a few of his responsibilities.[24]

[18] Ibid., no. 98.
[19] Ibid., nos. 52, 124, 126 and 129.
[20] Ibid., nos. 158, 159 and Appendix 4; *Regesta*, no. 528.
[21] *Cartulaire*, Appendix 5.
[22] *Regesta: Addimenta*, no. 68a
[23] *Regesta*, no. 10.
[24] Fass A, pp. 48–51.

In short, the liturgy – its existence and effective communication – was in the hands of the cantor.[25]

The liturgical authority of individuals such as Ansellus, Giraldus and Peter put them in a prime position to shape perceptions of history and identity. Liturgy, by nature commemorative and sacramental, mixes linear and cyclical dimensions of time; it remembers distinct events that have come and gone, but it also makes them immanent through liturgical reenactment that is not bound to sequence.[26] It is, in this sense, a mediator between past and present, conveying not the past itself, but an interpretation of it. This means that different liturgical uses and celebrations were 'practiced, living, singing models of time', and that cantors, as composers and organizers of the liturgy, may be understood as history writers, creators and stewards of models of the past.[27]

In addition to shaping perceptions of the past, the ritual performances overseen by cantors could transform the identities of worshippers. Anthropologists have long noted that ritual is transformative, a characteristic grounded in its nature as performance.[28] Ritual does not merely convey an idea or cause a belief; as Catherine Bell has aptly noted, 'Ritual is the thing itself. It *is* power; it acts and it actuates'.[29] Nathan Mitchell argues that this actuating power applies to identity: 'As performance, ritual redefines the self by embodying thoughts and emotions never before known, risked or felt. These coincide with (rather than are shaped or evoked by) the ritual performance.'[30] Liturgy, as ritual action, allows a worshipper not merely to assent intellectually to the views of reality or history that it advocates; rather, it instantiates those views in the bodies of participants, accomplishing an actual transformation of identity. Medieval cantors, then, as stewards of the liturgy, can be understood as having enormous potential to shape the identity of liturgical participants.

The twelfth-century cantors of the Holy Sepulchre possessed a particularly powerful liturgical tool for shaping history and identity in the new Office and Mass of the *Festivitas s. Hierusalem*. This novel feast, primarily built

---

[25] As there are identifiable cantors of the Holy Sepulchre, this work assumes that what can be known in general about the power of the office applies to them in particular, though it should be acknowledged that the cantor's duties were not always exclusively carried out by holders of the office.

[26] See, generally, Fass D.

[27] Ibid., p. 151.

[28] See, for example, the works of M. Douglas, *Purity and Danger: An Analysis of Concepts of Pollution and Taboo* (New York, 1966); V. W. Turner, *The Ritual Process: Structure and Anti-Structure* (Chicago, 1969), pp. 95–129.

[29] C. M. Bell, *Ritual Theory, Ritual Practice* (Oxford, 2009), p. 195 (italics in original).

[30] N. Mitchell, 'New Directions in Ritual Research', in *Foundations in Ritual Studies: A Reader for Students of Christian Worship*, ed. P. F. Bradshaw and J. A. Melloh (Grand Rapids, 2007), pp. 103–30 (p. 117).

out of existing liturgical material, was composed early in the century to commemorate a new miracle, the Crusaders' capture of the city. It was explicitly about the Crusades, the Franks and their relationship to Jerusalem. By overseeing its liturgical celebration, the cantors of the Holy Sepulchre were able to contribute to the 'reconstruction' of the city and its society, first, by presenting a coherent story of how the Crusade figured into the city's sacred history, and second, by helping worshippers become unified through a sense of identity generated through the liturgy.

But the cantor's influence can only be understood when the new Jerusalem feast's origin and development are properly understood. A charter of the Holy Sepulchre from 1130 to 1133 lists a feast for Jerusalem alongside Christmas and Easter as a day on which alms are to be distributed.[31] This suggests that the feast was adopted by the canons of the Holy Sepulchre by at least the third decade of the twelfth century. In fact the feast appears in the earliest known manuscript sources for the liturgy of the Holy Sepulchre – a sacramentary dating to between 1128 and 1132 and a sacramentary-evangeliary composed shortly thereafter.[32] Both have entries in their calendars on 15 July: 'Festivitas Hierusalem quando capta fuit a Christianis' and 'capta fuit a Francis', respectively. True to form, the first sacramentary records only the prayers of the Jerusalem Mass, while the second provides identical prayers but also the Gospel, Matthew 21. 10–17, the account of Jesus cleansing the Temple and healing the people.[33] The texts of a complete Jerusalem Office, along with a Mass with the introit *Letare Hierusalem*, appear in four early manuscripts, three of which were certainly produced in the Latin Crusader Kingdoms. The first, an ordinal copied for the use of the Templars in Jerusalem, is Vatican Library, MS Barb. lat. 659. In his extensive study of this manuscript, Sebastian Salvado argues that it was copied after 1173, reflecting a reworking of the liturgy of the Holy Sepulchre that took place between 1149 and 1153.[34] The second is an early thirteenth century ordinal of the Holy Sepulchre, Barletta, Archivio della Chiesa del Santo Sepolcro, MS s.n., which contains (among many other things) a copy of the breviary also preserved in the Templar ordinal.[35] In the sanctoral of these ordinals the feast is entitled, 'In Liberatione

---

[31] *Cartulaire*, no. 98.

[32] For the first, see Rome, Biblioteca Angelica, MS 477, with the canon of the Mass in Cambridge, Fitzwilliam Museum, MS McClean 49, fos. 70v–83v. For the second, see BnF lat. 12056. For further discussion, see Dondi, *Liturgy of the Canons*, pp. 61–63, 146–62.

[33] Rome 477, fol. 159r, contains prayers for a Mass titled *In festivitate civitatis s. Hierusalem*. BnF lat. 12056 provides the Gospel for the feast, Matt. 21. 10–17 under *In liberatione Ierusalem* (fols. 31v–32v) and the prayers under *Missa de Hierusalem* (fol. 250rv).

[34] Salvado, 'Liturgy of the Holy Sepulchre', esp. pp. 27–35.

[35] Barletta is an ordinal in the true sense, a compendium of the liturgy of the Holy Sepulchre which includes a breviary (fols. 33r–136r), a collectar (fols. 150r–212v)

sancte civitas Hierusalem'.[36] The third manuscript is a breviary appended to an abbreviated pontifical, compiled in Outremer in the twelfth century, Lucca, Biblioteca Arcivescovile MS 5.[37] Finally, the texts for the Jerusalem Mass and the hours of Vespers through Lauds appear under the title 'In Festivitas Sancte Hierusalem' at the conclusion of a thirteenth-century collection of histories of the First Crusade, BL Add. 8927, fols. 134r–135r.[38]

Together, these manuscripts suggest that there were at least three complete versions of the Jerusalem feast celebrated by the Holy Sepulchre in the twelfth century, each recasting Crusade history and each placing a different emphasis on the essential identity of the Franks. As it appears in the thirteenth-century collection of histories, the *Festivitas s. Hierusalem* focuses on the city's liberation, drawing on imagery associated with Advent – over three-quarters of its material explicitly refers to the city 'Jerusalem' or 'Sion', while just under half is borrowed from pre-existing Advent liturgy, including the Gospel, Matthew 21. 1–9, Jesus's triumphal entry to Jerusalem. Additionally, material from Epiphany and Dedication liturgies make up 15 and 10 per cent

and various other liturgical documents usually appearing in a pontifical or ritual. The breviary portion appears to have been copied from the same source as the Templar ordinal and therefore reflects the same time period (s. xii^med). The collectar, however, provides various additions and may reflect a slightly later period. A chronicle of the Crusades from 1097 to *c.* 1202 (the end of the chronicle is illegible) gives a *terminus a quo* of the early thirteenth century for the composition of the manuscript, and this date is confirmed by the thirteenth-century hand. This disorganization suggests the manuscript was probably not intended for liturgical use, rather being copied as a historical record of the rite of the Holy Sepulchre after the loss of Jerusalem: see C. Kohler, 'Un ritual et un bréviaire du Saint-Sépulcre de Jérusalem (XIIe–XIIIe siècle)', *Revue de l'Orient latin* 8 (1900–1), 383–500 (pp. 458–9). My thanks to Gaposchkin and Salvado for sharing photographs of the manuscript.

[36] In MS 659 the Mass is fols. 132r–132v and the Office fols. 101r–102r. In Barletta, the Office and Mass are fols. 109v–110v. The Barletta collectar, fols. 188v–189r, includes these additions for the feast: the prayer for the Vespers Magnificat, the full text of the prayer used for the Little Hours and the notation for the Magnificat antiphon for second Vespers.

[37] Buchthal and Wormald place the creation of Lucca 5 in Jerusalem, believing it to be the earliest manuscript of the Latin Kingdoms. Dondi describes it as breviary compiled in Caesarea around 1200 for Peter of Limoges, archbishop of Caesarea; she states that the breviary reflects the use of Chartres. Salvado dates the manuscript to between 1173 and 1228 and disagrees with Dondi concerning its production for the archbishop. However, all scholars seem to take the essential unity of the manuscript for granted, agreeing that it is was written in the Crusader kingdoms because it includes a chronicle of the Crusades (fol. 18v) and a petition for the patriarch in its litany (fol. 55r). See H. Buchthal and F. Wormald, *Miniature Painting in the Latin Kingdom of Jerusalem* (Oxford, 1957), p. xxx n. 5; Salvado, 'Liturgy of the Holy Sepulchre', p. 51; Dondi, *Liturgy of the Canons*, pp. 73–5, 181–8. My detailed analysis of this neglected source is forthcoming.

[38] Linder's fullest analysis of the feast is based primarily on this manuscript. See Linder, 'The Liturgy of the Liberation'.

of the borrowed material, respectively. The version in Add. 8927 is especially distinctive, drawing on Fulcher's *Historia Hierosolymitana* for its nine Matins readings – specifically, his account of the topography, siege and capture of Jerusalem. Add. 8927 also includes a new sequence for the Mass, 'Manu plaudant'.[39]

The *Festivitas s. Hierusalem* is essentially a celebration of an event. It is a story that presents the Crusading venture in epic terms, using biblical quotations and allusions to cast the conquest as the liberation of an enslaved Jerusalem (as foretold by Old Testament prophets) and the descent of the Heavenly City foreseen by the Apostle John. The chants of Vespers are a good example of the feast's dramatic quality, since they are structured as a tale of deliverance in which God and a personified Jerusalem are the main characters. The first antiphon introduces God, 'Behold! The name of the Lord comes from afar and his renown fills the world', quoting Isaiah 30. 27–28.[40] The next antiphon addresses Jerusalem: 'Jerusalem, raise your eyes and see the power of the king. Behold, the Savior comes to release you from bondage' (Isaiah 60. 4a).[41] Subsequent antiphons alternate according to this pattern, using Scriptural allusions to speak of God's impending Advent and to exhort Jerusalem to hope. The Vespers hymn, 'Urbs Hierusalem beata', highlights the significance of the city's liberation, describing Jerusalem as the 'vision of peace built in heaven out of living stones, and encircled by angels just as a bride for her companion' (cf. Apoc. 21. 2).[42] In this liturgy, then, the capture on 15 July fulfilled biblical prophecy of God's liberation of Jerusalem and heralded the marriage of the Lamb to his eschatological Bride, the New Jerusalem.

While the chants for Vespers thus focus on God's liberation of the city, the feast's liturgy more generally presents the Crusade as the prophesied liberation signalling the final descent of the Heavenly City. The liturgy's compiler makes this explicit in Matins in his use of readings from Fulcher of Chartres. These readings, woven together with chants alluding to scriptural promises of Jerusalem's salvation, unambiguously present the Crusaders and their deeds as the particular referents of sacred prophecy and vision. For example, when Fulcher's account of the moment when the Crusaders breeched the wall is repurposed as a Matins reading and paired with the responsory quoting Jeremiah 31. 5–7, 'Rise, Sion, turn to your God. Rejoice and be glad, Jacob, because your salvation comes in the midst of the nations', the juxtaposition presents the Crusaders as God's divine agents in his foretold liberation drama.[43] The rest of the feast's material likewise aids in

---

[39] Also in *AH*, XL, 71. See also Fass C for discussion of this sequence.
[40] Can 002527.
[41] Can 003606.
[42] Can 008405.
[43] Can 007033.

this representation of the conquest and the Crusaders as a foretold salvation. Likewise, the newly composed prose 'Manu plaudant' explains that the conquest is indeed the subject of ancient prophecy: 'Behold, your sons and daughters come from afar today, to you the gate of glory for pardon of their faults. Behold, due honor is rendered to the tomb, which the foreknowing prophet spoke of.'[44] At the same time, the Gospel of the feast likens the capture to Christ's Palm Sunday entrance, culminating in his Passion. The eschatological interpretation of the Crusade also continues to be emphasized, as in the Matins responsory, 'This is Jerusalem, the great city from heaven adorned just as a bride for the Lamb'.[45] In sum, the *Festivitas* focuses on the event of the city's capture, interpreted as the fulfilment of prophecy and vision – and it suggests that the Franks should understand themselves as divinely ordained liberators, heralds of the New Jerusalem descended from heaven.

The very different Jerusalem feast in the ordinals, the *Liberatio s. Hierusalem*, shares only half its chant and a third of its psalmody with the *Festivitas*, even when comparing only the hours that the two versions share. It also introduces a significant structural change, adding a procession after Prime with three stations: the west entrance to the *Templum Domini*, the point on the north wall where the Crusaders breached the city and the Aedicule in the Anastasis Rotunda of the Sepulchre.[46] This version of the liturgy focuses less on the event of the capture of Jerusalem itself, with only a third of its material explicitly mentioning 'Jerusalem' or 'Sion'. Instead, it is largely a celebration of God's nature as revealed *by* the events of the capture; the greatest portion of its material, just over a third, is borrowed from liturgy for Epiphany, less than a quarter from Advent and just over a tenth each from the Feast of the Trinity and the Dedication liturgy. The *Liberatio* is certainly still a commemoration, but focuses on using history to praise God, his righteousness, power and compassion. For instance, it shares a number of its Vespers antiphons with Add. 8927, which (as discussed) introduce the theme of God's foretold deliverance of Jerusalem. Yet, responding to these antiphons, the Vespers prayer in the *Liberatio* praises God for revealing the glory of the eternal Trinity,

---

[44] Translation taken from Fass C, pp. 154–5.

[45] Can 006803.

[46] The first station, 'in introitum templi', was likely at the west entrance, since the first chant sung at the station, the antiphon 'Pax eterna' (Can 004252) corresponds to the inscription which was placed over this entrance. See John of Würzburg, in *Peregrinationes tres*, ed. R. B. C. Huygens, CCCM 139 (Turnhout, 1994), pp. 79–141 (p. 94); Theodericus, in *Peregrinationes tres*, pp. 143–97 (p. 160). The point of the breech is marked with a red cross and the words 'Hic capta est civitas' on a map of Jerusalem in Cambrai, Médiathèque municipale MS 437 (c. 1140–70), reprinted in *Les Croisades: l'Orient et l'Occident d'Urbain II a Saint Louis, 1096–1270*, ed. M. Rey-Delque (Milan, 1997), p. 236. A optional station was held at the entrance to the Holy Sepulchre if the feast fell on a Sunday.

rather than simply thanking him for renewing the anniversary of the capture (as does the prayer of the *Festivitas*).[47] A different Gospel reading (Matthew 21. 10–17, as noted above) showcases the distinct emphasis on the revelation of God's character, suggesting that the Crusade was an example of God's righteousness and mercy, not merely his advent. Similarly, the chants of the *Liberatio*'s procession would have filled the city with the exaltation of God and his triumphs: On the way to the Temple, the Crusaders sang 'Blessed is the Lord God of Israel who alone performs miracles!' and 'What God is great like our God?'; at the wall they proclaimed, 'Thanks be to you God! Thanks be to you, truly one Trinity'; and before the Sepulchre, 'The Lord arose from this place!'[48]

The *Liberatio*'s focus on the capture as an epiphany, as the revelation of God's nature, presents the Franks as beloved sons entrusted with the Holy City and charged with representing God's glory. This is especially clear in the Matins readings: Isaiah 60–62, the Gospel of the day, and the credal 'symbol' of Leo III.[49] They begin with the capitulary also used in the *Festivitas*, 'Arise, shine, O Jerusalem, for your light has come' (Isaiah 60. 1–6), but continue through Isaiah 62, thus providing the entire extended prophecy. The Isaiah readings encourage Jerusalem to rejoice, since 'her sons will come from afar, and your daughters will rise up at your side' (Isaiah 60. 4b). This does not merely refer to the Crusading army converging on the city, as it would in the *Festivitas*, but to people dwelling within Jerusalem: 'Your people shall all be righteous; they shall possess the land forever, the branch of my planting, the work of my hands, that I might be glorified' (Isaiah 60. 21). These people are the Franks, who are 'oaks of righteousness' dwelling in the land (Isaiah 61. 3). Their righteousness will be a light to the nations, which will be a 'crown of beauty in the hand of the Lord' seen by all (Isaiah 62. 2). The Franks are the watchmen on the wall who will give the Lord 'no rest until he establishes Jerusalem and makes it the praise of the earth' (Isaiah 62. 6–7). In the *Liberatio*, then, the 'glory' of the Lord that will rise upon Jerusalem is not simply the city's liberation, but its inhabitation by its true sons and daughters, the Crusaders, righteous offspring blessed by the Lord.

In the third version of the Jerusalem feast, reflected in the Templar and Barletta ordinals, Crusade history and Frankish identity are given yet another distinct interpretation. This is a combined Jerusalem and Dedication feast: the

---

47 The prayer is 'Omnipotens sempiterne Deus qui dedisti famulis', the oratio *In Festo Sanctissime Trinitatis*. See *Les oraisons du missel romain*, ed. P. Bruylants, 2 vols. (Louvain, 1952), II, 219. The prayers of the *Festivitas* are discussed below.

48 For the first three, see Can 006249, Can 007498 and Can 002977; the fourth, apparently unique, is not recorded in the Cantus database.

49 This is a summary of Trinitarian doctrine sent by Pope Leo III to the Orthodox churches in the ninth century, printed in H. B. Swete, *On the History of the Doctrine of the Procession of the Holy Spirit from the Apostolic Age to the Death of Charlemagne* (London, 1876), p. 230.

15 July calendar entry in the Templar ordinal is the 'Liberatio s. Hierusalem' while the Barletta ordinal gives 'Dedicatio ecclesie Dominici Sepulcri' for the same day.[50] Within the sanctoral of the breviaries of both ordinals, however, the Jerusalem feast appears immediately before a Dedication Office and Mass with the heading 'The very same day, the Dedication of the Church of the Lord's Sepulchre which we solemnly celebrate according to the will and precepts of the Lord Patriarch Fulcher'.[51] Fulcher of Angoulême was patriarch of Jerusalem from 1146 to 1157, and on 15 July 1149, the fiftieth anniversary of the city's capture, Fulcher rededicated the Crusaders' newly constructed choir and altars.[52] The canons of the Holy Sepulchre thus appear to have celebrated a double feast from 1149 onwards.

Yet the rubrics of the Jerusalem Office indicate that the celebration of this double feast was in some ways limited. Thus, in the Templar ordinal between the final two antiphons of the procession, one rubric notes: 'Regarding this Liberation [feast]: We do nothing according to this new arrangement except the procession and early morning Mass, on account of the Dedication of the church.'[53] In keeping with this, the Templar ordinal heads the Jerusalem Mass 'early morning Mass' and the Dedication Mass 'great Mass'. Both ordinals also have a rubric at the conclusion of the Jerusalem feast: 'Only the early morning Mass of the Capture is sung. The procession is never diminished, however, but carried out festively.'[54] These details show that the Jerusalem feast was combined with the Dedication liturgy after 1149, specifically the Jerusalem Office was replaced with a Dedication Office, the procession was retained, the Jerusalem Mass became an early morning Mass and the High Mass was a Dedication. This accords with the testimony of John of Würzburg, who visited the city as a pilgrim sometime between 1150 and 1164.[55] Regarding 15 July he wrote:

> Eadem quoque die in eodem mense, licet longe iam anteriori tempore, cum iam dudum eadem sancta civitas sub dominatu Sarracenorum diversorum generum detineretur captiva, ab excercitu Christianorum est liberate. Ad cuius liberationis commemorationem eandem diem post consecrationis

[50] MS 659, fol. 4; Barletta fol. 16r.

[51] MS 659, fol. 102r; Barletta fol. 110v: 'Eodem die dedicatio ecclesia dominici Sepulchri quam sollempniter celebramus iuxta voluntatem et preceptum Fulcherii patriarche.'

[52] This according to an inscription placed in the Holy Sepulchre: for the text of the entire reconstructed inscription, see Linder, 'Like Purest Gold Resplendent', pp. 31–2.

[53] MS 659 fol. 101v: 'De hac liberatione, secundum novam institutionem, nihil facimus preter processionem et missam matutinale propter dedicationem ecclesia.'

[54] 'Missa matutinalis de captione tantum canitur, sed procession nunquam dimittitur, sed festive peragitur', MS 659 fol. 102; Barletta MS. fol. 110v; Barletta [peragitur]: ut prescriptum est *add.*

[55] Linder, 'Like Purest Gold Resplendent', pp. 43–4.

renovationem cum spirituali offitio reddunt celebrem in priori missa decantando, *Letare Hierusalem,* maiorem vero missam celebrant de dedicatione, *Terribilis est locus.*[56]

[At the time the Holy City itself was held in captivity under the power of Saracens of various kinds, it was set free by a Christian army. For the commemoration of this liberation, that same day, after the renewal of the consecration [of the church] through the divine rites, they continue the celebration in the mass by singing *Letare Hierusalem,* etc. Indeed, they celebrate the high mass – or more solemn service of the Dedication – which begins *Terribilis est locus.*]

Thus the feast celebrated by the canons on 15 July after 1149, and presumably until 1187, was a combined Liberation-Dedication. Accordingly, it would seem that the *Liberatio* was the version celebrated by the Holy Sepulchre prior to the mid-century, probably preserved in full in the breviaries on account of the conservative nature of the copying of liturgical books. (For the sake of convenience, my reconstruction of the relationship among these three versions of the feast is summarized in Table 15.1.)

With the three versions' differences in mind, then, we can turn to consider the development of the Jerusalem liturgy celebrated by the canons of the Holy Sepulchre. The earliest form of the feast was likely the *Festivitas s. Hierusalem* now preserved in Add. 8927. Of course, there is no calendar in the manuscript, nor any other external indication of the community to which the feast was attached, but the wording of the prayers of the Mass, revisions of prayers for the common Gallican *Missa in anniversario dedicationis basilice,* indicate that the *Festivitas* version was celebrated in Jerusalem on 15 July as a commemoration of the capture of the city.[57] Furthermore, the fourth prayer (*super populum*) is new composition, and it strongly suggests that the *Festivitas* was celebrated by the canons of the Holy Sepulchre and not another church in the city. It clearly refers to Christ's sepulchre at the conclusion of the prayer: 'grant to us, we pray, that through the august and glorious sepulchre of the same our Redeemer, we may merit to be raised from the grave to victory and achieve the blessedness of eternal happiness.'[58] Given the other internal evidence pointing to the circumstances of the feast's celebration, the most probable

---

[56] *Peregrinationes tres,* pp. 123–4; trans. A. Stewart, PPTS 5 (New York, 1971), p. 51.

[57] These revisions consistently replace references to the 'temple' with 'Jerusalem' or the 'Holy City', and they also replace references to celebrating the anniversary of the dedication with references to celebrating the anniversary of the day of the 'acceptio' of Jerusalem. For the original prayers, see *Concordances et tableaux pour l'étude des grands sacramentaires,* ed. J. Deshusses 3 vols. (Fribourg, 1982), II, p. 332, nos. 1085, 193 and 976.

[58] Add. 8927, fol. 135r: '… prebe nobis, quesumus, ut per venerabile atque gloriosum eiusdem redemptoris nostri sepulcrum, a vitiorum sepulcris resuscitari mereamur et felicitatis eterne gaudia consequemur.'

Table 15.1 The three stages of the 15 July feast celebrated
by the Holy Sepulchre in the twelfth century

Stages	*Festivitas sanctae Hierusalem*	*In Liberatione sanctae civitas Ierusalem*	Combined Dedication & Liberation
Date	1106–*c.* 1130	*c.* 1130–49	1149–87
MS sources	BL Add. 8927	Rome, Bib. Ang. MS 477 BnF MS lat. 12056 BAV MS Barb. lat. 659 Barletta, Santo Sepolcro, MS s.n. Lucca, Bib. Arc. MS 5	BAV MS Barb. lat. 659 Barletta, Santo Sepolcro, MS s.n. John of Wurzburg
Mass type	*Festivitas* (revised Dedication prayers)	*Liberatio* (new prayers)	*Dedicatio*
Office type	*Festivitas*	*Liberatio*	*Dedicatio*
Early Mass	–	–	*Liberatio*
Procession	–	after Prime	after Prime (*Liberatio*)
Gospel	Matthew 21. 1–9 (triumphal entry)	Matthew 21. 10–17 (cleansing the Temple)	Luke 19. 1–10 (Jesus visits Zacchaeus) Luke 6. 43 (Good and bad trees)
Matins readings	Fulcher of Chartres's *Historia Hierosolymitana*	Isaiah 60–62 Matthew 21. 10–17 'Symbol' of Leo III	Sermon of St Augustine *Quotienscumque* Luke 19. 1–10/ Luke 6. 43
Primary sources	Advent liturgy (76%) Epiphany liturgy (15%) Dedication liturgy (10%)	Epiphany liturgy (35%) Advent liturgy (22%) Dedication liturgy (11%) Feast of the Trinity (11%)	Dedication liturgy
Theological & historiographical concerns	The feast depicts the capture as the liberation of enslaved Jerusalem foretold by Old Testament prophets and the descent of the Heavenly City foreseen by the Apostle John	The feast is primarily a celebration of God's nature as revealed by the events of the capture	The feast portrays the city of Jerusalem as a kind of church, sanctified through the 'ritual' of the capture
Frankish identity	Foretold liberators and heralds of the New Jerusalem	'Watchmen on the walls' representing God's glory to the nations	Priests of the Lord, ministers of God

author of so straightforward a reference to the tomb of Christ was a liturgist writing for the Holy Sepulchre.

There are other reasons for thinking that the *Festivitas* was celebrated by the canons of the Holy Sepulchre. The work of Cristina Dondi has emphasized the liturgical pre-eminence of the Holy Sepulchre in Jerusalem, demonstrating that when the Templar and Hospitaller orders adopted a liturgical use, they followed that of the Sepulchre.[59] Furthermore, three of the four major shrine churches of Jerusalem in the twelfth century (Mount Sion, the *Templum Domini* and the church of the Ascension) were served by Augustinian canons from an early time, and it is possible (perhaps even likely) that these canons were in liturgical agreement with the Augustinian canons of the cathedral church, the Holy Sepulchre.[60] The possibility of liturgical agreement among these four major Augustinian establishments is made more probable by a document stipulating the mutual obligations of the churches upon the death of a canon.[61] Since the liturgical formation in Jerusalem's major secular churches thus tended toward agreement with the Holy Sepulchre, it is therefore unlikely that one of the other secular churches would create a rival version of the feast, in competition with the Holy Sepulchre's. Indeed, there is evidence that even the Benedictine establishments – such as church of the Assumption in Josaphat, the convent of St Mary Major and St Mary Latin in the Hospitallers' quarters – participated in the liturgy of the Holy Sepulchre during important processions and on high feast days, an observation which becomes all the more relevant in light of the aforementioned cartulary document paralleling Christmas, Easter and the Jerusalem feast.[62] The Holy Sepulchre should thus be understood as the church out of which the Jerusalem feast was written and revised, and all early versions of the feast, including that of the *Festivitas*, should be understood as most likely reflecting the Sepulchre's liturgical use.

The likely origin of the *Festivitas* in the Holy Sepulchre is reinforced by the circumstances under which liturgical books were produced in Crusader Jerusalem. There was only one known scriptorium in twelfth-century Jerusalem – the Holy Sepulchre's – and, lacking evidence for another scriptorium, we can tentatively conclude that most of the secular liturgical books used throughout the city (and certainly any new books) were produced,

---

[59] Dondi, *Liturgy of the Canons*, pp. 40–2.

[60] Indeed, even where there was independence of custom–as in the case of the funeral rite of the Augustianian house of Saint-Jean-en-Vallée–the house still adopted the liturgical texts of the cathedral church of the diocese, Chartres. See M. McLaughlin, 'The Twelfth-Century Ritual of Death and Burial at Saint-Jean-en-Vallée in the Diocese of Chartres', *RB* 105 (1995), 155–66.

[61] Hamilton, *The Latin Church*, p. 96. See MS 659, fol. 12v; Barletta fol. 138rv.

[62] Participation is indicated for the feasts of the Assumption, Palm Sunday, the *Cena domini* and Pascha: MS 659 fols 33r, 65rv, 69r, 76r; Barletta fols. 40r, 69v–70r, 73r, 78r.

repaired, modified or expanded there under the general supervision of the Sepulchre's cantor.[63]

Since the *Festivitas* was a feast of the Holy Sepulchre, the time during which it was composed and celebrated can be discerned with some degree of certainty. For the reasons discussed above, it could not have been in use between 1149 and 87, nor during the period immediately prior to 1149. Instead, the *Festivitas* is either an early twelfth century form or one developed after 1187. The general tone of the feast could support an early date; it is exuberant and triumphant, suggesting both the freshness of the Crusaders' success and that the city still belonged firmly to the West at the time of composition. Furthermore, since new liturgies for the liberation of Jerusalem were being spontaneously celebrated and officially promulgated by the Pope after 1187, it seems less likely that a revision of the feast of the liberation of Jerusalem, especially a revision in the direction of greater enthusiasm, would take place at the same time.[64] Indeed, BL Egerton 2902, a thirteenth-century sacramentary of the canons of the Holy Sepulchre, shows that the Jerusalem Mass was itself then revised to become a liturgy *for* the liberation: Egerton contains a calendar entry for 15 July, 'Dedicatio ecclesie s. Sepulchri et liberatio Hierusalem', but the Mass of the Jerusalem feast is now called the 'Missa pro libertate Hierusalem de manu paganorum', and the Gospel has been changed to Luke 19. 41, the account of Jesus weeping over Jerusalem.[65] The *Festivitas* thus seems very likely to be the earliest version celebrated by the Holy Sepulchre, composed sometime after 1106, when copies of Fulcher's *Historia* first became available.[66]

The approximate date of the revision of the *Festivitas* into the *Liberatio* can also be determined with some confidence. The sacramentaries' new prayers and new Gospel indicate that Mass of the feast was revised by the early 1130s, though the revision of the office appears to have been undertaken even earlier. This is suggested by Lucca MS 5, which contains an early twelfth century breviary appended to a late twelfth century collection of bishop's liturgy and other material. The first part of the manuscript, written in many different hands, presents liturgy reserved for a bishop intertwined with a Psalter and other material for the Office, as well as a petition for the patriarch of Jerusalem in the litany and a short chronicle of the Crusade ending with

[63] On the scriptorium of twelfth-century Jerusalem, see Buchthal and Wormald, *Miniature Painting*, pp. xxx–xxxi, 21–2.

[64] Linder, 'Individual and Community in the Liturgy of the Liberation of Jerusalem', in *Information, Kommunikation Und Selbstdarstellung in Mittelalterlichen Gemeinden*, ed. A. Haverkamp (München, 1998), pp. 28–34.

[65] BL Egerton 2902 fol. 93rv.

[66] *Fulcheri Carnotensis Historia Hierosolymitana (1095–1127)*, ed. H. Hagenmeyer (Heidelberg: 1913), pp. 42–8.

the capture of Tyre in 1124.[67] The breviary portion of the manuscript, written in a hand from the second quarter of the twelfth century, reflects a liturgical use with close ties in several instances to the Augustinian house of St-Jean-en-Vallée, Chartres, and it is notated with Chartrain neumes also dateable to the second quarter of the century.[68] But the liturgy of the Lucca 5 breviary is ultimately distinct from any known European use, and it may represent the Office liturgy celebrated by the canons of Sidon (or Tyre) in the first half of the century.

One important aspect of Lucca 5, suggesting its ties to the Holy Sepulchre, is a heretofore unidentified series of incipits of the Jerusalem office, copied on the last leaf of the material preceding the breviary. The chant programme indicated by these incipits corresponds to the *Liberatio* version, though lacking a title, office prayers and Matins readings.[69] Instead, the only instruction regarding the Matins readings appears at the conclusion of the set of incipits: 'Lectiones require in epiphania'. This lack of specificity is unlike other copies of the Jerusalem office appearing in later medieval manuscripts, such as the version preserved in Erfurt, which, while corrupted, does include the prayers and Matins readings of the *Liberatio*.[70] Thus the Lucca office could be an early intermediary form of the Jerusalem office, reflecting the point at which a liturgist had worked out a new chant programme without yet adding the prayers and readings to fully realize the *Liberatio*'s new vision. The instruction to use readings for Epiphany suggests that the liturgist is moving toward the *Liberatio* version, but since the incipits fail to identify Matthew 21. 10–17 as the Gospel text for the seventh Matins reading, the Jerusalem office preserved in Lucca could date from sometime prior to the composition of the sacramentaries.

There were therefore three complete versions of the Jerusalem feast celebrated by the canons of the Holy Sepulchre in the twelfth century – a version likely dating between 1106 and around 1130, another from *c.* 1130 to 1149 and a post-1149 version, while Lucca 5 demonstrates that an

---

[67] In my forthcoming analysis of this tangled opening, I identify the various sections and provide a paleographical study of each.

[68] The hand of the breviary closely resembles that of BnF lat. 2900, p. 58, the *De pignoribus sanctorum* of Guibert of Nogent written at Notre Dame de Nogent-sous-Coucy sometime between 1120 and 1124. The breviary hand also bears comparison to BnF lat. 1918, fol. 49, the *Opera Augustini* copied at St-Amand-en-Pevèle between 1107 and 1121. The neumes of Lucca 5 are very similar to those of Troyes, Médiathèque du Grand Troyes MS 894, an early twelfth century noted missal of the Benedictine abbey of St-Père-en-Vallée, Chartres. My study of the breviary is forthcoming.

[69] The Jerusalem Mass is written in the lower margin and appears to be a later addition. It reflects the Mass as described by John of Würzburg, in *Peregrinationes tres*, p. 139.

[70] UB Erfurt, Dep. Erf. CA. 8° 44, fol. 19r. My thanks to Professor Gasposchkin for sharing this material with me.

intermediate revision also existed, representing a stage between the first and second full versions. The early version, the *Festivitas*, presented the Franks as the foretold liberators and heralds of the New Jerusalem, while the second complete version, the *Liberatio*, reflected more on the theological import of the Crusaders' success and on the full prophetic message of Isaiah 60–62. Here the Franks are 'watchmen on the walls', beloved sons of Jerusalem entrusted with showing forth God's righteousness to the nations. The final form of the 15 July liturgy, as we have seen, interweaves the commemorative aspect of the earlier versions with a Dedication. Indeed, the choice of 15 July, a day that remembered the entire city, as the day on which to rededicate the Holy Sepulchre, the shrine which was the heart of the city, could hardly be coincidental, signalling that the writers responsible for the office had come to understand the entire city as a kind of church and themselves as its priestly citizens. The retention of the specific elements of the Jerusalem Mass and procession after Prime indicates this new understanding also, for those two elements parallel the structure of the medieval *Ordo ad benedicendam ecclesiam*, with its Dedication mass and sanctifying procession without and within the church.[71] Indeed, the Jerusalem procession served the same purpose as the dedicatory procession, which was to consecrate space through ritual attention. At the same time, the Jerusalem procession – with stations at places significant to the capture – served to integrate the event of the Crusade into the sanctifying ritual; the Crusade came to be understood as itself a ritual essential to Jerusalem's transformation into a kind of church.

If Jerusalem was a kind of church, made so by the Crusade, then the Franks were its clergy. According to the final version of the 15 July Jerusalem liturgy, the Franks were not merely liberators, or even witnesses, but something more: citizens of a type of the Heavenly Jerusalem whose task it was to dwell in the city as ordained minsters, bringing the nations into an encounter with a holy God. As the passage read at Matins for decades prior to the final transformation of 15 July liturgy had proclaimed, 'you shall be called the priests of the Lord; they shall speak of you as the ministers of our God'. And indeed, the final version of the Office would seem to realize that priestly role.

The figures behind these visions and identities were the cantors of the Holy Sepulchre. Bernardus, Peter and Bartholomeus presided over the combined form after the mid-century, and Giraldus (or possibly William) oversaw the transformation of the Jerusalem liturgy into this combined form after 1149. It was Ansellus 'de Turre', however, who may have been responsible for the initial creation of the *Festivitas* and then its revision into the *Liberatio*. If, as argued above, the *Festivitas s. Hierusalem* was composed

---

[71] *Le Pontifical romain au Moyen-Age*, ed. M. Andrieu, 3 vols. (Città del Vaticano, 1938) I, 176–95.

sometime after 1106, the Mass of the feast was apparently revised by the early 1130 and the Office was revised shortly before that, then it could be telling that all of these dates fall within the cantorship of Ansellus. This cantor was a Crusade enthusiast, one of the first to depart Europe for the Holy Land. Present at the siege of Jerusalem, he would have experienced at first hand the euphoria of the Crusaders' triumph. Furthermore, as a resident of Jerusalem, he was likely to have early access to Fulcher's text.[72] Finally, Ansellus seems to have had a reputation for independence and willfulness with regard to the administration of the liturgy; as Pope Calixtus II pointed out in a letter he sent to Patriarch Garmundus in 1121, Ansellus and the *succentor* William 'preside over the chorus of regular brothers, and instruct about the celebration of the divine office according to their own pleasure, by means of whatever person they choose'.[73] It would hardly be surprising, then, were Ansellus to be the liturgist responsible for the *Festivitas*.

Ansellus, perhaps assisted by the *succentor* William, may also have undertaken the first revision of the Jerusalem feast as well, for the first cantor did not remain independent and unconventional. The letter which Pope Calixtus sent to the patriarch was in fact a letter of chastisement, and in it the Pope threatened to remove both Ansellus and William from office should they refuse to abandon a secular way of life. One surmises that they submitted to reform, since both maintained their offices. Thus it is possible that the revision of the *Festivitas* carried out near the end of the 1120s was an extension of Ansellus's personal reform.

Regardless of the question of who composed the liturgy for the feast, and who was responsible for its various revisions, it was the cantors of the Holy Sepulchre who oversaw its performance throughout the century. In this way, these cantors exercised considerable influence over Crusade history and Frankish identity in twelfth-century Jerusalem. They were the ones who brought to Jerusalem the three versions of the 15 July feast, rebuilding the city in stages and potentially unifying the Franks around an evolving identity as liberators, watchmen and ministers.

---

[72] Fulcher, chaplain to Baldwin of Boulogne, moved to Jerusalem in 1100 when Baldwin became king, and he made it his home until his death in 1127. *Historia Hierosolymitana*, pp. 1–19.

[73] *Cartulaire*, no. 3.

16

Shaping Liturgy, Shaping History: A Cantor-Historian from Twelfth-Century Peterhausen

Alison I. Beach

August 27, 1134 was a momentous day for the Benedictine monastery of Petershausen.[1] It was the 139th anniversary of the death of the community's founder, Bishop Gebhard II of Constance (979–95), and after years of preparation the community stood ready to witness his canonization.[2] At the invitation of Abbot Conrad (1127–64), Bishop Ulrich II of Constance (1127–38) and the abbots of seven of the area's monasteries gathered to take part in the festivities. 'With tremendous joy and exultation, with hymns and praises', the sarcophagus containing Gebhard's relics was carried at the head of a great procession of clerics, monks and lay people, starting at the soon-to-be saint's old tomb, circling the entire monastic precinct and culminating with their placement with great honour in a newly prepared resting place in Petershausen's freshly restored basilica.[3]

---

[1] For historical background on Petershausen, see S. Appuhn-Radtke, ed., *1000 Jahre Petershausen: Beiträge zu Kunst und Geschichte der Benediktinerabtei Petershausen in Konstanz* (Constance, 1983); H. Walther, 'Gründungsgeschichte und Tradition im Kloster Petershausen vor Konstanz', *Schriften des Vereins für Geschichte des Bodensees und seiner Umgebung* 96 (1978): 31–67; F. Quarthal, ed., *Die Benediktinerklöster in Baden-Württemberg*, Germania Benedictina 5 (Ottobeuren, 1975), pp. 484–502.

[2] H. Maurer, *Das Bistum Konstanz, 2: Die Konstanzer Bischöfe vom Ende des 6. Jahrhunderts bis 1206*, Germania Sacra Neue Folge 42/1 (Berlin, 2003), pp. 142–3. While Bishop Conrad of Constance's canonization was confirmed by Pope Calixtus II in 1123, no such papal bull survives for Gebhard II. On the continued role of local bishops in awarding the title of saint in the early twelfth century through the translation of relics, see A. Vauchez, *Sainthood in the Later Middle Ages*, trans. Jean Birrell (Cambridge, 1997), pp. 22–7.

[3] *CP* 5.4: 'Anno a condito monasterio centesimo quinquagesimo secundo advenit Oudalricus episcopus et ex monasteriis patres septem invitati a Cuonrado abbate iam sepe dicti monasterii. Sed et turba clericorum et monachorum aliorumque fidelium affuit non modica, et cum immani gaudio et exultatione, cum hymnis et laudibus honorifice transtulerunt ossa et cineres beati confessoris Christi atque pontificis Gebehardi de loco prioris sepulchri et in sarchofago posita ambitum monasterii lustraverunt et postea cum magno honore in novo tumulo condiderunt.' For a German translation, see *Die Chronik des Klosters Petershausen*, ed. O. Feger, Schwäbische Chroniken der Stauferzeit 3 (Sigmaringen, 1978).

The occasion was clearly significant for all of the monks, lay brothers and religious women who comprised this dual-sex monastic community just across the Rhine from the city of Constance, but one among them stood at the centre of the day's liturgical events. Preparation had begun in the preceding months. There was an office for the new saint to compose, hymns and readings to choose, singers and readers to select and an order to set for the various processions. In the days just before, this monk would have presided over a dress rehearsal, checking the singing of the community's boys, readied for their role by his assistant, and correcting any errors in the music or in the pitch of the singers. On the day itself, he would have functioned as a kind of 'master of ceremonies', distributing the copes to all the members of the community in order of rank, ministering to the arriving bishop and intoning the chants.[4] This anonymous monk was Petershausen's cantor (*precentor* or *armarius*), a person of high rank within the hierarchy of monastic communities in the central Middle Ages, following only the abbot, prior and claustral prior in importance.[5]

According to the Constitutions of Hirsau, which had governed life at Petershausen since its reform in 1085, the cantor was ideally to be chosen from among the *nutriti*, those monks (or presumably nuns, in the case of a female community) raised from childhood within the monastery.[6] A *nutritus*, steeped in the liturgy – having lived its sounds, sights, rhythms, movements, gestures and postures over many years – would have gradually absorbed the deep training needed to manage the intricacies of the Mass and Office. By the central Middle Ages, the cantor was charged not only with the making of music and all other aspects of the celebration of the liturgy, but also with overseeing the work of the monastery's scriptorium and book collections.[7]

As many of the contributions to the present volume attest, the individual who held the office of cantor sometimes also took responsibility for keeping the *memoria* of his or her community. At communities associated with Hirsau, the cantor was specifically charged with keeping the memory of the dead

---

[4] Fass A, pp. 49–50.

[5] On the duties of the *armarius/precentor* in the late eleventh and early twelfth century in communities, including Petershausen, that followed customs patterned after those of Cluny, see Fass A, especially at pp. 47–51; and S. Boynton, 'Training for the Liturgy as a Form of Monastic Education', in *Medieval Monastic Education*, ed. C. Muessig and G. Ferzoco (London and New York, 2000), pp. 7–20 (pp. 8–10); on the role of the librarian/cantor in the Hirsau context, see also F. Heinzer, 'Hirsauer Buchkultur und ihre Ausstrahlung', in *700 Jahre Erfurter Peterskloster: Geschichte und Kunst auf dem Erfurter Petersberg, 1103–1803* (Regensburg, 2004), pp. 98–104 (p. 98).

[6] *Willehelmi Abbatis Constitutiones Hirsaugienses*, ed. P. Engelbert, CCM 15, 2 vols. (Siegburg, 2010), II, 113.

[7] For the duties assigned to Hirsau cantors, see *Willehelmi Abbatis Constitutiones*, II, 113–19; on the gradual evolution of the office of cantor from the early to the central Middle Ages, see Fass A.

by maintaining the necrology, the calendric list of the names of the departed for whom the community was expected to pray. This job entailed entering names in the home monastery's necrology, seeing to it that a list of those names was circulated periodically to affiliated communities for reciprocal prayer and entering names arriving from other houses.[8] Many cantors also wrote historical chronicles, maintained annals and composed the lives of saints of special importance to their communities. Some monastic cantor-historians such as William of Malmesbury and others profiled in this volume were prominent figures in their own time.[9] Others laboured anonymously. Some are identified in contemporary sources as cantor while others are only made visible through their performance of the duties associated with the office within their communities. Most left just faint traces of their activities, perceptible only through the careful study of the surviving texts and manuscripts that they used and produced.

I present a case here for identifying the impresario of the Translation of 1134 – the monk who served as Petershausen's cantor (in function if not also in title) from the 1130s to the 1160s – as the very same monk who had recently written the Life of Gebhard, and who would begin to compile the monastery's historical chronicle, the *Casus Monasterii Petrishusensis* in the years following. His reconstructed *œuvre* shows a twelfth-century cantor-historian at work, and complements the more spectacular cases from Malmesbury, Durham, Canterbury and elsewhere, bringing to light the interplay between liturgy, history and community identity at a more ordinary monastery in the central Middle Ages.

Hagiographer and chronicler

Although Petershausen's cantor-historian (hereinafter CHP) was a person of no great renown beyond his own community, he was the author of two surviving historical works. He completed the first of these, the Life of St Gebhard, before 1134, in preparation for the canonization.[10] This Life, which CHP modelled closely after the Life of St Conrad (written around 1123 by Udalschalk, Abbot of St Ulrich and Afra (*c.* 1125–49) for the bishop's canonization), survived the Middle Ages only in a single fifteenth-century

---

[8] *Willehelmi Abbatis Constitutiones*, II, 118; see also Fass A, p. 50.

[9] See especially the essays in this volume by Katie Bugyis, Margot Fassler, Paul Hayward, Charles Rozier, Sigbjørn Sønnesyn, Teresa Webber and Lauren Whitnah.

[10] University of Heidelberg, Codex Salemitani IX 9, fols. 1r–20r. For a digitized version of this manuscript, see http://digi.ub.uni-heidelberg.de/diglit/salIX9/0003; the Life was edited by G. Pertz in MGH SS 10:582–94; see also K. Spahr, 'Das Leben des heiligen Gebhard', in *Bewahren und Bewähren. Festschrift zur St. Gebhard-Tausendjahrfeier* (Bregenz, 1949), pp. 31–43.

manuscript.[11] It is in his second work, the *Casus monasterii Petrishusensis*, that he reveals himself as the author of the first, commenting that because he had already detailed Gebhard's life in another work, he now would touch on it only briefly.[12] His assertion that he had found a previously unknown epitaph for the bishop in 'an old book in the monastery of Stein', a community around thirty kilometres from Petershausen, suggests that he was accustomed, perhaps because of his status as cantor, to have access to the book collections of other monastic communities in the area, and this may have facilitated his research for both the Life and the Chronicle.[13]

Only a single copy of the Chronicle, preserved in University of Heidelberg, Codex Salemitani IX 42a, fols. 35r–98r, has survived from the twelfth century.[14] This text is primarily an autograph, written at Petershausen by CHP himself between *circa* 1136 and the 1160s.[15] His mature and regular Caroline minuscule can also be seen at work in a number of other manuscripts, including three necrologies, a martyrology, a Rule of St Benedict, a *computus* table and in the earliest surviving copy of the Office for St Gebhard. His engagement in the production of texts, and particularly texts related to the liturgy, offers further evidence for his role as cantor.

In addition to providing a scribal fingerprint for CHP, the Chronicle also offers textual evidence for its creator's interest in both the performance and material culture of the liturgy within his community. He anchors Petershausen's history in Gebhard's noble Alemannic ancestry, details his portentous birth by caesarean section, traces his path to the episcopacy and describes his foundation and endowment of Petershausen. But it is Gebhard's Translation that he highlights as the crowning event in the history of the community. Although CHP would later add an irregular series of folios and gatherings to the text in order to make room for additional notices about subsequent events, the Chronicle originally ended with the Translation,

---

[11] See the *Vita S. Cuonradi Constantiensis Episcopi*. MGH SS 4:429–36.

[12] *CP* 1.6: 'Cuius vitam quoniam alio opera ut potuimus executi sumus, nunc paucis attingemus'.

[13] *CP* 1.54: 'Sed et aliud epitafium inveni in antiquo libro apud Steinense monasterium de hoc Dei famulo conscriptum, quod se habet in hunc modum ...'

[14] A digitized version of the entire manuscript is available online through the University of Heidelberg: http://digi.ub.uni-heidelberg.de/diglit/salIX42a (accessed 19 June 2015). The Chronicle begins at http://digi.ub.uni-heidelberg.de/diglit/salIX42a/0083.

[15] Based on my own analysis of the manuscript, I agree with Franz Josef Mone, *Quellensammlung der badischen Landesgeschichte* 1 (Karlsruhe, 1848), p. 112; and Feger, *Die Chronik des Klosters Petershausen*, pp. 8–9, who both argued that the manuscript is the autograph of the author. For an argument that the manuscript is not the work of a single author-scribe, see Walther, 'Gründungsgeschichte und Tradition', pp. 37–9; and Irene Schmale-Ott, 'Der Bodenseeraum', in Wilhelm Wattenbach and Franz-Josef Schmale, *Deutschlands Geschichtsquellen im Mittelalter*, vol. 1 (Darmstadt, 1976), p. 28.

which stands alone in a section in the manuscript, heralded, like each of the five that lead up to it, with a decorative initial and incipit in red ink.[16]

He described in full detail the liturgical implements and vestments that Gebhard had provided to the monastery at its founding, lamenting their alienation, theft and destruction; the *custos* discovers the theft of a precious censer while preparing to celebrate Matins (*CP* 4.13); and an incompetent cellarer resorts to handing over valuable liturgical vestments to pay off outstanding debts (*CP* 4.15); the wrath of God rains down on Gebhard's successor, Bishop Lambert (c. 995–1018), in the form of maggots (*pediculi*) that pour out of his ears 'like a swarm of bees, and from each limb like a multitude of ants, until he breathed his last breath under this loathsome torment', for taking away, among other precious objects, 'two dorsals, two combs, one ivory comb adorned with gold, seven altar cloths, one hand-towel, one tapestry, one silver chalice, one golden stole...' (*CP* 2.4–5). And the only detail he recorded about Conrad's attendance at the Second Lateran Council in 1139 was that the abbot had brought two black cloaks that were used to make copes (*CP* 5.22).

He also detailed the renovations made to accommodate the intensified liturgy that the Hirsau reformers had introduced in 1085:

Et quia chorus erat brevis, quoniam gradus, per quos in sanctuarium ascendebatur, locum occupabant, gradus diminuit lapidum et numerum ampliavit canentium, et lapides abstulit atque homines pro eis in locum eorum constituit. Chorum quippe sanctuario pene coequavit, uno tantum gradu sanctuario supereminente, atque ita in choro stantibus locum dilatavit.[17]

[Because the choir was short, since the steps leading up to the altar occupied the space, [Abbot Theodorich (1085–1116)] had removed some of the stone steps and increased the number of singers—[and he thus] took away stones and put men in their place. Indeed, he made the choir almost level with the altar, which was only raised by one step, and he thus enlarged the space for those standing in the choir.]

---

[16] Book 4 ends on fol. 81v with the same *explicit* that signals the end of the prologue and all three of the previous books. The Translation then opens with its own *incipit*: 'Incipit de Translatione Beati Gebehardi Episcopi' ('Here begins the Translation of Blessed Bishop Gebhard') in the same format and with a decorative initial similar to those used for the Prologue and Books 1 through 4. See http://digi.ub.uni-heidelberg.de/diglit/salIX42a/0175. The creation of this book without a number would result in some confusion with the numbering of the subsequent books. With the ad hoc extension of the text following the Translation, the chronicler failed to indicate the beginning of a new book; the text simply continues with no further designation or rubrication. The end of this section (fol. 92r), however, was signalled with the *explicit* 'Here ends Book 5'. The confusion is immediately apparent when the *incipit* – on that same line – announces, 'Here begins Book Five'. See http://digi.ub.uni-heidelberg.de/diglit/salIX42a/0197.

[17] *CP* 3.7.

He then went on to note that 'ad hanc capellam ... omni die post vesperos et matutinos in honore sancte Marie solemniter procedit ibique post canticum et antiphonam atque orationem eius vesperos sive matutinos de omnibus sanctis et pro defunctis canit' ('solemnly processes every day to this chapel of the convent dedicated to St Mary and there, after the hymn, antiphon, and prayer of this Vespers or Matins, they sing the for all the saints and for the dead').[18]

Further, his discussion of Abbot Theodorich's accomplishments on behalf of the monastery suggests an individual with intimate knowledge of the community's book collections. He itemizes the manuscripts, both liturgical and non-liturgical, that the great reformer had procured for the monks:

> Missales libri quinque, quorum duo cum gradualibus, tres autem de sanctis et pro necessitatibus continentes. Liber evangeliorum unus, argento et osse decoratus. Libri lectionum duo. Officialis unus. Benedictionale unum. Graduale unum. Antiphonarium unum. Breviarium operis Dei. Liber consuetudinum. Gregorius super Ezechielem. Tertia pars moralium et quinta ex parte et sexta ex integro. Dialogus unus. Augustinus super Iohannem. Augustinus de consensu evangelistarum. Augustinus super primam partem psalmorum. Augustinus super epistolam Iohannis. Augustinus de opere monachorum, de bono coniugali, de virginitate, de viduitate, de orando Deo, de agone christiano in uno volumine. Item enchiridion Augustini. Flores Augustini. Augustinus de fide. Augustinus super quindecim gradus. Orienis super vetus testamentum. Regula sancti Benedicti. Pentateucum. Actus apostolorum. Exameron Ambrosi. Vita sancti Oudalrici. Matutinales libri duo. Omeliarum liber hiemalis.[19]

> [Five missals, two of which with graduals and three with sanctorals and for necessities; one book of the Gospels, decorated in silver and ivory; two lectionaries; one *Liber officialis*; one benedictional; one gradual, one antiphoner; a breviary for the Divine Office; a customary; Gregory's Commentary on Ezekiel; Book Three of the *Morals on Job*, part of Book Five, and all of Book Six; one copy of the *Dialogues*; Augustine's Commentary on John; Augustine's *On the Harmony of the Gospels*; Augustine's Commentary on the first part of Psalms; Augustine's Commentary on the Epistle of John; Augustine's treatises on the work of monks, good marriage, virginity, widowhood, praying to God and the suffering of Christ all in one volume; Augustine's *Enchridion*; a florilegium of works by Augustine; Augustine *On Faith*; Augustine on the Five Levels; Origen on the Old Testament; the Rule of Saint Benedict; the Pentateuch; the Acts of the Apostles; the *Hexameron* of Ambrose; the Life of St Ulrich; two matutinals; [and] a book of winter homilies.]

[18] CP 3.11.
[19] CP 3.49.

And he notes with the eye of a librarian that while some of these books had been sold, the majority of them still remained there.[20]

Apprentice at Wagenhausen, Cantor at Petershausen?

In his chronicle, CHP also offers an autobiographical detail that sheds light both on his possible apprenticeship for the role of cantor and on the dating and composition of a surviving manuscript from the monastery of Wagenhausen, a martyrology, necrology and Rule of St Benedict (Budapest, Széchényi-Nationalbibliothek Codex Latinus 514).[21] He states that he had been a monk at this small and struggling community, some thirty kilometres west along the shore of the lake and up the Rhine, under Abbot Folchnand (1105–19). Although the spiritual oversight of Wagenhausen was hotly contested in the late eleventh and twelfth century, Petershausen had charge of Wagenhausen both during the abbacy of Folchnand (who had served as a monk at Petershausen before he was sent to serve as abbot) and again from 1127 until the 1170s. Throughout this tumultuous era, Wagenhausen maintained a necrology, now preserved in Budapest MS 514, fols. 73r–88v. During Folchnand's abbacy, two scribes entered the names of the dead into this book, one of the duties, as noted above, that the Hirsau Constitutions specifically assigned to the cantor. The first scribe laid out the calendar itself, and entered the majority of the names. The second scribe, who alternated with the first, entered individual names more sporadically. While the first hand has not been identified, the second hand is that of CHP.[22] The pattern of interaction between the two, in which first hand and the second hand alternate in places, shows that both were active during the same period, suggesting the kind of interaction that one might expect from a cantor (Hand 1) and his assistant (CHP, Hand 2).[23]

---

[20] *CP* 3.49: 'Hos abbas Theodericus libros conscribi fecit, quorum aliqui iam venundati sunt, maior vero pars adhuc manet' ('Abbot Theoderich had these books copied; some of them were sold, but the majority remain').

[21] A. Vizkelety, *Mittelalterliche Lateinische Handschriften der Széchényi-Nationalbibliothek (Cod. Lat. 405–556)*, Fragmenta et Codices in Bibliothecis Hungariae 6 (Budapest, 2008), pp. 156–9.

[22] B. Meyer, 'Das Totenbuch von Wagenhausen', *Schriften des Vereins für Geschichte des Bodensees und seiner Umgebung* 86 (1968), 87–187 (p. 98); H. Tüchle, 'Ein Wagenhausener Nekrolog aus Petershausen', *Schweizerische Zeitschrift für Geschichte* 13 (1963), 196–205 (p. 203). Tüchle argued (p. 204), contra Meyer, that the necrology was produced at Petershausen between 1127 and 1134 and sent to Wagenhausen, probably in the hands of monks returning to take charge of the community after Bishop Ulrich deposed Abbot Uto and replaced him with Gebino. CHP was at Wagenhausen under Abbot Folchnand (c. 1105–19) and not under his uncle, Abbot Gebino (1127–35).

[23] Meyer, 'Totenbuch von Wagenhausen', pp. 97–8.

This necrology, however, is but one component of this composite manuscript, which was assembled from a variety of units dating from the ninth and the twelfth centuries. [24] One of these, written entirely by CHP himself, is a copy of the ninth-century Roman Martyrology of Usuard (fols. 7v–77v), supplemented with entries for three regional saints: Ulrich I of Augsburg (canonized in 993), Conrad I of Constance (canonized in 1123), and Gebhard II (canonized in 1134).[25] The inclusion of Gebhard in the Martyrology provides a *terminus post quem* of 1134, by which time CHP would already have left Wagenhausen for Petershausen, and possibly begun serving as cantor there.

The manuscript as it is now bound thus contains the hand of CHP at two distinct phases in his monastic career: as assistant to the cantor and as cantor. This juxtaposition can be explained by taking into account both CHP's movement from one community to the other and the likely trajectory of his monastic career. As a young monk at Wagenhausen, CHP seems to have served as assistant to the cantor, leaving traces of that supporting role in the community's necrology. The necrology, of course, remained at Wagenhausen after his departure for Petershausen. At some point later, between his arrival at Petershausen around 1119 and the 1130s, CHP took up the duties of cantor, which may have been a natural step for a monk who had been trained as a cantor's assistant. His transfer into the community would not have been an obstacle, as the Constitutions of Hirsau stipulate that a committed transfer with the appropriate skills could be assigned to the office.[26] In any case, CHP had presumably lived the Hirsau liturgy at Wagenhausen, where he may have even been a *nutritus*.

If he was, in fact, cantor, it may have been part of his job to provide needed liturgical texts to Petershausen's daughter houses. Liturgical books commonly moved from mother to daughter house, or from the house of the reformers to the house to be reformed. For example, Waltram, sent from Petershausen to serve as abbot (1138–46) of the newly founded daughter house Fischingen, brought with him a number of service books, including a missal, evangeliary, lectionary, *liber officialis*, benedictional, antiphoner, Psalter and Rule—all presumably copied from Hirsau-based models at Petershausen. It may have been in his capacity as cantor (or simply as

[24] Vizkelety, *Mittelalterliche Lateinische Handschriften der Széchényi-Nationalbibliothek*, pp. 156–9; H. Juhász-Hajdu and A. Bruckner, 'Zwei Handschriften aus dem Bodenseeraum in Ungarn', *Schriften des Vereins für Geschichte des Bodensees und seiner Umgebung* 86 (1968), 189–98 (pp. 190–6); Meyer, 'Totenbuch von Wagenhausen', pp. 94–5, 98, 163; Tüchle, 'Ein Wagenhausener Nekrolog aus Petershausen'.

[25] My attribution of this section of the manuscript to CHP is based on Meyer, 'Das Totenbuch von Wagenhausen', pp. 93–5, Vizkelety, *Mittelalterliche Lateinische Handschriften der Széchényi-Nationalbibliothek*, p. 157; and my own examination of the manuscript in Budapest in October 2014.

[26] *Willehelmi Abbatis Constitutiones*, II, 113.

scribe) and in connection with the restoration of Petershausen's oversight of Wagenhausen in 1127 that CHP copied the Wagenhausen martyrology, and also replaced the first folio (fol. 89) of the manuscript's ninth-century copy of the Rule of St Benedict. He seems also to have had some hand in producing a manuscript, Fischingen Pfarrarchiv C XV sig. 13, which contains a similar combination of texts (a martyrology, necrology and Rule) for Petershausen's new daughter house, Fischingen, founded in 1138. Unfortunately, this manuscript has gone missing in recent years and the few photographs that survive can provide only a limited basis for paleographical analysis. Albert Bruckner, who examined the manuscript and published images of several of its folios in the 1960s, attributed parts of it, including the Rule, to scribes at Petershausen.[27]

CHP also helped to meet the local need for manuscripts. Most of Petershausen's own liturgical books burned in the spring of 1159, when a massive fire destroyed the monastery. Some of the community's most treasured books, he lamented, were destroyed in the flames, among them 'a rather nice Rule containing the two martyrologies, one of the saints and the other of the dead'—a book that sounds very similar to those that had been sent to Wagenhausen and Fischingen.[28] These books had to be replaced if the monks were to begin again to celebrate the Mass and Office. CHP can be seen at work in the community's new necrology, University of Heidelberg, Codex Salemitani IX 42, for which he established the columnar layout and entered the base 'layer' of names.[29] He also transferred much of the information about donors and their associated feasts from the Chronicle, which had made it safely out of the fire, into the tops of the columns.[30] The lost martyrology was replaced by a new one, University of Heidelberg, Codex Salemitani IX 57, perhaps a gift from another community in the area.[31] From folios 53v to 56v, in

---

[27] My preliminary assessment of the identity of the scribe who established the layout for the necrology is based only on the description and photographs in A. Bruckner, *Schreibschulen der Diözese Konstanz: Thurgau, Solothurn, Klein-Basel, Bern*, vol. 10, Scriptoria Medii Aevi Helvetica (Genf, 1964), pp. 21–7. For its provenance at Petershausen, see especially pp. 26–7.

[28] *CP* 5.42: 'Tunc consumptum est principale altare cum omnibus ornamentis suis... capitulum, cuius omnes sedes utpote in sollemnitate pentecoste erant ornate variis velaminibus, et regula satis bona continens duo martyrologia, unum sanctorum, alterum defunctorum, et evangelia, et Ysidorus sententiarum ...'

[29] See http://digi.ub.uni-heidelberg.de/diglit/salIX42/0009.

[30] See, for example, CHP's hand at work on fol. 5r, where he enters the names and donations of Gerunc (left column) and Wolfirat (right column): http://digi.ub. uni-heidelberg.de/diglit/salIX42/0013.

[31] The hand in University of Heidelberg, Codex Salemitani IX 57 (http://digi.ub.uni-heidelberg.de/diglit/salIX57) bears a strong resemblance to those of Zwiefalten's contemporary female scribes, who seem to have specialized in copying liturgical books. While CHP notes in the Chronicle that Zwiefalten sent liturgical vestments (another specialty of Zwiefalten's religious women), they may later have sent

space left blank by the scribe of the martyrology, CHP copied a computational table, used to calculate the dates for Easter and other important feasts—a tool essential for the proper performance of the liturgy.[32]

Liturgical poet and composer

CHP also played a key role in the production of the rhymed office composed for Gebhard's feast. This office, preserved in its earliest form in University of Heidelberg, Codex Salemitani IX 42a, fols. 1v–10r, seems to draw its biographical material from CHP's Life of Gebhard. For example, the second antiphon of the first of the six nocturns for Matins—'Non consuete enixum . sed vulva matris constat excisum . Domino premonstrante quod ipsum scivit et ante'—shares the account of Gebhard's birth as detailed in the Life. The Life describes how, at the command of his dying mother, the premature Gebhard was cut from her womb upon her death and smeared with a protective coating of warm fat—a story that CHP would recount again a few years later in his chronicle.[33] The Life, which references Jeremiah 1. 5—'Before I formed thee in the bowels of thy mother, I knew thee: and before thou camest forth out of the womb, I sanctified thee, and made thee a prophet unto the nations'—and the antiphon share an understanding of this event as a sign of God's foreknowledge of Gebhard's great future in the church. CHP was also the scribe who copied the text of the office, including the hymns, antiphons and responsories with their accompanying neumes, as well as the readings.[34] While CHP's role as scribe does not prove that he composed the music for the office, it is certainly possible, and consistent with his likely role as cantor.

---

this manuscript also. On Zweifalten's female scribes, see A. Beach, '"Mathild de Niphin" and the Female Scribes of Twelfth-Century Zwiefalten', in *Nuns' Literacies in Medieval Europe: The Hull Dialogue*, ed. V. Blanton, V. O'Mara and P. Stoop (Turnhout, 2013), pp. 33–50. The inclusion of Gebhard in the martyrology provides a *terminus post quem* of 1134 for the copying of the manuscript.

[32] See http://digi.ub.uni-heidelberg.de/diglit/salIX57/0111.

[33] *CP* 1.6: 'Iunior igitur supra memoratorum fratrum, sed ornamentum eorum, Gebehardus ex defuncte matris [Diepirge] utero excisus et quibusdam fomentis obvolutus est usque ad tempus nativitatis, Deo eius vitam ad multorum salutem reservante. De talibus tamen excisis litere testantur, quod si vita comes fuerit felices in mundo habeantur' ('Therefore Gebhard, the younger of the aforementioned brothers, but their jewel, was cut out of the womb of his deceased mother [Diepirge] and he was wrapped in a certain poultice up until the time of birth, with God sparing his life for the salvation of many. It is written concerning such excisions that if the youth should survive, these things should be considered auspicious').

[34] See http://digi.ub.uni-heidelberg.de/diglit/salIX42a/0016.

Did CHP become Abbot Gebhard I (1164–70)?

Who was CPH? His chronicle offers the strongest clues. At various points in the text, he mentions a forefather (*avus*) Gebhard, who was a monk at Petershausen in the last decades of the eleventh century. He also repeatedly mentions his uncle Gebino (a diminutive form of the name Gebhard), a fellow monk who left Petershausen around 1127 to serve first as abbot of Wagenhausen (1127–34) and then of Fischingen (*c.* 1135–38).[35] The persistence of the name Gebhard/Gebino in the chronicler's family line suggests strongly that he was a descendent of the monastery's founder and thus related in some way to the powerful Udalrichinger counts of Bregenz, the ruling comital family of the Voralberg from the tenth to the twelfth century.[36]

CHP's noble lineage and familial connection to the founder is not surprising given the importance of the cantor in the central Middle Ages. This was such an important office within Hirsau communities that, according to Felix Heinzer, it often functioned as a springboard to the abbacy.[37] While it is not known if Conrad served as cantor prior to his election, it is a tempting suggestion, given that the abbot was remembered in the Chronicle as a poet and musician, and credited with copying the *Hexameron* of St Ambrose. Around the time that Conrad's successor took office, a new scribe-editor also took over the work of the Chronicle. It is possible that CHP was elected abbot in 1164 and served as Gebhard I (1164–71), a name strongly associated with CHP's family line. He may, of necessity, have left his decades old work-in-progress in the hands of a successor, who to judge by the similarity of their hands, may have been his assistant. If we estimate that CHP was born around 1095 and then served as assistant to the cantor at Wagenhausen until he was around 25, he would have been about sixty-nine at time when he became abbot—certainly a good old age in the twelfth century, but not an impossible one. If CHP did take up the office of abbot as Gebhard I, then this might help to explain why there is no person identified in Petershausen's necrology as *armarius* or *precentor*: he would have been remembered, in the end, as abbot.[38] This must remain, however, only an interesting possibility.

---

[35] *CP* 2.17, 3.28, 3.45, 4.32; on Gebino as Abbot of Wagenhausen and Fischingen, see *CP* 3.14, 3.15, 3.16.

[36] Walther, 'Gründungsgeschichte und Tradition', pp. 42–3; the *CP* is an important (though problematic) source for the history of the Bregenzer comital family. See B. Bilgeri, *Bregenz. Geschichte der Stadt: Politik, Verfassung, Wirtschaft* (Vienna, 1980), pp. 22–31.

[37] F. Heinzer, *Klosterreform und mittelalterliche Buchkultur im deutschen Südwesten*, Mittellateinische Studien und Texte 39 (Leiden, 2008), p. 389.

[38] The lack of individuals identified in Hirsau necrologies as *precentor* or *armarius* generally, requires further explanation. In my database of over 7,000 names from communities with connections to Hirsau, only two such individuals are specifically

Conclusion

Although it is not possible to educe his specific personal identity from the extant sources, CHP emerges from the surviving manuscripts produced at Petershausen as both a skilled and prolific copyist of liturgical books and as an historian. While he performed many of the duties that the customs of Hirsau assigned to the *precentor* or *armarius*, he is never identified with that title. Even so, with his clear engagement in both the liturgical life of the community and in imagining and preserving its history, he neatly fits the profile of the cantor-historian that stands at the centre of many of the chapters in the volume. Whether CHP was Petershausen's cantor in name or in function only, his surviving work illustrates the power of one individual – with both the skill and resources to deploy the powerful and interacting tools of *memoria* and *liturgia* – to shape the identity of a monastic community in the Middle Ages.

named: Adelheit *armaria* (22 May) and Gotscalchus *armarius* (17 August) – both from the monastery of Admont in Steiermark. See MGH Necrologia Germaniae 2. The near complete absence of identified cantors in Hirsau necrologies is puzzling in view of the apparent importance of the office within those reform circles.

Appendix 1
Manuscript Evidence for CHP's Activities as Cantor-Historian

Manuscript	Text(s)	Scribal Role	Authorial Role
University of Heidelberg, Cod. Sal. IX 42a	1 Rhymed Office for St. Gebhard (fols. 1v–10r)	1 Copied music and text of Office	1 Poet/Composer of Office (?)
	2 Chronicle of Petershausen (fols. 35r–98r)	2 Primary scribe	2 Author of Chronicle
Budapest, Széchényi-National-bibliothek Cod. Lat. 514	1 Martyrology of Usuard (fols. 7v–77v)	1 Sole scribe	1 Added entries for Ulrich, Conrad and Gebhard (?)
	2 Necrology (fols. 78r–88v)	2 Assisted with entry of the names	
	3 Rule of St Benedict (fols. 89r–166v)	3 Copied first folio of Rule (fol. 89)	
Fischingen, Pfarrarchiv C XV sig. 13 (missing)	1 Martyrology (fols. 1–110)	1 Scribe (?)	
	2 Rule of St Benedict (fols. 111–218)		
	3 Necrology (fols. 219–252)		
University of Heidelberg, Cod. Sal. IX 42	1 Necrology (fols. 4v–55r)	1 Set out columns, added names and donations (in arches above)	1 Drew on Chronicle for information about patrons
	2 Monastic Capitulary of 817 (fols. 55v–56r)	2 Scribe (?)	
University of Heidelberg, Cod. Sal. IX 57	*Computus* table (fols. 53v–56v)	Primary scribe	

17

The Roman Liturgical Tradition According to a Twelfth-Century Roman Cantor

Peter Jeffery

From the contents of this volume, one might get the impression that the cantor-historian was primarily a northern European phenomenon. Yet there is at least one known individual from southern Europe who composed a liturgical ordinal, performed liturgical music, studied liturgical history, wrote a chronicle of sorts and identified himself as a cantor. His name was Benedict, and he was a canon of St Peter's basilica at the Vatican in Rome. The book he wrote is entitled *Liber politicus* in the manuscripts. Paul Fabre, its modern editor, apparently thought this was a corrupt misspelling of *Liber polyptychus*, which would describe the book as many-sided, a polyptych or miscellany. Yet Fabre also thought this was a poor description of the book's actual content.[1] Another possible emendation is the one published by Jean Mabillon in the editio princeps: *Liber pollicitus*, apparently 'the promised book'.[2] I propose we assume that Benedict meant what he wrote, and that we should understand the title to mean, 'Book of the City', an attempt to render *Liber Urbanus* into Greek. *Urbanus* would in fact be an accurate title, since the entire book is about *Urbs*, the city of Rome.

There are three extant manuscripts. The twelfth-century manuscript in Cambrai is the closest chronologically, but the farthest away geographically, and Fabre considered it the least faithful copy of the text.[3] He preferred

---

[1] P. Fabre, ed., *Le Liber Censuum de l'église romaine, publié avec une préface et un commentaire*, tome I, Bibliothèque des Écoles françaises d'Athènes et de Rome, 2e série, vol. 6 (Paris, 1889–1901), Introduction, pp. 3–4. This volume was actually completed by L. Duchesne, whose name is not mentioned on the title page. The edition of the text itself will be found in P. Fabre, ed., *Le Liber Censuum de l'église romaine, publié avec une préface et un commentaire*, tome II, Bibliothèque des Écoles françaises d'Athènes et de Rome, 2e série, vol. 6.5 (Paris, 1905), pp. 141–74, 90–1. See Table 17.1 below for more exact information. A third volume of *Tables des matières*, ed. L. Duchesne, P. Fabre and G. Mollat, was published in 1952.

[2] Hence the work is better known as *Ordo Romanus XI*, from its position in J. Mabillon, *Musei Italici Tomus II, complectens Antiquos Libros Rituales sanctae Romanae Ecclesiae, cum Commentario praevio in Ordinem Romanum* (Paris, 1724), pp. 118–54; reprinted in PL 78, 1025–54.

[3] Cambrai, Bibliothèque municipale, MS 554 (512). LC, I, 3–4. A. Molinier, *Catalogue général des manuscrits des bibliothèques publiques de France: Départements 17: Cambrai* (Paris, 1891), p. 211.

the two fifteenth-century Roman manuscripts.[4] These two begin with a dedicatory epistle not found in the Cambrai MS, which has the following title:

> Benedicti Beati Petri Canonici Liber Politicus ad Guidonem de Castello tunc Cardinalem Sancti Marci, postmodum factus est Celestinus secundus.

> [*Liber politicus* of Benedict, Canon of Blessed Peter, to Guido of Castello, then Cardinal of St Mark, after that he was made (Pope) Celestine II.]

Guido de Castello was appointed cardinal priest of S. Marco, in what is now the Piazza Venezia, in 1134. He reigned as Pope Celestine II in 1143–44. Thus the epistle was written after 1134, and its title shows awareness of the papal election of 1143. More information about the dating comes from a chronicle of the popes that forms part of the *Liber politicus*. The chronicle ends with Pope Innocent II, who reigned in 1130–43 and is called 'dominus meus'.[5] Since the chronicle also mentions repairs that were made to the church of S. Maria in Trastevere in 1140, we can conclude that the *Liber politicus* was written between 1140, the time of the repairs, and 1143, the year Pope Innocent died and the dedicatee Guido was elected to succeed him. The chronicle in the Cambrai manuscript substitutes Pope Alexander III for Innocent II, indicating that this manuscript was written during Alexander's reign, 1159–81, by someone who had no hesitations about modifying the text.

Benedict's *Liber politicus* incorporated material from the canonical collection of Deusdedit, published in 1087.[6] Excerpts from the *Liber politicus* were subsequently incorporated into a work known as the *Gesta Pauperis Scolaris Albini*, evidently written after 29 October 1188, but before Albinus was appointed cardinal bishop of Albano, between 18 May and 6 June 1189.[7] The poor scholar Albinus tugs at our hearts with sad tales of how his parents died when he was young and left him an orphan,[8] but he did all right. Appointment as Cardinal Bishop made him one of the seven highest-ranking cardinals, and gave him the alliterative appellation Albinus of Albano. In

---

[4] Rome, Biblioteca Vallicelliana, MS F.73 and Vatican City, Biblioteca Apostolica Vaticana, MS latinus 5348. *LC*, I, 3–4. P. Salmon, *Les Manuscrits liturgiques latins de la Bibliothèque Vaticane 3: Ordines Romani, Pontificaux, Rituels, Cérémoniaux*, Studi e Testi 260 (Vatican City, 1970) p. 125 no. 424. Mabillon is less than perfectly clear about his sources, but refers to an 'alius codex' in the footnotes on pp. 141, 143, 'duobus codicibus' on p. 152 note a, and has an 'Additio ex cod. Valli-cellano' on pp. 153–4. Since the material on pp. 153–4 (sections 2 and 3 in Fabre's edition) also occurs in Vaticanus 5348, it would appear that Mabillon did not have the Vatican manuscript, but was using a different manuscript that did not contain sections 2 and 3.

[5] *LC*, II, 169; Mabillon, *Musei Italici*, p. 127.

[6] *LC*, I, 4. L. Kéry, *Canonical Collections of the Early Middle Ages (ca. 400–1140): A Bibliographical Guide to the Manuscripts and Literature* (Washington DC, 1999) 228–33.

[7] Vatican City, Biblioteca Apostolica Vaticana, MS Ottobonianus 5057 (late s. xii); *LC*, II, 87–137.

[8] *LC*, II, 87.

1192 some of Albinus's work was, finally, incorporated into the great listing of papal properties and rents known as the *Liber Censuum*, compiled by a certain canon Cencius, papal chamberlain, in 1192. Because of this, the only modern edition of Benedict's *Liber politicus* can be difficult to use, because it was published among the appendices to Fabre's edition of the *Liber Censuum*,[9] with some of Benedict's work appearing as sections within the *Gesta* of Albinus (see Table 17.1).

In any case it is clear that we are dealing with twelfth-century material, indeed material written between 1140 and 1143. As for Benedict, he describes himself in the dedicatory epistle as 'Benedictus, beati Petri apostoli indignus canonicus et Romane ecclesie cantor' ('Benedict, unworthy canon of blessed Peter the Apostle, and cantor of the Roman church').[10] Table 17.1 shows the contents of Benedict's *Liber politicus*, with section numbers and page numbers from Tome II of Fabre's edition, and page numbers from Mabillon's edition.

There has been some scholarly attention to item 1b, the ordinal for St Peter's;[11] the second and third items have been studied for their information about papal processions.[12] Attention has also been given to the remarkable folkloric practices described in the seventh item.[13] But it is clear that Benedict was not merely describing the practice of his own time. He must also have been a researcher, consulting Roman liturgical sources from earlier centuries. For example, Table 17.2 shows a passage from the ordinal that is clearly dependent on the eighth-century text known as *Ordo Romanus Primus*, the earliest description of how the pope celebrated stational Masses, as he visited one Roman church after another over the course of the liturgical year.[14]

On Easter morning, as the papal procession approaches the basilica of St Mary Major, a regional notary stands in Merolana street, waiting to

---

[9] *LC*, I, 1–600 (edition).

[10] *LC*, II, 141.

[11] For example: J. Dyer, 'The Double Office at St Peter's Basilica on *Dominica de Gaudete*', in *Music in Medieval Europe: Studies in Honour of Bryan Gillingham*, ed. T. Bailey and A. C. Santosuosso (Aldershot, 2007), pp. 200–19; J. F. Romano, 'The Ceremonies of the Roman Pontiff: Rereading Benedict's Twelfth-Century Liturgical Script', *Viator* 41 (2010), 133–50.

[12] S. Twyman, *Papal Ceremonial at Rome in the Twelfth Century*, HBS Subsidia 4 (Woodbridge, 2002); P. Montaubin, 'Pater Urbis et Orbis: Les cortèges pontificaux dans la Rome médiévale (VIIIe–XIVe siècles)', *Rivista di storia della Chiesa in Italia* 63 (2009), 9–47.

[13] M. Boiteux and I. Sordi, 'Cornomania e carnevale a Roma nel medioevo', *La Ricerca Folklorica* 6 (1982), 57–64; M. Harris, 'Claiming Pagan Origins for Carnival: Bacchanalia, Saturnalia, and Kalends', *European Medieval Drama* 10 (2006), 57–107 (pp. 90–5).

[14] Mabillon, *Musei Italici*, II, 1–16. The best edition is now: M. Andrieu, ed., *Les Ordines Romani du haut moyen âge 2: Les Textes (Ordines I–XIII)*, Spicilegium Sacrum Lovaniense: Études et documents 23 (Louvain, 1938), pp. 65–108.

Table 17.1 The contents of Benedict's *Liber politicus*

1a	*Epistola ad Guidonem de Castello* (*LC*, II, 141; *Musei Italici*, pp. 118–19)
1b	*Incipit de ordine Romane ecclesie et sacri Palatii dignitatibus* (ordinal for the liturgical year at St Peter's, including papal ceremonies; *LC*, II, 141–59; *Musei Italici*, pp. 119–53)
2	*Hec sunt festivitates in quibus papa debet coronari* (days on which the pope wears a crown; *LC*, II, 90, 165; *Musei Italici*, p. 153)
3	*Hec sunt stationes sancti Petri nocturnales* (days when the pope attended night office at St Peter's) and *Hec sunt sancti Petri diurne stationes* (days when the pope attended the day office at St Peter's; *LC*, II, 90, 165; *Musei Italici*, pp. 153–4)
4	(Untitled chronicle of the popes, with special interest in their liturgical innovations and matters related to St Peter's basilica; *LC*, II, 65–9)
5	*In ordinatione cardinalium et diaconorum et episcoporum qualiter agendum sit* (ordination rites for cardinals, deacons and bishops; *LC*, II, 90–1, 171)
6	*Incipit laudes festis diebus quando laudes canende sunt* (litanies to be sung at ordinations; *LC*, II, 91, 171)
7	*De laudibus Cornomannie* (popular customs and songs of the *schola cantorum*; *LC*, II, 171–4)
8	*Liber regionarius* (census of notable sites in Rome, found only in the Cambrai MS, possibly not originally part of Benedict's *Liber politicus*; *LC*, II, 175–7)

Table 17.2 Comparison of the *Liber politicus* with the *Ordo Romanus Primus*

Ordo Romanus Primus (*Ordines Romani*, pp. 71–2)	*Liber politicus* (*LC*, II, 152)
Die autem resurrectionis dominice, procedente eo ad Sanctam Mariam, notarius regionarius stat in loco qui dicitur Merolanas et, salutato pontifice,	Cum autem venerit in Merolanam, stat notarius ibi et alta voce dicit: *Jube, domne, benedicere.* Pontifex benedicit eum.
dicit:	Notarius dicit:
In nomine domini nostri Iesu Christi, baptizati sunt hesterna nocte in sancta Dei genitrice Maria infantes masculi numero tanti, feminae tantae.	*In ecclesia sancte Marie in hac nocte baptizati sunt tot masculi et tot femine.*
Respondit pontifex: *Deo gratias.*	Pontifex respondet: *Deo gratias.*
Et accipit a sacellario solidum unum; pontifex autem pergit ad stationem.	Et notarius accipit a sacellario unum bizantium.

313

address the pontiff. The actual words are slightly different in the two sources, but he announces how many males and females were baptized during the Easter Vigil the night before. The pontiff responds *Deo gratias* and the papal treasurer, known as the *sacellarius* or 'bag man', gives the notary a coin. In the eighth-century text this is a solidus, a gold coin with the emperor's image on it; in Greek it was called *nómisma*. This denomination was created by Emperor Constantine I in the fourth century and continued to be minted in Constantinople up to the reign of Emperor John I (969-76),[15] but the mint at Rome ceased stamping them out about the year 776.[16] In the twelfth-century *Liber politicus* the coin is no longer called a *solidus*, but instead is called a *bizantium*. Perhaps this is derived from the vernacular word *bisanti* or *bezant*, which was used in medieval Italy for gold coins minted in the Crusader kingdoms of the Middle East.[17] Benedict may have thought the oriental bezant of his time was equivalent to the coin used back in the eighth century, when Rome was under the rule of the Byzantine emperors. The change from *solidus* to *bizantium* cannot be explained by the current practice of Benedict's own time, because, elsewhere in Benedict's ordinal, the pope still uses *solidi* to pay officials for their ritual performances.[18] It is hard to be sure exactly what kind of *solidus* Benedict's pope would have used for this purpose, for the papacy did not mint its own money at the time Benedict was writing his ordinal (1140-3). Perhaps it was a coin bearing the likeness of one of the German monarchs who claimed the title of emperor. Or perhaps Benedict used the word *solidus* to represent one of its vernacular derivatives, like the French *sou* or Italian *soldo*, a word which was evolving toward its more general modern meaning of 'coin' or 'money'.[19] In any case, Benedict's account of a regional

[15] P. Grierson, *Byzantine Coins* (London,1982), pp. 8, 180; F. Füeg, *Corpus of the Nomismata from Anastasius II to John I in Constantinople 713–976* (Lancaster PA, 2007).

[16] On the Roman mint, with some examples of eight-century solidi printed there, see: P. Grierson, *Byzantine Coins* (London, 1982), pp. 169–70, and plates pp. 39–40; P. Grierson, *Catalogue of the Byzantine Coins in the Dumbarton Oaks Collection and in the Whittemore Collection 3: Leo III to Nicephorus III 717–1081*, Part I: *Leo III to Michael III (717–867)* (Washington DC, 1973), pp. 82, 87–91, 237–9, 271–5, 288–9, 296–7, 317–20, 327, plates VI, VII, XI.

[17] L. Travaini, *Monete e storia nell'Italia medievale* (Rome, 2007), pp. 92n, 248, 286, 325; P. Grierson, 'A Rare Crusader Bezant with the *Christus Vincit* Legend', *American Numismatic Society Museum Notes* 6 (1954), 169–78, and plate XVIII, 1–2; reprinted in P. Grierson, *Later Medieval Numismatics (11th–16th Centuries): Selected Studies* (London, 1979), item IX; P. Grierson and L. Travaini, *Medieval European Coinage with a Catalogue of the Coins in the Fitzwilliam Museum, Cambridge, 14: Italy (III) (South Italy, Sicily, Sardinia)* (Cambridge, 1998), p. 456.

[18] For example, *LC*, II, 150, left column line 35; p. 151 left column line 27; a wider variety of coins on p. 156 right column, p. 158 right column.

[19] 'No Popes [*sic*] are known to have issued coins from 983 to 1294' according to A. G. Berman, *Papal Coins* (South Salem NY, 1991), p. 47, and other sources. The Roman Senate began issuing *provisini* and *grossi* in 1184, according to *Corpus Nummorum Italicorum: Primo Tentativo di un Catalogo Generale delle monete medievali e moderne*

notary receiving a *bizantium* for announcing the number of Easter baptisms is not a description of an actual practice, but an imaginative interpolation derived from Benedict's reading of an early liturgical source.

We see more of Benedict as a historian in item 4 (see Table 17.1), his chronicle of the popes, in which he deals mostly with their liturgical innovations. Benedict's chronicle is clearly based on the *Liber pontificalis* and other familiar sources, but Benedict's use of his sources would receive a failing grade from any modern history teacher. Particularly strange is Benedict's section on Pope Gregory I (590–604),[20] which gives him credit for things that (according to the *Liber pontificalis*) were actually done by other popes. A sentence-by-sentence analysis of this section demonstrates his ways of working and suggests an underlying agenda.

Gregorius primus statuit ut quadragesimali tempore V feria ieiunium atque missarum celebritas fieret in ecclesiis, quod non agebatur.

[Gregory I decreed that, on the fifth feria in the time of Lent, a fast and a celebration of Mass be done in the churches, which was not being done (at the time).]

These words are taken from the *Liber pontificalis*, but from the life of Gregory II (715–31), for it was Gregory II, not Gregory I, who added the Thursdays of Lent to the Roman stational calendar.[21]

Hic constituit intra missarum sollempnia domini nostri Jesu Christi sancteque ejus genitricis, sanctorum apostolorum et omnium sanctorum martyrum ac confessorum perfectorumque justorum toto orbe terrarum requiescentium memoriam agere.

[He instituted that, during the solemnities of the Mass, a memorial be made of our Lord Jesus Christ and of his holy mother, of the holy apostles and of all holy martyrs and confessors and perfect just men resting throughout the world.]

coniate in Italia o da Italiani in altri paesi 15/1: Dalla caduta dell'impero d'occidente al 1572 (Rome, 1934; repr. Bologna, 1971), pp. 98–100. On the coinage of twelfth-century central Italy, see Travaini, *Monete*, pp. 44–53; P. Grierson, *The Coins of Medieval Europe* (London, 1991), pp. 93–6. On medieval meanings of the word *solidus* and its vernacular derivatives, see J. Belaubre, *Dictionnaire de numismatique médiévale occidentale* (Paris, 1996), pp. 132–3; Grierson and Travaini, *Medieval European Coinage*, p. 473.

[20] *LC*, II, 168–9.

[21] *LP*, I, 402. For comment see R. Davis, *Lives of the Eighth-Century Popes (Liber Pontificalis): The Ancient Biographies of Nine Popes from AD 715 to AD 817*, rev. ed., Translated Texts for Historians 13 (Liverpool, 2007), p. 8; J. F. Baldovin, *The Urban Character of Christian Worship: The Origins, Development, and Meaning of Stational Liturgy*, Orientalia Christiana Analecta 228 (Rome, 1987), pp. 122, 125, 128, 131 n. 14, 154.

This is derived from a statement in the *Liber pontificalis*, which actually says that Pope Gregory III (731–41) established an oratory at St Peter's basilica, full of relics of all these saints, in which both vigils and Masses were to be celebrated on their feasts, and in which Gregory III himself was eventually buried.[22] This oratory still existed in Benedict's day; indeed portions of Gregory III's inscriptions survive even now in the Vatican grottos.[23] For some reason Benedict refashioned the description of Gregory III's chapel into something 'instituted' by Gregory I.

The three statements that follow refer to innovations that were traditionally credited to Gregory I.

Hic augmentavit in precatione canonum 'diesque nostros in tua pace dispone' et cetera.

[He expanded (the text to be used) in praying the canons (of the Mass, by adding the words) 'and dispose our days in your peace' etc.]

The *Liber pontificalis* does indeed state that Gregory I added these words to the canon of the Mass.

Hic fecit supra corpus beati Petri et beati Pauli iugiter missas celebrari a cardinalibus.[24]

[He made for Masses to be celebrated continuously by cardinals above the body of blessed Peter and of blessed Paul.]

Gregory I is known to have rebuilt the area around St Peter's tomb so that an altar for Mass stood directly above Peter's body. The *Liber pontificalis* briefly mentions this, and says that Gregory did the same at the church of St Paul (Outside the Walls). Portions of Gregory's structures at St Peter's still exist.[25] But Benedict's *Liber politicus* says something new when it asserts that the Masses were to be said 'continuously by cardinals'. The term 'cardinal',

---

[22] *LP*, I, 417; *Lives of the Eighth-Century Popes*, p. 22.

[23] P. Jeffery 'The Roman Liturgical Year and the Early Liturgy of St. Peter's', in *Old Saint Peter's, Rome*, ed. R. McKitterick et al. (Cambridge, 2013), pp. 157–76 (pp. 161–3, and illustrations pp. 95, 157).

[24] *LP*, I, 312. R. Davis, *The Book of Pontiffs (Liber Pontificalis): The Ancient Biographies of the First Ninety Roman Bishops to AD 715*, rev. ed., Translated Texts for Historians 6 (Liverpool, 2000), p. 63. B. Botte, ed., *Le Canon de la messe romaine: édition critique*, Textes et études liturgiques 2 (Louvain, 1935), pp. 36–7.

[25] *LP*, I, 312; E. Kirschbaum, *The Tombs of St Peter & St Paul*, trans. J. Murray (New York, 1959), pp. 156–64, 190–2, with many photographs from the excavations of the 1940s–50s; D. J. Birch, *Pilgrimage to Rome in the Middle Ages: Continuity and Change* (Woodbridge, 2000), pp. 27–37; H. Brandenburg, 'Petrus und Paulus in Rom? Die archäologischen Zeugnisse, die Basilika S. Paul vor den Mauern und der Kult der Apostelfürsten: Ein Beitrag zur jüngsten Diskussion um die Präsenz der Apostol in Rom', in *Marmoribus Vestita: Miscellanea in Onore di Federico Guidobaldi*

meaning the 'principal priest' of a church, had been around for centuries, although in Benedict's time the Roman cardinals had not yet emerged fully as the Sacred College of papal electors.[26] But Benedict will have more to say about the liturgical duties of cardinals, and the word 'iugiter' ('continuously'), will be encountered again. Its meanings are difficult to understand from this passage alone.

Hic fecit Romanum cantum et ordinavit primicerium et scolam cantorum.

[He made the Roman chant, and he ordained a *primicerius* and a school of singers.]

The tradition that Gregory I 'made' the Roman chant and founded the Roman *schola cantorum* does not go back to the *Liber pontificalis*, though it was asserted in the ninth-century life of Gregory written by John Hymmonides the Deacon (*c.* 825–*c.* 882).[27] The word *primicerius*, meaning 'the first one [listed] on the wax [tablet]', was already used in the late Roman imperial court to apply to the chief notary;[28] it continued in use for the papal *schola notariorum*.[29] When Gregory the Great organized the defensors (aristocrats who served as patrons and attorneys) of the Roman church into a *schola*, the leader of this organization was also known as a *primicerius*.[30]

The origins of the *schola cantorum* are not so easily traced; we first hear of a *prior cantorum* in the seventh century.[31] A letter of Pope Paul I (757–67) to the Frankish King Pippin refers to a *prior scholae cantorum*.[32] However, in the first document that offers us concrete information about what the *schola cantorum* did, the eighth-century *Ordo Romanus Primus*, the person who leads

---

1, ed. O. Brandt and P. Pergola, Studi di Antichità Cristiana 63 (Vatican City, 2011), pp. 213–62.

[26] P. Jugie, 'Cardinal: Up to the Council of Trent', *The Papacy: An Encyclopedia*, ed. P. Levillain, 3 vols. (New York, 2002), I, 239–43; P. Jugie, 'Sacred College', *The Papacy*, III, 1356–8.

[27] *PL* 75, 59–242, with the claims about chant and the *schola* in Liber II.6–10, cols. 90–2.

[28] Theodosian Code 6.10.2, see C. Pharr, et al., *The Theodosian Code and Novels and the Sirmondian Constitutions*, The Corpus of Roman Law (Corpus Juris Romani) 1 (Princeton, 1952), pp. 129–30. A. Cutler and A. P. Kazhdan, 'Notary', and A. P. Kazhdan, 'Primikerios', *The Oxford Dictionary of Byzantium*, 3 vols. (New York, 1991) III, 1495, 1719–20.

[29] Thus it appears frequently in *Ordo Romanus Primus*. See also P. Rabikauskas, 'Notary, Apostolic', *The Papacy*, II, 1054–5.

[30] R. L. Poole, *Lectures on the History of the Papal Chancery down to the Time of Innocent III* (Cambridge, 1915), pp. 6–7, 12–20.

[31] P. Jeffery, 'Rome and Jerusalem: From Oral Tradition to Written Repertory in Two Ancient Liturgical Centers', in *Essays on Medieval Music in Honor of David Hughes*, ed. G. M. Boone, Isham Library Papers 4 (Cambridge MA, 1995), pp. 207–47 (pp. 227–30).

[32] *PL* 89, 1887; 98, 200; MGH Epp. III, 553–4.

the choir is known as the 'quartus scholae subdiaconus' ('fourth subdeacon of the *schola*'), implying that there were three people ranking above him who are not described as actually involved in the music performances. The fourth subdeacon's other title, *archiparafonista*,[33] seems to confirm that the three people above him did not actually sing, since it indicates he was the highest ranking of the *parafonistae*, the adult 'side-sounders' who stood next to the *infantes* of the *schola*.[34] However Benedict's terminology, in which the choir leader is called *primicerius*, reflects the practice of his own time, for his ordinal often refers to the singers as *primicerius cum scola* or *primicerius et cantores*.[35] In a twelfth-century music manuscript reflecting the use of St Peter's, the verses of the archaic Easter Week Vespers are alternately assigned to the *primicerius* and the *scola* [*sic*],[36] indicating that the choir leader was now known as *primicerius*.

> et docuit et ordinavit stationes propter penitentes, quas cum cantoribus et primicerio et regionariis faciebat, aliter in Quadragesima usque ad Pascha et aliter in Albis et in dominicis diebus et festivitatibus sanctorum.

> [and he taught and ordained stations for penitents, which they did with cantors and the *primicerius* and the regionaries, one way in Lent up to Easter and another way during the Easter season and on Sundays and feasts of the saints.]

The annual calendar of stations is attributed to Gregory I in the *vita* by John the Deacon,[37] and this belief is enshrined in the fact that the book of prayers for papal stational Masses was traditionally known as the Gregorian sacramentary.[38] On the other hand, the titles of Gregory's preserved sermons on the Gospels, which name the Roman church in which they were delivered, suggest that Gregory knew an earlier form of the stational calendar than the one enshrined in the sacramentary named after him.[39] Once again Benedict refers to the singers as 'the cantors and the *primicerius*', but his mention of the 'regionaries' sounds like an allusion to *Ordo Romanus Primus*, where each

---

[33] *Ordines Romani*, pp. 80, 31 n. 1.

[34] Ibid., p. 81.

[35] *LC*, II, 143 left column lines 19–20, 32–3, right column line 31; p. 144 left column line 31; p. 145 left column line 10, right column line 1; etc.

[36] BL Additional MS 29988, fols. 74r–76v, 77v. See M. Huglo, 'Le chant "vieux-romain": liste des manuscrits et témoins indirects', *Sacris Erudiri* 6 (1954), 96–124 (pp. 112–3). My opinion that this manuscript originated within the orbit of St Peter's will be spelled out in another publication.

[37] *PL* 75, 93–4.

[38] J. Deshusses, ed., *Le Sacramentaire grégorien: ses principales formes d'après les plus anciens manuscrits* 1, 3rd edn, Spicilegium Friburgense 16 (Fribourg, 1992), pp. 50–60.

[39] Baldovin, *The Urban Character of Christian Worship*, pp. 124, 151–2. See now Gregorius Magnus, *Homiliae in Evangelia*, ed. R. Étaix, CCL 141 (Turnhout, 1999), lix–lxx.

of the lower clergy was subordinate to one of the seven regional subdeacons of the city of Rome, and the notaries and defensors were also organized by ecclesiastical regions.[40] The statement that Gregory ordained the stations 'for penitents' echoes what the *Liber pontificalis* says about Pope Simplicius (468–83). However, what Simplicius was actually credited with instituting was not 'stations', but a particular way of staffing the basilicas of St Peter, St Paul and St Lawrence. Each of these would be served by priests from the local region who would rotate on a weekly basis, for the purpose of hearing confessions and baptizing.[41] On the other hand, Benedict's claim that stational Masses were celebrated 'one way' during Lent and 'another way' the rest of the year seems to follow the practice Benedict knew. His ordinal states that, on Ember Days, which had a penitential character, the pope 'cantat missam more quadragesimali' ['sings Mass in the Lenten manner']. The ordinal also recounts some practices that were only followed during Lent.[42] Benedict seems to have assumed that the practice of his own time extended back to Gregory I.

> Et statuit has antiphonas processionales in IIII^{or} tempora et in Quadragesima: 'Deprecamur te, Domine'; 'Multa sunt, Domine, peccata nostra'; 'Parce, Domine, parce populo tuo'. Et in letanias maiores alias antiphonas: 'Domine Deus noster' et ceteras.

> [And he instituted these processional antiphons on Ember Days and in Lent: 'Deprecamur te, Domine'; 'Multa sunt, Domine, peccata nostra'; 'Parce, Domine, parce populo tuo'. And on Major Rogations other antiphons: 'Domine Deus noster' and so on.]

Here again, Lent and the Ember Days are linked, this time by the same series of processional antiphons. There is a different series for the Rogation Days, another type of penitential day. The Rogation series, beginning with 'Domine Deus noster', is given in full in the ordinal, so that it was enough for Benedict to cite only its first antiphon here.[43] The other list is given in full here since it does not occur in the ordinal. There is no reason to attribute either list to Gregory beyond the belief that he produced the chant repertory.

> Et fecit sanctum Stephanum orphanotrophium Lateranis, ubi primicerius et cantores manerent, de quibus jugiter essent cum pontifice, et de episcopis,

---

[40] *Ordines Romani*, pp. 67–70.

[41] *LP*, I, 249: 'Hic constituit ad sanctum Petrum apostolum et ad sanctum Paulum apostolum et ad sanctum Laurentium martyrem ebdomadas ut presbyteri manerent, propter penitentes et baptismum: regio III ad sanctum Laurentium, regio prima ad sanctum Paulum, regio VI vel septima ad sanctum Petrum.' For translation see *Book of Pontiffs*, p. 43.

[42] *LC*, II, 144 left column lines 35–6; pp. 149–50, esp. p. 150 left column lines 4–6.

[43] *LC*, II, 155–6.

cardinalibus, diaconibus subdiaconibus, regionariis et de acolitis et cubiculariis, qui eum custodirent et essent ei bonum testimonium.

[And he made the orphanage of St Stephen at the Lateran, where the *primicerius* and cantors would live, some of whom would be with the pontiff continually, and some bishops, cardinals, deacons, subdeacons, regionaries and some acolytes and cubiculars, who would take care of him and be a good testimony to him.]

According to John the Deacon, Gregory founded two houses for the singers.[44] The one at the Lateran, which John mentioned second but Benedict mentions first, was also known as an orphanage; it seems to be of more recent origin than the house at St Peter's, which Benedict mentions second. Popes Stephen II (752–7) and his brother Paul I (757–67) are the earliest known alumni of the Lateran orphanage.[45] By Benedict's time it was evidently dedicated to St Stephen. As for the other clergy, who are listed in descending hierarchical order, it is interesting to see 'bishops, cardinals, deacons'. That means that, for Benedict, the word 'cardinal' by itself still implied 'cardinal priest', the main priest assigned to a church. Again we find the word 'continually'. It seems that the pope, who lived at the Lateran, was always accompanied by some cantors from the Lateran *schola*, who seem to have served the pope in shifts.

Et constituit sicut papa Gelasius ordinavit, ut essent per regiones de diaconibus, subdiaconibus, regionariis et notariis, ut si quod ecclesiasticum negotium oriretur in regione et diffinire non possent, representarent archidiacono ut ipse poneret finem.

[And he constituted, as Pope Gelasius had ordained, that there would be some deacons, subdeacons, regionaries and notaries (organized) by regions, so that if some ecclesiastical business arose in a (particular) region and they were not able to settle it, they could represent to the archdeacon that he should bring it to a conclusion.]

---

[44] *PL* 75, 89–90. J. Dyer, 'The *Schola Cantorum* and its Roman Milieu in the Early Middle Ages', in *De Musica et Cantu: Studien zur Geschichte der Kirchenmusik und der Oper: Helmut Hucke zum 60. Geburtstag*, ed. P. Kahn and A.-K. Heimer, Musikwissenschaftliche Publikationen: Hochschule für Musik und Darstellende Kunst Frankfurt/Main 2 (Hildesheim, 1993), pp. 19–40; J. Dyer, 'Boy Singers of the Roman Schola Cantorum', in *Young Choristers (650–1700)*, ed. S. Boynton and E. Rice, Studies in Medieval and Renaissance Music 7 (Woodbridge, 2008), pp. 19–36; J. Dyer, 'Roman singers of the later Middle Ages', in *Cantus Planus: Papers Read at the 6th meeting, Eger, Hungary, 1993*, ed. L. Dobszay, 2 vols. (Budapest, 1995), I, 45–64.

[45] *LP*, I, 440, 463; *Lives of the Eighth-Century Popes*, pp. 52, 79.

This summarizes the organization of the clergy described at the beginning of *Ordo Romanus Primus,* in which all the lesser clergy serve under the subdeacon and deacon of each region, but have the right to appeal decisions to the Roman archdeacon because he is 'vicarius pontificis' ('vicar of the pontiff').[46] It is not clear to what extent this system still functioned in Benedict's time, but it was formally abolished only by Pope Alexander VII (1655–67).[47] Why Benedict would attribute this system to Gelasius and Gregory is not clear. One manuscript of the *Ordo Romanus* attributes it to Pope Silvester (314–35); the *Liber pontificalis* ascribes the division of Rome into seven regions to as many as three popes: Clement I (first century), Fabian I (236–50) and Gaius (282–95).[48]

> Hic scripsit ordinem qualiter ecclesia regeretur et statuit ut quando pontifex extra Urbem iret, archidiaconus et archipresbyter cardinalis et primicerius representent vicem eius.
>
> [He wrote the order for how the church should be ruled, and he instituted that, when the pontiff goes outside the City, the archdeacon and cardinal archpresbyter and *primicerius* (of the notaries?) represent him.]

In the document by which Gregory set up the *schola* of seven defensors, establishing a certain Boniface as the first-ranking *primicerius,* Gregory 'per absentiam pontificis et sedendi in conuentu clericorum habere licentiam et honoris sui priuilegia in omnibus statuimus obtinere' ('established that, in the absence of the pontiff, they have the freedom of sitting in the assembly of the clergy and they retain the privileges of their honour in all things').[49] It is only later, in an epistle of Pope Martin I (649–53), that we find the statement that 'in absentia pontificis archidiaconus et archipresbyter et primicerius locum presentant pontificis' ('in the absence of the pontiff the archdeacon and the archpriest and the *primicerius* are present in place of the pontiff').[50] Again, a statement from a later pope is being attributed to Gregory I.

> Et fecit xenodochium sancti Gregorii juxta gradus beati Petri, et constituit ut tres cantores cum primicerio jugiter officiarent missam ad altare beati Petri, qui indutus pluviali et mitra et virga staret juxta altare cum secundo, tercio et quarto; et pro beneficio haberet sicut in privilegio ejus legitur.

---

[46] *Ordines Romani,* pp. 67–8.

[47] See the motu proprio *Nuper certis ex causis* of 26 October 1655 and *Alias nos* of 10 June 1657 in *Bullarum Diplomatum et Privilegiorum Sanctorum Romanorum Pontificum Taurinensis Editio,* XVI: *Alexander VII,* ed. A. Bilius et al. (Turin, 1869), pp. 86–7, 279–80.

[48] *LP,* I, 123, 148, 161; *Book of Pontiffs,* pp. 3, 8, 12.

[49] *S. Gregorii Magni Registrum Epistularum* VIII.16, ed. D. Norberg, CCL 140A (Turnhout, 1982), p. 535.

[50] *PL* 87, 201A; *LP,* I, 148, n. 4.

[And he made the hospice of St Gregory near the stairs of blessed Peter, and he instituted that three cantors with the *primicerius* would continually officiate Mass at the altar of blessed Peter. Vested with cope and mitre and staff he would stand by the altar with the second, third and fourth; and for a benefice they would have as stated in his privilege.]

Here Benedict mentions the other house for a *schola cantorum*, which stood by the stairs leading up to St Peter's basilica. It is not clear if a building still stood there in Benedict's time. What is interesting, though, is the statement that the *primicerius* and three cantors would officiate at Mass at the altar over St Peter's tomb. The number of four cantors reminds us that, in *Ordo Romanus Primus*, the choir leader is the fourth subdeacon of the *schola*, suggesting some unspecified role for the other three. In Benedict's text, however, the four are now bishops, vested in cope, mitre and staff – items which are never mentioned in *Ordo Romanus Primus*. Since they seem to stand by the altar together, it is less clear that the word *iugiter* in this case refers to a rotation. If Benedict knew or thought he knew of a privilege from Pope Gregory stating how much the four would be paid, that document remains unidentified

Et IIII cantores statuit ad sanctum Paulum et IIII ad sanctam Mariam maiorem, et IIII ad sanctum Laurentium foras murum pro servicio missarum cardinalium cum benefitiis ipsarum ecclesiarum. Et precepit primicerio et cantoribus ut nullo modo deviarent ab ordine quem docuit in Romana ecclesia.

[And he established four cantors at St Paul and four at St Mary Major and four at St Lawrence-outside-the-walls, for service at the Masses of cardinals, with benefices of these same churches. And he decreed to the *primicerius* and cantors that they deviate in no way from the order he taught in the Roman church.]

Thus Benedict believed that Gregory had also established four cantors at these three other Roman basilicas, who had learned an order of service taught by Gregory himself. This raises the question of what Benedict meant when he called himself 'cantor of the Roman church'. Was he one of four at St Peter's, or one of sixteen at the four basilicas? Was he a *primicerius*? The ordinal does not mention all these resident cantors when the pope arrives at one of the basilicas for stational Mass.

Precepit ut ad altare beati Petri nulla consecratio fieret nisi Romani pontificis; et quando pontifex facit consecrationem ibi, descendat ad sanctum Andream et ibi faciat consecrationem; postea revertatur ad missam.

[He prescribed that, at the altar of blessed Peter, no consecration would be made except by the Roman pontiff; and when the pontiff makes a consecration there, let him descend to St Andrew and make a consecration there; after that let him return to the Mass.]

'Consecration' here refers to the ordination of a bishop. Since only a pope could be consecrated at the main altar above the body of St Peter, Benedict's *ordo* directs that, on Ember Saturdays when a new bishop is to be consecrated, that pope should begin the Mass at the altar of St Peter, then move to the oratory of St Andrew and consecrate the new bishop there, then return to the altar of St Peter to complete the Mass.[51] The practice is not mentioned in sources earlier than Benedict, but it is mentioned, and attributed to Pope Gregory, by two later writers.[52]

> Et constituit IIII diaconos cardinales esse ad sanctum Petrum, qui legerent evangelia ad missam et predicaret unusquisque in ebdomada sua, et presbiter cardinalis ebdomadarius similiter esset ibi, propter penitentes et baptismum et propter missas peregrinorum ad altare sancti Petri.

> [And he established four cardinal deacons to be at St Peter, who would read the Gospels at Mass and preach, each in his own week. And similarly a weekly cardinal priest would be there, for the sake of penitents and baptism and for the sake of pilgrims' Masses at the altar of St Peter.]

The presence of a *presbyter hebdomadarius* at papal celebrations (not necessarily at St Peter's) is already attested in *Ordo Romanus Primus*,[53] though the rotation of four cardinal deacons is not. However the responsibilities of this cardinal priest, to hear confessions and perform baptisms, is clearly dependent on what the *Liber pontificalis* attributes to Pope Simplicius (468–83):

> Hic constituit ad sanctum Petrum apostolum, et ad sanctum Paulum apostolum, et ad sanctum Laurentium martyrem hebdomadam, ut presbyteri manerent ibi propter penitentes, et baptismum.

> [He established at St Peter the apostle, and at St Paul the apostle and at St Lawrence the martyr a weekly rotation, so that priests would remain there for the sake of penitents and baptism.]

Benedict's account of the liturgical innovations of Gregory the Great is a remarkable stew of contemporary practice, research into the liturgical tradition of *Ordo Romanus Primus*, historical information from texts that recounted Gregory's life and texts by or about other popes. The methodology is completely different from that of another Italian chronicler of the popes, the canonist Bonizo of Sutri (d. 1095).[54] In Book 4 of Bonizo's *Liber de Vita Christiana*, the account of Gregory I is based more closely on Gregory's

---

[51] *LC*, II, 144 right column.

[52] M. Andrieu, *Les Ordines Romani du haut moyen âge* IV: *Les textes (suite) (Ordines XXXV–XLIV)*, Spicilegium Sacrum Lovaniense 28 (Louvain, 1956), pp. 127–9.

[53] Ibid., p. 93.

[54] Kéry, *Canonical Collections*, pp. 234–7

own writings and on medieval writings about him.[55] Why was Benedict's approach so different?

One reason might be that Benedict simply assumed that most of the Roman liturgy was 'made' by Gregory – both what Benedict knew from contemporary practice and what he found in ancient sources like *Ordo Romanus Primus*. But I think he also had a view of the papacy as uniform in its teaching across time; and if this were the case, then it wasn't really necessary to identify which pope actually said or did what. There is some other evidence for such a view among Benedict's contemporaries. For one thing, nearly all the popes and antipopes of the eleventh, twelfth and thirteenth centuries took names that seem intended to emphasize the continuity of the papacy (see Table 17.3). Following the chaotic reign of Benedict IX (1032–55/6), who was deposed and restored twice, most popes chose a name from the early Christian period, followed by the numeral II, III or IV. Those who didn't, chose a traditional papal name: Leo, Stephen or especially Gregory. Indeed for over a millennium, between Pope Lando (913–14) and Pope Francis (2013–), no pope chose an original name, that is, one that had never been used before.

Something that happened near Benedict's time seems to illustrate the idea of treating multiple popes as if they were one larger-than-life personality. Pope Paschal II (1099–1118) moved the sarcophagus of Pope Leo I (440–61), to place it near the bodies of Popes Leo II (682–3), Leo III (795–816) and Leo IV (847–55), who had been buried together in Old St Peter's basilica. In 1607, during the building of the new basilica, Pope Paul V (1605–21) moved the bodies of all four to the altar known as Our Lady of the Column, though in 1714 Pope Clement XI (1700–21), reburied Leo I separately under his own altar a few feet away. It was in front of this altar of Leo I that Pope Leo XII (1823–9) also chose to be buried.[56] The place where the four popes Leo rested up to 1607 is still marked by a seventeenth-century fresco in the Vatican Grottos, on the ceiling to the right of the altar in what is now known as the Capella delle Partorienti.[57]

[55] Bonizo, *Liber de Vita Christiana*, ed. E. Perels (Berlin, 1930), with an appendix by W. Berschin (Hildesheim, 1998), p. 127.

[56] W. J. Reardon, *The Deaths of the Popes: Comprehensive Accounts, Including Funerals, Burial Places and Epitaphs* (Jefferson NC, 2004), pp. 40–1, 54–5, 61, 62–4, 229; V. Noè, *Le tombe e i monumenti funebri dei Papi nella basilica di San Pietro in Vaticano* (Modena, 2000), pp. 235–44, 257–66.

[57] For reproductions see: V. Lanzani, *Le grotte vaticane: memorie storiche, devozioni, tombe dei papi* (Vatican City and Rome, 2010), p. 48; Soprintendenza Speciale per il Polo Museale Romano, *Roma Sacra: Guide to the Churches of the Eternal City, Itineraries 26–27: The Vatican Grottoes*, ed. V. Lanzani (Rome, 2003), p. 88, plate 151.

Table 17.3 Popes of the eleventh through the thirteenth centuries

Clement II (1046–7)	Lucius II (1144–5)
Damasus II (1048)	Eugene III (1145–53)
Leo IX (1049–54)	Anastasius IV (1153–4)
Victor II (1055–7)	Hadrian IV (1154–9)
Stephen IX (1057–8)	Alexander III (1159–81) (replaces
Benedict X (antipope 1058–9)	Innocent II in the Cambrai
Nicholas II (1058–61)	manuscript)
Alexander II (1061–73)	Victor IV (antipope 1159–64)
Honorius II (antipope 1061–4)	Paschal III (antipope 1164–8)
Gregory VII (1073–85)	Callistus III (antipope 1168–78)
Clement III (antipope 1080,	Innocent III (antipope 1179–80)
1084–1100)	Lucius III (1181–5)
Victor III (1086–7)	Urban III (1185–7)
Urban II (1088–99)	Gregory VIII (1187)
Paschal II (1099–1118)	Clement III (1187–91)
Theoderic (antipope 1100–1)	Celestine III (1191–8)
Albert (antipope 1101)	Innocent III (1198–1216)
Silvester IV (antipope 1105–11)	Honorius III (1216–27)
Gelasius II (1118–19)	Gregory IX (1227–41)
Gregory VIII (antipope 1118–21)	Celestine IV (1241)
Callistus II (1119–24)	Innocent IV (1243–54)
Honorius II (1124–30)	Alexander IV (1254–61)
Celestine II (antipope 1124)	Urban IV (1261–4)
Innocent II (1130–43) (*dominus meus*	Clement IV (1265–8)
in Benedict's papal chronicle)	Gregory X (1271–6)
Anacletus II (antipope 1130–8)	John XXI (1276–7)
Victor IV (1138)	
Celestine II (1143–4) (dedicatee of	
the *Liber Politicus*)	

For Benedict's view of the liturgy, then, the most revealing word might be *iugiter*, 'continuously'. He saw the Roman liturgical tradition as uninterrupted. Whether textually reviving practices he had read about in ancient texts, describing the usage of his own time or recounting the innovations of the one multi-personality that was the Roman papacy, the liturgy was always a seamless whole, done over and over again without pause or even much change. We don't know how many people, if any, shared his title 'Cantor of the Roman Church'. But in his 'Book of the City' he sang the praises of the Roman church and its liturgical tradition better than anyone.

18

A Life in Hours:
Goswin of Bossut's Office for Arnulf of Villers

Anna de Bakker

Sometime in the 1230s, Goswin of Bossut, cantor of the Cistercian monastery of Villers-la-Ville, wrote a *vita* for a lay brother of his abbey, Arnulf. Goswin was an accomplished biographer, and the three surviving hagiographies attributed to him reveal an author as attentive to lyrical prose and scriptural allusions as to lively anecdotes displaying the virtues of his subject.[1] His stint as a hagiographer seems to have been undertaken at the behest of his abbot, William, who presided over the apex of a period of growth of Villers and was likely invested in promoting the monastery's status through the *vite* of several holy persons associated with it – in this instance, a *conversus* who had come to Villers some thirty years earlier and earned renown for the extremes of his penitential conduct as well as his generosity toward others. Goswin likely met Arnulf only toward the end of the lay brother's life, but his description is nevertheless vivid; over the course of two books, Goswin first lays out Arnulf's extraordinary exercises of self-mortification and then (as if to temper the somewhat grotesque image of Arnulf's physical sufferings) uses the second book to describe his charity, obedience and humility.[2]

Goswin's commemorative work did not end with the *vita*; a liturgical office for Arnulf also survives, presumably as part of the same hagiographical programme. In it, Goswin was able to use his skills as cantor to shape the memory of Arnulf in a different way. In writing an office for Arnulf, Goswin had a second mode for retelling the past, one with its own formal constraints as well as opportunities to emphasize and authorize new aspects of its subject. Careful study of this office reveals, first, the methods by which a cantor such as Goswin worked to transform a prose historical work into a

---

[1] In addition to Arnulf's life, Goswin has long been associated with the life of Abundus, a monk of Villers, and was proposed as the author of the life of Ida of Nivelles in 1947: see S. Roisin, *L'Hagiographie Cistercienne dans le Diocèse de Liège au XIIIe Siècle* (Louvain, 1947), p. 55. More recent work has confirmed that the similarities in style between the three *vite* make Goswin's authorship of all three 'all but proven'. See M. Cawley, *Send Me God: The Lives of Ida the Compassionate of Nivelles, Nun of La Ramée, Arnulf, Lay Brother of Villers, and Abundus, Monk of Villers, by Goswin of Bossut* (Turnhout, 2003), pp. 7–8.

[2] The *vita* exists in two editions: ed. D. Papebroeck, *AASS* (Antwerp, 1709) June, VII, pp. 606–31; (Paris, 1867), pp. 558–79. Citations refer to the 1867 *AASS*.

liturgical one and, secondly, the different images of Arnulf promoted through Goswin's two historical undertakings. Medieval history writing, particularly hagiography and chronicles, has been the subject of much recent scholarly study, yet it is uncommon to be able to see the process of liturgical-historical composition as clearly as Goswin's work allows. The office for Arnulf has the unusual virtue of being associated with a reasonably well-defined time and place, as well as with a *vita* by the same author. It is thus a rare witness to two individuals and their ties to the community at Villers: the holy man whose life was told in both prose and music, and the cantor responsible for shaping his memory.

Goswin's office for Arnulf survives uniquely in a modest *libellum* that is now Brussels, Bibliothèque royale de Belgique MS II 1658, alongside an office for Mary of Oignies.[3] It can be dated on paleographical and codicological grounds to the second quarter of the thirteenth century, probably not long after Arnulf's death in June 1228.[4] The two offices appear in reverse calendrical order, and numerous erasures and revisions appear throughout, the parchment is of uneven thickness and damaged in places, and the size of the folios as well as the size of the staff is variable, though the same scribe seems to have been responsible for both text and music. It thus seems possible that the manuscript, made of scrap parchment, was used by the composer to work out his ideas rather than to preserve a polished product for communal use. As the chief musician and rhetorician at the monastery at the time of Arnulf's death, it was presumably Goswin who gave the primary direction to this compositional undertaking. If so, his purpose is not entirely obvious; Mary's office seems to have been completed in some haste, suggesting a formal occasion which presented a deadline of some sort – but no clear possibilities present themselves. It seems likely that the Arnulf *vita* and office were both intended for 'a kind of local celebration within the order',[5] and that the office was composed roughly contemporaneously with the *vita* as an extension of the same commemorative project. The office thus allowed Goswin to recast the *vita* in a new mode, extracting and emphasizing portions of Arnulf's life according to what seemed most important for the community, allowing the juxtaposition of other texts to shape his meaning and employing the constraints and possibilities of various chant forms to promote history through musical means. Goswin was creating two parallel and interrelated narratives, one in prose and one in song.

---

[3] For more on Mary's office, see P. Mannaerts, 'An Exception to the Rule? The Thirteenth-Century Cistercian *Historia* for Mary of Oignies', *Journal of the Alamire Foundation* 2 (2010), 233–69. Mannaerts considers the revisions in that office to reflect 'the composer at work', and the same could be said of the Arnulf office.

[4] The manuscript is described by D. Misonne, 'Office liturgique neumé de la bienheureuse Marie d'Oignies à l'Abbaye de Villers au XIIIe siècle', in *Album J. Balon* (Namur, 1968), pp. 267–86.

[5] Mannaerts, 'An Exception', p. 248.

The historical context of both *vita* and office is relatively well documented. Goswin was cantor of Villers from roughly 1225 to 1260, while Arnulf entered Villers in 1202 and remained there until his death in 1228.[6] Villers, some twenty-five miles south of Leuven in the district of Liège, was a daughter house of Clairvaux, and in Goswin's (and Arnulf's) time it flourished under a series of charismatic abbots, some of whom would be promoted later in their careers to Clairvaux.[7] These abbots of the first half of the thirteenth century presided over something of a golden age of Villers, one which saw the foundation of two daughter abbeys and the regional blossoming of a remarkably varied hagiographical corpus.[8] The latter is a consequence of the Villers abbots' particular interest in promoting the spirituality not only of choir monks, but also of local communities of Beguines, nuns and lay people, as well as their own lay brothers.[9] Most of Arnulf's penitential activities, for example, took place during the abbacy of Conrad of Urach, who in his own novitiate had cultivated a relationship with a saintly lay brother at nearby Aulne.[10] Perhaps it was this early friendship with an unusual lay brother that made Conrad sympathetic to Arnulf's vigorous pursuit of self-mortification. Villers's *gesta* relate many anecdotes of other more or less contemporary lay brothers at the abbey, presented as examples of holy activity.[11]

Arnulf stood out among these other lay brothers owing to the extreme quality of his spiritual activities. As Goswin writes in the *vita*, after wasting his youth in 'levis moribus et verbis' ('trifling behaviour and speech'), Arnulf abruptly felt a calling to religion.[12] He spent two years in different religious circles in his native Brussels before deciding, at the age of twenty-two, to enter more fully into religious life as a lay brother at Villers. In his first year, however, Arnulf came to feel that life as a novice was much more lax than he had anticipated, and he therefore devised the first of his penitential practices: horsehair ropes tied so tightly against his body 'ut de carne eius putrefacta

---

[6] The precise dates of Goswin's cantorship are not known; see Cawley, *Send Me God*, pp. 7–8.

[7] See Cawley, 'Four Abbots of the Golden Age of Villers', *Cistercian Studies Quarterly* 27 (1992), 299–327.

[8] On the foundations, see *Chronica Villariensis monasterii*, ed. E. Martène and G.Durand, in *Thesaurus novum anecdotorum* (Paris, 1717), III, 1280. B. Newman, 'Goswin of Villers and the Visionary Network', in Cawley, *Send Me God*, p. xxx, discusses the hagiographic output.

[9] B. P. McGuire, 'The Cistercians and the Transformation of Monastic Friendships', *Analecta Cisterciensia* 37 (1981), 34–6.

[10] This episode, in which Simon predicts Conrad's ultimate rise to the rank of cardinal, is related in Caesarius of Hesterbach, *Dialogus Miraculorum/Dialog über die Wunder* iii.33, ed. N. Nösges and H. Schneidger, 5 vols., Fontes Christiani 86 (Turnhout, 2009), II, 614–16.

[11] Other than Arnulf, twelve lay brothers earn a notice in the *Gesta*, six of them named. See *Chronica Villariensis*, III, 1359–1374.

[12] *Vita* I.1.4, p. 559.

vermes ebullirent' ('that worms bubbled up from his rotten flesh').[13] Arnulf only ceased this activity as a courtesy to others who complained about the resulting stench, and he moved on to other less pungent forms of self-mortification. The rest of the first book of the *vita Arnulphi* is taken up with what has been called a 'virtual catalogue of self-torture', and 'a most extreme and detailed account of self-mortification, even by the standards of medieval hagiography'.[14] Goswin takes pains to note that all of Arnulf's superiors had given him permission to undertake all of these activities.[15] Indeed, since his disciplines ran counter to the usual policy that 'ordinis simplicitas sufficiat' ('simplicity of the order should suffice'),[16] and since these activities must have excused him from carrying out the normal duties of a lay brother, the support of his superiors must have been considerable. Modern readers have had more difficulty with this aspect of Arnulf's life, finding the memory of Arnulf 'distorted' by 'an excessive stress on [his] austerities' and cautioning not to 'get bogged down in the elaborate descriptions of torture in the first book'.[17]

Yet, if the office is any indication, this stress on Arnulf's austerities was especially important to Goswin. The longest of his hymn texts, 'Gaude mater ecclesia', offers a succinct story of Arnulf's life that is focused almost entirely on his penitential practices, from rolling in nettles and donning hair boots to wearing a vest made of hedgehogs (presumably with the spines facing inward). (The hymn, with relevant parallels from the *vita* and a translation, is given in Table 18.1.) This basic summary provided the essential account of Arnulf's life in the Villers *gesta*.[18] It presents these striking aspects of Arnulf's life as a kind of base layer for Goswin's project of memorializing Arnulf's saintliness.

Both the text and the music of 'Gaude mater ecclesia' appear to have been newly composed for Arnulf's feast, which perhaps accounts for its music having been written out in full (rather than merely one strophe, as was common for hymns in contemporary practice). Goswin's compositional strategy in this hymn seems to aim at imprinting the basic facts of Arnulf's

---

[13] Ibid. I.1.10, p. 560.

[14] Newman, 'Goswin of Villers', p. xl; J. France, *Separate but Equal: Cistercian Lay Brothers, 1120–1350* (Collegeville, 2012), p. 181.

[15] *Vita* I.3.21, p. 562.

[16] The particular policy of Abbot Charles of Villers, according to Caesarius, *Dialogus* vi.1, III, 1135.

[17] Cawley, *Send Me God*, p. 12; McGuire, 'Self-Denial and Self-Assertion in Arnulf of Villers', *Cistercian Studies Quarterly* 28 (1993), 241.

[18] Drawing on these sources, modern commentators have presented similar summaries of Arnulf's life. See, e.g., McGuire, 'Self-Denial', p. 259: 'Arnulf found his way from a middle-class family in Brussels to the great Brabantine foundation of Villers. ... He imposed pain on himself in order to be part of the world's pain and to act as intercessor.'

Table 18.1 'Gaude mater ecclesia'

Hymn*	Source text in the vita	Translation
Gaude, mater ecclesia, Pro Arnulphi presentia, Cuius sacra solemnia Celebrentur cum gloria.		Rejoice, mother church, for the presence of Arnulf, whose sacred feast is celebrated with glory.
Qui in Bruxella genitus Fertur de mediocribus Fuisse et fidelibus Ac honestis parentibus.	I.1.1: Fuit in ... Bruxella ... adolescens quidam, Arnulfus nomine, quem a mediocribus parentibus duxisse ferunt.	Who, it is said, was born in Brussels of middle-class parents, faithful and honest.
Hic in iuventutis flore Perfusus celesti rore Declinavit ab errore Mundi pro Dei amore.	Hic in primo adolescentie sue flore ... cepit erraticus viator incedere.	In the flower of his youth, sprinkled with celestial dew, he turned from the error of the world to the love of God.
In vicesimo secundo His etatis sue anno Iunctus fratrum collegio Fuit Villari optimo.	I.1.7: Anno etatis sue vicesimo secundo, venit ad monasterium Villariense.	In his twenty-second year, he was joined to the company of the brothers of Villers.
In sue conversionis Anno primo dirissimis Ligavit se tirunculus Christi tribus funiculis.	I.1.9: Fecit namque sibi furtim duos funiculos ... I.1.10: Fecit alium funiculum longiorem ...	In that first most difficult year of his conversion, the new follower of Christ bound himself with three cords.
Corpus suum pro Domino Crura pedesque satino Domavit cum cilicio Continue asperrimo.	I.3.17: ... caligas cilicinas in cruribus, et pedules cilicinos ...	He conquered his body for the Lord, his legs and his feet always in the roughest haircloth.
Percussitque cum ferula Carnem suam dirissima, Ad quam erat conglobata Ericii pellicula.	I.2.15: Fecit namque sibi ferulam ligneam agglutinans illi pellem ericii.	He hit his flesh with a very hard staff, to which was attached the pelt of a hedgehog.
Rusco quoque se et virgis Magnis cedebat ictibus Et volutavit in spinis Semet ipsum cum urticis.	I.2.15: Quotiescumque autem tam virgis quam rosco sive ferula ... cecidisset ... etiam ... nudum se volutabat in urticis.	He also struck himself with brush and sticks with great blows, and rolled himself in thorns and stinging nettles.

Table 18.1 *continued*

Hymn*	Source text in the vita	Translation
Catenis etiam tribus	I.3.19: Tres catenas	He also girded his flesh
Cinxit carnem sub vestibus	ferreas sibi acquisivit ...	with three chains under
Loricaque sub pellibus	I.3.20: Quesivit sibi	his clothes, and wore a
Ericiorum erat usus.	pelles ericiorum ...	cuirass of hedgehog pelts.
Nunc ergo sit altissimus		Now therefore let God
Deus atque benignissimus		most high be blessed by
In sui servi actibus		all, most merciful in his
Per omnia benedictus.		works to his servant.
Sit laus Patri cum Filio		Praise be to the Father
Sanctoque simul Paraclito		with the Son and to the
Nobisque donet Filius		Holy Paraclete, and may
Gratiam Sancti Spiritus.		the Son give us to grace
Amen.		of the Holy Spirit. Amen.

* *Hymni Inediti: Liturgische Hymnen*, ed. G. M. Dreves, *AH* 12 (Leipzig, 1892),
   no. 143, pp. 87–8.

life in the memory of the listener and singer. His technique here, as well as in the other Arnulf hymns and several antiphons, is to summarize some of the basic events of the *vita* and condense them in rhymed paraphrase. The repetitive and participatory aspects of hymns make them a good vehicle for committing things to memory – indeed, the hymn was one of the latest genres of chant to transfer from an oral tradition, one dependent for melodies on communal remembering, to a written practice.[19] The hymn's emphasis on penance is carried over from the *vita*, in the preface of which Goswin promises to spend the first book describing 'non solum corporales afflictiones sed etiam instrumenta afflictionem tantummodo' ('his bodily afflictions and the instruments with which he inflicted them').[20] Evidently these chapters formed the core of how Goswin wanted Arnulf to be remembered in the office, too, and the strophic aspect of the hymn gave him a convenient means of assuring that these afflictions would be committed to memory.

In other parts of the office, however, Goswin employs more rhetorically intricate tools to transform the prose *vita* into chant. The use of direct quotation allows him to preserve much of the *vita*'s prose, while also employing his skills to underscore specific aspects of Arnulf's larger story. In this office, Goswin limits the use of these quotations to five responsories, strategically placed at the beginning of Vespers and Matins and the end

[19] See S. Boynton, 'Orality, Literacy, and the Early Notation of Office Hymns', *JAMS* 56 (2003), pp. 99–168.
[20] *Vita* I.Pref.3, p. 558.

of each nocturn in Matins. Aside from a few occasional changes of diction, apparently for the sake of clarity while singing, the texts of these responsories are essentially taken word for word from the *vita*. Rather than simply being derivative, however, the melismatic nature of responsories allows Goswin to place considerable emphasis on specific portions of the text, stretching individual words over many of notes and, as it were, slowing down time to allow for concentration on certain ideas. Goswin uses this technique sparingly, preferring to save his longest melismas for final cadences, but on a few occasions he indulges in this type of melodic underscoring to strengthen particular themes. For example, the final responsory of the third nocturn – the

Ex. 18.1 Responsory 'Egressus igitur nobis'

Table 18.2 Third Nocturn, fourth responsory and verse

Text*	Source in the vita	Translation
Egressus igitur novus Christi tyrunculus cum Abraham de terra et de cognatione sua, ut iret in terram quam monstraverat ei Deus.	I.1.7: Egressus igitur novus Christi tyrunculus cum Abraham de terra et cognatione sua, ut iret in terram quam monstraverat ei Deus.	Christ's new little novice set out like Abraham from his land and kin, so he might enter the land that God had shown him.
V. Anno etatis sue vicesimo secundo reliquit parentes et valedixit seculo. [ut iret …]	Anno etatis sue vicesimo secundo, venit ad monasterium Villariense.	V. In the twenty-second year of his life he left his parents and bid farewell to the world. [so that …]
V. Gloria Patri et Filio et Spiritui Sancto. [ut iret …]		V. Glory to the Father and to the Son and to the Holy Spirit. [so that …]

* Brussels, Bibliothèque royale de Belgique MS II 1658, fol. 5r.

last of these direct quotations – presents Arnulf's entry as a 'little novice' (*tyrunculus*) into Villers. Goswin compares this to Abraham leaving his home and entering the Promised Land. The word *tyrunculus* receives moderately melismatic treatment despite being mid-sentence (see Ex. 18.1). The high-pitched melisma draws attention to Arnulf's status as a beginner, thus putting melody in the service of rhetoric.

Goswin also makes full use of the rhetorical structure inherent to a responsory, namely its internal repetition: the verse is framed by a kind of chorus, repeated a third time when a doxology occurs. The fourth responsory for the third nocturn, mentioned above, has such a doxology, and part of its text is emphasized through strategic repetition (see Table 18.2).[21]

The passage quoted from the *vita* uses a parallel structure to build from the comparison with Abraham to the conclusion of Arnulf's journey at the monastery of Villers. As it appears on the manuscript page, the responsory abandons this parallelism, replacing the clause about Arnulf's coming to Villers with one repeating his departure from his family. In performance, however, it becomes apparent how Goswin has adapted his rhetoric to the form of the responsory, since the repeated clause describes Arnulf's/Abraham's entry into 'the land God had shown him'. This clause gains additional meaning with each repetition; at first, it seems to refer primarily to Abraham's Promised Land, but when it is repeated after the verse it becomes

[21] See also Fassler's chapter in this volume where there is further discussion of the use of the form of the great responsory and its repeating sections to score rhetorical points.

more clearly about Arnulf, while after the doxology it becomes a kind of thanksgiving for the equation of monastery and Promised Land. Through both musical and structural aspects of the responsory, Goswin transforms his portrait of Arnulf, dramatically highlighting the saint's status as a new convert as well as the prominent place of Villers in the story. While the hymn focused on Arnulf as a disciplined and perhaps somewhat isolated penitent, in the responsory we thus find a community uniting around a *conversus* and affirming their own spiritual role in his story.

This focus on Arnulf's conversion, and on the role of Villers therein, is shared by the other responsories that quote from the *vita* – once even through reference to the conversion of St Paul, whose feast Arnulf shares.[22] The four responsories used in Matins present, in order, his origins and conversion to faith, his calling, his friendship with religious persons and separation from the secular world and, finally, his entry to Villers, all taken from the *vita*. The responsory for first Vespers disrupts this sequence, however, anticipating the Matins texts and drawing on a passage from the *vita* after Arnulf's entry to the monastery. This responsory thus gives a broader context for the specific events related in the Matins responsories – a placement perhaps suggested by the metaphors of birth and infancy employed by Goswin (see Table 18.3). As it appears in the *vita*, the passage used in the Vespers text is Goswin's interjected reflection on Arnulf's first penitential acts at Villers, those involving festering wounds incurred by tying ropes around his body. After narrating the details and circumstances of Arnulf's actions, Goswin allegorizes the instruments of his affliction by comparing them to the swaddling bands of Mother Grace, while also comparing the trials of his first year to spiritual circumcision. Goswin's treatment of the text in the office allows time for careful reflection on this complex collection of images; the melismas are some of the longest in the office, and the repetition is placed so that the responsory turns back from Arnulf's piercing cords to, once again, the nurturing mother. The responsories thus suggest how Arnulf's penitential practices should be understood: not as acts to be imitated literally, but as physical reminders of his spiritual grace.

The other aspects of Arnulf's spiritual grace are the subject of the second, and longer, book of Arnulf's *vita*, beginning with themes of charity, humility and patience in an account of Arnulf's interactions with (and prayers for) members of the monastery and the larger community. Arnulf's actions in this second book are generally more outwardly directed than those of the first, as he advises and (occasionally) reproves both clerics and laity, makes prophetic predictions and sends grace to those requesting it from afar. Such anecdotes make clear the respect in which Arnulf was held, at the same time as they justify Goswin's contempt for those who regarded the lay brother's spiritual

---

[22] The last responsory for the first nocturn, 'Cum autem placuit', is taken from *Vita* I.4, where, in turn, it is a quotation from Gal. 1. 15, which sometimes serves as the responsory for the feast of Paul (June 30).

Table 18.3 First Vespers, responsory and verse

Text*	Source in the vita	Translation
O vere felicem puerum Arnulphum, de quo nuper renato tam sollicita est mater gratia ut non solum nutriat eum lactis dulcedine, sed etiam myrratum vinum propinet ei ad bibendum, dum alligat eum in cunis infantie sue.	I.1.10: O vere felicem puerum, de quo recenter nato tam soliciter est mater gratia, ut non solum nutriat eum lactis dulcedine, sed etiam myrratum vinum propinet ei ad bibendum, dum alligat eum in cunis infantie sue tam pungentis fascia funiculi et cultro tam acutissimo carnalem in eo circumcidit lasciviam.	O truly happy child, Arnulf, recently reborn, for whom Mother Grace is so concerned that she not only feeds him with the sweetness of milk but also sets him with wine mixed with myrrh to drink, while she swaddles him in his infant cradle.
V. Carnalem in eo circumcidit lasciviam tam pungentis fascia funiculi et cultro acutissimo. [dum alligat ...]		V. She circumcises away fleshly lust in him with the bands of pungent cords and with the sharpest knife.

* Brussels, Bibliothèque royale de Belgique MS II 1658, fol. 1v.

ecstasies *in malo*.[23] Through this second book, Arnulf is presented not only as someone prone to extreme penance, but also as a sympathetic figure whose spiritual virtues were held in esteem by his community.

However, nothing from Book II of the *vita* appears in the office. Indeed, the office barely manages to cover the events of Book I (mostly through the aforementioned hymn), and it gives disproportionate weight to the very beginning of Arnulf's story – his upbringing and conversion. This preference for earlier episodes of Arnulf's life can be explained in both historical and rhetorical terms. At the time of Arnulf's death in 1228, Villers was under the guidance of Abbot William of Brussels (in office from 1221 to 1237), who seems to have been a great supporter of both Goswin and Arnulf.[24] Goswin became cantor under William's abbacy, and he mentions the abbot's role as commissioner for another of his works, the *vita* of Ida.[25] It seems likely that William gave an abbatial mandate to write Arnulf's *vita*, too, perhaps preferring to keep his role in it anonymous. This anonymous promotion of Arnulf would be in keeping with the kind of support he showed Arnulf while he was alive; for example, Goswin relates that under a certain abbot (*abbas quidam* – almost certainly William), Arnulf secretly asked permission to give

---

[23] *Vita* II.3.23, p. 570.
[24] For more on William, see Cawley, 'Four Abbots'; *Chronica Villariensis*, III, 1278–85; and J. Burton and J. Kerr, *The Cistercians in the Middle Ages* (Woodbridge, 2011), p. 158.
[25] Cawley, *Send Me God*, p. 29.

away food to the poor. The abbot allowed him to do so, but the secrecy of this arrangement caused problems for both when the almsgiving was reported by those less sympathetic to unauthorized charity.[26]

William also likely admired Arnulf's personal austerity. He is mentioned in the abbey's chronicle as having been particularly frugal in his use of food and clothing; one of the chief accomplishments of his successor was to finally acquire new clothing for the monks, something which the less materially concerned William had presumably avoided despite the monastery's income.[27] Arnulf's spiritual ambitions seem to have been cultivated under William's supervision, and in his later years Arnulf was allowed to be 'pene a cunctis forensibus curis liber' ('free from almost all outward cares') to pursue his life of prayer.[28] Many of the events of Book II seem to have taken place at this time. Abbot William was also noted for his engagement with lay brothers, local holy women and other members of the greater Villers spiritual community – the same sort of engagement seen in Arnulf's life, and which Arnulf was perhaps, as lay brother, better-placed to carry out than most of the cloistered monks.[29] If William's admiration was the driving force behind Arnulf's memorialization, the emphasis on Arnulf's origins could have served a political purpose. Like William, Arnulf hailed from Brussels, a fact mentioned five times over the course of his office. Given the alignment of Arnulf's and William's values, it seems as if one man of Brussels is standing in for another, with the praise of Arnulf's austerity serving to promote William's vision of the abbey. The emphasis on origins and separation from material comfort is not accidental; Goswin made sure that Arnulf's memory aligned with his abbot's ideals.

But neither William nor Goswin wanted Arnulf to be remembered only for his physical afflictions. Arnulf's other virtues are still present in the office, but in a different way; Goswin changes the means of representing Arnulf's character, but not his conception of that character. Just as Goswin adapted his prose for the responsories, he could also adapt the idea of spiritual virtues to the possibilities of quotation and juxtaposition in the office. In addition to citation and paraphrase, Goswin also worked to interweave biblical texts with the strictly biographical material of the *vita*, making deliberate use of biblical quotations in the remaining elements of the office. Almost every antiphon and responsory which is not directly about Arnulf himself is a quotation from the book of Ecclesiasticus. This does not seem to have been a common practice; there is no evidence for these antiphons and responsories in the usual Cistercian collections (or indeed in non-Cistercian ones), and little reason for Goswin to have written them out if they were well

[26] *Vita* II.1.8, p. 567.
[27] *Chronica*, p. 1285.
[28] *Vita* II.2.11, p. 568.
[29] France, *Separate but Equal*, p. 186.

known.[30] The selection and adaptation of verses from Ecclesiasticus for use in the liturgy appears to have been Goswin's work, or else it is a deliberate following of an otherwise unusual and unfamiliar model. A fondness for biblical allusion and citation is in keeping with his writing in the *vita*, where Ecclesiasticus is one of his more favoured books, but its use in the office is much closer to the text and much more consistent than any of his allusions in the *vita*.

The manner in which these texts are modified from their sources tends to be fairly consistent, and usually no more than a few words are changed. For example, in the third antiphon in the first nocturn of Matins, Ecclus 1. 18 is adapted to read: 'Religiositas custodivit et iustificavit cor viri sancti, et Dominus iucunditatem atque gaudium dedit ei' ('Religiousness kept and justified the holy man's heart, and the Lord gave him joy and gladness').[31] The few words that are changed – especially the shift from the biblical text's future tense (*custodiet, iustificabit*) to the office's perfect, and the added reference to the *vir sanctus* – help to make the verse apply to the present situation. Similarly, the abstract statements common to Wisdom literature have been modified to more concrete statements, using epithets which are themselves taken from elsewhere in Ecclesiasticus.[32] Thus in the fourth antiphon in the first nocturn, the generalized Ecclesiasticus 2. 9 – 'Qui timetis Dominum, sperate in illum' ('Ye who fear the Lord, hope in him') – becomes more concrete: 'Timuit Dominum vir venerabilis' ('the venerable man feared the Lord').[33] While in the *vita* Arnulf's virtues were illustrated through anecdotes demonstrating charity, humility, patience and obedience, the office relates his virtues through this series of Ecclesiasticus verses, which invoke his *humilitas, timor* and *religiositas*. Most remarkably, Arnulf – hardly a learned man – has become a *vir sapiens*, excelling in spiritual wisdom.[34]

The Wisdom-based verses may seem to abstract Arnulf's character, but there are ways in which this material, too, might have resonated with a community who knew Arnulf personally. For example, in the first nocturn the verses used for the first and last antiphon have even been modified slightly to make the whole nocturn begin and end on the word *opera* – not a major change, but one that might have been heard as a nod to Arnulf's status as a lay brother, working on the granges. The relationship of choir monks

---

[30] In contrast, in the office for Mary of Oignies he simply refers the cantor to the office for Mary Magdalene: see Brussels MS II 1658, fol. 9r ('... sicut de beata Maria Magdalena').

[31] Brussels II 1658, fol. 3v; cf. the biblical text: 'Religiositas custodiet et iustificabit cor; iucunditatem atque gaudium dabit.'

[32] The epithets such as *vir sanctus* are common in Wisdom literature, as well as in other medieval hagiographical works, but Ecclesiasticus is the only biblical book to contain six of the seven used. The seventh, *vir venerabilis*, is not biblical.

[33] Brussels II 1658, fol. 2v.

[34] Ibid., fol. 6r.

to the labourers who supported them was occasionally a tense one, and in other places occasionally erupted into revolts.[35] Consequently, Cistercian *exempla* literature often contrasted an ideally meek and diffident lay brother with a rebellious one who overstepped his bounds. Arnulf was neither of those things, making him a particularly complex character, potentially a model for choir monks and lay brothers alike. In this light, another aspect of Goswin's presentation of Arnulf becomes potentially significant; in two different antiphons, texts from Ecclesiasticus have been altered to include the phrases 'in medio fratrum suorum' and 'in fratribus suis', changes which introduce an emphasis on community not found at the corresponding points in the biblical text.[36] Only a few years later, a general statute would forbid lay brothers from referring to themselves as *fratres*, but here the term is being voiced by the choir monks who participated in the office to refer to one of their lay brethren.[37]

Goswin's use of scriptural quotations transforms Arnulf into something of an eternal figure, and in this respect it is useful to remember that the antiphons in which this abstraction is accomplished are further interwoven with psalms. Though the choice of psalms is of course prescribed by convention, the relationships between the psalms and antiphons are not inconsequential, since the antiphon presumably (at least in part) directed the interpretation of the psalm. This is perhaps most obvious in the first antiphon and psalm of the first nocturn, where the antiphon describes the *opera viri sancti*, and the psalm (Ps. 1) describes the actions of a different holy man, one who is blessed not to walk in the way of the wicked.[38] Similarly, Ps. 4 reflects on the good things due to those who hope in the Lord, and its antiphon in the

---

[35] On the economic and social relations of Cistercian monks and lay brothers, see B. Noell, 'Expectation and Unrest among Cistercian Lay Brothers in the Twelfth and Thirteenth Centuries', *Journal of Medieval History* 32 (2006), 253–74, and D. Zurro, 'We All Work in Common: Medieval Cistercian Lay Brothers in the Twelfth and Thirteenth Centuries' (unpublished PhD dissertation, University of Notre Dame, 2015).

[36] For the first, see the second antiphon in the second nocturn, Brussels II 1658, fol. 3v: 'In medio fratrum suorum erat vir prudens disciplinatus et non murmurabat cum corripet'; cf. Ecclus 10. 28: 'Vir prudens et disciplinatus non murmurabit correptus.' For the second, see the antiphon for None, Brussels II 1658, fol. 6r: 'In fratribus suis vir sapiens hereditavit honorem et nomen eius erit vivum in eternum'; cf. Ecclus 37. 29: 'Sapiens in populo hereditabit honorem, et nomen illius erit vivens in eternum.' McGuire, 'Self Denial', p. 255, detects a similar sense of the importance of lay brothers in Goswin's approach to the *vita*.

[37] Noell, 'Expectation and Unrest', p. 271. One wonders how many of the illiterate *conversi*, listening to the office from the side aisles, were able to appreciate that one of their own was celebrated not only not through scenes from his Life, but through the lens of biblical citations. (As Cawley, *Send Me God*, p. 166 n. 104, notes, the abbey church was not complete at this time, and the entire community would have been gathered in the first four bays of the nave.)

[38] Brussels II 1658, fol. 2r.

office echoes these sentiments by proclaiming that religion brings joy to the heart.[39] An apparently avid reader of the Old Testament, it seems likely that Goswin would have delighted in such juxtapositions, putting Ecclesiasticus and the psalms into conversation, and using the same sort of rhetorical back-and-forth as in his responsories. These psalms and Ecclesiasticus verses thus serve to give an Old Testament authority and gravity to Arnulf's biography, underlining his virtues rather than his suffering.

Taken together with the sections of the office derived from the *vita*, the Ecclesiasticus antiphons and responsories complete the picture of Arnulf as a saintly figure. While the texts taken from the *vita* supply a chronology of his life, conversion and self-affliction, the other chants provide a more metaphorical biography, one that takes place in the spiritual or eternal realm. Rather than attempting to describe Arnulf's virtues in so many anecdotes, Goswin has equated him with an abstract 'holy man' whose humility and wisdom made him an important member of the brotherhood at Villers.

Goswin's musical and rhetorical skill help to craft Arnulf into a complex figure who is capable of suiting different purposes. Arnulf's most striking traits, especially his severe penitential practices, are versified in the hymns, where they can be most readily memorized by participants in the liturgy. His origins and rejection of worldly things, however, are given at least as great an emphasis, likely because of the influence of Abbot William. These aspects of the *vita* are quoted directly and put into responsories that impart a certain solemnity and allow them to be appreciated by those considering Arnulf's life more deeply. Finally, Arnulf's connection to those around him is illustrated not, as in the *vita*, through any direct illustrative anecdotes from his life, but rather by weaving his hagiography with verses from Ecclesiasticus that put him in communion with eternal and holy virtues. The result is a varied portrait of a remarkable lay brother, complementing the prose of his biography – a skilful collection of music and texts which together compose a saint.

---

[39] Ibid., fol. 2v.

19

Writing History to Make History: Johannes Meyer's Chronicles of Reform

Claire Taylor Jones

A fifteenth-century manuscript from the Dominican convent of Adelhausen in southern Germany bears a brief account of the convent's history from the time of its founding to the Observant reform, so called because of the insistence on strict observance of the Order's Rule and Constitution.[1] After copies of the letters and bulls establishing the convent and incorporating it into the Dominican Order, the narrative begins by referring the reader to another chronicle. 'Das andechtig selig geistlich leben der heiligen swestern des wirdigen closters' ('The devout, blessed, spiritual life of the holy sisters of the worthy convent') was recorded in the early fourteenth century by Adelhausen's prioress Anna von Munzingen.[2] This text, however, concerns the aftermath of the nuns' descent into disorder and disobedience. From such remarkable holiness the convent had fallen so far that in 1410 God sent a fire that burned the convent to the ground as punishment for their willfulness. After begging for the means to restore their grounds and staying for years as guests in the convents of St Katherine and Klingental, the Adelhausen sisters finally went home. Yet the years spent in exile had made them used to commerce with the outside world, and upon their return to the rebuilt convent, the sisters failed to rebuild a spiritual life. Even after a divine admonition as extreme as the fire of 1410, the nuns persisted in their fallen way of life for another fifty years. The convent was not reformed until 1465, when a priest of the Dominican Order brought nuns out of Observant convents in Alsace and Basel to teach their sisters in the three Freiburg convents to live in enclosure

---

[1] See, in particular, E. Hillenbrand, 'Die Observantenbewegung in der deutschen Ordensprovinz der Dominikaner', in *Reformbemühungen und Observanzbestrebungen im spätmittelalterlichen Ordenswesen*, ed. K. Elm (Berlin, 1989), pp. 219–71; B. Neidiger, 'Die Observanzbewegungen der Bettelorden in Südwestdeutschland', *Rottenburger Jahrbuch für Kirchengeschichte* 11 (1992), 175–96.

[2] Freiburg im Breisgau, Stadtarchiv, B1 (H) 107, fol. 227v. In my transcriptions from the manuscript I have supplied abbreviated letters but have not otherwise altered or regularized the text. For more on the Adelhausen sisterbook, see J. König, 'Die Chronik der Anna von Munzingen nach der ältesten Abschrift mit Einleitung und Beilagen', *Freiburger Diözesan-Archiv* 13 (1880), 129–236; G. J. Lewis, *By Women, For Women, About Women: The Sister-Books of Fourteenth-Century Germany* (Toronto, 1996), pp. 10–12, 286.

and observe the Rule as devoutly as their fourteenth-century predecessors had done.

The story of Adelhausen's fall and reform is preserved in an autograph manuscript written at the convent by the reforming priest himself a little more than fifteen years after the reform and re-enclosure. Johannes Meyer (1422–1485) had spent the years after 1465 serving as confessor and reforming other Dominican convents throughout southwestern Germany and Alsace before returning to Adelhausen as confessor in 1482. Despite the fact that Meyer was not only present but also responsible for the events of 1465, he does not name himself and speaks only of 'ein priester unsers orden' ('a priest of our order').[3] Much of the account of the fire is constituted by contemporary letters of the mayor of Freiburg and the prioress of the convent, which Meyer copied out himself in the appropriate place chronologically. Furthermore, while the Latin documents concerning the convent's foundation are written in a different hand, Meyer's hand follows each with a brief German-language explanation of the document's contents. Meyer's narrative insertions in effect bind together several primary historical documents (bulls and letters) pertaining to important moments in the convent's history. More than recounting, this text preserves.

This history of Adelhausen represents the first in a series of short texts in Meyer's own hand which have been collected in the religious miscellany Freiburg im Breisgau, Stadtarchiv, B1 (H) 107. The texts comprise the last works of his life, composed from around the time he was reassigned to Adelhausen until his death in 1485. The four brief and likely incomplete works are German-language historical texts, two pertaining directly to Adelhausen and two with broader content. Meyer's propagandistic goals in furthering the Observant reform are clearly discernable in all four texts. He repeatedly mourns a Golden Age of the Order when all Dominicans observed the Rule and all nuns understood the Latin they sang.

Yet Meyer's attitude towards his contemporary female audience was more sympathetic than it initially appears. The chronicles in this manuscript misrepresent certain historical events and figures in an attempt to accommodate the concerns of his female readership. Furthermore, while Meyer certainly praises humility and piety in strict observance of the Rule, he also foregrounds women who took greater initiative in serving their convent, their Order and the Church at large. Concentrating on these late texts out of Adelhausen, I will argue that Meyer did not merely encourage devotion and obedience but also literacy and leadership among Dominican women. Through the exemplary women of the past, Meyer encouraged nuns in the present to engage actively in shaping the history of the Dominican Order.

---

[3] B1 107, fol. 232r.

The Observance began as a reform movement in the late fourteenth century within the mendicant orders and spread eventually to other monastic orders, as well.[4] The movement's guiding principle was a return to the monastic life as the founders had intended it to be pursued. What this meant in practice for female convents was a stricter enforcement of enclosure that went hand in hand with a liturgical reform and a renewed effort to improve Latin literacy. Despite the Dominican emphasis on higher education, the attempt to restore Latin literacy among the Dominican nuns was not meant to enable the women to participate in the intellectual life of the Order. Much more simply, it was feared that the nuns could no longer understand what they sang during the Office.[5]

The first female Observant Dominican convent was founded in 1397 at an abandoned site at Schönensteinbach near Colmar in Alsace. After the success of this first experiment, other convents were reformed by sending sisters from an already reformed convent to instruct their sisters in correct Observance. These delegations of reforming nuns brought both liturgical and devotional books with them in order to reinforce their own instruction.[6] The sisters who travelled as part of the reforming effort maintained long-distance friendships and mentoring relationships with the women in the convents where they had been in residence previously. St Katharina in Nuremberg reformed St Katharina in St Gallen entirely through letters which the St Gallen sisters collected into a handbook of the Observance.[7] Sister-city relationships sprang up, in which convents would send each other books or artwork as presents.[8] As more Dominican convents embraced stricter enclosure

---

[4] K. Elm, 'Reform- und Observanzbestrebungen im spätmittelalterlichen Ordens-wesen: Ein Überblick', in *Reformbemühungen und Observanzbestrebungen*, pp. 3–19.

[5] Ehrenschwendtner has examined the literacy of southern German Dominican nuns in depth in M.-L. Ehrenschwendtner, *Die Bildung der Dominikanerinnen in Süddeutschland vom 13. bis 15. Jahrhundert* (Stuttgart, 2004).

[6] G. Muschiol, 'Migrating Nuns—Migrating Liturgy: The Context of Reform in Female Convents of the Late Middle Ages', in *Liturgy in Migration: From the Upper Room to Cyberspace*, ed. T. Berger (Collegeville, 2012), pp. 83–100.

[7] This manuscript is now preserved in the Dominican convent of St Katharina in Wil. http://www.e-codices.unifr.ch/de/kaw/SrBuch/ (accessed 15 January 2015).

[8] A. Willing, *Die Bibliothek des Klosters St. Katharina zu Nürnberg: synoptische Darstellung der Bücherverzeichnisse* (Berlin, 2012), pp. lxxi–cii; S. Mengis, *Schreibende Frauen um 1500: Scriptorium und Bibliothek des Dominikanerinnenklosters St. Katharina St. Gallen* (Berlin, 2013), pp. 204–36. The St Gallen sisters sent works by Meyer to the Augustinian canonesses of Inzigkofen. W. Fechter, *Deutsche Handschriften des 15. und 16. Jahrhunderts aus der Bibliothek des ehemaligen Augustinerchorfrauenstifts Inzigkofen* (Sigmaringen, 1997), p. 120. Reformed Dominican and Clarissan convents within the same city also exchanged devotional objects. See A. Winston-Allen, 'Networking in Medieval Strasbourg: Cross-Order Collaboration in Book Illustration Among Women's Reformed Convents', in *Schreiben Und Lesen in Der Stadt: Literaturbetrieb im Spätmittelalterlichen Straßburg*, ed. S. Mossman, N. F. Palmer and F. Heinzer (Berlin, 2012), pp. 197–212; A. Winston-Allen, '"Es [ist] nit wol zu gelobind, daz ain

from the surrounding city they created, almost paradoxically, a thriving network of reformed convents, spread out over Alsace, German-speaking Switzerland and southern Germany, who maintained contact through written correspondence with their sisters in distant cities. These long-distance relationships, the selection of women reformers and the transportation of the reforming nuns to new communities was facilitated and overseen, of course, by Dominican friars, some of whom made names for themselves through their work.

In the third quarter of the fifteenth century Johannes Meyer had a hand in reforming many of the women's houses in south-west Germany and this zeal fuelled a vast literary output, albeit mostly as compiler.[9] Much of Meyer's œuvre consists of editions and translations of earlier works, including four of the nine surviving Dominican sisterbooks.[10] These works, produced during the fourteenth century, constituted histories of a single convent and record the lives of illustrious nuns with particular emphasis on visionary experience and miracles. In addition to editing these German texts, Meyer translated Latin works that he considered important for the Dominican Observance. In line with his interest in the sisterbooks, Meyer translated into German Gerard de Fracheto's *Vitae fratrum*, a collection of lives of prominent Dominican friars collected in the thirteenth century and on which the sisterbooks were largely modeled. In translating Humbert of Romans's *Liber de instructione officialium*, Meyer heavily adapted the descriptions of convent duties to the needs of nuns. In addition to transmitting and translating the works of others, Meyer profusely wrote chronicles both in Latin and German, largely as compilations from older Latin works, although he included material from both his own personal experience and the accounts of contemporaries. The most interesting of these is the *Buch der Reformacio Predigerordens*, the *Book of the Reformation of the Order of Preachers*, which recounts the history of the Observant reform, the first Observant convent at Schönensteinbach and a collection of exemplary lives for the sisters who will pursue strict Observance on the model of the sisterbooks.

Most interpretations of Meyer's relationship to and representation of women in his works rely on his programmatically selective editing of the sisterbooks, some of which survive both in their original form and in his edited version. Jeffrey Hamburger highlights how Meyer edits out more radical visionary material from the Adelhausen sisterbook and interprets

---

frowen bild so wol kan arbaiten": Artistic Production and Exchange in Women's Convents of the Observant Reform', in *Frauen - Kloster - Kunst: Neue Forschungen zur Kulturgeschichte des Mittelalters*, ed. J. Hamburger (Turnhout, 2007), pp. 187–95.

[9] For a survey of Meyer's life and works, see V. Zapf, 'Meyer, Johannes OP', in *Deutsches Literatur-Lexikon: Das Mittelalter*, ed. W. Achnitz (Berlin, 2012), cols. 754–62.

[10] R. Meyer, *Das 'St. Katharinentaler Schwesternbuch': Untersuchung, Edition, Kommentar* (Tübingen, 1995), pp. 65–72.

this as indicating opposition to private visionary devotion.[11] Reviewing Meyer's work on all four sisterbooks, Ruth Meyer identifies exemplarity as his guiding principle and points out that in the *Book of the Reformation* Meyer himself confirms Hamburger's evaluation of his practices.[12] In compiling the lives of Schönensteinbach sisters, Meyer reports having left out most of the visions because they are less useful to hear about than virtues and because it is easy to be deceived by false visions.[13] Anne Winston-Allen offers a more moderate picture of Meyer, noting his collaborations with prioresses in gathering information about the history of their convents. Yet she concludes that Meyer edited these same women out of reform history, downplaying their agency and emphasizing the initiative of male advisors.[14] This conforms to the short narrative with which I opened. Even though Meyer is not named, his divine calling is emphasized over any desire the Adelhausen nuns may have had to reform.

Yet understanding Meyer as a controlling, anti-visionary reformer obscures what he was trying to accomplish by missing the context in which he was working. Comparing Meyer's versions of women's stories to the female-composed originals will necessarily leave us disappointed, if only because they were composed 150 years later in a different cultural context.[15] Furthermore, modern scholars often view ecstatic behaviour as a vehicle for female agency, whereas Meyer was concerned with the reality of half-starved novices.[16] We should not interpret his injunctions and excisions as a negative attitude toward women but as concern for the nuns' physical health as well as their spiritual well-being.

Comparing Meyer's German translations for female audiences to their Latin male-oriented originals conveys a different picture. Meyer's translations deviate widely from the original in response to the needs and interests of his audience. His translation of Humbert of Romans's *Book of Offices* reorganizes

---

[11] J. Hamburger, *The Visual and the Visionary: Art and Female Spirituality in Late Medieval Germany* (Cambridge MA, 1998), pp. 427–67.

[12] Meyer, *St. Katharinentaler Schwesternbuch*, p. 67.

[13] Meyer, *Buch der Reformacio* III, 59.

[14] A. Winston-Allen, *Convent Chronicles: Women Writing About Women and Reform in the Late Middle Ages* (University Park PA, 2004), pp. 114–17.

[15] Winston-Allen makes this point and furthermore notes that, in comparison to his fifteenth-century male contemporaries, Meyer's position on female spirituality is remarkably mild; 'Rewriting Women's History: Medieval Nuns' Vitae by Johannes Meyer', in *Medieval German Voices in the 21st Century: The Paradigmatic Function of Medieval German Studies for German Studies*, ed. A. Classen (Amsterdam, 2000), pp. 151–2.

[16] In the *Book of the Reformation* Meyer mentions excessive fasting in particular as an *exemplum ex negativo* and admonishes his readers that 'an uf sechen ist zů haben zů den iungen und nüwen brůder und swöstren' ('the young and new brothers and sisters must be watched after'). Meyer, *Buch der Reformacio* III, 95. Note that it is not only women who are susceptible to devotional excess.

many of the official duties to reflect the differences between the hierarchical structures of male and female communities. His *Lives of the Brothers* cherry picks from the *Vitae fratrum* and Thomas of Cantimpré's *De apibus* only what he believes will serve and interest women. Even his Latin-language *Book of Illustrious Dominicans* includes a book devoted entirely to women's lives. Rather than writing women out of his texts, Meyer consistently writes them into genres that had been oriented towards men.

Meyer accomplishes this in a number of subtle ways in the texts collected in the Freiburg manuscript. These works seem to have been kept separately as works in progress and bound together, perhaps posthumously, as a single booklet before being bound in between two other codices.[17] The entire sequence of texts in Meyer's hand bears a continuous foliation from 1 to 100 that predates its inclusion in the larger codex and its renumeration as folios 225r–325r. The greater part of the texts comprising the rest of the miscellany are related to the liturgy, including hymn translations, sequence commentaries, office texts for saints Dorothy and Agnes and liturgical regulations handed down from the Dominican general chapter meetings. Although not a liturgical book itself, the miscellany gathers texts that promote not only correct observance but also knowledgeable spiritual engagement in liturgical practice.[18]

Their appearance in the manuscript suggests that these texts are much closer to drafts than to finished compositions. Empty spaces in between entries, numerous scribbles in the middle of lines and marginal additions in the same hand all contribute to the impression that these texts were works in progress. The collection of historical material pertaining to Adelhausen occupies part of the first quire with the rest left blank (225r–240r). The next two quires (240v–267v) are occupied by the *Chronicle of 1484*, so called because of the dated colophon in its prologue. This text begins with the death of Bernard of Clairvaux in 1153 and records significant religious events and notable people into the mid fourteenth century. The foundation of important Dominican women's houses in Germany as well as events of significance only to Adelhausen are integrated into the course of the history.

Meyer's prologue and the alphabetical list of Adelhausen nuns occupy most of two quires from 268r–287r. This list is not merely a reorganization and abbreviation of Anna von Munzingen's sisterbook but includes later nuns, as well. For example, Edelin de Ow is commemorated as having been

---

[17] A thorough description of the manuscript may be found in W. Hagenmeier, *Die deutschen mittelalterlichen Handschriften der Universitätsbibliothek und die mittelalterlichen Handschriften anderer öffentlicher Sammlungen in Freiburg im Breisgau und Umgebung* (Wiesbaden, 1988), pp. 342–9.

[18] C. T. Jones, 'Rekindling the Light of Faith: Hymn Translation and Spiritual Renewal in the Fifteenth-Century Observant Reform', *Journal of Medieval and Early Modern Studies* 42 (2012), 567–96.

prioress at the time of the reform in 1465. Following the sisters is a brief list of Dominican friars who ministered to the nuns of Adelhausen. The folio following this has been left blank except for a rubrication explaining that the space is for recording the names confessors, priests and lay brothers who died on the convent grounds. The quire and the collection of texts close with a note that the numerous gravestones on Adelhausen grounds memorialize the devout laypeople who supported the convent, before listing off miracles granted to Adelhausen sisters, albeit anonymously.

Two pages in a different hand have been inserted before the next quire picks up in Meyer's hand again. These pages bear a prologue and table of contents for the following *Chronicle of 1481*, which records the Masters General of the Dominican Order along with other notable Dominicans. This chronicle also takes its name from the date in the prologue, although it concludes with the death of Master General Salvus Cassetta in 1483. It is nevertheless clear from the variation in pen size and ink, as well as a brief insertion in a hand other than Meyer's, that the events between 1480 and 1483 represent later additions.[19] The final quire begins on 318r with a list of reformed Observant convents in German lands, followed by a list of Observant German men's houses, unreformed men's houses, unreformed women's houses and finally a list of convents that had either closed or transferred to other Orders, that is become canonesses or Premonstratensians. The old foliation ends with the text and the rest of the quire is blank.

However these texts came together, they were all produced some time in the four or five years before Meyer's death in 1485, the approach of which he appears to have been anticipating. In the prologue to the *Chronicle of 1481*, we read 'nu [ich] von kranckheit vnd alter wol mercken solt die nähe mÿnes endes' ('now that I may well see, from sickness and age, the approach of my end').[20] Towards the end of this chronicle, Meyer makes touching note of the commendation he received for his service from the Dominican Master General in 1482: 'Diser meister des ordens Salvus hatt mich úwern brůder jubilarium gemachet von wegen dz ich einhalbhundert jar in predier orden gewesen bin und von miner arbeit und sorg die ich in ettlichen clöstern getragen hab' ('This master of the Order Salvus acknowledged me, your brother, because I have been in the Order of Preachers for half a century and for the work and worry that I have borne in many convents').[21] After fifty

---

[19] C. Heimann, 'Beobachtungen zur Arbeitsweise von Johannes Meyer OP anhand seiner Aussagen über die Reform der Dominikanerkonvente der Teutonia, besonders der Natio Austriae', *Archivum Fratrum Praedicatorum* 72 (2002), 187–220 (pp. 201–2). Heimann also examines a number of other autograph manuscripts that bear Meyer's works in progress.

[20] B1 107, fol. 292r.

[21] Ibid., fol. 317r. Writing of Meyer's *Open Letter to Dominican Sisters*, Seebald notes that Meyer's self-description as 'your brother' suggests 'eine besondere Nähe bzw. Verbundenheit' ('an especial closeness or affinity') to his readership; 'Schreiben

years in the Order, these works represent his last service to the sisters not only in Adelhausen but throughout the Dominican convents of Teutonia. While it might be unsurprising that the texts pertaining to Adelhausen celebrate virtuous and exemplary women, both chronicles also reveal a cultivated interest in women's place in history and a commitment to women's place in the Order.

First and foremost, Meyer writes for his audience, that is to say, when he narrates events or describes people of great importance for the Order or even the Church at large, he focuses on aspects that would have been more important or more familiar to his female readership. For example, although he notes the dates of Thomas Aquinas's birth, entry into the Order and death, the only thing Meyer mentions Aquinas having written is the Office for Corpus Christi.[22] The nuns of Adelhausen were certainly familiar with this text even as the rest of Aquinas's work remained inaccessible to them. Three of the hymns from this Office are glossed and translated into German in an earlier section of the miscellany.[23] Therefore even those nuns with limited facility in Latin would presumably have been able to familiarize themselves with the content and meaning of the hymns.

While Aquinas gets rather short shrift, Meyer devotes an enormous amount of space to Albert the Great, perhaps largely because he was German but also out of local interest. Meyer writes that in the 1260s Albert presided over a consecration of priests in Strasbourg and consecrated the church of the Dominican convent in Basel as well as, closer to home, the parish church of the village Adelhausen.[24] Meyer also credits him with founding the convent of Paradies bei Soest and personally presiding over the enclosure of the nuns there.[25]

More interestingly, Meyer attributes to Albert a form of Marian devotion that sounds more mystical than scholastic.[26] He would often go into the garden or some other private place and, with heavy sighs and weeping eyes, sing songs to the Virgin. Meyer goes on to claim that Albert not only sang

für die Reform: Reflexionen von Autorschaft in den Schriften des Dominikaners Johannes Meyer', in *Schriftstellerische Inszenierungspraktiken – Typologie und Geschichte*, ed. C. Jürgensen and G. Kaiser (Heidelberg, 2011), pp. 33–53 (p. 40).

[22] B1 107, fol. 254r. For an overview of the extant liturgical manuscripts from the convent of Adelhausen, see H. Wachtel, 'Die liturgische Musikpflege im Kloster Adelhausen seit der Gründung des Klosters 1234 bis um 1500', *Freiburger Diözesan-Archiv* N.F. 39 (1938), 1–96.

[23] The hymns are 'Pange lingua gloriosi', 'Sacris sollemniis' and 'Verbum supernum prodiens' (AH 50, nos. 386–8) and appear on folios 82v–90v as 'O du menschlich zunge du besing', 'Die fröiden sigent zů gefügt' and 'Das öberst wort'.

[24] B1 107, fols. 258v–259r.

[25] Ibid., fol. 261r.

[26] For Albert's mariology, see M. Burger, 'Albert the Great – Mariology', in *A Companion to Albert the Great: Theology, Philosophy, and the Sciences*, ed. I. Resnick (Leiden, 2013), pp. 105–36.

privately in his devotion but also wrote sequences in honour of Mary, which are sung on Saturdays. The episode closes with the narration of a vision that is worth quoting at length.

> Hier um do er den schönen sequentz machet den man im predier orden singt an un[ser] lieben frowen tag: assumpcionis der also anfacht Salve mater saluatoris: Gegrüsset sÿest du mûtter unser behalters und kam an den verse Salve mater pietatis: Gegrüsset sÿest du mûter der gütikeit und sich ein wenig bedacht wie er den verse ordenlich volbrecht do satz er zů Et tocius trinitatis nobile triclinium und der gantzen drÿfaltikeit ein edele triskamer / Do erschein im die aller süssiste jungfrow Maria und sprach Danck sÿe dir lieber Alberte won also bin ich vor von nie keinem menschen gegrüsset worden.[27]

> [For this reason, when he was writing the beautiful sequence that we sing in the Dominican Order on the Feast of the Assumption that begins: 'Salve mater salvatoris' (Hail, mother of our savior), when he got to the verse: 'Salve mater pietatis' (Hail, mother of compassion), he thought a little how he could complete the verse appropriately. Then he added: 'Et totius trinitatis nobile triclinium' (and a noble treasury of the whole Trinity). Upon this, the sweetest Virgin Mary appeared to him and said: Thank you, dear Albert, because no one has ever before hailed me in that way.]

The attribution of Marian sequences to Albert may well be authentic, leaving to one side 'Salve mater salvatoris', although other medieval sources also ascribe this particular sequence to him. Meyer's contemporary Peter of Prussia, aware of this legend, explains in his *Vita beati Alberti* (1487) that this sequence belongs in fact to Adam of St Victor.[28] The thirteenth-century Dominican Thomas of Cantimpré recounts this miraculous appearance of the Virgin to the poet Adam in his *Bonum universale de apibus*, a text which Meyer knew and cites alongside Gerard of Fracheto's *Vitae fratrum* as one of his

---

[27] B1 107, fol. 262v. All sections (and only those sections) of the *Chronicle of 1484* concerning Albertus Magnus are printed in P. Albert, 'Zur Lebensgeschichte des Albertus Magnus', *Freiburger Diözesan-Archiv* N.F. 3 (1902), 283–98. The German is hastily written enough to be garbled. Albert supplied the missing abbreviations in his transcription. I have added nothing to the German but have translated according to what Meyer clearly means rather than what he wrote.

[28] A. Fries, 'Albertus Magnus Prosator', in *Albertus Magnus. Doctor Universalis 1280/1980*, ed. G. Meyer and A. Zimmermann (Mainz, 1980), pp. 141–65 (p. 141); M. E. Fassler, 'Who Was Adam of St. Victor? The Evidence of the Sequence Manuscripts', *JAMS* 37 (1984), 233–69. The sequence was already appearing in the late twelfth and early thirteenth centuries and could not have been written by Albert. For text and translations of the sequence, see Adam of Saint-Victor, *Sequences*, ed. J. Mousseau (Paris, 2013), pp. 178–83; J. Grosfillier, *Les séquences d'Adam de Saint-Victor: Étude littéraire (poétique et rhétorique), textes et traductions, commentaires* (Turnhout, 2008), pp. 415–20.

sources.[29] Meyer's version of the tale is more detailed and fanciful than Thomas's, in which Mary does not speak but merely inclines her head. Ironically, Meyer follows up this misattributed vision with a comment that he has written so much about Albert in order to combat 'untruths' that are circulating about him.

Whether Meyer knowingly recounted a story about Adam of St Victor as if it had been Albertus Magnus or whether he simply failed to notice the discrepancy between *De apibus* and the Albert legends, Meyer's motives in inserting the story are clear. He values liturgical piety and liturgical production over scholastic thought and expects the women of his readership to respond similarly. In all his works, Meyer concentrates on Dominicans from the province of Teutonia and evidently held a fondness for Albert as a son of German lands who became renowned throughout the Order. Imagining Albert's works of natural philosophy to be of little interest to nuns, Meyer paints a picture of the great bishop weeping over the composition of 'andechtiges gesang' ('devout song'), which he furthermore locates within the liturgical life of his readership.

Albertus Magnus is not the only figure to undergo unhistorical embellishment. Meyer feels compelled to mention the thirteenth-century controversy over *cura monialium* but is simultaneously unwilling to admit that any prominent members of the Dominican Order may ever have spurned their sisters. Although a decision to halt incorporation of women's houses was first made at the General Chapter in 1228, and the controversy was not officially settled with papal approval until 1267, Meyer chooses 1245 and the First Council of Lyon to expound upon the matter.[30] The reason for his choice is twofold: first, this moment represents the stage of the controversy at which the women themselves were most directly involved, and second, the women's engagement led to papal incorporation of numerous German convents into the Dominican Order, including Adelhausen.

Although in fact the Order had been struggling with its role in regard to women's houses for decades already, Meyer recounts that in 1245 it came to the sisters' attention that some of the brothers had petitioned Innocent IV that the nuns be disassociated from the Order. In response to this, numerous sisters 'sunder von tützschen landen' ('especially from German lands') were sent to the Council of Lyon on behalf of their home convents to petition the

---

[29] In this manuscript, he mentions *De apibus* as one of his sources for Jordan of Saxony's life (B1 107, fol. 294v).

[30] For expositions of the battle between the papacy and the Order over women, see E. T. Brett, *Humbert of Romans: His Life and Views of Thirteenth-Century Society* (Toronto, 1984), pp. 57–79; O. Decker, *Die Stellung des Predigerordens zu den Dominikanerinnen (1207–1267)* (Leipzig, 1935). U. Denne reviews this history with particular attention to its effect on Adelhausen in *Die Frauenklöster im spätmittelalterlichen Freiburg im Breisgau: ihre Einbindung in den Orden und in die städtische Kommunität* (Freiburg, 1997), pp. 69–72.

pope directly that they be confirmed in the Dominican Order. Protesting against the request of the brothers to be freed from *cura monialium,*

> do erworben sÿ durch gůtt güner vnd durch sich selb ... dz die swestern mit iren clöstern dem orden krefftenklichen worden incorporiert vnd vereÿnget / mit allen frÿheiten vnd gnaden des orden als vor ie vnd bas.[31]

> [through their own efforts and through good patrons they achieved ... that the sisters with their convents were officially incorporated and united with all the privileges and honors of the Order as ever before and after.]

Meyer attributes the success of the women's papal petition for inclusion to their own efforts and, in particular, to the sisters from German lands. After the account of the conflict, the grounds for it and its resolution at the Council, Meyer records that Adelhausen itself was confirmed on 12 June 1245. He notes that Adelhausen possesses no less than ten papal bulls from Innocent IV, two of which are copied at the head of the material pertaining to Adelhausen on folios 225v–227r. Meyer thus not only acknowledges the presence and effectiveness of women at the council but places representatives from Adelhausen at the historic event.

Innocent IV did declare in favour of the women in 1245 and the decision brought hordes of nuns demanding and receiving confirmation of their incorporation into the Dominican Order.[32] The women's active role in acquiring these privileges for their communities is recounted in a number of the sisterbooks.[33] Meyer only deviates from historical record when describing the attitude of the early Dominican Masters General to the care of the sisters. At the end of the entry on the Council of Lyon, Meyer refutes that Jordan of Saxony, the second Master General, 'den swestern nit ze vil geneigt sÿe gewesen' ('was not particularly inclined to the sisters') with a simple 'dz ist nit' ('that's wrong').[34] In matter of fact, Jordan of Saxony had overseen the initial decision to halt incorporation of women's houses at the General Chapter in 1228, although he believed that the friars should continue to oversee the houses already relying on them.[35] Meyer furthermore writes that

---

[31] B1 107, fol. 248r.

[32] Although the other Freiburg convents had not yet been founded, the event was of massive significance for Adelhausen's region. Of the seven convents in Strasbourg alone, six were incorporated in 1245. A. Leonard, *Nails in the Wall: Catholic Nuns in Reformation Germany* (Chicago, 2005), p. 17.

[33] Lewis, *By Women,* pp. 181–6.

[34] B1 107, fol. 248v.

[35] Decker notes that Jordan did not actively foster the foundation of new women's houses, despite extensive correspondence with a nun of St Agnes in Bologna (*Stellung,* p. 51). For more on this exchange, see G. Vann, *To Heaven with Diana! A Study of Jordan of Saxony and Diana d'Andalò with a Translation of the Letters* (London, 1960).

the women's cause was supported in 1245 by the current Master General, John of Wildeshausen, who brought his influence in the curia to bear on the decision. This can hardly be true, since the Order continued to fight against *cura monialium* with ordinances punishing friars for ministering to religious women.[36] Nevertheless, Meyer repeats in the *Chronicle of 1481* that John supported the incorporation of the women's houses.[37] The only Dominican who appears to deserve Meyer's praise in this regard is Hugh of St Cher, who exercised his authority not from within the Order but as cardinal and papal legate.[38]

Meyer's propaganda is more forced here than in his fanciful panegyric on Albertus Magnus. Writing in support of a reform that urged a return to the early life of the Order, Meyer is of course constrained to show that the early life of the Order included women. The entries for the 1240s make repeated reference to an initial observant spirituality among all Dominican brothers and sisters.[39] In outlining the history according to which his fifteenth-century female readers should reshape themselves, Meyer is confronted with the imperfections and animosities of an Order struggling with its female branch. Meyer chooses to write women into this history by painting all his male protagonists as sympathetic to the nuns.[40]

While the men's side of narrative must be finessed, Meyer can truthfully attribute agency and initiative to the early Dominican sisters. In the entry on the Council of Lyon Meyer does not name any women of Adelhausen who were particularly active in acquiring the papal bulls of incorporation but many women are commemorated by name elsewhere, especially for the foundation and reformation of their own and neighboring convents. For example, Meyer describes how Adelheit, countess of Freiburg, founded Adelhausen by petitioning the bishop of Constance for permission to remain enclosed on her own estate. He makes clear that Dominican friars played no role in her decision, since at the time there was no men's

---

[36] Ironically, such ministrations specifically included translating Latin works into the vernacular. Brett represents John as remarkably virulent in his opposition to the women; *Humbert of Romans*, pp. 63–5.

[37] B1 107, fol. 295r.

[38] Meyer notes Hugh's support of women on fol. 255v. Brett, *Humbert of Romans*, p. 65.

[39] For example, Jordan of Saxony left the Order 'in grosser geistlicheit der observantz jn allen clöstern der brüdern und swestern des gantzen ordens' ('in great holiness of observance in all the convents of brothers and sisters of the whole Order') and at the time of Adelhausen's incorporation 'wz observantz der geistlicheit in dem gantzen orden' ('observance of spirituality was in the whole Order') (B1 107, fols. 247v, 249r).

[40] Heinonen also ascribes conciliatory intent to Meyer in that he admonishes friars to responsibility in their care of nuns as much as he calls the women to obedience; 'Between Friars and Nuns: The Relationships of Religious Men and Women in Johannes Meyer's Buch der Reformacio Predigerordens', *Oxford German Studies* 42 (2013), 237–58 (p. 257).

convent in Freiburg. Friars had to travel from Strasbourg to provide for the Adelhausen sisters.[41] There is similarly no hint of brotherly intervention in the foundation of St Agnes in Freiburg by Berchta and her companions from Breisach.[42] Meyer notes that when a men's house was founded in Colmar in 1277, the prioress of Unterlinden, Hedwig, and her nuns greatly assisted the fledgling community of friars.[43] Far from relying on the support of men, women both establish their own communities and advise the friars in their foundations.

Meyer celebrates reforming prioresses as enthusiastically as founders of convents. In the *Chronicle of 1481*, Meyer commends a Gertrude who served as Observant prioress of St Katherine's in Nuremberg for forty years. During this time, he writes, she accepted 104 sisters into obedience and sent successful reforming parties to four different convents. Meyer resorts to bridal mysticism to express his admiration: 'Dis ist ein fruchtbari mütter gewesen die ir gemahel Christo so vil kindern geborn hatt selig si sÿ' ('She was a fruitful mother who bore so many children for her husband, Christ. May she be blessed').[44] He also praises Agnes, prioress of St Nicholas-in-Undis in Strasbourg, for having talked most of her charges into requesting reform.

When reform initiative is not credited to women, it is almost always laypeople, who request that the convents in their region be reformed and not Dominican friars. The greatest exception proves the disastrous attempt to reform Klingental, initially undertaken with all male and female convents in the city of Basel in anticipation of the Council to begin there in 1431. Unwilling to submit, Klingental managed to remove itself from the care of the Dominicans and under that of the bishop. The convent was returned to the Order for a second attempted reform that began in 1480 and failed with the expulsion of the Observant nuns already in 1482.[45] Regarding the initial reform, Meyer wrote simply that Klingental had left the order, before adding a marginal correction that 'der juristen / der bösen cristen' ('lawyers, bad Christians') had helped the nuns.[46] His entries on the second reform are so current that the remarks about its failure constitute a later addition. He records that almost none of the sisters wanted the reform, but innumerable Church officials insisted, 'ioch nit von predieren sunder von andern örden'

[41] B1 107, fol. 247r.
[42] Ibid., fol. 254r. These foundation histories are largely legend, as outlined in Denne, *Frauenklöster*, pp. 24–35.
[43] B1 107, fol. 260r.
[44] Ibid., fol. 310v.
[45] For an overview of this unfortunate history, see J.-C. Winnlein, '1477–1539: Les derniers combats pour l'Observance féminine en Haute Alsace', in *Dominicains et dominicaines en Alsace: XIIIe–XXe S.*, ed. J.-L. Eichenlaub (Colmar, 1996), pp. 37–52 (pp. 37–40).
[46] B1 107, fol. 309v.

('but not the Preachers, rather other Orders').[47] After adding the expulsion of the reforming sisters, Meyer comments bitterly, 'wz aber her us werde weist got' ('God knows what will come of this').[48] Simultaneously disapproving of the undisciplined sisters, Meyer seems to be asserting that the Dominicans would not force an entire convent into something the women did not want.

In addition to female Dominican leadership, Meyer includes other exemplary religious women, usually among lists of the notable people in a given era. For example, the very first entry in the *Chronicle of 1484* records the death of Saint Bernard in 1153. The rest of the entry consists of a list of important people who lived at the time along with their contribution to Christendom. After Peter Lombard, Peter Comestor and Hugh of St Victor, Meyer informs us that 'in tützschen landen wz Sant Hildegardis ein closterfrow ze pingen am rin / ein grosse prophetin / vnd in saxenland öch ein heilige closterffrow vnd prophetin / Elizabeth von Schönow' ('in German lands there was Saint Hildegard, a nun at Bingen on the Rhine and a great prophetess, and in Saxony there was also a holy nun and prophetess, Elisabeth of Schönau').[49] Meyer includes these two women in the list of luminaries living during the time of Bernard and importantly also identifies them as being German and Saxon respectively. Hildegard and Elizabeth not only represent famous and important women to be honored and emulated, but also renowned German nuns and therefore spiritual ancestors of Meyer's audiences from before the Dominican Order even existed.

Meyer continues to include important or exemplary women throughout the chronicle, demonstrating a particular interest in royal women who took the veil. He names a number of Hungarian princesses in St Elisabeth's family such as St Hedwig of Silesia, Margaret of Hungary and Elizabeth of Sicily. The relatives of Holy Roman Emperors also receive note. Rudolf of Habsburg, he says, had a sister in Adelhausen and Henry VII's sister Margaret was prioress of Mariental. The entries on these women are not extensive and often note little more than the date of their death and their royal connections. On the one hand, this can be read as indicating that the women's only importance consists in their male relations. On the other, since such familial connections are not noted for men, the only link connecting the Order's past to secular history resides with the women.

In addition to royal women, Meyer mentions notable mystics who were not necessarily Dominican. For example, he writes at length about Elisabeth of Spalbeek, mentioning both her stigmata and her trance states. Her life is recorded in 'ein schönes büchli' written by an abbot of Clairvaux, 'der ir heiligen gnade vil gesehen und eÿgenlich enphunden hatt' ('who had seen

---

[47] Ibid., fol. 316v.
[48] Ibid.
[49] Ibid., fol. 242r.

and experienced her holy grace firsthand').[50] Meyer evidently knew Philip of Clairvaux's *vita* of Elisabeth, but his decision to include a graphic depiction of her stigmata rings oddly.

In the *Chronicle of 1481*, Meyer focuses more exclusively on Dominican women. In a list of fourteenth-century personalities (including most notably Meister Eckhart) Meyer includes Elizabeth of Hungary (grand-niece of St Elizabeth of Hungary), Elsbeth Stagel, Elsbeth of Oye and Katherina von Gebersweiler. Meyer would have been familiar with the visions of Elizabeth of Hungary (a nun of Töß) and Elsbeth of Oye (from Ötenbach) from his work editing the Dominican sisterbooks.[51] The other two women are not only recorded by sisterbooks but are authors themselves. Elsbeth Stagel is credited with composing both the Töss sisterbook as well as the first half-destroyed version of the important Dominican mystic Henry Suso's life.[52] Suso is mentioned with Stagel but must wait another two folia before featuring in a short entry of his own.

Katherina von Gebersweiler composed the Unterlinden sisterbook, the only surviving sisterbook in Latin, and Meyer makes particular note of her learnedness.

> Katherina von gebenswiler priorin des closters genant Subtilia: oder in tützsch geheisen vnderlinden / der statt Colmar baseler bistům / ze mal ein wise clůge vnd wol gelerte jungfrow: als man wol mercken ist an iren schönen latinschen büchern / vnd epistelen / die sÿ nützlichen gescriben hatt.[53]

> [Katherina von Gebersweiler, prioress of the convent called Subtilia or in German Unterlinden in the city of Colmar in the bishopric of Basel. She was a wise, intelligent and well-educated virgin, as one may well see by her beautiful Latin books and letters, which she wrote to the benefit of others.]

Although Katherina is the only woman in these pages praised by name for knowing Latin, Meyer also comments elsewhere that the early German nuns were able to communicate with Dominican luminaries from other provinces

---

[50] Ibid., fol. 258r.

[51] W. Schneider-Lastin, 'Leben und Offenbarungen der Elsbeth von Oye. Textkritische Edition der Vita aus dem Ötenbacher Schwesternbuch', in *Kulturtopographie des deutschsprachigen Südwestens im späteren Mittelalter. Studien und Texte*, ed. B. Fleith and R. Wetzel (Berlin, 2009), pp. 395–467; *Das Leben der Schwestern zu Töß beschrieben von Elsbeth Stagel samt der Vorrede von Johannes Meier und dem Leben der Prinzessin Elisabet von Ungarn*, ed. F. Vetter (Berlin, 1906), pp. 98–120.

[52] For debate over her authorship, see D. Tinsley, 'Gender, Paleography, and the Question of Authority in Late Medieval Dominican Spirituality', *Medieval Feminist Forum* 26 (1998), 23–31. That Meyer, in any case, viewed Elsbeth as sole author is clear from his prologue to the Töß sisterbook. *Das Leben der Schwestern zu Töß*, p. 2.

[53] B1 107, fol. 302v.

in that language, most notably Peter Martyr, who apparently preached at Adelhausen.[54]

As in the list from the *Chronicle of 1484*, women fall after the men but are nevertheless included in the same paragraph and actually have more space devoted to them. This method of dealing with women's history represents somewhat of a departure from Meyer's earlier works in which he had for the most part dealt with the lives of men and women separately. In the *Book of Illustrious Dominicans* exemplary women are restricted to the sixth and final book and the *Book of the Reformation* devotes Book 3 to the lives of the Schönensteinbach sisters and Book 4 to the history of the male reformers. Furthermore, the women featured here are not only German nuns, but German *Dominican* nuns, all of whom contributed to the spiritual life of the order either through an exemplary visionary and devotional life or through their magisterial and expansive accounts of the holiness of their fellow sisters and even, in the case of Elsbeth Stagel, one of the brothers.

Meyer thus writes women into these final chronicles partially by (untruthfully) shaping that history into something more palatable and welcoming to women but also by commemorating both the women who influenced Dominican history and the women who recorded it. The sense achieved is that even, and perhaps especially, within enclosure, women can accomplish spiritual works that speak to audiences beyond the walls of their convents and even beyond their own time. Meyer does not idealize mere submissive obedience to male supervision but rather celebrates the women who took initiative in striving for spiritual perfection under the Dominican Rule. He presents these historical women as role models for enclosed nuns, assuring them that through their reform they were making history and that, by following the examples of the past, they could themselves become worthy of inclusion in such a chronicle – or, perhaps, write one themselves.

Meyer actively encouraged this kind of activity even earlier in his career. During the composition of the *Book of the Reformation*, he both interviewed elderly nuns at Schönensteinbach for their personal memories of the early Observance and solicited written accounts of the reform from the prioresses of other Observant convents.[55] In his *Open Letter to Dominican Sisters*, Meyer praises the prioress of Strasbourg convent St Nicholas-in-Undis for expanding his chronicle with more complete accounts of the reform for which she had also laboured.[56] In the *Book of the Reformation* Meyer had already asked of his readers that they carry on his work.

---

[54] Ibid., fol. 269r.

[55] Meyer describes interviewing the older sisters for their memories in Meyer, *Buch der Reformacio* III, 58. For the solicitation of written accounts, see Winston-Allen, *Convent Chronicles*, pp. 114–17.

[56] Printed in H. C. Scheeben, 'Handschriften I', *Archiv der deutschen Dominikaner* 1 (1937), 149–202 (p. 188).

doch beger ich von ainem yetlichen gotförchtigen menschen / der dis
büchli hört lesen / daz er us tů und zů setz / waz billich und recht ist / und
besunder ob hier nach kain closter unsers ordens in disen tüschen landen
werd reformiert / daz er daz selb och an daz end dis bůches schrib.[57]

[I ask of every God-fearing person that hears this book read that he expand
and add whatever is appropriate. Especially if any convent of our Order
in these German lands is reformed, he should write that at the end of this
book.]

Meyer conceives of his chronicles as open and, like the history they record, to
be shaped by future Dominican nuns.

The empty spaces left in the texts in B1 107 invite the readers to carry on
the work that Meyer would be unable to finish at the end of his life. After
the lists of Adelhausen nuns and the friars who ministered to them, Meyer
has left a folio blank except for the instructions: 'Hie na mag man bescriben
/ die bichvetter und ander brüder / sÿ siend priester oder conuersen die uf
dem hoff dis closters Adelhusen von zitt scheiden / und bÿ disem closter
begraben werden' ('Hereafter one may record the confessors and other
brothers, whether priests or lay brothers, who leave this world on the
grounds of this convent Adelhausen and are buried here').[58] The empty space
has a melancholy effect, given that in the prologue to the lists of names Meyer
anticipates his own approaching death. He is glad to be in Adelhausen, 'won
ich enphing vrkünd vnd zeÿchen: dz mir der tod nit fer syn mag / hier vm
begrifft mich der tod hie so ist es mir ein fröd in got / dz ich sol bÿ disen
gůtten gottes fründen bestattet vnd begraben werden' ('since I have received
a sign that my death may not be far. If death seizes me here, it will be a joy for
me in God that I should be laid to rest and buried with these good friends of
God').[59] Meyer did, in fact, die at Adelhausen in 1485 and was buried in the
convent church, although no one ever entered his name into his own book.
Still it seems as though, after a lifetime spent writing chronicles for women,
he was asking the women to write him into their history.

---

[57] Meyer, *Buch der Reformacio* V, 44.
[58] B1 107, fol. 288r.
[59] Ibid., fol. 268v.

Index of Manuscripts

General Index

Writing History in the Middle Ages